I0891437

THE SEA IN THE MIDDLE

THE SEA IN THE MIDDLE

THE MEDITERRANEAN WORLD, 650–1650

THOMAS E. BURMAN

BRIAN A. CATLOS

MARK D. MEYERSON

UNIVERSITY OF CALIFORNIA PRESS

University of California Press
Oakland, California

Library of Congress Cataloging-in-Publication Data

Names: Burman, Thomas E., author. | Catlos, Brian A., author. | Meyerson, Mark D., author.
Title: The sea in the middle : the Mediterranean world, 650–1650 / Thomas E. Burman, Brian A. Catlos, and Mark D. Meyerson.
Other titles: Mediterranean world, 650–1650
Description: Oakland : University of California Press, 2022. | Includes bibliographical references and index.
Identifiers: LCCN 2021054312 (print) | LCCN 2021054313 (ebook) | ISBN 9780520296527 (paperback) | ISBN 9780520969001 (ebook)
Subjects: LCSH: Mediterranean Region—History—476–1517—Textbooks. | Mediterranean Region—History—1517–1789—Textbooks. | BISAC: HISTORY / Europe / Medieval | HISTORY / Europe / Great Britain / Middle Ages (449-1066)
Classification: LCC DE94 .B87 2022 (print) | LCC DE94 (ebook) | DDC 909/.09822—dc23/eng/20211202
LC record available at https://lccn.loc.gov/2021054312
LC ebook record available at https://lccn.loc.gov/2021054313

Manufactured in the United States of America

25 24 23 22 21
10 9 8 7 6 5 4 3 2 1

To the memory of J. N. Hillgarth
1929–2020

On, si tu, fil, est amador de prudencia, ages saviea e sciencia, per la qual vules e sapies concordar prudencia e cautela, maestria, sens falsia e engan.

Therefore, son, if you are a lover of prudence, have wisdom and knowledge, through which you desire and know how to bring prudence and precaution, mastery, into concordance, without falseness and deceit.

—Ramon Llull, *Doctrina pueril* (1274–1276 CE)

CONTENTS

PREFACE

This is a new sort of course book for students and teachers interested in understanding the origins of the modern West. It is new because until very recently both scholars and the broader public have assumed that "the West" and "modernity" were phenomena that grew directly out of the cultures and societies of western Europe, and in particular, Britain, France, Germany, and the north of Italy. These were seen as the epicenters of the developments that gave shape to the modern West: first of all, the Hellenized Roman Empire, and then after the long parenthesis of the "Dark Ages," the Renaissance, the Reformation, the emergence of the nation-state, and eventually representative, constitutional democracy and the free-market economy. The past was imagined as a progression, whether guided by God or some imprecise Providence, out of primitivism and barbarity toward some ever-more perfect future. This is not so surprising, perhaps, when one considers that until recently our world has been dominated by these countries and their colonial heirs in the Anglo-American world, and that both the scholars who created this narrative, and the students who assimilated it, were natives of these nation-states, and identified in an intuitive and largely uncritical way with their values. It is a narrative that in retrospect could easily seem to be obviously true and was immensely appealing and self-validating. It was a narrative ground in presumptions, both historical and moral.

However, both society and scholarship have changed. The Anglo-European world can no longer presume to represent "the end of history," and, in any case, that same Anglo-European world is now made up of persons of diverse origins, genders, cultural backgrounds, and religious orientations, all of whom play crucially important roles in society and history. Indeed, this has long been the case; however, history was generally studied from the narrow perspective of upper-class white Christian men (and to a lesser extent, women), and the role of other groups was downplayed or dismissed—a historical exercise now dismissed as one focusing on "Dead White Men." But such a bias is not surprising, given that until the twentieth century power and prestige within both the academy and society as a whole lay largely in the hands of a narrow, privileged group of economically advantaged Christian European males. But, today, both the academy and society have been transformed, as men and women of diverse cultural, social, and ethnic backgrounds have become full participants in the scholarly enterprise—a fact reflected in the new demographic diversity of both scholars and students. Consequently, over the last half century or so, the way we do history has changed. Historical populations previously thought of as irrelevant to the grand narrative of "Western civilization"—peasants, the poor, women, Jews, and Muslims, to name a few—have become recognized as legitimate and important objects of study, whose role in the development of the modern world must be understood. This alone should be enough to provoke a reconsideration of how we conceive of and teach the development of Western society and culture, but there are other reasons, no less compelling, to do so.

First among these, perhaps, is the realization that the paradigm of the nation-state is simply not an appropriate framework for the study of the premodern period. European nationalism did not coalesce as a mode of identity until the nineteenth century, and it only emerged as an apparently valid historical category when scholars—whether deliberately or unconsciously—suppressed aspects of the past that appeared not to validate it and imposed anachronistic perspectives on the evidence they chose to use. Whereas previously, historians focused primarily on the writings and artistic expressions of the elite, they now also explore other sources—tax records, court and inquisition transcripts, objects of daily use, irrigation systems, folk literature and traditions, and so on—that were previously ignored or neglected because they did not seem likely to yield information relating to the history of "great men" and the national values these were believed to embody. New data, new technology, and new perspectives employed by historians and scholars of art, literature, and philosophy have led to serious reconsiderations of what constitutes the building blocks of our history, and in particular the value of the paradigm of the nation-state, for the period prior to the nineteenth century.

Other categorical distinctions that have been long presumed to be fundamental and undeniable—Europe versus Africa and Asia, the "Occident" versus the "Orient," Christian culture as opposed to Jewish and Islamic cultures, North versus South—have now been revealed to be if not ephemeral, at the very least, contextual, subjective, and relative in nature. Indeed, the very notion of "the West" has evolved, and for the purposes of this book, it will refer in broadest terms to the cultures and societies stretching west from the Indus to the Atlantic and from sub-Saharan Africa to the Baltic—those shaped by what might be referred to as Persian-Abrahamic religion. And this brings us to the Mediterranean.

Mediterranean Studies and Studying the Mediterranean

The Mediterranean is, of course, where Africa, Asia, and Europe meet, the sea around which the Roman Empire was once arrayed, and the region in which the Christian, Jewish, and Islamic worlds intersected and overlapped. Until the last few decades, this is how most scholars of history saw it. In the mid-twentieth century, however, a few historians, notably Shlomo Goitein, the pioneer of geniza studies,* and Fernand Braudel, an early environmental historian, began to study the region in its own right. Braudel's work was immediately influential in the development of Atlantic studies, a field that built upon the notion that a body of water, rather than a body of land, can frame a broad and meaningful historical analysis. For us, the authors of this book, the Mediterranean is not merely the sea, nor the islands and coast that surround it. It is a *region*, and like any region—it is an area bound by common features and characteristics, rather than a formally constituted and clearly defined zone. It has no borders that demarcate it. Rather than end at a definite point, the Mediterranean world fades, as it were, the farther one gets from its "center." In any case, the precise way in which "Mediterranean" is defined in any scholarly exercise depends on the context one is considering, and the characteristics one is focusing on. For Braudel it may have been "region of the vine and the olive," but it was much more. Thus, as the reader will see, our Mediterranean can include both the Middle East and Portugal, the Black and Red Seas, and trails off into central Africa, northern Europe, and Central Asia. In other words, the Mediterranean for us is not a *thing*, not a unity. Rather, it represents a whole spectrum of overlapping modes of identity, action, and expression in history, and of perspectives for understanding the history of the medieval world.

In the last decades of the twentieth century, scholars—and particularly medievalists—were turning back toward the Mediterranean. There were a number of reasons for this. First, the growth of comparative history encouraged historians in a range of fields to look beyond supposed national boundaries and to examine the influence that various cultures—particularly Islamic, Jewish, and Christian cultures—exerted on each other in the Middle Ages. Second, the importance of the Mediterranean as a cradle of commercial development encouraged historical approaches that set out to uncover networks of individuals and institutions that spanned the shores of the sea, and this spilled over into fields such as art history, intellectual history, and the history of science and technology. And finally, as scholars reexamined familiar sources

*These studies focus on the documents found in the Cairo *geniza*, a storage area discovered in a synagogue in Old Cairo that was the repository of thousands of discarded documents, most of which date from the tenth to thirteenth century. They have provided scholars with an intimate view of the life of the Cairo Jewish community, which was connected by trade to points across the Mediterranean and the Red Sea, and as far afield as India.

with fresh eyes, it became clear just how connected the worlds of Africa, Asia, and Europe, and of Islam, Christianity, and Judaism, were in the Middle Ages, and how crucial their influence on one another was in the formation of what would become modern Europe, Africa, and the Middle East. Many events and patterns that appeared to be anomalous, paradoxical, or inexplicable when seen through the narrow lens of European or Islamic history, could be revealed as coherent when viewed as part of a Mediterranean panorama. For many scholars of the Middle Ages—at least those who work in Mediterranean lands—it was becoming obvious that in many ways the region was central to the historical developments of the premodern West and deserved to be studied as such. For many historical questions, the Mediterranean is simply a more appropriate frame of reference than "Europe," "Africa," or "the Islamic world."

In 2000, when Peregrine Horden and Nicholas Purcell published their mammoth revision of Braudel's environmental approach, *The Corrupting Sea: A Study of Mediterranean History*, a new wave of Mediterranean studies was already gathering momentum, characterized by the establishment of centers, programs, and journals across Europe and North America. Whereas some of these initiatives relate to the modern Mediterranean or represent a repackaging of classics and the study of antiquity, most are focused on the Middle Ages and early modern era and are driven by the evidence that there was indeed a distinct premodern Mediterranean world that not only bridged, but encompassed the hinterlands that surrounded it, and the peoples who inhabited them. Since then, this impressively interdisciplinary scholarly movement has continued to gather force, as can be seen in the publication of special journal editions, volumes of collected essays, and monographs that take the Mediterranean as their frame, or engage in transregional comparative approaches. Academic research projects and conferences appear regularly under the Mediterranean rubric, and scholarly organizations with this orientation have proliferated, notably the Mediterranean Seminar (www.mediterraneanseminar.org), a forum for the development of research and pedagogy that counts nearly 2,000 scholars worldwide as associates, and serves as the fulcrum for a consortium of more than a dozen programs and centers around the world.

What is missing at this point is an accessible course book for teachers and students interested in this rewarding but challenging way of approaching the history of the West and the origins of modernity. As the first Mediterranean studies textbook, we hope *The Sea in the Middle* will constitute a useful framework for such a course, and will convey the complexity and importance of the region in this time, as well as the excitement and pleasure of studying it.

How to Use This Book

This book is designed to provide a tool for college and university teachers to lead a course on the political, cultural, intellectual, and economic history of the medieval or premodern West from a Mediterranean perspective. It is a starting point, and it is intended to present a narrative that incorporates the various peoples and faiths of the Mediterranean region, and to provide a knowledge base for the study of later developments in Europe, Africa, and the Middle East. Most scholars are trained in only one tradition or area, and so teaching the Mediterranean perspective is a daunting task. We hope that this book will enable teachers to build on their own specialized knowledge and incorporate it into a larger, comparative picture.

We have settled on a three-part chronology. The first part begins with the disintegration of the world of antiquity and coincides with the emergence of Islam. Running from about 650 CE to 1050 CE, it describes an Islamic- and Byzantine-dominated world. The period from 1050 CE to 1350 CE saw the collapse of the imperial/caliphal structures that had united the region, and a dramatic ingress of peoples from the continental peripheries, such as Franks, Turks, and Berbers. The Black Death and related crises of the mid-fourteenth century mark the next phase of our history, in which the Mediterranean remained central to the development of the West, but became more clearly contested between a European north and west, and an Islamic south and east. By 1650 CE, the Mediterranean was losing its character as the center of the Western world, thanks to the development of new oceanic trade routes to Africa, the Americas, and South and East Asia, the rise of northern Europe and the Safavid east, and the emergence of new notions of identity and society. By this time, the Mediterranean groundwork for modernity had been laid.

Each of the three chronological parts of the book begins with a brief overview, followed by four to six chapters that combine thematics with chronology. Two of the topical chapters in part 3 pull back to survey the entire period of this book. To sum up the political history of this region in a narrative form, or to review the plethora of dynasties, kingdoms, and rulers that rose and fell over the course of this thousand years, is beyond the scope of this book. What we aim to provide instead is enough information regarding the broad historical trends that shaped the Mediterranean and the various cultures and peoples who contributed to it, and to allow instructors to fit their own interests and specialized knowledge into what students will find is a complex, engaging, and refreshing view of the early history and development of the Western world. This approach entails its own challenges, and instructors may want to review the major events of each period before the students read each part. Having the class put together timelines could be a useful exercise. For each chapter a similar approach might be taken with major figures, movements, and institutions, which are not always defined in detail in the text.

The chapters themselves are divided into several larger sections each, most of which begin with exemplary "artifacts"—objects, texts, structures, or historiographical essays—which are analyzed with respect to the major themes of that section, and which we hope will provide a tangible jumping-off point for class discussion. The accompanying document reader is arranged to follow the textbook chapters. It presents short selections from contemporary primary sources, often several together on a related theme, along with questions for discussion. Both the artifacts and the documents in the source reader that complements this book are meant also to provide leads and possible topics for class discussion, research essays, or interpretive projects instructors might assign.

It has been both rewarding and challenging for us, the authors, to put together *The Sea in the Middle* and *Texts from the Middle*. We hope instructors and students alike will find it similarly rewarding and even enjoyable to delve into the rich and diverse past that forms the foundation of the modern world we live in today.

The Authors

THOMAS E. BURMAN (PhD, Centre for Medieval Studies, University of Toronto, 1991) taught at the University of Tennessee for twenty-five years before becoming Robert M. Conway Director of the Medieval Institute and Professor of History at the University of Notre Dame in 2017. His scholarly work focuses on the intellectual, cultural, and religious interactions between medieval Jews, Christians, and Muslims in the western Mediterranean. His first book, *Religious Polemic and the Intellectual History of the Mozarabs, c. 1050–1200* (Leiden: E.J. Brill, 1994), examined the learned culture of the Arabic-speaking Christians of Islamic Spain, while his *Reading the Qur'an in Latin Christendom, 1140–1560* (Philadelphia: University of Pennsylvania Press, 2007) traced the reactions of medieval and early modern Europeans to Islam's holy book, whether they read it in Latin translation or the Arabic original. The latter won the American Philosophical Society's Jacques Barzun Prize in Cultural History. His research has been supported by fellowships from the Rockefeller Foundation and the National Endowment for the Humanities. He is currently writing a book entitled *Ramon Marti, OP, the Peoples of Many Books, and Latin Scholasticism.*

BRIAN A. CATLOS (PhD, Centre for Medieval Studies, University of Toronto, 2000) is Professor of Religious Studies at the University of Colorado, Boulder and Research Associate in Humanities at the University of California, Santa Cruz. His work centers on Muslim-Christian-Jewish relations and ethno-religious identity in medieval Europe and the Islamic world, and the history of the premodern Mediterranean. In addition to many articles, he has written The *Victors and the Vanquished: Christians and Muslims of Catalonia and Aragon, 1050–1300* (Cambridge: Cambridge University Press, 2004), *Infidel Kings and Unholy Warriors: Power, Faith, and Violence in the Age of Crusade and Jihad* (New York: Farrar, Straus & Giroux, 2014), *Muslims of Medieval Latin Christendom, 1050–ca. 1615* (Cambridge: Cambridge University Press, 2014), and *Kingdoms of Faith: A New History of Islamic Spain* (New York: Basic Books, 2018). He has held several fellowships and won numerous prizes and distinctions. His work has been translated into ten languages. He is currently working on several projects, including *Paradoxes of Plurality,* which proposes a model for analyzing individual and group identity in the premodern Mediterranean. He codirects the Mediterranean Seminar, coedits the series Mediterranean Perspectives (Palgrave), and serves on numerous journal and monograph series boards.

MARK D. MEYERSON (PhD, Centre for Medieval Studies, University of Toronto, 1987) began his teaching career at the University of Notre Dame before moving to the University of Toronto in 1994, where he has supervised over twenty-five doctoral dissertations. His teaching and research focus on the history of Christian-Muslim-Jewish relations in premodern Spain and the Mediterranean, and on the history of violence. His publications include *The Muslims of Valencia in the Age of Fernando and Isabel: Between Coexistence and Crusade* (Berkeley: University of California Press, 1991), *Jews in an Iberian Frontier Kingdom: Society, Economy, and Politics in Morvedre, 1248–1391* (Leiden: E.J. Brill, 2004), and *A Jewish Renaissance in Fifteenth-Century Spain* (Princeton: Princeton University Press, 2004), runner-up for the National Jewish Book Award, USA, and for the Koret International Book Prize for the Best Book in Jewish History. Among his current projects are *Of Bloodshed and Baptism: Violence, Religion, and the Transformation of Spain, 1300–1614*, an anthropological history of violence within and between Christian, Muslim, Jewish, Converso, and Morisco communities. His research has been supported by the Social Sciences and Humanities Research Council of Canada, the Memorial Foundation for Jewish Culture, and the Harry Frank Guggenheim Foundation.

ACKNOWLEDGMENTS

This textbook project took shape over a long eight years of collaboration, and we, the authors, received indispensable feedback, suggestions, and help from so many people that we have undoubtedly lost track of all of them. Apologies to those who contributed but have been overlooked in this list. You know who you are, and we want you to know we are grateful.

Thanks are due to the Mediterranean Seminar, notably, codirector Sharon Kinoshita (University of California, Santa Cruz) and the many participants of the seminar workshops who read and provided feedback on drafts of the textbook and accompanying document reader. Thanks particularly to the University of Colorado, Boulder, the Medieval Institute at the University of Notre Dame, the University of Toronto, and the Marco Institute at the University of Tennessee, Knoxville for funding workshops at which we discussed and refined the manuscript.

Individuals we would like to thank include (in alphabetical order) Hussein Abdulsater (University of Notre Dame), Fred Astren (San Francisco State), Mohammad Ballan (SUNY Stony Brook), David Bocquelet, Remie Constable (of fond memory, late of the University of Notre Dame), John Dagenais (University of California, Los Angeles), Oren Falk (Cornell University), Abigail Firey (University of Kentucky), Alexandra Garnhart Bushakra (University of Tennessee, Knoxville), Claire Gilbert (Saint Louis University), William Granara (Harvard University), Dan Green (POM), Monica Green, Mayte Green-Mercado (Rutgers University), Daniel Gullo (Hill Museum and Manuscript Library), Harvey Hames (Ben Gurion University of the Negev), Demetrios Harper (Holy Trinity Orthodox Seminary), Peregrine Horden (Oxford University), Spencer Hunt (University of Notre Dame), Sergio La Porta (Fresno State), Danny Lasker (Ben Gurion University of the Negev), Mahan Mirza (University of Notre Dame), Lee Mordichai (Hebrew University of Jerusalem), Stephen Ogden (University of Notre Dame), Karen Pinto, Amy Remensnyder (Brown University), Gabriel Reynolds (University of Notre Dame), Denis Robichaud (University of Notre Dame), Teo Ruiz (University of California, Los Angeles), Cana Short (University of Notre Dame), Bogdan Smarandache (University of Toronto), Stefan Statchev (Arizona State University), David Wacks (University of Oregon), Lydia Walker (University of Tennessee, Knoxville), Kenneth Baxter Wolf (Pomona College), Fariba Zarinebaf (University of California, Riverside), and Nina Zhiri (University of California, San Diego).

It was Traci Crowell (then of Bedford/St. Martin's) who kickstarted this project, when she originally approached us to publish a Mediterranean textbook, at the precise moment that we had begun to discuss among ourselves. Several years later the University of California Press took on the project and brought it to completion, thanks to Lyn Uhl, who commissioned it, and Eric Schmidt and Cindy Fulton, who saw it through production. Kathy Borgogno did an excellent job tracking down images and coordinating cartography as did Marian Rogers with copy editing.

To these must be added the anonymous readers who reviewed the manuscripts at various stages of development and production both for Bedford/St. Martin's and UC Press.

Alongside those named above, Thomas E. Burman would like to thank in particular his wife, Elizabeth Raney Burman, for her constant, indeed enthusiastic, support during the many years of work on this project. Though it has been nearly thirty years since he finished graduate school, he would like to thank his doctoral supervisors at the University of Toronto, the late J. N. Hillgarth and the late George Michael Wickens, both of whom energetically encouraged him to work on a project that brought the Latin-Christian and Arab-Muslim (and Arab-Christian) worlds together. The outside reader for that dissertation was Thomas F. Glick (Boston University), who, like Hillgarth, had long been thinking about medieval Spain from a broad Mediterranean point of view, and whose pathbreaking work—and congenial friendship—has been a constant inspiration. He would also like to thank the History Department and Marco Institute at the University of Tennessee, Knoxville, and the History Department and Medieval Institute at the University of Notre Dame for their institutional support along the way, and especially his graduate students in courses on the Mediterranean. Those in a joint University of Tennessee and University of Kentucky seminar a half decade ago (taught on Zoom with his dear friend Abigail Firey) read and gave valuable feedback on the first part of the book. More recently, graduate students at Notre Dame have read earlier drafts of the whole manuscript and have provided useful comments and insights. Notre Dame faculty and graduate participants in the Religion and Pluralism in the Medieval Mediterranean Working Group, supported by the Medieval Institute, have been and continue to be a source of collegial learning and discussion. He thanks that group in particular for reading and commenting on the portions of the book for which he was primary author. Collaborating with Brian Catlos and Mark Meyerson on this project has been one of the great pleasures of his academic life. They have been a constant source of deeply learned insight, helpful and good-natured criticism, and deep friendship.

In addition to those named above, Brian Catlos would like to thank his wife and partner, Núria Silleras-Fernández (University of Colorado, Boulder), both for the feedback she gave on this project and for her patience in surviving yet another book project. For deep and enduring inspiration thanks are due to Thomas F. Glick (Boston University), Andrew Watson (University of Toronto), and of course the link that joins him with his collaborators, the late J. N Hillgarth (University of Toronto), to whom this book is dedicated. He is grateful to the University of Colorado, Boulder and the University of California, Santa Cruz for their support, particularly his colleagues in Religious Studies and the departments and programs at CU Boulder that support the CU Mediterranean Studies Group. Thanks are also due to the many scholars and graduate students who have taken part in the activities of the Mediterranean Seminar since 2007—encounters that have transformed and enriched his scholarly life and understanding of the premodern Mediterranean, and made this project possible. The Institució Milà i Fontanals (Consejo Superior de Investigaciones Científicas) has provided a summer research home, and a venue in Barcelona for our seminar events. Finally, he thanks his coauthors, Thomas Burman and Mark Meyerson—exemplary scholars and model collaborators—for their constancy, generosity, and support.

Mark Meyerson would like to thank, in addition to those named above, Jill Ross, Benjamin Meyerson, and Samuel Meyerson for their support and encouragement. Inspiration has come from so many scholars working in this burgeoning field of Mediterranean studies, but special acknowledgment goes to our late, great teacher, J. N. Hillgarth, to the late Frank Talmage (University of Toronto), and to Thomas F. Glick, whose work has been such a great stimulus since the 1970s. He would also like to thank colleagues in the Department of History at the University of Notre Dame, and the Department of History and Centre for Medieval Studies at the University of Toronto, for giving him the freedom and encouragement to teach Mediterranean-related courses, which were once regarded as novel. The Jackman Institute for the Humanities at the University of Toronto provided a congenial environment in which to write some chapters of this book. He would also like to thank his many students, undergraduate and graduate, whose enthusiasm and questions have spurred him to explore new (to him) corners of the Mediterranean and to consider interfaith relations from new perspectives. Finally, he would like to express his gratitude to his coauthors, Thomas Burman and Brian Catlos, for their immense learning, patience, and friendship, the best companions one could have for traveling through 1,000 years of Mediterranean history.

A NOTE ON CONVENTIONS

Who, Where, When...

There are many names in this book that may sound foreign and strange. For the most part we have used modern forms of people's names in the language those individuals used. Hence, *Marco* Polo, *Pere* the Ceremonious, *Suleyman* the Magnificent, and *Alexios* Komnenos. Exceptions are made for popes, saints, and emperors, and other individuals whose names are customarily given in English.

The first name-surname system we use in the Anglo-European world today only began to coalesce in the late Middle Ages and was not used uniformly. Last names began as references to one's place of origin, profession, some notable characteristic, or one's father or some important family ancestor. Arabic names are similar, but a little bit more complicated. They consist of several elements: normally a first name and a series of patronymics (e.g., *ibn* for "son of" or *bint* for "daughter of," in Arabic) that effectively chart the individual's genealogy, as well as titles, honorifics, and other components relating to place of origin or residence, profession, clan, tribe, or accomplishment. Sometimes a name is added to the beginning and prefaced by *Abu* or *Umm*, which can mean "father of" and "mother of" or used figuratively to indicate some remarkable characteristic. A given individual might be referred to by any of these. For example, the caliph of al-Andalus, 'Abd al-Rahman III, was 'Abd al-Rahman ibn Muhammad ibn 'Abd Allah al-Nasir li-Din Allah. He is typically referred to as "'Abd al-Rahman" or "al-Nasir" (but never "'Abd" or "Rahman"). The "III" is a modern addition; rulers were not typically referred to numerically in this era. The patronymic used in the plural (*banu*) can function like a surname, particularly if it relates to an ancestor regarded as illustrious or the founder of the family. For example, the Umayyad (Banu Umayya) caliphs who descended directly from the caliph Marwan (684–685) and who thus carried "ibn Marwan" as one of their patronymics were known together as the "Banu Marwan" (the sons, descendants, or clan of Marwan), or "Marwanids," in English. Names in Hebrew function in a similar manner.

Many names and terms referred to in this book are from languages such as Greek, Arabic, Hebrew, Persian, and Armenian that use alphabets different from the Latin alphabet we use for English. In each case we have used a simplified form of transliteration that avoids special characters. Because in most cases there are a number of different transliteration systems in use, in other publications you may find spellings of the same word or name that differ from the ones you find here.

For the most part we have referred to places by the name used by their modern inhabitants, except when there is a standard, modern American English equivalent. So, while you will read of Zaragoza (as opposed to Saragossa), Thessaloniki (as opposed to Salonika), and Lleida (as opposed to Lérida), you will find places like Florence, Fez, Mecca, and Jerusalem, rather Firenze, Fas, al-Makka, and Yerushalayim or al-Quds.

All dates in the text are provided in the calendar of the Common Era (BCE/CE)—a modern adaptation of the Christian Gregorian calendar (BC/AD) used since 1582. It is based on a solar year of 365.25 days that begins on January 1 and is counted from the notional birth-year of Jesus (now reckoned at 4 BCE). Previous to this the most common way of marking dates in Latin Christendom was the Julian calendar, which was the basis of the Gregorian, and in which the new year was reckoned from various dates (e.g., January 1, January 11, March 25, December 25) according to time and place. The Byzantines used various calendars, but preferred *Anno Mundi*—which, like the Hebrew calendar, began with Creation (5509 BCE and 3761 BCE, respectively). Other ethnic groups and religious communities—Armenians, Copts, Persians, Ethiopians—had their own solar calendars. The *hijri*, or Islamic calendar (AH), has a year of twelve lunar months counted from July 16, 622 CE, which is the date associated with Muhammad's departure for Medina (the *hijra*, or "emigration") and is held to mark the foundation of the Muslim community. Muslims refer to the period before this as *al-Jahiliyya*, "the Time of Ignorance." Because the *hijri* year is shorter than the solar year, they do not exactly coincide. Thus, one *hijri* year usually spans parts of two Common Era years; for example, 720 AH includes parts of 1320 and 1321 CE. Because it has fewer days and "moves" relative to the solar year, the *hijri* calendar is not practical for agriculture; hence, Muslims in this period often used the solar calendar of one of their subject peoples alongside the *hijri* calendar.

For Arabic and Hebrew we have used a simplified transliteration system without diacritics or special characters, and in which the Arabic 'ayn and hamza are both represented by the character ' (with initial hamzas omitted). The Arabic ta' marbuta is usually transliterated as "a" (although occasionally as "ah" as in *surah*). In most cases the names of dynasties and collectives that occur in Arabic and Persian have been Anglicized (e.g., Kharijites, Safavids) except in cases where the Arabized version has become part of the standard English lexicon (e.g., Sunnis, Shi'is).

Although this textbook can be read alone, readers are advised to use it conjunction with *Texts from the Middle: Documents from the Mediterranean World, 650–1650 CE* (University of California, 2022), a collection of primary source documents relating to the major themes discussed here. Cross-references to these texts can be found in this book and are noted as SEE SOURCEBOOK, followed by the chapter number and document reference.

INTRODUCTION

The Mediterranean: Land, Sea, and People

The Mediterranean was known to the Hebrews as "the Great Sea," "the Western Sea," or simply "the Sea," and to the Greeks as "the Sea of the Middle of the Earth." The Romans adopted this name as "Mediterranean," when they did not refer to it as "Our Sea" (Mare Nostrum)—an association Arab geographers acknowledged when they came to call it "the Sea of the Romans." As historians we are used to thinking of seas as dividing people, but from the time of even the remotest prehistory, the Mediterranean brought people together, through trade, travel, conquest, colonization, and migration. By the late Neolithic, systems of specialized production, distribution, and the storage of surplus had developed here, and as navigation improved, the shores and islands were linked both by regular long-distance and incremental local and regional trade. Under the Romans the sea would become the center of a complex commercial system in which high volumes of staples, natural resources, and luxury goods—not to mention people—circulated. In late antiquity this system—particularly the high-value and luxury trades—began to decline as a consequence of the general contraction of the Roman economy, but it would recover and expand under the Pax Islamica established from the ninth century in the wake of the Muslim conquests.

In the period covered by this book, the Mediterranean was not a region defined by linguistic unity, cultural homogeneity, or a common institutional framework, yet it was bound by overlapping networks of production, distribution, and commerce within a money economy, by a cosmopolitan urban culture, a common Abrahamic religious framework, a common Perso-Hellenic intellectual orientation, and a common set of literary languages, including Arabic, Latin, Greek, and Hebrew, that were used by the cultural elite across the region. Most importantly, the inhabitants of the Mediterranean shared a generally similar set of expectations as regards social and political interactions, and their acts were informed by the same general set of assumptions and presuppositions. It was a region characterized by religious difference, but also by integration: significant religious minority communities lived as legitimate subjects in the various principalities across the Mediterranean. It was a region that was profoundly integrated, even in the face of its political and confessional divisions—no less so, in its own way, than regions that we are accustomed to accepting as frameworks for historical inquiry, such as "Medieval Europe."

The Physical Environment

The Mediterranean was formed a little over five million years ago in the most spectacular flood in our planet's history. Previous to that it had been a low-lying dry depression (almost two miles deep at points) marking the boundary zone of the African, Eurasian, and Arabian tectonic plates, and cut off from the Atlantic by a mountainous ridge in what is now Morocco and Spain. When that ridge began to suddenly give way, water poured into the Mediterranean basin at a breathtaking rate; the entire sea—all four million cubic kilometers of water—cascaded in within a period of two years, and perhaps as little as two months. What was left was a salty, almost tideless sea, 2,700 miles from east to west at its longest point, and 1,100 miles from north to south at its widest, divided into a western and an eastern basin. Elongated and serpentine, its surface was pierced by the rocky peaks of pre-

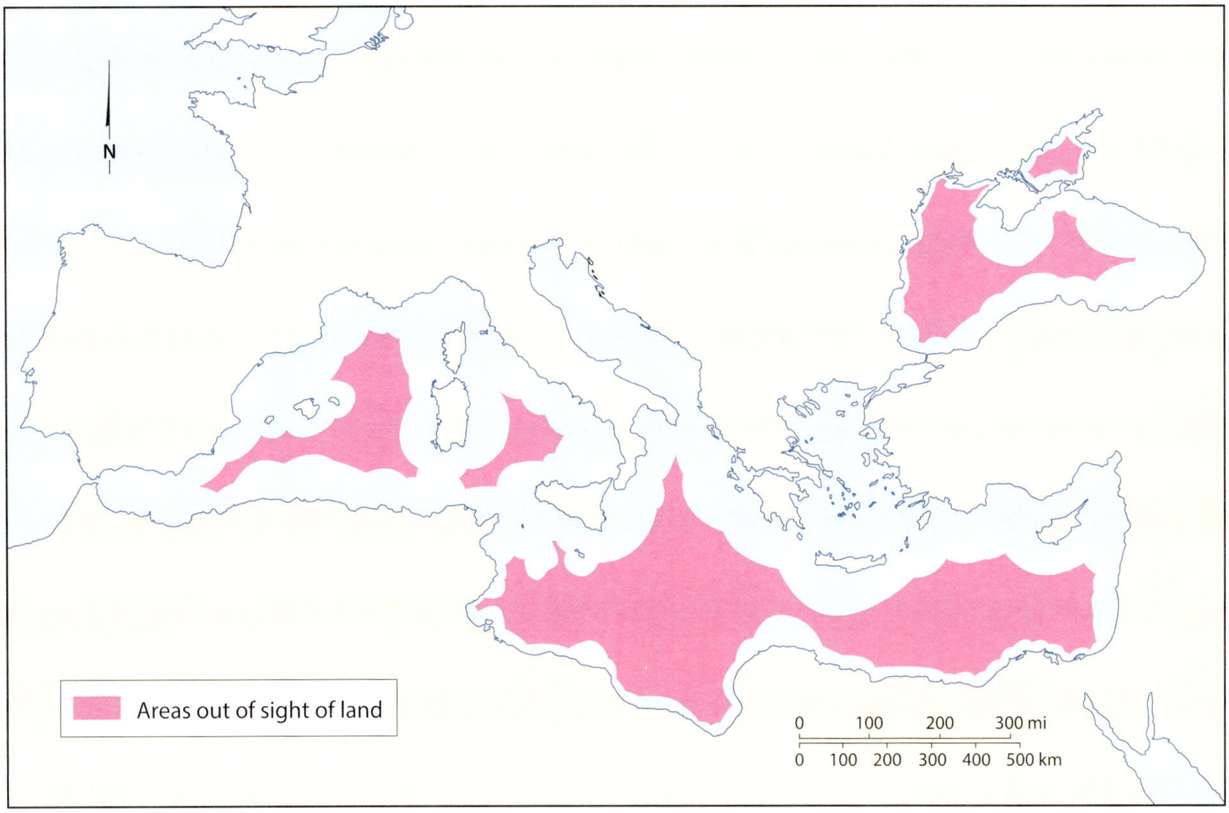

MAP 0.1 The Mediterranean: Lines of Sight. Republished with permission of John Wiley & Sons—Books, from Peregrine Horden and Nicholas Purcell, *The Corrupting Sea: A Study of Mediterranean History*, 2000; permission conveyed through Copyright Clearance Center, Inc.

historic mountain ranges, now islands. Much of the sea is quite shallow, and its sprawling shape and crenellated shoreline give it a high proportion of coast to area, and means that there are few points in the sea from where land cannot be sighted—a fact that facilitated navigation here and served to integrate the region since prehistoric times.

With the exception of the Nile, it is not fed significantly by rivers, but by a continuous inflow from the Atlantic and a smaller one from the Black Sea. The surface currents are predominantly westerly, with significant eddies, while the airstream is subject to dramatic shifts due to strong seasonal winds sweeping in from Europe, Africa, and Asia. The landscape is characterized by rapid changes in altitude and significant zones of volcanism and seismic activity. Generally, the climate is mildly subtropical, characterized by hot, dry summers and wet winters, and vegetation includes scrubby trees, including pines, oak, cypress, sycamore and fruit trees, shrubs, and grasses. Soil is generally thin and poor. Islands are home only to small game, while the continental hinterlands support larger herbivorous and predatory mammals. The chief exception to this panorama is the wetlands: most importantly, the Nile Delta, but also the mouths of the Ebro, Rhone, and Po, as well as other river outlets and marshlands on the coasts of Ifriqiya, Anatolia, and the Balkan Peninsula. Major bird migration routes cross the region, and in premodern times there was abundant marine life, including a rich variety of fish and crustaceans, and large species such as tuna, sea turtles, sharks, and even whales. As a whole it comprised a dense and highly fragmented physical environment consisting predominantly of an array of tiny microregions, each with marked variations of climate and vegetation, surrounded by continental hinterlands (Africa, Europe, and West Asia), each with distinct climate conditions and

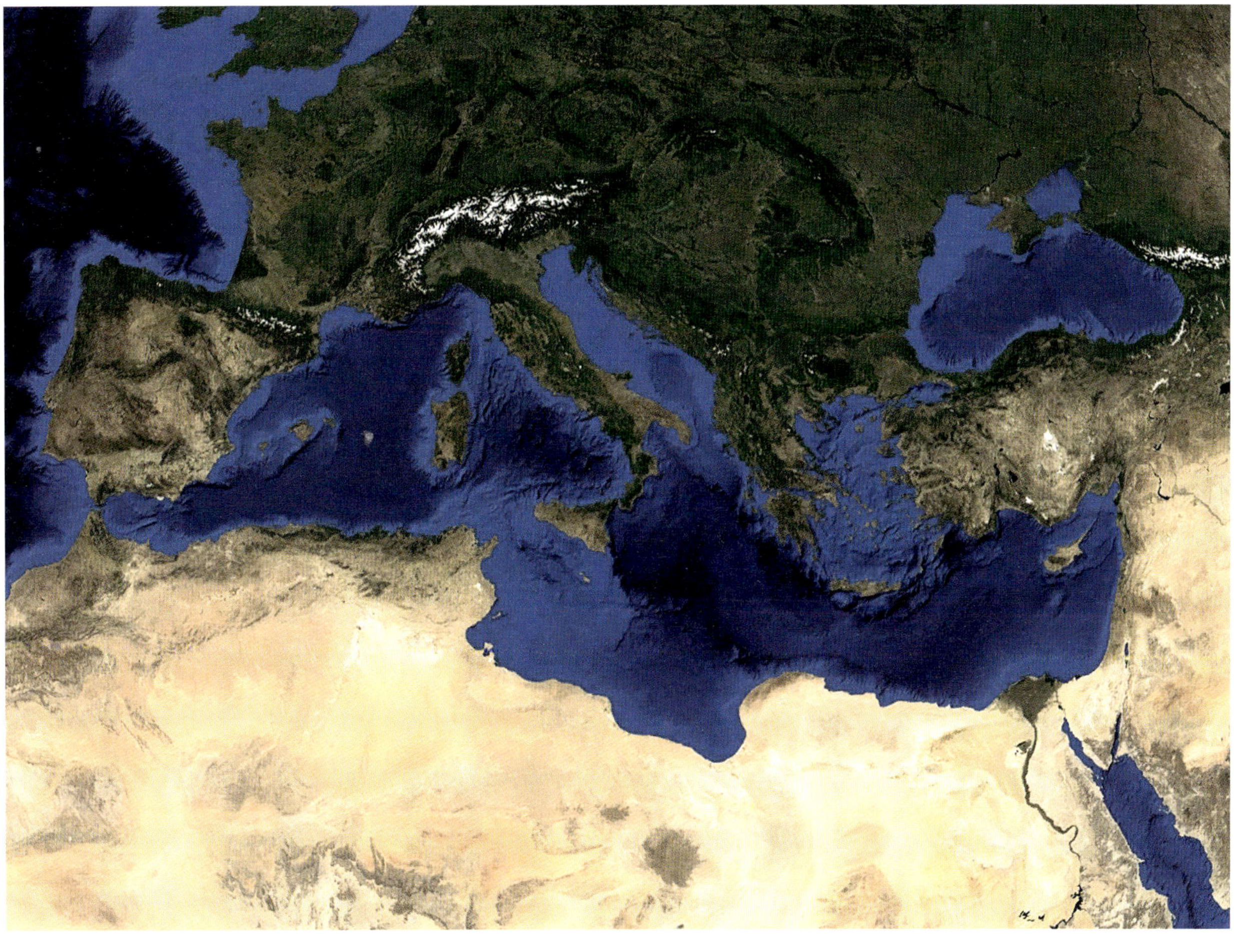

FIGURE 0.1 The physical Mediterranean, seen from space. Photo: NASA, modified by Eric Gaba, provided by Wikimedia Commons under Creative Commons License.

FIGURE 0.2 Exotic animals being transported for a hunt. Detail of a mid-fourth-century CE floor mosaic, Villa Romana del Casale, Piazza Armerina, Italy. Photo: Le Museé absolu, Phaidon, 10–2012, provided by Wikimedia Commons under a Creative Commons License.

abundant and varied natural resources. This, together with the ease of navigation around the sea, meant that from the Neolithic, the various microregions of the Mediterranean were able to develop specialized economies that were integrated through trade, which in turn stimulated the development of strategies and institutions for the storage and redistribution of surpluses, and enabled the region to support a population far greater than would have been the case had these micro-regions remained isolated. From the earliest times, the Mediterranean was a region profoundly integrated by trade, migration, acculturation, and exchange.

The Mediterranean in 650

The Sea in the Middle looked much different halfway through the seventh century than it had, say, two hundred and fifty years earlier in 400 CE. In that year, the centuries-old Roman Empire still ruled over all the lands surrounding the Mediterranean, but also territories at a great distance from it, such as England. It is true that by this point, the empire had long since been divided into two parts—a Latin-dominated western half, extending from the Balkans, Italy, and the middle of what is now Libya to the Atlantic Ocean, and a Greek-dominated eastern half that included Egypt, Syria, Anatolia, and the Greek heartlands—ruled over by two co-emperors. It is true too that there were real threats to the empire, not least from Germanic and Central Asian peoples who threatened Rome from the north. Indeed, already in the last years of the fourth century, Germanic Visigoths had begun a circuitous migration through the empire beginning in northern Greece, continuing through the Balkans, and, in the years after 400 eventually all the way through Italy across what is now southern France and into Spain. But the Mediterranean was still an entirely Roman sea, and Latin and Greek still dominated it as languages of daily speech, governmental administration, and learned discourse, just as they had for hundreds of years.

The coming two and half centuries changed this picture dramatically, as we will see if we take a tour around the Sea in the Middle in the year 650, beginning in the East, where the changes had been most dramatic and enduring. Foremost was the creation and rapid expansion of an Arab-dominated realm inspired by a religion that did not even exist in 400: Islam—a word meaning "submission (to God)." The Arabs had been a known quantity to the Romans—some had been long-time allies of Rome, while others were allies of Rome's great enemy to the east, Persia. But they had never seemed a real threat to Rome (or to Persia). Then, suddenly, the Prophet Muhammad (570–632) united the unruly Arab tribes under Islam and the Qur'an, which declared that God was absolutely one, and all must submit to Him. Soon after Muhammad's death in 632, a formidable Arab army, inspired by this new religion, and under the authority of his successors, called caliphs, struck out from Arabia. By 650 they had managed to conquer not only the Syrian and Egyptian territories that had long been under Roman control, but also almost all of the Persian Empire—both empires having been severely weakened by internal tensions and decades of warfare between themselves in the early decades of the century. However, the occupying Arab armies of this new empire, which is often referred to as the caliphate, constituted only a tiny percentage of the populations they ruled over. With the exception of some pagan groups, the followers of Islam, or Muslims (meaning "those who have submitted to God"), did not force those they conquered to convert to their faith, but allowed those they called the Peoples of the Book—Christians, Jews, and other monotheistic peoples—to continue to practice their religions as before, and to raise their children as Christians and Jews, as long as they recognized the political authority of Islam, and paid a special tax called the *jizya*.

This meant that while the new Muslim caliphate dominated much of the eastern and southern seaboard of the Mediterranean, the great majority of the population in these regions remained Christian and Jewish, and would remain so for centuries. However, neither of these groups was united. Over the course of the fourth and fifth centuries a series of theological disagreements erupted between Christian bishops and abbots regarding both the exact nature of Jesus as at once a divine and a human being, and the nature of the Trinity—all Christians believed that God was somehow at one and the same time both One and Three, in the form of the Father, the Son (that is, Jesus Christ), and the Holy Spirit. While the Trinitarian disagreements had largely been settled, the nature of Jesus has divided the Christians in the Middle

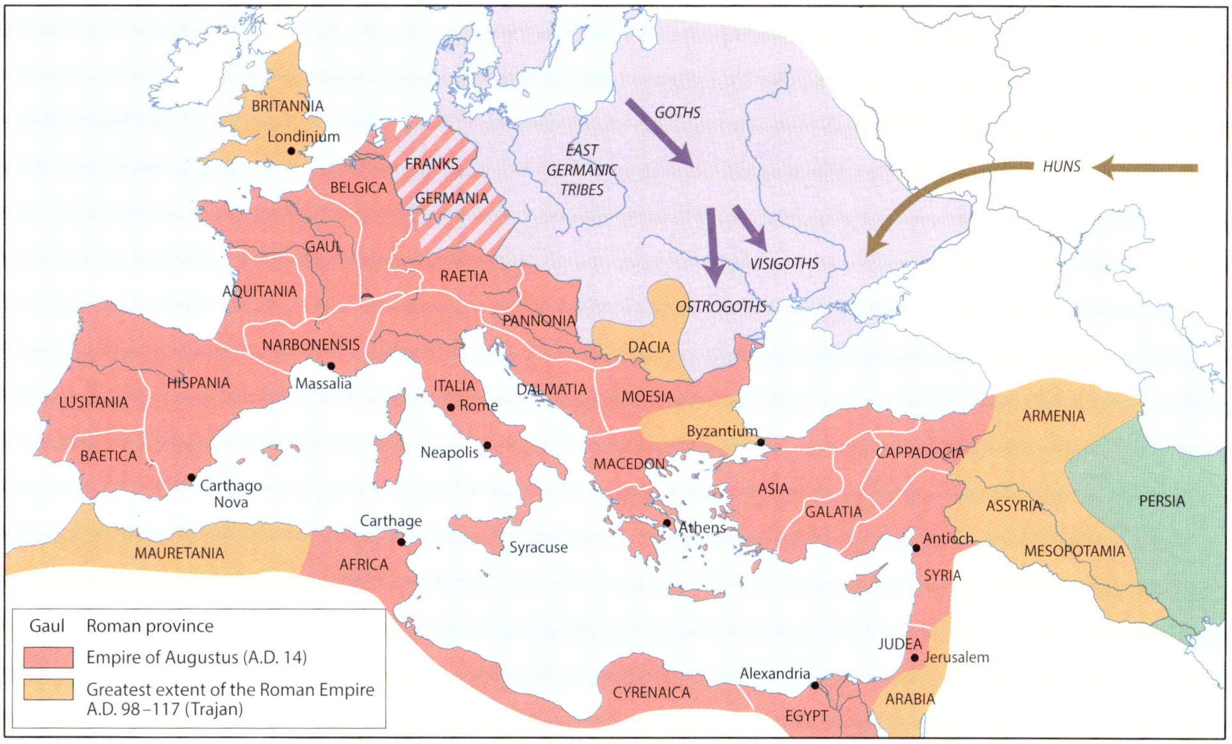

MAP 0.2 The Roman Empire. Original source unknown.

FIGURE 0.3 The Prophet Muhammad with the Black Stone of the Ka'aba. Miniature from a manuscript (1314 CE) of *The Compendium of Chronicles* of Rashid al-Din (d. 1318). The Picture Art Collection / Alamy Stock Photo.

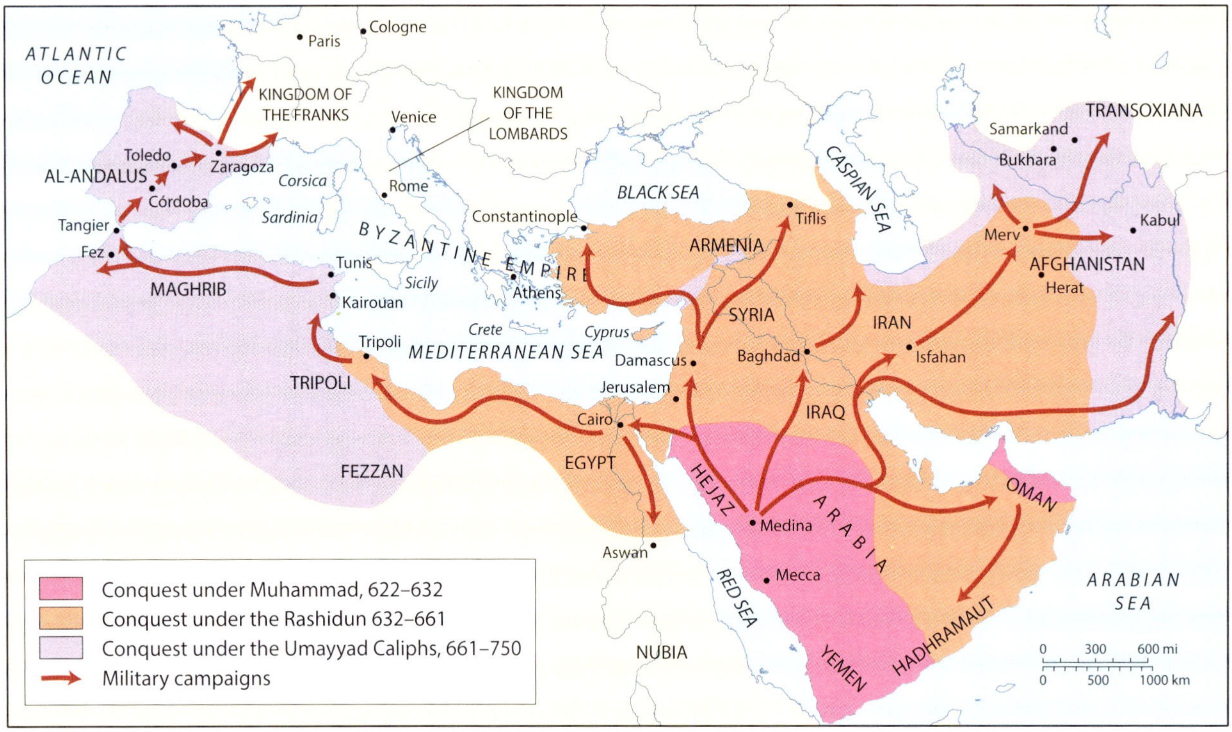

MAP 0.3 The Islamic Conquests. Original source unknown.

East ever since. There were, in fact, three major groups of Christians who disagreed among themselves about this issue, each with its own institutional identity and hierarchy of bishops and priests.

Likewise, the Jews living under Islam were divided between the Rabbanite Jews and the Samaritans. Rabbanite Jews were the ancestors of modern Judaism, whose learned leaders had finished compiling the Talmud, the vast supplement to the Bible that would shape the practice and theology of Jews all the way down to the present. The Samaritans, by contrast, adhered only to the first five books of the Hebrew Bible—their "Samaritan Pentateuch" has a number of small textual differences from the Rabbanite version—and maintained more of the ancient Hebrew religious hierarchy than Rabbanites did.

Moreover, while Greek had been the dominant learned language of the region for nearly a thousand years, other local languages had lived on as well. Most important were Coptic in Christian Egypt, alongside Syriac in what is now Israel, Palestine, Syria, and Iraq, Georgian in the Persian-occupied Caucasus, and Armenian in the Christian kingdom of Armenia, which would fall under Muslim control just a few years after 650. By the middle of the seventh century, all these languages had developed into thriving languages of Christian theology and worship, though Greek continued to be in use, as we will see, among one Christian sect in the early medieval Islamic world.

In conquering Egypt in particular, the Muslims had wrested away from Rome one of its wealthiest provinces. But that did not mean that the Roman Empire had ceased to exist, as we will see if we continue our tour north and west. Indeed, Rome survived, in a drastically changed form for centuries after the catastrophic loss of its southeastern territories. What endured was the descendant of the old Eastern Roman Empire, the Western Roman Empire having ceased to exist in the aftermath of a series of migrations of outside peoples over the course of the fifth century in the aftermath of the Visigothic meanderings from north of the Danube to Spain. The wealthier, more urban eastern empire managed to keep those migrating German and Central Asian peoples who had crossed the northern border of the empire out of its ter-

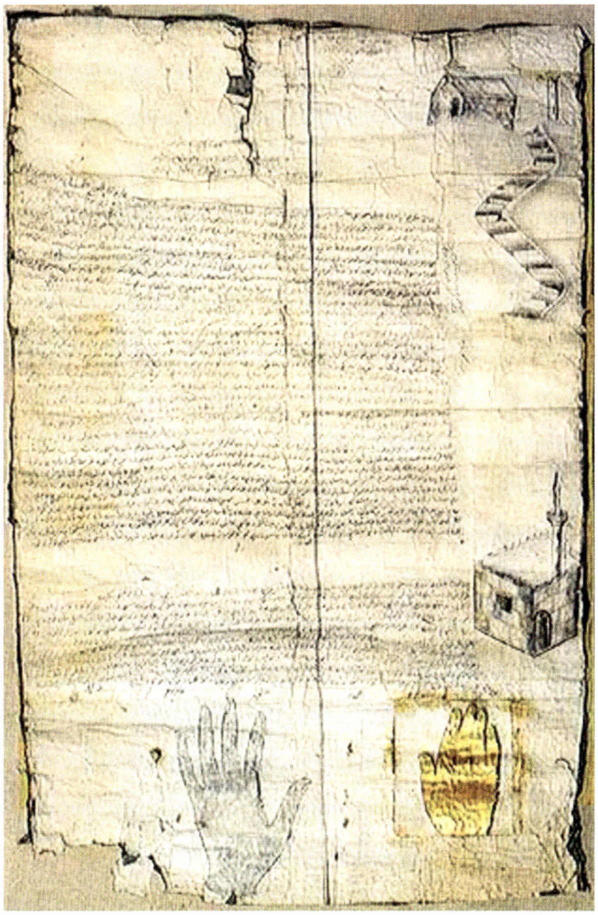

FIGURE 0.4 The Ashtiname (Covenant) of Muhammad to St. Catherine's monastery, sixteenth-century copy, Sinai, Egypt. The History Collection / Alamy Stock Photo.

ritories for the most part. Moreover, under the ambitious emperor Justinian (527–565), the Eastern Roman Empire had launched a vastly expensive and time-consuming attempt to regain the western Roman Empire from the Germanic kingdoms that had replaced it, with significant but partial success. At Justinian's death Rome once more included extensive parts of western North Africa and of Spain, as well as all of Italy. By the third decade of the seventh century, though, much of Italy had been lost to the incursions of the Lombards, another migrating Germanic people, and Spain had thrown off Roman control entirely. Furthermore, Slavic peoples, the ancestors of the modern Croatians, Serbs, Bosnians, and Macedonians, had migrated from north of the Danube down into the Balkans and western Greece, snatching those regions from eastern Roman control as well. Nevertheless in 650 the eastern Romans still possessed key coastal regions in the western Aegean, as well as all of Anatolia (what is now Turkey), Crete, a substantial part of the coast of North Africa, as well as several key islands in the western Mediterranean, including Sicily, Sardinia, and Corsica.

While the rest of North Africa would soon be lost to the expanding Arab-Muslim empire, the core lands of Greece and Anatolia, as well as Crete, Sicily, Sardinia, and parts of Italy would remain part of the Eastern Roman Empire well after 650. Though its emperors and people continued to consider themselves as Romans down until the empire's final demise in 1453, the eastern empire was now thoroughly Greek in speech, culture, and administration. While its church was still united with the Latin-speaking church of the lands of the former Western Roman Empire, the Latin and Greek branches had already begun growing apart in certain ritual practices, and these differences would grow over the centuries to come. The capital city, Constantinople, was one of the largest cities in the Mediterranean, and one of the most important trading hubs in the land- and seaborne trade that had been thriving in the region for millenia, and would continue to be so in the centuries to come. While this Greek-speaking empire was regarded for the rest of its history as *the* Roman Empire (in the face of an upstart Latin Holy Roman Empire), scholars refer to the medieval version of it by convention as Byzantium, or the Byzantine Empire. Byzantion was the original name of the city of Constantinople, which had been chosen centuries earlier as capital of the eastern empire, by Constantine I (306–337), who renamed it in his own honor.

Continuing our tour to the west, we come to the wedge of Slavic-controlled territory in parts of what had been Greece and the Balkans. This pagan, Slavic territory now separated Greek-Christian Byzantium from the territories of the old Western Roman Empire, where the Latin-speaking church of Rome held sway. Over the coming generations both Greek and Latin prelates and missionaries would seek to convert these pagan Slavs to their particular form of Christianity. Most eventually swore allegiance to the patriarch of Constantinople, the senior bishop of the Greek Church, rather than to the pope in Rome, the senior bishop of the Latin Church. While the

FIGURE 0.5 Saint Remy baptizing King Clovis, late-ninth-century ivory book binding. The History Collection / Alamy Stock Photo.

western part of this Slavic wedge occupied land that had been part of the old western empire, much of its destiny over the coming centuries would be bound up with Byzantium as a result of its confessional orientation.

Across the Adriatic Sea from these now Slavic territories lies the Italian Peninsula, which had been reconquered by Justinian I when he retook it from the German Ostrogoths, who had ruled it for more than a century. By the late sixth century, however, it was becoming ever more difficult for the Byzantine emperors to effectively intervene militarily here. Indeed, the Lombards, the last of the Germanic peoples to move into the old western empire, took advantage of this weakness and invaded Byzantine Italy in the last decades of the sixth century. They conquered all of the north, a region still called Lombardy to this day, and Tuscany, which together formed the Kingdom of the Lombards. Separate Lombard forces conquered much of Italy to the south of Rome, establishing the two independent Lombard duchies Spoleto and Benevento. The far south of Italy and all of Sicily, Sardinia, and Corsica remained, as we have seen, Byzantine territory.

Continuing our journey west, the enormous barrier of the Alps formed the boundary between the Lombard kingdom and the Frankish kingdoms. The Germanic Franks had moved into the Western Roman Empire in the fifth century and, under the rule of Clovis (ca. 466–511), who converted from paganism to Roman Christianity in 496, subjugated a large swath of territory that included large portions of modern France and Germany. His sons had continued his aggressive military campaigns, so that by the mid-sixth century theirs were the most dominant of the Germanic successor kingdoms that ruled over former western Roman lands, and remained so in 650. The Merovingians (the royal dynasty of Clovis and his descendants) followed Germanic custom in dividing their realms among their sons on their deaths, so that Frankish realms were often divided among several kings. In 650, however, only two Frankish kings—of Neustria and Austrasia, respectively—held sway in the Frankish realms. A subject Duchy of Bavaria (the Bavarians were another Germanic people who had settled in western Roman territories in the fifth century) recognized their overlordship, as did the Duchy of Aquitaine in what is now western France.

FIGURE 0.6 An Arian depiction of Christ's baptism with apostles in senatorial garb. Detail of a fifth-/sixth-century mosaic ceiling, Ravenna, Italy. Photo: © José Luiz Bernardes Ribeiro / CC BY-SA 4.0, provided by Wikimedia Commons.

The Visigoths, the Germanic people who had famously sacked Rome in 410, had soon after established a kingdom that dominated almost all the Iberian Peninsula and the Mediterranean coast of France, west of the Rhone. In the process, they pushed out another Germanic people, the Vandals, who crossed into North Africa. Their kingdom, which covered the coastlands of North Africa, Sicily, and the western Mediterranean islands, would be conquered by Justinian in 534. In Spain, only the Basques of the western Pyrenees, who like the Sardinians, had arrived in the Mediterranean thousands of years earlier, and whose unique language originated in the Neolithic, were not subjects of the Visigothic kings. In the same way that the Christians living under Islam were divided between three different sects in the middle of the seventh century, the Visigothic kingdom had been divided on religious grounds up until 589. The great majority of the former Roman population, who lived on under the royal authority of a small Visigothic elite, were Catholics in communion with Rome. The Visigoths themselves, however, like most of the Germanic peoples, including the Vandals and Lombards, had converted to a version of Christianity, called Arianism, that would be deemed a heresy by both Rome and Constantinople. Arians, whose origins went back to the third century, had taught that Jesus Christ, though the divine son of the Father, was not coequal or coeternal with the Father, but had been begotten at a particular point in history. At a church council in 589, the Visigothic king, Reccared (586–601), renounced Arianism, and made Roman Catholicism the only allowable form of Christianity in his realm.

This is a process that had happened at various times, with most of the Germanic peoples entering the Roman Empire as Arians and at some point converting to Cathol-

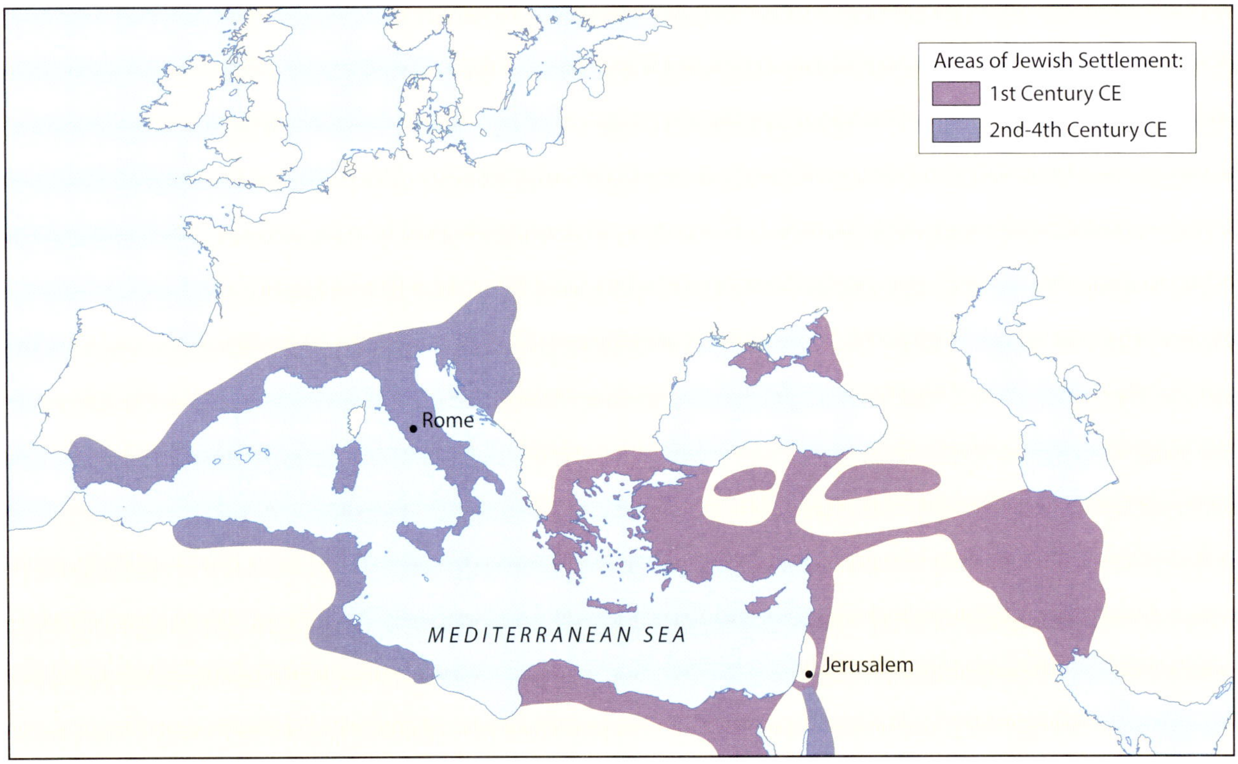

MAP 0.4 Jewish Settlement in Antiquity. Original source unknown.

icism, which was the religion of most of the people they ruled over. The exception were the Franks, who were still pagans when they moved into the western Roman lands, but who were forcibly converted to Catholicism by the same Clovis who did so much to expand their realms (and thereby began a close alliance between the Franks and the popes in Rome). Unlike the Christians under Islam in 650, then, those in the former Western Roman Empire were united in belief, and subject to the same hierarchy, whose head was the pope, though some of the Lombards remained Arian until about 680.

These Germanic successor kingdoms in what is now western Europe were by far the poorest regions in the Mediterranean in 650 (and would remain so for some centuries). The western half of the Roman Empire had never been as urbanized as the East, and over the course of the previous centuries, even those prosperous cities that did exist, such as Rome, began to lose population as the economy in the West became more and more agriculturally based, and much of the trade that had sustained urban centers vanished. In contrast, cities in both the Byzantine and the Islamic East, especially Constantinople, Antioch, and Alexandria, continued to thrive along with the dynamic trade that had long sustained them.

Our tour ends with North Africa. Directly across the Straits of Gibraltar at the southern tip of Spain, the Byzantine Empire still controlled a small area, including the Mediterranean cities of Septem (Ceuta) and Tangis (Tangier) as well as a large swath of the North African coast in what is now Algeria, Tunisia, and Libya centered on the ancient city of Carthage. In the areas not under direct Byzantine rule, there were a number of indigenous peoples. Some of these aligned with the Byzantines, often tenuously, while others were independent of Byzantium altogether. Those in what is now Morocco and Algeria the Romans referred to as Mauri and those in Tunisia and Libya (their province of Africa), they called Africans. The Arabs, who began to conquer the region in 647 referred to them all as Berbers—"barbarians." The coasts and some parts of the hinterland had been heavily

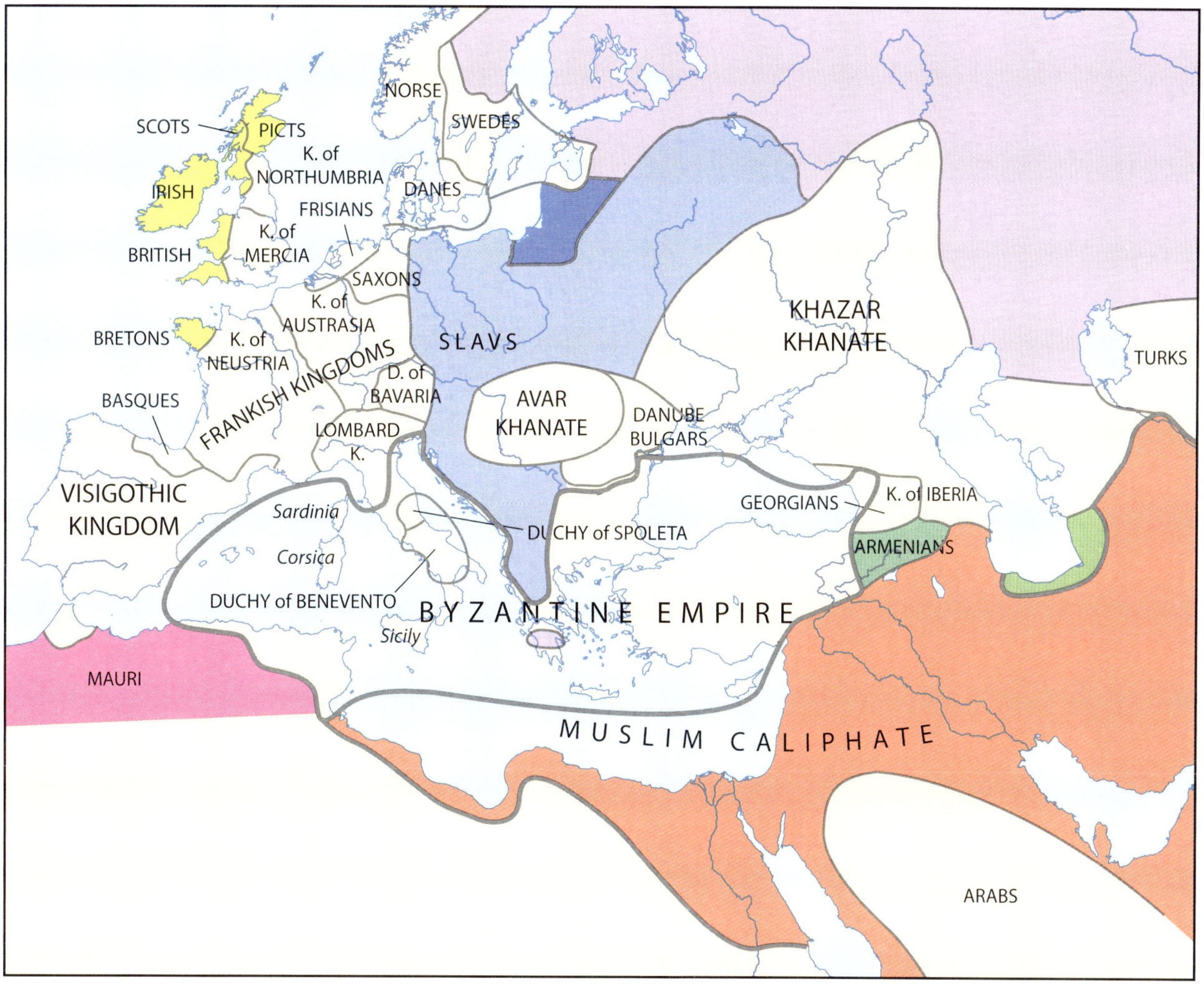

MAP 0.5 Peoples of the Mediterranean, ca. 650. From Colin McEvedy, "AD 650—The Byzantine Empire and the Arab Caliphate and Northern Europe," from *The Penguin Atlas of Medieval History* by Copyright © Colin McEvedy 1986, 1992. Published by Penguin Books 1986, 1992. Reproduced by permission of Penguin Books Ltd.

Christianized in the centuries before the collapse of the Western Roman Empire, and thus a network of churches survived both within Byzantine ruled territory and outside it, while some indigenous groups identified as Jews (although what this means is not clear).

In that connection, it should be added, finally, that Jewish communities lived in tiny minority groups in much of the Christian region of the Mediterranean as well, and would continue to do so for much of the Middle Ages. In general, they were legally less secure in Christian lands than within the Muslim caliphate, and this can be seen already in the seventh century with the Visigothic kings' periodic promulgation of harsh anti-Jewish laws, including forced conversion to Christianity, though Jewish communities survived in Spain to the end of the Visigothic period, and would later thrive there under Muslim rule.

Mediterranean Culture and Society in the Mid-Seventh Century

Although in some ways the Arabo-Islamic expansion represented merely yet another ingress of "barbarian" peoples into the imperial world of late antiquity, in important ways, it marked a new beginning. The Arabs and Islam were certainly transformed by the peoples they came to dominate and who gradually converted, but they were not absorbed culturally, religiously, or linguistically. In the centuries that followed, the lands around the Mediterranean would be either directly incorporated or economically and politically enmeshed with the emerging but still inchoate Dar al-Islam (House of Islam). Persia and the Mediterranean were once more united and integrated. Byzantium, battered and contracted, would survive the seventh century and recover, whereas the Germanic kingdoms of the central and western Mediterranean would be conquered by Muslims or remain principalities formally loyal to the Roman Church.

But the essential characteristics of the Mediterranean would persist. Since the dawn of history it had been a region of intense movement and interchange, and over the course of millennia, a succession of cultures and polities had come to shape the culture and society of the sea and its hinterlands, including Egyptians, Phoenicians, Greeks, and Romans, to name the most important. Rome was in many ways the great equalizer. For example, the Roman city of Volubilis in modern northern Morocco began as the capital of an indigenous kingdom, which came under the influence of Carthage, only to become provincial capital in 44 CE. On its paved and orderly streets, legionnaires from regiments as far afield as Britain and Armenia rubbed shoulders before moving on to other posts across the empire. Mediterranean cohesion was weakened by the wars, plagues, and political crisis of the sixth century, but would remerge after the eighth, largely as a consequence of the emergence of Islam and the revival of regional and transregional trade that it would set in motion.

As it was in 650 the Mediterranean remained a region connected by both incremental and long-distance trade and travel and with a relatively high proportion of urban population. It was still an aggregate of specialized and interdependent microregions, inhabited by culturally and demographically diverse populations. And the culture of the Mediterranean, both high and low, remained recognizable as such. The old commonalities were not swept away, but further enriched by the new influences and innovations brought in as a consequence of contact with the continental hinterlands of Africa, Asia, and Europe. It would remain, as it had been for millennia, the sea in the middle.

PART I

THE HELLENO-ISLAMIC MEDITERRANEAN (650–1050 CE)

The Making of the Helleno-Islamic Mediterranean

In the autumn of 643, an Arab general named 'Amr ibn al-'As conquered the city of Alexandria—on the coast of the Mediterranean Sea in the far north of what is now the Arab Republic of Egypt. At the head of an aggressive army of converts to the new religion of Islam, 'Amr himself had grown up in a predominantly oral Arab society that was rapidly being transformed through its adoption of this new religion and its holy book, the Qur'an. In a few centuries, Arabo-Islamic culture would become profoundly literate—indeed the leader in science, medicine, and philosophy in the Mediterranean basin—but when 'Amr marched into Alexandria he and his soldiers could only be in awe of the wealth and sophistication of this highly Greek city founded by Alexander the Great in the fourth century BCE. Beautiful Christian churches, Jewish synagogues, and civic buildings graced its wide boulevards, which were laid out precisely in a geometric grid. Most stunning of all, the ancient Alexandrians had built a massive causeway out to an island in the harbor and then built perhaps the tallest building in the ancient or medieval periods on that island: the Pharos, a huge lighthouse, as tall as the Statue of Liberty, that guided seafaring merchants traveling from all directions into Alexandria's double harbor.

Four centuries later in the mid-eleventh century, Alexandria—now Iskandariya in Arabic—was notably smaller in population, but remained an impressive, though now thoroughly Islamic, city. Arabic was the dominant language, and the city was dotted with mosques, some of them of enormous size. *Faqih*s, scholars of the practices and beliefs of Islam, now taught in the courtyards of these mosques, and five times daily the muezzins gave the call to prayer from their minarets so that faithful Muslims would know when to stop and bow toward Mecca.

At various times throughout the period between 650 and 1050, generals from the hinterlands beyond the Mediterranean, men much like 'Amr ibn al-'As, conquered many cities and regions surrounding that sea. Arab Muslims like 'Amr and his army, followers of the Prophet Muhammad, established a vast domain, called the House of Islam, that stretched from northern Spain, across North Africa, throughout the Middle East and all the way to the borders of India in little more than a century after the Prophet's death in 632. The dynasties of Umayyad (661–750) and 'Abbasid (750–1258), caliphs (from *khalifa*, "successor [to the Prophet]"), ruled from their capitals in Damascus and Baghdad, respectively. But other peoples were on the move too. In the Balkans, where Slavs migrating from the north had already created a wedge in late antiquity between the Latin- and Greek-speaking Mediterranean lands, Turkic Bulghars now arrived, forming a powerful kingdom that threatened the Byzantine Empire from the west. The Lombard (Long-Bearded) Germanic tribe displaced Ostrogothic/Roman rule in northern Italy, while late in this period, Turkic strongmen originating in Central Asia began conquering Arab-Muslim territory along the east coast of the Mediterranean.

These conquerors brought with them their own cultures. Across the southern Mediterranean, Arabic-speaking muezzins called Muslims to prayer just as they did in Alexandria, and poets and Qur'an scholars created a thriving Arabic literary tradition. As the Arabs moved east, moreover, they gradually adopted aspects of Persian culture and techniques of government, and these also made their way into Mediterranean lands, while the Lombards and Turks brought new warrior cultures to the settled, urban regions they occupied.

The geopolitical map of the Mediterranean had changed substantially, therefore, by the eleventh century. The Bulgarian migration in the Balkans exacerbated the division between the Latin- and Greek-speaking regions on the north side of the Mediterranean. The Arab-Muslim conquests, having already stripped the Byzantine Empire of its Syrian and Egyptian provinces, continued the rest of the way across North Africa, so that Byzantium was reduced to Greece, Anatolia, and the far southeast portion of Italy. These Muslim conquests continued north across the Straits of Gibraltar to include most of Spain within the caliphate. The European lands were still divided into separate, ethnically distinct kingdoms but

FIGURE P1.1 The Pharos lighthouse of Alexandria in a twelfth-century Persian manuscript, ca. 1475. Universitätsbibliothek Heidelberg / Moǧmal-ot-Tavārīḫ va'l-Qaṣaṣ / 273r.

were dominated now by two major realms, the Kingdom of France and the German Empire, a multilingual realm that included Slavic, Hungarian, and Italian speakers. By 1070, the influx of Turkic warlords into the Middle East contributed to the fracturing of the once united Muslim caliphate into a number of small, largely autonomous principalities—the Seljuk emirates in the Middle East, the Fatimid Caliphate in Egypt, and the former Umayyad Caliphate in al-Andalus (the Arabic name for Spain).

But in the face of all this change important continuities remained, and the city of Alexandria in 1050 provides clues as to why. For one thing, the enormous Pharos lighthouse, though damaged now by an earthquake in 956, still stood in the harbor, and an ancient, Greek-designed system of cisterns and canals continued to supply Alexandria's water. Still laid out in the careful Greek grid system, Alexandria's streets remained home to traders from all over the Mediterranean just as in antiquity, its harbors among the most thriving sites of commercial exchange in the world. While Muslims made up perhaps a majority of the population, the indigenous Christian population, the Copts, were still a very large presence, and thousands of Jews lived there as well, each group still using its own languages—Coptic for the Christians, Hebrew and Aramaic for the Jews. Moreover, in addition to carefully studying their own holy books, Muslim, Christian, and Jewish scholars in Alexandria were also reading ancient Greek science and philosophy.

Indeed, throughout the Mediterranean lands of the early Middle Ages, a great deal of the heavily Greek-inspired, "Hellenistic," culture of antiquity survived. In Byzantium the study of ancient Greek literature and philosophy continued unabated, while in the kingdoms of western Europe, ancient Latin thought—itself deeply dependent on Greek models—survived with similar vigor. Even in the now largely Arabic-speaking lands of Islam, systematic efforts to incorporate Greek medicine, science, and philosophy into Arabic through translation had reached their zenith by 1050, so that the names Aristu (Aristotle) and Aflatun (Plato) were as familiar to educated Muslims and Arabic-speaking Jews as they were to scholarly Greek and Latin Christians.

To understand why Hellenistic culture survived so effectively in the aftermath of the many conquests and invasions of the early Middle Ages, it is essential to bear in mind that all these conquering armies and the new, rudimentary administrations that they established were essentially small—though powerfully armed—occupation forces far outnumbered by the native populations under their control. Though the conquered natives did eventually assimilate to the newly dominant cultures—adopting the dominant languages, and often converting to the dominant religion—that process took centuries. For generations, therefore, Greek, Latin, Coptic, and Syriac Christians were the majority population of the House of Islam, while the Greek- and Latin-speaking natives of the Balkans introduced their Hellenistic ways to their Slavic overlords. All around the Mediterranean, Jewish communities thrived under Muslim or Christian rule.

By the time 'Amr ibn al-'As conquered Alexandria, moreover, that Hellenistic culture had itself changed in a significant way, and its legacy would fundamentally shape the Mediterranean for the duration of the Middle Ages. While Greeks and Romans and the peoples they conquered had originally been polytheists whose religions largely lacked written scriptures or complex theological content, both the rise of Christianity to dominance in the Roman Empire in the first centuries of the Common Era, and the course of philosophical speculation among the followers of Plato and Aristotle, had culminated in the striking ascendancy of monotheism, especially monotheism rooted directly or indirectly in the Hebrew Bible. By the seventh century, though there were polytheist pagan communities scattered here and there around the Mediterranean Sea, it was Christian bishops and monks and Jewish rabbis and scholars who were the most influential cultural figures, all of them deeply imprinted with Hellenistic culture. But their Hellenism was now at the service of strict monotheisms that would have been unrecognizable to the ancient Greeks and Romans, monotheisms that sought to carefully delineate proper belief and/or practice and to draw stark boundaries between themselves and outsiders. While the Arab House of Islam was dominant politically, militarily, and economically, across that great sea in the four centuries after 650, this scriptural, monotheistic Hellenism, which lived on as powerfully in the Arabo-Islamic empire as it did in the Christian regions, was the unchallenged religious and cultural force, and would remain so far beyond the chronological limits of this book.

CHAPTER ONE

The Legacy of Empire

Early in 638 CE an army assembled outside the gates of Jerusalem, the holiest city of Christendom and Judaism, and the most holy to Muslims, after Mecca and Medina—a place said to be the site of Abraham's aborted sacrifice of his son, Isaac. The remnants of the Byzantine army in Syria-Palestine had been routed at the Battle of Yarmuk in 634, and in the intervening years Arab horsemen had been raiding the region with impunity. That day, at the head of crowds of spear-bristling cavalry rode a figure garbed in a halo of sanctity: 'Umar ibn al-Khattab, warrior, general, and the second caliph (634–644), or "successor" of the Prophet as head of the Islamic "community," the *umma*. Nearing the city gates, the redoubtable warrior dismounted and entered Jerusalem in barefoot humility, and after greeting the Christian patriarch, Sophronius, visited the Church of the Holy Sepulcher and the Temple Mount, deliberately demurring from praying at the former in order to prevent the site from later being appropriated by Muslims. Finally, he issued a proclamation of tolerance to the Christian inhabitants in exchange for having opened their gates and submitted to the authority of Islam. This "Pact of 'Umar" guaranteed local Christians religious freedoms and personal security in exchange for staying loyal to their Muslim overlords and maintaining themselves as a clearly separate community in terms of language, custom and dress.

All of this is later legend and pious fiction. It was indeed at this time that Jerusalem surrendered, but it is all but certain that 'Umar was not present at the event, and it was very unlikely that he entered the city as described. Islamic historians, a century or two later, in an age when Muslims, Christians, and Jews were living increasingly intertwined lives in communities that were at times difficult to distinguish, developed evocative accounts of the event both to legitimize the role of the People of the Book in Islamic society and to mark them off as distinct and secondary peoples.

The fall of the Holy City was a potent symbol of the new world order, one in which Rome and Persia, exhausted and shattered, would see their territory subsumed in the new House of Islam. It occurred only decades after tradition claims that Muhammad (d. 632) himself had sent envoys to the emperors Heraclius (610–641) and Khosrau II (590–628) demanding they embrace Islam or suffer destruction. This was a threat that rang like prophecy: by the time of the death of 'Umar in 644, the Islamic world had engulfed the entire Middle East and much of the southern shore of the Mediterranean. A generation later Arab armies would be at the gates of Constantinople, and by the early 700s Muslim conquerors and marauders were settling in Visigothic Spain and the South of France. By this time Jerusalem had been reconfigured as the second center of the Umayyad Caliphate—an Arabic-speaking Islamic imperium with its capital at Damascus. The Dome of the Rock in the former and the Great Mosque in the latter—both constructed and decorated by Byzantine Christian artisans—served as the emblems of this new world order, one in which the caliphs imagined themselves effectively as the new Roman emperors.

The period between 650 and 850 CE marks the era in which the Mediterranean was nearly subsumed in the Dar al-Islam (House of Islam) and the Islamic world matured institutionally and politically, even as it fractured politically and ideologically. A resurgent Byzantium not only recovered Anatolia (modern Turkey) but expanded politically and culturally into the Balkans and

FIGURE 1.1 The courtyard of the Umayyad Mosque, Damascus, Syria. Photo by Spielvogel 1993, provided by Wikimedia Commons under the Creative Commons CC0 1.0 Universal Public Domain Dedication.

to the north of the Black Sea. This provoked stirrings along the periphery of the Mediterranean. Berber tribes on the fringes of the Sahara and Turkic nomads in Central Asia were drawn into the Islamic Mediterranean as converts and warriors, Bulghars and Slavs came into the Byzantine orbit, and Franks, Normans, and other Latinized Germanic peoples were organizing politically, economically, and religiously, having constituted their own Roman Empire alongside a Roman Church under the papacy that would claim universal sovereignty, first over all Christians, and eventually over all humanity.

The Age of Empires

The period between 630 and 1050 CE saw several waves of conquest and expansion within the Mediterranean. The first and most consequential was the initial Arabo-Islamic expansion, which began during the reign of the first caliph, Abu Bakr (632–634). By the 720s the former Persian Empire, the Byzantine territories of Syria-Palestine, Egypt, "Africa," and "Mauritania" (which would become Ifriqiya and al-Maghrib, "the West"), and the Visigothic kingdom of Hispania (al-Andalus), which included Septimania ("the Seven Cities" of southwest France), all came under Arab-Muslim domination. Pagan North African Berbers surrendered or were subdued and, as they converted, came to form the bulk of the Muslim forces in the West. In 718 the Umayyads' second and final siege of Constantinople failed, ending the direct danger to the empire, and in 732 Charles Martel's defeat of a raiding party near Poitiers temporarily checked Muslim probing and raiding into northern Europe.

Caliphate and Empire

Muhammad left no clear plan for the succession to the leadership of the Muslim *umma*, provoking a series of disputes involving members of his family, particularly his cousin and son-in-law 'Ali ibn Abi Talib, and the leading clans of Mecca, who belonged to the Quraysh, the same tribe as the Prophet. The first three caliphs, each elected by a council of grandees, were early converts and influential Qurayshis: Abu Bakr (632–634), 'Umar ibn al-Khattab (634–644), and 'Uthman ibn 'Affan (644–656). Simmering tensions over the nature of caliphal authority came to a head when 'Uthman was murdered by Egyptian rebels and 'Ali—who some claimed had been named successor by Muhammad—was finally proclaimed caliph (656–

Having subdued the non-Muslims of Arabia, in the 630s the Muslim Arabs turned northward and invaded Persia and Byzantium. Despite their small numbers they quickly brought most of the territory of these two empires under their control. A series of set battles crippled the weakened imperial armies, and thereafter the Muslims used the threat of violence and the offer of favorable terms of subjugation to obtain the willing if reluctant submission of native communities. Those who accepted became *dhimmis* (protected people), which guaranteed them certain rights and protections in exchange for recognizing the higher political authority of Islam and the Muslims. Towns were approached independently, and their inhabitants given the choice of surrender or battle, the loss of which carried the threat of enslavement and pillage. In reality, the Arabs were spread so thinly and had so little administrative experience that they needed the active collaboration of the peoples they conquered in order to maintain and consolidate their power.

The Pact of 'Umar (637–ca. 1130 CE)

According to legend—a later fiction—this pact of surrender was negotiated personally by the caliph 'Umar (634–644) and the patriarch Sophronius when Jerusalem fell in April 637, at a time when Muslim law had not yet been formalized. Because it was credited to 'Umar, an early caliph and Companion of the Prophet, the pact was regarded as a blueprint for the legal position of non-Muslims. However, it was not written down until much later, and undoubtedly reflects conditions and concerns of Muslims centuries long after the conquest. This version was recorded by the Andalusi philosopher and jurist 'Abu Bakr Muhammad at-Turtushi in the early 1100s in his book of regal advice, *The Beacon for Kings*.

> 'Abd al-Rahman ibn Ghanm related:
>
> When 'Umar ibn al-Khattab, may God be pleased with him, made peace with the Christian inhabitants of Syria, we wrote to him as follows:
>
> In the name of God, the Merciful and Compassionate.
>
> This is a letter to the servant of God, 'Umar, the Commander of the Faithful, from the Christians of such-and-such a city.
>
> When you came against us, we asked you for a guarantee of protection for ourselves, our offspring, our property, and the people of our religious community, and we undertook the following obligations toward you namely:
>
> We shall not build in our cities or in their vicinity new monasteries, churches, hermitages, or monks' cells, nor shall we repair, by night or by day, any of them that have fallen into ruin or which are located in the quarters of the Muslims.
>
> We shall keep our gates wide open for passersby and travelers.
>
> We shall provide three days' food and lodging to any Muslims who pass our way.
>
> We shall not give shelter in our churches or in our homes to any spy, nor hide him from the Muslims.
>
> We shall not teach our children the Qur'an.
>
> We shall not hold public religious ceremonies.
>
> We shall not seek to proselytize anyone.
>
> We shall not prevent any of our kin from embracing Islam if they so desire.
>
> We shall show deference to the Muslims and shall rise from our seats when they wish to sit.
>
> We shall not attempt to resemble the Muslims in any way with regard to their dress, as, for example, with the *qalansuwa*,* the turban, footwear, or the parting of the hair.†
>
> We shall not wear swords or bear weapons of any kind, or even carry them on our persons.
>
> We shall not engrave Arabic inscriptions on our seals.
>
> We shall not sell alcoholic beverages.
>
> We shall clip the forelocks of our heads.

* A rimless, fez-like hat worn by early Muslims.

† Early Muslim Arab men wore their hair parted in the middle, with two long braids, meant to evoke the horns that, according to tradition, Alexander the Great was said to have sprouted as a sign of his divinity.

We shall dress in our traditional fashion wherever we may be, and we shall bind the *zunnar** around our waists.

We shall not display our crosses or our books anywhere in the roads or markets of the Muslims.

We shall only beat our clappers in our churches very quietly.

We shall not raise our voices in our church services, nor in the presence of Muslims.

We shall not go outside on Palm Sunday or Easter, nor shall we raise our voices in our funeral processions.

We shall not display lights in any of the roads of the Muslims or in their marketplaces.

We shall not come near them with our funeral processions [or: we shall not bury our dead near the Muslims].

We shall not take slaves who have been allotted to the Muslims.

We shall not build our homes higher than theirs.

When I brought the letter to 'Umar, may God be pleased with him, he added: "We shall not strike any Muslim."

We accept these conditions for ourselves and for the members of our religious community, and in return we are to be given protection. If we in any way violate these conditions which we have accepted and for which we stand surety, we forfeit our covenant of protection (*dhimma*) and shall become liable to the penalties for rebelliousness and sedition.

Then 'Umar, may God be pleased with him, wrote to him: Confirm what they asked, but add two clauses which I make conditional upon them in addition to those which they have made conditional upon themselves. They are: "They shall not buy anyone made prisoner by the Muslims," and "Whoever strikes a Muslim with deliberate intent shall forfeit the protection of this pact."[1]

The Treaty of Tudmir (713 CE)

In fact, all through the era of conquest local commanders continued to negotiate treaties on their own authority on an ad hoc basis. When the Muslims invaded Hispania (al-Andalus) in 711 under the command of Musa ibn Nusayr (himself possibly the son of a Christian or Persian slave and prisoner of war), they crushed the Visigothic army in a single battle, and then proceeded from region to region to obtain the submission of surviving local strongmen. This treaty was concluded by Musa's son, 'Abd al-'Aziz, with Theodimir (Tudmir, in Arabic), a local Visigothic potentate who ruled a small area on the Mediterranean coast. This version of the treaty was recorded by the Andalusi religious scholar and geographer Ahmad al-'Udhri in the eleventh century. Several later versions exist, but are nearly identical.

In the name of God, the Merciful, the Compassionate. This is a charter from 'Abd al-'Aziz ibn Musa to Tudmir, son of Ghandaris, establishing a treaty of peace that [Tudmir] shall be under God's pact and under His covenant, and under whatever He sent His Prophets and His messengers to bring. He shall be under the protection of God—may He be praised and glorified!—and under the protection of Muhammad—may God bless him and grant him peace! No evil shall be done to him or to his followers of any kind. They shall not be taken captive, nor shall they be separated from their wives and their children. They shall not be killed, their churches shall not be burned down, and they shall not be coerced in matters of religion. Their peace agreement applied to seven cities—Oriola, Mula, Lorca, Valentilla, Alacant, Hellín, and Elx—provided that he not fail to observe the treaty, that what has been bound shall not be loosed, that he honor what we have imposed on him and obligated him to do, and that he not conceal information from us that he has acquired. It is also incumbent upon him and his followers to pay the annual tribute [*jizya*]. The tribute imposed upon every free man is: one *dinar*, plus four bushels of wheat, four of barley, four liquid measures of vinegar, two of honey, and two of oil. Slaves each pay half that. Witnessed by 'Uthman ibn 'Ubaydah al-Qurashi, Habib ibn Abu 'Ubaydah al-Qurashi, Sa'dan ibn 'Abd Allah al-Rab'i, Sulayman ibn Qays al-Tujibi, Yahya ibn Ya'mur al-Sahmi, Bishr ibn Qays al-Lakhmi, Ya'ish ibn 'Abd Allah al-Azdi, and Abi 'Asim al-Hudhali. Written in the month of Rajab 94 [April 713][2]

It is striking that the Treaty of Tudmir, which allegedly postdates the Pact of 'Umar by nearly a century, is so much more brief and simpler. Nor does it make reference

* A belt traditionally worn by some Eastern Christians.

to many of the conditions outlined in the pact. It is also clearly a bilateral treaty, outlining the obligations of both conqueror and conquered. Nevertheless, the two documents share a similar spirit, and a notion that non-Muslims should submit to the political authority of Islamic rulers. Both are also represented as agreements between the subject community or its leadership and the conquerors.

Discussion Questions

1. What do these two documents tell us about the nature of power and the position of the Muslims vis-à-vis their new subjects in the eighth century and in the twelfth century?
2. What sorts of expectations did the conquerors and conquered have?
3. To what extent is "religion" or religious identity a factor in these agreements?
4. What do these agreements tell us about the societies and economies Arabs brought under Muslim rule in the first century of Islam?

Further Reading

Burns, Robert I., and Paul E. Chevedden, *Negotiating Cultures: Bilingual Surrender Treaties in Muslim-Crusader Spain under James the Conqueror.* Leiden: Brill, 1999. Pp. 202–3, 231–32.

Cohen, Mark R. "What Was the Pact of Umar? A Literary-Historical Study." *Jerusalem Studies in Arabic and Islam* 23 (1999): 100–157.

Levy-Rubin, Milka. *Non-Muslims in the Early Islamic Empire: From Surrender to Coexistence.* New York: Cambridge University Press, 2011.

Tritton, A. S. *The Caliphs and Their Non-Muslim Subjects: A Critical Study of the Covenant of 'Umar.* London: F. Cass, 1970.

Notes

1. Cohen, 106–8.
2. Burns and Chevedden, 231–32.

661). In this era of the "Rightly Guided," or universally acknowledged caliphs based in Medina, Byzantine Syria and Palestine (638), and Egypt (646) were rapidly conquered together with the Persian Empire of the Sasanids (651). Islam began to coalesce as a religious and political system, as Arabs colonized the lands of Persia and much of the eastern and southern shores of the Mediterranean.

But these successes exacerbated divisions within the *umma* and 'Ali faced rebellions from rival claimants, notably Muhammad's kinsmen, the Banu Umayya, who had dominated pagan Mecca and whose power base was Syria. One of these, Mu'awiya ibn Abi Sufyan (the son of the former leader of pagan Mecca, Muhammad's most intractable enemy), would declare himself caliph (661–680) and set out avenge the murder of his kinsman, 'Uthman, provoking a civil war. The two sides met at the Battle of Siffin (657), which ended in stalemate after a significant contingent of 'Ali's forces declared that no man was above God's judgment and left the field. 'Ali turned to wage war on these Kharijites ("Splitters" or "Leavers"), only to be murdered by a Kharijite assassin four years later. By 683 Mu'awiya's son, Yazid (680–683), had neutralized 'Ali's family and the other caliphal contenders and suppressed the Kharijites. Now unchallenged, the Umayyad Caliphate, based in Damascus and oriented toward Rome, would oversee the drawn-out subjugation of North Africa (647–709), the conquest of al-Andalus (711), and continuing expansion toward Central Asia and the Indus Valley. Attempts were made to conquer Constantinople in 674–678 and 717–718, but without success. SEE SOURCEBOOK I:1 AND SOURCEBOOK I:2.

In 750 the caliphate fell victim to a rebellion led by sympathizers of the family of 'Ali in southern Iraq and discontented Arab magnates and converts in Khorasan, and a Persian-oriented caliphate was established under the 'Abbasid dynasty. A new capital was founded at Baghdad in 762, ushering in what is often called the Golden Age of Islam. Al-Andalus became the refuge for the surviving Umayyad faction, whose emirate (princedom), based in Córdoba, dominated the Iberian Peninsula and expanded into the Maghrib. A second phase of Islamic conquest in the Mediterranean took place between about

800 and 950 CE in which the islands of Mallorca and Menorca, Sicily, and parts of Italy, Malta, and Crete were taken, and Byzantine Cyprus became a tributary. Enclaves were established at Bari in Italy, and at Fraxinetum in Provence, and raids were carried out as far north as Switzerland. These conquests were undertaken as independent initiatives of local leaders; the 'Abbasids focused on expanding eastward into the rich lands of Central and South Asia, and neither Constantinople nor Western Christendom was targeted for conquest.

The 'Abbasid caliph was the titular head of the Muslim community, but by the 880s the Dar al-Islam was made up of functionally independent princedoms ruled by breakaway dynasties of governors that acknowledged the authority of Baghdad only as a formality. Egypt and Syria were ruled by the Turkic Tulunids (868–905), Ifriqiya by the Arab Aghlabids (800–909), and al-Andalus by the surviving Umayyads (756–1008). The provinces of the East were ruled by a succession of competing Persian and Turkic dynasties, notably the Samanids (819–999) of Bukhara and the Ghaznavids (977–1186), each of which dominated the Oxus Valley, Afghanistan, and much of modern Iran and Pakistan. The façade of Islamic unity would finally be shattered with the declaration of the Shi'i Fatimid Caliphate in Ifriqiya in 909 and the Umayyad Caliphate of Córdoba in 926, each defying the claims of universal authority of the weakened 'Abbasid state. The Fatimids conquered Egypt in 969, and their capital of Cairo became the nexus of the lucrative trade between the Indian Ocean, the Horn of Africa, and the Mediterranean. Their rivals, the Umayyads of al-Andalus, expanded into the Maghrib and toward the Sahel—the grasslands on the southern fringes of the Sahara—accessing the rich goldfields of Ghana.

MAP 1.1 The Mediterranean, ca. 650.

Not long after the 'Abbasid revolution, Charles the Great (Charlemagne), King of the Franks (768–814), who ruled most of what is now France and much of central Europe, took control of Septimania and the Lombard kingdom of Italy, incorporating them into what would come to form a new Roman Empire. The imperial title belonged to Byzantium, but the presence of a woman on the throne, the empress Irene (797–802), provided a loophole, and Pope Leo III (795–816) crowned Charles as "Augustus" and "Emperor of the Romans" on Christmas Day 800. In an 813 treaty Byzantium referred to him noncommittally as "Emperor of the Franks." As "Augustus," the title he preferred, Charles claimed sovereignty over not only Latin Europe, but also the Muslim-ruled Holy

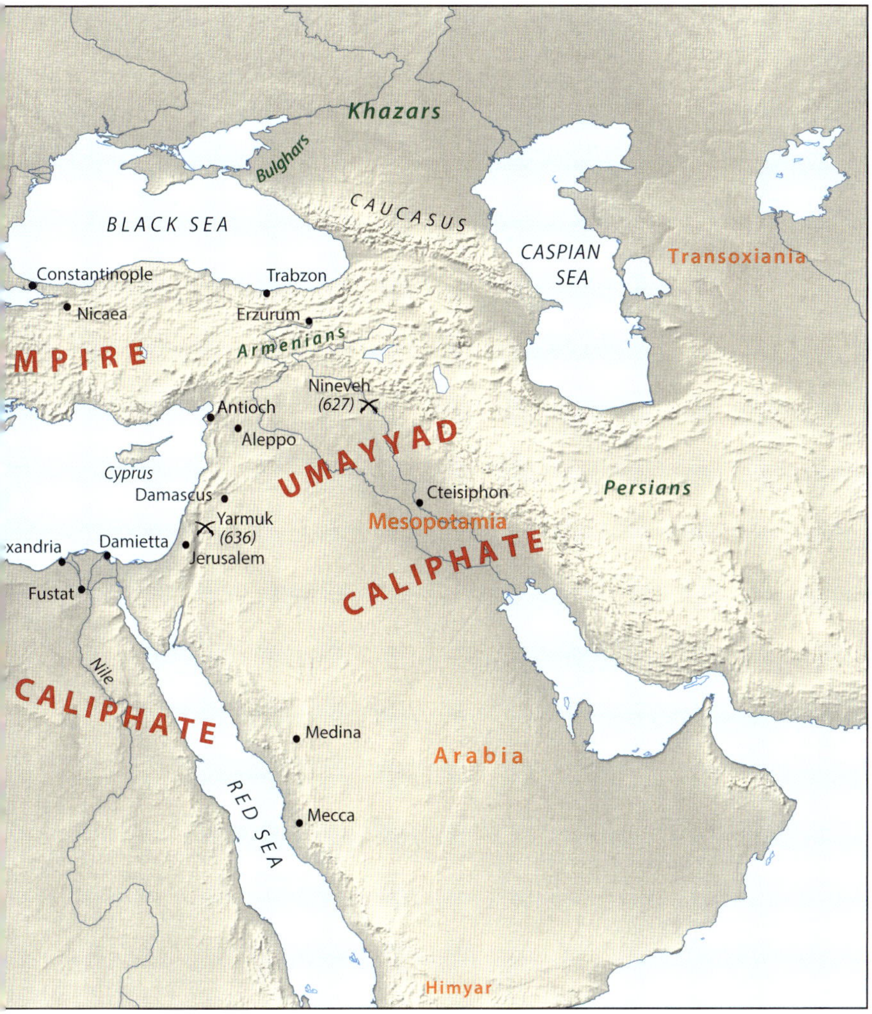

badly mauled in an attack by Basque forces in Roncesvalles Pass.

The two incidents would be conflated in the French Crusade-era epic, *The Song of Roland,* in which monstrous and treacherous "Saracens" ambush the rear guard of Charlemagne's army, and total disaster is only averted by the hero Roland, who blows his horn, Olifant, to summon reinforcements, with such force that it kills him. But far from reflecting intractable religious conflict, the actual events reflect how readily Christians and Muslims (whether Charlemagne and the Arab rebels, or the Arabs and the Basques) were willing to join together to face common enemies.

In any event, Charlemagne's preoccupation was not the conquest of Islamic Spain, but to establish control over Germanic northern and central Europe with the collaboration of the Roman Church. His Carolingian (from Carolus, Latin for Charles) Empire laid the institutional foundations of what would become the medieval Latin West, but was short-lived. Charles passed the title on to his son Louis the Pious (813–840), but Louis split his lands among his divisive sons, who pushed the empire into civil war. As a consequence, Latin Christendom shattered into a mosaic of independent kingdoms, duchies, and counties, and the imperial title and project lay dormant.

At the time of Charlemagne's coronation, Byzantium—the "real" Roman Empire—controlled little more than modern Greece, the Balkan coasts, much of Anatolia (modern Turkey), and part of northern Syria. Southern Italy and Sicily remained Byzantine too, though the latter would be conquered in 902 by Muslim forces originally summoned as allies by a rebellious Byzantine general. In the Balkans the empire had been contending with "barbarians"—first Slavs, then a succession of Central Asian "pony peoples." From the late seventh century Avars and Bulghars arrived in the Balkans and began to mix with

Land, and made an unsuccessful incursion into Islamic al-Andalus.

In the 770s a coalition of local Muslim leaders in northern Spain, threatened by the establishment of an emirate in Córdoba by the Umayyad refugee 'Abd al-Rahman I (756–788), proposed a joint attack with Charlemagne against the *amir.* But when the Frankish king's forces arrived at Zaragoza, the Muslim conspirators balked, leading Charlemagne to take his army northward to assert his authority over Christian Pamplona before crossing back to France. Crossing the Pyrenees, his army was pursued and harassed by forces from Zaragoza, and

FIGURE 1.2 A silver *denarius* minted at Frankfurt (812–814 CE), featuring Charlemagne as "Charles Emperor Augustus." INTERFOTO / Alamy Stock Photo.

the Slavic population, establishing a pagan khanate. In the 900s this now-Christian Bulghar Empire dominated the Balkan Peninsula. Several attempts were made to conquer Constantinople, including a planned attack in 924 in conjunction with the Fatimid Caliphate. In the 900s, under the Macedonians (867–1056), a dynasty of Armenian origin, Byzantium turned the tables, attacking Bulgaria, aided by the Kievan Rus from north of the Black Sea, leading ultimately to the conquest and dissolution of the Bulgarian Empire by Basil II "the Bulghar-Slayer" (976–1025) in 1018.

In the centuries of upheaval following the rise of Islam, Byzantine Anatolia had come under the control of Armenian and Caucasian princes, who identified variably as Christian (whether Armenian, Byzantine, or other) or Muslim. The Macedonian emperors gradually forced them into the imperial fold and at least superficially into the Byzantine Church. The Kievan Rus converted in the late 900s, while a Kingdom of Georgia, with an independent church, was established between the Black and Caspian Seas. The empire continued to spar with the 'Abbasid Caliphate, and by 1050 had extended its control into the Caucasus and down along the Syrian coast.

A New Order

Like the Romans, Greeks, and Hebrews, who classified outsiders as "barbarians" ("babblers") or *goyim* (the nations), the Arabs of the seventh century conceived of a world divided between the righteous, civilized, and legitimate (themselves) and everyone else, *al-'ajam* ("barbarian"—that is, non-Arabic speaking). For Muslims, conquest was rationalized as the duty to extend to all humanity the opportunity to live under God's law. The Arabic word for conquest, *fatha* (pronounced FAT-hah), means "an opening up." Hence, Muslims saw a world divided between the Dar al-Islam and the Dar al-Harb (Abode of Warfare). This was complicated by the fact that Jews and Christians, their predecessors as worshippers of the God of Abraham, were considered People of the Book—possessors of revealed but corrupted scriptures, and adherents to erroneous but legitimate creeds (a category soon broadened out of practical necessity to include Zoroastrians, and even polytheistic Hindus). Thus, from the outset, the Dar al-Islam was religiously diverse. Jews and Christians were seen initially as fellows in a larger "community of believers," whose place was to live under the tutelage of Islam as *dhimmis* (protected peoples)—second-class but lawful subjects. Only "polytheists" and "idolators"—for the most part pagan Arab and Berber nomads—were to be obliged to convert to Islam or fight to the death.

The practical demands of conquest required compromises. The Arabs lacked institutions and were few in number. And while they could cow the vulnerable populations of the post-Roman Mediterranean into submission, they lacked the resources to garrison discontented native populations, or an institutional framework for administering the complex territories that they had taken charge of, and therefore they needed the collaboration of the people they conquered. Thus, their general strategy was to meet and defeat a region's organized forces—as with the Byzantines at Yarmuk in 635 and Sbeitla (Tunisia) in 647, the Persians at al-Qadisiyya in 636, and the Visigoths at Guadalete in 711—and then approach each town or locale and demand the locals surrender or face conquest and enslavement. Local elites were given assurances that their authority would be maintained, and that communal legal rights and religious liberties would be respected, in exchange for submission to the conquerors, recognition of the superior jurisdiction of Islam, and the payment of tribute. Of course, the conquests were destructive, traumatically violent events—churches, temples, and palaces were systematically looted, bloody battles were fought, resistors put to the sword, and both commonfolk and captives of war carried off as slaves. SEE SOURCEBOOK 1:3.

The treaties themselves were negotiated on an ad hoc basis by individual commanders and the precise terms varied considerably. The tenuousness of Arab control in the first century is illustrated by the fact that when cities did resist or revolt, as did Alexandria, they were not punished but managed to renegotiate more amenable terms of submission. In an established pattern of Mediterranean imperialism, the goal was not to transform or destroy these societies but rule over them. Arab settlers generally lived apart, quarantined in garrison towns to prevent their absorption into local society, and conversion of conquered peoples to Islam was generally discouraged, as it would dilute the power and wealth of the Arab Muslim ruling caste and reduce the special tax obligations subject communities carried.

Under the new regime the upper-level Byzantine elite in Syria-Palestine was eliminated, displaced by the Umayyads, who had deep roots in the area, although in the countryside change was hardly perceptible except for an increase of Arab Bedouin. Indeed, what had been a declining Byzantine province saw increased prosperity as it became the center of the caliphate, and the heterodox Syriac Churches were liberated from Byzantine domination. In Egypt, Byzantine ("Melkite") and indigenous Coptic Christian communities remained the overwhelming majority, the latter depended on to administer the complex fiscal and agricultural infrastructure. Local administrative elites remained largely intact.

In Ifriqiya and the Maghrib, Byzantine control was tenuous and limited to the declining and isolated coastal cities where rival factions struggled for control, some taking the Arab invaders as allies. The interior was home to pagan, Jewish-, or Christian-identifying tribes. One group from the Zanata nation identified as Jewish and was led by a female "sorceress" named Dihya. These Berbers (barbarians)—a term applied by Arabs to all of the non-Romanized indigenous North Africans—offered spirited resistance to the invaders, who took half a century to conquer the region, a process made possible only by the progressive incorporation of vanquished tribes into the Islamic faith and Arab army. Even after they converted, however, Berbers continued to be subject to abuse and ethnic discrimination, including arbitrary enslavement. Here, in Ifriqiya and the Maghrib, little by way of urban elites or infrastructure survived, and Christianity, once very robust, quickly declined.

In 711, Muslim forces, now consisting overwhelmingly of converted Berbers under the leadership of Tariq ibn Ziyad (likely a freed Berber slave, and the namesake of Gibraltar: Jabal Tariq or "Mount Tariq"), crossed to Spain. According to tradition, he was aided by "Count Julian," perhaps a disgruntled Byzantine governor of Ceuta, and by Spanish Jews resentful of Visigothic repression. At the Battle of Guadalete King Roderic's (710–711) forces were annihilated, thanks in part to the collusion of supporters of the previous king, Witiza, who had been pushed from power. Most of the Iberian Peninsula fell rapidly, as surviving Visigothic warlords and residual members of the Ibero-Romano elite, such as the Banu Qasi ("the clan of Cassius") at Zaragoza, became Arab clients and eventually converted to Islam. These converts were indispensable to establishing Muslim rule here, but were pushed out of power in the 850s by a new ethnic Arab elite. Those bishops who did not flee the invasion also helped smooth the transition to Islamic rule. As across the Islamic Mediterranean, the church provided administrative infrastructure crucial to the success of Arab dominion.

Despite the ideal of a single *umma*, the Arab Muslims did not constitute a united "people." Pre-Islamic clan rivalries continued, framed as a struggle between Qaysi (northern Arabian) and Yamani (southern) tribes. The conservative Meccan elite, represented by the Syrian-based Umayyad clan, were strongly drawn to Byzantine models of rule. They seized the caliphate in 661, but were resented by the earlier converts and less-powerful Arabs, who had favored the failed bid of 'Ali to succeed the Prophet as the first caliph. Although overthrown by the Umayyads, 'Ali had developed a strong power base in southern Mesopotamia that remained fiercely loyal to his descendants. And while the Arab tribal divisions that had characterized identity in the early Muslim world faded, ethnic tensions remained, both between Arabs and non-

Arab Berbers, Persians, and Turkic peoples, and between urbanized communities and nomads.

All of this set the stage for the split between Sunni "traditionalists" and the Shi'i, or members of the "Party of 'Ali," precipitating the 'Abbasid revolution of 750. The causes of the revolt were several. Syria was the center of Umayyad political power, which caused resentment in southern Iran and Iraq, now the most populous, dynamic, and wealthy region of the Dar al-Islam. Pious Muslims were scandalized by Umayyad worldliness and by their attraction to Roman/Byzantine culture; they criticized the clan for aspiring to be "kings." Some believed that authority over the community should rest with the descendants of Muhammad—this was the origin of Shi'ism. At the same time, the large numbers of Sunni converts in Khorasan (northern Persia), who had come to comprise the bulk of the army, resented Arab domination. The various discontents banded together to violently overthrow the Umayyads and place al-Saffah (750–754), a descendant of Muhammad's uncle al-'Abbas (a closer blood-relative than the Umayyads), on the throne. The Umayyad family was hunted down and massacred—only one prince, the son of a Berber slave-woman, 'Abd al-Rahman, managed to escape, and eventually took power in al-Andalus. Under the 'Abbasids, the epicenter of the Islamic world shifted east, setting the stage for an incredible political and cultural florescence.

MAP 1.2 The Mediterranean, ca. 800.

After the revolution the Sunni 'Abbasids repressed Shi'ism, which splintered and went underground. Influenced by Persian traditions, it became increasingly esoteric and millenarian in spirit, elevating the figure of 'Ali to that of near equal of Muhammad, and attributing supreme religious authority to an Imam (prayer leader) descended from him through his daughter Fatima (d. 632), a wife of 'Ali. For their part, the perennially ungovernable Arab nomads who were attracted to nonconformist creeds, such as Kharijism and Qarmatianism, violently rejected all caliphal authority. The Qarmatians—a radical Shi'i sect—would establish a sort of utopian republic in Bahrain, sustained by slave labor and raiding 'Abbasid lands. Such was their disdain for the establishment that in 930 they sacked Mecca and Medina, massacring pilgrims and carrying off the Black Stone of the Ka'aba, which they held hostage for about twenty years.

Détente and Diplomacy

Unlike the Mediterranean lands that the Arabs had conquered and would transform into dynamic commercial

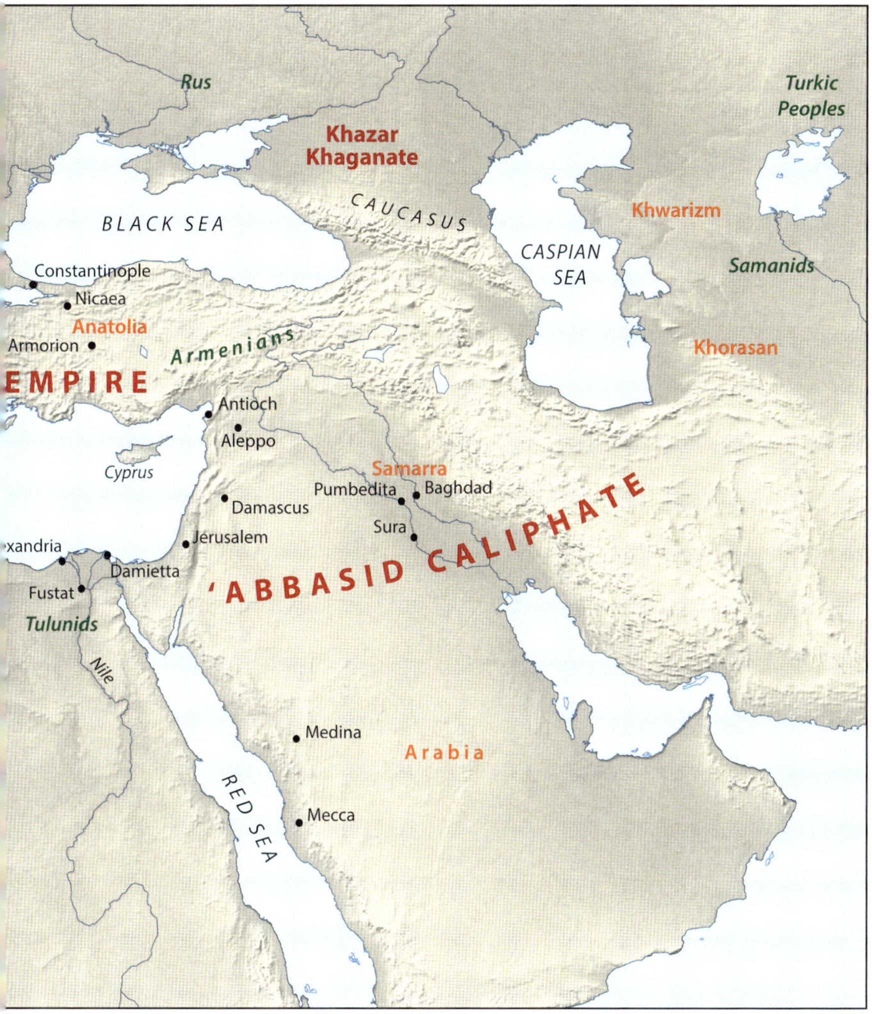

ern Italy in 961, taking the title Emperor of the Romans a year later. He clashed with the Umayyads of Córdoba over the issue of Muslim raiders in Provence, but to no effect. His successor, Otto II (973–983), continued to push south in Italy to the increasing dismay of the Byzantines, until he was stopped in 982 by Muslim forces from Sicily. His death a year later and ensuing succession problems unraveled the Ottonian project in Italy and southern Europe by the beginning of the eleventh century, leaving little imprint in the Mediterranean. The empire survived north of the Alps as a patchwork of autonomous principalities ruled over by a clutch of interrelated magnate families who controlled the imperial succession to their own ends. In 1027 the imperial title would pass to the Salian dynasty of southern Germany, and by the late 1100s their efforts to flex imperial power and intervene in Italy would bring them into collision with a papacy engaged in its own process of institutional consolidation and political expansion.

Thus, by the second half of the tenth century, it seemed a new status quo had been established in the Mediterranean, with the major players being the (Sunni) Umayyad Caliphate of Córdoba, the (Shi'i) Fatimid Caliphate of Egypt, the (Sunni) 'Abbasid Caliphate of Baghdad, the Roman (Byzantine) Empire, and the papally supported Germanic Roman Empire in the northwest. Within the fissures between these great powers a dizzying number of semi-independent polities and peoples coalesced, exploiting the political and economic opportunities borne of their political rivalries and commercial connections. In Ifriqiya and Sicily the Berber Zirids and Arab Kalbids came to power. Southern Anatolia and Syria were ruled by Armenian and Arab princes. Italy was contested by the trading republics of Pisa, Amalfi, Venice, and Genoa, and the Papal States and Lombard counties. A string of petty Latinate principalities—Asturias/

societies, Latin Christendom—with the exception of some Italian port towns—remained economically underdeveloped, and barely urbanized, populated overwhelmingly by a poor and disenfranchised peasantry. In the 900s, in the northwest of Europe, the feeble kings of France struggled to exert authority over what had been Charlemagne's western domains, while two regional new powers were emerging in the tenth century: the Normans, converted Vikings who had settled in northern France, and the Burgundians, a military clique and the vanguard of monastic reform, through the Order of Cluny.

Germanic Europe was briefly unified under the Saxon king Otto I (936–973), who went on to conquer north-

León, Pamplona/Navarre, and the Catalan, Occitan, and Provençal counties—stretched from the Atlantic to the Alps across the north of Spain and the shore of the Mediterranean.

The great empires were in principle mutually hostile but were not in a position to take decisive military action against each other. Consequently, the exercise of diplomacy and "soft power"—coercion and indirect influence—characterized their relations. The Christian-Muslim divide notwithstanding, there was an atmosphere of congenial pragmatism, and the most intractable struggles were between polities of the same religious orientation, who thus presented the greatest challenge to each other's legitimacy. Hence, Byzantium and Córdoba tended to align against the Franks, who themselves courted Byzantium's enemy, the 'Abbasids. As enemies of Baghdad, the Fatimids sought out the Byzantines, although when the Bulghars appeared ascendant, the Fatimids courted them to undermine Byzantium. Alliances (at times only on paper) often crossed confessional lines, and diplomacy (together with trade) linked the various corners of the Mediterranean world, integrating imperial powers with the smaller heterodox principalities along their perimeters. In this era Islam, which in principle did not admit the legitimacy of non-Muslims regimes, normalized the establishment of peaceable relations with infidels through the legal concept of Dar al-'Ahd (the zone of legitimate truce), or by characterizing their non-Muslims allies as tributaries rather than equals.

MAP 1.3 The Mediterranean, ca. 1000.

Insurgents and rebels were regularly welcomed in imperial courts—whether Andalusis in Frankish lands or Armenians in Egypt. The practice of demanding political hostages from one's clients—often a child of the ruler—further narrowed the gap between distinct empires and cultures. Children raised in luxury at foreign courts could come to identify more closely with their hosts than with their own. Political marriage was used as a diplomatic tool between kings of different faiths, doctrinal restrictions against interfaith unions notwithstanding. For example, the petty princes of Christian Spain sent their daughters to marry into the aristocratic courts of al-Andalus; hence, the kings of Pamplona were not only politically dependent on the Umayyads of Córdoba, but were their kin. In general, petty dynasties on the imperial fringes formed alliances and intermarried with their counterparts with little regard to religious orientation. SEE SOURCEBOOK 1:4.

Diplomatic exchanges also helped establish cultural ties, some long-lasting, others ephemeral. The 'Abbasid

caliph Harun al-Rashid (768–809) famously sent gifts (including an elephant and a clock!) to Charlemagne after the Frankish king had sent envoys in 798 to negotiate an alliance. In the 920s the Bulghars' alliance with the Fatimids against Byzantium was stymied only by Constantinople's payment of a large bribe to Cairo. In happier times, the Fatimids and Byzantium shared authority over the patriarch of Jerusalem, and pledged mutual relief in time of famine. In the 930s Constantine VII (913–959) sent gifts to 'Abd al-Rahman III of Córdoba, including 140 columns for the caliph's new palace, and a copy of Dioscorides's medical treatise, followed by a Greek monk to translate it. Such episodes were part of a continual to-and-fro among the empires and lesser principalities clustered around the Mediterranean. SEE SOURCEBOOK 1:5.

Clergy were often chosen as ambassadors. The Byzantine missionary Saint Cyril (namesake of the Cyrillic alphabet) was sent to the Bulghars, to Baghdad, and to the Jewish Khazars of the Caucasus in the 800s. Such missions may have had a religious dimension, but conversion was not necessarily their aim. For envoys, diplomacy could be a path to clerical advancement. Reccemund (or Rabi' ibn Ziyad), an Andalusi Christian courtier, was made a bishop by 'Abd al-Rahman III after his mission to Otto I's capital at Aachen in the 950s. Otto sent the monk John of Gorze to al-Andalus, where he made contact with Mozarabs (Arabized native Christians, from *must'arib*, "would-be Arabs"). Members of religious minorities—especially Islamicate Jews—were often employed as envoys, on account of either their linguistic abilities or their "neutral" status. The Andalusi *nasi* (prince), Hasdai ibn Shaprut—physician, rabbi, and caliphal customs official—not only served as a diplomat for Córdoba to the Christian Spains, but having positioned himself as a patron and protector of Jews across the Islamic and Byzantine Mediterranean dispatched his own envoy to Constantinople, hoping to make contact with the Jewish Khazar khanate to the east.

For their part, merchants often accomplished what force of arms could not, thanks to the allure of sophistication and civilization they bore with them. Traders pushed the imperial influence far beyond the borders of Byzantium and the caliphates, awakening a taste for the luxuries and wealth of the Mediterranean world in the "barbarian" peoples of distant continental hinterlands. In Europe, first Norsemen and Slavs, and eventually Normans and Burgundians, in Central Asia, Turkic horsemen, and in Africa, Berber tribes of the Atlas Mountains and of the southern edges of the Sahara would

FIGURE 1.3 The Bulgarian khan Simeon exchanges envoys with the Fatimid caliph, from a twelfth-century Sicilian manuscript of the *Synopsis of Histories* by John Skylitzes (d. 1101). Photo provided by Hispanic Digital Library, Biblioteca Nacional de España, CC-BY-4.0 International License.

all be gradually transformed from barbarian traders, raiders, and swords-for-hire into converts, clients, . . . and conquerors.

Faith and Power

Two countervailing forces bound the various Christian and Islamic kingdoms and empires that ringed the Mediterranean in the first four centuries of Islam. The Romano-Persian imperial model, with its claims to universal authority and divine sanction, was undermined by practical demands of ruling the region. The Mediterranean was an aggregate of ethnically and religiously diverse societies characterized by sophisticated commercial and agricultural economies, which no ruler could realistically aspire to control completely. Both Byzantium and the 'Abbasid Caliphate claimed unique authority over their respective confessional communities, but this did not reflect reality. By the tenth century such claims would be formally contested—in Christendom by the papacy and the Holy Roman Empire and in the Dar al-Islam by the rival Fatimid and Umayyad Caliphates. Not only did each Mediterranean empire rule over communities of nonbelievers, each congregation of believers had members scattered across various empires.

Religious Authority

The model for Christian religious organization was the secular administration of the Roman Empire—a single hierarchy of provinces (archbishoprics) and municipalities (dioceses) under the authority of the emperor. Doctrine was formulated by the upper clergy and transmitted from the top down to the faithful. The senior clergy included the patriarchs—the bishops of the most prestigious sees (Alexandria, Antioch, Jerusalem, and Constantinople)—together with the pope (the bishop of Rome) and the abbots of the most influential monasteries. Byzantium was a theocracy and as high priest, an emperor could, in principle, command the faithful what to believe and how to worship, and the maintenance of religious orthodoxy was seen as a foundation of imperial legitimacy.

The Byzantine Church had virtually no independent political power, and little role in a well-developed administrative apparatus staffed by educated laymen, and bishops and patriarchs could be in principle appointed and deposed by imperial order. The two ecumenical councils held between the eighth and twelfth centuries, Nicaea II (787) and Constantinople IV (869–870), were vehicles of imperial policy—Irene's restoration of icon worship and Basil I's removal of the powerful patriarch Photios, respectively. That said, when an emperor was weak or determined to fight the currents of popular piety the political cost could be considerable, as religious disagreements could mobilize would-be rebels among the military elite and played into the hands of a papacy seeking to challenge the emperors' religious authority.

Papal authority was also limited. From 537 to 753 the papacy was under Byzantine control. Martin I (649–655), a pope who defied imperial authority, was deposed and arrested on charges of aiding the Muslims in North Africa. After the 750s the papacy began to break away, and in 800 recognized Charlemagne as emperor while making its own claim for sovereignty over the kings in the former western empire. This was based on the popes' claim to be Christ's representative on Earth (as the successor of the Apostle Peter, the first bishop of Rome), the prestige of Paul's martyrdom, and on the "Donation of Constantine," a forged decree purportedly granted by the first Christian emperor in the 310s. In reality, even the papacy's religious authority was yet to be clearly delineated. The wider church was almost entirely under the control of the monarchs and the upper nobility, who treated monasteries and bishoprics as private patrimony; and despite the papacy's pretensions, until the eleventh century it was largely a local institution of limited power, controlled by powerful Roman families. That said, leading clergy and lay rulers did look to the popes to resolve disputes, ratify religious policy, and legitimize their titles.

The Latin and Greek Churches remained in principle a united communion, but the Greek East and Latin West had grown apart religiously, culturally, and politically. In 1054 this breach would be formalized with the schism and mutual repudiation of the two churches sparked ostensibly by a dispute over the wording of the Nicene Creed. This split coincided with the growing military capacity of the Latin West. Within decades the Byzantines had been pushed out of Italy and Norman forces

Prior to the mid-eleventh century the Mediterranean was a region of empires, each claiming but not exercising universal authority, each modeling its authority on the precedent of Rome, and each anchoring its legitimacy in religious claims. Imperial claims were reinforced in literature, laws, court ceremony, architecture and through the construction and dissemination of imagery. In these examples, taken from the Byzantine Empire of the Macedonian dynasty, the "Roman" Empire of the German Ottonians, and the early caliphate of the Arab Umayyad

FIGURE 1.4 The emperor in the Psalter of Basil II, Constantinople, ca. 1000 (enhanced image). FLHC 11 / Alamy Stock Photo.

FIGURE 1.5 The emperor in the Gospels of Otto III, Reichenau, ca. 1000. The History Collection / Alamy Stock Photo.

dynasty, images of the ruler reflect the priorities of each imperium and its competition for and engagement with the legacy of Rome.

The Psalter of Basil II

Basil II, the "Bulghar-Slayer," reigned for nearly half a century over the Byzantine Empire, subduing his rebellious subjects and reestablishing the empire as the major power in the eastern Mediterranean and Anatolia. After a brief war, a ten-year truce was signed with the Fatimids in 1000. Basil was recognized as sovereign of the caliphate's Christian population, and the caliph as the authority over the empire's Muslims. Later, southern Crimea was taken and the Armenian kingdoms were subdued. Basil was most famous for destroying the Bulghar khanate, a campaign in which, according to later legend, he blinded 99 out of every 100 of the 15,000 prisoners he took at the Battle of Kleidion in 1014. Basil's reign represented the height of Byzantine power since the era of Justinian.

This image is from a deluxe liturgical book produced in Constantinople. Basil appears, statue-like and standing on a plinth, in the garb of a Roman general, receiving a lance from Archangel Michael, and a pearl-studded crown from Archangel Gabriel as "protector of the world," with Jesus holding another above his head. His red boots are a symbol of imperial power, and by his side is a sheathed sword. He resembles military saints, six of whom flank him in imitation of the medallions of the four evangelists, Mary, and John the Baptist that sometimes are presented with Jesus. A poem below describes the scene and notes, "The martyrs are his allies for he is their friend. They cast down those lying at his feet." The figures below are likely not conquered Bulghars, but Basil's various subjects performing the prostration of formal submission (*proskynesis*) to the emperor. It is followed by a folio with scenes from the life of King David, providing a further royal and biblical association.

The Gospels of Otto III

Otto III (996–1002) inherited the Kingdom of Germany at age three in 983, and was under the tutelage of regents (including his mother, Theophanu, and grandmother, the dowager-empress, Adelaide of Italy) until he came of age in 994. In 996 he claimed his father's titles of King of Italy and Roman Emperor, and would spend his short reign trying to subdue Rome. He suffered Viking attacks, and the Slavic territories east of the Elbe were lost, but Otto saw the conversion of the Hungarians to Latin Chris-

FIGURE 1.6 'Abd al-Malik (685–705) on the "Standing Caliph" *solidus*, Damascus, 694–695 CE. ©Historical Views / agefotostock.

tianity under King (Saint) Stephen in 1000. Otto III saw himself as a successor to Charlemagne and Constantine, and sought to reestablish the lost glory of Rome. He made Rome the capital of his empire, cultivated ancient and Byzantine influences, and aspired to establish a theocratic state under his authority. His motto was For the Restablishment of the Roman Empire. In reality, he was hated by his Italian subjects, and unable to overcome the political instability that characterized his reign; his death, childless at twenty-one, split the empire and plunged it into a succession crisis.

The Gospels of Otto III contains the four Gospels as well as other material. It was produced at the scriptorium of the royal monastery at Reichenau (in the German Alps). The illumination, an imitation of an earlier representation of Otto II, shows the emperor being brought offerings by the four provinces—from left to right, the Slavic Lands, Germany, Gaul, and Rome—personified as submissive queens. Otto is flanked by barons and clerics. He is presented as static, imperious, and impassive, like the ancient statues of seated emperors this portrait was modeled on, his direct yet unfocused gaze recalling contemporary depictions of Christ as Pantocrator (Lord of All). He wears the imperial crown (held today at the Imperial Treasury at the Hofburg Palace in Vienna), and holds a scepter topped with a bird (recalling both the imperial eagle and the dove of the Holy Spirit) and the crossed orb, a symbol of universal dominion that went back to the early Roman Empire.

The "Standing Caliph" *Solidus*

'Abd al-Malik ibn Marwan, the fifth Umayyad caliph (685–705), came to the throne at the age of about forty, facing Byzantine aggression, rebellions, and a rival claimant to the caliphate. In 689 he signed a truce with Justinian II (685–695 and 705–711) of Byzantium, but war broke out in 692 when the caliph began sending tribute in the form of gold coins he had minted (a violation of the Byzantine prerogative). 'Abd al-Malik made significant military advances in the West, defeating the Byzantines at Carthage in 679, and he subdued Syria, the Arabian Peninsula, and Iraq. In addition to issuing gold coinage, he oversaw a precise reedition of the Qur'an, and built the Dome of the Rock in Jerusalem. His reign laid the groundwork for the on-going success of the Umayyad dynasty.

This 4.5 gram gold *solidus* (a Roman coin measure) reflects this imperial turn. The face features a full-length, personalized portrait of 'Abd al-Malik. One can distinguish his single eyebrow, large nose, and cleft lip. The "buggy" eyes are typical of contemporary portraits, representing kohl eyeliner. Dental problems left the caliph with breath so bad he was known as "the fly-killer." With his long hair, parted Arab-style, falling over his shoulders, dressed in royal brocaded robes, a whip hanging over his right shoulder, and hand ready on a sheathed sword, he strikes a confident, threatening stance, reflecting his recent military successes over Byzantium. The portrait may have been modeled on a previous coin of the Byzantine emperor, and resembles a contemporary caliphal statue found at a palace in Jericho. (Coins modeled on Sasanid designs and featuring the caliph as Persian emperor were minted in Iraq.) A modified Muslim profession of faith, "There is no god but God—He has no associate—Muhammad is the Prophet of God," surrounds the figure. The reverse inscription reads, "In the name of God, this *dinar* was struck in the year 76."* The object on the steps is a modification of a Byzantine coin motif that features a crucifix. Eliminating the crossbar removed the Christian connotation while maintaining the coin's familiar appearance, which would have inspired confidence in 'Abd al-Malik's subjects in Syria and Palestine. The image may be a spear, or a column—an allusion to the caliph as "the pillar of Islam." Similar coins were issued in silver and copper. In 705 this coin design was abandoned in favor of one that had no pictorial elements, but simply Arabic inscriptions. However, this was not a consequence of pious Islamic rejection of imagery; rather, it arose out of the failure to find a symbolic vocabulary that resonated with both the Roman and the Persian peoples of the caliphate. Thus, the newly designed Arabic coins served to help reinforce the emerging Arabo-Islamic culture and reinforce the unity of the Dar al-Islam.

*Dinar is the Arabic term for denarius, the Roman silver "penny."

Discussion Questions

1. How do the three images each engage with the legacy of Rome, and to what extent do they reflect the particular circumstances of the rulers?
2. How does religion figure in each of these objects?
3. What do the common symbols and elements tell us about the exercise of power in the Mediterranean at this time?

Further Reading

Foss, Clive. "Arab-Byzantine Coins: Money as Cultural Continuity." In *Byzantium and Islam: Age of Transition*, ed. Helen Evans and Brandie Ratliff, 136–43. New York: Metropolitan Museum of Art, 2012.

Garrison, Eliza. *Ottonian Imperial Art and Portraiture: The Artistic Patronage of Otto III and Henry II*. Farnham: Ashgate, 2012. Pp. 6–72.

Spatharakis, Iohannis. *The Portrait in Byzantine Illuminated Manuscripts*. Leiden: Brill, 1976. Pp. 20–26.

Stephenson, Paul. "Images of the Bulgar-Slayer: Three Art Historical Notes." *Byzantine and Modern Greek Studies* 25 (2001): 44–68.

Treadwell, Luke. "Abd al-Malik's Coinage Reforms: The Role of the Damascus Mint." *Revue numismatique*, 6th series, 165 (2009): 357–81.

were attacking Greece with the aim of conquering the empire.

Outside the Byzantine Empire, the heterodox (or heretical) Coptic and Syriac Orthodox Church and the Church of the East were thriving under Islamic rule, each headed by its own patriarch, who oversaw an independent hierarchy of bishops. Likewise, the Georgian and Armenian Churches maintained their independence, as did the Bulgarian Slavic Church, even after the victories of Basil II.

In the Islamic world, the caliphs, as the successors of the Prophet Muhammad, could claim universal religious authority, although from the time of the Umayyads, they rarely interfered in doctrine. With Islam's emphasis on equality and individual responsibility, religious authority and law were grounded not in the dictates of a caliph or clergy, but in the consciences of the members of the community of believers as expressed by the loose collective of pious learned Muslims known as the *'ulama'* (from *'ilm*, "learning"). There was no formal hierarchical "clergy" in Sunni Islam, and thus it did not lend itself to the imposition of doctrine or the establishment of rigid orthodoxies. Members of the *'ulama'* (like rabbis in Judaism) were regarded by believers as being pious, erudite, and judicious. Some were appointed as official magistrates, but the authority of each *'alim* rested in his reputation among the people (not unlike pastors in modern Evangelical denominations). Because the test of faith was simply the recognition of God as unique and Muhammad as His Messenger, Muslims had wide latitude in formulating specific beliefs. Thus, the emergence of distinct Sunni, Shi'i, and Kharijite Islams was not seen as an existential threat.

The religious authority of Muslim rulers was largely limited to the appointment of religious officials, such as *qadis* (judges), whose general views reflected their own. Rulers who dictated doctrine might be branded as illegitimate by the *'ulama'*. In the 880s, the 'Abbasid caliph al-Ma'mun (831–833), for example, faced revolt after imposing his own rationalist Mu'tazilite theology on his subjects. An exception was the Fatimid regime, in which the Caliph and Imam coincided in the same divinely sanctioned individual. These caliphs did promulgate doctrine and did maintain a sort of clerical hierarchy, but their religious authority applied only to those Isma'ili Shi'i who followed them—a small minority—and not to the rest of their Sunni Muslim subjects.

Because Islam provided a legitimate place for religious minorities, caliphs also appointed or controlled the heads of these communities under their rule. Christian bishops and patriarchs and the Jewish exilarch in Baghdad functioned as influential civil servants and political administrators in these Islamic regimes, subordinate to but not quite controlled by the caliph. But these minority communities were also diverse. Judaism was characterized by rival sects, with the dominant Rabbanites set against Karaites and Samaritans. Similarly, the mutually hostile Christian churches jockeyed against each other for influence and prestige before the caliphs.

Imperial Courts

The conceptual distinction we so readily make today between church and state was not a generally a feature of Mediterranean societies, although it can be traced to developments in Latin Christendom toward the end of this period. In Byzantium, the emperor, or *basileus,* was an autocrat, and law was an imperial prerogative, tempered by custom, but only marginally influenced by the church. Justinian's sixth-century *Code of Civil Law* provided a framework that was augmented by subsequent imperial digests and decrees, including the *Ecloga* of Leo III (717–741), which entrenched the notion of equal citizenship and public law. Under Basil I and Leo IV (866–912), Justinian's code was further updated and translated into Greek as the *Basilika* (Royal Law), reflecting an acknowledgment of the disappearance of the old Roman imperial administrative structure, and that the culture and language of the empire had become Greek.

The sacred person and the court of the emperor were the center of both patronage and prestige. However, the succession itself was not strictly hereditary. Once a dynasty was established (typically through a military coup), successors were drawn from among the imperial family, based on prestige, merit, and the preferences of palace factions. Heirs were sometimes crowned when still infants in order to ensure continuity. This flexibility enabled stronger candidates to come to the fore, but engendered a dynamic in which co-emperors and regents (male or female), generals, and courtly cliques could undermine the integrity of the institution and the stability of the empire.

Empresses, who sometimes ruled as regents or co-emperors, exercised functionally independent power at court, and had their own networks of patronage. For example, Empress Irene, the wife of Leo IV (775–780), served as regent and co-regent of her son Constantine VI (780–797), ultimately blinding and deposing him when he tried to push her from power, and taking sole control until her death in 802. Later, Zoë (1028–1050), the daughter of Constantine VIII (1025–1028), came to power at age fifty and disposed of her first husband, Romanos III (1038–1034), in order to marry her lover, Michael IV (1041–1042). When Michael's nephew came to power as Michael V (1041–1042), he exiled Zoë, but she was brought back by public acclaim to co-rule with her sister, Theodora III (1042–1056), after which she installed as co-ruler a new lover, Constantine IX (1042–1055), under whom the empire spiraled into chaos and decline.

The imperial administration was divided into ministries, organized into bureaus, and staffed by professional lay administrators, among whom eunuchs (typically castrated as boys by their families in the name of career advancement) came to play an ever-more prominent role as both military commanders and household administrators. Leading military families and provincial rulers (frequently the same) endeavored to marry into or otherwise infiltrate the palace, and from the tenth century official and honorary court positions were granted increasingly to foreign warriors, which caused tensions with the native nobility. Emperors and empresses were successful at reining in the independent ambitions of court functionaries and imperial officials by ensuring rank and office depended on their goodwill. Interruptions in succession or the existence of rival claimants for the throne provided the opportunities for leading families to seize the throne and supplant the ruling dynasty. At bottom, imperial power rested to no small extent on the wealth of the empire, and the court's capacity to generate and distribute high volumes of tax revenue in the form of hard cash. That power would endure only as long as the good times did. SEE SOURCEBOOK 1:6.

Ideally, civil authority was separate from military power in the provinces. In the seventh century, as a response to Arab and pagan aggression, the emperors reorganized the provinces into military districts (*themes*), appointing generals as civil governors and cultivating a broadly participatory military culture in which a reserve of landowning commoners became a significant element. With the domination of the Balkans and Anatolia in the tenth century, the *theme* system was expanded, and Armenian families flooded the court and upper administration, many converting from Armenian to Byzantine Orthodoxy and adapting to Greek culture, at least superficially. At the same time tax concessions (*pronoia*) were granted to aristocrats in exchange for providing soldiers—a process that has been characterized as similar to feudalization. Thus, the wealth and power of the provincial military elite expanded and became hereditary, undermining the free status of the peasantry, who drifted into dependence, losing ownership of their lands and military privileges.

Under Basil II in the early 1000s, Byzantium appeared at its height—a centralized empire under the rule of a soldier-*basileus;* but in reality, it was becoming an aggregate of semiautonomous provinces defended by a narrowing military class, and peopled and ruled by an array of nations, including Armenians, Arabs, Bulgarians, Italians, and Slavs, whose elites adapted the official Greek culture and Orthodox religion of the empire, but whose folk remained religiously and ethnically distinct. After Basil died childless in 1025, the crown passed to his elderly brother, Constantine VIII, who proved unable to control the palace, which plunged into destabilizing intrigue under Zoë and her successors.

The caliphs of Islam could not aspire to be autocrats. For the most part, the articulation of law—like the elaboration of doctrine—lay in the hands of the *'ulama',* who by the ninth century had developed four distinct schools of legal interpretation, all of which were considered valid by Sunnis across the Islamic world. At the same time, political power (*sultan*) came to depend almost entirely on military capacity, which was increasingly to be controlled by ambitious palace functionaries and rebellious provincial governors and military commanders, who withheld revenues, founded local dynasties, and acted as de facto kings, thus undermining the real power of the caliphs.

The palace culture and administration of each of the three caliphates were highly organized, based on the institutions of Sasanid Persia, which were adapted first by the 'Abbasids, and spread to Fatimid Egypt and Umayyad Córdoba. A thriving commercial economy and access to abundant gold and silver provided the basis for a culture of patronage that sustained the power of the monarchs. Polygamy, together with the latitude permitted in choosing heirs under Islamic law, provided for a larger pool of successors, but also spurred competition among family factions, not infrequently led by powerful and financially independent royal wives. A greater threat were palace cliques, whether led by eunuchs, generals, or local clans, who took over key positions, such as *wazir* (prime minister) or *hajib* (chamberlain), and worked to marginalize the caliphs in all but name. In a complex, cash-driven economy, administrative and fiscal officials wielded great power. Hence, a preference for employing members of out-groups in these positions—whether *dhimmis*, foreigners, or heterodox Muslims—members of communities who could not overtly challenge the legitimacy of the sovereign, and who were to some extent dependent on and vulnerable to his whims.

By 800 Arabic was the official, sacred, and main spoken and literary language of the Islamic Mediterranean; local tongues (Greek, Syriac, Coptic, Persian, and Latin) had survived in the administration during a century of transition, but now persisted generally only as liturgical languages and minority vernaculars. Islam was making significant inroads in the conversion of native peoples, and these converts began to claim their place among the *umma* and in doing so transformed Islamic society and culture. In the 'Abbasid lands the literary movement called *shu'ubiyya* reclaimed the prestige of Persian culture, criticizing Arabs as barbaric. Traditional Arabic tribal identity no longer drove politics, and the economic and political prestige that lineage had previously carried was reduced to an imprecise status—a dynamic that also reinforced the caliphs' position as direct rulers over all their subjects, whether Muslim or *dhimmis*. As in Byzantium, a comparatively literate and legally free populace provided the pool for the secretaries and bureaucrats who staffed the ministries, offering a means of integration for non-Arabs and non-Muslims in the structure of power, stimulating social mobility, and reinforcing the open and meritocratic character of the government.

Through the 900s a Persian-style kingship attracted both Byzantium and the Islamic caliphates and was characterized by the increasing isolation and veneration of the ruler, who came to be presented as a distant, otherworldly figure, ensconced in a palace-city surrounded by eunuchs, slaves, and functionaries, and accessible only through official intermediaries. Constantinople was home to the massive Sacred Palace of the emperors, while the foundation of self-contained palace-cities, including 'Abbasid Samarra (836), Umayyad Madinat al-Zahara (936), and Fatimid al-Qahira (Cairo, 973) reflect this trend in the Islamic world. This development increased royal prestige but sowed the seeds for decline, as it isolated monarchs and emboldened the palace and military elites, who increasingly wielded true power. When factions within these domestic elites clashed, the result was the civil wars that brought down the Umayyad and Fatimid Caliphates and crippled the 'Abbasids and Byzantium.

Christianity on the Edge

The Latin Mediterranean was an exception to these trends. Neither the Frankish nor German "Roman Emperor" nor the papacy had the power to impose their authority unilaterally on a politically divided Western Christendom. As the nobility preferred to see it and in accordance with barbarian tradition, kings were merely war leaders—"firsts among equals"—and they sought to undermine royal power. But hereditary, sacralized kingship was promoted by the monarchy and church as a counter to instability. However, even on an abstract level, Latin Christendom was not unified, and not all European kings acknowledged the Frankish or Germanic "Roman Emperor" as their sovereign.

Out of necessity, the church and secular rulers gradually developed a codependent relationship in which the emperors (and kings) came to all but monopolize military force and secular power, which they used at times to support and protect the church. For its part the church provided a literate institutional framework and vouchsafed the religious (and therefore, political) legitimacy of the rulers. It provided court chaplains, medics, and chroniclers; the upper clergy served as lords, contributing taxes and leading troops in war; and the papacy served as a mediator in disputes among kings and as a moral and religious guarantor of royal policy. Clergy constituted Europe's primitive financial administration, and, together with the upper nobility and the royal bodyguard, clerics constituted the bare-bones royal courts of the time (the *familia* or "household").

But the church and the nobility were not two clearly delineated camps—the upper clergy were almost without exception members of the upper nobility, and many wore the helmet of a lord as well as the miter of a bishop or abbot. Important abbots and bishops were typically the children of powerful noblemen and, as landholders, were also secular lords and even war leaders. Their loyalties often lay with their families rather than the church, and many had little vocation and were personally corrupt. The only thing that kept church land from being reabsorbed by the aristocracy was the requirement of clerical celibacy. While it was often ignored in practice, it meant powerful churchmen could not legally pass the titles and properties of the church down to their children or create clerical dynasties. This was one of the reasons kings granted lands to abbots and bishops; it could be seen as an act of charity and piety, but it also prevented land from getting in the hands of noble families who might challenge a king's authority. Thus, neither popes nor kings could make a claim to singular authority. In this near-subsistence economy, the lack of cash meant that kingship was, by necessity, itinerant, because tribute had to be consumed in kind. Peasants paid taxes in the form of food, and kings and nobles moved around to consume it. Wealth was difficult to accumulate and harder to transport. The economy here was simply too underdeveloped and close to subsistence to support an autocratic or bureaucratic regime or a working system of codified public law.

From the fifth to seventh century the Germanic barbarian nations—the Franks, Visigoths, Burgundians, and Lombards—who took over the crumbling western empire, each promulgated law codes that combined their particular customary practices with Roman law, following the principle that rights were apportioned according to the ethnic identity of the individual. Of these, the Salic Law of the western Franks would prove the most influential, as it was imposed or adopted by neighboring groups to the east and formed the core of the Carolingian legal system, which sought to impose a standard law within the empire governing such matters as criminal offenses, civil disputes, and inheritances. Alongside this, the church enacted laws relating to matters of faith and morality based on the decrees of ecumenical councils, supplemented haphazardly by promulgations of local synods of bishops and papal decrees. Church law provided the only region-wide legal framework but was vague and difficult to enforce in this period.

In any case, there was little by way of a functioning public or state administrative structure, given that Roman institutions, urban culture, and commerce had all but disappeared. Charlemagne countered this by empowering the church and upper clergy as agents of his empire and instituted the office of the *missus dominicus.* These royally appointed roving "lordly envoys"—typically teams of one cleric and one lay courtier—were dispatched across the realm to administer justice to even the lowest of subjects and to brake the abuses of local potentates. With the decline of this office under Charlemagne's successors, authority once more became personal, and members of the clans who made up the professional warrior elite were confirmed as local rulers, dukes, and counts, in exchange for providing military service. This elite lived off an un- or semi-free agricultural workforce, which constituted the foundation of the elite's prosperity.

This was a world of lords and peasants, and the power and title of a nobleman depended on how much land he controlled and whom he owed loyalty to and received protection from. In the time of the late Roman Empire the rural Latin West had been populated by slaves and free farmers. As Roman institutions declined and the empire became less secure, free citizens commended themselves to powerful rural landholders (*domini,* "lords") as sharecropping *coloni* in exchange for protection, suffering a gradual loss of rights. Meanwhile, rural slavery declined, both because the great Roman estates (*latifundia*) maintained by enslaved workers had largely disappeared, and because purchasing, supporting, and controlling slaves was expensive and difficult. In seventh- and eighth-century Italy and Spain, royal laws were promulgated in response to the problem of runaways. Consequently, lords preferred to divide their estates into individual plots, granting some to free peasant families and others to slaves. Slaves who cleared new land were sometimes rewarded with manumission, and the children of slaves who married free women were free, but such freedom often carried labor obligations to the former owners. In any event, temporary and permanent judicial and debt slavery continued in the Latin West, and a substantial slave population remained in Europe through the tenth century.

Cash had all but ceased to circulate, so peasants of whatever status, now increasingly referred to as serfs (from *servus,* "slave" or "servant"), usually owed a share of their produce as rent and were often obliged to perform certain labor services for the lord. As violence and insecurity increased in the countryside in the tenth century, some lords began to take advantage of the peasants' need for land and protection—from predatory local knights or foreign raiders—by tying them perpetually to the land through legal arrangements and imposing greater taxes and labor obligations on them. As royal power declined in the 900s a wave of encastellation, in which local lords constructed castles and forts for their own protection against rival nobles, to better resist the monarchy, and to intimidate their peasantry, began in the north and extended southward into Languedoc and Provence, and eventually Italy and Christian Iberia.

Seignorial or lordly relationships were the bedrock of economic and social life at the local level. Power was patrimonial, based on a family's landholdings. Noble lords, for their part, forged multilayered and crisscrossing bonds of personal loyalty (vassalship) with each other and the knights in their service. Vassals made personal pledges of military service to their lords in exchange for protection and recognition of their authority over their own lands. There was no functioning notion of citizenship or of geographic or national political identity. Politics was shaped, rather, by family identity and personal bonds of loyalty to powerful people in a manner not unlike the relationships between Arab tribesmen and their clients.

Until the 900s, nobles often divided their lands equally among their children, and it was not uncommon for women to hold lordships. However, this practice diluted the wealth of a family by repeatedly subdividing it, leading to political fragmentation, land hunger, and family infighting, and encouraged a culture of predatory petty lords whose security depended on relationships of vassalage and marital alliances with their neighbors. When primogeniture was adopted in northern Europe beginning around 1000, it enabled noblemen there to amass larger patrimonies and greater power. In the following centuries northern Europeans used this advantage to conquer territory in the Christian Mediterranean, particularly Languedoc and Provence.

Italy, the contested frontier zone of the Latin, Byzantine, and Islamic worlds, was somewhat exceptional; here, a relatively dense population helped to sustain urban life and commerce, and the absence of an effective central power meant that individual towns and regions were able to improvise. Some towns, particularly ports that were able to establish trading relationships with the wealthier lands of Islam and Byzantium, managed to shake off seignorial rule and establish themselves as oligarchical republics of notionally free citizens.

Geopolitics and Faith

From the outset Islam was shaped by religious and political struggle initially against the pagans of Arabia. As these latter were subdued or converted, the traditional biannual raiding custom of the Arab nomads was Islamicized and merged with the Qur'anic notion of *jihad* (moral struggle), providing a religious rationalization for political expansion against Byzantium and Persia, and the acquisition of land, slaves, and booty to be shared among the Arab Muslims (with one-fifth going to the Prophet or caliph). By the early 700s the Mediterranean frontiers of the Dar al-Islam were stabilizing, and relations with non-Muslim neighbors normalized. Nevertheless, the ideal of waging military *jihad* against the infidel remained compelling. Al-Mansur, the usurping chamberlain of Umayyad al-Andalus (977–1002), used it to great effect in the late 900s—as a way of providing an outlet for the military, appeasing the *'ulama'*, galvanizing public opinion, reinforcing his own credentials as ruler, and keeping the neighboring Christians down. He personally led some fifty-seven such raids. Indeed, any attacks on non-Muslims, whether in France and Italy in the 800s or the pagan fringes of the Sahara in the 900s, invited being cast as religious struggles, even though any concerted or systematic attempts to conquer the Byzantine and Latin worlds had long been abandoned.

The greatest religio-political struggles in the Islamic world were against fellow Muslim theological and political dissenters, whether heretical rationalist Mu'tazilites, revolutionary Shi'is, insubordinate Kharijites and Qarmatians, or dissident Umayyads or 'Abbasids (as the case may have been). Such conflicts were not only qualified as religious, but were executed with unflinching brutality, quite in contrast to the benign indifference generally shown to the docile *dhimmi* population. In the 900s the three caliphates strenuously advocated *jihad* against each other, but this was carried out largely through proxies.

In the Christian world a similar relationship between geopolitical agendas and religious choice can also be observed as the various pagan groups chose to convert to either Arian, Latin, or Byzantine Christianity. Adopting a particular creed implied subordination to its self-declared authorities, whether emperor or pope. It was because of this that Christian rulers insisted so emphatically on their subjects' orthodoxy—hence, the imperative for foreigners who moved into the court ambit of Constantinople to become Byzantine Orthodox. As Byzantine imperial ideology crystallized in the tenth century members of the dissenting churches (notably the Syriac and Armenian) were the target of discriminatory laws—preventing advancement in the imperial administration, prohibiting marriage with Byzantine Christians, and implementing policies to socially isolate and economically disadvantage them. Ultimately these faiths were proscribed within the empire.

The empire also cultivated a culture of holy war in response to the Arab invasions of the seventh and eighth centuries and as a consequence of the religious element of Byzantine kingship. This was useful for galvanizing subjects not only against the Muslim threat, but against any non-Orthodox enemies, such as the heretical Paulician Armenians—a gnostic Christian sect that attacked Byzantium with the aid of the 'Abbasids in the 800s. Each regiment in the Byzantine army had an official singer, whose role it was to harangue the soldiers, leading the hymns they sang as they marched into battle for God and emperor. Remarkably, this impulse did

FIGURE 1.7 Ivory icon with Saint Demetrios, perhaps used as a standard carried in battle, Byzantium, 950–1000 CE. The Metropolitan Museum of Art, New York, The Cloister Collection, 1970, 1970.324.3, Open Access CCo.

not translate into a determination to reconquer the Holy Land and wrest it from Islam. This would have been well within reach in the tenth century, but the emperors simply had other priorities.

In Latin lands a notion of holy war also developed, rooted in principles outlined in Saint Augustine's (d. 430) concept of "just war." Christian kings who fought against pagan rivals were rewarded with sainthood, and Charlemagne framed his expansion versus the pagan Saxons as a religious war, but as his efforts to dominate Christian lands show, it was territorial expansion that motivated him. Some clerical historians portrayed the Muslim invasion of Spain and France as holy wars—encouraged, no doubt, by the Muslims' propensity to loot churches and monasteries—but for the most part contemporary chroniclers portrayed these as political events and viewed the Arabs as little different from any other group of foreign invaders. It was only in the eleventh century, when the Latin nobility was in a position to expand aggressively into the Islamic world, that Western Christendom developed a coherent doctrine of holy war.

Byzantines, Latins, and Muslims all shared in a providential view of history they inherited from the Hebrew Old Testament. Christians in particular tended to imagine themselves as the "new Israel"—God's chosen people, whether suffering His wrath as a consequence of their failings or striking against His enemies (in which context Muslims became the "Amalekites" or "Edomites" of Old Testament terminology). If the subject Christians of the Islamic world shared such sentiments, however, they were obliged to be more discrete, lest they violate the spirit of their submission to Islam under *dhimma* and risk their lives. The mid-ninth-century "voluntary martyr" movement of Córdoba was a singular episode of religious resistance—one that was apparently not supported by the majority of the martyrs' coreligionists. Most Christians, including most of the church leadership, appeared remarkably content under (or at least resigned to) Islamic rule. Jewish minorities, who could not realistically aspire to sovereign power or look to rescue from foreign coreligionists, continued to view themselves as the true Israel, whom God would eventually redeem.

In this period the expanding Islamic world's optimistic sense of divine Manifest Destiny was reflected in its confident embrace of cosmopolitan culture. Here, the upper classes energetically sponsored the appropriation of the learning and cultures of the subject peoples and non-Muslim foreigners, including philosophy, science, medicine, music, and literature. The cultivation of knowledge became a mark of prestige and power not only for the caliphs, but for the members of the upper elite who sought to emulate or displace them and served as a medium for the assimilation of non-Arab peoples into an Islamicate cultural environment. The integration of Muslims, Christians, Jews, Zoroastrians, and others (particularly South Asians) contributed to the emergence of a vital Islamicate culture that blossomed in Baghdad in the

'Abbasid period, and in other Islamic courts from Córdoba to Cairo beginning in the ninth and tenth centuries. From there it would extend through the Mediterranean and deep into Europe and Africa, laying the foundations for the transformation of the West.

By the tenth century the three competing caliphates ('Abbasid, Fatimid, and Umayyad of Córdoba) and the three empires (Byzantine, Bulgarian, and "Holy Roman") bore significant resemblances. A common trait was the devolution of civil authority in the provinces to local military leaders, who acted increasingly as independent sovereigns. As the more compact and cohesive imperial powers of the era—Byzantium and the three caliphates—began to unravel after the year 1000, regional principalities around the peripheries broke away, initiating an age of dynamic competition in the Mediterranean, which provided opportunities for previously marginalized groups, including indigenous converts, Berbers, Jews, Armenians, Lombards, slaves, and "infidels," to take on greater and more formal political roles within the empires. A parallel can be observed in the Jewish Mediterranean, when the power of the exilarchy (the king-in-exile, established in the time of the Babylonian captivity) declined with that of the caliphate that was its sponsor, and regional communities became formally independent of Baghdad.

In spite of political fragmentation, however, this Islamic caliphal world continued to function like a united "empire" culturally and economically. Because law derived from the *'ulama'* and not from each ruler, regime change at the top had little effect on the practice of Islamic law or the legal cohesiveness of the Islamic world, political divisions notwithstanding. Commerce was not necessarily interrupted by political conflict, and the Dar al-Islam constituted, effectively, a massive free-trade zone. Likewise, Arabic remained the dominant spoken and written language throughout Islam (for Christian and Jews, too), so scholars, officials, merchants, and seekers-of-fortune continued to circulate from west to east and back with ease. And thanks to the prestige of the Qur'an and the person of the Prophet, Arabo-Islamic social customs and cultural traditions provided a common framework from the shores of the Atlantic to the banks of the Indus. This was true not only for the Muslims of the Dar al-Islam, but also for its Jews, who had adopted Arabic as their vernacular and assumed many of the outward social customs of the Arabo-Islamic world, and whose legal culture also spanned the region unaffected by political divisions.

CHAPTER TWO

Mediterranean Connections

In 1047 Nasir Khusraw—poet, scientist, and philosopher-theologian, and a former financial official of the Seljuq *amir* (prince) of Khorasan (in northern Iran)—set out for Cairo to study Fatimid theology. After making the pilgrimage to Mecca and Medina, in mid-August 1047 he witnessed one of the great ceremonies of the capital, "the Opening of the Nile." The annual ritual in which the floodgates were opened was one of great solemnity and celebration. In his *Safar-nama*, or "Book of Travels," Nasir recounts in Persian how the regiments of the caliph's army, including Bedouin Arabs, Berbers, central Africans, Turks, and Persians, and other mercenaries and slaves, ride out in formation on horse- and camelback, together with a parade of infantry. Also on display are princes from across the eastern Mediterranean and beyond: Persia, Byzantium, Georgia, Nubia, Yemen, and the Caucasus. To the tumult of drums and trumpets, out rides the caliph, the living Imam, on a lavishly saddled mount, shaded by his broad imperial parasol and surrounded by an honor guard decked out in silk and bejeweled brocade. Behind him follow the various ministers and high officials of his palace, together with the most important clergy of all the faiths. Through the avenues they rode, past banners of silk embroidered with calligraphy praising the caliph. The streets were jammed with city folk: Sunni and Shi'i Muslims, Rabbanite and Karaite Jews, and members of the various Christian faiths. Finally arriving at a spacious pavilion shaded by yet more silken Byzantine tapestry, the caliph dismounted and taking up a spear, cast it at the levee holding back the river's waters. As workers with picks attacked the earthen dam, water began to gush forth, and the crowd erupted in cheers. It would be another year of abundance and prosperity.

The ancient Greco-Persian historian Herodotus had called Egypt "the gift of the Nile," and 1,500 years later the river and the complex irrigation systems that it fed watered the verdant fields that fed Fatimid Cairo's population of several hundred thousand. The river also sustained the cotton crop that drove the Egyptian textile industry and served as a highway connecting Egypt to sub-Saharan Africa—an important source of slaves, spices, and valuable exotica. Through its access to Red-Sea and Mediterranean ports, Cairo became the center of trade networks that reached across the Mediterranean, into the Near East, and to East Africa, India, and beyond. The power and wealth of the caliphate and the cosmopolitanism of Cairo were, therefore, consequences of the bounty of the Nile and the city's geographical location on the edge of the Mediterranean and as the junction of Europe, Africa, and Asia.

Conflict and Integration

The Mediterranean world was one of both endemic conflict and profound integration. At bottom, Mediterranean societies were organized for warfare. The military vocation brought the greatest prestige, wealth, and social mobility; and the threat of violence, whether external or from domestic elites, both reinforced social hierarchies and fostered a sense of community. Conflict was at times inspired by and expressed in terms of religious difference, but mundane competition among rival military elites and aristocracies for control of particular populations and territories, and the revenue and prestige that these holdings generated, drove hostilities more frequently. Muslims and Christians fought against their

From the seventh to the early eleventh century Cairo emerged as one of the three great imperial capitals of the Mediterranean (alongside Córdoba and Constantinople), and was perhaps the most populated, wealthy, and diverse of the three. It was home to significant populations of Muslims, Christians, and Jews of very nearly every tradition, and of peoples from across North Africa and the Near East, sub-Saharan Africa, Byzantium, Persia, and even parts of the Latin world. It was an important center of trade linking these regions with each other and with the Indian Ocean. In 969 it was founded as the capital of the Fatimid dynasty, making it not only the center of a major political and economic empire, but of Isma'ilism, a particular interpretation of Shi'i Islam, ruled over by a divinely appointed caliph/*imam* descended from the Prophet via his daughter, Fatima. The evolution of the city's landscape provides clues regarding the wealth of the dynasty and their understanding of political and religious authority.

The Evolution of Greater Cairo

The site, just south of the Nile Delta, had been settled since Pharaonic times; and by 100 CE a settlement had grown up around the fortress known as Pi-Hapi-n-On (or "Babylon," in Greek), which by the sixth century had become a thriving city. In 643 the Arab conqueror 'Amr ibn al-'As established a garrison settlement or *misr,* called al-Fustat (the Tent), centered around a mosque, and beside the existing town. But Arab dependence on local administrators led to the settlement of non-Muslims here. The city functioned as the administrative center until the 'Abbasid revolution. The 'Abbasid governor established a new garrison town nearby, centered on a new mosque, and called al-'Askar (the Army). In 868 a new governor arrived, a Turkic slave-soldier named Ahmad b. Tulun. He founded a new garrison and administrative settlement, called al-Qita'i (the Fiefs), and built a new mosque here for the army, which was made up increasingly of sub-Saharan Africans. In 935 the Tulunids were supplanted by a new dynasty of governors, the Ikshidids, who moved the army and administration back to al-'Askar. Through all of this and beyond, Babylon-Fustat remained the economic and industrial heart of the city, a crowded, cosmopolitan mix of shops and high-rise apartment buildings, in which people of all faiths and backgrounds moved and intermingled. Through the eleventh century, the financial bureaucracy remained largely in the hands of Coptic Christians, and Jews were prominent in credit and commerce, notably the trade of high-value luxury goods (such as pearls and gems) from the Persian Gulf and India. The city had a sophisticated cash economy: wageworkers typically had contracts, apartments could be rented, loans were available, and letters of credit were used to safely transfer funds across the Dar al-Islam, and even to the Christian Mediterranean.

In 969 the brilliant Fatimid commander Jawhar "the Sicilian," the son of a Slavic slave, arrived and conquered the city on behalf of the caliph al-Mu'izz (953–975). He founded a new city, al-Qahira (Cairo), honoring the caliph as "the Conqueror," but also referring to the god and planet Mars, associated with war and consonant with the astrological omens of the day of his victory. This was established as a self-contained and isolated, walled palace-city, some distance to the north. Inside, a new mosque was built, a mosque-school, al-Azhar, and two great palaces (one for the caliph, the other for the *wazir* and bureaucracy) with a massive military parade ground between. Each ethnic contingent in the army was provided with a separate quarter within the walls, except "the Blacks," who were quartered outside. No other residents were allowed, and no one could enter the palace-city mounted, except the caliph. The lands around the city, claimed by the ruling family as their own, soon attracted merchants and settlers, and a city grew up around al-Qahira, the rents from which provided tremendous income to the dynasty. Under the all-powerful Armenian general and *wazir* Badr al-Jamali (d. 1094), massive new walls and gates were constructed. Subsequently, the messianic caliph, al-Hakim, constructed a new mosque.

Nasir Khusraw's Travel Account

The Persian traveler Nasir Khusraw traveled the length of Egypt, an experience he recorded in his *Book of Travels.* Cairo, which he visited in 1046, left him greatly impressed.

> I estimated that there were no less than twenty thousand shops in Cairo, all of which belong to the sultan (Caliph). Many shops are rented for as much as ten *dinars* a month, and none for less than two. There

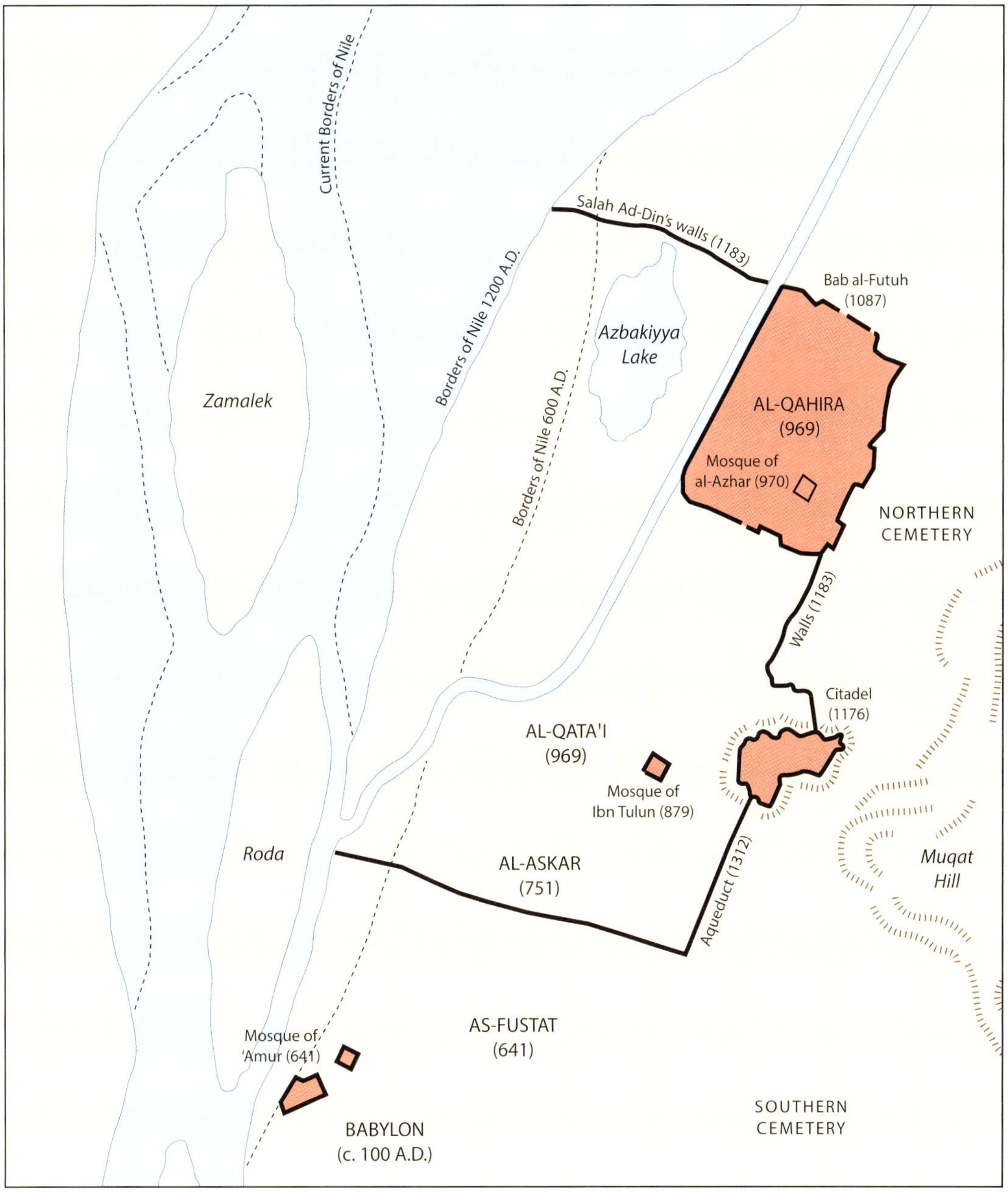

MAP 2.1 The Evolution of Greater Cairo. Original source unknown.

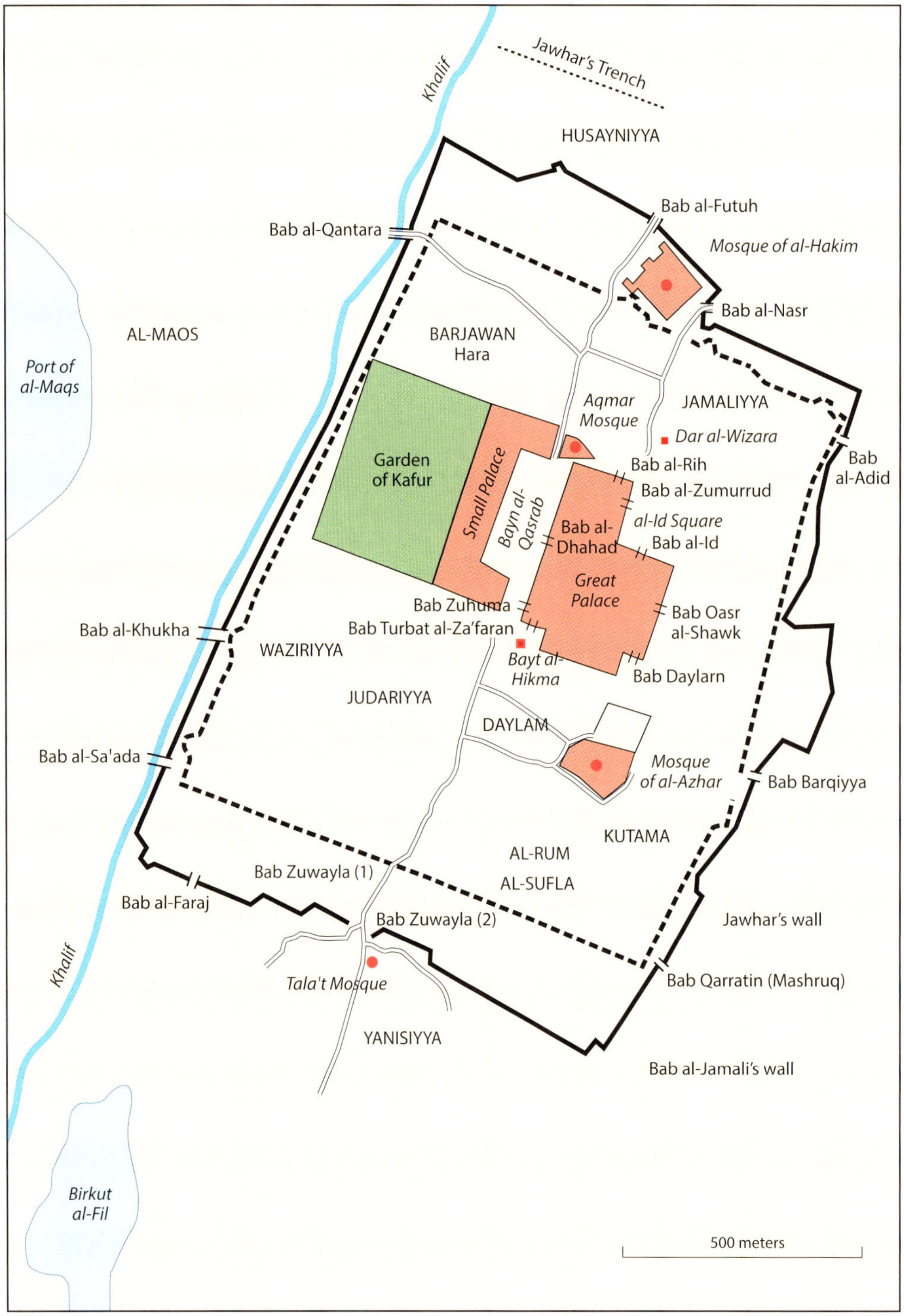

MAP 2.2 A Detail of the Fatimid Imperial City. From *Cairo* by André Raymond ©Librairie Arthème Fayard, 1993.

is no end of caravanserais [inns], bathhouses, and other public buildings—all property of the sultan [and] there are eight thousand buildings belonging to the sultan that are leased out, with the rent collected monthly. . . .

They say that twelve thousand hired servants work in the palace, in addition to the women and slave girls, whose number no one knows. . . .

In the midst of the houses in the city are gardens and orchards watered by wells. In the sultan's harem are the most beautiful gardens imaginable. Waterwheels have been constructed to irrigate them. There are trees planted and pleasure parks built even on the roofs. . . .

When one looks at the city of Old Cairo [Babylon] from a distance, it looks like a mountain. There are some houses which have fourteen floors, and others which have seven.[1]

Discussion Questions

1. Why was it seen as necessary to found so many new settlements?

2. How could Cairo's prosperity survive so many revolts and regime changes?

3. What forces would have led to the integration of Cairo's diverse population, and what sorts of problems might this have caused?

Further Reading

Goitein, S. D. "Cairo: An Islamic City in the Light of the Geniza Documents." In *Middle Eastern Cities: A Symposium on Ancient, Islamic, and Contemporary Middle Eastern Urbanism*, ed. Ira M. Lapidus, 80–96. Berkeley: University of California Press, 1969.

———. *Letters of Medieval Jewish Traders*. Princeton: Princeton University Press, 1974.

"Jamiʿ al-Azhar." *Archnet.org*. https://archnet.org/sites/2311.

Nasir-i Khusraw. *Naser-E Khosraw's Book of Travels = (Safarnama)*. Trans. M. Thackston. Albany: Bibliotheca Persica, 1986.

Staffa, Susan Jane. *Conquest and Fusion: The Social Evolution of Cairo, A.D. 642–1850*. Leiden: Brill, 1977.

Note

1. Nasir-i Khusraw, 56–60, 67.

own coreligionists as much or more than they fought each other.

Over the course of the seventh to eleventh century, as the Mediterranean became more prosperous and more cohesive as a region, it exercised an ever-stronger pull on the "barbarian" peoples of the continental hinterlands. Typical of the codependent relationship that often develops between dynamic nomadic peoples and institutionally sophisticated sedentary groups, the Mediterranean continued to attract less-developed warrior peoples from its periphery, whether Arabs, Berbers, Viking Norsemen, and Slavs in the eighth and ninth centuries or Magyars, Normans, Berbers, Turkic Central Asians, and Sub-Saharan Africans in the tenth and eleventh. As they were drawn into the region, these peoples all contributed to its evolving political and cultural landscape. But they did not fundamentally transform it, and, in fact, they served as vectors for the outward dissemination of Mediterranean culture and the extension of Mediterranean trade networks far beyond the shores of the sea.

The complexity of the Mediterranean economy and the region's high population density meant that prosperity and stability depended to no small degree on the maintenance of existing economic relations and administrative institutions, and the preservation of the established social order. Conquest, even when it implied a significant religious or cultural reorientation (as with the Muslim conquests or the Crusader occupation of Palestine), was often limited at first to the elimination or absorption of the conquered military aristocracy and royalty. Local elites tended to collaborate with conquerors, as generally their own position and privilege were not challenged, and their skills and knowledge were necessary for the continuing function of the economy and collection of revenue, while rulers realized that they could increase their power in the domestic sphere by skillfully manipulating the various ethnic and religious communities under their rule. Mediterranean peoples could easily arrive at arrangements of accommodation because they shared a broadly common cultural ori-

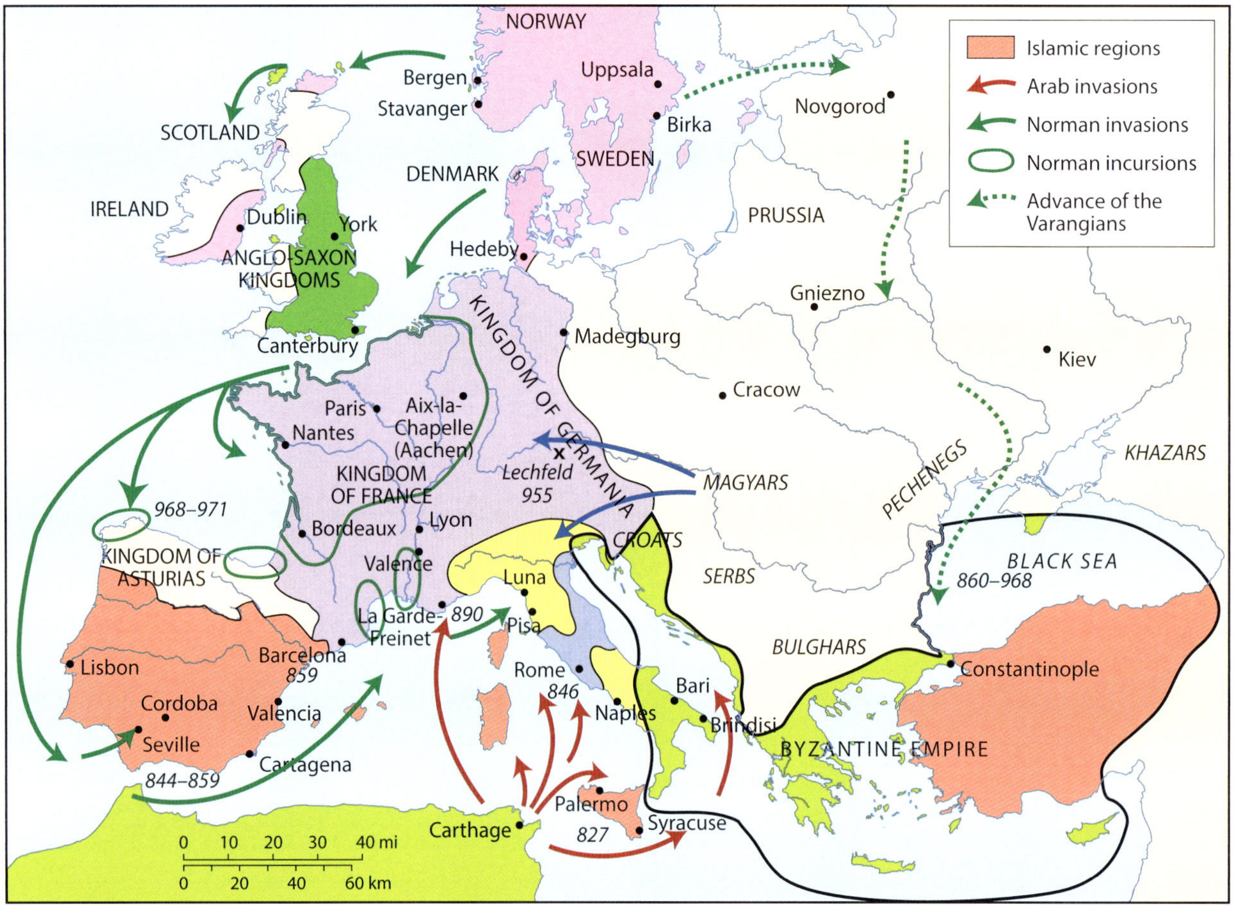

MAP 2.3 Invasions and Migrations, 800–1000. Original source unknown.

entation defined by Perso-Abrahamic religion, Roman institutions, Greek thought, and common folk-values as regards gender roles, slavery, honor, and folk beliefs. This "mutual intelligibility" provided a middle ground in which different peoples could engage in relationships of collaboration, subjugation, and domination, on terms that were both understandable and acceptable to all parties (if reluctantly, to some). Relationships of clientage, conversion, and slavery acted as bridges between these communities and encouraged mutual influence, as well as providing the means for newcomers to integrate into Mediterranean society, whether through conflict or collaboration. Thus, we can see in this period the continuing evolution of a Mediterranean culture—not as a formal construct, but as a common repertoire of responses to the challenges and opportunities posed by the geographical, social, and economic environment of the region.

Warfare and Warriors

By the late seventh century the old legionary system of a paid, professional army had been abandoned in the Roman Empire, and a new military developed in Byzantium that combined a relatively small, permanent imperial army with the popular armies of the *themes*. The latter were dominated by a heavy infantry—swordsmen recruited from among peasant farmers—together with heavy cavalry of the provincial military aristocracy. The imperial force was professional and included also light infantry archers. Logistical infrastructure was provided by the treasury. It was a regimented and trained force, apparently capable of carrying out formal tactical maneuvers of considerable precision and discipline, while the provincial reserves provided defensive depth to the empire. On campaign, the imperial and provincial armies would combine; frequently emperors personally fought in command of these forces, and usurpers and would-be usurpers were usually former generals. A number of the many surviving Byzantine military manuals were apparently written by emperors.

In both the Balkans and Anatolia, clients, proxies, and mercenaries—often of Armenian or Bulgarian origin—were used as border forces (*akritai*), whether integrated within or serving alongside the army of the empire. These were less dependable than Byzantine troops, but allowed the empire to respond to the tactics of their adversaries in kind; such service also provided a means for integration of outsiders in the Byzantine elite. The heroic ballad of the half-Greek, half-Arab Digenis (Two-Blooded) Akritas, compiled in the twelfth century and based on earlier oral sources, reflects the cultural and religious ambiguities of the military elite of the borderlands.

The empire's great wealth also sustained a professional, standing imperial navy, whose forces were also supplemented by private and church-owned vessels. Domination of the northeastern Mediterranean was favored by the development in the late seventh century of "Greek fire," a petroleum-based incendiary (like napalm) used to great effect in sea battles. In the 900s, mercenaries became increasingly important, of whom the Rus were an important source. To protect the emperor as much from domestic intrigues as outside threats, the Varangian palace guard was founded, recruited mainly among Norse Vikings, but also Anglo-Saxons and Rus. Together with the decline of the popular armies of the *themes* and Leo IV's (886–912) militarization of provincial governorships, these trends represented a "privatization" of the armed forces in the empire and a decline of civil authority in the provinces. They were a suitable response to immediate challenges, but laid the groundwork for Byzantium's military and political crises of the mid-eleventh century. SEE SOURCEBOOK 2:1.

Initially, the Islamic forces consisted of a tribally organized army (*jund*)—a highly mobile force of light cavalry—in which, in theory, all Arab men served and were compensated according to their status in the *diwan* (a registry of Arab clans). In the early years of Islamic rule old tribal divisions undermined the unity of Arab forces and led to episodes of conflict. In the late 600s large numbers of converted Berber tribes in the West and Persian and other peoples in the East transformed the army and created new tensions that fueled internal conflict through the 800s. In traditional Arab armies, discipline and tactical coordination presented a challenge, contrary as they were to the individualistic ethos that characterized "barbarian" societies. Unlike the Arabs of the Persian Gulf, those who moved into the Mediterranean had no maritime tradition, and thus subject Christians in Egypt and Ifriqiya were instrumental in operating the Muslim navies that developed in this period. The caliphs tried to maintain central control over their armies and separate military and civil jurisdictions, but were obliged in practice to cede semiautonomy and hereditary rights to the military governors of vulnerable frontier provinces. Muslim rulers exploited the predatory and competitive nature of ungovernable nomadic tribes by recruiting them as proxies and clients. Central Asian nomads were particularly sought after as highly mobile mounted archers.

By the 900s, in order to undermine the political power of the Arab elite the caliphs were recruiting mercenaries and purchasing slave-soldiers in large numbers, including Berbers, pagan Slavs, Christians in al-Andalus, and Armenians and Turkic peoples in the 'Abbasid and Fatimid Caliphates. The Fatimids also recruited heavily among central Africans. This had the effect of both integrating outsiders into the Muslim political culture—often in the face of stiff resistance from Arab- or Persian-identifying local elites and populace—and of extending the religious influence and economic reach of the Dar al-Islam into the non-Muslim lands where these slaves and soldiers were recruited. The power of these foreign military cliques was checked by competition among them, which astute rulers deliberately manipulated.

Foreign slave-soldiers (*mamalik*, sing.: *mamluk*, whence Mamluk), who were isolated and utterly dependent on their owners, became important components of the military, especially of caliphal bodyguards. Prized for their absolute loyalty, they showed little compunction in wielding violence against restive local Muslim populations whom they had no affinity to. In ninth-century al-Andalus, for example, the Hurr– or "Silent Ones" (so

FIGURE 2.1 Warriors from the *Urgell Beatus*, Catalonia, tenth century. Photo provided by Wikimedia Commons under the CC-PD-Mark | PD-Art License.

called because they could not speak Arabic) were made up of converted "Slavic" slaves and captured Christians. As in Byzantium, dependence on mercenaries and the "privatization" of military authority contributed to the weakening of central power and bred competition and internal conflict among a military elite that was increasingly detached from both the rulers and the populace. Some rulers resorted to *iqta'*, which granted a locale's tax revenue to a warlord—often a foreigner—in return for military service. As occurred in Byzantium with the institution of the *pronoia*, those who received such tax concessions felt little attachment to their subjects, and tended to exploit them, while neglecting infrastructure maintenance, and thus undermining the fabric of state and society.

In Frankish lands the introduction and diffusion of the stirrup, which allowed more effective use of the horse, helped spur the transition away from infantry—whose favored weapons were the axe and spear—toward a dedicated elite of *milites* (knights), who developed a distinct mode of heavy cavalry tactics centered on the coordinated charge. This was part of a gradual process of technological, social, and cultural evolution, which was favored by and encouraged the development of a closed, hereditary military class, which became politically independent in the absence of central authority following the collapse of the Carolingian Empire in the 800s. Kings and emperors, as well as magnates (including bishops and abbots), each had their own household guard, but depended on bonds of vassalage (a personal, feudal obligation) to bring together larger forces. As in the case of tribal armies, discipline and coordination were a challenge because of the informal and personal nature of authority, and the emphasis on individual valor and feats of courage. There were no effective organized navies in Latin Europe, and logistics and the funding for military campaigns were borne by the nobility themselves. This military class was sustained by a large population of servile peasant (*serf*) farmers; warriors recouped the costs of military service through the plunder and the appropriation of conquered lands. From the 900s, the growth of the military class, coupled with land shortages and the allure of wealth, began to draw Frankish and Norse warriors to the Mediterranean, particularly to Byzantium.

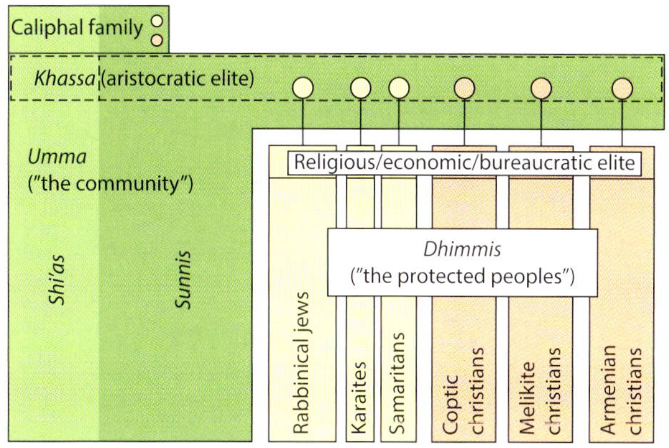

FIGURE 2.2 Religious identity and social prestige in the Fatimid Caliphate. Courtesy Brian A. Catlos.

The Ordering of Society

One of the characteristics that set the Byzantine and Islamic Mediterranean apart was the complexity of its social order. In the underdeveloped Latin lands of the tenth century, for example, society was divided between "those who work, those who fight, and those who pray," the latter two estates dominated by a self-conscious aristocracy of birth. The prestige and power attached to noble lineage were extremely important, but beyond this there was only a vague sense of ethnic identity (and for the most part little by way of vernacular literary cultures for it to be anchored in). In this world of personal power and overlapping bonds of obligation, title did not necessarily translate into authority. In principle, the emperor or a king was at the top of this pyramid of dependent relationships, but given that an individual might hold numerous lordships in different territories and carrying different obligations, a king could be in some contexts the vassal of another nobleman or another king. For example, through much of the Middle Ages, the kings of England held the title Duke of Normandy, and, as such, were in some contexts considered vassals of the kings of France. Nor were a king's possessions necessarily territorially contiguous, given that royal authority was based on a patchwork of vassal relationships rather than a clearly defined geographical territory. Even single towns were sometimes split among multiple lordships. Thus, overlapping bonds of lordship and vassalage were common, and the power of kings and magnates to command subordinates was limited. This was very much a rural, agrarian world—until the eleventh century—and outside of Italy, urban society was barely organized, with the exception of small Jewish enclaves that were cultivated by secular and ecclesiastical rulers in order to foster commerce. Otherwise, commercial and artisanal classes in Latin lands enjoyed little influence or prestige.

Despite the importance of trade (particularly domestic trade), commerce was not looked on as a prestige profession in Byzantium. By the tenth century the markers of prestige were ethno-religious identity (Greekness), rank or class, and imperial office. Members of the elite, or at least those who operated in the imperial ambit, were expected to adopt Greek identity—the language and Orthodox faith of the emperors—at least outwardly. In the provincial setting this could be a liability, as it could place one in opposition to one's own constituents who might identify with heterodox churches and with other linguistic cultures (e.g., Slavonic, Armenian, Syriac, or Arabic), thus undermining the authority of Greek Orthodox governors. It was not uncommon for elite individuals to "commute" between cultures, depending on the environment or situation they found themselves in. Class was hereditary, particularly within the aristocracy, but military and bureaucratic service provided an entrée and a means of social mobility. It was not unheard-of for a soldier of peasant origins to rise through the ranks, or even to become emperor. In addition, the thriving urban environment sustained a substantial "middle class" population of functionaries, merchants, and artisans.

Byzantium's large slave population consisted primarily of war captives and, particularly after the tenth century, Slavs brought in by Russian traders. But it also included Byzantine children who were sold to relieve family debts. Constantinople became a major center of this trade. Slaves were used primarily in the household environment and craft sectors. Individual aristocrats might own thousands. Castrated slaves were highly valued, but not all eunuchs were unfree—neutering a child provided him with a path into aristocratic and imperial service and greater family prosperity. Toward the end of this period, slavery and clientage became blurred; emancipated slaves typically remained members of their former owner's household network.

As for non-Christians there was an important Jewish community in Byzantium, including both Rabbanite Jews and Karaites. They endured considerable legal and popular hostility, and occasional decrees of forced conversion were promulgated in the 800s and 900s. Some Jews worked as farmers but were most active in the textile and silk trades. The community at Constantinople was robust, but southern Italy was the center of Byzantine-Jewish cultural and intellectual production. Few Muslims in this period lived under Byzantine rule, although there was a small community in the capital and undoubtedly some in the eastern provinces.

Islam was in theory a classless society of Muslim equals and of *dhimmi* communities, who lived under separate but subordinate legal regimes and had distinct rights and obligations. However, three broad classes of Muslims can be discerned: the *khassa* (an open, semihereditary aristocracy), the *'amma* (free common folk), and enslaved Muslims. Slaves, however, had rights under Islamic law and were considered persons; they could not be mutilated or killed arbitrarily and could own their own property. Conversion did not guarantee manumission, but, in principle, free Muslims could not be enslaved. As in Byzantium, slavery was primarily a household affair, although slaves were also used in the military and in craft industry, and occasionally—as in southern Iraq and Bahrain—for mass agricultural labor. The practice of polygamy together with the acceptability and popularity of concubinage led to a particular demand for female slaves, who were in no position to resist sexual assault by the owners. Wealthy men might maintain scores of unfree women. Favored concubines who bore their owner an heir could be rewarded with property, emancipation, and marriage. Because male domestic slaves lived within the intimate confines of their owners' homes, eunuchs were in high demand. But prohibitions against mutilating both slaves and free Muslims meant that eunuchs had to be captured and castrated in the distant pagan periphery and shipped to market. This demand for slaves first stimulated a Latin trade in pagan Slavs, and then drew Muslim merchants into central Africa and the Caucasus.

Tribal and ethnic affinities were also important; those sedentary folk who identified as "Arabs," including the descendants of converts, tended to look down on nomadic peoples including Arab Bedouins, but in particular, Berbers and dark-skinned central Africans. Free newcomers to the Islamic world, including Persians, Turks, Berber peoples, and Armenians, tended to remain as cohesive communities, adding an ethnic element to the social landscape. In the Persian Gulf, Africans were imported en masse for agricultural work, but otherwise Blacks typically came individually as military slaves and concubines, and also coalesced socially as a consequence of discrimination they suffered. That said, some Black slaves and ex-slaves rose to the pinnacles of power in the administration, or as royal or aristocratic wives and concubines.

Unlike in the Roman legal tradition, under Islamic law women owned, inherited, and controlled their own property, even after marriage, and had clearly established, if somewhat lesser, legal rights than men. Female aristocrats and high-status slaves were often highly educated and could amass tremendous wealth through inheritance, gifts, and their business ventures. Although they were excluded from formal authority, many exerted influence from behind the scenes through their own patronage networks or as regents.

For example, in 1036 the Fatimid caliph al-Zahir (1021–1036) died, leaving his seven-year-old son, al-Mustansir (1036–1094), as heir. Real power was held by the new caliph's mother, Rasad, one of the many Sudanese slave-girls al-Zahir had purchased from the Karaite Jew Abu Sa'd al-Tustari. As the mother of the heir, she had been lavished with properties and incomes, and became independently powerful, and it was she who would be pulling the strings of power until the 1060s. Placing her former master, al-Tustari, in charge of her finances, she set out to consolidate her hold by concentrating power in the person of the *wazir*, whom she could appoint. Her first choice was Yusuf al-Fallahi, a converted Jew. But al-Fallahi courted the Seljuq regiments of the caliphal army in 1048 and incited them to murder al-Tustari. Rasad had al-Fallahi put to death, and appointed a new protégé, Abu Muhammad al-Yazuri, a Sunni Muslim, as *wazir* in 1050, until his execution in 1058. Under her reign large numbers of Sudanese slave-soldiers were purchased to offset the influence of the Seljuq and Berber contingents of the Fatimid army. This exacerbated ethnic tensions that ran parallel to palace and army rivalries, and for many years the Sudanese and Seljuq regiments battled each other, wreaking havoc in the capital and pushing the volatile caliphate into anarchy.

Rasad was, in fact, one of several women rulers in the Fatimid world. The princess Sitt al-Mulk (reputedly a Christian, like her mother) is thought to have arranged the assassination of her brother, the messianic caliph al-Hakim (996–1021), reigning afterward as regent for her nephew, al-Zahir (1021–1035). In Yemen, the Fatimids' allies, the Sulayhid dynasty, were also known for their powerful queens. One of these, Sayyida bint Ahmad, earned widespread praise over seventy-one years of rule, first as regent for her husband, then for her son, and finally in her own right, from 1094 to 1138. She had been given formal religious authority by al-Mustansir, who declared her head of the Isma'ilis in Yemen, and she went on to effectively found the Tayyibi branch of Isma'ilism.

But, as in the Byzantine Empire, for a woman to strive for public authority was risky and potentially destablizing. In late tenth-century al-Andalus, Subh, a former Christian slave and wife of the Umayyad caliph al-Hakam II (961–976), conspired to keep their son, Hisham III (1026–1031), under her tutelage. She was betrayed by a co-conspirator, the *hajib* Muhammad ibn Abi 'Amir al-Mansur, who seized power and confined her in her palace. His efforts to establish a parallel and parasitic dynasty of *hajib*s under the cover of the caliph ultimately failed, but precipitated the fall of the Umayyad Caliphate of Córdoba.

As a whole, Islamic society was strikingly fluid and meritocratic. Birth was not an absolute impediment to upward mobility, and even some slaves gained renown and authority as religious scholars and men of letters, or wielded great power and accumulated great wealth as caliphal household officials, commanders, and governors. Even the religious divide that theoretically ensured the superiority of Muslims was often blurry. After the first century and a half of Islamic rule *dhimmi*s had not only acculturated outwardly to Arabo-Islamic social norms, but could rise to the highest ranks in caliphal administration, with some eventually converting to protect their position. In Egypt, the fiscal administration was run largely by Coptic Christians, and Greek and Armenian Christians were important in the army. Jews also gained position and power across the Islamic world as administrators. As in the case of prestige professions, such as that of court physician, members of minorities were not necessarily prized because their community held a monopoly on skill, but rather precisely because they were politically disadvantaged and vulnerable and would be less like to poison or betray their king. In any event, wealthy people wanted to be attended by the best physicians, whoever they happened to be.

Because Muslim rulers saw the main political threat as coming from fellow Muslims, this contributed greatly to an environment of apparent "tolerance," as it encouraged the elevation of non-Muslims into positions of power. As was the case for openly powerful women, the opportunities enjoyed by these non-Muslims were seen by some pious men as a violation of the divine order and contrary to the spirit of Islam, and could be used to justify repression by rulers or violence by rebellious demagogues and their followers. On the whole, however, in this period Jewish and Christian communities enjoyed stability and security thanks to their important roles in local economies and their "constitutional rights" as *dhimmi*s enshrined in Islamic scripture and law. SEE SOURCEBOOK 2:2.

City Life

For the most part, cities in Latin lands had been abandoned or shrank with the collapse of the Roman Empire. Formerly urban walled spaces were sometimes turned over to agriculture. Obsolete civic and religious structures were quarried for materials or, like the amphitheaters in Nîmes and Tarragona, converted into the fortified nuclei of primitive settlements. Not much of formal town life remained outside of Italy, and urban institutions and infrastructure survived most strongly in Rome, which thanks to its prestige and the notional presence

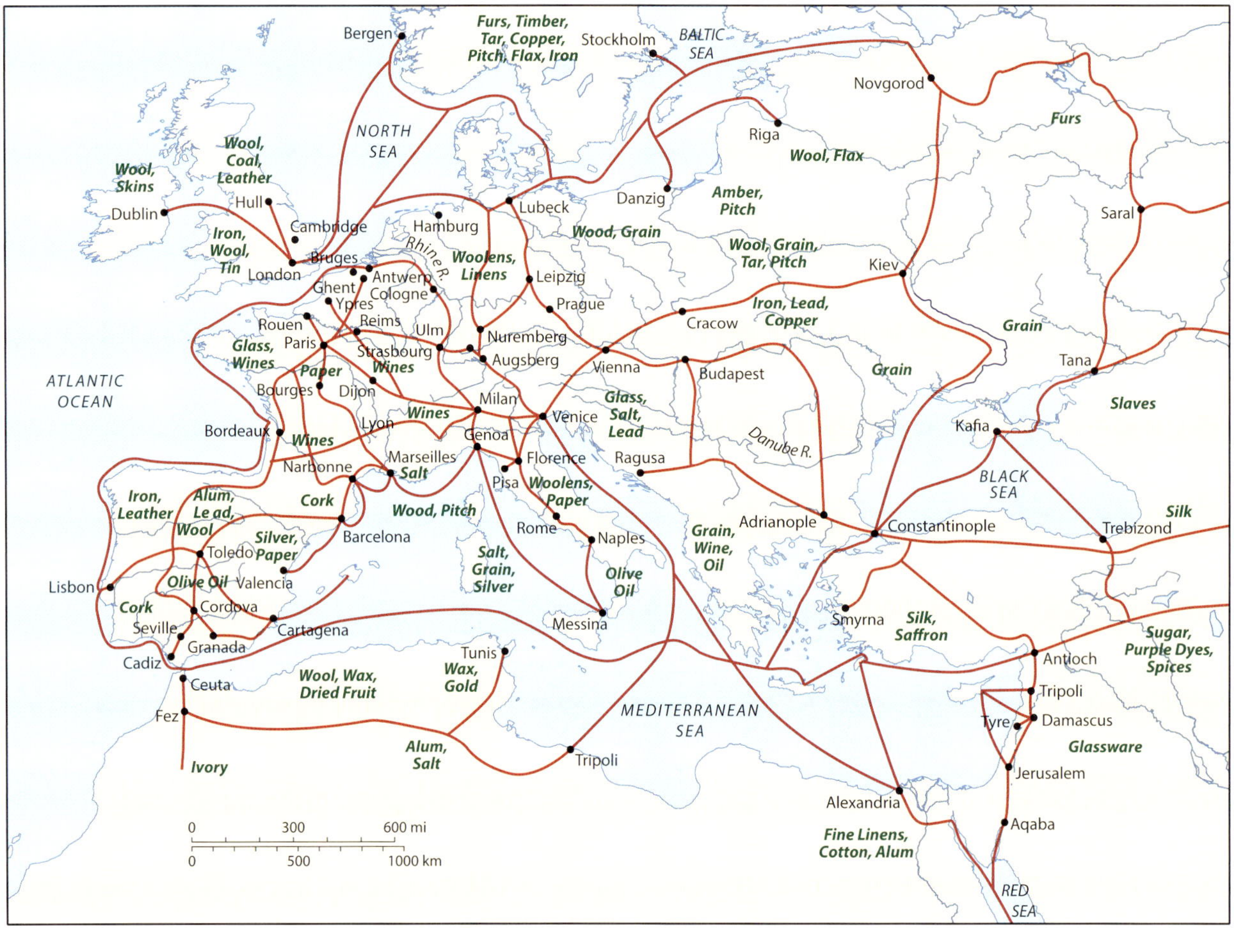

MAP 2.4 Trade between Europe and the Mediterranean, ca. 1000. Original source unknown.

of the papacy, retained at least the outward manifestations of civic life and organization. It was also likely the largest Latin city, with a population of perhaps 50,000. In the eighth and ninth centuries, Italian ports, including Amalfi, Pisa, Genoa, and Venice, stimulated by trade between the wealthy Islamic world and the resource-rich European hinterland, became the centers of a new urban society, which was oligarchical in organization and modeled itself outwardly on the institutions of republican Rome. By the late tenth and eleventh centuries, powerful Latin lords, such as the counts of Barcelona and Provence, recognized the value of this approach, and encouraged the growth of port towns such as Barcelona and Marseilles, while secular and ecclesiastical lords farther north established small urban Jewish colonies to provide credit and stimulate trade. But prior to 1000 in the Latin West, rural monasteries, as centers of education, services, and exchange, often filled the economic and cultural roles typically played by towns and cities.

The Roman city lived on in the Byzantine heartland, where urban life had continued largely uninterrupted by catastrophic change, and where strong centralized power had ensured the survival of commerce, public life, and a large commercial and artisanal class. The capital, Constantinople, was the uncontested metropolis, the location of the court and the patriarchate, and the economic hub of the empire. The area around the ancient forum was the site of the massive Great Palace, and Justinian's Hagia Sophia (Holy Wisdom) remained the largest church in Christendom. A second palace, Blachernae, dominated the northwest of the city. Roman civil facilities, such as the hippodrome, and fortifications were maintained and expanded. Together with its huge population, the city's location at the crossroads of Europe and Asia and between the Black Sea and the Mediterranean and its strongly defended port guaranteed its place as both entrepôt and market. Ancient inland provincial capitals, such as Nicaea (Iznik), Iconium (Konya), and Theodosiopolis (Erzerum), served as regional economic and administrative nodes, but cities with ports, notably Thessaloniki, Trabzon, and Antioch (Antakya), became increasingly important in the tenth century as Mediterranean and Black Sea trade intensified.

Counterintuitively, it was the nomadic Arabs who were responsible for the greatest wave of urbanization the Mediterranean had seen since the age of the Romans. Although they settled in some former Roman cities, such as Damascus and Zaragoza, for the most part the Arabs established new garrisons, often alongside existing cities, such as al-Fustat (the Tent), beside Babylon-in-Egypt (Old Cairo). As these grew, they eventually subsumed the earlier settlements. Later, caliphs established self-contained palace cities, such Baghdad and Cairo, usually a short distance from the existing metropolis—to insulate them from the restive populace and the prying eyes of the religious authorities. Provincial capitals followed a similar pattern of development, especially when these became the capitals of independent kingdoms or emirates. Port cities were also either revived, like Alexandria and Palermo, or established anew, like Almería and Mahdia.

In time, the caliphal capitals, Baghdad, Cairo, and Córdoba, became true metropolises with populations possibly exceeding one million, and the larger port cities, like Palermo, may have reached a quarter of that. Such growth was made possible by the emergence of a mobile, money-driven commercial economy fueled by the injection of African gold and sustained by the cohesive regional framework of exchange provided by the Arabic language and Islamic law. The economic specialization this facilitated, together with advances in agricultural production and trade, enabled the region to sustain a population many times denser than that of the near-subsistence economies of the Latin lands.

Islamic cities had a distinct structure from their classical antecedents. The heart of civic life was the congregational mosque, where ideally the entire local community gathered for Friday noon prayer, where the public treasury was kept, the *qadi* (magistrate) held court, and notaries gathered. Close by was the *qasaba* (casbah) or *qasr*—the fortress that was the seat of the governor, king, or caliph, and the home of the garrison and the civil administration. Also near the mosque were the covered markets (*qaysariyyas,* from Caesar)—centers for retail trade and wholesale distribution, as well as small family-run craft workshops. Cemeteries, often the only public urban open spaces, except for mosque courtyards, lay on the outskirts. Public hospitals, fountains, inns, baths, and other service establishments funded by notables or supported as pious foundations (*awaqf,* sing. *waqf*), akin to modern nonprofits, dotted the city. The public administration (controlled by the rulers) maintained cisterns and substantial food stores for defensive purposes and to avoid shortages. Streets were swept and human waste gathered and sold as fertilizer, and main avenues were lit at night. A police force (*shurta*) kept order, while city life was under the watchful eye of the *muhtasib,* a quasi-religious, quasi-civic public morality official whose responsibilities included catching cheating merchants and pursuing Peeping Toms.

The grids of the broad, straight Roman roads were abandoned or built over. Islamic cities usually developed organically, as aggregations of clan-based neighborhoods, typically with their own mosques, and utilities, as well as churches and synagogues. Over time this was diluted by mobility and conversion; and Muslims, Christians, and Jews lived together in mixed neighborhoods. The narrow, winding lanes were designed with the region's occasional but torrential rainfalls in mind, and needed to accommodate only foot and donkey traffic rather than chariots or carts. Cities were walled for defense, taking advantage, where possible, of existing Roman fortifications. Larger cities were surrounded by sprawling suburbs, often with their own congregational mosques; the suburbs would eventually be walled in.

With their conquest of the Mediterranean and Near East, the Arabs were faced with the need to create urban commercial institutions, including mechanisms for enforcing rules of commerce and trade that were crucial to maintaining prosperity. As in other cases, they began by making use of a Byzantine precedent, here the *agoranomos,* or "market inspector." This post, which dated back to classical Athens, and was charged with the supervision of weights, measures, and commercial practices, and policing fraud, became common across the classical Hellenistic world, and was eventually adopted in the Sasanian Empire as the *rab suqa* ("market master," in Aramaic). With the Islamic conquest of Persia, the office survived as the *sahib al-suq* ("market master," in Arabic).

As Islamic law and theology matured in the ninth century, the notion of making a moral accounting before God and of commercial accounting (both known as *hisba*) came to be seen as correlative. Thus, the domain of the officer, now called the *muhtasib,* included the enforcement of morality in the public sphere, including the market, building regulations, relations between men and women, and so on. By the eleventh century these officials could be found across the Islamic world, including the Maghrib and al-Andalus. In the twelfth and thirteenth centuries, when Christian powers conquered Islamic Spain, they too lacked a tradition of urban administration, and the *sahib al-suq* or *muhtasib* was adopted as the *zavazoque, zalmedina,* or *mostassaf*—a commercial official with purely secular functions, which spread even into Christian-ruled territories that had never been under Muslim rule.

The lavish spending at royal courts and on building projects stimulated domestic manufacturing and service economies. Thus, the Islamic Mediterranean cities were centers of production and distribution and comprised sizable markets themselves. The prosperity of their citizens generated taxes for the public treasury, and rulers amassed personal wealth through rents collected on urban properties that they owned. The palaces of caliphs, aristocrats, and leading functionaries were centers of cultural production and of learning, and private libraries were regarded as status symbols. The very wealthy also established extensive parks and gardens, either on the outskirts of cities or on rural estates. In the tenth century the Islamic Mediterranean stood out not only because it contained several major metropolises, but because of the dense network of secondary cities, both inland and coastal, which contributed to a robust, dynamic, diverse, and decentralized economy of exchange that was not dependent on the stability, durability, or patronage of a particular political regime, and that could easily adapt to changing conditions and survive political fragmentation and upheaval.

Connection and Exchange

Together with the physical characteristics of the Mediterranean, and its location between three distinct continental hinterlands, the development of Islamic urban society and the reestablishment of Byzantine power in the late ninth and tenth centuries were the conditions that drove the tremendous wealth and prosperity that characterized the region in the decades up to and following the year 1000. Increased trade, agricultural production, and dense population, as well as access to hinterland resources and markets, were the engines that drove economic development, demographic growth, and cultural transformation. The Arabic language and Islamic law, and to a lesser extent Byzantine institutions, provided frameworks for exchange, contact, and credit on a regional scale, independent of political divisions. The establishment of bimetallic currency (silver and gold) in the Islamic world gave considerable flexibility to the Muslim economy and helped establish its currency as the preferred means of exchange throughout the region and beyond. Copper pennies (*falus,* from the Latin *fallis*) lubricated small-scale commerce. Access to considerable supplies of precious metal (particularly gold, from central Africa) enabled taxes to be collected as cash, and wealth to be amassed, stored, and transported in large quantities. The legal and religious cohesiveness of the Islamic world enabled merchants, particularly Muslims and Jews, to transfer cash safely and rapidly through the medium of letters of credit—which could be easily and safely carried to and cashed in distant lands. The ubiquity of currency and a relatively high index of literacy, together with a cultural disposition in Islam toward commercial activity (Muhammad himself had been a merchant), helped develop a cash-based market economy that even the lower classes engaged in. Regional specialization stimulated efficiency and commercialization in agriculture.

By the mid-900s, however, there were signs of an impending environmental crisis, at least in the eastern Mediterranean, where more frequent cold spells and droughts provoked regional famines, which put stress on administrative institutions that had developed in the boom years. Episodes of civil unrest became increasingly common in Fatimid and 'Abbasid lands, as did military uprisings, and the raiding of nomads became

ARTIFACT THE *RIBAT-FUNDUQ* OF SOUSSE (SUSA): MILITARY, COMMERCIAL, AND RELIGIOUS INFRASTRUCTURE IN THE ISLAMIC MEDITERRANEAN

In the ninth century, monastery-fortresses known as *ribats* were constructed along the periphery of the Islamic world, particularly in the West. They served both as bulwarks for defense and as jumping-off points for raids, where pious-minded ordinary Muslims could serve as warriors for a time in the service of Islam and thus fulfill their military duty of *jihad*. Some were built by local rulers and governors, others were built privately. The *ribat* has been characterized as similar to the Christian monastery, and has been suggested as an inspiration for Crusade-era military orders. The frontiers of the Islamic world were also nodes of commerce, and in times of peace or when the frontiers shifted, *ribat*s might serve as *funduq*s (fortified inns for travelers and traders, also known as *caravanserais* or *khans*), religious schools (*madrasas*), or convents of Sufis.

Sousse

Founded by the Phoenicians, seized from the Romans by the Vandals, and later serving as a Byzantine provincial capital (Justiniapolis), Sousse was positioned as the natural trade outlet for the rich inland agricultural zone of coastal North Africa. It was conquered by Muslims in 647 and destroyed. In 821 the Aghlabid governor, Ziyadat Allah, built the *ribat* to replace an earlier 'Abbasid structure of 771; in the decades that followed, the town grew such that a larger fortress (844) and a congregational mosque (850) were needed. It thrived through the mid-eleventh century, when the region was sacked by the Bedouin Banu Hilal and Banu Sulayman tribes, sent by the Fatimids to punish the rebellious Zirid governors of Ifriqiya. Sousse appears in the *geniza* documents as an important center for Jewish traders.

FIGURE 2.3 Southeast view across the courtyard of the *ribat* of Sousse (Tunisia). dbimages / Alamy Stock Photo.

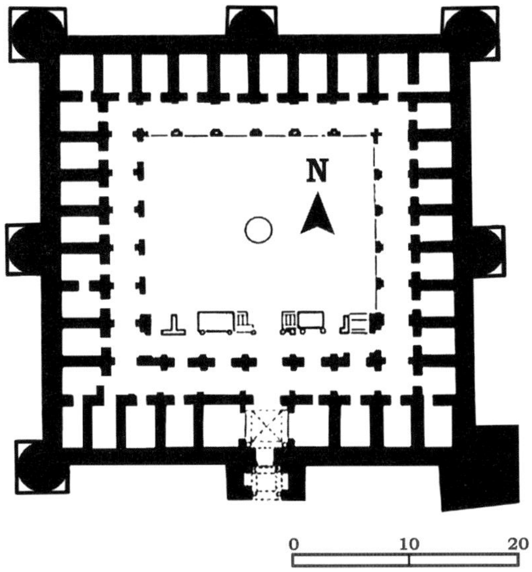

FIGURE 2.4 Floor plan of the *ribat*. ©Historical Views / agefotostock.

The eleventh-century Andalusi intellectual 'Abd Allah al-Bakri, the greatest geographer of the Islamic West, wrote:

> The town of Sousse ... is guarded by the sea on the three sides ... surrounded by a strongly built stone wall ... Sousse is entirely built of buildings of cut stone, and has many markets which sell an extraordinary abundance of merchandise and fruit. The meat sold here is the best in the world.... Around Sousse there are many fortresses, *ribats*, and other places where the pious gather. Inside the town is the "Ribat of the Guard," a building as big as a town and surrounded by a strong wall; it serves as a refuge for men who practice devotion and good works.... There are many weavers in Sousse, and they make a thread of which each *mithqal* of weight is worth two *mithqals* of gold.* It is here that the fullers embroider the fine cloth of Kairouan.[1]

The *Ribat* of Sousse

The *ribat* of Sousse is the oldest surviving building of its type and is conserved largely as it was built in the early 800s. Its architectural style was broadly inspired by Byzantine precedents, and much *spolia* (recycled classical material), including columns and vaults, was used in it. Square in plan, its walls each measure 38 m in length and 14 m in height, and are topped by broad 1 m tall battlements. The main entrance was once closed by a heavy gate and features arrow slits and slots for dropping stones on attackers. Inside, a spacious courtyard is surrounded by thirty-three rooms that served as residential quarters and for prayer and study. Two stone staircases lead up to a second story with smaller cells and a prayer hall. Three corners of the building are girded by circular towers four stories high, and on the southeast corner a fortified bastion serves as the foundation for a ten-story watchtower, styled after contemporary 'Abbasid minarets.

The *ribat* here was founded as a functioning fortress. Ziyadat Allah intervened in Sicily in 827 at the invitation of the renegade Byzantine admiral Euphemius; the invasion was launched from Sousse, under the command of an aging religious scholar, Asad ibn al-Furat, the *qadi* of Kairouan, who in a rather curious and unmilitaristic harangue of the troops on their departure, cried out:

> I swear, O soldiers, that I have not been appointed to this command by my father, or my grandfather, nor do I know of anyone to whom such a thing has happened, for I have been given this appointment because of my achievements with the pen, not the sword. I urge you all to spare no effort, no fatigue, in searching out wisdom and learning! Seek it out and store it up, add to it, and persevere through all difficulties, and you will be assured of a place both in this life, and in the life to come!

After Sousse was fortified with walls in 859 the *ribat* lost its military importance, and became a hospice for the faithful and pilgrims, and possibly functioned as a *funduq*. *Ribats* sometimes became places of refuge for religious dissidents or opportunists of dubious vocation.

The *Funduq* of Sousse

The word *funduq* is derived from the Greek *pandocheion* (inn), and denotes a fortified accommodation for mer-

---

* The *mithqal* was a unit of 4.25g, a weight that corresponded to that of the gold *dinar*—a coin based on the Roman silver *denarius* coin (penny).

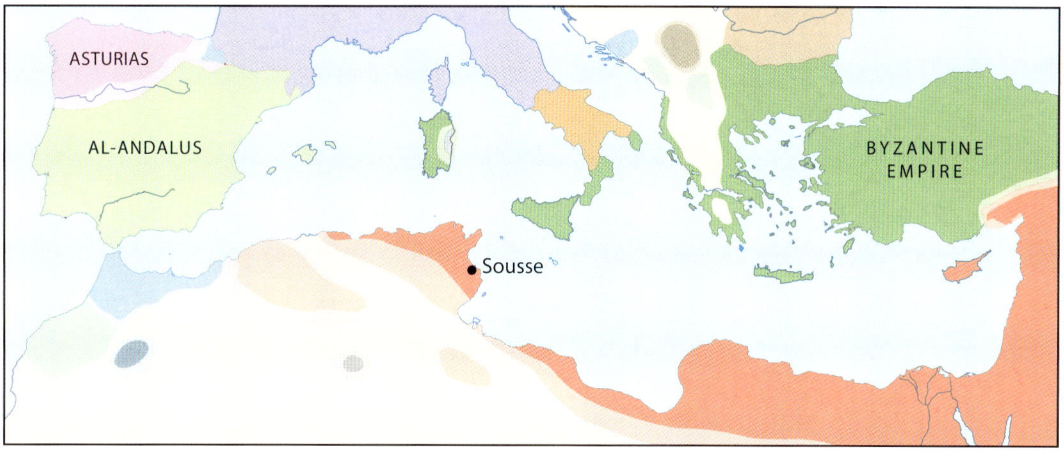

MAP 2.5 Sousse in the Mediterranean, ca. 1000 CE. Drawn from "History of Europe" series. Reproduced with permission of Euratlas.com.

chants, their pack animals, and their cargo. *Funduqs* had a square floor plan similar to the *ribat*: larger rooms on the ground floor served as stables and for storage, while cells on the upper floor served as living quarters. They provided protection and a place of encounter for traders, and facilitated the collection of duties and taxes. The common presence of *funduqs* in towns and along routes was crucial for the development of trade across the Islamic world. As in the case of *ribats*, some *funduqs* were established by rulers, but many were private foundations endowed as religious trusts. Later, non-Muslim traders in Muslim cities and ports were assigned special dedicated *funduqs* that functioned in a manner analogous to embassy compounds.

Both the *funduq* and the *ribat* were responses to the conditions of the medieval Mediterranean and were crucial to economic development, religious culture, and military defense and expansion. *Ribats* provided an opportunity for the inhabitants of an increasingly urbane Islamic world to fulfill their obligation to wage holy war, while *funduqs* constituted an important element of economic infrastructure and promoted long-range cultural diffusion and cohesion.

Discussion Questions

1. What does the *ribat* of Sousse suggest about the relationship between religion, politics, and commerce in the Islamic Mediterranean? How is its location important?

2. What elements of Islamic culture and society would have been conducive to the establishment of these types of foundations?

3. Why was there nothing equivalent to the *ribat* or *funduq* in Christian Europe? Or was there?

Further Reading

Broadhurst, J.C. *The Travels of Ibn Jubayr.* London: Cape, 1952. Pp. 345–46 (for a former *ribat* in Norman Sicily).

Constable, O. Remie. *Housing the Stranger in the Mediterranean World: Lodging, Trade, and Travel in Late Antiquity and the Middle Ages.* Cambridge: Cambridge University Press, 2003.

Kennedy, Hugh. "The *Ribat* in the Early Islamic World." In *Western Monasticism ante Litteram: The Spaces of Monastic Observance in Late Antiquity and the Early Middle Ages,* ed. H. Dey and E. Fentress, 161–75. Turnhout: Brepols, 2011.

Khalilieh, Hassan S. "The Ribât System and Its Role in Coastal Navigation." *Journal of the Economic and Social History of the Orient* 42 (1999): 212–25.

"Ribat Sousse." *Archnet.org.* https://archnet.org/sites/3762.

Scales, P.C. "The Ribat: The Archaeology of a Muslim Religious Community, Spain." *Boletín de arqueología medieval* 7 (1993): 65–75.

Note

1. Adapted from al-Bakri, *Description de l'Afrique septentrionale* (Constantine: Braham, 1900), 83–88.

more aggressive. This was a prelude to the profound demographic and political transformation that would get underway in the mid-eleventh century, and would transform the region and mark the end of the age of the caliphates and the beginning of the end for the Byzantine Empire.

The region was also endowed with an impressive physical infrastructure—the legacy of the empire and Rome's large-scale use of mass slave labor. The shores of the Mediterranean were where the Roman road network was thickest, featuring major "interstates," as well as an array of smaller highways linking provincial towns and cities. The Via Domitia, for example, connected Rome to Cádiz (originally ancient Phoenician Agadir) in the extreme west, crossing both the Pyrenees and the Alps. Roman bridges were also crucial; their sturdy and sophisticated construction enabled them to survive in serviceable form through centuries of neglect, and they continued to provide nexuses for trade and transportation. Another important legacy was the complex and redoubtable fortifications that surrounded Constantinople, and other eastern Mediterranean cities, as well as the hydraulic infrastructure, although Roman aqueducts had fallen into disuse in those parts of the empire where city life declined in the fourth through eighth century. Abandoned Roman cities were an important source of *spolia* (reused decorative and construction elements), and recycled Roman columns and sarcophagi could be found adorning and supporting mosques, churches, and palaces around the Mediterranean.

The prosperity, wealth, and integration of the region stimulated movement, resettlement, and colonization. Regional diasporas of Jews, Armenians, Normans, Berbers, and Black Africans gave rise to economic, political, and cultural networks that crossed political and confessional boundaries. This dynamism, together with the demand for resources and raw materials for this deforested and mined-out region, also drew in new populations from the surrounding hinterlands, and pushed the boundaries of Mediterranean civilization outward. From the mid-eighth century Islam, for example, was no longer "spreading by the sword," but by trade—reaching Sumatra by the late 600s, gaining ground in Central Asia after the Battle of Talas (against the Chinese Tang dynasty) in 751, and establishing itself politically in the Niger region and the Horn of Africa by the 900s. Byzantium's expansion into the Volga followed a parallel course. The capitals and bustling ports of Byzantium and the Islamic world became centers of cosmopolitanism, and with the exception of the Latin lands, even the countryside of the Mediterranean was ethnically and religiously diverse.

Farm and Field

Food production was the most important sector in every premodern economy, no matter how urbanized. The disintegration of the Roman economic and political system in the fourth through seventh century was characterized by the abandonment or decline of large, grain-producing plantation estates across the region, as both demand for food and distribution networks declined. North Africa and Syria-Palestine experienced widespread rural depopulation and, in some areas, desertification. Nomadic herders became more important and encroached on previously arable lands here and along the southern shore, although complex, large-scale irrigation systems continued to function in Egypt and in Mesopotamia. This phase of abatement was not a consequence of the rise of Islam, but of the ecological and political crises that preceded it. Arabo-Islamic expansion was a consequence rather than a cause of the decline of the classical Mediterranean, and it was the rise of Islam that laid the groundwork for the reestablishment of urban culture and region-wide trade.

Muslims disseminated irrigation techniques that originated in Persia and North Africa, such as the *qanat* (a type of subterranean well network), and communal canal systems that reflected the tribal organization of Arab and Berber societies. These sophisticated irrigation practices, which were able to emulate the monsoon conditions of the Indian Ocean zone, enabled the dissemination of a range of new cereal crops, as well as the intensification of market gardening, and the introduction of vegetables, trees, fruits, and nuts from as far afield as India and central Africa. Together, irrigation and fertilization increased yields dramatically, constituting a "green revolution." As in Byzantium, agronomy and animal husbandry manuals were produced in the Islamic world from the tenth century, some by Christian authors. One tenth-century almanac ("The Calendar of Córdoba") was written by the

FIGURE 2.5 Workers in the vineyard, from an eleventh-century manuscript, the *Geoponika*, a Byzantine agronomy manual of the tenth century. The History Collection / Alamy Stock Photo.

Andalusi courtier and bishop Reccemund/Rabi' ibn Ziyad. SEE SOURCEBOOK 2:3.

In the Dar al-Islam the commercialization of agriculture and the proprietary nature of land tenure encouraged experimentation, unlike in the Latin world, where semi- or unfree peasants farmed their plots collectively. Large-scale husbandry was generally not integrated with farming; herding remained largely the vocation of nomads. Certain breeds, such as Barbary and Arabian horses and merino sheep, were disseminated throughout the region, as camels and dromedaries had been in the previous millennium.

Although in some grain-producing areas large rural estates survived, in the rural Islamic world, as in Byzantium, free smallholders came to dominate agricultural production and rural land ownership. Whereas these tended to be independent "yeoman farmers" in the empire, in the Islamic world it seems that land and irrigation rights were often held by extended families. But there was a wide variety of rural tenancies, including sharecropping, wageworking, and private and family ownership. The strong profit motive encouraged families and individuals with means to diversify their activities to include farming, herding, craft, and speculative investment, breaking down the distinction between peasant and townsman and further stimulating social mobility.

The introduction of new food crops, together with the availability of spices from East Africa, South Asia, and beyond, transformed the cuisine and culture of the Islamic Mediterranean and filtered into Byzantium and Latin Italy and Spain. The introduction or extension of the cultivation of nonfood crops and products fed both trade and industry. Egypt, for example, remained an important center of cotton production, and mulberry trees gradually spread through the Mediterranean from Byzantium as the closely guarded techniques of silk production were leaked or appropriated. The Mediterranean oak, though not well suited for timber, produced charcoal and cork, and hosted kermes beetles, the eggs of which were crushed to produce valuable red dye.

The changes in Mediterranean agriculture were only one aspect of a larger process of cultural transformation originating in the Islamic world. The musician, composer, gastronome, and style maven Abu 'l-Hasan 'Ali ibn Nafi (d. 857)—known better as Ziryab (Blackbird) because of his African origins—who emigrated from Baghdad to Córdoba in the early 800s, is credited with transforming the popular culture of al-Andalus and Europe by introducing Perso-Islamic high style to the Islamic West. While a court musician of Harun al-Rashid, he had developed a unique style on the *al-'ud* (the forerunner of the lute and guitar), and was unparalleled as a singer and composer. Departing a Baghdad that was spiraling into chaos, he headed to Aleppo, then west to Aghlabid Ifriqiya. Finally, he was welcomed to al-Andalus in 822 by the *amir* 'Abd al-Rahman II (822–852), who endowed him with a generous pension and lands and made him a favorite at court.

Whereas previously, slave girls had been sent east to Persia or Arabia to be trained and refined, Ziryab founded a music and singing school in Córdoba based on his own style, from which his students, both free men and female slaves, then fanned out across the Islamic West. He is also credited with modernizing Andalusi hairstyles and fashion, introducing seasonal wear and antiperspirant. In addition, he brought new recipes from the East, as well as the use of tablecloths and the practice of eating in courses. This was precisely the era in which al-Andalus was becoming conscious of and emerging from its provincialism, and Ziryab represented everything that was sophisticated about the 'Abbasid East. His life reflects the high premium Muslim rulers placed on cultural sophistication and how Mediterranean networks facilitated cultural innovation and the dissemination of styles and fashions across the region.

In the nearly cashless Latin West, on the other hand, hereditary servile or semiservile rural tenancy was the general rule; it was monasteries, with their gardens and autonomously managed estates, that tended to serve as centers of innovation. Peasants could not sell land, which they did not own but held—usually as scatterings of small parcels—from their lords in exchange for labor dues and a portion of the harvest in kind. This brought stability, but also rigidity, and social mobility was low and innovation slow. Italy and the Iberian Peninsula were exceptions. Italy's relative prosperity and decentralized political landscape increased opportunities for producers to diversify and experiment. In Spain the dangerous and underdeveloped frontier with al-Andalus (often described as "deserted," but meaning without seignorial control) provided a space where entrepreneurial peasants could escape lordly dominion and settle new territory as free men. Some lords, notably monasteries, began to use long-term collaborative arrangements to entice peasants to clear new land for vineyards and arboriculture, and as a means of colonization.

In contrast with the Latin West where the role of warrior and ruler was combined, in Islamic lands civil and military administration were meant to be independent, except in militarized frontier zones. In the Islamic West the *hisn-qarya* (fortress-village) settlement pattern combined locally supported or "state"-run public defense facilities with settlements of free villagers in a nonseignorial arrangement. As free subjects, Muslim farmers owed few if any labor dues; taxes were paid in cash in accordance with Qur'anic prescriptions, along with a whole range of extracanonical levies rulers imposed on their subjects in contravention of Islamic law. In Muslim Syria-Palestine, however, as in Byzantium, by the tenth century, peasants seem to have been losing autonomy and were facing declining prosperity. Although local lords in the Greek and Islamic East never gained judicial rights over their subjects, "feudalizing" tax-farming arrangements encouraged exploitation by a mercenary elite and introduced an intermediary authority that eroded the status of peasants.

Commerce and Craft

Commerce and craft had suffered a similar decline to organized agriculture in the sixth and seventh centuries, particularly in the western Mediterranean, and for many of the same interrelated reasons: political disintegration, climate change, population decline, and plague. But commerce—particularly low-value but intense local trade—did not disappear, and it was the emergence of Islam as

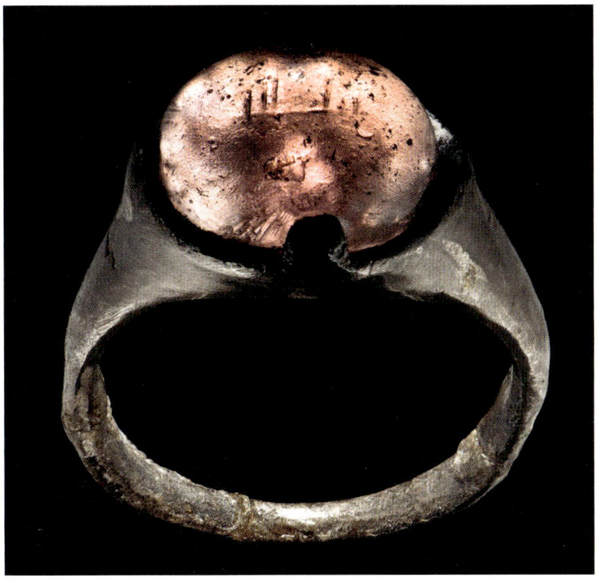

FIGURE 2.6 A ring with the inscription "for/to Allah" in Arabic, found in a Viking-era woman's burial; Birka, Sweden, ninth century CE. Image courtesy of The Swedish History Museum/SHM. Photo: Ola Myrin, CC-BY-4.0.

a political and cultural power that reestablished long-distance trade and stimulated local and regional commerce both within the Dar al-Islam and across confessional lines. By the ninth century, there were reports of the Radhanites—Jewish traders from Persia—ranging into Frankish lands and as far east as China. Tenth-century Jewish traders' letters from the Cairo *geniza* reveal family networks that linked the Islamic and Christian Mediterranean with India.

As members of a relatively small and closed community with a high index of literacy and social cohesion and an independent legal and religious culture, Jews were able to create cohesive long-distance trade networks in the absence of state power. But they were not unique. For many of the same reasons, Armenian merchants would eventually come to dominate inland trade in the East. In any event, Muslim merchants were far more numerous and important in the Islamic world in this period, and native Christians participated in trade as well. Norsemen also traded (and raided) across the Mediterranean, and into the Islamic world, as did the peoples on the border of the Islamic and Byzantine Mediterranean, such as Rus, Turkic peoples, Franks, and Berbers. Notable hoards of 'Abbasid coins have been unearthed in Scandinavia. Such was this influence that the eighth-century Anglo-Saxon king Offa of Mercia (757–796) minted gold coins that featured a garbled Islamic declaration of faith in Arabic on one side! Byzantine commercial culture, for its part, seems to have been oriented more toward the internal market—leaving longer-distance trade largely in the hands of foreign merchants—although certain products, notably silk, were important export items. SEE SOURCEBOOK 2:4.

Long-distance trade was not confined to luxury commodities, such as the spices and gems that came across the Indian Ocean. Rather, it was the demand for key commodities and food staples that drove it. From the ninth century, slaves and timber from northern and eastern Europe were brought into the Islamic Mediterranean by Jewish, Frankish, and Norse merchants, together with furs and other animal products. In the tenth century, central Africa became increasingly important as a source of plentiful and cheap gold and slaves, as well as ivory, spices, furs, and other exotica. Domestic commerce included locally produced foodstuffs, cloth and clothing, glassware and porcelain, and other craft items and decorative objects. Contemporary records list hundreds of types of items that were traded. Some industries, like paper, depended on proximity to large populations centers (to supply rag); others, such as tanning, to hinterlands with large-scale nomadic or seminomadic herders. The Islamic world had both, and thus became an important exporter. For all the emphasis historians put on long-distance luxury trade, the large population base and the many urban centers of the Byzantine-Islamic Mediterranean created local markets for a regional trade that dwarfed long-distance commerce in volume and value.

In Byzantium, crafts and professions were organized into state-controlled guilds, a legacy of the Roman era, and these functioned as a means of collecting customs and tax revenue, and for elite members to maintain their privilege. There were no formal guilds or corporations in the Islamic world. In principle everything was owned by a person and therefore subject to the rigid and egalitarian inheritance laws that were prescribed by the Qur'an. However, the establishment of enterprises as *waqf* or *hubus* (pious endowments) could shelter property from these laws and from tax obligations and enable it to be passed down through generations undivided among heirs. This was not dissimilar to the strategies used by noble families in Latin lands to conserve wealth—where they founded and endowed monasteries that would be ruled over by their descendants, who would thus preserve family influence by sheltering patrimony under the protection of the church.

The scale of commerce in the Islamic world and the lack of any social stigma attached to it encouraged the emergence of an extremely robust and powerful merchant class, which included both Muslims and non-Muslims. Wealthy but vulnerable Christians and Jews provided an important financial reserve for Muslim rulers, as these could be easily pressed into making gifts or loans to the state or could be subject to piously rationalized confiscations without exciting any opposition from the rulers' Muslim subjects. Among Muslims it was merchants who became the most active and influential members of the *'ulama'*. As such, they posed both a counterbalance and a threat to the caliph or prince who wielded secular political authority (*sultan*). In times of political instability, the merchants'/clerics' combination of populist moral authority and economic power enabled them to press their agendas ahead of those of their rulers—an advantage that became clear as central power across the Islamic world broke down after 1000 CE and these merchants/clerics at times overthrew their rulers in favor of new princes or to establish local oligarchical republics.

Long-distance trade was both a means by which the reach of the Mediterranean world was extended, and a means by which new peoples and commodities were drawn into it. For example, the city of Sijilmassa, located in the eastern shadow of the Atlas Mountains and on the northwest edge of the great Saharan sand sea, connected to Aoudaghost, thousands of kilometers to the south, and then on to Ghana. Thus, it emerged by 900 as the main northern caravan terminus on one of the main north-south routes that connected the gold-rich sub-Saharan region to the Mediterranean.

Muslim traders carrying salt and craft goods south from here returned with slaves, exotica, including ivory, skins, and animals, and the high-quality and abundant gold of the Niger River region and Akan forest. It was this gold that drove the prosperity of the Caliphate of Córdoba and the local Berber dynasties who ruled as clients of the Umayyads until the decline of the latter in 1008. Such was Sijilmassa's prosperity in the tenth century that merchants there wrote checks to each other to the value of tens of thousands of dinars. It was here—the economic hub of the Islamic West—that 'Ubayd Allah al-Mahdi (909–934) took refuge before establishing himself in Ifriqiya and declaring the Fatimid Caliphate. Throughout the Middle Ages Sijilmassa remained a prize for any group who sought to dominate the Maghrib, but by the sixteenth century, when European ships had reached the West African Gold Coast, it had declined, and lay in ruins.

The traffic along the route southward from Sijilmassa exposed the pagan nomadic tribesmen to Islam, including the Berber Almoravids, who raided and guarded the caravans, and as these warriors converted they inserted themselves politically into the western Mediterranean, conquering the Maghrib and al-Andalus shortly after 1050. This route was also the conduit for the peaceful conversion, or semiconversion, of the ruling classes of central Africa and of their integration into the Arabo-Islamic world. This process culminated in the eventual establishment of Timbuktu and Djenné as centers of Islamic learning, and the rise of the Kingdom of Mali under Mansa Musa (ca. 1280–1337). It was the gold of the Akan and the Niger delta that would attract Portuguese navigators a century later and provided an early stimulus for the European "Age of Discovery." Similar routes to the east connected central Africa to Ifriqiya, while in Egypt, the Nile and the Red Sea and Indian Ocean coasts were conduits for trade and vectors for Islamicization.

The tremendous commercial dynamism of the Islamic world was due to a number of factors, first among which was the formal legal, linguistic, and cultural homogeneity that was a feature of the ninth- and tenth-century Pax Islamica. Because it emerged organically out of scriptural rather than "state" law, Islamic law functioned across political divisions. The lack of rigid class structures, the individualism and egalitarianism of Islam and its openness to outsiders and infidels, together with a lack of corporate institutions that could stifle innovation, created an extremely dynamic entrepreneurial culture. Easy access to capital, thriving internal markets, and the development of sophisticated credit mechanisms were also important. Together with a variety of types of partnerships that shared risk and capital, credit mechanisms developed

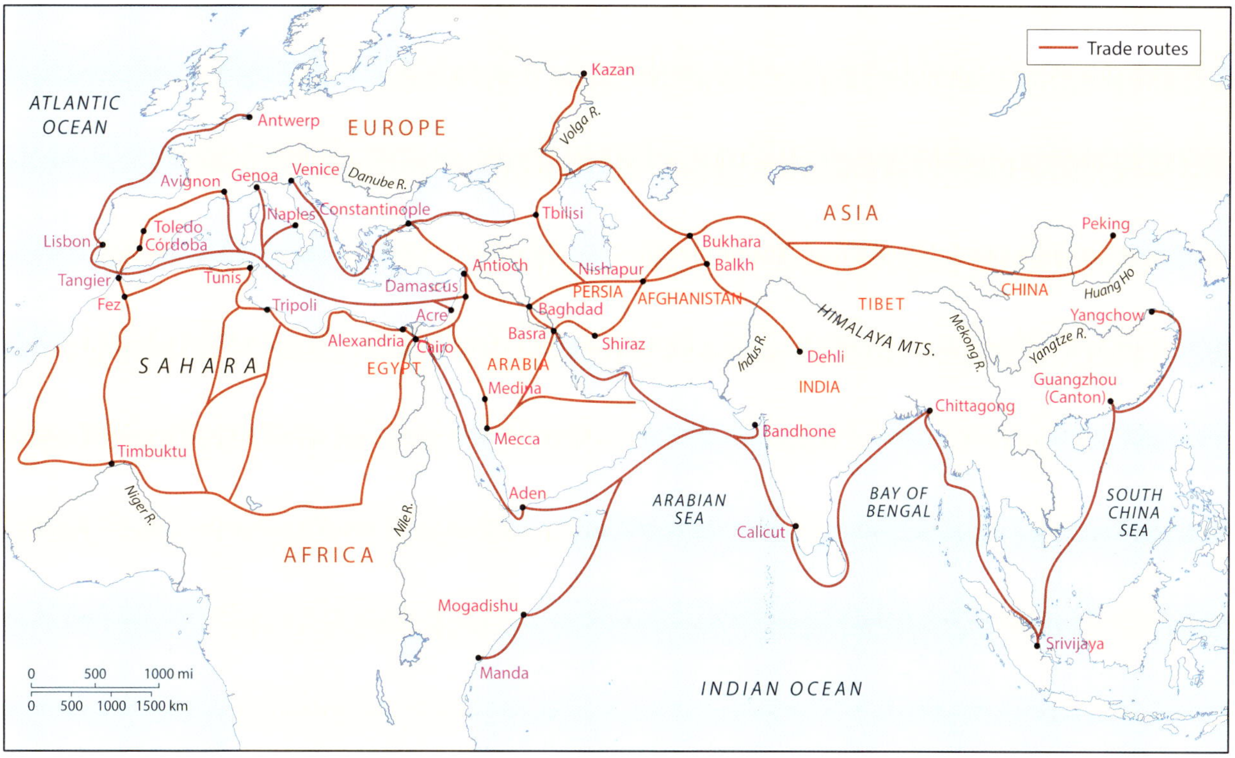

MAP 2.6 Islamic Trade Routes, ca. 1050. Original source unknown.

as a consequence of the legal and moral consensus that bound the region, and the importance of reputation and trust in commercial success. The robust caliphal states (and Byzantium) of the ninth and tenth centuries also played a role in spreading commerce. Organized efforts to enforce peace and order on land and sea reduced the risk of trade and travel, and networks of *funduq*s (*pandocheia,* in Greek) and *caravanserais* provided port facilities and infrastructure for overland trade, as did working postal (and intelligence) services. In the Byzantine and Islamic world the literary and scientific patronage of the elite encouraged the elaboration and circulation of works of geography, notably the Arabo-Islamic literary genre "Routes and Kingdoms," which describes towns from the Atlantic to Central Asia together with their commodities and resources and the directions and distances between them. SEE SOURCEBOOK 2:5.

People and Places

Movement in the Mediterranean was undoubtedly primarily related to commerce, but the long-distance luxury trade that historians so often focus on was only part of this. Both sea and land routes traversed the Mediterranean, and each had advantages and disadvantages. Seasonal currents and winds circumscribed sailing routes, even though oared power continued to be used. Muslims popularized the maneuverable *dhow,* a small boat with a triangular sail capable of sailing upwind; the magnetic compass; and advanced astronomical navigation. Sea travel was relatively cheap for moving cargo, but risky, as losses tended to be total. Land routes were less dependent on season, but bandits were a danger. In both cases, local, regional, and long-distance trade combined with the incremental trade, or cabotage, that moved goods and people around the Mediterranean in short hops from port to port.

This integration of long-distance and local trade not

only served to economically integrate the region, but facilitated the establishment of small expatriate trade communities in port towns and landlocked trading centers—an important medium for the dissemination of culture, folk practices, and varieties of religious belief, and a demographic force that helped transform the cities and regions of the Mediterranean, as foreign trading and craft elites became established, married into local populations, and gained influence in new locales. Merchants were often men of learning, and served also as missionaries and as envoys, spies, and agents of foreign powers. Economic opportunity, particularly in the socially mobile and urban Islamic world, but also in Byzantium, brought peasants from the countryside to town, nomads to settled areas, and seekers of fortune from the provinces to the capitals and back, all of which contributed to the rich cultural ferment of the Mediterranean, and served to disseminate learning, technology, and commodities.

Religious pilgrimage—an established custom in Christianity, Islam, and Judaism—also drove the circulation of people into and throughout the region and was closely linked to trade. As the memoir of Egeria, a woman from northwest Spain attests, Christians from across the Mediterranean had been visiting the Holy Land since the late fourth century. The decline in pilgrim traffic from Latin lands after the fifth century reflected the economic decline there, but by 1000 the region was recovering, and Latins were once again coming as religious tourists to the Holy Land. Muslim authorities provided protection to pilgrims (such as they could) subject to payment of an entry tax. Occasional episodes of a repressive nature, such as the Fatimid caliph al-Hakim's destruction of the Church of the Holy Sepulcher in 1004, represented minor interruptions.

Rome, the seat of the papacy, and local sites associated with relics and martyrs, and pre-Christian sacred places, were also destinations; the Catholic doctrine of absolution and penance, which gelled in the eleventh century, encouraged the petition of saintly intervention via relics and shrines. The purported discovery of the remains of Saint James the Apostle (later recast as "the Muslim-Killer") in Iria Flavia in the far northwest of the Iberian Peninsula was the germ of the "Route of Santiago." After the mid-eleventh century this would become the major Latin pilgrimage route, with tendrils reaching through Europe. It would serve as a major economic and cultural artery and an ideological focal point for Christian expansion into Muslim Spain. In Byzantium, Constantinople, with its concentrations of relics relating to Christ's Passion and the Virgin, and Thessaloniki, the cult site of the soldier-saint Demetrios, together with local holy sites, displaced Jerusalem as preferred destinations.

For Muslims, the highly choreographed annual pilgrimage to Mecca (the *hajj*) was to be completed once in one's lifetime (wealth and circumstance permitting). By 700 Mecca's importance as a market had declined, but the *hajj* remained an important stimulus for trade outside of the Arabian Peninsula. Islamic eschewal of sainthood notwithstanding, the tombs of Companions of the Prophet, local holy men, the Virgin Mary, the Old Testament Prophets and Patriarchs, and appropriated Christian saints and figures of classical mythology also drew devotees. Jewish pilgrimage fit this same general pattern, particularly in the East, where the tombs of Prophets and Patriarchs, as well as important rabbis and sages, attracted supplicant visitors. Trans-Mediterranean pilgrimage among Latinate Jews would intensify in the late eleventh century, as Latin-Christian traffic increased. Members of all three religious groups appropriated and recast holy sites from classical mythology, including sacred springs, groves, and rocks. The traveler Ibn Hawqal (d. 988) visited Sicily in 972, reporting that Aristotle's coffin was hung from a chain in the great mosque of Palermo and that Christians would pray to it for rain.

The larger migrations that took place in the period prior to 1050 CE also contributed to the transformation of the Mediterranean. The Arabs provide the most obvious example of the impact this could have on culture and society. Few Arabs reached the western Mediterranean, and here migrations of Berber peoples in large numbers, particularly to al-Andalus, and later to Sicily, had a significant impact. Earlier Berber migrants appear to have assimilated to the new Arabicized Andalusi culture, while later arrivals tended to maintain strong social and cultural links with clan members in North Africa. Once the Dar al-Islam coalesced, it became a zone in which ethno-religious groups originating in the region or beyond, including Turkic peoples, Jews, Persians, and central African Blacks, circulated and settled. Byzantium operated in a similar fashion in the Balkans and

Black Sea area. Moreover, the centralized and authoritarian character of imperial rule enabled transportation of whole peoples to be carried out as policy (such as the mass resettlement of heretical Paulician Armenians in Thrace and Balkan Bulghars in Anatolia in the tenth century). Like Jews in the West, Armenians, who included Christians of various denominations and Muslims, were mobile on both sides of the confessional frontier in the East and found opportunities in the breakdown of imperial and caliphal power in the decades following 1000 CE. Some groups immigrated to the Mediterranean in response to the military needs of the region's rulers, whether temporarily, like the Norsemen, or permanently, like the Seljuqs. Across the Mediterranean, warfare produced captives, often in large numbers and including women and children; their sale and dispersal constituted mini-diasporas, and captive women had an impact on their host societies via their role in the household and as mothers that has been underestimated by historians.

The net effect of these various modes and scales of movement and resettlement was the enrichment of Mediterranean culture and society by the introduction of outside influences, and homogenization through contact and acculturation. They were also the basis for the formation of professional, intellectual, technical, religious, and family networks that spanned the region, and often crossed confessional lines; these acted as potent vectors for acculturation and innovation in a whole range of fields. Next to communal affiliation and personal political or familial loyalty, place became an important nexus of identity. The natural solidarity felt by inhabitants of the same town or region could, in many contexts, override differences of ethnicity or religious identity. As the Mediterranean drifted into climatic and political crisis after the year 1000 CE, movement within and to the region intensified. The next phase of Mediterranean history, roughly 1050 to 1350 CE, would be defined both by the emergence of new indigenous elites and compact political entities, and by the increasing ingress of groups from the European, African, and Asian hinterlands. The political fragmentation of the Mediterranean was both a cause and a consequence of the intensifying competition between these groups.

CHAPTER THREE

Conversion and the Consolidation of Identities

In 851 a wealthy Christian named Isaac appeared before a Muslim judge in Córdoba, the capital of the Umayyad emirate of al-Andalus, and, after feigning a desire to convert to Islam, let loose a barrage of blasphemies against the Prophet Muhammad and the Islamic faith. He deliberately left the Muslim authorities little choice but to condemn him to death in compliance with Islamic law. Isaac was the first of some fifty Christians who were executed at the hands of the Muslim rulers over the next nine years, some deliberately, some less willingly. By this time the Christians of the Iberian Peninsula had been living under Muslim rule for 140 years, since Muslims conquered the peninsula in 711, seizing it from its Catholic Visigothic rulers. The new Muslim rulers had granted the subjugated Christians the freedom to practice their religion and to regulate their internal and family affairs in accordance with the laws of the Catholic Church. However, as a result of increasing social interaction with Muslims, service in the Umayyad government, and exposure to the Muslims' rich Arabic culture, literate Christians had been abandoning the Latin language and culture for Arabic, and perhaps a quarter of the Christian population had converted to Islam. The militant Christian martyrs hoped that their dramatic, public proclamation of their faith would stem the tide of this quiet, gradual cultural and religious transformation. Isaac, an Umayyad government official fluent in Arabic, was ironically an embodiment of Christian acculturation; his later retreat to a monastery and suicidal attack on Islam, however, were hardly typical. The martyrs' movement petered out as a result of pressure from the Umayyad authorities and from moderate Christian leaders worried about how the zealots' actions were antagonizing the Muslims. As Isaac and his fellows feared, Arabization and Islamization continued; by the twelfth century around 80 percent of the Christians of Muslim Spain would embrace Islam.

By 1050, the conversion of the majority of the Christian population to Islam was well underway throughout the Muslim-ruled lands of the Mediterranean, though at varying rates. It was for the most part a gradual process, unmarked by coercion on the part of the dominant Muslims or the extreme reactions of anxious Christians, such as the Córdoban martyrs.

Christian reactions to Muslim conquest and rule varied partly because Christians were not a homogeneous, united group, neither before nor after the advent of Islam. Christians were divided by political allegiance, theological niceties, and language. When the Muslims arrived on the scene the Greek Byzantine emperor and Byzantine Church espoused the Catholic or "Orthodox" theology on the nature of Jesus Christ articulated at the Council of Chalcedon (451), namely, that Christ was a person who possessed two natures, divine and human. They faced opposition from Miaphysite subjects of the empire in Syria and especially Egypt who maintained that Christ had only a single, divine nature and who expressed their faith in the Syriac and Coptic languages, respectively. Farther west, in the Germanic kingdoms that had supplanted the Roman Empire, the language of church and government was Latin. Most Christians were Catholic, acknowledging the spiritual authority of the pope in Rome; however, the Lombard rulers in Italy were still Arians, a sect that differed with Catholics on the position of Christ the Son in the Trinity.

Whether living under the dominion of the new Muslim rulers or under Christian regimes, Christians throughout the Mediterranean had to adjust to the immense political and religious changes precipitated by the rise of Islam. The Christians who survived under Muslim rule as Christians would do so largely as Arabic speakers; when melded to their particular theologies, their unique political and linguistic status would result in sectarian identities and ecclesiastical structures distinct from those of the churches in Christian states. In its much reduced size and straitened circumstances, the Byzantine Empire could no longer be a realm that encompassed a broad range of Christian sects and ethnicities; it would instead increasingly emphasize its Greek Orthodoxy for religious and political purposes. At the same time, the Latin Catholic Church, centered on papal Rome, would gradually distance itself from the Byzantine emperor and Greek Orthodox Church because of theological and political controversies and the inability of the Eastern emperor to provide it with protection against its several enemies.

Like Christians, Jews in Muslim states were attracted to Arabo-Islamic culture, and many of them—though proportionately fewer than Christians—would convert to the faith of the new masters. Yet the Jews' position as ostensible political neutrals in a sea encircled by competing Muslim and Christian states enabled them to make the most of Muslim domination of the Mediterranean through the creation of commercial and scholarly networks that extended to all shores. Jewish acculturation and mobility within the expanse of the Muslim world would significantly shape Jewish identity and culture.

Muslim Conquest and Christian Conversion

Christian conversion to Islam is a poorly understood process, in part because it was mostly quiet and uneventful, with the Muslim rulers usually observing the Qur'anic maxim "There is no compulsion in religion" (2:256). Conversion began slowly in the years following the conquest. Initially it was not encouraged, for the Arab-Muslim ruling elite of the Umayyad state based their authority and fiscal regime on the distinction between themselves and non-Muslim taxpayers, who bore a heavier tax burden. Conversion accelerated under the 'Abbasids, who, on the one hand, promoted Islam and emphasized the equality of all Muslims, Arab and non-Arab, and, on the other, sporadically enforced the restrictions of the *dhimma* pact and thus increased Christians' sense of vulnerability. In the ninth and tenth centuries, conversion snowballed as Christians became ever more intertwined with the growing number of Muslims, until it began to taper off in the eleventh century, once the bulk of Christians had converted.

Within this general framework, a number of social, economic, and cultural factors help to explain why Christians opted for Islam. Aside from these more mundane factors, religious conviction was certainly significant, though it is hard to document. What is easier to document are the efforts of committed Christians to persuade their wavering fellows to resist the allure of Islam. That their endeavors so often failed had important consequences, not only for the diminishing Christian communities but also for Muslim states and societies that had to integrate so many new Muslims.

Slaves, Spouses, and Clients

The stipulations of the *dhimma* pact guaranteeing Christians religious freedom and communal autonomy obscure messier entanglements that brought Christians over to Islam in the early postconquest years. The Muslims enslaved large numbers of Christians in the course of their expansion, before the *dhimma* regime was firmly in place. Many slaves accepted the religion of their masters, who tended to manumit them (that is, release them from slavery) as an act of piety. Muslim masters, moreover, had the right to have sexual relations with their female slaves. The children born of this legal concubinage acquired the status of their Muslim fathers: they were free and Muslim. By law, the enslaved mothers had to be freed on the death of their masters, even if they had not converted; still, in most cases they would have become Muslim.

The Muslims' impressive conquests convinced many Christians, free and enslaved, that the victors enjoyed divine favor. Islam became a religion of prestige. Among the Berbers of North Africa entire tribes therefore embraced Islam; most Christian Arab tribes in Syria and Mesopotamia also converted fairly rapidly. The garrison towns founded by the conquerors attracted many lower-class Christians seeking conversion in the hope of improving their circumstances, perhaps especially to

The construction of the Dome of the Rock probably began in 691, and was rapidly completed, on the orders of the Umayyad caliph 'Abd al-Malik (685–705). The lavishly decorated, domed octagonal building was set atop the empty Temple Mount (known to Muslims as the "Noble Sanctuary"), where the second Jewish Temple, built by King Herod, had stood until its destruction by the Romans in 70 CE.

According to some Jewish traditions, the Ark of the Covenant had been placed on the Rock that the Dome would enshrine; other traditions identified the Rock as the site where Abraham prepared to sacrifice his son Isaac. In early Muslim tradition, however, the Rock was the place from which God had risen to Heaven after finishing the creation of the universe. Yet the *'ulama'* later rejected this tradition because of its anthropomorphic representation of God. By the eleventh century the Rock was firmly associated with the Prophet Muhammad's mystical Night Journey to Jerusalem and Ascension to Heaven, alluded to in the Qur'an (surah 17), even though the Dome of the Rock had not originally been intended to commemorate these events.

The Dome of the Rock, rather, was meant to signal 'Abd al-Malik's triumph over rival claimants to caliphal authority and, most importantly, Islam's triumph over Judaism and especially Christianity. Its construction likely grew out of a larger plan of the caliph Mu'awiya (661–680) to transform Jerusalem into a Muslim center. Jerusalem had been Christian demographically and architecturally since the reign of the emperor Constantine (306–337), and Jews had been excluded from the city by the Byzantine authorities. In the late seventh century the city housed a

FIGURE 3.1 Exterior of the Dome of the Rock, Jerusalem. Photo by Diego Delso, delso.photo, provided by Wikimedia Commons under the Creative Commons Attribution-Share Alike 3.0 license.

small Muslim population and a fledgling Jewish community whose residence the Muslim rulers permitted. The Dome's specific location in a city sacred to all three faiths, as well as the inscriptions and mosaics that adorned the Dome, at once expressed Islam's transcendence of the two rival monotheisms and its fulfillment of Abrahamic prophetic tradition.

Muslims built the Dome of the Rock on the Temple Mount so that it would dominate the Christian city, particularly the Church of the Holy Sepulcher and its dome of the Anastasis, which commemorated the death, burial, and resurrection of Christ, and the no-longer-surviving Church of the Ascension. Although Muslims were unaware that the Herodian Temple had stood on the Temple Mount, they did know of King Solomon's Temple and understood that, for Christians, the location of the Church of the Holy Sepulcher facing the rubble-strewn Temple Mount symbolized Christianity's triumph over Judaism. The construction of the Dome of the Rock on the site of the Jewish Temple was not meant to raise the profile of Judaism but to position Islam as the religion that fulfilled it while pointedly putting Christianity in its place.

The Dome of the Rock's inscriptions, which contain Qur'anic passages, give special attention to the relationship between Islam and Christianity and emphasize Jesus's status as a prophet but not as the son of God. An interior inscription reads (Qur'an 4:169–71):

> O ye People of the Book, overstep not the bounds in your religion; and of God only speak truth. The Messiah, Jesus, son of Mary, is only an apostle of God, and his Word which he conveyed into Mary, and a Spirit proceeding from Him. Believe therefore in God and His apostles, and say not 'Three'. It will be better for you. God is only one God. Far be it from his glory that He should have a son.

The inscriptions, like the one on the north gate, also express the universality of Muhammad's prophetic mission (Qur'an 9:33): "He it is who has sent His messenger with the guidance of the religion of truth, so that he may cause it to prevail over all religion, however much the idolaters may hate it." The inscriptions can be seen to have had a missionary intent, inviting unbelievers, especially Christians, to accept the third and final revelation granted to Muhammad. Yet their principal audience was certainly Muslims, the people who would have entered the Dome of the Rock. From the inscriptions the adherents of the new faith would have learned of Islam's political and theological superiority, what distinguished it from the Jewish and Christian faiths it had superseded, and how to counter Christian arguments.

FIGURE 3.2 The Rock inside the Dome of the Rock. Half of a stereoscopic image in the G. Eric and Edith Matson Photograph Collection of the Library of Congress, Prints and Photographs Division, Washington, D.C. LC-DIG-matpc-05029.

The Dome of the Rock's sumptuous mosaics reminded viewers of the Umayyads' power and their surpassing of their Byzantine rivals. The employment of craftsmen who had worked on the mosaics of Byzantine monuments in the region enabled the Umayyads to use Byzantine artistic styles for their own purposes. The crowns and jewels that are prominent in the mosaics were meant to represent trophies of the Byzantine and Persian rulers whom the Muslims had defeated. The trees covered with jewels, scholars think, were supposed to evoke Solomon's Temple and palace, or visions of paradise in a city, Jerusalem, which was associated with the end-time by all three faiths.

When the Crusaders conquered Jerusalem in 1099, they thought that the Dome of the Rock stood on the site of King Solomon's Temple; they converted it into a church. Salah al-Din, however, reconsecrated the Dome as an

FIGURE 3.3 The Dome of the Rock overlooking the Church of the Holy Sepulcher. Ryan Rodrick Beiler / Alamy Stock Photo.

FIGURE 3.4 Interior mosaic with Arabic inscription and hanging crowns and jewels. ©Historical Views / agefotostock.

Islamic shrine when he retook the city in 1187. In modern times the Dome has become a UNESCO World Heritage Site. Since the Israeli capture of east Jerusalem from Jordan in the 1967 War, Muslim authorities have administered the Temple Mount as a religious trust (*waqf*).

Discussion Questions

1. What different meanings might the Dome of the Rock have had for the Muslim, Christian, and Jewish residents of, or visitors to, Jerusalem at the end of the seventh century, and how might these meanings have changed over the subsequent centuries?

2. How effective would the Dome of the Rock have been as a missionary tool, and why might its messages have been especially important for recent converts to Islam?

3. What kind of impact might the changing configuration of architectural space and of new monumental structures have on relations between distinct groups in a religiously plural society?

Further Reading

Grabar, Oleg. *The Dome of the Rock*. Cambridge: The Belknap Press of Harvard University Press, 2006.

———. *The Shape of the Holy: Early Islamic Jerusalem*. Princeton: Princeton University Press, 1996.

Johns, Jeremy, ed. *Bayt al-Maqdis: Jerusalem and Early Islam*. Pt. 2. Oxford: Oxford University Press, 1999.

Peters, F. E. *The Distant Shrine: The Islamic Centuries in Jerusalem*. New York: AMS Press, 1993.

Raby, Julian, and Jeremy Johns, eds. *Bayt al-Maqdis: 'Abd al-Malik's Jerusalem*. Pt. 1. Oxford: Oxford University Press, 1992.

escape the heavier taxes imposed on non-Muslims. The Muslim rulers' fiscal demands indeed fomented sporadic rebellions among the Coptic peasantry in Egypt between 725 and 832. The harsh suppression of the rebellions induced numerous despairing peasants to convert to Islam.

Conquest, early enslavement, and the opportunities associated with a triumphant faith dovetailed with social and legal practices that facilitated the incorporation of Christians and Christian converts into Muslim kinship structures. The society of the Arab-Muslim conquerors was composed of tribes, that is, of malleable kinship groups constituting political communities. Early on, Arab tribesmen demonstrated considerable flexibility in dealing with converts. Converted and freed slaves established a relationship of clientage with their former masters and family. Because tribal concerns influenced much of Islamic social life, the adoption of an Arab tribal name, and sometimes genealogy, provided ties that could be crucial for the converts' Muslim identity. Such manumitted clients (*mawali*, sing.: *mawla*), as well as the offspring of slave mothers, and the mothers themselves, were integrated as members of Muslim families and tribes.

Free Christians who converted also sought to become *mawali* of Arab patrons. In the Umayyad period many clients, of both free and slave origin, quickly penetrated Arab-Muslim society. They served in the army in considerable numbers, with some receiving positions of command. Other neo-Muslims held posts in civil government: *mawali* often ran the fiscal administration in Egypt in the first half of the eighth century, and regularly governed North African provinces. Others played a prominent role in intellectual life. Abu Hanifa (705–767), the founder of the Hanafi school of law, whose great-grandfather was a freed convert, continued to identify as a *mawla*. Yet many Arabs, concerned about the potential threat of neo-Muslims to their prestige and authority, discriminated against *mawali* for their servile, non-Arab origins. Nevertheless, *mawali* had a clear and legitimate place, which rendered Muslim society less alien and more attractive to other potential Christian converts, especially poorer Christians hoping to improve their lot.

Arab Muslims consolidated their authority—and demonstrated the honor of their tribe, people, and faith—by marrying women of elite Christian families. Marital alliances pacified the defeated aristocracy, who hoped in this way to secure their own position under the new regime. After the Muslim conquest of Visigothic Hispania, for instance, the family of the former king Witiza (d. 710) reportedly managed to maintain its high social status through the successive marriages of one of its women, Sara, to two leading members of the Arab army. Sara's descendants would become prominent Arab families in Muslim Seville, with some bearing the moniker Ibn Qutiyya, "son of the Gothic woman." Such elite Christians set an example followed by lower-status Christians. The emerging Islamic laws upheld Arab tribal honor while extending Islam: Muslim males could marry *dhimmi* women, not vice versa; the offspring, in this patrilineal society, would be Muslim, like their father. As the Christian community in a particular region lost its women to Muslim families, the Muslim community would have increased dramatically in proportion, thanks particularly to the legality of polygamy, which allowed men to take four wives.

The Christian wives of Muslim men, however, were not required to convert or to sever ties with their natal families and communities. Thus, they functioned as key intermediaries between Muslim and Christian communities, and interfaith unions came to be at the center of social networks in which the families and friends of the Muslim and Christian spouses mingled. The Muslim children of these mixed marriages, raised by Christian or formerly Christian mothers in a Muslim household, were often bilingual, in Arabic and the local vernacular, and bicultural. They were able to circulate more easily in both Muslim and Christian societies, and they broadened the range of social, cultural, and religious contacts between the societies. The social and kinship networks in which Muslims, neo-Muslims, and Christians were enmeshed became ever wider and denser, and conversion proceeded apace.

Arabization and Islamization

Christians' conversion was tied to their acquisition of the Arabic language and the cultural norms of their Arab-Muslim rulers, narrowing the cultural distance between themselves and the Muslims, who then saw them more sympathetically. After the Umayyad caliph 'Abd al-Malik made Arabic the language of government, any Christian wishing to serve in the administration or associate with the Muslim elite had to learn the language of the Qur'an. Under the 'Abbasids, Arabic became the vehicle of a fresh and vibrant intellectual tradition. Harun al-Rashid and his successors sponsored the translation of Greek, Syriac, and Persian scientific and philosophical texts into Arabic, which enabled Muslim scholars to make significant advancements on the Hellenic and Persian legacy. Most of the translators were Christians, the most notable being Hunayn ibn Ishaq (808–873), an Arab Christian and Syriac speaker who became the physician of the caliph al-Mutawakkil (847–861) and headed a circle of translators that included his son Ishaq and his nephew Hubaysh. Although the intellectual culture that they contributed to was distinctively Arabic and Islamic, it proved tremendously alluring to literate Christians, who were drawn not only to scientific works but also to Arabic poetry and belles lettres.

With the entrenchment of Arabic, Christians of Syria-Palestine had largely lost the ability to use Greek for literary and theological purposes by the ninth century, although Syriac lasted longer. In Egypt Christians still wrote in Coptic in the thirteenth century, but Arabic was the principal language of their church, and had long been the vernacular of the laity. In tenth-century al-Andalus Christians translated sacred texts into Arabic because Latin was no longer spoken. Generally, Arabic became the language of everyday speech, especially in the cities where Christians had the most contact with Muslims. Its acquisition became economically essential, especially after Muslims came to dominate Mediterranean commerce in the early 800s. SEE SOURCEBOOK 3:1.

From the reign of 'Abd al-Malik onward, Muslim rulers also promoted Islam through the construction of major mosques, such as the Great Mosque of Damascus, built over the city's Christian church, and by ensuring that converts were relieved of the poll tax (*jizya*). The 'Abbasids put greater emphasis on the distinction between Muslims and non-Muslims, and under their rule the '*ulama*' elaborated Islamic law and grappled with theological questions that applied to Muslims of all backgrounds. This inculcated a deeper sense of what it meant to be Muslim, but also what it meant to be non-Muslim, thereby provoking an ambivalence toward Christians that tipped over into popular Muslim hostility. Muslim rulers sometimes expressed their piety by removing public symbols of Christianity, such as the cross, by increasing taxes on the church, or, as in the anomalous case of the Fatimid caliph al-Hakim, destroying churches and persecuting Christians. Such negative pressures also prompted Christians to convert. In the Maghrib a mix of acculturation, spiritual attraction, and possibly coercion led to the almost complete absorption of the Christian communities by the twelfth century. Here, the emigration of the Christian clerical leadership had apparently deprived local Christians of the intellectual and institutional resources needed to resist Islamization.

Christian Resistance

Some Christians were alarmed by the Arabization of their communities, fearing that acculturation presented a slippery slope to conversion. They realized that Islam's monotheism, its acknowledgment of the revealed character of Judaism and Christianity, and its recognition of Jesus as one of God's messengers blurred the differences between the two faiths and made it easier for Christians to abandon their own. Concerned Christians responded in several ways to this threat.

One tactic was to halt Arabization by encouraging study of Christian texts in their original languages. The priest Eulogius and the layman Paul Alvarus, vociferous admirers of the Córdoban martyrs, tried to spark a Latin cultural revival in Muslim Spain by importing from the Christian north Latin manuscripts of classical and early Christian authors and by teaching Christians Latin poetry. They proved to be less successful than the Egyptian Copts and Syriac Christians at maintaining the literacy of their brethren in their scriptural language.

Another tactic that was apparently more effective was to write polemical texts that attacked Islam and apologetic texts that defended Christianity against Muslim criticisms. Whether writing in Arabic or in their native tongue, Christian apologists often demonstrated detailed knowledge of Islam and the Qur'an. Some apologists rejected Muhammad's prophethood, given that, unlike Jesus, he had performed no miracles. Others upheld Christian doctrines rejected in the Qur'an, such as the Trinity, and countered the Muslim argument that Jewish and Christian scriptures had been corrupted. Still others, such as John of Damascus (652–749), a Syrian Christian who had served in the Umayyad government before retreating to a monastery, characterized Islam as a "heresy" because it recognized Christian scripture as revealed, but rejected the indispensable doctrine of Jesus's divinity.

Christian writers targeted Arabizing coreligionists for cooperating with Muslims or emphasizing Jesus's prophetic status instead of insisting on his divinity. They wanted Christians to declare their faith unambiguously, and some did just that by choosing the monastic life. The Córdoban martyrs of the 850s took this to an extreme, publicly proclaiming Christianity while blaspheming Islam, and thus provoking their own executions. There were martyrs in the East, but they were mostly individuals who were executed for having lapsed into Christianity after converting to Islam. A number of the Córdoban martyrs, as offspring of mixed marriages, had experienced identity crises, which they tried to resolve by self-destructively provoking Muslim violence. Flora, for example, was the daughter of a Muslim father, who died early in her childhood, and a Christian mother of noble descent, who illicitly raised her and her sister as Christians. When Flora's devout Muslim brother denounced her before the local *qadi* (judge) for apostasy, she declared her Christian faith. She later incurred the death penalty because she and a companion named Maria, the daughter of a Christian man and a Muslim woman who had illegally converted to Christianity, publicly defamed the Prophet Muhammad in the *qadi*'s court. Ultimately, the only lasting result of the martyrs' suffering was their commemoration in a series of texts meant to inspire other Christians to resist.

The Impact of Mass Conversion

Islamization manifested itself most palpably in the form of mosques, palaces, and markets, with their specific "Islamic" style, that replaced or dwarfed existing Christian structures. A defining feature of the Muslim city was the congregational mosque, which was meant to accommodate the entire local Muslim population for the Friday prayer. Substantial Christian conversion was one factor prompting the periodic enlargement of these mosques. The Great Mosque in Umayyad Córdoba thus underwent its most dramatic expansion in the late tenth century, nearly tripling in size during the reigns of al-Hakam II

FIGURE 3.5 Great Mosque of Córdoba, Spain; aerial view. Photo: Toni Castillo Quero, provided by Wikimedia Commons under the Creative Commons Attribution-Share Alike 2.0 Generic license.

and the *hajib* al-Mansur. New construction in cities met the needs and reinforced the identity of expanding Muslim populations, which themselves became more ethnically diverse as various Mediterranean peoples adopted the faith of the conquerors.

Through all of this, converts required direction on how to live a proper Muslim life. This came from the *'ulama'*, who served as models of upright conduct and religious learning, and who addressed the complexities of daily life through their legal rulings. Thus, converts and their descendants constituted a growing proportion of the masses whose needs the *'ulama'* addressed, and came to join the ranks of the *'ulama'* themselves. 'Ali ibn Ziyad (d. 799), who played a key role in bringing the Maliki school of law from Medina to North Africa, was the son of a Christian convert from Tripoli.

The spread of the Islamic faith created new political challenges that neither the Umayyad nor the 'Abbasid empire could ultimately overcome. The Umayyads, who governed as the Arab rulers of an Arab kingdom, could not maintain legitimacy in the eyes of disgruntled non-Arab Muslims. The 'Abbasids who ousted them were members of the sacred family of the Prophet Muhammad, through the line of his uncle 'Abbas, and hence girded their rule with the symbolism of Islamic legitimacy that even non-Arab Muslim subjects respected. Yet the 'Abbasids too were victims of Islam's success, for by the late ninth century the caliphate had begun to fragment, its provinces governed by dynasties who either professed only nominal allegiance to the caliph or none at all. As the caliphs came to rely increasingly on armies of foreign converted slave-soldiers largely of Turkic origin and without roots in local societies, Muslims across the caliphate felt alienated from the Arab caliphal elite. In the

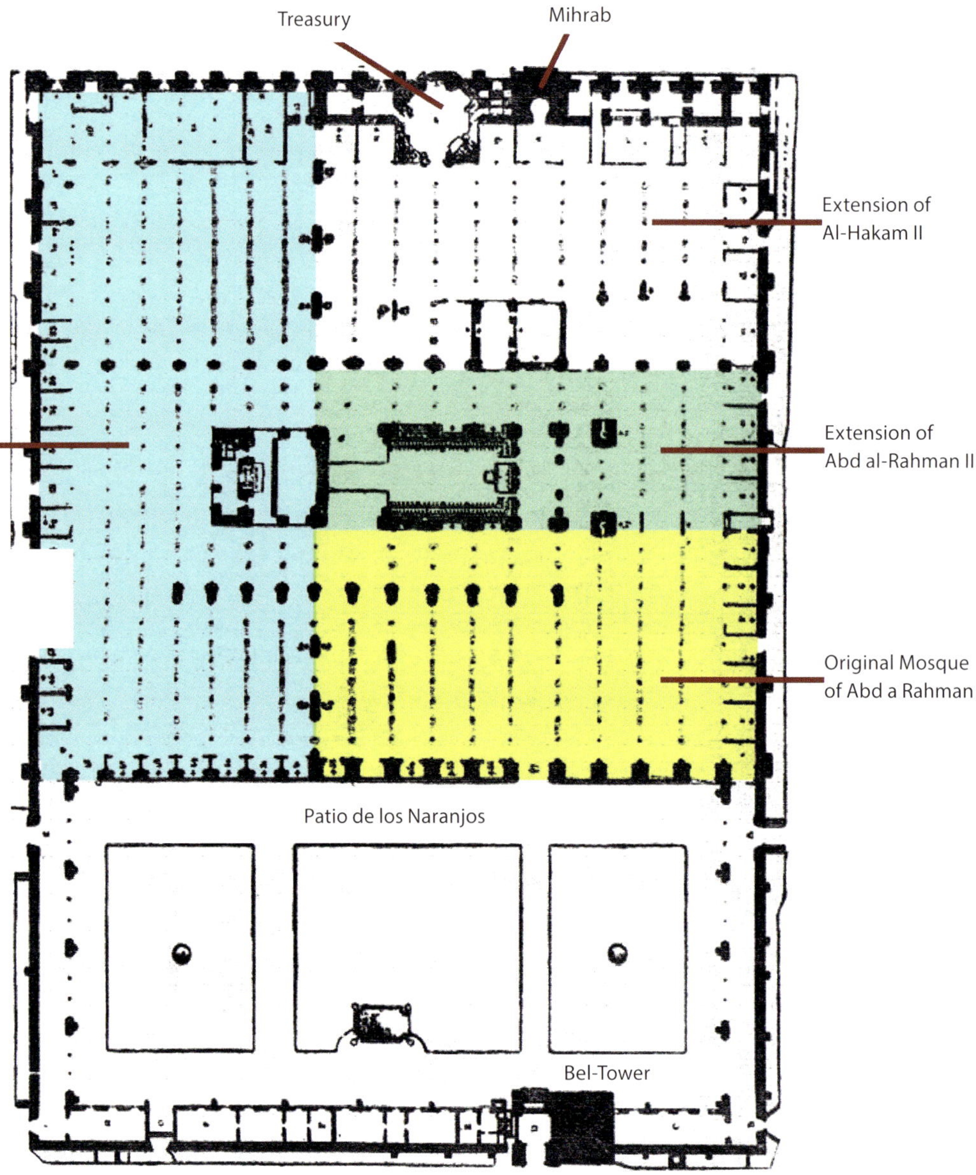

FIGURE 3.6 Great Mosque of Córdoba, floor plan. ©Historical Views / agefotostock.

provinces, converts and their descendants contributed to the development of regional variants of the overarching Arabo-Islamic culture. Soon, indigenous Muslim elites emerged who either seized power themselves or lent their support to foreign rulers, some of them 'Abbasid officials who had come to identify with local interests.

Many rulers based their authority on religious charisma or descent from the Prophet; this political discourse was a response to the deepening faith of the non-Arab local elites and masses whose support they needed. Berber leaders, for instance, often espoused Kharijite doctrines, insisting that the leader (*imam*) be chosen on the basis of his learning and piety, irrespective of ethnic background, and that political authority be dependent on the upholding of Islamic principles. The Rustamids (777–909) of Tahert were a Kharijite dynasty, eventually removed from power by the Fatimids, the Shi'i dynasty that claimed descent from 'Ali. It was precisely in the period of the political disintegration of the 'Abbasid Caliphate—from 945 to 1050—that divisions between Sunni and Shi'i Islam formalized and hardened. Indeed, the 'Abbasids in Baghdad and the Umayyads in Córdoba were prompted to more explicitly define Sunni Islam in response to threats from Shi'ism. This Islamic sectarianism could not have found its political expression without the enthusiasm of the masses of converts whose religious sensibilities Islam had irrevocably altered, and vice versa.

Byzantine Christianity and the Eastern Churches

Eastern Christians reacted to the Muslims' rapid conquest of Syria-Palestine and Egypt in the 630s in the manner that contemporaries often interpreted cataclysmic events: as divine punishment for their own sins, or, as some Miaphysites maintained, a scourge sent against the "heretical" Byzantine Orthodox Church for having persecuted them. Many vainly hoped that the conquest was temporary and God would eject the Arab invaders through the agency of resurgent Byzantine forces. For generations to come, however, Christians who lived under Muslim rule would adapt and forge new ecclesiastical identities in Arabizing societies. The Byzantine Empire, though greatly diminished and on the defensive, was still able to draw on spiritual resources no less formidable than the walls encircling Constantinople to withstand the Muslim threat. After the mid-800s Byzantium would take the offensive and bring many new souls into the Orthodox Church, particularly among the Bulghars and Slavs of the Balkans.

The Imperial Church under Siege

The Muslim conquests changed the place of the Byzantine emperor and church in the Christian world. Beyond the borders of their reduced domains, the emperors could not hope to enforce their claim to be divinely appointed rulers over all of Christendom. Although the popes in Rome continued to recognize the emperor in temporal affairs, imperial power waned even in this sphere. The sixth-century influx and settlement of polytheistic Slavs in the Balkans had rendered communication between Constantinople and Rome more hazardous; Muslim advances in the Mediterranean exacerbated the problem.

In this politically fragmented Christendom, the patriarch in Constantinople could more aggressively counter assertions that the Roman pope, as the successor of Saint Peter, should hold supreme authority. The patriarch's authority was unchallenged within the Byzantine Empire because the non-Chalcedonian churches that had rejected his authority were now all under Muslim rule, and the remaining Christians were largely Greek. But with Byzantium turning inward, clashing papal, patriarchal, and imperial claims only accelerated the divergence of the Greek East and the Latin West.

Byzantine Christians regrouped around the emperor and the Orthodox Church. There had long been a close relationship between the church and the secular government in the eastern empire in which the emperor controlled patriarchal appointments and influenced theological decisions. During the seventh and eighth centuries the identification of lay interests with clerical concerns heightened as the Byzantine authorities endeavored to preserve Orthodoxy by suppressing deviant belief and practice. Now viewing themselves more as Orthodox Christians than as Romans, Byzantine Christians believed that divine favor and the survival of Byzantium hinged on their adherence to theological positions enunciated by the patriarch of Constantinople and the emperor. For them, it was not just a matter of maintaining political independence: their eternal salvation was at stake.

From this perspective, the survival of Constantinople was crucial. Not only was it the imperial capital and the seat of the patriarch, it was a "New Jerusalem," a city under the protection of God and the Virgin Mary that would, Byzantines believed, play a key role in Christ's Second Coming. Since Constantinople could not match the Christian associations of the real Jerusalem, relics of Christ and the saints were gathered from all over the Mediterranean into its many churches, including the great Hagia Sophia.

The patriarch of Constantinople sat at the top of the Orthodox ecclesiastical hierarchy; beneath him were metropolitan bishops who governed the empire's ecclesiastical provinces, and under these came their many subordinate bishops. These bishops disseminated theologi-

The emperor Justinian I (527–565) ordered the construction of Hagia Sophia, or Holy Wisdom, in 532, after suppressing a rebellion against imperial authority in Constantinople, during which the original fourth-century church was burned down. The building of the Great Church, as it came to be called, was part of Justinian's program to reestablish one united Orthodox Roman Empire in the Mediterranean through military conquest, legal reform, the rooting out of Christian heresy and paganism, and sponsorship of imperial architecture, especially ecclesiastical architecture. Built in less than six years and unparalleled in its size and splendor, Hagia Sophia was meant to be and became the center of ritual for the imperial regime, a church worthy of adorning the imperial capital Constantinople, the New Rome.

Through its many windows the church was suffused with light, which contemporaries understood to symbolize wisdom and Jesus Christ, the Word of God and source of salvation. As the historian Procopius described it, the worshipper was made to feel the divine presence:

> You might say that the [interior] space is not illuminated by the sun from the outside, but that the radiance is generated within, so great an abundance of light bathes this shrine all around. . . . And so the visitor's mind is lifted up to God and floats aloft, thinking that He cannot be far away, but must love to dwell in this place which He himself has chosen.[1]

Later generations of Orthodox worshippers were no less affected by the magnificence of Hagia Sophia. For the patriarch Germanos (715–730) "the church is an earthly heaven in which the super-celestial God dwells and walks about. It represents the Crucifixion, Burial, and Resur-

FIGURE 3.7 Hagia Sophia. Photo: Arild Vagen, provided by Wikimedia Commons under the Creative Commons Attribution-Share Alike 3.0 Unported license.

FIGURE 3.8 Mosaic above the south entrance door into Hagia Sophia. Photo: Myrabella, provided by Wikimedia Commons under the Creative Commons CC0 1.0 Universal Public Domain Dedication license.

rection of Christ."[2] The church was the stage upon which the Orthodox liturgy was enacted; the principal actors were the clergy led by the patriarch and the emperor. The emperor was, significantly, the only layman admitted into the church's sanctuary, where the clergy performed Mass. The tenth-century *Book of Ceremonies* details the emperor's entry after elaborately choreographed processions to and through the church:

> The patriarch [first] goes into the sanctuary. . . . When he [the emperor] is about to go in the metropolitans [bishops] stand holding the holy doors, and when they push them towards the emperor a little the emperor kisses the crosses fixed on them and goes into the sanctuary. . . . After praying there [at the portable imperial altar] he goes up and receives communion from the hands of the patriarch. . . . After the emperor has received communion, the emperor and the patriarch both make obeisance before each other.[3]

Viewing the cooperation of emperor and priesthood under the church's great dome, onlookers received the message that both powers were essential for upholding a Christian empire. The ceremonies in Hagia Sophia legitimized the power of the emperor as the defender of Orthodoxy who was at the top of the earthly hierarchy, and so closest to God in Heaven.

While the role of Hagia Sophia as the theater of imperial Orthodoxy remained constant, the church's decorations did change over the course of the centuries, most notably in the ninth and tenth centuries, after the close of the era of iconoclasm, the imperial prohibition of images of God and the saints. Hagia Sophia originally lacked such images, but with the official restoration of the veneration of icons in 843, decorating the Great Church in the capital with figurative mosaics was deemed crucial for establishing the norms of church decor and worship throughout the empire. The walls of Hagia Sophia were gradually covered with images, some of which accentuated the connection between the emperor, the Orthodox Church, and God and his mother, the Virgin Mary.

This late ninth-century mosaic over the south entrance door into Hagia Sophia, for instance, shows the enthroned Virgin and Christ Child flanked on the left by Justinian I offering a model of the church and on the right by Constantine I (306–337) presenting a model of Constantinople, the city that he had made his imperial capital. The mosaic thus links Hagia Sophia to the founders of the city and the church, and places both city and church under the protection of Jesus and Mary.

FIGURE 3.9 Mosaic above the ceremonial entrance. Photo: Myrabella, provided by Wikimedia Commons under the Creative Commons CC0 1.0 Universal Public Domain Dedication license.

Another example is this mosaic from around 900, which was located above the church's ceremonial entrance, where the emperor and the patriarch entered together. It depicts an unnamed emperor prostrating himself in an act of homage before an enthroned Christ surrounded by roundels of the Virgin Mary and the Archangel Gabriel. Though it is thought that the mosaic portrays a penitent Leo IV (886–912), who had contracted a marriage that violated church law, Robin Cormack observes that there was nothing humiliating about an emperor showing obeisance to Christ, the King of Kings. The viewer would recognize that the emperor, the only layperson permitted to enter the church's sanctuary, was closest to God. The emperor's display of piety and humility made him a more suitable ruler in the eyes of his Christian subjects.

A church of such majesty could hardly remain immune to the political changes experienced by the city that housed it. After capturing Constantinople in 1453, the Ottoman sultan Mehmed the Conqueror converted Hagia Sophia into a mosque. The seat of the patriarch then moved to the Church of the Holy Apostles. The secular republic of Turkey under Mustafa Kemal Ataturk made Hagia Sophia a museum in 1934; it later became a UNESCO World Heritage Site. In July 2020, however, the president of Turkey, Recep Tayyip Erdogan, ordered the redesignation of Hagia Sophia as a mosque, stirring up an international controversy that is indicative of this monument's great meaning.

Discussion Questions

1. How did the sacred space of the church of Hagia Sophia function as a site for the articulation of imperial political power?
2. Situated in the capital of an empire often assailed by Muslim and pagan Slavic enemies, how did Hagia Sophia serve as a source of inspiration for the citizens of Constantinople?
3. How would the Great Church have impressed foreign visitors and diplomats from, say, papal Rome or from Muslim, Slavic, or Frankish (Carolingian) domains?

Further Reading

Cormack, Robin. *Byzantine Art*. 2nd ed. Oxford: Oxford University Press, 2018.

———. *Writing in Gold: Byzantine Society and Its Icons*. London: George Philip Publishers, 1985.

Krautheimer, Richard. *Early Christian and Byzantine Architecture*. 4th ed. New Haven: Yale University Press, 1986.

Notes

1. Cyril A. Mango, *The Art of the Byzantine Empire, 312–1453: Sources and Documents* (Englewood Cliffs, NJ: Prentice-Hall, 1972), 74, 76.
2. Cormack 2018, 33.
3. *Constantine Porphyrogennetos: The Book of Ceremonies*, trans. Ann Moffatt and Maxeme Tall (Leiden: Brill, 2012), 64, 67.

cal doctrines and canon law articulated by the patriarch and the clerical elite in Constantinople, and propagated the message that Christian salvation was closely linked to imperial rule. Ascetic holy men and monks were also important. They inspired Christians with their austerity and deep piety, and provided spiritual guidance. Members of elite families expressed their devotion by endowing monasteries or becoming monks themselves. The Byzantine Church did not develop monastic orders; rather, most monasteries followed some version of the rule of Saint Basil (330–379), which emphasized communal worship, biblical study, and service to the wider community through the operation of schools and hospitals. Byzantium, in short, metamorphosed into a spiritual fortress.

Iconoclasm and Orthodoxy

Yet Byzantine Christians hardly felt secure. The harrowing Umayyad siege of Constantinople in 717–718, followed by devastating Muslim campaigns in Anatolia in the 720s, left demoralized Christians looking for ways to please God and end their suffering. The solution, decided on by Leo III (717–741) in 726 and followed by his son Constantine V (741–775), was iconoclasm, the prohibition of Christian veneration of icons, formally promulgated at a church council in 754.

Icons were images of Christ, Mary, and the saints painted on wooden panels or made of mosaic that were hung in churches, public places, and private houses. Viewed as intercessors between man and God, they were a focus of Byzantine popular devotion. As early as the 600s, Jews had criticized such image worship as a violation of the Second Commandment against idolatry, but even more significant was the Islamic rejection of sacred figural art, reflected in 'Abd al-Malik's Dome of the Rock, which was decorated with nonfigurative mosaics and Qur'anic inscriptions, and Yazid II's (720–724) decree ordering the destruction of Christian iconography. The contrast between the victorious armies of Islam and beleaguered, icon-worshipping Byzantium was evident. Indeed, by the 720s, clergy and soldiers in the frontier provinces were voicing the opinion that God was punishing the empire for the veneration of images.

The emperors' iconoclastic policies were controversial. The patriarch Germanos resigned in 730, and many monks resisted the assault on traditional observance. Constantine V responded by publicly humiliating monks, forcing them to marry, and closing some monasteries. The popes denounced iconoclasm on theological grounds but maintained their political loyalty to Emperor Leo, who nonetheless retaliated by depriving the Roman Church of territories in southern Italy, Dalmatia, and the Balkans. In the event, Byzantine military successes, which were assisted by the upheaval of the 'Abbasid revolution, validated iconoclasm, at least for a while. However, after the 'Abbasids resumed more vigorous attacks, in 787 the empress-regent Irene convoked the Council of Nicaea II, which restored icon veneration.

A new military crisis, this time in the Balkans, set the stage for the "second iconoclasm." In 811 the Bulghar khan Krum (802–814) defeated a Byzantine army, killing the emperor Nicephorus and threatening Constantinople, and as a bid for redemption Leo V (813–820) reinstituted iconoclasm. The results, however, were less impressive. In 827 the Aghlabids from Ifriqiya began their conquest of Byzantine Sicily, and Crete was taken by an expedition of rebellious Andalusi Muslims fleeing Umayyad reprisals in Córdoba. In 838, Muslim forces captured Amorion, a city in western Anatolia. Finally, another empress-regent, Theodora, had the veneration of icons reintroduced at a synod in 843. It also instituted a new ceremony, the Feast of Orthodoxy, which was to be celebrated annually, at first in Constantinople and then throughout the Byzantine world. In it Orthodoxy as defined at Nicaea II was acclaimed, and heresy, including iconoclasm, condemned. The growing weakness of the 'Abbasid Caliphate seemed to confirm the wisdom of these decisions.

The long controversy over iconoclasm was largely a Byzantine concern, a symptom of an inward-looking and besieged empire. Relations with other Chalcedonian churches either were strained or grew more distant, but the patriarchate in Constantinople emerged from the episode a stronger institution, esteemed as the great defender of Orthodoxy. Its power would increase in tandem with Byzantine expansion in the coming years, giving the papacy in Rome a more formidable ecclesiastical opponent. SEE SOURCEBOOK 3:2.

FIGURE 3.10 Chludov Psalter (ninth century) depiction of the whitewashing of an icon of Christ, likened to the Crucifixion. The Picture Art Collection / Alamy Stock Photo.

Eastern Christians beyond Byzantium

One significant consequence of the Muslim conquests in the eastern Mediterranean was that the various Christian denominations now living outside Byzantium fully developed their ecclesiastical identities under Muslim rule and increasingly formulated their distinct theological positions in Arabic. The Muslim authorities, by organizing their non-Muslim subjects in accordance with their religious affiliation and permitting them to retain their religious leaders, helped perpetuate the divisions between denominations. Each Christian sect had its own hierarchy, monasteries, and liturgical language.

The Orthodox Christians under the caliphate, or Mel-

FIGURE 3.11 St. Catherine's Monastery in Sinai, Egypt. Photo: Joonas Plaan, provided by Wikimedia Commons under the Creative Commons Attribution 2.0 Generic license.

kites, actually had little contact with their brethren in Constantinople from 750 to 1050, the crucial centuries of their church's development. The Melkites, distinguished from the Greek Orthodox by their adoption of Arabic and for whom Greek remained only a liturgical language, were dispersed from Alexandria to Baghdad. Their main intellectual center was Jerusalem, with its patriarchal see and nearby monasteries. In the mid-eleventh century, when Constantinople established a protectorate over the Melkite Church in Jerusalem with the permission of the Fatimids, who had occasionally appointed its patriarch, a cultural division emerged between the Greek-speaking hierarchy and the Arabic-speaking laity. The Maronite Christians of Lebanon adhered to the same Chalcedonian theology as the Melkites, though their church evolved separately. In 1182, just five years before the fall of Crusader Jerusalem, they entered into communion with the papacy.

Almost all Miaphysite Christians, who dissented from the Christological formulation of Chalcedon—called Jacobites by their rivals, after the Miaphysite bishop of Edessa Jacob Bar'adei (d. 578)—resided within the caliphate. Here, they had more freedom to consolidate their institutions and elaborate and defend their doctrines than they had possessed when faced with the interference of the Byzantine Church. There were a number of Miaphysite churches, each with its own hierarchy and distinct liturgical language. The Miaphysites in Syria-Palestine worshipped in Syriac; their fellows in Egypt, the Copts, whose patriarch resided first in Alexandria and after 1077 in Cairo, used a Coptic liturgy. The Ethiopian Church, founded in the fourth century, had been a province of the Coptic Church since the sixth. Although by the ninth century the religion of the Muslim traders who settled on the East African coast was attracting a growing number of adherents, the Ethiopian kingdom, with its capital at Aksum, remained Christian. The metropolitan of its church, the *abuna*, was always an Egyptian appointed by the Coptic patriarch. Ethiopians worshipped in their written language, Ge'ez, into which they had translated the Bible and their liturgy from the original Greek by the seventh century.

Armenian Christians were for the most part Miaphysites, though there were some Armenian adherents of Chalcedonian Orthodoxy, especially among those who had migrated to Byzantium in reaction to the 'Abbasids' settlement of Muslims in their homeland. A formal schism developed between the Armenian and Byzantine Churches in the tenth century, when there were two independent Armenian kingdoms. Whether under Muslim rule or Byzantine rule or independent, Armenians used the Armenian rite in their churches.

Yet another group of dissenters from the Chalcedonian language about the natures of Jesus, though in a way quite different from the Miaphysites, were the Christians who would come to be referred to as the Church of the East, though they were known pejoratively as Nestorians in the Middle Ages. They flourished especially in Persian lands but in other parts of the Middle East as well (and even in Central and East Asia). They used Syriac as their liturgical language, but, like Christians elsewhere in the Middle East, they adopted Arabic for other purposes.

Once they became fluent in Arabic, Melkite and Miaphysite scholars as well as those from the Church of the East living under Muslim dominion translated Greek and Syriac biblical manuscripts and texts from the early Church Fathers into Arabic, work that was essential for strengthening the Christian identity of their communities, and some participated vigorously in the intellectual life of 'Abbasid Baghdad in the ninth and tenth centuries. Throughout the caliphate Christians composed original theological works in Arabic, developing a vocabulary to articulate Christian theological concepts as well as the Greek philosophical ideas that were so critical for their arguments. Christian apologists wrote in Arabic either to defend Christianity against its Muslim detractors or to advance their particular interpretation of Christianity against Christians of other denominations. The Melkite Theodore Abu Qurrah (755–830), for example, produced treatises that expounded Melkite doctrine, defended it against the Miaphysites, and championed Christian veneration of icons as a crucial expression of Christian faith in an Islamic environment.

Christianization of the Balkans

In the Byzantine Empire, where the emperor was perceived as a divinely appointed instrument for spreading the Orthodox faith, imperial success was measured in terms of territorial expansion and the acquisition of believers for the church. Byzantine "reconquest" of Muslim-held territory resulted in few lasting spiritual gains, but in the Balkans, where spiritual conversion preceded political conquest, the Byzantine Church achieved much.

The dominant power in the Balkans in the mid-ninth century was the pagan Bulghar khanate, a state dominated by Turkic Bulghars who ruled over Slavs and Greeks, including many Christians. To the west of it lay the pagan Slavic state of Moravia. The rulers of both states, the Moravian Rastislav (846–870) and the Bulghar Boris (852–889), realized their paganism exposed them to aggression from the Christian Byzantines and Carolingians and so expressed a willingness to receive missionaries in 862. They set in motion complex maneuverings involving the Orthodox and Latin Churches and the imperial powers that eventually brought about the conversion of their subjects.

In order to offset a Frankish-Bulghar alliance, Rastislav turned to the Byzantine emperor Michael III (842–867), who sent a mission to Moravia under the leadership of Cyril (d. 869) and Methodius (d. 885), Slavic-speaking brothers from Thessaloniki. Soon, the Bible and the liturgy were translated into Old Church Slavonic, a literary form of the Slavic language written in "Cyrillic" (modified-Greek) script. Notwithstanding the pope's approval, German Catholic clergy managed to arrest Methodius, expel his disciples, and restore the Latin liturgy by 885. Moravia's alliance with Byzantium also ended. Followers of Cyril and Methodius, however, introduced the Slavonic liturgy into Catholic Croatia where it was used by some Slav congregations.

Khan Boris had meanwhile agreed in 862 to accept Christianity from the German Church as a means of counteracting Byzantine pressure. Emperor Michael III responded the next year with an invasion of Bulgaria, which prompted Boris to renounce the German alliance and convert to the Orthodox faith. Yet Boris wished to obtain as much independence as possible for himself and the nascent Bulgarian Church; thus in 866 he again turned to the Frankish king Louis the German and to the pope, playing them off against Byzantium.

Boris found more room to maneuver on account of a major dispute that had erupted between Rome and Constantinople when Pope Nicholas I (858–867) intervened in the appointment of the patriarch of Constantinople. Initially supporting the emperor's candidate, Photios, in the hope that the emperor would return to papal jurisdiction the lands emperor Leo III had removed, the pope turned against Photios in 863 when he did not receive the expected concessions. The pope and the patriarch then excommunicated each other in 866–867.

The upshot of Boris's intricate negotiations was that in 870 the Bulgarian khanate returned to the Orthodox Church. Yet, as Boris hoped, the Bulgarian Church gained autonomy and its own archbishop. Two of Methodius's Slavic disciples, Clement and Nahum, used Slavonic to evangelize and to train indigenous priests; it eventually replaced Greek as the liturgical language. While the Bulgarian Church retained its Slavonic identity, the khanate would be annexed by Byzantium in 1018. The Serbs also became Orthodox and adopted the Slavonic rite, probably before they attained independence from Bulgarian rule circa 931 and theoretically became vassals of Byzantium. In the Christianized Balkans, as in Islamic domains, distinctive regional churches survived by virtue of the shared ethnicity and liturgical languages of their members.

Byzantine Orthodoxy penetrated northward into Slavic Russia, becoming the official religion there after Prince Vladimir I of Kiev (980–1015) received baptism, probably in 988, as a condition of his marriage to Basil II's sister Anna. Although the new faith spread slowly, the reign of Vladimir's son Jaroslav (1015–1055) saw the establishment of a Russian ecclesiastical hierarchy headed by the archbishop of Kiev, who was usually a Byzantine Greek appointed by the patriarch in Constantinople. The Russian Orthodox Church adopted Byzantine canon law, but, instead of Greek, it used the Old Slavonic liturgy introduced from Bulgaria and Serbia and theological works translated into Old Slavonic.

The Latin Church in the West

By the time Muslim conquerors reached the western Mediterranean most of the Germanic kingdoms occupying the lands of the defunct Western Roman Empire had long been undergoing a process of conversion to Christianity. The head of the growing Catholic Church in the West was the bishop of Rome, the pope. Yet the dissolution of the old Roman world, with its capital in Rome, weakened any claims to authority over the Christian world that the popes might make. The Byzantine emperors, whose political power and notion of an imperial prerogative in religious affairs seemingly positioned them to defend the popes but also to limit their authority, ultimately proved too distant and too embattled in the East to do either one.

The popes therefore looked northwest to the new power, the Frankish Carolingian dynasty, for protection. The papacy's alliance with what was to be a new Roman Empire helped it to secure its territorial possessions and institutional base in central Italy. Papal cooperation with the Carolingians and other secular rulers who were intent on extending the boundaries of Latin Christendom to the north and east at the expense of pagan peoples and on furthering the Christianization of their subjects enhanced papal authority. The rulers of the newly conquered regions would look to the pope for legitimacy and increasingly devout Christians throughout the Latin West would turn to the pope for spiritual guidance. By the mid-eleventh century an expansive and religiously coherent Latin Christendom, with a reforming papacy at its head, possessed the material and spiritual resources to assert itself confidently in the wider Mediterranean arena. It would confront a Byzantine Empire and an Orthodox Church that had successfully pursued their own plans of conquest and conversion.

The Survival of Papal Authority

As the successors of Saint Peter, the popes claimed to have inherited the powers and primacy in the Christian world that Christ had bestowed on Peter (Matthew 16:18–19). Furthermore, as Gelasius I (492–496) first claimed, since priestly authority was concerned with immortal souls, it was superior to kingly authority; the emperor's role therefore was to act as the executive arm of the papacy and to guard the church. This at least was the papal theory. In reality, the papacy was weak and imperiled. The Arian Lombards had been the dominant power in Italy since the late sixth century. Arianism was based on the doctrines of the fourth-century Alexandrian priest Arius, who had asserted that Christ the Son was not coequal and coeternal with God the Father, thereby denying the essential divinity of Christ. The condemnation of Arius's position and formulation of the orthodox Nicene Creed at the Council of Nicaea II had not prevented Germanic peoples from adopting Arianism. The Lombards eventually converted to Catholicism in 698, but did not abandon their ambition to capture Rome. The Byzantine emperors, while willing to acknowledge the pope's precedence among the patriarchs, did not agree with the Gelasian idea of the papal-imperial relationship. They were not in a position, however, to intervene in spiritual affairs in the West as they did in Byzantium. In the temporal sphere, the Eastern emperors still retained control over Sicily, and parts of Italy, but, with their hands full in the East, none had visited Rome since 663.

The growing Lombard menace precipitated the momentous shift of the papacy's political alliance from Byzantium to the Franks. In 751 the Lombard king Aistulf conquered Ravenna and then threatened Rome. Lacking Byzantine protection, Pope Stephen II (752–757) concluded an alliance with the Frankish king Pippin III (741–768). Having defeated Aistulf in 755–756, Pippin returned Ravenna and other lands that Aistulf had captured in central Italy to the pope. When the Lombards struck back, Pippin's successor Charlemagne intervened in 773, defeating the Lombards and making himself their king, while renewing his dynasty's alliance with the papacy. On Christmas Day 800, in St. Peter's church in Rome, Leo III (795–816) crowned Charlemagne emperor. The pope had much to gain: a permanent protector and a new Roman emperor in the West who could legitimize and safeguard papal possession of former Byzantine territories in Italy.

The popes were now sovereign lords of what were, in effect, the Papal States. Revenue from these possessions allowed for the development of a more elaborate papal administration that included a papal chancery and archives, a legal staff for handling cases related to ecclesiastical affairs, and a financial department. The administrative staff consisted of members of the Roman elite who had once served in the Byzantine administration in Italy. When the popes, who also came from noble Roman families, were elected by the clergy and people of Rome, they announced their election and promised their loyalty to the Carolingian emperors; they no longer needed to have the Byzantine emperor sanction their election. The papal alliance with the emperors in the West represented a new north-south axis of political and spiritual power around which an expanding Latin Christendom would consolidate its identity. SEE SOURCEBOOK 3:3.

Expansion and Conversion

The institutional development of the papacy and the growth of its authority hinged to a significant extent on the expansion of Latin Christendom and the deepening piety of the laity—there were, in other words, more Catholics and more who cared about papal rulings on spiritual matters. Yet often it was not the popes who directed the Latin Church's expansion and the dissemination of its teachings but lay rulers and missionaries who subsequently obtained papal approval of their actions. But missionary work was dangerous, and military conquest was sometimes needed to facilitate pagan conversion. Long before the pope crowned him emperor, Charlemagne conducted harsh campaigns against the Saxons and, after defeating their leader Widukind in 785, imposed Christianity on them. Yet in the expansion of the Latin Church into much of northern and eastern Europe the prime movers were local pagan princes. Attracted by the power and cultural prestige of a Christian world more sophisticated than their own, these princes adopted Christianity and were followed by their people. Harald Bluetooth (950–986) in Denmark, Olaf Tryggvason (995–1000) in Norway, Miesco I (960–992) in Poland, and Geisa I

(972–997) in Hungary all established autonomous Catholic churches subject to the pope. Conversion brought about an increase in both royal and papal authority.

The pope was at the pinnacle of an expanding ecclesiastical hierarchy in which bishops played a key role. Indeed, the creation of new bishoprics marked Latin Christendom's expansion; even when lay rulers took the initiative in establishing them, papal approval was essential. In their dioceses bishops ordained parish priests, promoted educational endeavors, and mediated with the political authorities, many exercising considerable political power themselves. Bishops also judged cases in accordance with a still developing canon law, which was based on the decrees of church councils and popes. Although there were limits to papal authority, the churches within Europe's hundreds of dioceses were all united in their use of Latin as a liturgical language and their growing conformity to the rite of Rome.

The uniformity of Christian worship in the Latin West was advanced by the Carolingians. Charlemagne and his clerical advisers, led by the Englishman Alcuin (d. 804), obtained liturgical books from the papal court; these, the Latin Vulgate Bible, and many other religious texts were copied in the thousands by scribes at monastic, cathedral, and court scriptoria. Charlemagne's legislation required cathedrals and monasteries to have schools for educating the clergy who were responsible for instructing the people in the basic tenets of Catholic doctrine. Under the Rule of Saint Benedict of Nursia (d. 543), which was promoted by emperor Louis the Pious (814–840), monastic communities would live in obedience to their abbot and divide their daily activities between private prayer, study, and manual labor, which in the ninth century increasingly meant copying books. The number of Benedictine monasteries continued to grow, as did the property under their control, so that monasteries came to play an important role in Europe's agricultural expansion and regional trade as well as in its spiritual and cultural development.

Adopting a life of prayer and penance as a monk or a nun was the greatest expression of lay piety, but laypersons also showed devotion by endowing monasteries with land, in exchange for the monks' prayers for their souls and those of their kin, or offering their sons and daughters to a life of religious service. Monasteries and secular churches housed the relics of saints and were the sites of shrines to saints, where people flocked on the saints' annual feast days, seeking their protection, miraculous cures, or intercession before God on their behalf.

Common patterns of worship contributed to the emergence of a coherent Latin Catholic identity in the West. This identity was, to be sure, more diffuse and varied than the Greek Orthodox identity of Byzantium's inhabitants. Still, as a result of the combined efforts of popes and Carolingian emperors, the cultural unity of Latin Christendom would be built on a firm foundation, one strong enough to survive turbulent times.

Reform and Schism

During the late ninth and tenth centuries, following the breakup of the Carolingian Empire, the papacy and the Western Church suffered from the interference of the lay nobility in ecclesiastical affairs. With the weakened Carolingians unable to shield the Italian Peninsula and Rome from Muslim raiders from Sicily, ninth-century popes built fortifications, negotiated anti-Muslim alliances with southern Italian princes, and commanded fleets. The papacy became a prize that Roman noble factions contested; later ninth- and tenth-century popes were consequently an unimpressive lot. Pope Sergius III (904–911), for instance, was elected with the support of the powerful layman Theophylact, a commander of the Roman militia and papal financial adviser, and then arranged the murder of his predecessors, Leo V (903) and the "antipope" Christopher (904–905). Theophylact's daughter Marozia later engineered the election of her illegitimate son as Pope John XI (931–935).

Throughout Europe, clergy and laity alike, victimized by Viking, Hungarian, and Muslim invaders or by predatory Christian nobles, turned to local lords for protection. But aristocratic protection corrupted the church. Local lords gained the power to appoint bishops, abbots, and the priests of parish churches on their own estates, often making their choices on the basis of political expediency. Sometimes they put ecclesiastical offices up for sale, a practice known as simony that violated canon law, with the result that high clergy at times had little vocation. Nevertheless, the spiritual authority of the papacy endured. Universal reverence for the see of St. Peter, regardless of the man who occupied it, made Rome the place from which widespread reform could be most effectively promoted—if only the right popes were elected.

Reform movements were in fact growing within the church, and they enjoyed the support of some lay powers. Monastic reform began when Duke William III of Aquitaine founded the monastery of Cluny in 910. The new Cluniac order, which spread rapidly throughout Latin Christendom over the course of the tenth and eleventh centuries, was directly subordinate to the pope and free from lay control. Departing from the model of autonomous Benedictine monasteries, the Cluniac order was centralized and disciplined, with the one abbot in Cluny governing the priors of hundreds of individual monasteries. The Cluniacs reinvigorated Benedictine monasticism and placed greater emphasis on communal liturgical worship and intellectual labor than on private prayer and agricultural work.

Kings and emperors of the German Ottonian dynasty also supported reformers. In 1046 Henry III (1039–1056) intervened in a disputed papal election and appointed reforming popes from Germany and Lorraine. One of them, Leo IX (1049–1054), put the papacy at the head of the reform movement and began the formation of what many historians label a papal monarchy. In 1059, under Nicholas II (1059–1061), leading churchmen, later institutionalized as the College of Cardinals, assumed the sole responsibility of electing the pope, excluding all laymen, including the emperor, from the process. Leo and his successors, most notably Gregory VII (1073–1085), worked to put an end to simony, clerical marriage and concubinage, and the role of the secular authorities in local church affairs. Gregory's initiatives would come to be known as the Gregorian Reform. The new papal assertiveness inevitably caused conflicts with kings and emperors, particularly over which power would appoint new bishops. The resulting Investiture Controversy would dominate relations between popes and secular rulers in the coming centuries. Still, in Latin Christendom none doubted the principle of universal papal spiritual authority.

The patriarchs in Constantinople, however, had other ideas. They had long differed with the Western Church on certain ritual and theological issues—notably the wording of the Nicene Creed—but what especially rankled in the mid-eleventh century was the reformed papacy's aggressive assertion of its primacy in the Christian world. Matters came to a head after the Norman conquest of Byzantine lands in southern Italy. In 1050 Pope Leo IX attempted to make the Greek clergy there acknowledge him as their ecclesiastical superior, which elicited vociferous criticism from the patriarch, Michael Keroularios. When the pope sent an embassy led by Cardinal Humbert of Silva Candida to Constantinople in 1054 to discuss a possible papal-Byzantine alliance against the Normans, the uncompromising Humbert clashed with and excommunicated Keroularios. The patriarch responded in kind. Though not recognized as a permanent schism at the time, the Catholic and Greek Orthodox Churches henceforth largely went their separate ways. Military force would soon lend papal pretensions more weight.

An Islamo-Judaic Mediterranean

Jews had the unique experience of being a religious minority in both the Christian and the Muslim states of the medieval Mediterranean. The Jews had since the first century CE necessarily become accustomed to coping with the social and cultural challenges of living under non-Jewish rulers, most recently in the Christian Roman Empire and in the Zoroastrian Sasanian (Persian) Empire. The Muslim conquest of the Middle East and much of the Mediterranean world nonetheless created new circumstances and challenges as well as new opportunities for Jews.

Having rejected the messianic claims of Jesus and the prophecy of Muhammad, Jews suffered from their status as "unbelievers" in polities whose fundamental source of identity was Christianity or Islam. Their status as one of the Peoples of the Book under Islam, however, made for conditions in Muslim lands that were often better than those in an insecure Byzantium or in the emergent kingdoms of the Latin West. The Jews, moreover, benefited economically and culturally from being ostensive political neutrals in a region contested by Christian and Muslim rulers, and from their strong connections to the commercial networks of the Islamic world.

The large majority of the Jewish population resided in the lands the Muslims conquered, and their most important religious leaders and institutions were located in Iraq. Jewish communities flourished in the Muslim world, engaging in synchronous cultural and economic developments with Muslims that were so striking and profound that it is no exaggeration to characterize the Mediterranean of the tenth and eleventh centuries as Islamo-Judaic.

The important role that Jews played in the commerce of the Mediterranean and wider Muslim world rendered them attractive immigrants to rulers in an underdeveloped western Europe who wished to promote trade in their domains. Jewish settlement thus spread gradually northward from the shores of the Mediterranean into the lands of the Franks, as far north as the Rhineland towns of Mainz, Speyer, and Worms.

Rabbinic Judaism was consolidated in this period as the scholars of the Iraqi Talmudic academies, the principal interpreters of the Babylonian Talmud, widely disseminated their legal opinions and helped make the Babylonian Talmud the text that would govern Jewish life throughout most of the diaspora. Finalized by 650 CE, the Babylonian Talmud was a compilation of biblical interpretation and legal discussion, and was itself based on the Mishnah (ca. 200 CE), a codification of rabbinic teaching and law.

There was of course significant cultural variation among the far-flung Jewish communities of the Muslim and Christian worlds, the result of Jewish adjustment to and immersion in the cultures of the different societies in which they dwelt. As in the case of Christians living under Muslim rule, the Jews' Arabization sometimes led to their adoption of Islam. In fact, the earliest Jewish converts, though few in number, were members of Arabian Jewish tribes and already Arabic speaking. Among the Jews of Christian realms, for whom the dominant culture was less attractive, voluntary conversion was relatively less frequent.

Jewish Status under Christianity and Islam

The status of Jews in early medieval Christian realms was based on Roman law and the writings of the Church Fathers. The Roman emperors' toleration of Judaism as a licit religion had persisted after the empire became Christian, though the law code compiled by the emperor Theodosius II (408–450), which would be influential in the Germanic kingdoms in the West, used pejorative language in reference to Judaism and included measures, such as barring Jews from employment in the imperial service, that were designed to maintain Christian superiority over Jews. The code of the Eastern emperor Justinian I (527–565) was harsher than the Theodosian Code, but it still upheld the Jews' right to practice their faith.

The Church Fathers, many of whom wrote when Christianity was an embattled faith in competition with Jews and pagans, fashioned a negative image of Jews and Judaism that was intended to validate Christianity while denigrating the faith in which it originated. Through their interpretation of the Old Testament, the scripture Christians shared with Jews, the Fathers endeavored to demonstrate that it foretold the coming of Jesus as the Messiah and that the Jews—the "Old Israel"—had been superseded by Christians—the "New Israel"—for having rejected or, according to some Fathers, even having killed Jesus. Saint Augustine (354–430), whose views shaped papal Jewish policy, asserted that on account of the Jews' repudiation of Jesus, God had punished them with dispersion and servitude among the nations. Yet the Jews, according to Augustine, had a function in the divine plan as witnesses to the truth of Christianity and to the replacement of the old Law of Moses with the new covenant of Jesus. The Jews therefore were not to be killed but should persist until the end-time, when they would convert. Following Augustine, popes discouraged forcible baptism of Jews.

Muslim writers concerned themselves far less with the Jews and their Torah and did not feel compelled to justify their faith at the expense of Judaism. Even though the Prophet Muhammad had clashed with the Jews of Medina, which resulted in negative Qur'anic statements about Jews, Muslim writers did not dwell on these episodes because, unlike the crucified Jesus, Muhammad had triumphed. Muslims avoided controversies over the interpretation of revealed scriptures by arguing that Jewish scripture had become corrupted over time, unlike the Qur'an, the final, unadulterated revelation. Since Jews, like Muslims, insisted on the absolute oneness of God, Muslim polemicists focused more on Christianity with its "polytheistic" Trinitarian theology.

Jews in Muslim lands benefited from being not the only religious dissidents. Christians were far more numerous and, as potential allies of Christian princes, posed more of a political problem for the Muslim authorities. *Dhimma* legislation did not single out Jews, and in these early centuries Jews were rarely subjected to persecution. Some Jews, like Hasdai ibn Shaprut in al-Andalus, or Ya'qub ibn Killis in Fatimid Egypt, attained influential positions in Muslim government.

In Christian realms, where Jews were the only religious minority, they endured more hardship on account of the actions of insecure Christian rulers. In Byzantium Leo III and the usurper Romanos Lekapenos (920–944) called for the conversion of Jews in efforts to gain political support by imposing religious uniformity. Such conversions were temporary, however, since subsequent emperors reaffirmed Judaism's legitimacy. The Visigothic rulers of Spain, who had only converted from Arianism to Catholicism in 587, passed harsh anti-Jewish legislation through much of the seventh century, hoping to win ecclesiastical and popular support and to enhance their often shaky authority. The Muslim conquest of 711 undoubtedly improved the Jews' situation; according to later sources, Jews actively supported the invaders.

In the domains of the Franks, the Jews' experience was more tranquil. Ruling according to the traditions of Roman law, the Carolingians did not oppose the Jews' practice of their faith and created a special Christian official, the "master of the Jews," to oversee Jewish affairs in the empire. The emperors granted privileges and protection to Jewish merchants to foster their commerce and settlement. Some clergymen, most notably Bishop Agobard of Lyon (816–840), expressed anxiety about Jews mingling with and exercising religious influence over unlearned Christians and inveighed against Jews trading, owning, and possibly converting pagan and Christian slaves to Judaism. Clerical agitation, however, did not result in much harm to the Jews. SEE SOURCEBOOK 3:4.

The Consolidation of Rabbinic Judaism

The Muslim conquerors unified the Jews of the Mediterranean and Middle East within their vast domains and allowed for the continuation of the rabbinic academies existing in Palestine and Iraq. The 'Abbasids' relocation of the center of caliphal power to Iraq in the mid-eighth century increased the influence of the Jewish institutions of a region where Jews had resided since the Babylonians transplanted them there, mostly as captives, in 597 and 586 BCE. The exilarch (head of the exiles), theoretically the leader of all Jewish communities in the 'Abbasid empire, was appointed by the caliph. His real administrative authority, however, did not extend beyond Iraq and Iran. More important were the heads of the rabbinic academies, the *geonim* (sing. *gaon*). Originally located in Sura and Pumbedita, the academies moved to Baghdad in the ninth century. Residing in or near the 'Abbasid capital was one factor that enabled the *geonim* and the Babylonian Talmud to achieve primacy over the rabbinic leadership in Palestine and the Palestinian Talmud. Since the *geonim* were the chief interpreters of the Babylonian Talmud, local rabbis from throughout the Islamic world sent them queries on matters of religious law. Through their authoritative answers, called *responsa*, the *geonim* exerted great influence on world Jewry. In the ninth century, moreover, the *geonim* compiled a prayer book that became the standard liturgy for Jews everywhere.

The authority of the *geonim*, however, did not go unchallenged. The Karaite sect, which clearly emerged in the ninth century, repudiated the authority of the Talmud and its rabbinic interpreters. By the tenth century Karaite communities were widely established, especially in Egypt and Palestine. Despite their religious differences, Karaite and Talmudic, or "Rabbanite," Jews sometimes intermarried. Rabbanite Judaism would overcome the challenge of the Karaites only gradually.

Even among Rabbanite Jews the authority of the *geonim* diminished in the tenth century, for just as various political and cultural centers rose throughout the Muslim world as the power of the 'Abbasids in Baghdad waned, so too did vibrant centers of Jewish culture emerge in places such as Qayrawan in Tunisia, Cairo in Egypt, and Córdoba in Spain to rival the rabbinic academies in Iraq. Yet on account of the ongoing migration of Jews, including Rabbanite scholars, from the Islamic East to the Mediterranean, these new regional Jewish subcultures were all united in their common adherence to a Jewish lifestyle centered on the Babylonian Talmud. By the mid-eleventh century the academies in Iraq were on their last legs, and obeisance to the *geonim* was no longer necessary or practical.

The activities of Jewish merchants contributed to the cultural unity among Jewish communities both when gaonic authority was at its height and afterward. Many

Jews moved to Muslim cities for economic opportunities, and some became key players in the Muslim-dominated commercial networks that extended from India to Spain. Like their Muslim counterparts, with whom they sometimes formed partnerships, Jewish merchants were often scholars as well. Even when they were not, they frequently had connections with the rabbinic academies and facilitated the flow of gaonic correspondence throughout the Jewish world. Jewish traders also increasingly migrated to the Muslim West before and after 'Abbasid decline in the tenth century while maintaining kinship and commercial ties with the East. Political boundaries between competing Muslim and Christian realms were not an impediment to Jewish merchants and the merchandise and religious learning they carried. In fact, as a result of the cultural and commercial links that southern Italian Jews had with the East, the Judaism of the Babylonian Talmud spread northward through Italy and to the Rhineland over the course of the tenth century.

Acculturation and Conversion

Among the Jews of the Muslim world, just as among Christian *dhimmis*, Arabic became the language of daily parlance, replacing Aramaic in Iraq and Palestine, Aramaic and Greek in Egypt, Latin and Berber in northwest Africa, and Latin in Iberia. By the tenth century Jews were writing theological works in Arabic, though they continued to use Hebrew for studying Torah, reciting daily prayers, and writing liturgical poetry, and Aramaic for the study of the Talmud. Arabized Jewish scholars enthusiastically immersed themselves in an intellectual milieu made compelling by the availability of Arabic translations of Hellenistic philosophical and scientific texts. Jewish philosophers and physicians studied and exchanged ideas with Muslim counterparts and teachers.

Such cultural immersion in some cases led to conversion to Islam. Jews participating in a *majlis*, interfaith theological discussions that took place in tenth-century Baghdad and Fatimid Cairo, reportedly converted because of the Muslims' elegant arguments concerning the prophecy of Muhammad. The Jews' perception of Islam as monotheistic—compared to their view of Christianity as an idolatrous faith—facilitated their adoption of it once they had been convinced of Muhammad's prophetic status. For Jewish officials in Muslim governments, conversion could help them attain their highest ambitions. Ya'qub ibn Killis (930–991), born in Baghdad, began his career as a Jewish representative of merchants in Palestine and ended it as a Muslim *wazir* in the Fatimid court. Everyday social contact and comfort with Muslims, made possible by residential mixing and partnerships between traders and artisans, must also have encouraged Jews to embrace Islam. Forced conversions, or conversion as a consequence of degradation and despair, were rare in this early period. And when coercion was involved, as in the reign of the Fatimid caliph al-Hakim, the converts were permitted to return to Judaism after his death.

Still, proportionate to the masses of Christians who gradually adopted Islam, fewer Jews converted. First of all, the Jews were long accustomed to minority status and to lacking political power; if anything, the Muslim conquest improved their circumstances. Generally, Jews did not marry Muslims, and the Muslim conquerors saw little to be gained by marrying the daughters of relatively powerless Jews. Given that they were rarely targeted by Muslim polemicists and that they feared antagonizing their rulers, Jews produced little anti-Muslim polemic. In the few extant polemical works, Jews argued against the Muslims' claims that the later revelation of Muhammad had abrogated the Torah. In some instances, Jews took the inspiration provided by Arabo-Islamic culture and diverted it toward Jewish cultural endeavors that helped to strengthen Jewish identity. Immensely influenced by Arabic poetry, which played an important role in Muslim public life, and aware of the great pride that Muslims had in the Arabic language and literary tradition, Jewish poets deliberately cultivated Hebrew poetry in order to demonstrate that they could compose poetry in their own biblical language that was just as elegant as the Muslims'. The Andalusi Jewish courtier Hasdai ibn Shaprut patronized poets such as Menahem ben Saruq (ca. 920–970) and Dunash ben Labrat (ca. 920–990), forerunners of a "golden age" of Hebrew poetry in the next two centuries. SEE SOURCEBOOK 3:5.

In the early medieval Latin West there was little in the way of high culture that Jews wanted to explore. Christianity posed a threat because it disputed the Jews' interpretation of their own Bible. Jews therefore wrote works to refute Christian claims and even circulated a scurrilous life of Jesus, the *Toledot Yeshu*, which poked fun at Jesus's divinity and the virginity of Mary. Bishop Agobard's worries about the Jews' religious influence on Christians are indicative of the situation in this period. Indeed, a deacon at the Carolingian court named Bodo secretly converted to Judaism in 839, and feigning a pilgrimage to Rome, fled to Muslim Spain. Here, he sold his fellow travelers into slavery, and, with the name Eleazar, engaged in a polemical debate with Paul Alvarus, who was possibly of Jewish origin himself and would later become one of the most vocal supporters of the martyrs of Córdoba.

CHAPTER FOUR

Peoples of the Book Reading Their Books

Sa'adyah ben Joseph (882–942) lived in a world of books. As the most influential Jewish thinker of the early Middle Ages, the Torah—the Hebrew Bible—was central to his faith, but he only read that scripture in conjunction with a huge assemblage of later Hebrew and Aramaic Jewish texts called the Talmud. Since he lived at the heart of the Islamic world, he was also immersed in a vast number of Arabic works, especially philosophical and theological ones, some written by Jews, others by Christians and Muslims. Sa'adyah, moreover, vigorously defended his wide reading. In a treatise called the *Book of Beliefs and Opinions,* he argued that it was necessary to read Torah in the company of the Talmud because "there are Biblical commandments that entail qualities that are left unexplained [in the Torah], for example, the method used to prepare fringes, or build the booths for Sukkot [an important Jewish festival, agricultural in origin]."[1] The only source for this further information was guidance handed down through the ages—what Sa'adyah called "tradition"—guidance that supplements what the Torah says, and that, he insisted, is exactly what the Talmud is.

Strikingly enough, this great rabbi also recognized that "all the community of monotheists"—Jews, Christians, and Muslims—agreed that such "tradition" was a valid source of religious knowledge. He could not have been more correct. Although all Mediterranean monotheists had their specific holy books—the Hebrew Bible, the Christian Bible, the Qur'an—that possessed unique authority in their communities, they overwhelmingly read those books in conjunction with a larger set of texts that they saw as essential to understanding their religions as well. When the Peoples of the Book read their holy books in the medieval Mediterranean, they did so with a lot of other books alongside them.

To understand the religion and culture of medieval Jews, Christians, and Muslims, therefore, we must recognize that, as Sa'adyah ben Joseph suggested, they were all actually Peoples of Many Books, who, in this way, had much in common with each other. Not only was the content of their holy books similar, but their approaches to reading them were too. They shared alike in a culture of commentary that had roots in antiquity, and, either directly or indirectly, their understanding of their holy books was shaped by a key strand of ancient philosophy called Neoplatonism. Everywhere in the Mediterranean, moreover, one of the key jobs of learned scholars was to preach. Though we lack much evidence for how the uneducated majority understood the religions they were taught, they participated in these bookish religions in concrete ways. For one thing, they often wore passages of their holy books on their bodies in the form of amulets!

Yet, despite these commonalities, there were real differences between the religious cultures of the Mediterranean. At some points their sacred texts conflicted outright, and other aspects of their scholarly and religious cultures—such as language and alphabets—tended to magnify these differences. The educational institutions, moreover, that sustained these bookish cultures were almost always tied directly to one religion or another: Jews studied at Jewish schools, Muslims with Muslim teachers. Despite participating alike in a common scriptural monotheism, therefore, it is clear that Jewish, Christian, and Muslim religious authorities worked hard to draw boundaries around their own religions so that it was clear who was in and who was out, though such

Throughout the period from 650 to 1650 only a small percentage of people in the Mediterranean could read, and therefore it is tempting to conclude that the holy books that were at the core of Judaism, Christianity, and Islam were available—and important—only to the educated elite. But just as ancient Egyptian pagans wrote magic incantations or prayers to gods or goddesses that they wore around their necks to ward off evil, so monotheists jotted down passages of their scriptures that they placed in small containers that they wore as amulets, believing that these would protect them from Satan, heal their illnesses, or bring them good fortune.

About eight inches high and six inches wide this piece of papyrus from Egypt is creased, with one vertical line dividing it in half, and four horizontal ones. This indicates that it was folded up into a packet about one inch by four inches, probably to be worn around the neck as such an amulet. The text is a combination of Bible verses written in Greek, including Psalm 78:23–24 and Matthew 26:28–30:

FIGURE 4.1 Sixth-century Greek-Christian amulet. Photo ©Historical Views / agefotostock.

FIGURE 4.2 Eleventh-century Muslim amulet. The Metropolitan Museum of Art, New York, Gift of Nelly, Violet and Elie Abemayor, in memory of Michel Abemayor, 1978, 1978.546.32, Open Access CC0.

> Fear you all who rule over the earth.
>
> Know you nations and peoples that Christ is our God.
>
> For he spoke and they came to being, he commanded and they were created; he put everything under our feet and delivered us from the wish of our enemies.
>
> Our God prepared a sacred table in the desert for the people and gave manna of the new covenant to eat, the Lord's immortal body and the blood of Christ poured for us in remission of sins.

Radiocarbon analysis dates the fragment to between 574 and 660 CE. Its recent discoverer points out that the text was not copied by a priest or someone transcribing verses directly from a Bible: "The amulet maker clearly knew the Bible, but made lots of mistakes: some words are misspelled and others are in the wrong order. This suggests that he was writing by heart rather than copying it."[1]

This eleventh-century strip of paper, also from Egypt, is about 9 inches long and 3.5 inches wide. Rather than being written by hand, the text here has been block printed, a technology that Islamic civilization borrowed from China long before it was ever used in Europe. The upper portion consists of the seal of Solomon—the six-sided star supposedly on the face of Solomon's signet ring, an image common in medieval Jewish tradition, but borrowed by Islam, enclosed in a square. The Arabic inside the star reads: "Authority belongs to its owner." The white Arabic on black background around the star contains a set of Qur'anic phrases: "God be praised! Praise to God! There is no god but God." The lower text block begins with "In the name of God, Most Gracious Most Merciful," a phrase that begins nearly every surah of the Qur'an, this followed by invocations in the Qur'an's many names of God, and then a series of Qur'anic verses such as 2:1 ("Behold the Book! No trace of doubt in it. A guide to the pious.") and 3:1 (God! There is no god but He! Ever-Living, Everlasting."). Parts of this lower portion are indecipherable, but it is notable that it contains some of the so-called mysterious letters of the Qur'an—letters that appear, usually in groups that do not spell any known Arabic words, at the beginning of many surahs. In this case we have the opening mysterious letters of the second surah, *A-L-M*, which were known for their talismanic power.[2]

Discussion Questions

1. Why would people think that an amulet would be efficacious?
2. Is this magic or religion?
3. What do these artifacts tell us about shared religious practices in the medieval Mediterranean?

Further Reading

De Bruyn, Theodore. *Making Amulets Christian: Artefacts, Scribes, and Contexts*. Oxford: Oxford University Press, 2017.

Schaefer, Karl R. *Enigmatic Charms: Medieval Arabic Block Printed Amulets in American and European Libraries and Museums*. Leiden: E. J. Brill, 2006.

Notes

1. "One of World's Earliest Christian Charms Found," http://www.manchester.ac.uk/discover/news/one-of-worlds-earliest-christian-charms-found/.
2. Schaefer, 193–96, ill. pl. 47.a–c.

boundaries were often crossed, and the less educated frequently found them hard to see.

God's Books

While there were books in the ancient world that had supreme cultural authority, such as Homer's *Iliad* among the Greeks, the core texts of the civilizations of the medieval world possessed even greater prestige, since they were, for their followers, God's own books. For Jews and Christians the books of the Bible were written by human authors but inspired directly by the Creator. For Muslims God Himself was the author of the Qur'an, His own Arabic words delivered to the Prophet Muhammad by the angel Gabriel. These scriptures had a common religious vocabulary—there is one God who requires obedience from his followers and is a just and merciful judge—but they conflicted with each other at points too, sometimes angrily. That each religion venerated its holy book as it appeared in a specific language written in a specific alphabet made the differences among the religions seem even greater than they were.

A Common Religious Vocabulary

In a passage that Muslim (and non-Muslim) scholars never tired of discussing, the Qur'an pronounced that "as for the believers, for the Jews and Christians . . . who believe in God and the Last Day, and who do righteous deeds, these have their wage with their Lord" (Qur'an 2:62). Whatever else it might mean, this famous verse vividly exemplifies some of the fundamental similarities in religious language among the religions of the book. The Jewish and Christian Bibles and the Qur'an did all equally proclaim that God is one. In the Gospel of Luke, for example, Satan, while tempting him in the wilderness, offered Jesus dominion over the whole world if he would do homage to him, to which Jesus responds: "It is written, 'Worship the Lord your God, and serve only him'" (Luke 4:8). But in this passage from the Christian Bible, Jesus was simply quoting a verse of the Hebrew Bible (Deuteronomy 6:13) in which Jews were given the same instruction. This shared monotheism of the Mediterranean's holy books was something that, for the most part, all Jews, Christians, and Muslims recognized about each other. Indeed, the Arabic word for "God" in the Qur'anic passage above is Allah—the most common word for "God" in the Islamic tradition. But its literal meaning, "the (one) God," made Allah a term that all monotheists used: when the countless Christians and Jews living in the medieval Islamic world spoke about, or prayed to, God in Arabic (something they commonly did) they called him Allah too.

Jews, Christians, and Muslims also believed in what the Qur'anic verse above calls "the Last Day." To be sure, they had different ideas about the details. Yet Mediterranean monotheists all agreed that at some point this world would pass away, all the dead would be resurrected, and an age of justice and peace would be established. The Hebrew Bible taught that on that day "O dwellers in the

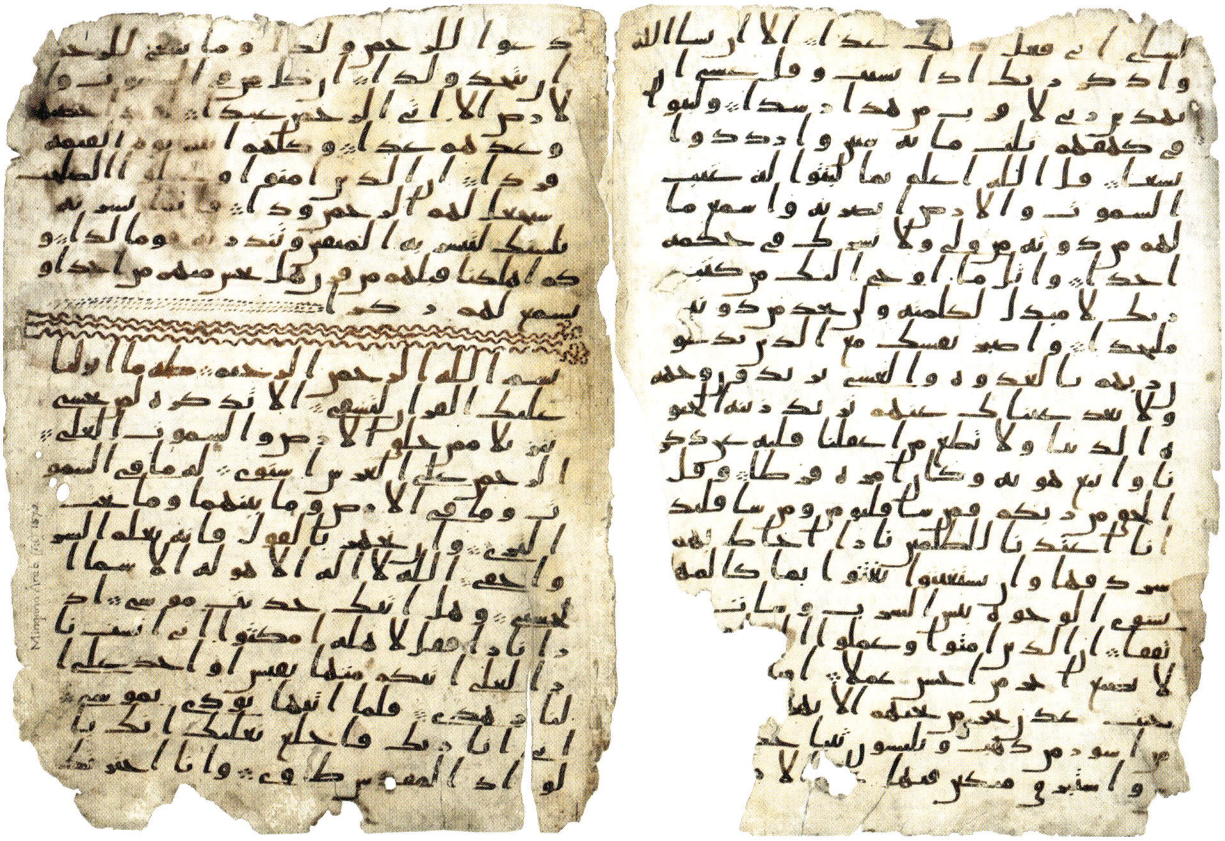

FIGURE 4.3 Two pages of one of the oldest manuscripts of the Qur'an, 568–645. Photograph provided by Wikimedia Commons under the Creative Commons |Public Doman license.

dust, awake and sing for joy . . . the earth will give birth to those long dead" (Isaiah 26:19), a sentiment that carried over into the Christian New Testament, which stressed that Jesus will serve as judge of all nations on that "last day" (John 12:48). For Muslims too this "day of resurrection" or "day of religion" as the Qur'an often called it (74:1, 6; 1:3) would be a day of judgment. Indeed, like Christians, many Muslims believed that Jesus—revered as a prophet in Islam—would stand before all people as judge, though others said Muhammad would play this role. On a deeper level, this common belief in what Jews called "the World to Come" was part of a shared religious understanding of history—that it was a drama that moved in one direction, toward a heavenly future where, as Isaiah the prophet said, "the wolf shall live with the lamb; the leopard shall lie down with the kid" (Isaiah 11:6). SEE SOURCEBOOK 4:1.

That the "last day" would be a day of judgment was the corollary of another common requirement of these holy books—the doing of "righteous deeds." The Qur'an movingly called on Muslims to spend their wealth not just for their own families, but for the "orphans, the poor, and the needy wayfarer" (Qur'an 2:215), actions that Jesus had thoroughly approved of in the Christian Bible (Matthew 6:2–4). Once again, though, the same ethical standard appears throughout the Hebrew Bible, as at Deuteronomy 24:21: "When you gather the grapes of your vineyard, do not glean what is left; it shall be for the alien, the orphan, and the widow."

Conflicting Beliefs

Indeed, the scriptures of Jews, Christians, and Muslims are so similar that it was not unusual then (or now) to mis-

FIGURE 4.4 Christ as judge, separating the sheep from the goats, Church of Apollinare Nuova, Ravenna, sixth century. Bridgeman Images.

take a passage of one for verses of another. A Christian bishop named Iliya I (d. 1049), who lived in the Islamic world in what is now Turkey, quoted passages from the Qur'an (2:28, 3:156) while writing about the Trinity when he thought he was quoting the biblical account of Moses at the Burning Bush (Exodus 3:1–10). Nevertheless, the Qur'an denounces the Christian belief in a divine son of God—"Lord Supreme! Neither begetting nor begotten" (112:1–3)—one of many statements in these holy books that attacks other people's religion. There were differences after all. When the Christian Bible painted a picture of Jesus as the Jewish Messiah, who is the very Word of God (John 1:1, 14) who died sacrificially for all humanity's sins (Hebrews 9:28), it departed strikingly from the Hebrew Bible, which foretold a human Messiah, an anointed king who would restore all Jews to Israel and overthrow all tyranny (Isaiah 11:1, 4, 12). The Qur'an, on the other hand, had much to say about Jesus the Messiah too—and even taught, like the Christian Bible, that he was born of the Virgin Mary—but insisted that he was merely a human prophet.

Moreover, the Christian and Muslim scriptures rambunctiously accuse other monotheists of evil practices and wrongheaded beliefs. For Jesus in the Christian Bible, the contemporary Jewish teachers called Pharisees, who were the intellectual and religious ancestors of medieval and modern rabbis, were hypocrites: "Now you Pharisees clean the outside of the cup and the dish, but inside you are full of greed and wickedness" (Luke 11:39). While the Qur'an praised the Jewish prophets, it nevertheless denounced Jews as killers of the prophets God had sent—most especially Jesus—and for breaking their covenant with God by falling back into idolatry (4:153–57). Though the Qur'an described Christians as those closest to Muslims in belief and admired the humility of Christian priests and monks (5:82), it attacked Christian belief in the Incarnation and Trinity unstintingly (4:171). While the Hebrew Bible, written before the beginnings of Christianity and Islam, could scarcely attack either by name, it likewise castigated believers in false gods such as Baal (1 Kings 18:18–21).

Our Holy Book, in Our Holy Language

The scriptures of Judaism, Christianity, and Islam, therefore, despite their similar religious vocabulary, explicitly differed from each other—and not just in matters of detail. Their material forms, moreover, tended to magnify these quarrels. Take language. In the Qur'an God pronounced that the Islamic holy book had a specific linguistic form: "We have sent it down as an Arabic Qur'an" (12:2). But the same could be said for the other holy books—they existed in a particular language for a particular religion. Other than a few parts, the Jewish Bible—by far the longest of these holy scriptures—was in Hebrew of a sort that no one even among the Jews spoke as a mother tongue by the seventh century. While Christians treated the Jewish Bible as their own, adding on top of it the rather slender (Greek) New Testament, the Jewish Bible was not a Hebrew book for them. Greek Christians read the Jewish scriptures in a translation called the Septuagint that Greek-speaking Jews had produced in antiquity. Latin-speaking Christians read the whole Bible—both the Hebrew and Greek parts—only in various Latin translations, most notably Saint Jerome's fourth-century version called the Vulgate, which he completed in 405 CE. Very large communities of Syrian, Armenian, and Egyptian Christians, moreover, read their Bibles exclusively in their own languages: Syriac, Armenian, and Coptic. SEE SOURCEBOOK 4:2.

For everyone in the medieval world, then, holy scripture was intimately connected with the specific language of a specific religious community. And not only were the

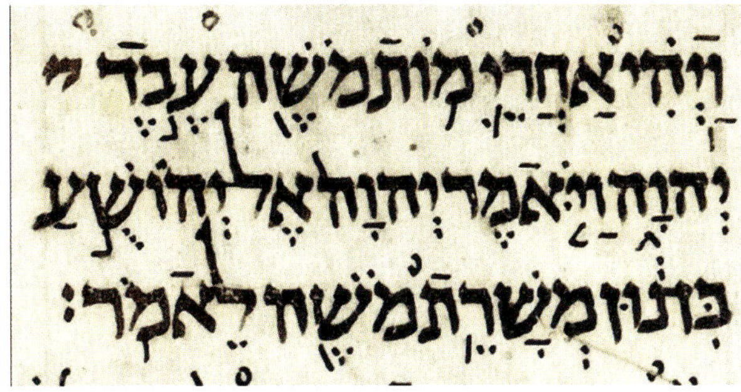
ויהי אחרי מות משה עבד
יהוה ויאמר יהוה אל יהושע
בן נון משרת משה לאמר:

FIGURE 4.5 Close-up of book of Joshua in the Aleppo Codex. Photograph provided by Wikimedia Commons under the Creative Commons | Public Doman license.

languages different, but so were the alphabets, which themselves took on a divine quality. Even though Hebrew and Arabic, for example, are closely related languages, and indeed the alphabet of one was used in certain circumstances to write the other, without some amount of study each looks completely unintelligible. The same is true of Greek and Latin.

Jews, Christians, and Muslims, therefore, other than those who were bi- or multilingual, found each other's holy texts completely opaque linguistically, and these linguistic and alphabetic walls extended outward from their scriptures to their cultural, educational, and religious traditions. Latin Christians wrote about their Latin holy book in Latin using the Latin alphabet, while Muslims everywhere elaborated on the Qur'an in Arabic using the Arabic alphabet. Eventually languages other than Latin, Greek, Hebrew, and Aramaic (the language in the ancient Middle East that was spoken by Jesus) were used for written purposes within these holy languages' spheres of dominance, but when Jews wrote any other language—Aramaic, say, or Arabic or even Persian or Berber—they did so using Hebrew letters, while Muslims wrote Persian and Turkish and even Spanish in Arabic letters. This is why the languages of western Europe all use a common alphabet today: they were all parts of the Latin-Christian world where writing in Latin script was next to godliness.

Holy Books and Scholars

Within each religious tradition, a highly educated scholarly class was the main preserver and interpreter of the holy book. Unsurprisingly in cultures informed by scriptures that they deemed the very Word of God, the elite level of education was intended to produce sophisticated interpreters of the sacred text, and much of their own scholarly work consisted of writing commentaries on those holy texts, commentaries that often contained quite original insights and ways of reading.

Education and Institutions

To become a fully educated scholar of a sacred text required years of education. In Byzantium, for example, students had to pass through a three-stage curriculum. At the elementary level, a humble teacher of rather low social status gave children instruction in reading, writing, and simple arithmetic. After learning the Greek alphabet, they would then study the most basic elements of grammar—how to conjugate verbs and inflect nouns, and would be put to work copying age-old maxims such as "Accept the counsel of a wise man." In the second stage, a highly educated teacher called a *grammarian* would not only immerse them in the rest of Greek grammar, but teach them how to read the classical (non-Christian) literature of Greek antiquity. Finally, at the advanced stage, Greek students would study with a *rhetorician,* who taught them how to write persuasive and elegant literary works and to deliver them orally.

While the languages of instruction varied by religion and culture, all Christian, Jewish, and Muslim scholars passed through an educational curriculum rather similar to this, with its own set of authoritative textbooks, though neither Jewish nor Muslim students regularly read the pagan literature as both Greek- and Latin-speaking students did. While many students learned in small informal schools with a single teacher, especially in the early stages of education, over time a complex range of institutions evolved. The Islamic world provides many examples. At the basic level, Muslim students often began at about age seven to learn to write Arabic and read the Qur'an in a school called a *maktab* or *kuttab* (both from the Arabic root meaning "to write"). For much of the early Middle Ages, the higher levels of Islamic education all occurred at mosques where more advanced students would undertake study of Qur'anic interpretation and the enormous body of Islamic traditions about Muhammad, his Companions, and the prophets collectively called the Hadith. By the tenth century, still another educational institution developed, the *madrasa* (from the Arabic verb meaning "to study"). Supported typically by an endowment given by a pious donor, *madrasa*s would eventually become the most important centers for Islamic education, where up to twenty elite students could both live and study with the leading intellectuals of the Islamic world.

Moreover, for Christians throughout the Mediterranean monasteries were important educational centers. Following the examples of holy hermits who devoted themselves to prayer and meditation on scripture in the Egyptian and Syrian deserts, particularly pious Christians created communities of monks or nuns who vowed to live celibate lives of obedience to a spiritual master called an abbot or abbess. While the earliest Christian hermits were not always even literate, these communal monasteries became centers of intense literacy and biblical reading. In the Latin-speaking world, a short guidebook for monastic life (*Rule of Saint Benedict,* ca. 530) written by an abbot named Benedict of Nursia (ca. 480–547), came to regulate most monasteries by the tenth century, and required that all monks spend a third of their day in what he called *lectio divina,* "divine reading," of the Bible or early Christian writings. As a result, Latin-speaking monks had to be literate when they joined monasteries or had to be educated within monastic walls after entering. Greek-speaking monks in the East were allowed more variation in communal monastic life, as were those in the many Syriac- and Coptic-speaking Christian monasteries in the Islamic world. But, as in Latin monasticism, literacy was normally essential. Eastern monasteries also, therefore, were centers of learning. SEE SOURCEBOOK 4:3.

Among the most elaborate educational institutions of the early medieval Mediterranean (fl. 589–1038) were the rabbinical academies in Palestine and Iraq, like the one that Sa'adyah ben Joseph led in the tenth century, where rabbis studied the vast collection of Jewish oral tradition, recorded in what is known as the Talmud. Like the Islamic *madrasa*s and Christian monasteries, the two most important rabbinical academies, Sura and Pumbedita near Baghdad, had substantial endowments that allowed both scholar-teachers and students to be paid stipends so that they could devote themselves to Talmudic study. While some students studied at the acad-

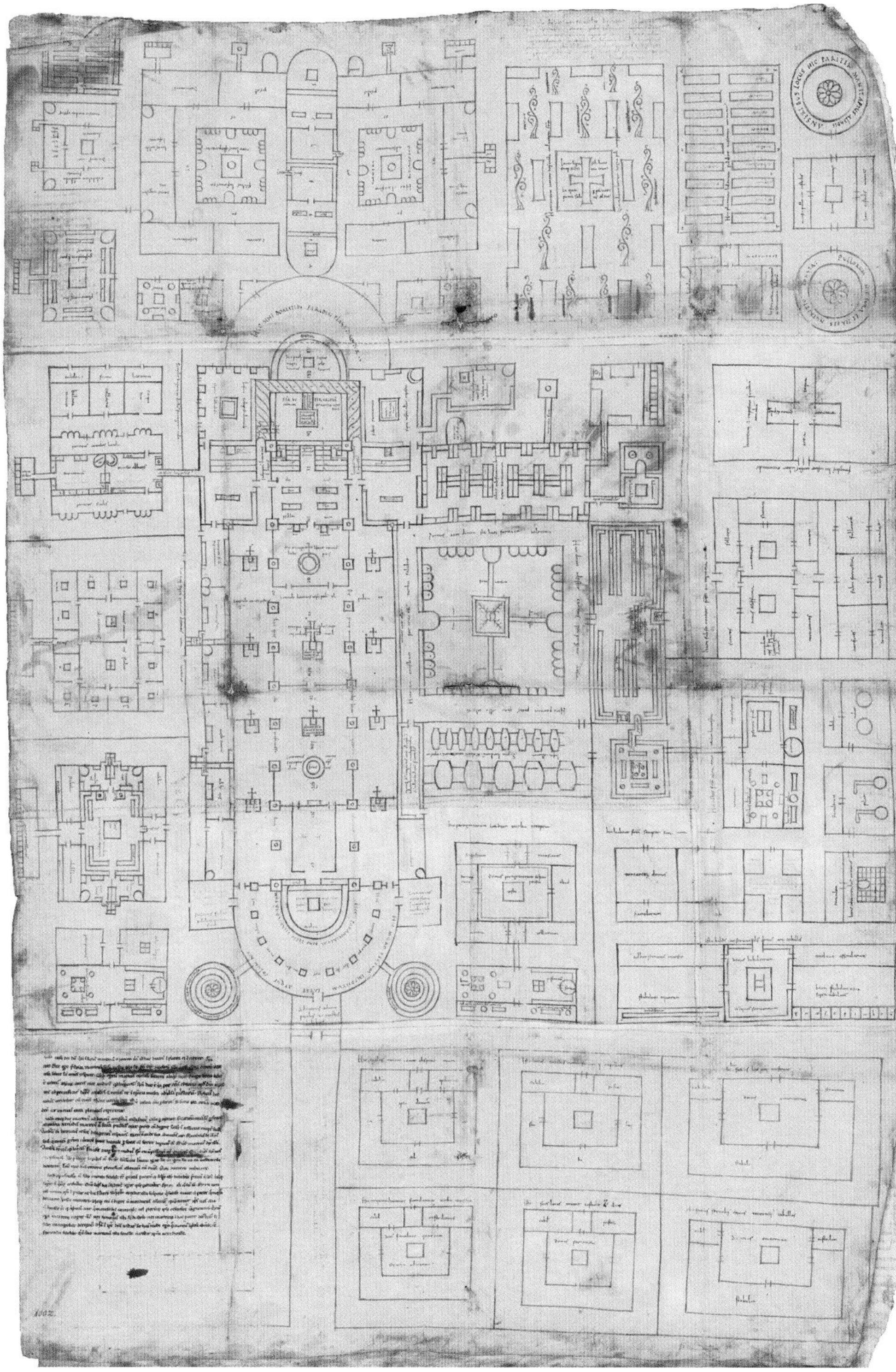

FIGURE 4.6 Close-up of the monks' cloister in *Plan of St. Gall*, ca. 820–830. Photograph provided by Wikimedia Commons under the Creative Commons | Public Doman license.

emies year-round, moreover, many were in residence only during the months of Adar (February/March) and Elul (August/September) and carried on their studies on their own in their hometowns during the rest of the year. During these two so-called *kallah* months, some seventy scholar-teachers sat facing the academy's *gaon* (head) during study sessions, and were joined by as many as 400 students as tractates of the Talmud were carefully recited and explained. By 650 CE, the Talmud had already reached its full development, and the authority of the learned rabbis who had memorized and studied it was significant. As authorities on the Talmud, *gaons* prepared written responses to questions posed to them by Jewish leaders throughout the region. They did so after consulting with the other rabbis in the academies, though they sent their *responsa* out under their own names. Eventually, the *gaons* were recognized as the final arbiters in any dispute among Talmudic Jews.

The Compulsion to Comment

By the seventh century CE, the kingdoms and empires that emerged from Roman civilization were heirs not only to ancient civilizations that had long venerated certain texts but also to age-old traditions of interpreting them. Ancient scholars had written often massive commentaries on texts ranging from Aristotle's scientific and philosophical works, to the great Latin poet Virgil's epic poem, the *Aeneid,* to the Hebrew and Greek Bibles. Medieval scholars continued and intensified this practice, to such an extent that, while other genres of literature were certainly written, it is helpful to think of early medieval culture as a culture of commentaries.

At Christian, Jewish, and Muslim educational centers, scholars wrote sophisticated commentaries through which they read their scriptures. Byzantine scholars were fond of compiling *catenae* or "chains" of the teachings of the great Greek-Christian biblical interpreters. These were collections of key passages of those earlier scholars' commentaries on important parts of the Bible. So focused were early medieval Byzantine intellectuals on the content of these "chains" of earlier passages, that some complained that no one read the Bible itself any longer. Likewise, those scholars who wrote in Latin in the West, such as Bede (ca. 673–735), a monk living far off to the north on the border of Scotland and considered the most learned Latin scholar of the eighth century, wrote long commentaries on books of the Bible that depended heavily on late antique Latin authorities.

In the Jewish tradition, this commentary culture had already developed to a very high level by 650. On the one hand, standard commentaries for many books of the Hebrew Bible were already circulating. On the other, the massive compilation known as the Talmud, consisting of originally oral teachings in Hebrew called the Oral Torah and late antique rabbinical discussions of them in Aramaic, functioned broadly as a commentary on the Hebrew Bible as well. It had been compiled in two forms, the longer called the Babylonian Talmud, the shorter, the Palestinian Talmud (after the regions where they were produced). In either version it served (and serves), as one modern scholar put it, as the "lens" through which the Jewish people across time have understood their holy book.

In the Islamic world, the culture of commentary developed only after the seventh century, and, as in the Jewish tradition, did so in two different ways. First of all, as the Islamic empire expanded dramatically in the century after Muhammad, Islamic rulers encountered a range of new situations that the Qur'an, itself a relatively short book (shorter than the Greek New Testament, and much shorter than the Hebrew Bible), did not address. Since Muslims believed from an early period that God's law must govern all aspects of life, this posed serious difficulties. Early Muslims began to recall the sayings and actions of the Prophet Muhammad that could be useful both in understanding the Qur'an itself, but also in addressing circumstances that the Qur'an did not. Individually these accounts were called *hadith*s (narrations), and collectively are known as the Hadith. For a long time these *hadith*s circulated only orally, but a handful of Muslim scholars, most notably al-Bukhari (810–870) and Muslim Ibn al-Hajjaj (ca. 817–875), carefully combed through what they said were hundreds of thousands of these, and wrote down only those few thousand that they deemed to be entirely authentic. Like the Talmud for Jews, then, the huge collections of *hadith*s served as a kind of supplement and commentary on the Qur'an for Muslims, and have been used ever since as sources of teaching on the

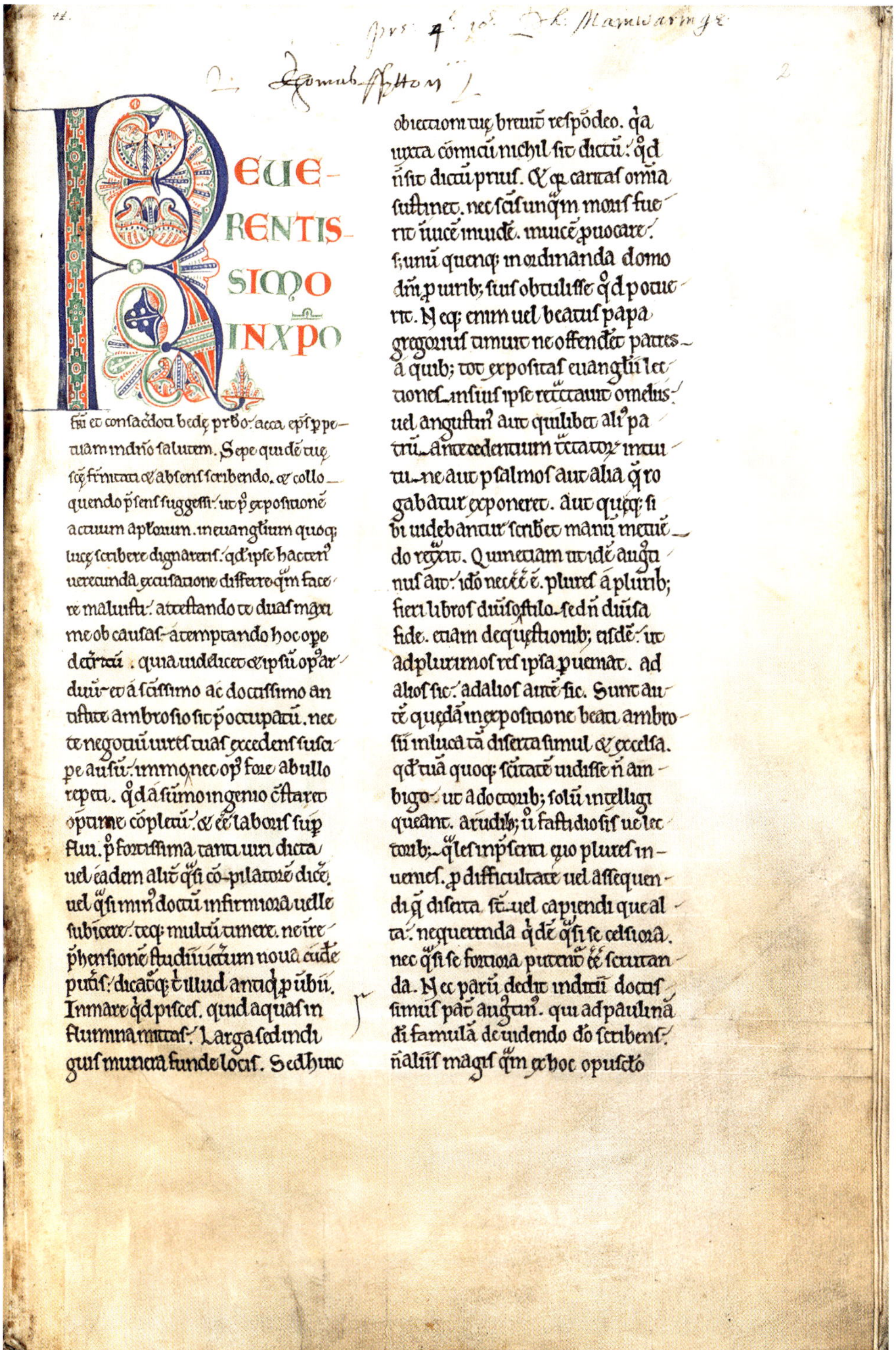

FIGURE 4.7 The beginning of Bede's commentary on the Gospel of Luke in a twelfth-century manuscript. © Historical Views / agefotostock.

practices and beliefs of Islam that are nearly as authoritative as the Qur'an. SEE SOURCEBOOK 4:4.

Many Muslim scholars, beginning soon after Muhammad's lifetime, also devoted enormous energy to expounding the meaning of the Qur'an directly, often verse by verse. Doing so required, as it did for Jewish and Christian scholars, everything from explaining the meaning of unusual words or apparently ungrammatical sentences to identifying people mentioned in the holy text to deriving practical moral guidance. One of the key sources of explanatory material for the Qur'an was the body of Hadith itself, so Qur'anic commentators often quote individual *hadiths*. But they also turned to the beloved poetry of the pre-Islamic Arabs to explain the Qur'an's language. Perhaps the culmination of early medieval Qur'anic commentary—and a work that is still widely read by Muslim scholars today—is the huge commentary by Muhammad ibn Jarir al-Tabari (839–923) called *The Comprehensive Demonstration in Interpretation of the Qur'an*. SEE SOURCEBOOK 4:5.

Scriptural Scholars and Everyone Else

At no point between 650 and 1050 was more than a tiny percentage of the population of any Mediterranean civilization able to read and write (though in some areas almost all Jewish males had some ability to read). It is tempting to conclude, therefore, that this elaborate culture of commentary was of no relevance to everyone else. This is certainly not true. While only a tiny class of religious leaders had the education to produce books, the majority of the population were consumers of them, in one way or another. Far more than in our age (though podcasts and audiobooks are changing this), people read books by listening to them. In the Islamic world we have many accounts of public reading, including of a vast historical work written by the same al-Tabari whose commentary became so influential.

Indeed, the Mediterranean world was ambivalent about the written nature of its holy books. Being able to recite a holy book by memory was not only very common, but, especially among Muslims and Jews, the only truly authoritative way of possessing and teaching it. Muslims who had memorized the whole Qur'an could add a special title to their name: *hafiz*, "preserver," of the Qur'an. The rabbis who taught the Talmud in Baghdad recited its lengthy subdivisions (called tractates) from memory, and insisted that the Talmud as a whole (an enormous, multivolume work in modern printed editions) should be preserved and passed on only orally. But Christian monks and bishops likewise knew much of the Bible, and most especially the Psalms, by memory, and often quoted them from memory when they wrote. The Mediterranean was a sea of books to be sure, but these books survived as much in memory as on the written page, and were delivered as often to their readers in oral as in written form.

A key function of religious leaders, moreover, was preaching the message of their holy books to broad audiences of believers and unbelievers. In the Christian world in this period, it was typically bishops who had sufficient education to preach effectively, though in the prosperous city of Constantinople, even laymen and emperors can be found preaching in the years around 900 CE. On the edges of Christendom, it was often missionary monks—such as the eighth-century English evangelist to the Netherlands and Germany, Saint Boniface (ca. 675–754), who preached the gospel.

Indeed, it was in preaching that Mediterranean holy books jumped outside their sacred learned languages such as Greek and Arabic. Where Islam was spreading into Iran, missionaries such as Musa ibn Sayyar al-Aswari (fl. 738) translated the Qur'an into Persian while preaching, and Abu Hafs al-Nasafi (d. 1142) even composed a rhyming Persian translation of Islam's holy book to make it even more memorable for Iranian converts. Saints Cyril and Methodios actually invented the first alphabet for the Slavic languages for their translation of the Bible into Slavonic. Jewish preachers in the Middle East had begun addressing their listeners in their spoken language of Aramaic in the ancient period, and preached in vernacular languages such as Arabic and Persian wherever they lived.

One sign that the oral recitation of scripture and the preaching of its message had an impact is the fact that Mediterranean people believed that holy books—or at least passages from them—had nearly magical powers. Irish monks in the seventh century brought a copy of the Psalms into the fields in spring to encourage the rain to fall. Scholars at the rabbinical academies in Baghdad responded to questions about the age-old practice of wear-

FIGURE 4.8 Images of Saint Boniface baptizing and his martyrdom from eleventh-century manuscript. The Picture Art Collection / Alamy Stock Photo.

ing amulets containing passages of the Hebrew Bible, something that was just as widespread in the Islamic world. Muslims often carried small cases or cylinders around their necks that contained narrow strips of paper on which Qur'anic phrases or verses were written. Such amulets—whether worn by Jews, Christians, or Muslims—were widely thought to ward off evil or sickness.

Holy Books and Greco-Roman Thinking

Mediterranean scholars were educated to have an intimate knowledge of their holy books, and a great deal of their scholarly work focused on explaining the meaning of those sacred texts. Yet we also find them perpetuating the thought of the pagan Greeks and Romans who had dominated the Great Sea long before the rise of scriptural monotheism. The same monks and priests who studied the Bible so intently also continued to preserve and read the works of Homer and Virgil, even writing commentaries on them, just as they did on the Christian Bible. Jews and Muslims did not cultivate Greco-Roman literature to the degree that Christians did, but they were the leaders in the early Middle Ages in preserving and developing another key legacy of the pagan past: Greek science and philosophy. Moreover, while Jews, Christians, and Muslims in the Islamic world broke out of their linguistic boxes when they read and wrote philosophy—they all did so in Arabic—Latin and Greek Christians remained monolingual, even when they read ancient literature.

Homer and Virgil among Medieval Christians

We would not be able to read Homer and Virgil had it not been for early medieval Christian monks and scholars. The earliest manuscript copies of most of the great works of Greek and Latin literature, it turns out, are from the ninth century CE, well after the disappearance of the pagan civilizations that gave birth to them. But not only did monks copy and read such works, the works served—as we saw above—as standard parts of the educational curricula of the medieval Christian world. There were at least two reasons for this. First, key late antique Christian writers such as Gregory of Nyssa and Augustine of Hippo had themselves been immersed in Greco-Roman literature, and had argued that the study of pagan texts was, at least to some extent, essential for Christian thinkers. Second, in literate Christian clerical circles, Latin and Greek eloquence was essential, and the works of classical authors such as Homer and Cicero were by common consent considered the best models of such eloquence, despite being written by pagans. Indeed, there are a number of copies of Virgil's *Aeneid* from the early medieval period that preserve the notes that Christian readers wrote in the margins as they read, and anonymous Carolingian scholars wrote guidebooks for understanding Rome's epic. To make such works more palatable, monastic readers typically interpreted them through a Christian lens, making the exploits of Hercules and Aeneas into Christian morality tales.

Much the same situation existed for pagan Greek literature in Byzantium. A ninth-century churchman, Ignatios the Deacon (d. after 874), for example, alluded to Homer and quoted classical proverbs repeatedly in his surviving correspondence, and in two letters discussed minute questions of ancient Greek poetic meter with remarkable understanding. Indeed, Byzantium offers the most remarkable examples of the systematic study of ancient Greco-Roman literature in the early Middle Ages. Photios (ca. 810–893) is most well known as the influential patriarch of the Greek Church in the late ninth century, but he also wrote a huge work (1,600 pages long in a modern edition) called the *Bibliotheca* (Library) in which he summarized and commented on 280 works of ancient Greek literature, many of which have since been lost.

The Neoplatonic Heritage

By 650 CE careful philosophical reflection—using reason, that is, to understand not only how the cosmos works, but what humans must do to live a meaningful, happy life—was already at least 1,000 years old in the Mediterranean lands. By late antiquity, the dominant philosophical school in the Mediterranean was Neoplatonism, a revival and intermixing of the ideas of the two greatest Greek philosophers, Plato and Aristotle. Early medieval scholars—Islamic, Jewish, and Christian—preserved and read their works, even writing commentaries on them. The same rabbis, priests, and *imams* who studied the Bible and the Qur'an so intently often found

For Jews, Christians, and Muslims in the Mediterranean world, the Hebrew Bible, Christian Bible, and Qur'an were God's books, but this scarcely meant that scholars read no others. Not only did crowded bookshelves of commentaries grow up around these sacred texts, but intellectuals turned to many other texts to help make sense of their experiences of the world, and many of these texts had been written hundreds of centuries previously by pagan Greeks or Romans. In this intellectuals were continuing the practice of certain ancient Jews and Christians. Philo the Jew (ca. 25 BCE–50 CE), for example, had read widely in Neoplatonic philosophy by Jesus's time.

Indeed, a full 200 years before the rise of Islam, Augustine of Hippo (354–430), a pagan Roman convert to Christianity who would become one of the most influential thinkers in Christian history, had not only read widely in Greco-Roman pagan literature before converting, but continued to be deeply influenced by it after becoming a Christian bishop and theologian. In a passage of his famous autobiography, *The Confessions*, he pointedly discussed how much basic Christian teaching he had learned directly from the same Neoplatonists that Philo had admired, without really needing to read the Gospel accounts—and how much not. In the passage that follows he explores how much of the message of two famous Christian Bible passages, John 1:1–14 and Philippians 2:6–11, was anticipated by Neoplatonist writings.

Augustine of Hippo, *Confessions* 7.9

> First you* wanted to show me how you 'resist the proud and give grace to the humble' (1 Pet. 5:5), and with what mercy you have shown humanity the way of humility in that your 'Word was made flesh and dwelt among' men (John 1:14). Through a man puffed up with monstrous pride, you brought under my eye some books of the [Neo]platonists, translated from Greek into Latin.† There I read—not of course in these exact words, but with entirely the same sense and supported by numerous and varied reasons—'In the beginning was the Word and the Word was with God and the Word was God. He was in the beginning with God. All things were made by him, and without him nothing was made. What was made is life in him; and the life was the light of men. . . .' Further, 'he was in this world, and the world was made by him, and the world did not know him.' But that 'he came to his own and his own did not receive him; but as many as received him, to them he gave the power to become sons of God by believing in this name,' that I *did not* read there (John 1:1–12).
>
> Again, I read there that the Word, God, is 'born not of the flesh, nor of blood, nor of the will of the flesh, but of God.' But that 'the word was made flesh and dwelt among us' (John 1:12–14), I *did not* read there. In reading the Platonic books I found expressed in different words, and in a variety of ways, that the Son, 'being in the form of the Father did not think it theft to be equal with God,' because by nature he is that very thing.‡ But that 'he took on himself the form of a servant and emptied himself, was made in the likeness of men and found to behave as a man, and humbled himself being made obedient to death, even the death of the Cross so that God exalted him' from the dead 'and gave him a name which is above every name, that at the name of Jesus every knee should bow . . . and every tongue should confess that Jesus is Lord in the glory of God the Father,' (Phil. 2:6–11)—that these books *do not* have.[1]

Byzantine scholars had preserved countless ancient Greek texts, and were educated to read them directly. Like Augustine, many Byzantine intellectuals cultivated an interest in the Neoplatonic philosophers, whose works seemed so useful in explaining Christian beliefs and cultivating Christian piety and mysticism, but some read far more widely. The great theologian and patriarch of Constantinople, Photios (ca. 810–893), made his way through a vast library of ancient Greek literature, and recorded his observations about the texts in his *Bibliotheca*. In the excerpt

* I.e., God, to whom Augustine addresses most of *The Confessions*, as if in prayer.

† Modern scholars do not know who the pagan Neoplatonist Augustine refers to here was, or which Neoplatonic books he gave Augustine.

‡ I.e., God.

below, he comments on Herodotus (ca. 484–425 BCE), the ancient Greek "father of history."

Photios, *Bibliotheca*

> Read the nine books of the *History* of Herodotus, in name and number identical with the nine Muses. He may be considered the best representative of the Ionic, as Thucydides of the Attic dialect. He is fond of old wives' tales and digressions, pervaded by charming sentiments, which, however, sometimes obscure the due appreciation of history and its correct and proper character. Truth does not allow her accuracy to be impaired by fables or excessive digressions from the subject.
>
> He begins his history with Cyrus, the first king of Persia, describing his birth, education, manhood, and reign, and goes down to the reign of Xerxes—his expedition against the Athenians, and subsequent retreat. Xerxes was the third who succeeded Cyrus, the first being Cambyses, the second Darius. . . . Darius was succeeded by his son Xerxes, with whom the history concludes, although it does not go as far as the end of his reign. Herodotus himself, according to the evidence of Diodorus Siculus,* flourished during these times. It is said that, when he [i.e., Herodotus] read his work, Thucydides,† then very young, who was present with his father at the reading, burst into tears. Whereupon Herodotus exclaimed, "Oh, Olorus!‡ how eager your son is to learn!"[2]

While very little of Greek philosophy and science—apart from certain Neoplatonic works like those read by Augustine—had been translated into Latin before the eleventh century, cutting off early medieval Latin intellectuals from much of that heritage, caliphs and other influential leaders in Arab-Muslim society paid bi- and trilingual scholars, many of them Christians, to translate much of it into Arabic. By the tenth century, therefore, Muslim thinkers had not only digested much of Greek philosophy and science, but built on it creatively. In the final excerpt, al-Farabi (ca. 872–950), one of the greatest of these Muslim philosophers, discusses how Aristotle (384–322 BCE), the pagan Greek scientist who lived fully 1,000 years earlier, understood the basic elements of which the cosmos was constructed and how they related to each other. Virtually all Jewish, Christian, and Muslim thinkers in the Mediterranean subscribed, by the way, to Aristotle's ideas about this.

Al-Farabi, *The Philosophy of Plato and Aristotle*

> Then [Aristotle] investigated afterwards what one ought to call these elements if they are pure, having the essence belonging to them alone (without their contrary being in any way mixed with them), and are most extreme in the powers in virtue of which they are elements. He did not find names by which to call them, and found the generally accepted names to be the names of the substrata that belong to these elements mixed with others. Whereupon he inquired about the species of the 'elements' that have generally accepted names, and whenever the local motion of one of these species was close to being the local motion of a certain element, or its sensible qualities close to being the qualities of a certain element, he transferred to the sum of that element the name of the corresponding species. He called the body that is together with [that is, next to] the heavenly bodies, *Fire;* and he made it known that it is not this fire that we have. For *fire* is applied to flame and ember by the multitude, not to anything else. But since the movement of flame, especially, is a movement that aims, as it were, at burning air in order to ascend above it, he therefore called the body floating over the rest of the elements (that is, that which has one of its two surfaces contiguous to the concave of the heavenly bodies) by that name *Fire*. He called the body that is below it by the name *Air,* that which is below it by the name *Water,* and that which is in the center by the name *Earth*. All the elements are associated [that is, mixed together] in the body that is in the center, that is, earth; that is required theoretically and is evident by observation. Since mixture is of two types, *Earth* is mixed with the rest of the elements in both of the two types. *Water* also is mixed with *Earth* and *Air* in both ways; its mixture with Fire is not noticeable, however; yet it is required that it be mixed with it also. *Air* is inferior to *Water* in this respect, and *Fire* is inferior to them all in its mixture with the others. These, then, are things of which [Aristotle] made an exhaustive investigation.[3]

* A first-century BCE Greek historian whom Photios had also read.

† Thucydides (ca. 460–400 BCE) was a Greek historian in the generation after Herodotus.

‡ I.e., Thucydides's father.

Discussion Questions

1. What do these excerpts suggest about the range of uses to which Mediterranean scriptural monotheists put ancient Greco-Roman learning?

2. How would you describe the attitudes toward ancient pagan thinkers that we find in these excerpts?

Further Reading

Adamson, Peter. *Philosophy in the Islamic World*. Oxford: Oxford University Press, 2016.

Marenbon, John. *Medieval Philosophy: An Historical and Philosophical Introduction*. Abingdon: Routledge, 2007.

Treadgold, Warren. *The Nature of the Bibliotheca of Photios*. Washington, DC: Dumbarton Oaks/Harvard University Press, 1980.

Notes

1. Saint Augustine, *Confessions*, trans. Henry Chadwick (Oxford: Oxford University Press, 1991), 121.

2. Photius, *Bibliotheca* 60, trans. J.H. Freese, http://www.tertullian.org/fathers/photius_03bibliotheca.htm.

3. Al-Farabi, *The Philosophy of Plato and Aristotle*, trans. Muhsin Mahdi (New York: Free Press of Glencoe, 1962), 110.

Neoplatonic thought valuable in explicating their monotheistic beliefs.

Summarizing Neoplatonism—a highly complex system of thought—is difficult, but for early medieval monotheists, two features stood out. On the cosmic level, Neoplatonists argued that the source of all things was a transcendent being called the One whose very nature was to abound in goodness, beauty, and truth. The pagan philosopher Plotinus (205–270 CE), a key founder of Neoplatonist thought, describes the One that we search for to "make over our soul" as "the Good," the creator ("Generative of all"), "higher still" than the intellect, and "unique in form or, better, formless, existing before Form was, or Movement or Rest."[2] From this superabounding One Neoplatonists believed that a Divine Mind, often called the Word, emerged, and from the Divine Mind, a World Soul emanated. This World Soul was the origin of all material reality, including humans. Second, the point of life for humans was to return to their ultimate origin in the One in this life by learning to rise up, through living a life of self-denial and meditation, to direct, mystical experience of the One. SEE SOURCEBOOK 4:6.

It is not hard to see why many Jews, Christians, and Muslims found these ideas attractive, since they seemed to be a rational, external confirmation both of monotheism, the One standing for the God of scripture, and of a way of life that would culminate in the experience of God. Though there were, of course, important and obvious differences, this all sounded a lot like what the Jewish and Christian Bible as well as the Qur'an seemed to teach. Christians were particularly fascinated by the Neoplatonic triad of the One/Divine Mind/World Soul, which seemed so reminiscent of their doctrine of the Trinity. Indeed, ancient Jewish and Christian thinkers had embraced so many Neoplatonist ideas as their own that in many ways Neoplatonism had become an essential part of the scriptural monotheism that dominated the entire early Middle Ages.

Neoplatonism in the House of Islam

Though Islam was a new religion in the seventh century, the House of Islam was nevertheless the site of the most remarkable cultivation of that Greek, Neoplatonic heritage in the early Middle Ages. Indeed, having conquered the heavily Hellenized Middle East, Islamic political and intellectual leaders, especially in the ninth and tenth centuries, systematically fostered the translation of a vast range of ancient Greek and Syriac works of philosophy into Arabic. By early in the tenth century, therefore, Arab-Muslim scholars possessed a fully equipped Neoplatonic library, and Greek philosophy was flourishing among not only Muslims, but also Jews and Christians living in Muslim lands.

Like ancient Jews and Christians, Muslims found that Greek philosophical terminology and ideas were handy in defending their faith, and thus was born a whole theological tradition of philosophical and religious discourse

FIGURE 4.9 Tenth-century manuscript of Homer's *Iliad* accompanied by explanatory commentary. © Historical Views / agefotostock.

FIGURE 4.10 Sculpture of a philosopher, perhaps Plotinus. Historic Collection / Alamy Stock Photo.

called *kalam* (argument). A key issue of *kalam,* for example, was how to justify Islamic belief in the one God described in the Qur'an in a way that did not contradict reason. This was not easy, since the Qur'an spoke about God in ways that seemed to attribute thoroughly human qualities to him—he is described, for example, as having not only sight and hearing, but even hands (e.g., 38:76). Muslim theologians soon developed arguments using the Aristotelian logic favored by Neoplatonists to show that God is indeed utterly transcendent, as reason required, but that he had certain attributes such as omnipotence, knowledge, and vision that corresponded to the qualities attributed to him in the Qur'an.

Neoplatonic thought showed up in two other ways in the Islamic world as well. By the ninth century, a significant ascetic movement called Sufism had developed, many of whose adherents dedicated themselves to mysticism—to the direct, personal experience of God in this life, something that, as we have seen, the pagan Neoplatonists deeply desired as well. It is no surprise, then, to discover that the thought of many Sufi mystics had a Neoplatonic character. Early Sufis, such as the Andalusi thinker Ibn Masarra of Córdoba (883–931), argued that such passages as the enigmatic "Light Verse" (24:35)—"God is the light of the heavens and the earth. His light is like a niche in which is a lantern, the lantern glass... its oil almost aglow, though untouched by fire.... He wills and strikes parables for mankind. God has knowledge of all things"—justified an allegorical reading of the Qur'an that emphasized direct spiritual experience of God.

From the tenth century on, some Muslim scholars became interested in studying Greek philosophy not so much as a tool in defending Islam or in experiencing God directly, but as a coherent, independent system of thought. Such scholars eventually had their own title—*faylasuf,* from the Greek word for "philosopher"—and the most famous examples from this period are al-Farabi (ca. 872–950) and Ibn Sina (or Avicenna, 980–1037). Both daringly reworked the Neoplatonism they had inherited. Al-Farabi, for example, elaborated extensively on both Aristotelian logic and theories of cognition ("knowing"). Ibn Sina explicated the whole of Aristotle's systematic thought, which had tended to be deemphasized by Neoplatonists, but welded it onto certain key Platonic themes in ways that would make him, as we will see in chapter 9, the most influential philosopher in the entire medieval Mediterranean.

We should not be surprised to find that in the multireligious House of Islam the boundaries between religions became hazy when it came to the study of philosophy. *Falsafa* (i.e., Greek philosophy) and Sufism were not exclusive to Muslims. Among the most important works of Jewish spirituality and mysticism, *The Duties of the Heart,* written in 1040 by the Andalusi rabbi Bahya ben Joseph ibn Paquda (fl. 1050–1090), was the fruit of what one scholar has recently called an intense "Sufi-Jewish dialogue."[3] Likewise, among the most important teachers of the Muslim philosopher al-Farabi (ca. 872–950) were the Christian *faylasufs* Yuhanna ibn Haylan (d. 910) and Matta ibn Yunus (ca. 820–940), and among his students, the practitioner of Christian *kalam,* the *faylasuf* Yahya ibn Adi (893–974).

الشيخ الفاضل ابي زكريا يحيى ابن عدي
البصري عالم من علما النصارى المسيحيين لان
تلك البلاد البصره وما معها يسمون نصارتها بمثل
هذا الاسما وقوله الشيخ ابي زكريا انما هو تعظيم
في حق الرجل كونه من العلما واما تسميتهم يحيى
وعدي ويونس وعلي وعمار وعيسى ومثل ذلك
فليس في ذلك شناعة لان عادة اهالي تلك
البلاد يسمون مثل هذه الاسما وهم نصارى مسيحيين
علما افاضل نيح الله نفوس الماضيين منهم في
فردوس النعيم

FIGURE 4.11 Manuscript of works by the Arab-Christian philosopher Yahya ibn Adi, copied 1654. © Historical Views / agefotostock.

Neoplatonism in Latin and Greek Christianity

Latin- and Greek-Christian thinkers also cultivated Neoplatonism in the early Middle Ages, but in less intense and systematic ways. This is particularly true of the Latins in the poorest region of the Mediterranean whose very language reflected a lack of sophisticated philosophy or theology. The Latin word *philosophus* (philosopher) in this period simply referred to a wise or perceptive person or a school master or monk (indeed *philosophia*, "philosophy," could mean "monastic life"), not a practitioner of systematic, rigorous philosophy. There was no Latin word for "theology" or "theologian" at all—these terms would only develop in the later Middle Ages. Nevertheless, we do find Latin scholars practicing something akin to the *kalamic* theology of the Islamic world—using, that is, Greek philosophical tools and concepts to defend and explain Christian belief.

The courts of the Carolingian rulers played a key role here. One of Charlemagne's most important advisers, the English monk Alcuin (735–804), tirelessly advocated the study of Aristotelian logic, a key element in the Neoplatonic curriculum. Charlemagne's grandson, Charles the Bald, put one of his court intellectuals, the learned Irish scholar John Scotus Eriugena (ca. 815–877), who, uniquely in this period, knew Greek, to work on translating into Latin the works of a late antique Christian Neoplatonist known as Pseudo-Dionysius, which had been sent as a present from the Byzantine emperor. Not only did this introduce a whole new current of Neoplatonism to Latin readers, but it also inspired Eriugena to write his own massive Neoplatonic interpretation of Christianity called the *Periphyseon*. Nevertheless, while this work was a masterpiece of philosophical theology (but the subject of real criticism by contemporary and later Christian thinkers), in this relatively poor culture, which did not even have precise terms for philosophy or theology, it is not surprising that Eriugena had no students or followers who continued his remarkable work.

The Greek-Christian intellectual world, while by no means as dynamic as the Islamic, was more philosophically energetic than the Latin. In part this was a question of resources. Greek-Christian scholars could read the ancient Greek philosophers directly, most of whose works were unavailable in Latin in the early Middle Ages. Not only, therefore, was the study of Aristotle's logic an essential part of Byzantine education, but intellectuals such as Photios in the ninth century, and the learned courtier Michael Psellos (ca. 1018–1078), read a whole range of Greek philosophers. Psellos, for example, even turned to pagan Neoplatonism to explain what Jesus meant when, puzzlingly, he asked, "Why do you call me good? No one is good but God alone" (Mark 10:18). More so than Latin-Christian or Arab-Muslim thought, moreover, Byzantine theology was profoundly mystical in orientation. Not surprisingly, then, Neoplatonist ideas about how the human soul can encounter the One show up repeatedly in the widely influential works of Symeon the New Theologian (949–1022). In his Hymn 25, he describes the direct experience of God as "swirlings of the flame": "But, Oh what intoxication of light, Oh, what movements of fire! / Oh, what swirlings of the flame in me, miserable one that I am, coming from You and Your glory!"[4]

Interpretation, Unity, and Power

The sea of books that was the Mediterranean contained within it a sea of readers and listeners and a sea of interpreting scholars, all of them reflecting on holy books that, while inspiring to believers, were often difficult to understand. Inevitably a pressing question arose for these Peoples of the Book: What happens when interpreters disagree on the meaning of the holy text? While there may have been exceptions, almost no intellectual in the Mediterranean lands thought that religion was merely a private matter—that everyone could believe whatever they wanted and should be left alone to do so. This meant that mechanisms to determine proper belief and enforce it were essential. Some of these, especially among Christians, had already developed in the late antique world, but Muslims had to formulate such mechanisms in their entirety in this period. While Jewish, Christian, and Muslim religious authorities could enforce right belief (orthodoxy) and right practice (orthopraxy), sometimes quite brutally, we should not conclude that these orthodoxies and orthopraxies were merely rigid systems of conformity. Indeed Rabbanite Judaism, Catholic/Orthodox Christianity, and Sunni Islam—the dominant religions of the medieval world—were successful not only through enforcement by powerful institutions and powerful people, but also because they were highly complex and surprisingly flexible entities that, while "anathematizing"—declaring heretical—some ideas, allowed for considerable variation of practice and belief in other areas.

Councils, Creeds, and *Filioque*

By 650 CE Christianity—Greek, Latin, Syriac, and Coptic—had long since developed into a religion unusually preoccupied with defining right practice and right belief, and had, as a result, gone through periods of bitter conflict. These major conflicts, however, were almost entirely in the past, and, ultimately, Christians had come to agree that the authority to define right belief resided with the bishops of the church, each of whom had been installed in his position by other bishops in a chain

Various mechanisms developed over time among all the Mediterranean Peoples of the Book to determine right practice and belief in rather general terms—and this is the subject of the section that follows. But in specific cases Jews, Christians, and Muslims often had difficulty working out what God's will might be, and needed to consult expert opinion. For Jews and Muslims this uncertainty led to much the same practice: requesting in writing a judicial opinion from a leading religious scholar, who, if he chose, might issue such an opinion, likewise in writing. In the case of Jews, the request was usually sent to one of the heads of the Talmudic academies in Iraq, while among Muslims it could be addressed to any highly regarded scholar. Modern scholars refer to a Jewish opinion of this kind as a *responsum* (pl. *responsa*), while the standard Arabic term for a judicial opinion, *fatwa,* is used in all languages to refer to the Muslim version. A large number of both survive from the Middle Ages.

Often such requests—whether Jewish or Muslim—dealt with concrete legal matters arising from the nonstop commerce that flowed across the Sea in the Middle.

A *Responsum* of Sa'adyah ben Joseph (882–942)

Written originally, like many of his *responsa,* in Arabic, this legal opinion of the great scholar Sa'adyah ben Joseph, with whom this chapter opened, survives only in a later Hebrew translation, and concerns a business partnership between two merchants called Simon and Levi who have accepted funds from two investors, Reuben and Judah. At issue is not only the liability of the investors for the merchants' debts, but also the use of a conditional curse called a *gezerah* in place of an oath in God's name. The request for Sa'adyah's judgment reads in part as follows:

> Reuben gave Simon and his partner Levi funds to use in a profitable business, and Judah also gave them funds. And Simon and Levi paid Reuben an appropriate amount of the profit on a regular basis. And later Reuben wished to withdraw his capital and Simon and Levi returned it to him and he was repaid in full. And subsequently the king confiscated all the assets of Simon and Levi together with Judah's funds which they had in their keeping. Judah then sued Reuben and told him: 'You are the partner of Simon and Levi, so return my funds for you are obligated to give them to me.' Reuben said: 'I was not their partner but had an investment with them and have already been repaid by them and I have had no connection with them for some days,' and Simon and Levi acknowledge this. And nevertheless some people arranged a compromise between them, and Reuben swore to Judah by means of a gezerah that he is not in possession of any funds belonging to Simon and Levi and they are not partners, and this was satisfactory to Judah. And later... he changed his mind and sued Reuben a second time, saying 'Swear to me by the Torah because I have heard that you do not consider a gezerah to be a binding oath.' Would it please our master to instruct us as to whether Reuben is obligated or not.

Sa'adyah responded as follows:

> If what transpired between Reuben and Simon and Levi and Judah is as described in this question, Judah has no claim on Reuben on account of Simon and Levi, inasmuch as the two partners who handled the funds are Simon and Levi, but Reuben and Judah are the investors, and no connection is created between them because of this... for, according to the law, both Reuben and Judah are lenders and depositors only, not partners... and since it is known that half the funds of an investment are treated as a loan and half as a deposit... the investor of the money is exempt from any claims against the one who handles the funds, because one who deposits funds with another is not liable for the debts of the one who holds the funds and a lender is not liable for the debts of his debtor..., it is clear that Judah was legally in the wrong to claim from Reuben the debts that Simon and Levi owed him....
>
> And as for Judah who arraigned Reuben once again, after he had accepted a gezerah that was not required of him, and who said, 'Swear to me by the Torah for I have heard that you do not consider a gezerah to be an oath,' his words are flawed in many ways: for one, he had already received from him more than his due... yet he imposed a gezerah; and sec-

> ondly, in wanting to make him swear on the Torah and failing to realize that the gezerah was on the Book and thirdly, he imagines that the gezerah is only effective against a person who considers it an oath, whereas it is indeed effective against anyone who lies, whether he considers it an oath or not.[1]

A *Fatwa* on a Jewish Silk Merchant in North Africa

A well-known Muslim legal scholar, Abu 'Abd Allah al-Mazari (d. 1141), was consulted by the *qadi* of Gafsa (in what is modern Tunisia) who had received a complaint, most likely from a Muslim, about a Jewish trader who was suspected of offering silk for sale that had been procured by unlawful means. Al-Mazari instructed him to follow the normal procedure for cases in which an accuser could not corroborate his claim with eyewitness testimonies or indisputable proof:

> [Al-Mazari] was asked by a *qadi* whom he named that a Jew was brought before him who had silk that he wanted to sell, and which was said to be messed up and torn in such a way as to cause suspicion that it had been taken as plunder from a certain caravan that he mentioned. The Jew, now, brought a group of people from Gafsa who testified that [he] was trustworthy and not one to fall under this kind of suspicion. The silk was impounded pending the [al-Mazari's] reply.
>
> He [al-Mazari] replied: if the suspicion based on the messed-up and torn state [of the silk] has not been substantiated, and trustworthy witnesses or a group of people whose outward behavior is pious and who are not the kind to collude to lie have testified that it is not like this Jew to purchase what has been attributed to him, and moreover what is required by his status is to avoid the like of this [behavior], he will be summoned to take an oath that he did not receive it from someone who had robbed the caravan to which the one who expressed doubts had referred or any other one. If he accepts, the *qadi* is bound by the answer. The Jew will deliver the oath in the synagogue, in the spot that he holds most in awe, by God than whom there is no other god, that the silk referred to is not from the caravan that was seized and that he only bought it from someone who sold it to him in a lawful manner, and that he had no knowledge of any suspicion or swindle attaching to it.
>
> He who is present at his oath-taking in said terms in the place referred to will add to his testimony "in such-and-such a month of this-and-this year."[2]

Discussion Questions

1. These two opinions focus on what we would now think of as secular legal matters. Why in the context of the medieval Mediterranean is it not surprising that the petitioners turned to religious scholars for their views on these issues?

2. What do these opinions tell us about the interactions both *within* and *between* religious communities in the medieval Mediterranean?

3. What assumptions do the Jewish and Muslim opinions share?

Further Reading

Goldish, Matt. *Jewish Questions: Responsa on Sephardic Life in the Early Modern Period*. Princeton: Princeton University Press, 2008.

Gómez-Rivas, Camilo. *Law and the Islamization of Morocco under the Almoravids: The Fatwās of Ibn Rushd al-Jadd to the Far Maghrib*. Leiden: E.J. Brill, 2014.

Mann, Jacob. *The Responsa of the Babylonian Geonim as a Source of Jewish History*. New York: Arno Press, 1973.

Notes

1. Sa'adyah ben Joseph, "A Responsum of Sa'adyah ben Joseph (882–942)," adapted from Brody, *Sa'adyah Gaon*, 119–20.

2. Al-Mazari, "A *Fatwa* on a Jewish Silk Merchant in North Africa," adapted from Camilla Adang, "A *Fatwā* by al-Māzarī (d. 536/1141) on a Jewish Silk Merchant in Gafsa," in *Jewish-Muslim Relations in Past and Present: A Kaleidoscopic View*, ed. Josef W. Meri, Studies on the Children of Abraham 5 (Leiden: Brill, 2017), 167.

stretching back directly to Jesus's twelve disciples—what Christians called *apostolic succession*. But what happened if one bishop disagreed with another about the meaning of the Bible? While bishops of more prestigious and older dioceses could be called on to adjudicate such disputes, ultimately the basic Christian beliefs on key issues like the Incarnation (God made flesh in the human person of Jesus) and Trinity (three manifestations of one God—Father, Son, and Holy Spirit) had to be hammered out in meetings, called church councils, of the bishops of all of Christian Europe. It was at such councils in the fourth century CE that the definitive statement of Christian belief called the Nicene Creed (325 CE) had been written.

This basic pattern for defining right belief—bishops define Christian orthodoxy in councils in which secular rulers often interfered—remained in force right through the Middle Ages. The dispute in the early Middle Ages between Latin and Greek Christians over the so-called *filioque* clause of the Nicene Creed exemplifies both how it functioned, and how sometimes it did not, in this period. In defining the relationship between the members of the Trinity, the bishops at Nicaea had specified in the creed that the Holy Spirit "proceeded from the Father." From the late sixth century on, beginning in Spain, Latin Christians began inserting the phrase "and from the Son" (*filioque*) immediately after, so that the Holy Spirit was deemed to proceed from both Father and Son. By the ninth century, "and from the Son" was commonly said throughout the Latin-Christian regions of Europe, and after the year 1000 had been adopted in Rome as well. The Greek Church, upon learning in the early ninth century that Latin monks in Jerusalem were chanting the creed with "and from the Son," objected strenuously—because no general, so-called *ecumenical* (universal) council (like that at Nicaea) had ever approved this addition to the creed. As it happens, this dispute over "and from the Son" was and remains the only substantive doctrinal disagreement between the Roman Catholic and Greek Orthodox Churches, which have been divided over this issue since the mid-eleventh century, when the Byzantine and Roman Churches mutually excommunicated each other over it.

The People of the Sunna and the Shi'i *Imam*s

If the *filioque* dispute exemplified how a late antique pattern of determining Christian orthodoxy continued (mostly) to function in the early Middle Ages, the new religion of Islam had to devise such a pattern entirely anew in this period. The most important context in which this happened was the bloody period of civil war (656–661) fought primarily between those who believed Muhammad's cousin and son-in-law 'Ali (656–661) should lead the now enormous House of Islam and the Umayyad caliphs (661–750), who had been selected by a council of Islamic leaders to govern. Over time this political split between the majority, who accepted the Umayyad dynasty, and the proponents of 'Ali (in Arabic, the "Party of 'Ali" = *Shi'at 'Ali*, hence "Shi'i") took on a religious cast as each side developed different theories of religious authority to justify their position, and then further differences in belief and practice developed as well.

For the Shi'is ultimate interpretive authority belonged to Muhammad and his descendants through 'Ali whom they referred to as *imams* (leaders). By virtue of their family connection to the Prophet, Shi'is believed God had given the Shi'i *imams* special insight into right belief and the authority to adjudicate religious disputes. Initially, different Shi'i groups identified specific descendants of 'Ali as successive *imams*, though by 873 the majority came to believe that at some point the true *imam* went into hiding and would return at the end of time as the Mahdi (the Rightly Guided") who would restore order and bring justice for the persecuted Shi'i Muslims before the end of the world. Shi'i religious practice, while sharing much in common with that of other Muslims, came to emphasize commemoration of the murders of 'Ali and his son al-Ḥusayn, and the continuing oppression of the Party of 'Ali.

Over against the development of Shi'i notions of religious authority, the Umayyad regime and its supporters—as well as the 'Abbasid dynasty (750–1258) that succeeded it—gradually came to locate supreme authority in Islamic religion in the "practice" or "pathway"—the Sunna—of the Prophet Muhammad. The basic principle of the Sunna is that when uncertainty arises regarding the practices or beliefs of the Islamic community, the solution must be sought in the Qur'an itself, and, if not

FIGURE 4.12 Shrine of Imam al-Ḥusayn in Karbala, Iraq. Photo Karar Alasadi, Creative Commons Attribution-Share Alike 4.0 International License.

available there, in what Muslims remembered of Muhammad's own actions and views as preserved in the Hadith. Those who were deeply knowledgeable of the Qur'an and Hadith, the learned *faqihs* (from Arabic *fiqh,* "law"), must be consulted on such questions. They in turn issued opinions—*fatwas* (rulings)—that those in positions of authority, who usually asked for the views of more than one scholar, could follow. Over the course of time those opinions that stood up to the criticism of other scholars came to be recognized as part of the Sunna. This meant that ultimately the criterion for what was obligatory in belief and practice for these *Sunni* Muslims was a consensus of learned scholars from four established schools of Islamic legal thought: Hanafi, Maliki, Shafi'i, Hanbali. Each had been founded by an Islamic scholar and each was considered equally valid in the Sunna, though they differed from each other in many matters of detail. While the majority of Muslim scholars, for example, forbade the consumption of alcohol based on key Qur'anic verses, *faqihs* of the Hanafi school of law were lenient on this issue, and, unlike the other schools, also allowed ritual prayers to be said in a language other than Arabic.

Rabbis and the Authority of the Talmudic Academies

Judaism also experienced disputes across the Mediterranean. For one thing, the centers for Talmudic study and Jewish scholarship were in Iraq and Palestine, a great distance, say, from Qayrawan in Muslim North Africa or the Rhineland cities of Latin-Christian Europe, places that had important Jewish communities. Not surprisingly, it was quite difficult for rabbis in Jerusalem or Baghdad to enforce their views in such remote communities. Furthermore, by no means did all Jews recognize the notion of an authoritative Talmud that supplemented the written Torah.

For one thing the already age-old division between Rabbanite Jews and Samaritans existed right through the Middle Ages (and all the way to the present). The Samaritans rejected all of the Hebrew Bible except the first five books (in a slightly different version, which they wrote in their distinctive, archaic Hebrew script), and they preserved some of the ancient biblical offices—high priest, priests, and Levites—that had fallen out of use among the Rabbanites. They adopted Arabic very soon after the conquest (writing it also in their own distinctive script), and were well known to Arabs as physicians.

More significantly for Rabbanite Jews, in the eighth century, a Palestinian rabbi named 'Anan ben David (715–795 CE) wrote a treatise called the *Book of Commandments* (ca. 770) that strenuously denied the authority of the Talmud, and in the ninth century and later, Benjamin al-Nihawandi and others who claimed 'Anan's legacy, and who referred to themselves as Karaites (which means something like "biblicists"), continued his attacks. Fundamentally this was a dispute—in the bookish culture of the medieval Mediterranean—over which books were the most important. For those who adhered to the Talmud, called the Rabbanites, the Hebrew Bible could only be understood properly through the lens of the massive Talmudic assemblage of texts. For Karaites, the Bible alone was sufficient guidance in all matters.

Karaites gained real strength in some areas of the Jewish world, including Palestine and Jerusalem, into the eleventh century and beyond. Not surprisingly, some Rabbanite leaders, especially Sa'adya ben Joseph, the tenth-century *gaon* of the rabbinical academy of Sura in Iraq, worked strenuously to combat Karaite views. He wrote polemical tracts directed specifically against them, but also criticized Karaism here and there elsewhere in his many writings. But in general the leaders of the Talmudic academies paid little direct attention to the Karaites, who seem not to have proselytized among Rabbanite Jews. Rather, Rabbanite leaders like Sa'adya ben Joseph focused their attention on building up their authority among the Mediterranean Jewish communities that did recognize the Talmud.

Orthodoxy and Plurality

During the early medieval period, therefore, the Mediterranean's Peoples of the Book devised and sustained mechanisms to control how their holy books were interpreted, leaving this responsibility in the hands variously of bishops and church councils, learned *faqih*s, and prominent rabbis such as the *gaon*s, and these groups were often successful in stifling dissent, not uncommonly through the armed help of secular rulers. Yet it would be a mistake to imagine that the orthodoxies that eventually predominated—Latin Catholicism, Greek Orthodoxy, Sunni Islam, and Rabbanite Judaism—were rigid religious traditions and nothing else. In fact, their long-term survival, like that of any religious movement, was a result as well of their flexibility and ability to accommodate difference.

Indeed, within each tradition, certain kinds of variety were institutionally established. Christian monasticism had originated in late antiquity as a movement of protest against the opulence of the mainstream church. Bishops, therefore, often saw celebrated monks as rivals to their own authority. But monasticism—especially communal monasticism—had many admirers within the mainstream church too, including powerful bishops who argued that, properly managed and controlled (by bishops, of course), monasteries could be a legitimate part of Christian society. In effect, therefore, the church offered the faithful two very different forms of acceptable Christian life—that of the married layperson and that of the celibate monk or nun. Mainstream Sunni Islam came to recognize that each of the four different schools of religious-legal thought was valid, though, as we have seen, they differed from each other in many matters of detail.

Furthermore, the authoritative libraries of these religions of many books were themselves full of apparently conflicting statements and paradoxes upon which debate could never be put to an end. The Eucharist or Mass, at which bread and wine were transformed into the body and blood of Jesus, had long since become the central ritual event of Catholic and Orthodox Christianity. Yet there were endless questions about how this transformation happened, which culminated in a vigorous "Eucharistic controversy" in ninth-century Latin Europe. The vast Talmud was itself far more an anthology of unresolved debates on key aspects of Jewish practice than a comprehensive set of answers. It thus inherently stimulated still further debate. Early Sufis, far more of whom were mainstream Muslim believers than scholars have long thought, argued for an allegorical reading of the Qur'an that emphasized direct spiritual experience of God. But other mainstream Muslim scholars strenuously maintained that such esoteric Qur'an interpretation would destroy the coherence of Sunni Islam.

Diversity of opinion, even dissent, therefore, often flourished in the early medieval Mediterranean, whether in the anti-Talmudic writings of 'Anan ben David and later Karaites; in the rationalist, antireligious poetry of the nominally Muslim Syrian Abu al-Ala al-Ma'arri (d. 1058); in the thoroughgoing (and heavily criticized) Neoplatonist theology of the eleventh-century Byzantine John of Italos; or in the trenchant hostility to the mainstream schools of Islamic jurisprudence of the Andalusi polymath Ibn Hazm of Córdoba (d. 1064). Indeed, out of such diversity complex greatness could emerge, as two thinkers from the very end of this period exemplify. SEE SOURCEBOOK 4:7.

Anselm of Canterbury (d. 1109) was an Italian monk trained in French monasteries who became an English archbishop. But he was also a philosopher, and, in an unprecedented embrace of pure logic, he propounded the so-called ontological proof for the existence of God (God is "that which no greater thing can be thought") that has never ceased to fascinate, perplex, outrage, and inspire philosophers. Abu Hamid al-Ghazali (d. 1111), while holding the most prestigious post in the most prestigious *madrasa* in Baghdad, lost his faith and, abandoning his professorship, fled into the company of the oft-criticized Sufis for nearly a decade. But he eventually returned to the elite world of the *madrasas*, faith intact, and wrote a thick synthesis of Islamic law, theology, philosophy, and Sufism called *Bringing the Religious Sciences to Life* that made him the most beloved Islamic thinker from his time into the twentieth century. Both Anselm and al-Ghazali lived within regulated systems of orthodoxy and orthopraxy, and both received their share of criticism for their ideas. Yet even modern totalitarian regimes have not been able to stamp out diversity of thought, despite all the resources and brutality of the well-funded police state. The profoundly weaker instruments of premodern religious control could never have quashed diversity of opinion entirely (even if they had wanted to) or stamped out the creativity of such original thinkers, especially when they held in their hands such powerful tools as their holy books and the assembled further texts—those powerful bookish lenses—through which they read them.

Notes

1. Sa'adyah ben Joseph, *Sa'adyah Gaon's Commentary on Genesis [Perushei rav sa'adyah gaon livereshit]* (New York, 1984), 13–15 (Arabic), 181–84 (Hebrew translation), as quoted in Robert Brody, *Sa'adyah Gaon* (Oxford: The Littman Library of Jewish Civilization, 2013), 33.

2. Plotinus, *The Enneads* 6.3, translated by Stephen MacKenna, as anthologized in Algis Uzdavinyis, *The Heart of Plotinus* (Bloomington, IN: World Wisdom, 2006), 210–11.

3. The quotation is from the title of Diana Lobel's *A Sufi-Jewish Dialogue: Philosophy and Mysticism in Bahya Ibn Paquda's "Duties of the Heart"* (Philadelphia: University of Pennsylvania Press, 2007).

4. C. J. deCatanzaro and George Maloney SJ, *Symeon the New Theologian: The Discourses* (New York: Paulist Press: 1980), 24.

PART II

AN AGE OF CONFLICT AND COLLABORATION (1050–1350 CE)

The Mediterranean from the Edges

On October 2, 1187, the defeated Frankish-Palestinian lord Balian d'Ibelin presented the keys to Jerusalem's Tower of David to the victorious Kurdish prince al-Malik al-Nasir Yusuf ibn Ayyub—better known to history as Salah al-Din (or "Saladin"). Less than three months earlier, this sultan of Egypt and Syria had annihilated the army of the Crusader kingdom of Jerusalem, including the forces of the Templar and Hospitaller knights, at the Battle of the Horns of Hattin. Now the Holy City—the site of the ancient Jewish Temple, the scene of Christ's passion, and the launch pad for Muhammad's "night flight" to Heaven—was once again under Muslim rule. The Latin conquest of the city on July 7, 1099, by a force of Burgundian, Norman, and Provençal Crusaders and their Genoese allies, had been a bloodbath, culminating in the deliberate massacre of thousands of defenseless Muslim, Jewish, and Eastern Christian inhabitants. By contrast, whether out of expedience or magnanimity, Salah al-Din spared the surrendering Franks. Thousands suffered the terrible fate of enslavement, but those who had the means were permitted to ransom themselves for cash. And so it was, in autumn 1187 a column of refugees led by Balian and the Latin patriarch of Jerusalem wound its way westward to the port of Tyre, one of the few remaining Latin possessions in the Holy Land. Soon after, the Dome of the Rock and al-Aqsa mosque were resanctified, and Jerusalem was transformed once more into the city of Muslims, Jews, and Eastern Christians it had been before the Frankish conquest.

Long held up as a central event in the Middle Ages, and as evidence of the violent collision of Islamic and Christian civilizations, the recapture of Jerusalem was, in fact, not the watershed it is often made out to be. It did not mark the conclusion of the Crusades, nor was any concerted attempt made by a unified Latin Christendom to retake it by force afterward. Although the Crusade era did see an increase of communal violence across religious lines and the intensification of religious rhetoric aimed at "infidels," both the Crusader conquest and Salah al-Din's recovery were symptomatic of the process of economic, cultural, and social engagement of the Christian and Islamic worlds that played out in the Mediterranean region from the mid-eleventh to the mid-fourteenth century.

Internal political tensions and environmental stress had led to the collapse of the caliphal/imperial order in the mid-eleventh century. As had been the case with Persia and Rome in late antiquity, the failure of these empires—Byzantium and the three caliphates—was both a result and a cause of the arrival of "barbarian" outsiders into the Mediterranean world, this time Turks, Arabs, Berbers, and various western European peoples the Arabs referred to generically as al-Ifranj (the Franks). Each was drawn into the region from its underdeveloped, sparsely populated, and environmentally stark fringes. Some, such as the Seljuq Turks and Berber Almoravids, were recent converts to Sunni Islam, while Arab Bedouin lived on the margins of the caliphal world and were not fully integrated into the cosmopolitan Islamicate culture that had developed there. As for the Franks, northern Europe had long been "officially" Christian, but it was only in the century or so previous to this era that Europe converted in a deep sense or that the faith had reached the "rustics" of the countryside, or the pagans of the north. In other words, each of these groups evinced the zeal of the recently converted, further heightened by the fact that each originated in a relatively undiversified, rural environment. They came from lands of extreme—and their worldview was shaped by the stark binaries of good versus evil, life versus death, and the faithful versus the infidels.

Yet the military energy and moral determination of these peripheral peoples proved impossible for the urbane Mediterranean world to contain. Thus, the period from roughly 1050 to 1350 can be characterized as one in which the Mediterranean was shaped from the edges by "barbarians," for whom it became an object of desire and an arena of competition. Recruited first as mercenaries, they infiltrated the imperial administrations that had sought to take advantage of their martial prowess, ulti-

FIGURE P2.1 A miniature showing Muslims and Franks at the Battle of the Field of Blood (1119), from *The History of the Voyage to and Conquest of Jerusalem* (France, 1337). © Tallandier / Bridgeman Images.

mately pushing the empires to fracture and disintegrate. In the Islamic world, the caliphate of Córdoba imploded in a generation-long civil war sparked by tensions between Berber mercenaries and indigenous Arab-identifying Muslims. The enfeebled ʿAbbasid dynasty was taken under the protection of Seljuq warlords in 1055, leaving the caliph as a mere figurehead. The Fatimid Caliphate would survive until it was dissolved by Salah al-Din in 1171, but had long been riven by factionalism between sub-Saharan African, Berber, Arab, and Armenian blocs in the army and government, and by hostile Sunni and Shiʿi factions. Christendom fared little better. The Ottonian Holy Roman Empire collapsed under the weight of incursions by the Norse and Magyars, disobedient local lords, and the extinction of its royal lineage in 1024. Byzantium spiraled into a disarray encouraged by Slavic and Armenian elements in the army and palace, before being dealt a near death blow by the Seljuqs at the Battle of Manzikert in 1071. The empire would briefly restabilize under the Komnenoi dynasty, only to be smashed in 1204 by Venetian and Frankish forces, whose Fourth Crusade, aimed ostensibly at conquering Egypt and retaking Jerusalem, concluded with the sack of Constantinople and the partition of the Christian Byzantine Empire.

These predatory factions, whether military or mercantile, did not represent national movements rooted in a particular land or language, but rather, families and their networks of client groups, aggregated through patronage and opportunism. Their territorial ambitions were open-ended and region-wide. A single kin group or cluster, such as the Frankish Angevins or Normans of the Hauteville clan, the Turkic Seljuqs or Mu'minid Almohads, or an oligarchical republic, like Venice or Genoa, might control lands scattered across the Mediterranean, extending its power by a combination of conquest, commerce, diplomacy, and marriage. Whatever larger "civilizational struggles" between Christianity, Judaism, and Islam may be observed, and the rhetoric of holy war notwithstanding, policy was driven by expedience. Christian and Muslim powers found themselves as allies against their own coreligionists as often as they fought each other. Political conflict between princes of rival faiths could be easily framed in terms of Crusade or *jihad*, but even wars between rulers of the same faith were frequently justified on religious terms when political rivals could be characterized as heretics or false believers. And yet, this fragmented, contested Mediterranean was remarkably cohesive—a legacy of the previous imperial/caliphal period. Even as the political dominance of the Muslim and Byzantine worlds declined, Islamic law and culture and imperial Roman political cultures provided frameworks for regional cohesion, and through this period of conflict, the various shores became ever more deeply embroiled politically and commercially. For the most part, newcomers sought to integrate themselves in these structures or co-opt rather than destroy them.

Rulers and religious authorities struggled to harness the tremendous forces at work in this period. The Byzantine emperors failed, and the empire never fully recovered from the partition of 1204. Although Constantinople was reestablished as the capital of a Greek Orthodox empire in 1261, most of Anatolia had been lost to Turkic warlords, Greece was dominated by Latin adventurers, and in 1346 a new Serbian Empire was established in the Balkans. Meanwhile, the remnants of the Komnenoi dynasty established a rival empire-in-exile at Trabzon, in the eastern Black Sea. The pagan Mongols, who sacked Baghdad and ended the 'Abbasid Caliphate in 1258, provoked a reordering of Muslim western Asia. In the aftermath, the Mamluk or slave regime of Egypt claimed guardianship over a caliph-in-exile, but by this time, the Almohads of Morocco had already appropriated the supreme title of Islam, a claim that would be revived in 1256 by their successors, the Hafsids of Tunis.

In the Latin West, these centuries of prosperity saw a revival of Roman law, which both kings and popes endeavored to turn to their own purposes, and the establishment of new religious orders and secular institutions. The papacy came to imagine itself as a universal monarchy, putting it at odds with the Greek Church, from which it split in the Great Schism of 1054, and with the Holy Roman emperors and other kings of Europe, who rejected papal supremacy and worked to undermine and co-opt ecclesiastical institutions. The church's struggle to impose its will on Christendom, while expanding Christianity's reach through mission and crusade, proved too great a task, and in 1309 the popes fled Rome for Avignon, becoming hostages under the "protection" of a French crown, which under the Capetian dynasty would rise from near irrelevance under Henri I (1027–1060) to being the leading power of Latin Christendom under Philip IV (1285–1314).

Early in this period, improving climate and technological advances fueled a dynamic of increased food and craft production, population growth, and social mobility. The increase of wealth created new markets for both staple and luxury goods, and helped spur European engagement with the Mediterranean and the Byzantine and Islamic worlds. Cities grew, becoming better connected and more cosmopolitan, as traders and travelers circulated and settled throughout the region in larger numbers. As a result, this was an era of tremendous growth, in which trade flourished, and in which the distant continental hinterlands of Europe, Africa, and Central Asia were drawn into the Mediterranean world. In the East, beginning in the 1070s a prosperous and sophisticated empire of Khwarazm took control of the main cities of the Silk Route, which connected China and India to the region. In sub-Saharan Africa, contact with Muslim trans-Saharan merchants led to the foundation of an Islamic empire of Mali in the 1230s. By the thirteenth century northern European kingdoms had become connected to the Mediterranean through routes up the Rhone and the Rhine.

It was not only commodities and technologies that were disseminated, but a myriad of texts, styles, and ideas that transformed thought and culture, particularly in comparatively underdeveloped Latin Christendom and sub-Saharan Africa. The dissemination of Helleno-Persian thought as adapted and refined by Islamic scholars was crucial, most importantly the adaptation of Aristote-

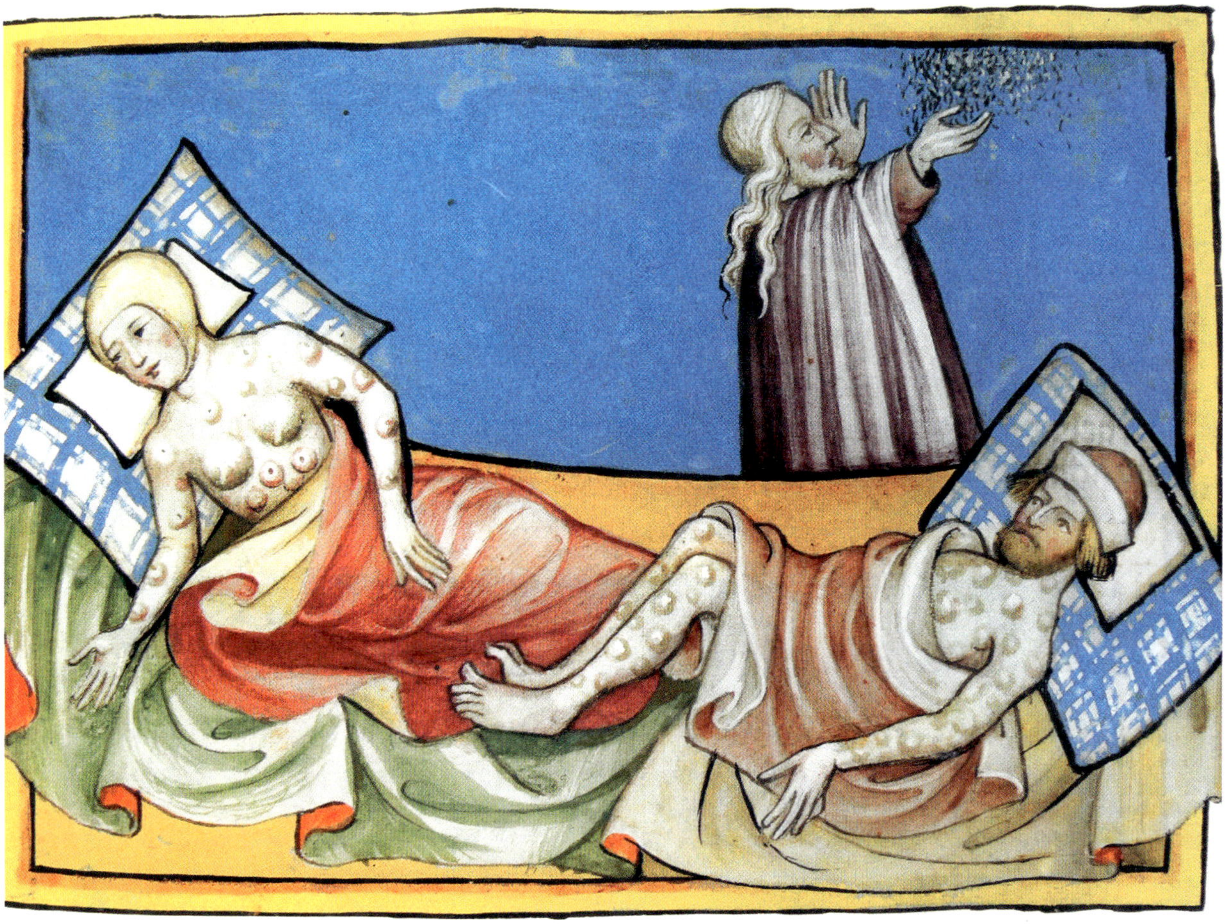

FIGURE P2.2 Two wealthy victims of the Black Death, from the Toggenburg Bible (Swizerland, 1411). Pictures from History / Bridgeman Images.

lian thought to Abrahamic monotheism, which provoked revolutions and reactions in Christian, Jewish, and Islamic learned culture. Ordinary people became consumers both of new products and of new ideas, including heterodox religious beliefs that established religious authorities would brand as heretical. Manicheism—the ancient Persian dualistic religion that once rivaled Christianity—reappeared in the Balkans as Bogomilism and in the western Mediterranean in the form of the Cathar heresy, while popular piety and mysticism found outlets in Islamic Sufism, Jewish Kabbalah, and the mendicant (or begging) orders in the Latin West. Members of rival religions optimistically engaged each other in debate, disputation, and polemic, energized by the conviction that reason could establish the undeniable truth of their own faiths, while others sought a higher esoteric truth that could not be contained by a single creed. New intellectual institutions developed—celestial observatories and teaching hospitals in the Islamic world, and universities in the Christian West. All were formally religious in orientation, but served also to reinforce the political agendas of rulers and provide an educated administrative class.

The rising tide of popular piety, together with increasing literacy, led to the development of vernacular literatures in the Latin West, which broke the monopoly of Latin on literacy, and planted the seeds of national identity in these lands. The Byzantine and Islamic spheres also saw the emergence of new or revived literary traditions among Berbers, Copts, Persians, and Armenians, in the shadow of Greek and Arabic, while among Mediterranean Jews, Hebrew evolved, heavily influenced by Arabic, and reemerged as a secular literary and scientific language.

Then, in the first half of the fourteenth century the exuberant optimism and expansion that characterized the Mediterranean of the 1100s and 1200s came to a crashing halt. The favorable climate that since the 1050s had permitted the expansion of agriculture, the growth of population, and the emergence of specialized economies began to cool. The 1320s saw crop failures, famine, and unrest. The same culture of commerce that had fueled the prosperity and integration of the larger Mediterranean world had also left it vulnerable to disruption, and the same long-distance trade that had opened up new global horizons would precipitate a crisis of apocalyptic proportions. Carried west by the Mongols in the late 1340s, within the space of a few years the Black Plague would devastate the Islamic Near East, the Mediterranean, and Christian Europe, with mortality rates in some areas reaching well over 50 percent. Economies were devastated, social bonds shattered, and religious institutions were put to the test, heralding a century-long era of civil unrest, warfare, and spiritual disillusionment that would transform both the Mediterranean and the larger world of the West.

CHAPTER FIVE

Holy and Unholy War

It was the morning of April 13, 1204, and the imperial capital was in flames. Crusader forces —Frankish knights and their Venetian allies—had breached the towering walls that had kept Constantinople safe for the previous 800 years, and were camped in front of the Blachernae palace. The emperor, a usurper named Alexios V Doukas (1204), who had ordered his predecessor, the Latin puppet Alexios IV Angelos (1203–1204), strangled two months earlier, had secretly fled the city the night before, taking with him what treasure he could carry. Despite this, desperate Greek forces had rallied, and in reaction, the Latins had set fire to the buildings between themselves and the defenders.

As the city went up in flames and native resistance crumbled, Crusader forces swept through the panicked neighborhoods, killing without quarter, raping women—even nuns—and looting or destroying anything of value they found. Neither churches, nor libraries, nor homes, nor great public works were spared—even the tombs of emperors and saints were sacked. Much was simply wrecked: ancient statues were cast down or melted for their bronze; reliquaries were smashed for their jewels and the saintly bones within them, chalices and furnishings were carried off, and the great gem-encrusted altar of the Hagia Sophia was torn apart. The Venetian forces showed somewhat better discipline, refraining from wholesale destruction, but methodically claiming the best of the imperial booty, crating it up lock and stock and shipping it home. They took most of the cash too: some 200,000 silver marks' worth, to the Franks' 100,000, in compensation for providing the fleet that made the conquest possible.

The city, only recently the glory of Christendom, was left a charred shell. It would never fully recover. The imperial title, coveted by Frankish kings since the era of Charlemagne, was taken hostage. A council of Venetian grandees and Latin magnates partitioned the already-fragmented empire, and bestowed the crown on Baldwin of

FIGURE 5.1 Queen Tamar of Georgia (d. 1213). Detail from a fresco in the Vardzia Monastery, Vardzia, Georgia, thirteenth century CE. Magdalena Paluchowska / Alamy Stock Photo.

Flanders (1204–1205), a Crusade leader. Enrico Dandolo (1192–1205), the doge, the all-powerful elected leader of the council of Venice, had turned down the honor, preferring power to prestige. He took three-eighths of the imperial territory, plus part of the capital. But little of the empire remained. The Doukas family had fled to Epirus (modern Albania) and established a separate state. Another Crusader, Boniface of Montserrat, was crowned king of Thessaloniki (1204–1207). A relative of the Angelos family, Theodore Lascaris (1205–1221), declared himself emperor in Nicaea, which would soon come to dominate the west of Anatolia. And far in the East on the southern shore of the Black Sea, a descendant of the Komnenoi dynasty that had ruled in the final period of twelfth-century glory, declared himself emperor at Trabzon. Most of Anatolia, the former Byzantine heartland, was dominated by Seljuq Turks and their Sultanate of Rum (Rome), although in the East an independent Georgian kingdom thrived under its queen, Tamar (1184–1213), and the south was under the control of the Latin-allied Armenian Kingdom of Cilicia, which would survive until 1375. The new Latin Empire itself, mostly confined to modern Greece, quickly fractured into mutually hostile lordships, which were forced to contend with each other and a revived Bulgarian Empire on their northern frontier.

MAP 5.1 The Mediterranean, ca. 1100.

Although the Crusades had been launched in 1095 with the avowed goal of defending the Eastern Churches against Seljuq oppression, in many ways, it was the sack of Constantinople in 1204, rather than the conquest of Jerusalem in 1099, that marked the natural culmination of the movement, and that epitomizes the forces that began to transform the Mediterranean beginning in the early eleventh century. It was after this conquest that the pope could at last claim uncontested dominion over the Catholic-Orthodox Church. Framed as a holy war and aimed ostensibly at the recapture of Jerusalem and the conquest of Egypt, this Fourth Crusade soon became the victim of economic forces, namely, the determination of Venice to dominate the eastern Mediterranean, countering its rival, Genoa, and taking revenge on the Greeks for the anti-Latin uprisings that had gripped Constantinople in the last decade of the 1100s. Although it was charged with rhetoric of holy war, this was a Crusade in which Islam played virtually no part, and fellow Christians were seen as infidels. As the Fourth Crusade shows, it was political and economic priorities that drove conflict in this era, while religious ideology served as a means for justifying the struggles between competing powers. However, conflict does not preclude collaboration, and it

can stimulate acculturation and innovation even among enemies. Thus, this was also a period of profound integration, as economic interests and the growth of trade forced the regional players to collaborate even in the face of their differences.

Pilgrims and Predators, ca. 1050–1150

Today we are acutely aware of the dramatic effect climate change has on everything from politics to culture. Nearly a thousand years ago climatic trends played a crucial role in the decline of the caliphal/imperial order of the eighth to tenth century, and the transformation of the Mediterranean and the larger West. These changes, however, were not uniform. Two contrary but simultaneous trends affected the eastern and southern Mediterranean and the northwest and tilted the balance of regional power toward Latin Europe.

A Climate of Change

In the lands of the East, stretching from Egypt and Byzantium across Persia, a cooling and drying trend began in the late 900s, becoming progressively more acute over the following century. The immediate effect was a series of crop failures and famines. The complex urban societies of these lands depended on a steady and abundant food supply; once this was disrupted, urban institutions and regional commercial economies began to fail, taxation systems came under pressure, and social and political unrest and religious discontent followed. By the second quarter of the eleventh century the Byzantine Empire, the Fatimid Caliphate, and the 'Abbasid Caliphate in the East were all in the grips of crisis. The breakdown of central power emboldened native Mediterranean groups previously marginalized under imperial rule to carve out their own polities, including Armenians and Georgians in Anatolia, Italian city-states, and the Christian princes of the north of the Iberian Peninsula. Within the imperial ambit political divisions and social tensions—sometimes expressed as communal violence aimed at rival ethnic or religious groups—became more common.

The weakening of urban institutions and the agricultural economy provided an opening for the nomadic pastoral peoples who lived on the periphery to expand their influence. No longer held at bay by the structures of imperial/caliphal power, and less affected by the climatic turn, these raiders infiltrated imperial territory, attacking towns and disrupting trade and agriculture, further exacerbating the crisis. On the other hand, the activities of these nomadic peoples helped stimulate continental

It was not until the Frankish expansion into the Islamic Mediterranean of the eleventh century that Latin Europe and the Islamic world began to engage with each other on a broad scale. Although the factors behind this engagement were economic, political, demographic, and religious, and relations between Christian and Muslim principalities were collaborative as well as hostile, official chroniclers—who were for the most part men of religion—had an interest in presenting both Crusade and *jihad* as civilizational struggles.

Accounts of Council of Clermont (1095)

The launch of the Crusades is traditionally attributed to a speech made by Pope Urban II on November 27, 1095, during the Council of Clermont. Here, the pope called on the nobility of Latin Europe to stop fighting each other and, instead, go to the aid of the Christians of Byzantium who were under attack by the Seljuq Turks. The council had been convened to address matters relating to the Gregorian Reform of the church, and Urban's "call to Crusade" appears as almost an afterthought—not even recorded at the time by anyone present. The accounts we have were composed with the benefit of hindsight—all date from after 1100, at which point the Frankish forces had conquered Jerusalem and established a kingdom there.

From *The Deeds of the Franks* (Anonymous, ca. 1101)

> And so Urban, Pope of the Roman See, with his archbishops, bishops, abbots, and priests, set out as quickly as possible beyond the mountains and began to deliver sermons and to preach eloquently saying: "Whoever wishes to save his soul should not hesitate humbly to take up the way of the Lord [to Jerusalem], and if he lacks sufficient money, divine mercy will give him enough." . . . And . . . little by little, through all the regions and countries of Gaul, the Franks, upon hearing such reports, forthwith caused crosses to be sewed on their right shoulders, saying that they followed with one accord the footsteps of Christ, by which they had been redeemed from the hand of hell.[1]

From *The Jerusalem History* (Robert of Rheims, ca. 1107)

> From the confines of Jerusalem and the city of Constantinople a horrible tale has gone forth and very frequently has been brought to our ears, namely that a race from the kingdom of the Persians, an accursed race . . . has invaded the lands of those Christians and has depopulated them by the sword, pillage and fire; it has led away a part of the captives into its own country, and a part it has destroyed by cruel tortures; it has either entirely destroyed the Churches of God or appropriated them for its own religion. They destroy the altars, having defiled them with uncleanliness. They circumcise the Christians and the blood they either spread upon the altars or pour into the vases of the baptismal font. When they wish to torture people by a base death . . . [a long list of gory tortures is enumerated]. . . . On whom therefore is the labor of avenging these wrongs and of recovering this territory incumbent, if not upon you? You, upon whom above other nations God has conferred remarkable glory in arms, great courage, bodily activity, and strength to humble the hairy scalp of those who resist you.[2]

The *Book of the Jihad* of 'Ali b. Tahir al-Sulami (1105)

An expert in Islamic law from Damascus, al-Sulami heard refugees' accounts of the massacres committed by the Franks at the conquest of Jerusalem (1099), and it was he alone of contemporary Muslim observers who attributed a religious or "civilizational" motive to Crusader aggression, going so far as to conflate the Byzantines and Franks as a united force. However, his call for a unified Muslim *jihad* in response went all but ignored until the Seljuq warlord 'Imad al-Din Zanki saw it is a means of galvanizing support in Syria in the 1140s.

> [On account of the Muslims' poor government and immorality] God dispersed their unity, split up their togetherness, threw enmity and hate between them and tempted their enemies to snatch their country from their grasp, thus curing their hearts of their faults. A number of the enemy pounced on the island

of Sicily, while the Muslims disputed and competed, and they conquered in the same way one city after another in al-Andalus. When the reports confirmed for them this country [Syria] suffered from the disagreement of its masters and its rulers' meddling, with its consequent disorder and disarray, they confirmed their resolution to set out for it, and Jerusalem was declared their dearest wish.

They looked out from [Syria] on separated kingdoms, disunited hearts and differing views laced with hidden resentment, and with that their desires became stronger and extended to whatever their outstretched arms could desire. They did not stop, tireless in fighting the jihad against the Muslims. The Muslims were sluggish, avoiding fighting them and reluctant to engage in combat until the enemy had conquered more than their greatest hopes had conceived of.[3]

The *Alexiad* of Anna Komnene (ca. 1148)

Anna Komnene (1083–1153), the daughter of Emperor Alexios I, also recorded her impressions of the Crusaders and their motives in her biography of her father. It was Alexios's request for help against the Seljuq invasion that is often credited as prompting Urban's "call." As a Byzantine Anna Komnene did not recognize the Crusaders as Christian champions against Islam.

Peter [the Hermit]* had in the beginning undertaken his great journey to worship at the [the Church of] Holy Sepulchre [in Jerusalem], but the others (and in particular Bohemond)† cherished their old grudge against Alexius and sought a good opportunity to avenge the glorious victory which the emperor had won at Larissa.‡ They were all of one mind and in order to fulfil their dream of taking Constantinople they adopted a common policy. I have often referred to that already: to all appearances they were on pilgrimage to Jerusalem; in reality they planned to dethrone Alexius and seize the capital.[4]

The *Chronicle* of Matthew of Edessa (1113–1140)

Matthew of Edessa (d. 1147) was a monk in the Armenian Orthodox Church. Armenian Anatolia had been dominated in turn by Byzantines, Seljuqs, and Franks, all of whom were considered agents of the devil or instruments of the wrath of God by Matthew and his coreligionists. Although he initially portrayed the Franks as divinely appointed rescuers of Armenia from the Turks, by 1117 his opinion had changed.

And so little by little [Baldwin]§ systematically toppled all of the Armenian princes; in this way, more than the Persian race, he persecuted the Armenian princes who had been left by the furious race of the Turks. He proscribed them all with great oppression, he toppled the entire principality of Goł Vasil,¶ he put to flight all of the ranks of nobility... many other handsome princes were killed in prison and by torture and in chairs; and there were many whose eyes had been put out, hands cut off and noses slit; they castrated them and, having raised them up on wood, killed [innocent children] in order to have their parents punished. And such innumerable and unspeakable deeds [were done]; [the Franks] reduced the land to ruin and destruction with unjust torments, always in order to take treasure unjustly.[5]

Discussion Questions

1. What motives are ascribed to the Crusaders and their enemies by the different authors and why?
2. What common threads run through these descriptions?
3. How does religion figure in these accounts?

Further Reading

'Ali ibn Tahir al-Sulami. *The Book of the Jihad of 'Ali ibn Tahir*

* Peter the Hermit was the popular preacher who rallied masses of common folk to march on Jerusalem in the aftermath of the Council of Clermont. In 1096 his "People's Crusade" reached Constantinople, but was wiped out by the Seljuqs after crossing over to Anatolia.

† Bohemond of Taranto, the son of Robert Guiscard, had long battled Byzantium. In 1098 he seized Antioch, reigning as prince from 1098 to 1111.

‡ In 1082 Alexios staved off the Norman conquest of northern Greece by defeating Bohemond of Taranto at Larissa with the aid of Seljuq soldiers.

§ Baldwin of Bouillon was a Burgundian Crusader who later became King Baldwin I of Jerusalem (1100–1118). Invited by T'oros of Edessa (1094–1098) to push back against his Seljuq overlords, Baldwin seized the throne, and established the County of Edessa.

¶ Goł Vasil was an Armenian lord who also served in the Byzantine court and army.

al-Sulami (d. 1106): Text, Translation, and Commentary. Trans. Niall Christie. Farnham: Ashgate, 2017.
Andrews, Tara L. *Matt'eos Urhayec'i and His Chronicle: History as Apocalypse in a Crossroads of Cultures.* Leiden: Brill, 2017.
Anna Komnene. *The Alexiad.* Trans. Edgar Robert Ashton Sewter. Harmondsworth: Penguin, 2009.
Chevedden, Paul E. "The Islamic View and the Christian View of the Crusades: A New Synthesis." *History* 93 (2008): 181–200.
Christie, Niall, and Deborah Gerish. "Parallel Preachings: Urban II and Al-Sulamī." *Al-Masaq: Islam and the Medieval Mediterranean* 15 (2003): 139–48.
MacEvitt, Christopher. "The *Chronicle* of Matthew of Edessa: Apocalypse, the First Crusade, and the Armenian Diaspora." *Dumbarton Oaks Papers* 61 (2007): 157–81.
Peters, Edward. *The First Crusade: The Chronicle of Fulcher of Chartres and Other Source Materials.* Philadelphia: University of Pennsylvania Press, 1998.

Notes

1. August C. Krey, *The First Crusade: The Accounts of Eye-Witnesses and Participants* (Gloucester: Smith, 1958), 28–30.
2. Dana Carleton Munro, *Urban and the Crusaders* (New York: AMS Press, 1971), 5–8.
3. al-Sulami, 206–7.
4. Anna Komnene, 319.
5. Andrews, 131–32.

trade into sub-Saharan Africa, Central Asia, South Asia, and Southeast Asia, where Islamic religion and institutions spread through the medium of merchants and native converts, thereby integrating these areas into Mediterranean trade and cultural systems.

Northern and western Europe, however, experienced the "Medieval Optimum": a warmer, wetter climate trend that increased agricultural productivity by lengthening the growing season and making previously unproductive land (such as higher altitude areas) arable. Innovations in technology, including the diffusion of the horse collar (from China), which enabled horses to be used as draught animals, the heavy plow, which could turn rich soil, improvements in water and windmills, advances in land reclamation, and the introduction of new crops, particularly nutrient-rich legumes, all increased food output. The net effect was a dramatic rise in population and productivity. The sparsely populated European interior was colonized, thanks in part to the emergence of two new centralized monastic orders in Burgundy: the order of Cluny (910) and the Cistercians (1098). Cistercian houses in particular became nodes of economic stimulus both in the interior and along the frontiers as they cleared forests and integrated unruly borderlands into the Latin Christian world.

Increased efficiency prompted a move away from subsistence farming, facilitated the emergence of a craft sector, and enabled peasants to move off the farm and into towns. The growth of towns helped spur the development of commerce by providing both markets and centers of production and distribution. Taxes could be paid increasingly in cash instead of kind. Wealth became portable, allowing the nobility to move to towns and become rentiers and consumers. In the twelfth century annual trade fairs appeared, notably in the Champagne region. These linked northern Europe to the Mediterranean, with raw materials moving south, and finished goods and exotica, some originating in central Africa and the East, sent north. Commerce, relatively underdeveloped in Latin Europe, was stimulated by the lending activities of Jews, who were not constrained by religious laws against offering credit at interest to Christians; by the activities of Italian merchants, who served as intermediaries with the Byzantine and Islamic worlds; and by the discovery of new deposits of silver in central Europe after 1200.

This emerging prosperity was a springboard for political and religious developments. The kings of Latin Europe turned to the precedents of Roman law as they sought to impose their will on a landed nobility that was determined to resist the rise of monarchical power. As Christianity finally reached the rural masses and as townsfolk became more sophisticated and demanding, the papacy and clergy were forced to develop an institutional apparatus through which the church could govern the religious lives of the faithful effectively. They built on the Peace of God movement that had been established as early as

989 to reduce the violence endemic to Europe, gradually systematized canon law, and attempted to address the moral failings of the clergy, who were frequently corrupt and lacked vocation. The Gregorian Reform, named after Gregory VII (1073–1085), and spearheaded by the rigidly corporate order of Cluny, brought the popes into open conflict with the kings and Holy Roman emperors. The resulting power struggle, known as the Investiture Controversy—because it related to who (king or pope) held the authority to appoint bishops—drove the papacy to develop an explicitly imperial agenda, and contributed to the creation in the 1100s of a new form of military monasticism.

The military orders, the first among which were the Hospitallers (1099) and Templars (1119), were founded by knights to protect pilgrims to the Holy Land. These warrior-monks, sworn to serve the papacy, quickly grew into independent military forces crucial to the defense of the Holy Land. Soon, more such orders were founded across the Latin West, including the order of Calatrava in Castile and the Teutonic Knights in the Germanic northeast, with the aim of fighting for Christendom on the Islamic and pagan frontiers. Patronized by kings, they became major seigniorial powers, important creditors and economic players—thanks in part to their capacity to guard and transport cash. Soon, they escaped the control of the papacy and the kings, and followed independent agendas, competing against each other to the ultimate detriment of the Crusader kingdom they had been founded to protect.

Latin Europe's growth also produced social and religious tensions. The rise in population engendered large masses of landless poor, who—energized by their deepening faith—flirted with apocalyptic and revolutionary religious ideologies. Rising Christian consciousness and prosperity fed a growing preoccupation with salvation, which led the faithful to embark on pilgrimages, whether to the Holy Land, Rome, or other sites of saintly veneration, either as a means of performing the penance required by Catholic doctrine, or simply out of wanderlust. Anxieties regarding Christ's foretold return, exacerbated by the passing of the millennium (the thousand years since his death), and compounded by a growing sense of worldly injustice, crystallized as a conviction among many that the world was on the verge of an apocalyptic transformation. Finally, the growing noble class, whose capacity to wage war was constrained by the church's Truce of God (1027), yet under pressure to acquire land, began to look hungrily at the lands of Byzantium, Islam, and the pagans, which were not protected by the papacy. These various trends coalesced in 1095, when Cluniac pope Urban II (1088–1099) promised the knights of the Latin West salvation should they embark on the rescue of their "brethren who live in the East," who had been attacked by the Seljuq Turks. Almost immediately the declared goal of the venture became the liberation of Jerusalem from Islam. The era of the Crusades was launched.

However, Christian-Muslim conflict was only one element of the Crusades, not unlike the *jihad* waged by various Muslim groups in the same era. Crusading was to an important extent the religious expression of political and economic agendas that were rooted in the larger processes that were transforming both the Mediterranean and the entire West. The Franks, like the Turks and Berbers, were part of the latest wave of "barbarians" drawn into the power vacuum of the Mediterranean from its less developed fringes.

The Collapse of the Islamic West

In the year 1000 the Umayyad Caliphate of Córdoba was to all appearances at the height of its power: a highly populated, extremely wealthy, and urbanized commercial imperium that ruled directly or indirectly over all of the Iberian Peninsula and most of northwest Africa. However, serious structural weaknesses underlay its façade of strength. The dynasty had been usurped by the *hajib* (court chamberlain) Muhammad ibn Abi Amir (or "al-Mansur") whose dictatorial tendencies had alarmed the established elite and the religious authorities. Al-Mansur, like the caliphs before him, had imported large numbers of Berber mercenaries to serve in his army and government, exacerbating ethnic and political tensions in the caliphate. After his death in 1002 it took only seven years until the caliphate imploded in a civil war that saw widespread Berber-Andalusi violence, and left al-Andalus and the Maghrib splintered into more than a score of petty, regional kingdoms, ruled over by Berber warlords, local potentates, and palace slaves. When the dust of the two-decade civil war settled, the Umayyad line was effectively extinct, and al-Andalus was dominated by eight or so *taifa* ("splinter") kingdoms, each of which struggled against the others for supremacy on the peninsula.

The Christian principalities on the northern periphery of the caliphate were also locked in bitter rivalry, but took advantage of the *taifa* kingdoms' weakness to plunder them or lock the Muslim princes into costly tributary relationships. This was the beginning of the era later cast as the Reconquista, or "Spanish Reconquest." Religious and political motives are nearly impossible to disentangle, but it was clear that the Christian kingdoms were on the ascent, and thus their princes invoked the spirit of holy war to reinforce their own legitimacy and encourage solidarity among their subjects. It was then that Saint James, whose purported resting place in northwestern Spain was becoming Latin Europe's most popular pilgrimage site, was transformed into Santiago Matamoros—"Saint James the Muslim-Killer"—the patron saint of the Christian "Empire" of León. Its rulers claimed descent from the pre-Islamic Visigothic kings of Hispania, and therefore sovereignty over all of Christian and Muslim Iberia.

In fact, political entanglement led to economic interdependency, wherein Christian kings provided soldiers in return for tribute from the *taifa* kingdoms, and much of that tribute returned to the *taifa* kingdoms in the form of purchases of crafts and commodities. Thus, when Christian powers began to conquer Muslim territory in the late eleventh century, the goal was not to expel Muslims, but merely to displace their ruling class. Hence Alfonso VI of Castile and León (1065–1107) would present himself in Latin as "Emperor of All the Spains," or "of the Three Religions" (Christianity, Judaism, and Islam), or in Arabic as "Emperor of the Two Religious Communities." Similarly, individuals who were later held up as religious warriors and heroes of the Reconquista, most notably the outlaw nobleman Rodrigo Díaz de Vivar, "El Cid," were, in fact, adventurers with little regard for goals loftier than the acquisition of territory and plunder.

Despite their vulnerabilities, the *taifa* kingdoms remained extremely prosperous, and their rulers aspired to both material wealth and cultural sophistication as an expression of their legitimacy. Poets, scientists, and scholars found them generous and eager patrons, which led to a period of incredible cultural output and innovation in virtually every scholarly field. Jews participated actively in this flurry of creativity; they wrote mostly in Arabic, but increasingly in Hebrew. This so-called golden age was possible because Jews were highly integrated in the power and economic structures of many *taifa* kingdoms. These kings had become effectively secular rulers, who left religious matters in the hands of the *'ulama'*, and therefore had little hesitation to employ Jews and Christians in the highest positions in their administrations.

The most successful Jewish courtier was Isma'il ibn Naghrilla (d. 1056), the all-powerful prime minister of the *taifa* kingdom of Granada, ruled over by the Zirids, a clan of Sanhaja Berbers from Ifriqiya, and populated by many Jews. A polymath widely admired for his skill in Arabic, he served as tax collector and (by his account) general of the *taifa* kingdom. Completely integrated into the Islamicate aristocratic culture of al-Andalus, he composed voluminous poetry, both sacred and profane, in Arabic and Hebrew, ran a renowned academy of Jewish thought and letters, fought on behalf of Rabbanite Jews against the Karaites, and was hailed as *ha-Nagid* (prince) of the Jews of al-Andalus. When his son and successor, Yusuf, was killed in a popular uprising in 1066 along with other members of the Granadan Jewish community, this was a symptom both of Muslim-Jewish religious tensions and of integration. Yusuf had been plotting to overthrow the ruling dynasty and take control of the kingdom himself. Although Yusuf had been the subject of anti-Jewish rhetoric, his death and the violent outrage that accompanied it were predictable consequences of contemporary politics. By way of analogy, when the Norman chancellor of Sicily, Maio de Bari, was deposed in 1160, a furious mob attacked his family and the palace officials that supported him, torturing them to reveal where Maio had hidden his treasure. SEE SOURCEBOOK 5:1.

In North Africa it was not Christian princes who took control of the former Umayyad territories, but the al-Murabitun (Almoravids)—fierce desert warriors, likely named for the veils they wore to protect their faces and as a sign of their community. These pagan tribesmen had been drawn into the caliphal orbit by raiding and protecting the caravans that snaked from Morocco down through the western Sahara toward the gold fields of Ghana. Their conversion to Islam in the 900s provided them with a moral platform for the conquest of northwest Africa beginning in the 1040s, while their rigorous Sunni orientation encouraged the *'ulama'* to collaborate and provide them with an institutional framework. Notwithstanding their Sunnism, they were proudly Berber; it would be generations before members of the dynasty spoke Arabic alongside their native Tamazight.

The dramatic rise of these self-proclaimed holy warriors attracted the attention of the *'ulama'* of al-Andalus, many of whom were members of the commercial class. These were increasingly alarmed by the *taifa* kings' decadent free-spending ways, particularly their submissive relationship to the Christian princes whose soldiers they used to attack each other. In order to sustain their opulent courts and pay the heavy *parias,* a tribute or "protection money" the Christians demanded, the *taifa* kings levied ever-heavier and illegal taxes on their subjects. Exhausted by decades of turmoil, and frustrated by their own lack of influence, the *'ulama'* lobbied the Almoravids to intervene, and were soon joined by the *taifa* kings themselves, who feared their own elimination after Alfonso VI's conquest of Muslim Toledo in 1085.

The Almoravids crossed over to al-Andalus in 1086 and dealt a stunning defeat to Alfonso VI, and four years later—armed with *fatwa*s from leading authorities in the East—returned to depose the *taifa* kings and take al-Andalus. But their empire, with its capitals at Marrakesh and Seville, would be short-lived. The Andalusi people quickly cooled on their ostensible saviors. Ultimately, the Almoravids could not turn the military tide against the Christians. They governed as a heavy-handed ruling caste, reviving popular anti-Berber sentiment, and their rigorous, legalistic Islam alienated both cosmopolitan Andalusis, and common folk, who were drawn increasingly to mysticism. The Almoravids would be brought down by another Berber religious-revolutionary movement: the Almohads (al-Muwahhidun, or "Monotheists"), who conquered Marrakesh in 1147 and landed in al-Andalus two years later, just as Latin forces were seizing several key cities. The southern Almoravids, who had colonized West Africa, and spread Islam there, collapsed a few decades later.

The Contest for the Central Mediterranean

Change in the central Mediterranean was heralded by the arrival of the five sons of a minor Norman lord, Tancred d'Hauteville, in Italy in the 1030s. The peninsula was divided among petty principalities and urban republics jostling against each other and a papacy under control of a corrupt local family, the Theophylacti. The Ottonian collapse in 1024 had left northern Italy in the hands of local lords, while the central part was under control of the popes and native Lombard princes. Much of the east and south was held by Byzantium, together with the Dalmatian coast of the Adriatic, while Sicily was under the shaky grip of the Kalbids, an independent Arab dynasty. Along the Italian coast were a number of independent maritime urban republics—Amalfi, Genoa, Pisa, and Venice—that were gaining prosperity through trade with the Islamic world and Byzantium and evolving into important naval powers.

The d'Hautevilles, led by the brothers Robert Guiscard ("the Clever") and Roger Borsa ("the Purse"), distinguished themselves as warriors. Initially they served rival Lombard lords and participated in Byzantium's failed reconquest of Sicily, but quickly turned against their masters. By 1071 Robert had established a duchy of Apulia and Calabria that ruled most of southern Italy. Pushing the Byzantines out, he followed up by invading the Balkans with the ultimate goal of seizing the empire. His successes threatened both Byzantium and Venice, leading the empire and fledgling maritime power to join forces. Meanwhile Norman mercenaries had joined Armenian insurgents in Anatolia; after Robert's death in 1085, his son Bohemond enlisted with the Frankish Crusaders, and ultimately seized Antioch, establishing an independent princedom.

Invited first as allies of rival Muslim warlords, Robert and Roger determined to conquer Sicily. After taking Palermo in 1072, Robert left the conquest of the island to his brother. Roger took the title count (1071–1101) and over the course of twenty years managed to bring the island under his power, fending off relief forces sent from Ifriqiya. His son, Roger II (1105–1154), shook off the regency of his mother, Adelaide del Vasto (regent 1101–1112), at age sixteen, took over the family possessions in southern Italy, waged war against Byzantium, the papacy, and the

Lombard lords, and was crowned king of Sicily in 1130 against the will of Pope Innocent II (1130–1143). He presided over a diverse kingdom, inhabited mostly by Arabic-speaking Muslims, and Greek-speaking Orthodox, with a Latin military and clerical elite, and a small community of European settlers.

The king and his successors were very much enamored of Muslim culture and became active patrons of Islamic art and Arabic literature, constructing glittering palaces, churches, and gardens in a distinctive hybrid Latinate-Byzantine-Islamicate style. They spoke Arabic, staffed their palace with Muslim domestics, and entrusted the administration to "the palace Saracens"—a clique of eunuch former slaves, many of central African origin, who administered the kingdom in Arabic, managed the treasury, and commanded the fleets, all the while not so secretly continuing to practice Islam. Palermo was immensely wealthy, generating as much income as the entire contemporary Norman conquest, the kingdom of England (taken in 1066 by the Norman duke William the Conqueror). This prosperity depended on Sicily's commercial relationships with the Islamic Mediterranean, notably Zirid Ifriqiya and Fatimid Egypt. Diplomatic relations among the three were extremely close, facilitated by Armenian families who had settled across the eastern Mediterranean and by networks of palace slaves. SEE SOURCEBOOK 5:2.

The Zirids, Sanhaja Berbers who had served as Fatimid governors in Ifriqiya, had broken away in the early eleventh century. In response, the Fatimids had encouraged the Banu Hilal, a Bedouin Arab clan that had settled in Egypt, to attack. These are described as wreaking havoc on agriculture and sedentary society and crippling the Zirid economy, although their arrival was likely as much a consequence of environmental changes that were undermining the region. By the 1100s Ifriqiya had gone from being a supplier of food to a consumer, and it was Norman Sicily that benefited—taking in African gold, slaves, and exotica for Sicilian grain. The allure of this trade encouraged the Normans to attack and conquer the central Mediterranean islands, including Malta, and eventually the coast of Ifriqiya, where they defeated the Zirids, and tenuously claimed—against great native resistance—the title Malik Ifriqiya (King of Africa).

Roger II died in 1154, and within a decade the central Mediterranean was in flux. As the Fatimid Caliphate tilted into civil war, the Normans turned against it, attacking its ports, Alexandria and Damietta. Meanwhile, Sicilian naval power was eclipsed by the rising might of the Italian republics, while a robust Byzantium under the Komnenoi blocked Norman ambitions in the Adriatic and Aegean. Ifriqiya was lost in 1160, conquered by the Almohads—the same Berber insurgents who had brought down the Almoravids.

Violent palace factionalism plagued the reign of Roger's son, William I (1154–1166), and the regency of his dowager, Marguerite of Navarre (1166–1171). Latin clergy and Frankish elements at court rose up against the palace Saracens, sparking retaliation against the the latter and sectarian violence. Marguerite of Navarre's son, William II (1153–1189), who came of age in 1171, struck back against the rebel nobility and Byzantium, sacking Thessaloniki. His Christian and Muslim forces massacred thousands, but were turned back before reaching Constantinople. When William II died childless in 1189, and his illegitimate cousin, Tancred (1189–1194), claimed the throne, the fate of the dynasty and its Muslim allies was sealed. By the mid-twelfth century a resurgent Latinate empire, now referred to as the "Holy" and ruled by the German king Frederick Barbarossa (1152–1190), attempted to reassert control over Italy. The urban republics and the papacy resisted the ambitions of Frederick's Hohenstaufen dynasty, but his heir, Henry VI (1191–1197), would overcome them and in 1194 go on to take Sicily, which he claimed through his wife, Constance, a daughter of Roger II. His son Frederick II (1198–1250)—who would become emperor in 1220—would make it his base. Frederick was a notorious Arabophile who depended on his Muslim subjects as soldiers; in 1224 in response to their restlessness, he transported Sicily's Muslims, now numbering only a few thousand, to a colony at Lucera, a town in central Italy,

By this time, Genoa and Venice had become the dominant central Mediterranean powers, with Amalfi and Pisa in decline (Amalfi having been crippled by Pisa, and Pisa at war with Genoa). Both had become rich through commerce, and by serving as private navies and logistical providers for the Crusaders and Byzantium. In the meantime, through a mixture of piracy, gunboat diplomacy, and negotiation, they had secured a scattering of colonial possessions and footholds in the major African and Levantine ports, thus coming to dominate the trade in African and Asian goods that made their way to northern European markets, and to control important quantities of capital.

Crisis in the Eastern Mediterranean

Between the death of Basil II in 1025 and the coup of the general Alexios Komnenos (1081–1118), the Byzantine throne had been occupied by thirteen Macedonian princes, princesses and in-laws, and usurping generals. Instability intensified the political crisis of the empire. Georgians and Armenians in Anatolia shook off Byzantine rule, generals revolted, and from the 1050s the empire faced incursions from the Normans in the West, the Seljuqs from the East, and pagan Pechenegs and Cumans coming into the Balkans from the Volga region, where they had crippled Byzantium's allies, the Kievan Rus.

Of these groups, it was the Seljuqs—a clan of nomadic herders belonging to the Ghuzz peoples originating in the Khazak steppes north of the Caspian Sea—who had the most impact. They had been exposed to Sunni Islam as mercenaries in the Persianate empire of the Ghaznavids, which dominated the fertile lands of northern Iran, Afghanistan, and the Oxus valley. Like the Almoravids, the Seljuqs combined an intuitive military vocation with the zeal of new converts. They were sought after as soldiers by Muslim rulers, and also fought as *ghazis* (holy warriors) against pagan nomads in Central Asia. By 1050 they had supplanted their Ghaznavid masters, and moved into the heartland of the caliphate—now in decline and dominated by the Buyids, a dynasty of Shi'i warriors and *wazirs*. Here, the Seljuqs determined to restore the rightful Sunni order by bringing the caliphate under their protection.

Recruited by the caliph al-Qa'im (1031–1075) to counterbalance the Buyids, the Seljuq leader, Tugril Beg, took Baghdad in 1055, establishing the Great Seljuq Sultanate under the umbrella of 'Abbasid legitimacy. Tugril's successor, Alp Arslan ("Heroic Lion"; 1063–1072), consolidated Seljuq rule by enlisting Persian administrators to manage the new regime. Chief among these was Nizam al-Mulk (Pillar of the Kingdom), whose administrative and educational reforms in the service of Seljuq legitimacy were laid out in his seminal Persian-language political treatise *Siyasatnama* (The Book of Government). Although the Seljuqs' self-declared aim was the restoration of Sunnism, and consequently, the overthrow of the Shi'i Fatimids, after taking Persia they found themselves facing vulnerable Byzantium. An incursion into the Anatolian central plateau led to the destruction of the imperial army and the capture of emperor Romanos IV Diogenes (1068–1071) at the Battle of Manzikert in 1071. In the aftermath, Seljuq forces swept westward, nearly reaching Constantinople, encouraging subject peoples to throw off Byzantine dominion, and—according to tradition—prompting the new emperor, Alexios Komnenos, to dispatch a request to certain noblemen in the Latin West for military aid. It was this letter that was said to have moved Urban II to enjoin the Latin knights to go east to rescue their Christian brethren, thus launching the Crusades.

Would that it were so simple. At this point, fifty years after the Great Schism, the Byzantine and Roman Churches hardly saw each other as brothers. Nevertheless, Urban II's "call to crusade" at the Council of Clermont in 1095 reverberated across the Latin West, both for religious reasons and because it provided an ideological framework for a Latin expansion into the Byzantine and Islamic Mediterranean that was already underway as a consequence of the demographic, political, and economic changes that were prompted by the Medieval Optimum.

The first to take up Urban's call were the masses of poor landless peasants, worked up by messianic popular preachers. An unruly mob from northern France made its way via Germany to the Holy Land with apocalyptic fervor, attacking Jewish communities and looting Christian lands as they went. The establishment was horrified, and in Hungary King Kálmán unleashed his troops (which included Muslims) on this "People's Crusade." This venture came to an unhappy end, when after crossing over to Asia from Constantinople in fall 1096, they were slaughtered by Seljuq forces. Next came the knights of the "First Crusade"—mutually hostile contingents originating in Burgundy, the north of France, and Languedoc, together with Normans from Italy—all of whom assembled at the gates of Constantinople in late 1096 and early 1097. The aim of the Crusade had now

FIGURE 5.2 The Accession of Malik-Shah, from Rashid al-Din's *Compendium of Chronicles*, Persia, 1314 CE. Photo: Jami al-Tawarikh provided by Wikimedia Commons under the Creative Commons CC0 license.

crystallized as the conquest of Jerusalem, the Holy City, and its participants saw themselves as "armed pilgrims" undertaking a journey to the Holy Land to fight for Christendom in penance for their sins, and in the service of the Lord. The word "Crusade" would not be coined until the thirteenth century.

But in the twenty-five years since Manzikert, the situation in Anatolia had changed. The succession of Alp Arslan's son, Malik Shah ("King King" in Arabic and Persian; 1072–1092), was contested by family members, prompting his assassination and that of Nizam al-Mulk in 1092, and splintering the Seljuq unity. The Sultanate of Rum, based at Konya and in control of much of western Anatolia, established a cool peace with Constantinople, and sparred with the various Armenian and Turkic principalities of the region, while Syria and Palestine coalesced as a hot frontier between the Fatimids and the Seljuqs, with independent Turkic lords holding Aleppo, Mosul, Antioch, and Damascus, and the Fatimids ruling Jerusalem and the territories to the southwest.

For Alexios Komnenos, the arrival of the Franks in 1098 posed a dilemma; many were openly hostile to him—particularly the Normans—and he was anxious that any land they conquered be returned to the empire. Consequently, to their great resentment, he made the Crusaders swear oaths of loyalty as a precondition for allowing them to cross to Asia, and secretly contacted the Fatimids to advise them of the Franks' approach. By the time the Crusader forces reached Antioch in 1097, its various factions were effectively at war. A contingent of Burgundians under Baldwin of Bouillon split off, responding to a call from an Armenian, T'oros of Edessa, for aid. In short order, T'oros was deposed and murdered and Baldwin took his throne, establishing the County of Edessa. Antioch itself was conquered in June 1098 after a harrowing nine-month siege, which further exacerbated tensions among the Crusaders, who suffered fatigue, disease, and starvation, and nearly abandoned the attack. Here the importance of the maritime republics was proved. Genoa kept food and other key supplies arriving at the siege camp, saving the campaign but driving the Crusaders ever deeper into debt with the exorbitant prices charged.

To the anger of the Crusade leadership, Robert Guiscard's son, Bohemond of Taranto, claimed the city as his own, establishing an independent Principality of Antioch in defiance of Byzantium in 1098. As the rest of the Frankish forces continued south toward Jerusalem, they cut a path through central Syria and the Lebanese coast, looting and killing, and even committing acts of cannibalism. Local Arab and Seljuq warlords and Fatimid governors did their best to weather the onslaught, either resisting or offering support, but did not form a unified Islamic coalition against the Crusaders. To the locals, the Franks did not appear as an existential threat to Islam, rather as just another contingent of invaders, who could be expected to integrate into the patchwork politics of the region.

The siege of Jerusalem would change this. The city had become a neglected backwater, ravaged by Bedouin raiders and fought over by Seljuqs and Fatimids for many decades. It maintained an important Jewish community and was the seat of the (Fatimid-appointed) patriarch of Jerusalem, but it held only symbolic significance for Muslims, and Byzantium showed little interest. Thus, the Franks' single-minded obsession surprised the defenders. Crusader forces encircled the city on June 7, 1099, and when the walls were breached in mid-July, the Fatimid garrison negotiated its own evacuation, leaving the Muslim inhabitants to their fate. For the Franks, the Holy City was to be cleansed of Muslim impurity by the methodical, deliberate, and joyous slaughter of its inhabitants, including women and children. Because the Franks tended to perceive the Eastern Christians here also as infidels they too bore the brunt of violence and discrimination. Many of the Jewish community evaded death only by ransoming themselves, having sold their Torah scrolls to their coreligionists in Ashkelon.

In the aftermath, the Franks conquered what remained of Palestine, as well as the Lebanese and Syrian coasts. Two more Latin principalities were established: a Burgundian-dominated Kingdom of Jerusalem, and a Provençal-ruled County of Tripoli. Like their Seljuq rivals, however, the Crusaders did not comprise a united front, and for all their initial zealotry, the rival factions soon found themselves at war with each other and Byzantium, all the while courting Muslim neighbors as allies. SEE SOURCEBOOK 5:3.

From the beginning, the Crusader principalities were vulnerable. They had a small population base and depended on settlers and soldiers coming from the West to fight on their behalf. Genoa and Venice, whose naval and mercantile support was key to Latin survival here, exploited their own importance by extracting important trading privileges that undermined the power of Latin rulers. In any event, the Italians' goal was the establishment of profitable trade relations with Byzantium and the Muslim powers farther east, and not necessarily the maintenance of strong Frankish principalities or the waging of potentially disruptive religious wars.

The Kingdom of Jerusalem was established as an ethnic state in which only Franks (as opposed to all Christians) enjoyed full rights, and in which Latins displaced Greek and Syriac Orthodox clergy. In 1100 Baldwin of Bouillon, Count of Edessa, became the first king, and having died childless was succeeded by his cousin, Baldwin II of Bourq (1118–1131). Baldwin II had three daughters, Melisende (1131–1153), who would reign as co-ruler and, later, queen-regent, and Alice and Hodierna, whom he married to the prince of Antioch and the count of Tripoli, thus laying the groundwork for the unification of the Latin principalities. However, the succession of these strong-willed and capable women further destabilized the Latin East. They refused to bend to the will of their husbands and children, fomenting factionalism, thus providing an opportunity for the rebellious nobility of the kingdom to weaken the monarchy. In the meantime, the military disadvantage the Franks suffered because of their small numbers was offset by the establishment of the Templars and Hospitallers, military-monastic orders that answered to the papacy and became important as defenders against outside attack, and as a counterweight to the Latin nobility.

Once established, the Crusader states and their Muslim neighbors achieved a remarkable degree of accommodation. It would be wrong to see the Kingdom of Jerusalem as merely some beleaguered and isolated Frankish outpost surrounded by a throng of hostile Muslim powers. Trade and military treaties were established, notably between Jerusalem and Damascus, and Antioch and Aleppo, and some areas were co-ruled by Muslim and Christian princes. In Byzantium, Alexios was succeeded by his son John II (1118–1143), and John by his son, Manuel (1143–1180). Under their rule, the empire recovered, and once more became the dominant regional power, enforcing a fragile peace and maintaining both Frankish and Seljuq compliance through the threat of military retaliation. Popular Muslim sentiment, however, was building against the Franks, stoked by popular preachers. 'Imad al-Din Zanki, a Ghuzz warlord who held Aleppo and Mosul as *atabeg* (father-prince; 1127–1146) for the Seljuqs, discerned that Syrian unity was a necessary precursor to victory over the Franks, and that *jihad* could be used to galvanize popular support. He failed in his attempt to take Muslim Damascus, but did conquer Crusader Edessa in December 1144—the first territorial victory over the Crusaders. Although Zanki would be murdered two years later, Nur al-Din, his son and successor as *atabeg* of Aleppo (1146–1174), would follow his strategy, and lay the groundwork for the defeat of the Franks.

The Contested Mediterranean, ca. 1150–1250

Although the Crusade's formal goal—the conquest of Jerusalem—had been achieved in 1099, the movement showed no signs of slowing, and through the mid-twelfth century Latin military and mercantile powers continued to aggressively expand into Byzantine and Islamic spheres, not only in the East, but across North Africa and the Iberian Peninsula, as well as into the pagan lands of northeastern Europe. The economic, demographic, and political forces behind this movement could not be contained, driving Latin colonial expansion, irrespective of whatever ideology may have been used to justify it.

The End of the Fatimids and the Kingdom of Jerusalem

When the Franks arrived in Palestine in 1099, the Fatimid regime was suffering from a similar fate that had weakened both the Umayyads and the 'Abbasids. The caliphs had been eclipsed by a shadow dynasty of functionaries—in this case, that of Badr al-Jamali (d. 1094), a freed slave of Armenian origin, who had become the leading general, and his son, al-Afdal Shahanshah ("King of Kings"—the title once taken by pre-Islamic Persian emperors), who succeeded him as *wazir* (1094–1121). Badr had taken control of the caliphate in 1073, bringing with him large numbers of Armenian troops and refugees, both Christian and Muslim. He had reestablished stability, but the army remained highly factionalized by ethnic cleavages, and tensions would flare into a series of civil wars and uprisings after al-Afdal's death. Thereafter, the caliphs were little more than props. The resulting instability encouraged foreign powers, including the Normans, Italian traders, and Frankish Jerusalem to attack Egypt. In 1163 after the assassination of another Armenian *wazir,* Ruzzik ibn Tala'i, war broke out between two rivals, Dirgham and Shawar, who appealed for aid, to the Franks and the Seljuqs respectively, ultimately precipitating a brief Frankish occupation of Cairo, and subsequently, the overthrow of the caliphate in 1171.

The wheels had been set in motion twenty-five years earlier by Zanki's conquest of Edessa, which provoked an immediate and enthusiastic reaction from the Frankish West in the form of the Second Crusade. It was preached aggressively by the Cistercian abbot Bernard of Clairvaux (d. 1153)—an eloquent supporter of the military orders, and an advocate of expanding the Crusade against anyone, whether Muslim, pagan, or Christian, who did not recognize papal authority. Although joined by luminaries, including Conrad III of Germany (emperor, 1138–1152), Louis VII of France (1137–1180), and his queen, Duchess Eleanor of Aquitaine (1137–1204), the campaign was a disaster. The Crusaders refused to attack Nur al-Din, and instead chose the more glamorous but strategically senseless target of Damascus, Jerusalem's ally. There, the Frankish forces were routed, and this betrayal drove the populace to seek Nur al-Din's protection in 1154. With Syria thus united, Nur al-Din promoted a *jihad* ideology aimed at expulsion of the Franks and the reconquest of Jerusalem, the sanctity of which he actively promoted. It was only the threat of Byzantine reprisal that held him at bay.

Meanwhile, the Frankish kingdom tilted into conflict, fueled by a series of problematic royal successions, the scheming of native Latin magnates, disruptive Crusaders from the West, and the machinations of the Templars and Hospitallers, who not only saw each other as rivals, but cultivated local Muslim powers, notably the Shi'i Assassins, as allies. The Fatimid civil war, together

Surrounded by salty marshes within the no-man's land between the Catholic Holy Roman Empire and the Orthodox Byzantine Empire and with access to the Byzantine and Islamic Mediterranean, in the 1100s Venice emerged as a commercial, military, and imperial republic. It was ruled over by a quasi-elected/quasi-hereditary duke (*doge*), and St. Mark's Square (*Piazza San Marco*)—dominated by St. Mark's Basilica and the Palace of the Doge—was the symbolic and administrative center of the city and of the maritime empire it developed.

St. Mark's Square

There has a been a palace and church in St. Mark's Square since the early ninth century, although the present fortified palace was begun in 1340. The basilica was founded to house the remains of the apostle Mark (legendarily smuggled by Venetian merchants out of Alexandria in a barrel of pork and cabbage to foil Muslim customs inspectors) in the 800s, but today's cruciform Byzantine-Italian style church topped by five domes was begun in the late eleventh century. The vast interior (241 × 170 feet) is lavishly decorated with Byzantine-style gold ground mosaics. The church was not a cathedral, and there was no bishop of Venice; rather, the basilica was the private chapel of the doge, and the city's leading clergyman was the *primicerio*, appointed by him. The square also featured the *campanile* (a renovated, ancient bell tower), administrative offices, and warehouses. Sometime in the twelfth or thirteenth century two towering granite columns were added in the square's lagoon-side annex, one topped with a lion symbolizing Saint Mark the Evangelist, and the other with a figure of Saint Theodore standing on the back of a vanquished sea dragon.

Spolia

The incorporation of *spolia*—building materials and decorative elements plundered in conquest or taken from ancient ruins—is prominent in St. Mark's Square. Such recycling (a widespread and ancient tradition in the Mediterranean region) had both a practical and a symbolic dimension. Constantinople had been a storehouse of ancient art and Christian religious treasures since its founding as the imperial capital in 325. Following the imperial capital's conquest in 1204, Venetian authorities

FIGURE 5.3 Gentile Bellini, *Processione in Piazza San Marco*, 1496. Photo: Didier Descouens, provided by Wikimedia Commons under the Creative Commons Attribution-Share Alike 4.0 International license.

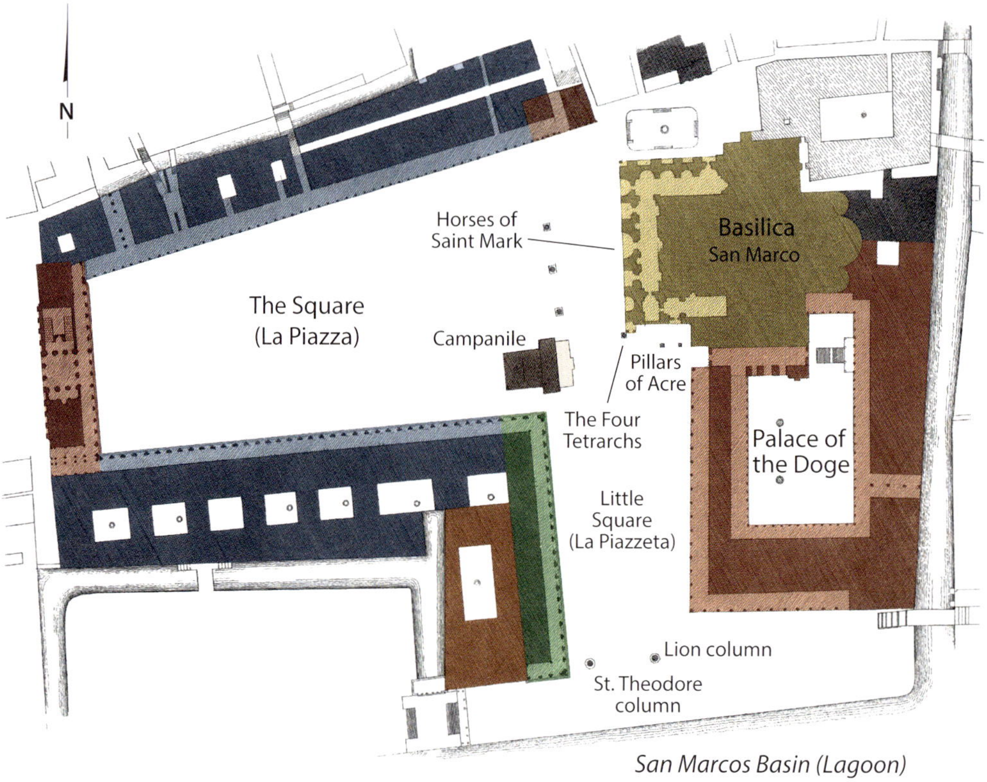

FIGURE 5.4 Plan of St. Mark's Square. Image: Wikimedia Commons under the Creative Commons Attribution-Share Alike 4.0 International license, provided and previously altered by Venicescapes, further altered for this use.

together with the Frankish Crusaders sacked the city, dismantling churches, palaces, and civic buildings, and crating off large quantities of cash, precious metal and gems, religious and secular furnishings and accessories, works of art and decoration, and architectural elements.

Three notable examples include the portrait of the Four Tetrarchs, the Horses of Saint Mark, and the "Pillars of Acre." The statue of the Tetrarchs (joint rulers of the empire under Diocletian) was carved from purple porphyry around 300 and until 1204 sat in a public square in Constantinople. After its appropriation it was set into a southwest corner of the basilica's façade, next to the palace of the doge. Close by are the so-called Pillars of Acre, each carved in elaborate low relief with Byzantine motifs. Long believed to have been a trophy from Venice's victory over Genoa at Acre in 1258, they were, in fact, plundered from a sixth-century church in the imperial capital. Not far away sits the Pietra del Bando or "Stone of Proclamation," a low stub of an ancient porphyry column that the doges used as a platform for broadcasting decrees. The Horses of Saint Mark comprise a group of copper/bronze chariot horses likely dating from the second or third century that probably graced the Hippodrome of Constantinople. Taken in 1204, fifty years later they were installed on the upper part of St. Mark's façade over the main doors. However, not all of the Byzantine objects were, in fact, plunder—some were purchased, while others were actually made in Venice but so as to appear Byzantine.

Relics

Prior to the 800s the city's patron saint was the dragon-slaying Theodore of Amasea, but the abduction of Mark's relics brought greater prestige to the city. Over the centuries a large collection of relics was assembled, many of which were looted from Constantinople in 1204 or later.

FIGURE 5.5 A sketch showing the *piazzetta* (little plaza), basilica, and palace in St. Mark's Square, ca. 1400. Image: *The Book of Ser Marco Polo, The Venetian: Concerning the Kingdoms and Marvels of the East* (London: J. Murray, 1871), page xlviii. Hathi Trust Digital Library, digitized by Internet Archive, original from The Getty Research Institute.

FIGURE 5.6 The portrait of the Four Tetrarchs, next to the "Porta della Carta," in St. Mark's Square. Photo: Nino Barbieri provided by Wikimedia Commons under the Creative Commons Attribution-Share Alike 3.0 license.

FIGURE 5.7 The Horses of St. Mark's Basilica. Photo: Tteske provided by Wikimedia Commons under the Creative Commons Attribution-Share Alike 3.0 Unported license.

FIGURE 5.8 The "Pillars of Acre." Photo: Peter J. StB.Green, provided by Wikimedia Commons under the Creative Commons Attribution-Share Alike 3.0 Unported license.

These included the relics of Saint Lucy (which had been taken from Syracuse by the Byzantines in 1039), Saint Simeon (also said to be in Zadar, Croatia), Saint Anasthasius, Saint Zachary (the father of John the Baptist), the arm of Saint George, the skull of John the Baptist (also said to be at Damascus, Sabastiya, Rome, Amiens, and Munich), Saint Paul the New Martyr, Saint Helen (the empress), Saint Nicholas (partly also at Bari), Saint Barbara, Paul of Thebes (the first hermit), Isidore of Chios, and many others. Other saintly relics, as well as items associated with Christ, including a fragment of the True Cross, thorns from Christ's crown, drops of his blood, a nail from the Cross, and the knife used at the Last Supper, were acquired later. Held in gilded and bejeweled reliquaries, saintly remains were stored in the crypt of St. Mark's and other churches of the city, to be brought out for public display on auspicious occasions.

Discussion Questions

1. Why would Venice engage in a program of accumulating relics? What purposes could these serve?
2. What factors might have affected the selection and placement of Byzantine objects and relics? And why would even those purchased be presented as plunder?
3. How did the display of *spolia* advertise Venice's imperial power, and to whom?

Further Reading

Buckton, David, et al. *Venice*. Milan: Olivetti, 1985.

Mack, Rosamond E. *Bazaar to Piazza: Islamic Trade and Italian Art, 1300–1600*. Berkeley: University of California Press, 2002.

Maguire, Henry, and Robert S. Nelson. *San Marco, Byzantium, and the Myths of Venice*. Washington, DC: Dumbarton Oaks, 2010.

Mathews, Karen R. *Conflict, Commerce, and an Aesthetic of Appropriation in the Italian Maritime Cities, 1000–1150*. Boston: Brill, 2018.

Perry, David M. *Sacred Plunder: Venice and the Aftermath of the Fourth Crusade*. University Park: Penn State University Press, 2015.

with the Latin monarchy's chronic lack of cash led King Almaric (1163–1174) to intervene in Egypt. In response, Nur al-Din dispatched a Kurdish commander, Shirkuh, to take control of the caliphate. When Shirkuh died in 1169, he was succeeded as *wazir* by his nephew, Yusuf ibn Ayyub. Once secure in Egypt, Yusuf, who would be known to history as Salah al-Din, declared the caliphate dissolved in 1171. Soon after, the last Fatimid caliph, the eleven-year-old al-'Adid (1160–1171), died.

Alarmed by Salah al-Din's ambitions, Nur al-Din prepared to move against him but died while preparing to invade Egypt in 1174. Immediately, Salah al-Din moved to dispossess his heirs, and in short order took control of both Egypt and Syria, as well as Arabia. With Byzantium locked in dynastic intrigues and an increasingly fraught relationship with Genoa and Venice, it was no longer in a position to impose peace, and, therefore, the Kingdom of Jerusalem's days were numbered. Still, Salah al-Din took his time, and to reinforce his support among the notoriously fickle Seljuq troops used court poets and biographers to consciously cultivate a persona that perfectly combined the attributes of pious *jihadi* and an Arab war-

FIGURE 5.9 Warriors fighting on horseback. Miniature from a Fatimid manuscript, twelfth century CE. Museum of Islamic Art, Cairo, Egypt / Bridgeman Images.

rior of old. In 1187 he sprang the trap, luring the army of Jerusalem to a total defeat at the Horns of Hattin, overlooking the Sea of Galilee. In the months that followed he conquered the city of Jerusalem and almost the entire kingdom, leaving only a handful of coastal enclaves under Frankish control. Although touted as a pan-Sunni movement, Salah al-Din's aim, like Nur al-Din's, was to put his own family in power. Like Malik Shah, he relied on a brilliant native administrator, the former Fatimid functionary al-Qadi al-Fadil, to run his regime. After Salah al-Din's death in 1193, his descendants, the Ayyubids, would rule Syria and Egypt for the next seventy years.

Reaction from the Latin West to the conquest of Jerusalem was swift, and a Crusade (the Third) was launched to great fanfare by Henry II of England (1154–1189), Philip II Augustus of France (1180–1223), and the emperor Frederick Barbarossa (1152–1190). However, Barbarossa drowned while crossing a river in Anatolia, and Henry II's successor, Richard the Lionhearted (1189–1199), was determined to use the campaign against his Christian rivals, particularly Philip Augustus. On the way to the Holy Land, Richard attacked Norman Sicily, and sacked Byzantine Cyprus. After leading a daring attack that retook the port of Acre, and slaughtering thousands of Muslim prisoners in cold blood, Richard proposed to wed his sister, Joanna, the widow of William II of Sicily, to Salah al-Din's brother, al-ʿAdil, rather than marching on Jerusalem. This would be impossible under church law unless al-ʿAdil were to convert, and so Richard secured a ten-year truce and returned home, having sown violent intrigue among the Latin lords of the East. Forced to continue by land after a shipwreck near Venice, he was captured crossing Austria and imprisoned for over a year by the emperor Henry VI. When he was freed in 1194 through the intervention of his elderly mother, Eleanor of Aquitaine, the ransom bankrupted the Kingdom of England—a land the French-speaking Richard disdained. He had lived there only one year as an adult, and apparently never even learned to speak the language.

Later attempts to recover the Holy City proved no less superficial. The Fourth Crusade resulted in the destruction of Byzantium in 1204, and the Fifth Crusade, which included a Seljuq-Frankish alliance and the participation of Georgian forces, was decisively defeated after seizing the port of Damietta in Egypt in 1221. The emperor Frederick II's Sixth Crusade was not so much a war as a public relations exercise and a round of diplomacy with the ever-weaker Ayyubids of Egypt. In 1229 Frederick was crowned king in Jerusalem and received partial control of the city and other locales for a ten-year period. Finally, in 1249 (Saint) Louis IX of France (1226–1270) landed a massive force and captured Damietta. However, a year later the Christian army was nearly annihilated by the Turkic Mamluk slave-soldiers who now dominated the Egyptian army, and Louis himself taken prisoner, freed after pledging a massive ransom and to go home.

By now Jerusalem had once more become irrelevant, despite its symbolic importance. The trade that drove Latin engagement with the Islamic and Byzantine world largely bypassed Syria, and in the eastern Mediterranean diplomacy was the principal means of European expansion. By 1260 the Ayyubid dynasty of Salah al-Din had failed, a victim of interfamily intrigues in Syria, a coup by the same Mamluks who had defeated Louis—and the arrival of a new wave of invaders from Central Asia: the pagan Mongols, who would usher in a new era in the Mediterranean and the West.

The Fall of Byzantium and Rise of the Trading Republics

Initially, the Komnenid dynasty brought good government and good fortune to Byzantium. Alexios and his successors, John II and Manuel—strong, capable emperors, who each ruled for decades—could not reverse the damage done by the Seljuq invasion, but nevertheless reestablished the empire as the preeminent power in the eastern Mediterranean. In the mid-1100s John and Manuel managed to bring the Turkic, Armenian, and Frankish principalities of Anatolia and the Holy Land under control through a combination of military action, diplomacy, and threat. So great was the prestige attached to the imperial title that Turkic warlords did not even conceive of overthrowing the empire; rather, they sought its validation through recognition of their own sovereignty. Successes were achieved similarly in the Balkans as far north as Hungary. However, the greatest threat came from the Latin West, in the form of predatory noblemen thirsting after the prestige of the imperial title, an increasingly muscular papacy, and uncompromisingly mercenary Italian trading states. The singular prestige of the imperial crown, which the Komnenoi deliberately promoted, retained an awesome power that Latin rulers and noblemen were eager to partake in, thus enabling the emperors to skillfully use patronage and marriage into the dynasty as a policy instrument. The challenge was to use it judiciously, preventing non-Greeks from gaining too much authority, and avoiding exciting a reaction by the native Byzantine elite. Manuel's marriage in 1161 to Princess Maria of Antioch would violate these principles and help precipitate the end of not only the dynasty but the empire itself.

Byzantium's relationship with the Italian trading republics was even more delicate. The history of these port cities begins in the early Middle Ages, as they exchanged much needed raw materials from Europe for exotica and finished goods coming from the Islamic and Byzantine worlds. Contacts with the sophisticated but increasingly vulnerable powers of the eastern and southern Mediterranean encouraged their expansion. Trading, warfare, and piracy were not clearly delineated, and these towns developed hybrid fleets capable of all three. Meanwhile, the political fragmentation of Italy provided them the independence to develop social and institutional structures suited to an urban and commercial environment, while their domination of Latin sea trade fueled a prosperity that was further stimulated by the spurt of European growth that began after 1000. It was at this time that they began carrying pilgrim traffic to the Holy Land. By the second half of the century, trade, warfare, and pilgrimage had merged as Latin knights on the return leg of their journeys to the East helped Italians raid the North African coast. Foreshadowing the Crusade movement, in 1087, Pisa and Genoa sacked Mahdia, in Ifriqiya, with the blessing of Pope Victor III (1086–1087), who offered the absolution of sins in exchange for fighting the infidel almost a decade before Urban II did the same at Clermont.

During the First Crusade, Genoese and Pisan fleets provided naval support and carried in supplies and reinforcements, taking advantage of their presence in eastern waters to raid Byzantine islands and coastal towns. Their assistance did not come cheap. They took a heavy profit on the goods and people they carried, and typically demanded exclusive trading privileges and one-third ownership of any port city they helped to conquer, thereby laying the foundations of their future colonial enterprises. Independent of Crusader armies, when diplomacy failed, they used violence or the threat of attack to secure privileges and tribute in eastern Mediterranean ports. For their part, Muslim and Byzantine authorities came to appreciate dealing with Italian traders—who provided access to new European markets for goods passing through these ports, stimulated local trade and craft production, and ensured them a measure of naval protection. Nevertheless, the Italians' determination to extract the most favorable terms reduced the benefit to their hosts, while the rivalry between the perennially warring republics often caught local powers in the middle.

These tendencies crystallized in Byzantium, which, as an extensive territorial power with a large population and sole access to the Black Sea, became a prime object for both Genoa and Venice. The Byzantine emperors tried to retain the initiative by playing them against each other, alternately favoring them with privileges. However, this undermined the trust of the republics in Byzantine leadership, and whichever trading city happened to be on the outs sowed anti-Greek sentiment among the Frankish elite and clergy in the hopes of gaining support in the West. Moreover, the Catholic Franks considered the Byzantine Orthodox schismatics, and were well aware that the empire had a history of allying with Muslim powers against Crusaders when it suited them. The empire for its part was becoming more dependent on the Franks and the Italians. Frankish knights were taking on an increasingly important role in the Byzantine military, while the efficacy of the Italian navies had led the empire to largely abandon its own naval program in the later 1100s, effectively "privatizing" it and allowing Genoese and Venetian fleets to provide maritime defense. This led to short-term savings, but left Byzantium vulnerable and dependent.

When Maria of Antioch became empress in 1161, the fortunes of the Franks in the Byzantine court rose, and all the more so after Manuel's death in 1180, when the dowager became the guardian of her eleven-year-old son, Alexios II (1180–1182). Reacting against the growing Latin influence under Maria, the populace of Constantinople and members of the ruling dynasty supported a renegade uncle, Andronikos Komnenos, who seized the throne in 1182. He put Maria, Alexios, and the leading Latin courtiers to death, and encouraged a massacre of the Genoese and Venetian residents. Such excesses prompted nobility and clients across the empire to rise up, and in 1185 Andronikos was overthrown and publicly tortured and murdered in a popular revolt led by the general Isaac Angelos. Over the next two decades violent infighting among the Angeloi dynasty further destabilized the empire, and led the young emperor Alexios IV, who had been deposed by his uncle Alexios III (1195–1203), to appeal to the Frankish West for aid, making impossible promises of rich material rewards and reconciliation between the Greek and Latin Churches were they to restore him to the throne.

He found an eager reception. The Venetians were thirsty for revenge and to reestablish their presence in Constantinople, the Frankish nobility dreamed of plunder and of finally taking the imperial crown, and Innocent III (1198–1216) saw a chance to reunite the church under papal authority. Moreover, the Crusaders who had gathered already for a Fourth Crusade, had become indebted to Venice, and in exchange for release from these obligations agreed to secretly steer the Crusade away from its intended target, Egypt, first to the city of Zara (modern Zadar) in Croatia, which the Crusaders seized for Venice from the king of Hungary, and then on to Constantinople. And so it was, that in 1204 the Christian empire established by Constantine the Great, which had weathered nearly a millennium of history, was brought down by Crusaders whose goal was ostensibly to protect it. For the next half century Constantinople would be the capital of a much-reduced Latin Empire, co-ruled by Frankish nobility and the Venetian republic. Meanwhile, various Byzantine claimants to the throne established rump states in the former imperial territories, the Balkan kingdoms broke free, and new influxes of Turkic peoples pushed into Anatolia. SEE SOURCEBOOK 5:4.

Papacy and Empire

The conquest of Constantinople can be seen as the natural consequence of developments in the Latin West, particularly the emergence of the Latin Church as a centralized institutional and political power. The Gregorian Reform of the mid-eleventh century, the development of a coherent body of canon law, institutions for collecting church taxes, the emergence of centralized monastic orders, and the establishment of a papal *curia,* analogous to a royal court, seemed to put the papacy on a path to claiming universal sovereignty, not only over Latin Christians, but the entire world. This immediately put the church at odds with secular rulers, notably the Germanic emperors, who fought against the papacy over the right to appoint bishops, which from the church's perspective was a religious matter, and from the kings', a political one. SEE SOURCEBOOK 5:5.

With its near monopoly on literacy and education, and with the tremendous territory bishops and abbots controlled as lords, the church's authority was seen as a threat to monarchs. In this "investiture controversy" each fought with the weapons at their disposal: the papacy by threatening disobedient kings with excommunication or the interdiction of their kingdoms (which would imperil their subjects' salvation by suspending the church's activities) and by mobilizing rebellious noblemen and towns; and the emperors by force of arms and by appointing their own, rival "anti-popes." Although these disputes would continue through the Middle Ages, in 1122 a compromise was reached between Calixtus II (1119–1124) and the emperor Henry V (1111–1125), which confirmed the church's prerogative to appoint bishops and abbots in exchange for those prelates ceding their secular power to the kings. In the meantime, the papacy had continued to develop the institutional apparatus of a monarchy. The imperial papacy reached its apogee with Innocent III (1198–1216), a dedicated reformer, who aggressively employed Crusades to pursue papal policy, and who became the feudal lord of kingdoms, including Sicily, Aragon, Portugal, Hungary, Ireland, and England.

Only four years after Innocent's death, the empire struck back in the form of *stupor mundi*—"the wonder of the world"—Frederick II, king of Sicily (1198–1250), who as the "Holy Emperor" from 1220 ruled over a broad swathe of territory from the Mediterranean to the Baltic, and claimed the crown of Jerusalem. A warrior and man of culture—rationalist, Arabophile, reformer of laws, and founder of the first secular university (at Naples)—Frederick's power provoked the reaction of Innocent IV (1243–1254), who found allies among the rebellious towns of Italy (the "Guelphs," who faced off against "Ghibellines" loyal to the emperor) and the landed nobility of Germany. To the papacy, Frederick was nothing less than "the Antichrist," and it waged a war against him until this death in 1250. Four years later, Frederick's Hohenstaufen dynasty would fail—an apparent victory for the papacy, but one that would prove short-lived.

This struggle took place against the backdrop of the demographic and economic boom of the Medieval Optimum, which saw the rise of towns and of a commercial and artisanal middle class, neither of which fit into the established conception of a society comprised only of warriors, priests, and peasants. For monarchs, towns could boost prosperity and serve as a counterweight against the nobility, which was determined to resist the royal centralization, but they were also difficult-to-govern and potentially rebellious nodes of resistance.

The population increase both benefited and threatened the papacy. The emerging middle class provided a pool of clergy capable of running the new, corporate church, but was, by virtue of its increasing sophistication, inquisitive, critical, and demanding both in terms of the meaning of scripture and doctrine, and the church's role in society. Ordinary people were now reading more scripture and expressing greater and more informed concern for their

FIGURE 5.10 The emperor Frederick II meets the Ayyubid sultan al-Kamil, from *New Chronicle*, Florentine, ca. 1348 CE. The Picture Art Collection / Alamy Stock Photo.

own salvation, as well as a critical attitude to what they perceived as the failings of a corrupt, worldly, and disengaged church.

This was manifested in outbreaks of popular dissent. The Waldenses, or "Poor Men of Lyon," emerged in the 1170s as a Bible-study group among Rhone valley cloth workers who lamented the church's lack of pastoral work, and quickly spread into the towns of northern Italy and the Rhine. When they began publicly preaching in defiance of local bishops, the Waldenses were branded heretics, and systematically rooted out and driven underground. A further threat emerged in a group that took root in Languedoc around the same time, the "Good Men." This religious movement, which appears related to ancient Manicheism, was a dualistic Christian religion—one that envisioned creation as a battleground between a god of good and a god of evil, and the material world as inherently corrupt. Catharism (or "Albigensianism") resembled Armenian Paulicianism, and Balkan Bogomilism, and was possibly brought to Languedoc by Crusaders and pilgrims returning from the Holy Land.

This religion of the "Good Men" constituted an alternative Christianity with a distinct theology, which therefore denied any legitimacy to the Latin Church. It was popular among both common folk and the local nobility, who saw the church as corrupt and its theology as unrealistic, and who resented the papacy's increasing demands for taxation. When Count Raymond VI of Toulouse (1194–1222), himself a Catholic, refused to stamp out the heresy in his lands, Innocent III launched a Crusade in 1209. Like Innocent's Fourth Crusade, this soon turned into a baldfaced political enterprise. The twenty-year campaign, distinguished for its brutality and the atrocities deliberately committed against common folk, was little more than a pious rationale for predatory northern French noblemen under the leadership of the sadistic Simon de Montfort to conquer Languedoc. De Montfort's death in 1218 did not bring an end to the war, and the war did not bring an end to Catharism; however, it paved the way for the intervention of Louis VIII of France (1223–1226), and Languedoc's annexation in 1258 under the authority of Louis IX, vastly expanding the French king's territory and wealth. The last Cathar tried and executed as a heretic went to the stake in 1321.

An immediate effect of the new popular piety and the heresies that it spawned was the establishment by Innocent III of a new type of religious order—the Mendicants, or "Beggars." Unlike monks, whose goal was ascetic isolation and the spiritual battle against evil, these friars ("brothers") were urban and very much engaged with the world. Espousing poverty, and dedicated to pastoral work, their appeal was that they resembled in many ways the heretics they were determined to counter. The Franciscans or "Lesser Brothers," founded by a charismatic Italian preacher named Francis of Assisi in 1209, sought to emulate the lives of the disciples of the gospel, preaching to and caring for the urban masses neglected by the established church. The Dominicans or "Preachers" were founded five years later by the Spaniard Dominic de Guzmán, with the aim of converting Cathars. Both became phenomenal successes and would soon dominate both the new universities of Europe and the papacy. The Franciscans came to favor a mystical, revolutionary Christianity, of such extremes that some branches would be branded heretics. The Dominicans became the intellectual instrument of doctrinal conformity. The Inquisition was run by Dominicans with papal support in Languedoc to aggressively root out grassroots heresy in the aftermath of the military conquest of the region.

The foundation of the Mendicants represented the church's efforts to maintain a spiritual grip on a rapidly changing world. Through its engagement with the Mediterranean, Latin Europe became aware of a much wider, diverse, and sophisticated world—one that challenged Western Christians' conception of themselves as being at the center of creation. In this period the church wrestled with its relationship to Judaism, the challenge posed by a clearly more advanced Islamic culture, the transformation of European society, and the papacy's own transformation into a monarchy. Even before the war against the Cathars, Rome had been accused of misusing Crusade as an implement of raw power—a charge that became difficult to refute as penance became monetized through the practice of crusading by proxy (that is paying someone to crusade on one's behalf) and the outright sale of the absolution of one's sins in the form of "indulgences." By the mid-thirteenth century, the European monarchies would eclipse the papacy as the promotors of Crusade. Crusading would continue into the sixteenth century, but it had clearly become an instrument of secular rulers in the service of their political agendas. By having a military campaign qualified as a Crusade, kings could lawfully appropriate church taxes to their cause, as well as provide religious incentives for their warriors.

The Contest for the Western Mediterranean

These various trends can be seen in Latin Christendom's collision with the Islamic world in the western Mediterranean. Here, as in the East, the forces at work were rooted more in processes internal to Islamic and Christian societies than in any supposed "clash of civilizations." Much as the Norman warriors had infiltrated Italy in the eleventh century, Burgundian nobleman and clergy had insinuated themselves into the Christian principalities of the Iberian Peninsula, here with the complicity of local princes, who were in need of military aid, and the institutional support of the Latin Church, particularly the Cluniac and Cistercian monastic orders. These Burgundians were drawn by the prospect of land and plunder, and the goal of extending the dominion of Latin Christianity both into Muslim lands and over the indigenous Mozarabic Church. Indeed, the peninsula became something of a laboratory of Crusade and papal sovereignty. Even before Urban II's call to crusade, indulgences had been promised to knights who fought Islam here, and by the thirteenth century, the papacy had positioned itself as liege lord of Portugal and Aragon. The mid-twelfth century saw a string of military successes by Christian kings: Portugal took Lisbon in 1147 with the aid of Crusaders en route to the Holy Land, Almería was captured by Castile-León with the aid of Genoa in the same year—both campaigns notable for the deliberate slaughter of the native populace—and the Crown of Aragon took Tortosa with the Genoese and Templars in 1148, and Lleida in 1149 with Hospitaller support.

These gains came as a consequence of the collapse of Almoravid power. Native Andalusi warlords had been resisting the Almoravids since their arrival by forging alliances with Christian powers, but within a decade or two there was also considerable grassroots resistance. Ultimately, however, it was a rebellion in North Africa that undid the regime. A nativist Berber movement had emerged among the tribes of the Atlas Mountains under a messianic holy man named 'Abd Allah ibn Tumart (d. 1130), who declared himself in 1121 to be the Mahdi, or "Rightly Guided One," who would usher in a new age of righteousness. These Almohads harnessed the discontent of the Almoravids' North African subjects, conquering the capital of Marrakesh in 1147. That year, Ibn Tumart's righthand man, 'Abd al-Mu'min (d. 1163), proclaimed a new universal caliphate under the rule of his own family. With the wealth of the western Saharan gold routes behind him, within a decade he had brought the Muslim West from Ifriqiya to al-Andalus under his power, exterminating the Almoravid dynasty and doggedly pursuing their remaining loyalists to Mallorca and on to Ifriqiya.

It was a truly revolutionary movement. Rather than constituting a Sunni revival, like that of the Almoravids or Seljuqs, the Almohads championed what was effectively a new, pure, and mystically informed version of Abrahamic monotheism that combined various recent developments of the Muslim faith. They saw their *tawhid,* or "doctrine of unity," as superseding not only Judaism and Christianity, but previous versions of Islam. Mosques were reconsecrated and their *qibla,* or "direction of prayer," changed from Mecca to the star Canopus (toward which the Kaaba is oriented). Any non-Almohads were considered "infidels," and were subjected to official repression and even forced conversion.

But Almohad dominion was to prove as fleeting as that of the Almoravids had been. In al-Andalus and North Africa the regime faced resistance and revolt, both from the local Muslim warlords, Almoravids in Mallorca, and from the general populace, the bulk of whom did not subscribe to the Almohad creed. In any event, the purity of their religious mission was almost immediately diluted by the practicalities of politics. The military threat at home obliged the Almohads to employ Christian mercenaries in ever greater numbers, and by the time the regime collapsed in the 1220s, there were some 12,000 Christians living in Marrakesh, served by their own bishop. But commerce was the great leveler. The markets of Latin Europe had become indispensable to the success of the Andalusi and Magrhibi economy and the trans-Saharan trade that together constituted the foundations of Almohad power and prosperity. Thus, for all the Almohad rhetoric of *jihad* and Latin Crusade posturing, the Almohad era saw an intensification of economic integration and political collaboration among Christian and Muslim powers in the western Mediterranean. SEE SOURCEBOOK 5:6.

As the Almohad Caliphate crumbled in the 1220s the Christian rulers of the Iberian Peninsula were poised to seize the advantage. In the 1220s and 1230s in a series of campaigns designated as Crusades, Portugal, Castile and León, and the Crown of Aragon together conquered almost all that remained of Islamic Spain, including the Balearic Islands, leaving only a handful of semiautonomous protectorates, and a compact, independent sultanate of Granada in the far south (called the Nasrid Sultanate, after its founder, the local warlord Muhammad ibn Yusuf ibn Nasr, who ruled from 1232 to 1273). In many of these conquered territories, substantial numbers of native Muslims were induced to remain in their lands as Mudejar (stay behinds), with the promise of broad privileges of legal autonomy, and guarantees of personal freedom and religious liberty. Many Jews had fled al-Andalus to the Latin north during the Almoravid and Almohad periods, and many now returned as colonizers for the Christian kings. The Christian powers also made in-roads into North Africa, but a series of Mudejar revolts around the middle of the thirteenth century, coupled with the rise of the Marinids in Morocco and the establishment of the remnants of the Almohad regime in Tunis as the Hafsid dynasty, helped put a brake on Latin expansion there. By 1250 a new equilibrium had been tenuously established, and for the next century it would be commerce as much as combat that would shape Muslim-Christian-Jewish relations across this reintegrated Mediterranean.

CHAPTER SIX

A Connected Sea

Such a sight had never been seen, even in cosmopolitan Cairo. It was July 1324, and ranged around the three great Pyramids under the blank-eyed stare of Abu 'l-Haul ("The Fearsome One," the Sphinx), lay a sprawling encampment of tents housing some 10,000 slaves, soldiers, attendants, and noblemen, and one prince: Mansa Musa ("King Moses") of Mali. They had made the 4,000-mile trek from west-central Africa to the Egyptian capital as one leg of a journey in fulfillment of the Islamic obligation to perform the *hajj* pilgrimage to Mecca. To finance the trip and to spread his good reputation, Musa had come with a caravan of thousands of camels carrying some fifteen tons of gold. He was so lavish in his generosity that the price of gold temporarily dropped in Egypt. After an audience with al-Nasir Muhammad (1310–1341), the Mamluk sultan, Musa proceeded to the Holy Cities, Mecca and Medina. On his return he brought with him a number of Sunni religious authorities, a Shi'i missionary, and the Granadan poet Abu Ishaq al-Sahili, who is credited with designing Musa's new palace and the great mosque at Timbuktu.

Mansa Musa was not the first king of Mali to make the *hajj*. Spurred by contacts with Muslim traders bringing salt, bronze, beads, and craft goods, and with the Almoravids, who attempted to dominate the area, by the eleventh century Islam was established in the Sahel, the savannah on the southwestern rim of the Sahara. By the late eleventh century a Muslim kingdom of Ghana had emerged, and indigenous Soninke merchants spread Islam southward into the forests of the Niger region. Many Africans came north as slaves, and significant numbers of Ghanaian troops, it seems, fought in the Almoravid army against Christian Castile. In the mid-1200s, after Ghana had begun to decline, Sundiata Keita of Mali (ca. 1235–1255) converted to Islam and founded an empire that would stretch across western and central Africa and control much of the lucrative gold trade. Under his successors Mali would become integrated into the Mediterranean commercial system and cultural sphere, becoming the most important source of gold for the growing European economy, and leading the empire to expand farther south toward the gold-rich Akan forest. In a manner analogous to Christianity in the pagan north of Europe a few centuries earlier, Islam provided a means for the regional elite here to establish a ready-made institutional framework. For some time, it was fundamentally a courtly and urban phenomenon. Large-scale conversion would come only gradually, giving rise to an Islamic culture that would represent a fusion of indigenous and imported traditions.

A similar process was going on to the east in the emerging sultanate of Kilwa, on the Swahili coast in what is now Tanzania. Here, it was the long-established trade originating along the Nile and around the Horn of Africa, and connections to Indian Ocean commerce, that brought Islam and sedentary culture. In the last decade of the 1200s a small kingdom founded on the East African coast by Yemeni Arabs in the tenth century was superseded by the native Mahdali dynasty, who enlarged its territory and established firmer ties with the wider Islamic world. The second ruler, al-Hasan ibn Sulayman (1310–1333) was, like Mansa Musa, a great patron of learning and culture, who actively sought to deepen contacts with the Mediterranean north. He built palaces, fortresses, and mosques, minted coins, and patronized foreign *'ulama'*. Like his counterpart in Mali, he was legendary for his largesse.

These developments in sub-Saharan Africa, like those in the Mediterranean's European and Central Asian hinterlands, reflect both the expansion and the deepening integration of the Mediterranean world in the period from 1050 to 1350. This was set in motion by environmental changes, but driven largely by commerce, as Europeans, Africans, and Asians all fought for their place at the Mediterranean table. It had profound implications for the development of culture and of social life across the region, and laid the foundations for the European expansion into Africa and the so-called age of discovery that would be underway by the late fifteenth century.

MAP 6.1 The Mediterranean, ca. 1200.

Conflict and Integration, ca. 1250–1350

In the thirteenth and early fourteenth centuries the Latin Mediterranean became the battleground for a clutch of royal and noble dynasties, together with urban republics, that expanded in a hodgepodge across the region, acquiring territory and royal titles in a complex chess-like game of conquest and political marriage played among themselves and against outsiders. In this highly fragmented Mediterranean many dynastic and urban imperia possessed scattered territories and titles that were constantly fluctuating, as a result of marriage alliances, split or contested inheritances, and internal intrigues and uprisings.

Transregional Dynasties

The death of Frederick II in 1250 augured the end of the short but glorious Hohenstaufen dynasty. His son Conrad, who had held the much-diminished and almost-landless title of king of Jerusalem as well as that of Italy, succeeded as king of Sicily and Germany, but died in 1254. His two-year-old son, Conradín (1254–1258), soon faced a challenge from his own uncle and regent in Sicily, Manfred (1258–1266), and then from a resurgent papacy under Clement IV (1265–1268).

Clement recruited Charles, the count of Anjou and Provence, and the head of the Angevin branch of France's Capetian dynasty, to take the throne of Sicily (1266–1285) as a papal vassal and eliminate the Hohenstaufens with the backing of Louis IX and the support of a Crusade, thus prompting a two-year war in Italy between the two families and their supporters among the cities and magnates of the peninsula. After killing Manfred in battle in 1266 and hanging a captured Con-

radín in 1268, Charles was left king of Sicily (including Naples and southern Italy). Ten years later he became also prince of Achaea (in Greece). For the following century Naples remained under Angevin rule, and in 1308 Hungary's throne was acquired by Charles's great-great grandson, Charles Robert (1308–1342). Although the Angevins would retain possessions in France, the central Mediterranean, and central Europe through the 1300s, their position was weakened over the course of that century by another cadet branch of the Capetian family. The Valois came to the French throne after Charles IV (1322–1328) of France and Navarre died without a male heir, and they chipped away at the Angevins' power through marriage claims and military action.

However, the Angevins had already faced a serious challenge from a rival family to the west. In 1137 Count Ramon Berenguer IV (1131–1162), the ruler of Barcelona and the Catalan counties (including Roussillon, in modern France), was betrothed to Petronila, the infant daughter of Ramiro the Monk, king of Aragon (1134–1137). In 1162 their son, Alfons the Troubadour (1164–1196), would become the first ruler of the Crown of Aragon—a dynastic aggregate centered on Barcelona that would become a major Mediterranean power. By 1250, the Crown, under the long rule of Jaume (James) the Conqueror (1213–1276) had taken Islamic Mallorca and Valencia, and forced Muslim Menorca into clientage. Jaume successfully harnessed the military energies of his landed nobility, the growing peasant population, the skills of native and foreign Jews, and the commercial proficiency of the Catalan merchant class to create a versatile colonial enterprise that, unlike those of his rivals, did not depend on the Italian trading republics for a navy or logistics. Like his Aragonese predecessors, he was careful to preserve the viability of the Muslim territories he conquered by encouraging the native population to remain in their lands as legitimate, but second-class subjects—even in the face of Muslim revolts that gripped Valencia in the second half of the century. SEE SOURCEBOOK 6:1.

Under his successors, the Crown expanded in the Mediterranean. Jaume's son, Pere (Peter) the Great (1276–1285), engaged in gunboat diplomacy with Tunis, which was under the rule of the Hafsid family, an offshoot of the extinct Almohad regime. He conquered the coastal islands and become a protector of the dynasty against other Christian powers—including a crusading Louis IX of France (1226–1270). In 1282 with popular support, he seized the island of Sicily from Charles of Anjou, prompt-

The political and economic integration of the larger Mediterranean world is reflected in the affinity for common symbols of power and prestige and the appreciation for rare materials and sophisticated craftsmanship—a reflection of the informal yet potent Mediterranean culture that transcended or underlay differences of ethnicity and faith. Designs, motifs, and themes that were originally rooted in particular cultures came to be universally recognized as prestigious, whether their original signification was forgotten or celebrated, as can be seen in the types of objects that moved around the Mediterranean world.

The Eleanor Vase

This 22-inch-tall cut-crystal vessel with gold mountings was likely carved in Persia, either during the late Sasanian (sixth–seventh century) or 'Abbasid (ninth–tenth century) period. The crystal itself likely originated in Madagascar, carried by Malagasy merchants and picked up by Muslim traders on Mayotte (from the Arabic, "The Island of Death"), in the Comoros Islands, just to the northwest. From Persia it may well have come to Egypt, perhaps taken during the brief Fatimid occupation of Baghdad in 1058, if not earlier. Financial crisis in eleventh-century Egypt led to parts of the Fatimid treasury being pilfered or sold off across the Islamic world and Byzantium. In response to a famine in 1058 the *taifa* king of Denia sent food to the Fatimids, who reciprocated with valuable treasures, initiating a series of gift exchanges. Once in Denia, the vase may have passed to the Banu Hud, the kings of Zaragoza, when they absorbed that kingdom in 1076. Decades later, with the aid of the populace, the Almoravids dislodged the last of the Banu Hud, 'Abd al-Malik 'Imad al-Dawla, from Zaragoza. Taking refuge with his library and treasures in his castle at Rueda in 1110, 'Imad al-Dawla joined forces with the Aragonese ruler, Alfonso the Battler (1104–1134), and helped defeat the Almoravids at the Battle of Cutanda in 1120. Alongside him fought Duke William IX, "the Troubador," of Aquitaine, to whom it seems 'Imad al-Dawla presented the vase as a gift. It eventually passed to William's granddaughter, Eleanor of Aquitaine, who presented it as a gift to her new husband, Louis VII of France (1137–1180) in 1137. Louis commended it to the church—perhaps in hopes of getting a child by Eleanor—through his adviser, Abbot Suger, who was compiling a rich treasury at the royal abbey of Saint-Denis as part of his program to enhance the prestige of the Capetian kings. Suger added the gilded and bejeweled mount, which features a Latin inscription outlining the provenance of the vase.

FIGURE 6.1 The "Eleanor vase." © INTERFOTO/agefotostock.

> As a bride, Eleanor gave this vase to King Louis, Mitadolus ['Imad al-Dawla] having given it to her grandfather, the king having given it to me, and Suger having given it to the Saints.[1]

The vase is currently in the Louvre.

FIGURE 6.2 The "Innsbruck bowl." © De Agostini Picture Library / De Agostini Editore / agefotostock.

The Innsbruck Bowl

This enameled gilded copper bowl, about 8.5 inches across and 2 inches deep, is something of a mystery. Flurries of vegetal designs, interspersed by a dancing girl, acrobat, and musician, palms (or "trees of life"), and rondels featuring mythical beasts, surround an image of Alexander the Great. Alexander is taking flight, harnessed to two griffins, which he goads into flight by holding two skewers of meat just above them and out of their reach (as in the third-century Greek *Alexander Romance*, which was widely translated from Persia to the Atlantic).* The exquisite workmanship is evidently Byzantine, the motifs are

* The "tree of life" or "tree of knowledge" is a common and ancient folk motif and myth meme in western Asia and the Mediterranean that connects various elements of the universe.

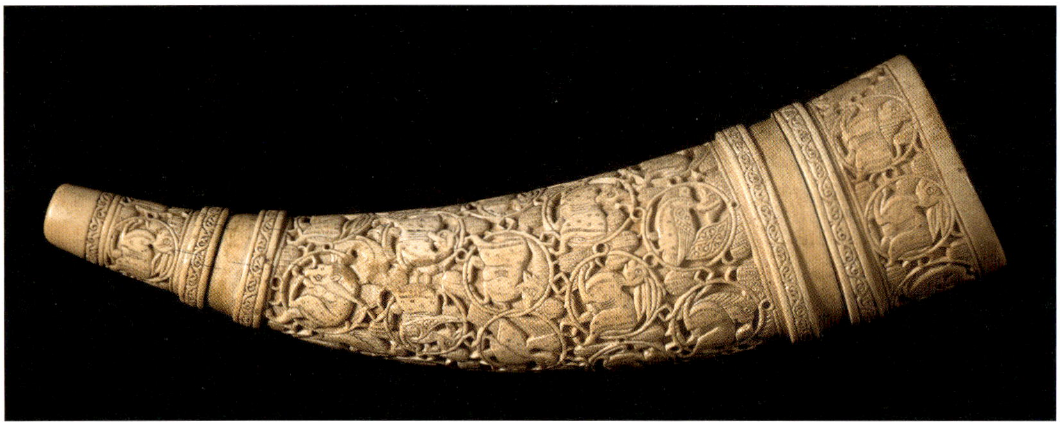

FIGURE 6.3 Ivory *olifant*, eleventh–twelfth century CE. Photo: bpk Bildagentur / Museum for Islamic Art / Jürgen Liepe / Art Resource, NY.

both European and Near Eastern, but the Arabic inscription reads:

> The great prince and army commander, the fortified [by God], the victorious, Nasir al-Din Rukn al-Dawla, saber of the community of believers, splendor of the nation, leader of armies, crown of kings and sultans, slayer of infidels and polytheists, Alp Sevinch Sunqur Beg Abu Sulayman Da'ud, son of Artuq, sword of the Commander of the Faithful.[2]

The bowl also displays a Persian inscription that is undeciphered.

The individual has been identified as Rukn al-Dawla Abu Sulayman Da'ud, a Turkoman ruler who held the small principality of Hasankeyf in southeastern Anatolia from 1114 to 1142. Some have suggested that the dish was made in "culturally hybrid" Georgia, where Byzantine craftsmen could have applied their techniques to Islamicate and Persian objects; however, given its extremely high quality, a more likely hypothesis, perhaps, is that it was manufactured in the royal workshops of Constantinople and intended as a gift by the emperor to a client and ally, who as a Muslim could not be granted a crown as was customary, and so received a regal object that acknowledged his legitimacy but did not put him on an equal footing with Christians.

It is currently in the Tiroler Landesmuseum Ferdinandeum in Innsbruck, Austria.

Olifants

Elephant horns, or *olifants,* had long been used in the Mediterranean and Near East as ceremonial instruments, as well as in warfare and for hunting. Fatimid expansion into central Africa in the eleventh century brought new supplies of ivory, and Islamic Sicily became a principal center for the production of elaborately carved tusks that became popular across the region. As exotica associated with heroics that figured often in epic and folktales, they had a certain magical aspect. Under Norman rule production expanded to serve northern European markets, notably Norman England. As production diversified, non-Muslim craftsmen outside Sicily (e.g., Amalfi and Venice) also manufactured *olifants,* sometimes of "knock-off" quality—making it difficult to date them or specify their site of origin. Scores found their way first into noble courts, and then church treasuries as donations. Some feature explicitly Christian imagery, either as a gesture to the export market or added later.

This horn, about 20 inches long and 4.5 inches wide, and currently in Berlin's Pergamon Museum, is one of about twenty surviving *olifants* classified as "Fatimid." It was likely produced in Sicily or southern Italy in the eleventh or twelfth century under either Muslim or Christian rule. The decoration, typical of high-quality *olifants,* is based on motifs common in Egyptian and Near Eastern textiles, and features rondels containing animals associated with mythology and the hunt, intertwined by vegetal designs.

An early mention of an *olifant* occurs in the *Song of Roland* (see chapter 1), where he blows his massive horn of the same name. In the twelfth-century epic *Aspremont,* Roland receives his horn, Olifant, together with his sword, Durendal, and his horse, Veillantif, as spoils after killing the Muslim king, Aymes, who was attacking Charlemagne.

Discussion Questions

1. What qualities endowed these items with a value or prestige that transcended ethnic or religious divisions?

2. What do the symbols and motifs suggest about "Mediterranean culture"?

3. Why would nonreligious items such as these be prized and collected by the church?

Further Reading

Beech, George T. "The Eleanor of Aquitaine Vase, William IX of Aquitaine, and Muslim Spain." *Gesta* 32 (1993): 3–10.

Hoffman, Eva. "Pathways of Portability: Islamic and Christian Interchange from the Tenth to the Twelfth Century." In *Late Antique and Medieval Art of the Mediterranean World,* ed. Eva Hoffman, 317–47. Malden, MA: Blackwell, 2007.

Redford, Scott. "How Islamic Is It? The Innsbruck Plate and Its Setting." *Muqarnas* 7 (1990): 119–35.

Shalem, Avinoam. *The Olifant: Islamic Objects in Historical Context.* Leiden: Brill, 2004.

Steppan, Thomas. "The Artukid Bowl: Courtly Art in the Middle Byzantine and Its Relation to the Islamic East." In *Perceptions of Byzantium and Its Neighbors, 843–1261,* ed. Olenka Z. Pevny, 84–101. New Haven: Yale University Press, 2000.

Notes

1. George T. Beech, "The Eleanor of Aquitaine Vase: Its Origins and History to the Early Twelfth Century," *Ars Orientalis* 22 (1992): 75, for the Latin, retranslated here.

2. Helen C. Evans, William D. Wixom, and Metropolitan Museum of Art (New York), *The Glory of Byzantium: Art and Culture of the Middle Byzantine Era, A.D. 843–1261* (New York: Metropolitan Museum of Art, 1997), 422.

ing the pope, Martin IV (1281–1285)—a creature of the Angevins—to call a crusade against Aragon, recruiting France, which had its own designs on Tunis, and Pere's brother, Jaume, who ruled Mallorca (1276–1311), to the cause. The Crusade was defeated with the aid of Muslim soldiers from Christian Valencia, and Sicily remained under the control of the family, although no longer ruled from Barcelona after 1295. Under a series of long-reigning monarchs, over the following half century the Barcelona dynasty expanded by military action and marriage, conquering Menorca, Sardinia, Corsica, and parts of southern Italy. In the early 1300s Catalan *almogàvers,* soldiers of fortune, constituted as the Great Catalan Company under the command of the Italian admiral Roger de Flor, seized the Duchies of Athens and Neopatria in Greece. Catalan merchants, meanwhile, established an important presence in Constantinople, Alexandria, Damascus, Muslim Granada, and the ports of North Africa.

The Struggle for the Straits of Gibraltar

By 1250 the Almohad Caliphate had imploded. In Iberia, this came as a consequence of local uprisings in al-Andalus by native Sunni warlords who rejected the Almohad creed and foreign dominion, and allied with the Christian powers, Aragon, Portugal, Castile and León. What remained of Islamic Spain after 1250 was a small sultanate of Granada, which Castile claimed formally, although with limited effect, as a vassal. In the Maghrib the Almohads were brought down by the Marinids, Berber herdsmen (whence "Merino" wool), and other local rebels, while the Hafsids, a branch of the Almohad Mu'minid dynasty, established a much-reduced caliphate in Tunisia.

The Christian powers of Iberia characterized their wars against Granada, the Marinids, and the Hafsids as crusades, and occasionally acted in near unison, but, as often as in the western Mediterranean, the various Christian and Muslim powers allied with each other against their coreligionists. Granada and Tunis did their best to exploit Christian weaknesses and rivalries—playing the various kingdoms, trading republics and the papacy against each other, and sheltering rebellious Christian

FIGURE 6.4 A fresco showing Jaume I of Aragon taking counsel during the conquest of Muslim Mallorca in 1229 from the palace of the Caldes family; Barcelona, 1285–1290. National Museum of Catalan Art, Barcelona, Spain. Funkyfood London–Paul Williams / Alamy Stock Photo.

noblemen, many of whom crossed the Mediterranean to serve as mercenaries in Muslim Africa. Instability in Christian Iberia continued through the fourteenth century. Although Castile and León had been united since (Saint) Fernando III of Castile (1217–1252) claimed the Leonese crown in 1230, the kings' power was undermined by both the landed nobility and the ever-more independent towns; and war and intrigue between Castile, Portugal, and Aragon continued.

Over the course of the mid-thirteenth to the mid-fourteenth century, the Marinids consolidated their rule in Morocco, and launched a number of attacks against both Granada and Castile. Control of the Straits of Gibraltar and Atlantic-Mediterranean shipping was the focus of these campaigns. The dynasty saw the value of military innovation and pioneered the use of cannon in the West; crucially, however, they failed to maintain a navy, which led them to become dependent on Genoa for logistical support. In 1340 the sultan Abu al-Hasan (1331–1348) personally launched an invasion aimed at retaking Tarifa from Castile, but suffered a crushing defeat on land and sea by a Christian coalition at the Battle of Rio Salado—effectively ending Marinid ambitions in Spain. The Hafsids also failed to develop a competitive navy, and focused on commerce rather than conquest. Between their privileged access to central African gold and exotica, and their need for imported wheat, the caliphs forged an array of treaties with Sicily, Aragon, and Christian port cities across the central and western Mediterranean.

In 1270 Louis IX headed a massive Crusade the first objective of which was the conquest of Tunis. Dysentery swept through the siege camp at Carthage, killing many, including the king himself, bringing the mission to an ignominious end. In the early 1300s internal political strife would weaken the Hafsids, culminating in the conquest of Tunis by the Marinids in 1348. After 1350 the dynasty would reemerge and experience a second century of prosperity and expansion. Although the control of the straits would continue to be disputed in the following centuries, the Christian powers of the Iberian Peninsula, Portugal and Castile-León, carried the military and political advantage and would eventually seize several of the major North African ports.

Renaissance Men

Despite continuous political upheaval, whether between rival cities, or factions who declared loyalty to the papacy (Guelfs) or the Holy Roman Empire (Ghibellines), and the constant intervention of outside powers, northern Italy entered a period of economic dynamism and prosperity. Although some regions were ruled by either lay or ecclesiastical lords (including the papacy), the characteristic political arrangement that developed here was the commune—anchored in urban identity and citizenship, and dominated by oligarchies made of powerful families who had acquired fortunes as landowners, merchants, industrialists, or bankers. After 1250 important industries developed here, including cloth manufacture and leatherworking (both depending in part on trade with the Islamic world for raw materials), glass blowing, and papermaking. These industries provided a foundation for the tremendous expansion of commercial relations with both northern Europe and the Islamic world—despite repeated papal embargoes forbidding trade of a long list of "strategic materials" with Muslim powers. Over the next century, Italian trade in the East would expand, thanks in part to the rise of the Mongols and their domination of western, central, and eastern Asia. In the 1260s Genoa established a trading colony at Kaffa in the Crimea on the northern shores of the Black Sea; in 1271 the Venetian Marco Polo would embark on a trip that would lead him (he claimed) to China and back around Southeast Asia and India. Demand for "spices"—rare goods including not only edibles, like pepper, cinnamon, and cloves, but a whole range of plants and gems from India and Southeast Asia, and silk and manufactured goods from China—brought not only Italian merchants, but missionaries and diplomats east, leading to the establishment of a considerable European presence in the Mongol lands, including permanent consulates.

Pisa, Genoa, and Venice had all benefited from the death of Frederick II, and the respite from the claims over northern Italy by the "Holy Roman emperors." While Pisa mostly confined its activities to the western Mediterranean and Venice to the eastern, Genoa's activities brought it into conflict with both. A decisive victory over Pisa gave Genoa the upper hand after 1280, by which time it had opened up a route through the Straits of Gibraltar that brought its galleys to England and northern Europe. In the East, conflict between Venice and Genoa was not conclusive, although Venice was more successful at acquiring colonies in the Adriatic and Aegean. Prosperity was not confined to ports, and inland centers such as Pavia, Milan, Bologna, and Siena also benefited. Florence developed into Christian Europe's leading center for banking, and its currency, the *florin*, became the dominant money in the Mediterranean by 1350. The urban elites of northern Italy vied for power and prestige, giving rise to the transformative cultural wave known as the Renaissance, which embraced an idealized vision of ancient Roman culture and humanistic values. But the rise of these powerful families was also a destabilizing force, leading to open feuding within cities, which opened the way for interventions by outside powers, and increasingly acrimonious class divisions that undermined republican institutions, and tilted some cities into despotism.

With the Holy Roman Empire (the Germanic empire's designation since 1254) in crisis, the papacy's political power grew, although it did not match its pretensions. In 1302 Boniface VIII (1294–1303) promulgated *Unam Sanctam*, a bull that declared the pope sovereign over "every human creature," and yet by 1309 unrest had forced the papal court to decamp from Italy and take refuge in Avignon, in Provence. It would remain in this "Babylonian Captivity" until 1376, coming under increasing influence of the kings of France, who had been gradually extending their territorial domains southward. Louis IX had annexed Languedoc in the aftermath of the Cathar Crusades, and although Provence remained nominally independent, French influence was strong. While the French kings remained formally committed to crusade to bolster their claims as protectors of the church, they were too embroiled in struggles against European rivals and in economic difficulties. In order to address the latter, the Capetian kings alternated between expelling and readmitting Jewish communities, thereby appropriating the profits of Jewish credit under the guise of piously motivated retaliation for their usury. In 1288, the Angevin king of Naples, Charles I, expelled the Jews from his kingdom, England's Edward I followed in 1290. In 1307 Philip IV struck at the papacy and increased his treasury by turning on the Templars. Philip brought the knights up on trumped-up charges of apostasy, idol worship, and sodomy, executing the leaders and seizing the order's property in France. After Clement V (1305–1313) dissolved the Templars in 1312, other European kings followed suit. The rival Hospitaller order survived, establishing an independent territorial base on the island of Rhodes by 1310, although in continental Europe it came increasingly under the control of secular rulers.

From the Decline of Byzantium to the Rise of the Ottomans

The Venetian-dominated Latin Empire of Constantinople was brought down in 1261 by Michael Palaeologus, co-emperor of Nicaea (1259–1282), and his Genoese allies; but Byzantium, now comprising only western Anatolia and eastern Thrace, would never recover its pre-1204 glory. Mainland Greece would remain contested by various Latin powers and the Byzantine Despotate of Epirus. As Byzantine Anatolia unraveled, the emperor waged war in the West using Greek and Turkic troops, and finally staved off Latin aggression by submitting the Orthodox Church to the papacy in 1274. This gained him legitimacy in Latin eyes, but provoked popular and clerical unrest, resulting in the excommunication of the emperor and his patriarch by a synod of Greek bishops. The eastern Balkans saw the consolidation of a new Bulgarian Empire that had emerged in the 1180s, and claimed to have superseded Constantinople as the centre of Orthodox Christianity, while conflict in the western Balkans between Venice and Hungary provided an opportunity for Serbia to emerge as an imperial power. Here, in 1346 King Dušan the Mighty (1346–1355) proclaimed himself emperor, thus challenging both Constantinople and the revived Bulgarian Empire. Meanwhile, in eastern Anatolia, the Empire of Trabzon maintained its claims to the imperial title, while the Armenian kingdom in Cilicia sought to strengthen ties with the Latin West, notably the Kingdom of Cyprus—the last vestige of the Crusader Kingdom of Jerusalem, now ruled over by the French Lusignan family—and by allying with the pagan Mongols, whose arrival in the mid-thirteenth century transformed the Middle East.

FIGURE 6.5 A scene with soldiers, from an Armenian manuscript of the *Alexander Romance*, fourteenth century CE. The Picture Art Collection / Alamy Stock Photo.

"Mongols" is a generic name for the nomadic, pagan Central Asian nomads who circulated through the steppes west of China and north of the Himalayas, trading livestock, hides, and horses and serving as intermediaries in the land trade between China and the Mediterranean. In the late 1100s a prophet-like warrior named Temüjin united the Mongol tribes under his rule, taking the title Chinggis Khan ("Universal Emperor"; 1206–1227) and launching a wave of conquests that would create a land empire that stretched from the China Sea to the shores of the Mediterranean. Infamous for their brutality and deliberate and exemplary destruction of towns and cities, the Mongols devastated the urban and commercial centers of Khorasan including Bukhara (in 1220) before proceeding to Baghdad. They took the caliphal capital in 1258, unceremoniously murdering the 'Abbasid caliph, al-Musta'sim (1242–1258), and mercilessly sacking the city. It was said that the Tigris River ran black with the ink of the thousands of books cast into its waters. Meanwhile, another group had moved northwest, overrunning the Volga Rus in the 1220s and driving into Russia and eastern Europe. Attacking Hungary and the Balkans in the 1240s and 1250s, they crippled the Second Bulgarian Empire.

In Anatolia the Mongols encountered a cluster of Turkic and Armenian principalities, alternating between affiliation and conflict with Byzantium, whose imperial dignity held these lesser princes in awe. In Syria the Mongols struck the divided realms of Salah al-Din's heirs, the Ayyubids. Aleppo fell in 1260, and Damascus would be briefly seized in 1300; each suffered considerable destruction. The savage violence of the Mongols may have been exaggerated by chroniclers, but clearly they did severe damage to social, economic, and cultural infrastructures. On the other hand, the arrival of these seemingly unstoppable pagan hordes awoke the interest of the papacy, which dispatched missionaries deep into Central Asia with the hope of converting them. Local Christian powers, like Armenia and Cyprus, supported the Mongol campaigns against Ayyubid and Seljuq princes. Their appearance helped feed the myth of "Prester John" in the Latin West. Held to be a descendant of one of the Three Magi of the Gospels, Prester John was imagined to rule over a vast and powerful Christian kingdom in the East, from where he brings an army to rescue the failing enterprise of Crusade in the Holy Land. But, like the prospect of Mongol conversion to Christianity, Prester John was revealed to be a fantasy. In 1295 the Ilkhans—the Mongol dynasty ruling in Baghdad—converted to Islam and launched a cultural and commercial renaissance across the former 'Abbasid lands. Prester John never appeared. SEE SOURCEBOOK 6:2.

Thirty-five years earlier, in 1260, the Mongol reputation for invincibility had been punctured at the Battle of 'Ayn Jalut, south of the Sea of Galilee. Here, the Egyptian sultan Qutuz (1259–1260) routed an Armenian-supported Mongol force—a defeat the Mongol ruler, Hülegü (1256–1265), was prevented from avenging due to infighting among the various Mongol rulers. Qutuz was a member of the Mamluk (Slave) dynasty that had seized Egypt. After the death, childless, of the Ayyubid sultan al-Salih (1240–1249), his powerful widow, the former slave, Shajar al-Durr, took the throne with the support of the slave contingents who dominated the army. However, when the Syrian Ayyubid princes threatened to rebel as a consequence, a clique of Mamluk commanders deposed and murdered her. Referred to as "Bahris" because their garrison was a fortress set in the Nile (*bahr* means "river"), they would rule Egypt until 1382.

The Ayyubids had built their army by purchasing large numbers of Turkic and Caucasian boys, who were then converted to Islam and raised in spartan and regimented barracks. Scrupulously loyal to the regime and deeply bound to each other, they felt little connection to the populace. In a space of decades, the Mamluks imposed their rule on Syria and western Arabia, staving off the Mongols, and finally bringing an end to the Latin presence with the conquest of Acre in 1291. For all of their fearsome anti-Crusader rhetoric and their repression of Syrian and Lebanese Christians whom they saw as complicit with the Franks, the Mamluks cultivated commercial contacts with Latin powers, and Italian and Catalan traders had an important presence in Alexandria and Damascus. Their domestic policies were less liberal; Coptic Christians came under increasing pressure—particularly those in the administration—even as they flourished linguistically and culturally. Moreover, the Mamluks' carefully maintained identity as foreigners, coupled with their expansion of the *iqta'* tax-farming system, led to the increased exploitation of common and rural folk, and ultimately sapped their economy. To bolster their legitimacy in 1261 they acclaimed a nephew of the murdered al-Musta'sim as caliph in Cairo, and for the next 250 years they installed increasingly distant 'Abbasid family members as powerless figureheads.

The Mongol advance of the early 1200s had pushed increasing numbers of Central Asian Ghuzz nomads into Anatolia. Mongol forces decisively defeated the Seljuqs and their allies from Trabzon and Armenia at Köse Dağ in 1243, and for the next half century would dominate Anatolia from their stronghold at Erzurum. But with the Mongols in decline in the 1300s, one of these Ghuzz clans, the Osmanli, or "Ottomans," established a sultanate under Osman I (ca. 1280–1323) just east of Constantinople in 1299. Over the course of the next half century the Ottomans under Osman and his son, Orhan (1323/4–1362), subdued the various neighboring Turkic sultanates, and raided Byzantium. In 1331 they took Nicaea (now Iznik) as their capital. Unlike their Seljuq predecessors, the Ottomans coveted the title of "Roman Emperor" themselves. In the 1340s they began to intervene directly in Byzantine politics, provoking a dynastic struggle that further destabilized the already feeble empire and the volatile Balkans, and provided the opportunity to begin their campaigns of conquest in European Thrace in the 1350s. The second and definitive conquest of Byzantine Constantinople was only a century away.

MAP 6.2 The Mediterranean, ca. 1300.

Mediterranean Connections, ca. 1050–1350

Political and religious divisions, warfare, raiding, and piracy notwithstanding, the Mediterranean of 1050 to 1350 became increasingly integrated as a region and more firmly connected with ever more far-flung hinterlands. This was an era of migration. New peoples arrived on Mediterranean shores, those already in the region circulated and resettled, whether out of opportunity or by force, and travelers, missionaries, and diplomats struck out far across the three continents. Much of this movement was driven by trade, as well as the will to conquer, but religion and intellectual impulses spurred the circulation of pilgrims and missionaries. With either Jerusalem or the Holy Cities of Arabia imagined as the center of this ever-broadening world, the Mediterranean remained both conceptually and practically the crossroads of Africa, Asia, and Europe.

Routes and Kingdoms

The notion that European civilization somehow uniquely embodies curiosity and the enterprise of exploration is a modern Anglo-European myth. During the caliphal period intrepid (mostly Muslim) travelers not only crisscrossed the Dar al-Islam and Mediterranean shores but struck deep into Africa and Central and East Asia and fanned out across the Indian Ocean to Southeast Asia. A handful journeyed to Latin Europe, but this was an inhospitable land, with little to offer them, given that Latin and Jewish traders came south with northern goods.

Muslim scholars relied on the worldview of Ptolemy of

Alexandria (fl. ca. 150) whose spherical Earth was characterized by seven longitudinal "climates"—which affected both physical geography and the characteristics of their human inhabitants. Over the first three Islamic centuries this abstract conception was fleshed out by scholars and the observations of travelers who composed a genre of geographies named after the seminal *Book of Routes and Kingdoms* by the Andalusi geographer 'Abd Allah al-Bakri (d. 1094). These gazetteers described the major features and resources of the lands around the Mediterranean, together with itineraries linking major towns and cities, including distances, descriptions of the commodities found, and snippets of history, myth, legend, and advice. The genre reached its apogee with Muhammad al-Idrisi, a Moroccan educated in al-Andalus, who emigrated to the court of Roger II of Sicily. Under the king's orders, he compiled a description and atlas of the world—including Europe, Asia, much of Africa, India, and Oceania—as well as a mechanical silver planisphere in the 1160s.

This was also an era in which first-person travel memoirs—a genre known as the *rihla* (journey)—became popular in the Islamic world, written by travelers who embarked on the *hajj* or who traveled to seek their fortunes or in pursuit of knowledge. An Andalusi pilgrim, Muhammad ibn Jubayr, traveled to Egypt, Arabia, and Syria and back through Frankish Palestine and Norman Sicily in the 1180s, leaving rare firsthand glimpses of Muslim life in these Christian territories. His fellow countryman Abu Hamid al-Gharnati (the Granadan) had set out eastward a half century earlier, making the lower Volga his base, and settled for a time in Christian Hungary, where he served as a liaison for Muslim soldiers there and an unofficial envoy. In the 1180s the Persian al-Harawi composed a guide to the Muslim sacred sites (as well as some Christian and Jewish ones) in the Holy Land and around the Mediterranean. Around 1200 a former slave, the Byzantine-born Yaqut al-Rumi ("the Roman"), who was based at Baghdad and Aleppo, used his commercial journeys, which took him from Alexandria to Khwarizm, as the basis for several geographical and ethnographical works, notably his encyclopedic *Gazetteer of Lands*. The genre reached its height with Muhammad ibn Battuta (1304–1377) of Tangiers, who financed his travels through trade and occasional stints as a courtier and Islamic judge. In his old age he dictated accounts of his adventures and the peoples he encountered across Byzantium and Central Asia, through India, Southeast Asia, and China, across Arabia and down the east coast of Africa, and finally to

Although land travel remained perhaps the primary mode of transport and transportation on both the northern and southern shores of the Mediterranean, it was sea travel that bound together the Mediterranean economy, society, and culture. Despite the risks involved, sea travel was normally faster, safer, and more efficient in terms of moving commodities. With land nearly always in sight in the Mediterranean [see map 0.1], navigation was usually carried out along the coasts and from island to island (a practice known as *cabotage*), taking advantage of daytime shore breezes and the protection of land. Navigation was a skill passed down orally, and charts and instruments were rudimentary. Speed depended on wind and currents and varied between 1 and 5 knots per hour. Longer journeys could take weeks, but landfall was not normally more than a few days away. Whereas open-water navigation was possible all year round, in winter storms, rain and fog rendered coastal sailing rather dangerous.

Until the late eleventh century Andalusi, Fatimid, and Byzantine navies controlled the seas, but by the twelfth century it was Christian shipping from Italian republics, such as Venice, Genoa, Pisa and Amalfi, as well as Barcelona, Marseille, and other European ports that dominated the trade routes, carrying goods and passengers from both Christian and Muslim lands, although the Almohads and Marinids had navies, and the Ottomans would later develop a major fleet.

To the Sea in Ships

The introduction of the lateen (triangular) sail by the fifth century allowed ships to sail into the wind and contributed to the decline of the oar-powered ships of the classical age. By the fourteenth century Italians were combining lateen and broader square sails to make fast and maneuverable multimasted ships. Oared galleys required considerably larger crews and were usually reserved for warfare and military transport. The two most common ship types in the Mediterranean through the fourteenth century were round ships and galleys.

Most round ships had a length-to-beam ratio of about three to one and were powered by a single or double mast. A typical ship might measure 33 × 98 feet and have two or three decks. The round, stout shape maximized cargo capacity but rendered round ships slow, aggravated by the fact that they could only sail with favorable winds. Larger and slimmer versions, known as *navas*, were favored for military use, often adding a third mast, sometimes with a square sail.

The fast and maneuverable Byzantine *dromon* was a descendant of the great galleys of the classical period. Most seem to have been *biremes*, approximately 100 feet (30 m) in length, with two banks of rowers, perhaps 120 in total, together with the ship's crew and marines. Armaments included grappling hooks, heavy crossbows, Greek fire, and wooden "castles" for defense.

FIGURE 6.6 A Catalan *nau*, or roundship, ca. 1400 CE. Illustrated by David Bocquelet, Naval Encyclopedia. Image courtesy of the artist.

FIGURE 6.7 A Byzantine *dromon*, 800–1400 CE. Illustrated by David Bocquelet, Naval Encyclopedia, Image courtesy of the artist.

FIGURE 6.8 A ship sailing in the Persian Gulf, from an illuminated manuscript of *The Assemblies* of al-Hariri (d. 1122 CE), illustrated by al-Wasiti (1237 CE). © Fine Art Images / Heritage Image Partnership Ltd / Alamy Stock Photo.

Life on Board

Shipboard space was at a premium, and as a consequence, individuals of different social classes, ethnic origins, and religious communities found themselves living in an enforced intimacy—one compounded by the dangers faced by passengers and crew, including storm, shipwreck, and piracy. Few could swim. Personnel might consist of the owner or shipmaster, one or two captains or pilots, helmsmen, a quartermaster, first mate, accountant, lookout, and other crew members tasked with managing the

FIGURE 6.9 Almohad galleys as illustrated in the thirteenth-century *Cántigas de Santa María*, an illuminated collection of hymns in Galician credited to Alfonso X, king of Castile and Léon. Science History Images / Alamy Stock Photo.

sails, rigging, and so on, together with young boys apprenticing these various roles. Passengers might include men and women of various social ranks and conditions, from nobles to slaves. The largest ships might carry 1,000 passengers or more, who lived and slept on deck with their possessions and who may have had no more than 10 square feet of living space each. Privacy would have been minimal and conditions fairly squalid by modern standards. Prior to the twelfth century Jews and Christians often traveled on Muslim vessels, and afterward, Muslims and Jews on Christian vessels.

In 1184/85 when the Andalusi traveler Ibn Jubayr sailed from Acre in the East to Cartagena in the West on Genoese ships, the trip took six months (including one shipwreck), of which about sixty-five days were at sea. Muhammad ibn Battuta, who traversed not only the Mediterranean but the Indian Ocean in the 1300s, lost his fortune and his family at sea on more than one occasion and was forced to start from scratch. Contemporary memoirs and works of fiction recount the dangers of sea travel. Those captured by pirates might be held for ransom or sold into slavery. Salvage rights encouraged some people to profit from victims of shipwreck, who would be expected to pay the costs of their rescue, or might simply be enslaved by their rescuers. Unprotected women and children were vulnerable to physical and sexual abuse. The dead would be buried at sea, often unceremoniously and with little regard to ritual needs. Merchants could lose their entire fortune should their cargo be lost or taken at sea. On the other hand, sea travel provided opportunities to accumulate knowledge, prestige, and riches that would otherwise be impossible, and to see marvels and exotica unimaginable to those who never left land.

Discussion Questions

1. What effect would living in close quarters at sea have on how people saw others of different faiths and ethnicities?

2. How might a shipwreck survivor left with little or nothing rebuild his or her life in a strange and foreign land?

3. What complications, for themselves and for others, might result from someone dying or simply being lost at sea?

Further Reading

Broadhurst, Ronald J. C. *The Travels of Ibn Jubayr.* New Delhi: Goodword Books, 2001.

Kahanov, Yaacov, and Iskandar Jabour. "The Westbound Passage of Ibn Jubayr from Acre to Cartagena in 1184–1185." *Al-Masaq* 22 (2010): 79–101.

Kinoshita, Sharon. "Travelers and Texts." In *A Cultural History of the Sea,* ed. Margaret Cohen, vol. 2, "The Medieval Age," ed. Elizabeth Lambourn. London: Bloomsbury, forthcoming.

Kogman-Appel, Katrin. *Catalan Maps and Jewish Books : The Intellectual Profile of Elisha Ben Abraham Cresques, 1325–1387.* Turnhout: Brepols, 2020.

Malain, Nikki. "Live by the Sea, Die by the Sea: Confronting Death and the Dead in Medieval Liguria, 1140–1240 C.E." In *Dealing with the Dead: Mortality and Community in Medieval and Early Modern Europe,* ed. Thea Tomaini, 221–52. Leiden: Brill, 2018.

Waines, David. *The Odyssey of Ibn Battuta: Uncommon Tales of a Medieval Adventurer.* London: I. B. Tauris, 2010.

Mali—where he was scandalized to see slave women and young Muslim girls walking about topless.

By the mid-twelfth century Latinate Jews and Christians traveling on religious or cultural pilgrimage produced several works. The anonymous *Book of Saint James* (ca. 1145) provided a stop-by-stop guide for Christian pilgrims heading to Santiago de Compostela, and a number of descriptions of Jerusalem and the Holy Land were written by Latin pilgrims. Around the same time, the Navarrese traveler Benjamin of Tudela (d. 1173) left an account of Jewish communities he visited from Narbonne to Pumbedita in Iraq, while Samuel ben Samson from Languedoc memorialized his journey to Muslim Jerusalem and Palestine in 1210. SEE SOURCEBOOK 6:3.

The missionary impulse drove Christian travelers to the Islamic East and beyond. The Florentine Dominican friar Riccoldo da Montecroce spent years studying Arabic in Baghdad and roaming the Islamic East working as a muleteer in the 1280s and 1290s, while the Flemish Franciscan William of Rubrück left an account of his journey to the Mongol tent city of Karakorum in 1253 and his failed attempt to convert the khan Möngke (1251–1259) to Christianity. Most famous is Marco Polo's vivid if dubious memoir describing his twenty-four years of travel to China—where he claimed to have worked as a Mongol functionary—to India, and back. The Latin imagination was fully unleashed with *The Travels of Sir John Mandeville,* a best-selling hoax travelogue, in which the author claimed to have set out in 1322 and traversed the Near East and India, encountering all manner of strange plants, animals, and monstrous peoples. Transcontinental trade had existed for millennia, but it was the establishment of Pax Mongolica—"Mongol Peace"—across the length of Asia in the 1250s that transformed the incremental trade of the Silk Roads into a route that a single traveler could traverse in relative security.

This period, then, was one of intense mobility across and beyond the Mediterranean—with merchants, pilgrims of all faiths, missionaries and preachers, relic-hunters, and curiosity seekers plying the land and sea routes that crisscrossed the seaboard and stretched far out into its hinterlands. Muslim, Jewish, and Christian scholars moved throughout the region in search of masters, often rubbing shoulders and exchanging ideas in the cosmopolitan port towns and courts of the Mediterranean world. This was also an era of resettlement—Latin peasants were drawn from northern Europe to conquered Islamic lands in Iberia, Sicily, and the Levant; Central Asians rippled into Anatolia and the eastern Mediterranean; and Berber and sub-Saharan peoples moved north toward the southern shores of the sea. Latin rulers in the western Mediterranean encouraged Jews to settle in their newly conquered territories, even as they faced expulsion at the hands of the kings of France and England. Christian and Muslim mercenaries and adventurers, including royal princes, sojourned, often for years, in the service of infidel rulers. Latin merchant cities established trading colonies and settlements around the Mediterranean and Black Seas and on the islands within them, while in Byzantium and Latin Christendom, noblemen and noblewomen were uprooted and transplanted as they claimed far-flung noble or royal titles, or were sent off in marriages intended to consolidate their dynasties, or churchmen were assigned as bishops or abbots in foreign lands. Royal brides, who typically brought their own household retinues, served as an important medium for the dispersion of local tastes and traditions and the leavening of a broadly coherent Latin-Christian secular and religious culture.

Not all movement was voluntary. Slavery remained important in both the Islamic and Christian worlds. Cross-confessional warfare, raiding, and piracy saw prisoners of war and captive civilians abducted and carried to far-off lands. Legal and religious institutions developed to aid the manumission of captives, but many never returned—some pressed into hard labor, others as household slaves, with some, whether they converted or not, remaining in their new lands as freed subjects. Female captives typically pressed into domestic service were an important vector for informal cultural transmission through their role in their owners' households.

Conquest, rebellion, and revolution also provoked mass movement and cultural dissemination, not only through colonization, but by the deliberate dislocation of conquered peoples. The rise of the religiously rigorous Almohads in Iberia and the Maghrib in the late 1100s provoked a local Jewish diaspora toward Latin Europe and the Islamic East. In the following century an uncompromising Castilian military campaign and the uprisings of subject Muslims it triggered in southern Spain led to the exile of Andalusi populations to North Africa. In the 1280s the Mamluk sultan Qalawun (1279–1290) subdued the Holy Land and Levant, pushing out Maronite and Armenian Christians he viewed as Frankish allies, whereas a century and half earlier heterodox Druze and Nizaris (the "Assassins")—both offshoots of the Fatimids—had taken refuge in the same area, where they allied with Frankish powers against their Sunni Muslim enemies.

On the Road

Although we tend to associate the Mediterranean with sea travel, travel by land was just as important. Surviving Roman roads and bridges provided a framework for land transportation, although in the Islamic world, a shift away from wheeled cart traffic to camel, donkey, and human-powered transport reduced the importance of well-maintained roads. Land transport was less affected by weather and seasonal change than sea routes, and although there were risks of mishaps, whether at river crossings or on account of bandits or hostile local regimes, in many ways it was less risky. Routes connected inland cities, ran parallel to the coasts, and crossed the deserts and steppes of North Africa and western and central Asia. Merchants traveled in caravans for safety—larger ones like the great *hajj* convoys were like mobile cities, including travelers, merchants, soldiers, and members of the elite, together with slaves, servants, and family and household members. Travel was slow—perhaps eight miles per day—and was often done at night to avoid heat, with caravans camping at towns along their route, or at wells, oases, or caravanserais that were constructed along trade routes. Also known as *khan*s or *funduq*s, these were fortified inns—constructed as private initiatives or by rulers seeking to stimulate trade—where merchants could shelter their merchandise and animals. Rivers also served as inland routes, but these are rare in the Mediterranean region, and only a few—the Nile, the Ebro, the Rhine, the Po, and the Volga on the Black Sea—carried significant trade.

Shipping routes crisscrossed the sea, and pilots tended to follow routes that kept land in sight, whether along coasts, or island hopping. *Cabotage* was preferred to long-distance point-to-point navigation, with ships making landfall at ports all along their route, unloading and picking up commodities and passengers as they went. Coastal navigation mitigated the limiting effects of seasonal wind and sea currents and effectively separated the sea into two navigational zones divided by the axis formed by the Italian Peninsula and Ifriqiya. Seafaring was risky; loss

FIGURE 6.10 The Byzantine navy deploying "Greek fire," ca. 821; from a twelfth-century Sicilian manuscript of the *Synopsis of Histories* by John Skylitzes (d. 1101). Photo provided by Hispanic Digital Library, Biblioteca Nacional de España, CC-BY-4.0 International License.

of ship or life was not uncommon. Few people, even sailors, could swim, and the sea represented a chaotic and unpredictable force in the popular imagination. Nevertheless, transporting goods by sea was much faster than by land. A north–south crossing might take a week, while sailing from Barcelona to Alexandria, nearly the length of the Mediterranean, no less than fourteen days.

Ships were of varying propulsion and design and tended to be outfitted both for transport and defense. On the one hand shipping was vulnerable to piracy, and on the other merchants often combined raiding with trading. Narrow and relatively shallow-draft oar- and sail-powered galleys of ancient design dominated in the early Middle Ages and were used for military purposes into the early modern era. The dissemination of the triangular lateen sail from the fifth century forward improved ship speed, particularly upwind. By the eleventh century, ships were getting wider and deeper, with greater cargo capacity, influenced by the shorter, rounded *coca* (cog) and caravel designs from northern Europe. Oars became less important, with multiple sails providing power. By the twelfth and thirteenth centuries heavier, fully rigged three-mast ships were common. Wooden "castles" were added to the fore and aft of ships for defense, and to increase storage and passenger capacity, evolving eventually into the galleons of the sixteenth century, which incorporated these into hull design and featured multiple square and lateen sails.

Ships were constructed privately or in royal enterprises sponsored by Byzantine emperors, Muslim caliphs and princes, and eventually Latin kings and urban oligarchies. By the thirteenth century, royal and state arsenals (meaning "shipyard," from the Arabic *dar al-sina'a,* or "workshop") were found across the Latin Mediterranean. Before the advent of gunpowder, naval warfare was carried out much as infantry warfare, by ramming or grappling enemy ships, before engaging in close combat. Archers and large, ship-mounted crossbows enabled action at a distance, while Byzantine and Islamic navies used "Greek fire"—a rudimentary flame-throwing system to defend their ships with great effect.

Travel by sea carried considerable risk as a consequence of weather and pirates, helping stimulate partnership and investment arrangements to lower or distribute risk. Ships traveled in convoys to provide security in the event of accident or attack. Crews were often mixed, and Christian, Muslim, and Jewish merchants traveled on the same ships. Life aboard was cramped and squalid, which together with ever-present dangers forced passengers and crew of diverse faiths and ethnic backgrounds into intimate collaboration and necessary compromise, bound by their common fate and shared vulnerabilities. One by-product of this was *lingua franca*—apparently an informal, unwritten pidgin common to merchants and sailors. SEE SOURCEBOOK 6:4.

Prior to the twelfth century, navigation was performed by observation, the accumulated knowledge of currents and coastlines by shipmasters, taking bearings from the night sky, and instruments like a simple compass (from the thirteenth century) and the *kamal* or *qiyas*—rudimentary devices for calculating latitude from the stars. The sextant and astrolabe, used to cross the long distances of the Indian Ocean, were rarely used in the Mediterranean. Shipboard maps and navigational manuals (*rahmani,* in Arabic) from this era have not survived.

Between 1150 and 1350 Byzantine and Islamic dominance of the sea gave way to Latins, thanks to the collapse of the caliphal/imperial order and Latin sailors' adaptation of three innovations: the enclosed magnetic mariners' compass, accurate portolan maps illustrated with compass lines, and portolan manuals with detailed navigational instructions. Between the fall of the Almohads in the 1200s and the rise of the Ottomans in the 1400s Latin navies dominated the sea, and Latin merchant ships carried most cargo and passengers, including Muslims and Jews traveling within the Islamic Mediterranean. On his pilgrimage of the 1180s, Ibn Jubayr traveled on Latin ships.

At port and on land routes, merchants lodged in *funduq*s, which continued to be built in the Islamic Mediterranean, as well as Christian lands. By the thirteenth century, the term referred also to the self-contained merchant colonies-cum-embassies that Muslim authorities required foreign Christians to lodge in. Here they were subject to their own laws—each merchant republic or kingdom maintained its own *funduq*s—and were not subject to the legal restrictions placed on *dhimmi*s. The rare Muslim merchants who visited Latin lands stayed in separate *funduq*s, or lodged with local Muslims, if possible, whereas foreign Jewish merchants lodged with local communities. Like ships, port towns were by nature highly cosmopolitan, and provided an important zone for acculturation and exchange—it is no accident that these were sometimes the settings for informal or formal religious disputations and proselytizing, such as when Genoese merchants disputed against Jews at Ceuta (1179), and Mallorca (1286), or when the Mallorcan layman Ramon Llull was nearly stoned to death by a crowd of Muslims when he preached publicly at the port of Bijaya (in modern Algeria) in 1314.

Markets and Merchandise

By 1100 the population in Latin Europe was growing such that urban life and economic specialization could support domestic markets, and with the gradual reintroduction of cash, a market for luxury and manufactured goods. Although the region remained overwhelmingly agrarian, the move away from a "feudal" consumption economy enabled noblemen and kings in some regions to become rentiers who could live in towns away from their estates. They could then accumulate capital that could be used for purchasing or investing—a transformation that was kick-started by the Italian republics' engagement with the Islamic and Byzantine Mediterranean. The expansion of Latin power into Islamic Spain, North Africa, Sicily, the Holy Land, and Byzantine Anatolia and Italy brought plunder and, in some cases, a lucrative flow of tribute. New influxes of silver (from Germany) and gold (from the Islamic Mediterranean) further fueled trade.

Generally, the Latin West ran a trade deficit with the Mediterranean, and much of the cash paid in tribute by Muslim principalities returned to them in the form of purchases of finished goods, including ceramics, textiles—particularly silk—and leather goods. In the 1100s craftsmen in the Islamic world were creating ceramics, ivory boxes, and other goods specifically for the Latin export market. An example of these are the elaborately carved elephant tusks known as *olifants,* which were first made in the Islamic world, before becoming fashionable in the twelfth-century Latin West. Islamicate motifs were adapted for this new market, and the result is that it is often impossible to say where or by whom surviving *olifants* were manufactured.

Up to the 1200s Byzantine and Islamic craft and industrial production far outstripped the Latin world in terms of both quantity and quality. This is reflected, for example, in the fact that western European words for "leather-worker" or "shoemaker" (e.g., the Old French *cordewan,* whence the English *cordwainer*) mean "from Córdoba."

Until the 1200s the silk industry was dominated also by Byzantines and Muslims, and even after a Latin industry developed in Greece, the Levant, Sicily, and Spain, the quality of Islamic silk workmanship remained superior, as was the case with wool and cotton production and finishing up until at least the fourteenth century. Although Latins certainly minted coins, including in gold, high-quality Islamic coins—such as the Almoravid "Morabitun," and the Almohad "Mazmudi"—and their Christian imitations remained the standard for international trade in the western Mediterranean, until the rise of the Florentine *florin,* and the Venetian *ducat* in the mid-1200s. The value of once highly regarded Byzantine gold coins declined with the fortunes of the empire after 1050, suffering a series of debasements and reforms.

A commodity Latins were particularly interested in were relics, purchased, plundered, or stolen from churches and holy sites in Byzantium and the Levant. Relics were an investment that could pay larger dividends both in prestige and in generating donations to their host churches. The sheer volume of saintly remains that appears at this time reflects what was certainly an "industry" dedicated to producing new remains of long-dead saints. Up to fourteen churches claimed to hold the circumcised foreskin of Jesus, while the head of John the Baptist could be found in the Great Mosque at Damascus, in Sabastiya (Palestine), Rome, Munich, and Amiens, in France (having been looted from Constantinople by Crusaders).

Slaves continued to be an important commodity across the Latin and Christian Mediterranean. In the Muslim world, sub-Saharan Africa and the Caucasus had become the primary sources for slaves. In the 1100s and 1200s Latins enslaved Muslims though raiding and conquest, but after the early 1300s, as Latin military expansion slowed, Greek and Turkic slaves came to dominate. Although slave-ownership was widespread, the slaves themselves seem to have remained for the most part in Latin Mediterranean lands, and there was no significant export trade to northern Europe.

The Islamic and Byzantine Mediterranean faced distinct challenges. Relations between sedentary agriculturalists and urban dwellers and nomadic herders were crucial for the development of prosperity here. It was an uneasy symbiosis in which town dwellers provided food staples, finished craft goods, and new technology to the nomads, who supplied meat, hides, wool, and military protection to the urbanites. This relationship was a source of cultural dynamism and innovation, but also of instability. Ibn Khaldun (1332–1406), the Tunisian historian often described as the father of sociology, developed a theory that saw history as a process of conflict between nomadic and settled peoples, in which warlike nomads, fortified by *'asabiyya* (group solidarity), coalesced to overthrow complacent sedentary regimes. Once in power the group in question would settle down into individualistic decadence, and dissipate its own *'asabiyya,* only to be conquered by the next group of barbarians—a cycle that typically spanned only three generations. These relations between settled peoples and nomads—who gradually accepted Islam and were drawn into the sedentary world—were instrumental in Islamic overland trade, notably the establishment of trade routes across the Sahara that brought the African gold that drove prosperity of the Islamic Mediterranean.

However, as in the early period it was local and regional trade that drove the Mediterranean economy and most impacted policy. Commerce in indispensable staples, such as grain, sugar, and salt, was fundamental and contributed to a regional unity that overrode confessional frontiers. The need for grain for urban populations bound the economic and political destiny of Christian Sicily to Muslim Ifriqiya in the twelfth century and beyond, and drove expansion into the northern shores of the Black Sea, which became a breadbasket for Byzantium. The highly varied microregions of the Mediterranean stimulated specialization and exchange. Some commodities, like mastic (a resin used for medicine and cooking), alum (for fixing dye in cloth), and murex (snail shells for purple dye), could only be found in specific locales, while other valuable products, like sugar and saffron, could only be cultivated in certain areas. Silk manufacture, confined at first to Byzantium and certain Islamic lands, was treated like a state secret, which slowed down its dissemination, although by the late 1200s workshops had been established as far north as Paris. The urbanization and connectedness of the Mediterranean region encouraged the development of specialized craft production and the refinement of technical skills in specific locales, such as working with filigree (decorative embroidery done in metal thread), given that products could be effectively distributed across the region and beyond. Trade and economic exchange knew no borders in the medieval Mediterranean, integrating individuals of various faiths and ethnicities in chains of supply, production, and distribution, and defying confessional boundaries between Christian and Muslims regimes.

Strategies and Structures, ca. 1050–1350

The economic and political integration of the Latin, Byzantine, and Islamic Mediterranean in the period between 1050 and 1350 was characterized by dynamics of both coercion and collaboration. This was an era of conflict and colonization, and of organized violence often framed as religious struggle, whether between Islam and Christianity, Christianity and Judaism, or rival Islams and Christianities. Newcomers who arrived from the continental hinterlands quickly found themselves obliged by dint of the interdependent Mediterranean economy to "acclimatize" to the regional sociocultural environment, and established mutually beneficial relationships with "infidel" regimes. This acclimation served as a catalyst for the development of institutional and legal structures that bridged the various confessional zones, and ultimately for the reconfiguration and reorientation of the Mediterranean economy toward an increasingly dynamic and dominant Frankish Europe.

Colonization, Commerce, and Culture

Colonization took several forms in this period, including warfare and conquest, movements of settlers and colonists, and commercial expansion. Not all military activity can be characterized as colonization, and much merely entailed the displacement of an existing monarch or upper nobility by another drawn from within the same broad cultural and religious community. However, even when, for example, the Hohenstaufens under Emperor Henry VI took Sicily from the Normans, they would have brought with them members of their household, nobility, and clergy. This was not a migration, but nevertheless had a cultural impact. Princesses, who were often married to foreign kings, also served to disseminate culture through their entourages.

Others came in larger numbers—such as the Burgundians and other "French" peoples, who moved into the Iberian Peninsula and the Latin East and came with numbers of Frankish settlers in tow; the Seljuqs (and eventually the Mongols and Ottomans), who were accompanied by significant numbers of soldiers and settlers of various Turkic extractions; the Almoravid and Almohad movements, each of which involved the circulation and settlement of Berber tribes in new lands; and the Venetians, who established substantial colonies, such as at Crete. In some cases, the impact of this settlement was transitory, as with Latin settlement in the eastern Mediterranean and Ifriqiya; at other times colonized regions were permanently and dramatically transformed, as in Turkic Anatolia or Latin-dominated al-Andalus.

The population boom of the Medieval Optimum helped to push Latin expansion in the Islamic Mediterranean, but by the mid-twelfth century the supply of settlers was running low. This forced rulers to actively recruit colonists among the increasingly emancipated serfs of Latin Europe by advertising generous terms of liberty and municipal self-government, to use Jews as settlers, and to induce Muslim townsfolk and farmers to remain in their native lands under Christian rule. This can be seen most clearly in the Iberian Peninsula, where the pace of conquest in the twelfth and thirteenth centuries far outstripped the availability of colonists, with the result that Christians ruled over areas populated by free Muslims substantially, or even in the majority.

In the 1100s in order to attract settlers both from their own territories and from the wide Latin world to the expanding frontier, rulers in northern Spain began to grant generous charters that freed common folk from noble control. This created a free population that was expected to participate in urban militias and to serve in the king's campaigns, but also to engage in raiding and pillage against neighboring Muslim lands. Many offered freedom even to escaped criminals and serfs once they had lived in these towns for a year and a day. Here, the practice of warfare provided a means for former peasants to enrich themselves and gain noble status through feats of arms and by acquiring loot. This contributed to something of an "Old West" environment, where raiding, cattle and sheep rustling, and the killing or capture of infidels were carried out as organized campaigns or

Successfully navigating in both coastal waters and the open sea required a tremendous amount of skill and knowledge, most of which was passed down orally. Navigational instruments were rudimentary prior to the fifteenth century, effectively limited to the compass and the *kamal* (for calculating latitude), with the latter superseded by the mariners' astrolabe in the thirteenth century. Since antiquity pilots had also used *peripli*—written notes describing routes, ports, and hazards—but none survive from before the 1400s. They may have used shipboard maps or charts, but none have survived. Extant maps tend to be deluxe versions, produced for members of the elite and not necessarily intended for actual travel; however, they do provide us with clues as to how contemporaries saw the world and where the Mediterranean fit in it.

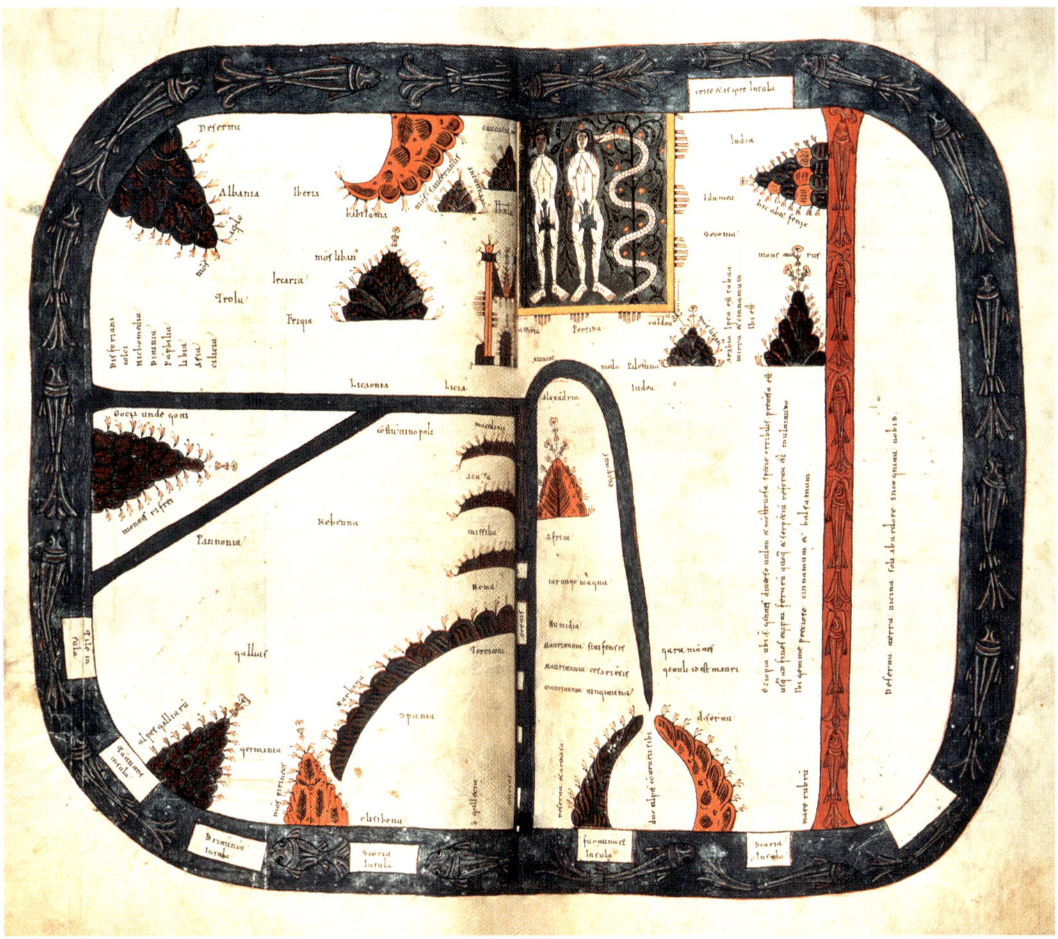

FIGURE 6.11 World map from the Beatus of Liébana, Castile, 1091–1109 CE. British Library, London, UK © British Library Board. All Rights Reserved / Bridgeman Images.

FIGURE 6.12 Reconstitution of al-Idrisi's world map by the German cartographer Konrad Miller (1929), shown upside down. Rotated upside down by PHGCOM. Photograph provided by Wikimedia Commons under the Creative Commons |Public Doman license.

V.
IV.
III.
II.
I.
IDRISI vom Jahr 1154 n.Ch.

FIGURE 6.13 The "Catalan Atlas," Mallorca, 1375 CE. Bibliothèque nationale de France. Photograph provided by Wikimedia Commons under the Creative Commons |Public Doman license.

The Silos Apocalypse World Map (1091–1109)

This map is found in a manuscript completed between 1091 and 1109 at the monastery of Silos in northern Spain. The manuscript is an edition of an eighth-century "Commentary of the Apocalypse of St. John," by the Spanish monk Beatus of Liébana. The map represents the inhabited world and is based on classical notions of the globe, as summed up by the Spanish encyclopedist Isidore of Seville (d. 636) in his *Etymologies*.

> The globe derives its name from the roundness of its circle, because it resembles a wheel. . . . Indeed, the Ocean that flows around it on all sides encompasses its further reaches in a circle. It is divided into three parts, one of which is called Asia, the second Europe, the third Africa.[1]

As for the Mediterranean, Isidore noted:

> The Great Sea is the one that flows from the Ocean out of the west, turns to the south, and finally stretches to the north. It is called "great" because the other seas are smaller in comparison with it. This is also called the "Mediterranean" because it flows through the "middle of the land" (*media terrae*) all the way to the East, separating Europe, Africa, and Asia. . . . And just as the land, though it is a single thing, may be referred to with various names in different places, so also this Great Sea is named with different names according to the region.[2]

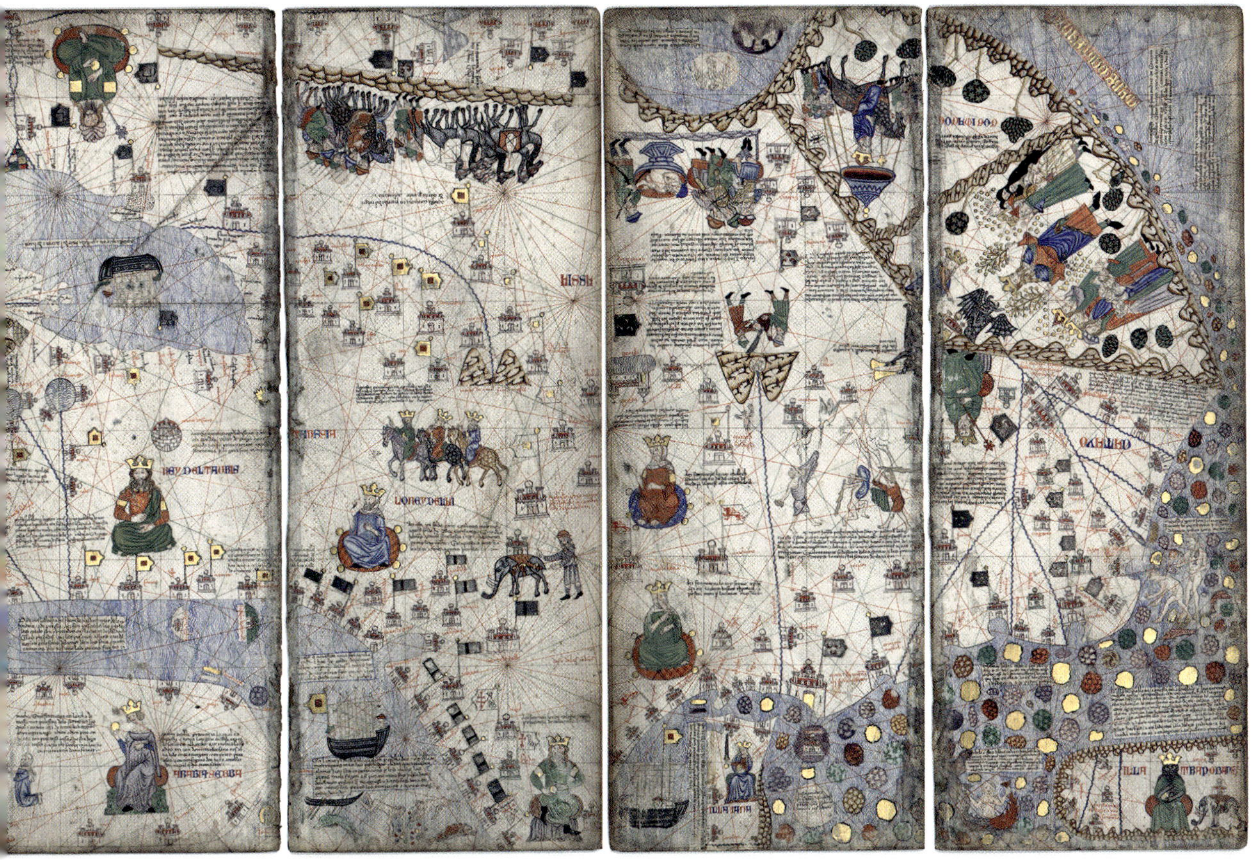

The map is oriented with the East at the top and the Mediterranean in the middle, fed by the Nile, and with the Don and its tributary, the Danube, connecting with the ocean. Jerusalem, the only city identified, is near the center, and the Garden of Eden can be seen at the top center. The Red Sea is colored red, and fish can be seen in the oceans and seas. Several mountain ranges are featured, as are islands, including Great Britain and Ireland. Few other details are included.

The Map of Roger (1150/60s)

Among the many Muslim scholars attracted to the court of Roger II of Sicily was Muhammad al-Idrisi (d. 1164/65?), a geographer, botanist, and poet born in Ceuta, Morocco, and educated at Córdoba. At Palermo he was commissioned by the king to compile a deluxe illustrated geography and a map of the world engraved on silver. According to al-Idrisi,

> [Roger] wished that he should accurately know the details of his land and master them with a definite knowledge, and that he should know the boundaries and routes both by land or sea and in what climate they were and what distinguished them as to seas and gulfs together with a knowledge of other lands and regions in all seven climates.[3]

Known commonly as the *Kitab Rujjar* (Book of Roger), this Arabic and Latin text included seventy regional maps, and was based on the work of the Ptolemaic school of geography of Baghdad, as well as on the writings of other geog-

FIGURE 6.14 The "Catalan Atlas," detail (enhanced), 1959 copy of 1375 original. Photograph by Library of Congress, Geography and Map Division, provided by Wikimedia Commons under the Creative Commons 3.0 license.

raphers and travelers. It was a popular work, circulating widely in Arabic and Latin in the centuries that followed.

The map is oriented with the south at the top (customary in the Islamic world), and is densely marked with cities and towns, rivers, mountain ranges, and other features labeled by name and rendered in detail. The illustration here is a nineteenth-century collage reproduction of the individual regional maps.

The Catalan Atlas (1375)

This deluxe world map is attributed to the Jewish cartographer Abraham Cresques (d. 1387) of Mallorca and his son, Jahuda, and was commissioned by King Pere the Ceremonious of Aragon and later presented to Charles V of France, who had requested the best map Pere could provide. It was drawn on parchment, which was attached to six large wooden boards. Mallorca was an important center of cartography and navigational technology, in which Jews played an important role. After the pogrom of 1391 Jahuda converted to Christianity and went on to serve at the naval academy founded by Henry the Navigator of Portugal.

Catalan Atlas, (enhanced) detail

The western parts of the map imitate contemporary *portolans*, or navigational maps, that include compass bearings for navigation, combined with a traditional world map. The areas of Africa and Asia were fleshed out by late medieval travelers' accounts. Important towns and cities and geographical features are marked. Flags denote kingdoms and principalities. Detailed illuminations and annotations in Catalan illustrate important natural features, local commodities, travelers, ships (including Chinese junks), caravans (including the Polo brothers'), exotic creatures, and personages, such as Mansa Musa and biblical figures.

Discussion Questions

1. If not used for travel, what purpose did these maps serve and for whom?

2. What does the relative size and position of the Mediterranean tell us about its place in the cultures that produced these maps?

3. Can the choices of what is represented on these maps be seen as reflecting larger social, economic, or cultural shifts?

Further Reading

Harley, J. B., and David Woodward, eds. *The History of Cartography*. Vol. 1, *Cartography in Prehistoric, Ancient, and Medieval Europe and the Mediterranean*. Vol. 2, *Book One: Cartography in the Traditional Islamic and South Asian Societies*. Chicago: University of Chicago Press, 1987, 1992.

Kogman-Appel, Karin. *Catalan Maps and Jewish Books: The Intellectual Profile of Elisha Ben Abraham Cresques, 1325–1387*. Turnhout: Brepols, 2020.

———. "Fictive Travel and Mapmaking in Fourteenth-Century Iberia." In *Maps and Travel in the Middle Ages and the Early Modern Period*, ed. Ingrid Baumgärtner et al., 136–64. Berlin: de Gruyter, 2019.

Pinto, Karen C. *Medieval Islamic Maps: An Exploration*. Chicago: University of Chicago Press, 2016.

Talbert, Richard J. A., and Richard W. Unger. *Cartography in Antiquity and the Middle Ages: Fresh Perspectives, New Methods*. Leiden: Brill, 2008.

Notes

1. Stephen A. Barney, *The Etymologies of Isidore of Seville* (Cambridge: Cambridge University Press, 2006), 285.

2. Barney, 277–78.

3. S. Maqbul Ahmad, "Cartography of al-Sharīf al-Idrīsī," in *The History of Cartography*, vol. 2, book 1, *Cartography in the Traditional East and Southeast Asian Societies*, ed. J. B. Harley and D. Woodward (Chicago: University of Chicago Press, 1994), 159.

private initiatives, and further nurtured the ideal of the Christian Reconquest of Spain that was coalescing at this time. Such opportunities to acquire freedom and plunder attracted settlers from across Christendom and led to the development of what some historians have characterized as a "society organized for war."

Indirect colonization was also common. The small dynastic states and urban republics of the postcaliphal Islamic Mediterranean were vulnerable to the strong-arm tactics of Latin princes and trading cities, which under threat of attack and the promise of protection, could force these weaker states into tributary relationships, often as a prelude to outright conquest. A similar dynamic can be observed in the Seljuq and Ottoman expansions into Anatolia and Syria. Occasionally, territories found themselves under the "co-dominion" of more than one colonial power. For example, in the Orontes valley of Syria and north of the Sea of Galilee in the 1100s, Frankish and Seljuq lords came to arrangements whereby both would extract revenue and rule over the same rural communities simultaneously.

Although the age of caliphal power had passed by the mid-eleventh century, and the Islamic Mediterranean was fractured and under attack by foreign Christians and Muslims, the structures of Islamic law and the robustness of the Arabic language, neither of which depended on the power of a state, continued to provide a coherent legal and cultural framework for commerce and diplomacy that bridged the region. Traders and travelers, like Ibn Battuta in the fourteenth century, could still move from the Atlantic coast to Central Asia, and even beyond, speaking only Arabic and subject to the same Islamic laws and broadly similar cultural expectations. Although Byzantine law was by definition limited to the zones under imperial control, Greek and the broad Byzantine culture provided a similar element of cohesion on the northern shores of the eastern Mediterranean. The Latin world lacked such a degree of cohesion, despite the fact that Latin served as a common language, and the church, through the papacy and canon law, provided a degree of institutional and legal unity.

Whereas in the Islamic Mediterranean in this period Arabic remained effectively the single language of literature and administration among Muslims, in the Latin West, local Romance vernaculars evolved into literary and eventually administrative tongues. This process further accelerated with the foundation of universities in the 1100s and 1200s and the development of secular bureaucracies. Basic literacy and numeracy spread to non-clergy of the lower classes because they were a prerequisite for trade. By the late 1200s not only business contracts, but many royal and municipal records were kept in local languages in the Iberian and Italian Peninsulas and the South of France. Popular literature, including poetry, history, fiction, and autobiography, were written in local Romance, beginning with the Occitan poetry of the twelfth-century troubadours, and on to the *Song of the Cathar Wars* (1213), Ramon Llull's Mallorcan novel *Blanquerna* (ca. 1283), and the Archpriest of Hita's Castilian *Book of Good Love* (1330). Dante's *Divine Comedy* (ca. 1320) and Petrarch's sonnets of the early 1300s were both written in Italian dialects, and by the mid-fourteenth century the humanist movement with its strong vernacular imprint had spread across the Latin Mediterranean.

The Latin world had a strong tradition of secular lawmaking, wherein each prince legislated for his own realms—a trend that was intensified in the 1200s as monarchs invoked imperial-style privilege and promulgated systematic law codes modeled on Roman precedents. Church law, on the other hand, was meant to be universal, but in many ways the papacy resembled another monarchy in its approach to both establishing laws and bending them out of convenience. For example, the embargoes popes had promulgated since the 1170s forbidding the shipment of strategic commodities (including foodstuffs, arms, and so on) to the Islamic world were often ignored or could be evaded through the purchase of exemptions. Like secular rulers, the papacy and many bishoprics cultivated trade and diplomatic relations with Muslim powers in spite of church laws to the contrary. Thus, the popes and the ideologically rigid Almohads corresponded and exchanged embassies in the period around 1200, and in the 1250s economic concerns led Alexander IV (1254–1261) to intervene against the bishop of Tarragona's planned crusade against Hafsid Tunis.

The Latinate and Islamic legal and linguistic cultures that dominated the Mediterranean may have rested on distinct ideological and institutional foundations, but they were not essentially incompatible. Through colonization and trade and tributary relationships these two spheres blended; the common cultural and theological traditions of the Mediterranean rendered their traditions "intelligible" to each other and provided common ground for collaboration. For example, Muslim and Christian princes generally did not dispute each other's legitimacy, but recognized themselves and their peers as all ruling "by the grace of God"—the same God of Abraham each worshipped according to his own faith. They referred to each other as "friends," and spoke of their "love" for each other. These may have been diplomatic niceties, but they reflect the concessions of legitimacy that were the foundation of Mediterranean diplomacy, and—together with the fractured nature of Christian legal culture—served as a catalyst for the development of an informal body of "international law" governing trade and maritime security that bridged Christendom and the Dar al-Islam.

Collaboration and Credit

Diplomacy (and espionage) was carried out by various means and agents. Trusted merchants could serve as formal or informal envoys to foreign powers, whether carrying letters, conveying petitions, gathering intelligence, or facilitating the ransom and return of captives and prisoners of war. Because of their "unofficial" status, merchants could often move widely and discretely, coming into contact with different types of people in the places they visited. Noblemen and warriors also served as envoys—the common chivalric values and vocation of the military aristocracy bridged cultural divisions between Latins, Byzantines, and Muslims and made it possible for knights to establish personal bonds even with infidels. The much-romanticized amicable exchanges between Richard the Lionhearted and Salah al-Din at the siege of Acre in 1192 are one example of this widespread dynamic. Thus, the Muslim and Christian mercenaries who served in infidel courts across the Mediterranean provided another diplomatic and intelligence channel as well as a vector of acculturation. Men of learning, who in each of the three faith communities were typically also men of religion, were preferred as envoys, thanks to their intellectual and cultural sophistication and their high level of linguistic proficiency—crucial for drafting delicate diplomatic correspondence. Clergy also embodied a prestige recognized even across religious lines; hence, the success of monastic orders, such as the Trinitarians and the Order of Mercy, in freeing captives held in Islamic lands. Region-wide networks of diasporic communities, including Armenians (in the eastern Mediterranean) and Jews (in the West), favored these peoples' recruitment as diplomats. Many Christian rulers used Arabic-speaking Jews as envoys to Muslim courts—a lucrative niche that Jewish courtiers endeavored to safeguard.

Diplomacy, including that related to trade and nautical security, was rooted in a regional understanding of maritime law that derived from Romano-Byzantine precedents that had been codified in the Rhodian Sea Law (ca. 800), which governed matters such as commercial transactions and partnerships, jettison, shipwreck, salvage, and piracy. Muslim jurists made adjustments to bring it in line with *shari'a* law. Irrespective of political and religious divisions, the various parties around the Mediterranean had a strong interest in maintaining order on the seas, while retaining the right to legitimate warfare and privateering. This broad legal consensus was supplemented by individual treaties between rulers aimed at opening up favorable trading conditions and protecting their subjects from capture at sea. Hence, it was in this period that ships began the custom of flying flags indicating their political affiliation. By the thirteenth century Christian royal law codes also incorporated nautical provisions, and specific maritime law codes were promulgated at Barcelona, Messina, and Genoa. As the Catalan mercantile domain expanded in the fourteenth century, the Barcelona customs were spread through the establishment of "maritime consulates" across the region. This coincided roughly with the creation of stock or commodity exchanges in ports and inland cities across the Latin Mediterranean.

As part of the larger "commercial revolution" affecting Latin Europe, merchants, craftsmen, and laborers began to organize in self-governing guilds and religiously framed confraternities in order to control and protect prices, technology, and production. Given that technical knowledge was regarded as a form of patrimony, these organizations typically ran parallel to family and kin networks. Outside of corporations, strategies developed for establishing and governing limited partnerships, known as *commendas,* and for investing in and insuring commercial endeavors. Contracts were governed generally by "common law," which like the church's canon law coalesced in twelfth-century Bologna out of Roman precedents before spreading across the Latin West. At a time when institutions were relatively weak, however, it was traders' need to maintain their reputation as honest and trustworthy individuals that also helped reinforce agreements. This has been noted particularly in the Islamic Mediterranean with some historians crediting Jewish traders' region-wide social cohesion and the importance of maintaining a good reputation as a major element in Jewish success in long-distance trade prior to the evolution of European contract law and institutions. SEE SOURCEBOOK 6:5.

This communal cohesion, together with the religious prohibition of Christians lending at interest to other Christians, was the foundation of Jews' near monopoly over credit in the Latin world prior to the thirteenth century, when rulers and churchmen nurtured Jewish urban communities in order to stimulate commerce. In spite of the church's prohibitions and royal laws limiting usury, however, both Jews and increasingly Christian lenders devised schemes to disguise the illegally high interest rates they charged. Canon law notwithstanding, by the end of the thirteenth century Christians, including clergy and ecclesiastical foundations, were actively engaged in lending and speculative activities such as tax-farming, leaving Jews vulnerable to popular and official repression, as they came to be seen as economic competitors. The crises and crop failures of the early 1300s exacerbated tensions, as increasingly indebted Christians blamed Jews for their financial predicaments. Islamic law posed similar restrictions vis-à-vis charging interest to Muslims, but work-arounds had developed early, and Islamic jurists, many of whom were themselves members of the commercial class, were disposed to interpret the law in such a way that made lending at interest possible, and also developed a legal apparatus for a whole array of investment, partnership, land lease, and sharecropping arrangements.

In the Latin world, longer-term multiphase ventures might be formalized as a firm or company (*compagnia*), which specialized in commerce or lending, and which was often linked to the governmental (and thus, military) apparatus of the state. In the 1330s the Bardi company—one of the two leading banks of Florence—

FIGURE 6.15 Caricaturized Jewish moneylenders from Alfonso X of Castile's *Cántigas de Santa Maria*, Castile, 1270s–1280s CE. Biblioteca Monasterio del Escorial, Madrid, Spain / Tarker / Bridgeman Images.

had assets more than five times greater than those of the English crown. New bookkeeping techniques, such as "double-entry" accounting, were adopted, as was the "letter of exchange," which facilitated the safe transfer of funds between distant locales. Similar developments had already taken place in various forms in the Islamic world, and these at times provided models for European innovations, even when the latter were couched in Romanized legal vocabulary. In theory, Islamic law, which is rooted in individual responsibility, is not amenable to the existence of corporations; but institutions, such as the pious endowment (*waqf* or *hubus*), which could include agricultural and commercial enterprises, hospitals, schools, and baths, functioned effectively as firms. What did not occur in the Islamic world was the tight coordination of political power and commercial energies that came to characterize Latin Christendom and laid the foundation for European mercantile colonialism, which would mark the period beginning in 1350.

The Reorientation of the Mediterranean Economy

The increasing robustness of the Latin European economy between 1050 and 1350 was a major factor in the reorientation of Mediterranean trade in this era. Latin Europe became a complex urbanized society of producers, consumers, and merchants. As access to new reserves of precious metal were opened up, whether from mining, plunder, or tribute, currency came back into common use, further lubricating the Latin economy. Despite the military conflict that often characterized Frankish-Islamic relations, the Latin and Muslim spheres became increasingly integrated and codependent economically. In practice, papal injunctions against trade with the Islamic world were as ineffective as church prohibitions against usury. The rise of the Mongols also benefited the Latin world, both by opening up the land routes across Asia and by damaging the competing economy of the Islamic East. Although trade remained bilateral through this period, the balance shifted in favor of the Latin world. In the Islamic eastern Mediterranean, increasingly dependent on foreign trade for staples, and sapped by the abuses of the *iqta'* system, wages fell, prompting popular unrest, which sometimes targeted *dhimmis* as scapegoats.

Whereas at the beginning of this era the chief axis of commerce in the Mediterranean ran east to west from Muslim Egypt to Islamic Spain, by 1300 the north–south axis, controlled by Christians, was edging toward dominance. The importance of Muslim port cities declined as they became way stations on trade routes rather than the principal centers of production and consumption. The opening of routes through the Straits of Gibraltar to the North Sea exacerbated this trend, given that long-distance trade could now bypass Mediterranean lands.

However, by the first decades of the fourteenth century, there were indications that the Latin economy was in trouble. The Medieval Optimum was giving way to a cooling trend in Europe, which, together with the over-farming of marginal lands, would contribute to a series of crop failures and famines in the 1320s. The aristocracy's eager embrace of the rentier culture, characterized by perpetual contracts that did not factor in price fluctuations, left them vulnerable to economic upheavals and, especially, to inflation. When prices rose, the value of rents fell, impoverishing the nobility and benefiting the peasantry. In 1337 war broke out between the Plantagenet dynasty (the branch of the Angevins that held the throne of England from 1154) and the Valois dynasty (a branch of the Capetians) over control of France. This "Hundred Years' War" would eventually engulf almost the entire Latin West. In 1345 it would claim among its casualties the great Florentine banks of the Bardi and Peruzzi families—victims of a massive default of war loans made to Edward III Plantagenet (1327–1377), king of England. By 1350 the Mediterranean economy in general, and the Latin economy in particular, had become overextended, overleveraged, and vulnerable; the famines, plague, and wars that struck in midcentury pushed the economy of the Western world into crisis, and provoked a whole series of political, economic, social, and cultural transformations both across the Mediterranean and deep into its continental hinterlands.

CHAPTER SEVEN

Mediterranean Societies

Waves slapped against the sides of the ship bobbing in the surf in a little cove on the edge of Palermo as a stream of chests and crates were hurriedly loaded onto the swaying deck. Suddenly, hushed voices in Sicilian and Arabic gave way to shouted orders to raise anchor and prepare sails, and the rowers paddled out to sea. Those chests were full of treasure, and at the boat's helm was Peter el Caid—"the Commander"—chamberlain, royal admiral, and confidant of Margaret of Navarre, the queen-regent of Sicily.

By birth a Berber from Jerba (an island off Tunisia) named Ahmad, Peter, was likely enslaved at about age ten when the Normans took the island in 1135. Castrated, baptized, and incorporated into the royal household as one of the "palace Saracens"—the crypto-Muslim eunuchs who ran Roger II's kingdom—he rose quickly, serving as an officer in the *diwan* (the financial administration) by 1141. Known for his generosity and easy manner, Peter accumulated friends and allies, together with considerable wealth and property. By 1159 he was serving William I as admiral, leading an unsuccessful attack on Almoravid Mallorca, perhaps in an attempt by William to curry favor with the Almohads, who were rolling relentlessly eastward toward Norman Ifriqiya. Soon after, he was sent with a massive fleet to relieve the Almohad siege of Mahdia. Here, some sources claim, Peter inexplicably and deliberately withdrew, leading to the massacre of the Norman garrison, and the Almohad conquest of the Norman Kingdom of Africa. Nevertheless, Peter's fortunes continued to rise at court.

When William I's dependence on the palace Saracens provoked a revolt by the nobility in 1160, the king was briefly captured, and his son and heir was killed along with many of the eunuchs. Once order was restored, William and the eunuchs took violent revenge on the aristocracy, further polarizing the kingdom. Appointed master chamberlain, Peter—known as "Baron," and "Perroun" in Latin and Greek (both corruptions of the French for "Little Peter")—was put in charge of the prosecutions. Riding around the island and mainland counties with a large contingent of knights and archers, he pressed the nobles back into loyalty to the king with a combination of threats and bribes.

On William's death in 1166, his son, the Arabic-speaking, thirteen-year-old William II, inherited the throne under the tutelage of his mother, the Spanish-born Margaret of Navarre. Facing resistance from the local magnates and even her own kinsmen, the queen appointed the now-manumitted Peter—according to a contemporary chronicler, "like all the palace eunuchs . . . a Christian only in name and appearance, but a Muslim by conviction"—as her right hand. His work would have had him in close contact with the kingdom's ally, Fatimid Egypt, and its rivals, the Almohads. There was ample opportunity to play a double game. As his wealth and patrimony grew, Peter adopted children, and likely patronized the Sicilian Muslim community.

Although the rank and file of the army largely supported Peter, the Latin magnates chafed at the "feminization" of Margaret's court and at the status of a castrated former slave. Plots against Peter simmered, and as Margaret's grip on power wavered, he made his move. Packing up as much treasure as he could carry, including, it was rumored, the crown jewels, he set off by night with a cadre of trusted eunuchs, sailing south to Ifriqiya. Here, he interviewed with the Almohad caliph, 'Abd al-Mu'min, pledging his support and openly returning to Islam under the name Ahmad al-Siqilli. Next, he headed to Morocco to take up a commission as admiral under the caliph's son and successor, Yusuf, for whom he built up the Almohads' war fleet and pursued the remnants of the Almoravid regime in the Balearics and Africa. Serving until at least 1185, he never attacked his former kingdom, and likely helped broker the Almohad-Norman peace of 1180. Such was their esteem for him that Margaret and her circle refused to believe Peter's treachery and continued to defend his honor. But his defection empowered her enemies and accelerated her political demise and that of the Norman dynasty in 1194, and the establishment of the Hohenstaufens under Emperor Henry VI.

Peter's career constitutes a window onto the complex politics of identity in the multiconfessional, multicultural Mediterranean of the era of the Crusades. Peter, himself a victim of organized violence—enslaved and mutilated, robbed of his family, gender, religion, and identity—rose to the pinnacle of power in a Christian kingdom, while all but openly practicing Islam—a capital crime. But neither his foreign origin, his infidel inclinations, nor the stain of slavery prevented his talents from being recognized and rewarded, although they also served as ammunition for his enemies. In the end, he was clever enough to stay one step ahead, using his skills to reinvent himself and reach equal heights and greater prestige in the service of the enemies of his former lords.

The Politics of Diversity

Because of its geographic variety, its economic integration, and its long tradition of movement and exchange, the Mediterranean had always been a region in which peoples of different faiths, customs, and traditions were obliged to work and live side by side. The conquering newcomers drawn into the power vacuum resulting from the collapse of the imperial/caliphal order proved no exception. None had the power to conquer the whole region, and for those few who managed to seize control of a substantial part of it, their control tended to be tenuous and fleeting. Although many saw the natives of the lands they conquered as infidels, they quickly found that disturbing the delicate, integrated ecosystem of the Mediterranean economy reduced their revenue and diminished their power. As a result, most realized very quickly that they needed to adapt to the diverse environment of the Mediterranean, if they hoped to remain in power, and that included granting legitimacy to and establishing rights for the infidels under their rule.

Law and Legitimacy

The Arabs had grappled with this challenge since the rise of Islam, and thus the status of *dhimmis* was first articulated under Muhammad. However, the Qu'ran offered only vague principles, and it would be rulers and jurists who elaborated the details of *dhimma* over the following centuries. Thus, the so-called Pact of 'Umar became increasingly elaborate, emphasizing the curtailment of non-Muslim rights, ritual humiliation, and restrictions on public religious observance. While the core principles of *dhimma* were rarely challenged, the legal conditions varied dramatically from place to place—at times *dhimmis* were well integrated, at other times they were marginalized and vulnerable. Much depended on local conditions, including the social and economic equilibrium between Muslims and *dhimmis*, the threat of outside (infidel) attack, and the relative power of the religious elite. Powerful, confident *'ulama'* tended to be committed to the "letter of the law"—which is to say, limits might be strictly enforced, but *dhimmis* would be given protection. This can be seen in Almoravid Spain, when the religious elite—adherents of the "conservative" Maliki school—did not hesitate to order the mass exile of Mozarab Christians who collaborated with outside powers, but also demanded the removal of a local governor who illegally abused Christians' rights.

These conditions are best observed in "living" legal documents—the collections of *fatwas*, or legal opinions, promulgated by jurists, and manuals of *hisba,* or "moral accounting," composed by *muhtasibs*, or urban morality officers, part of whose charge was policing the boundaries between religious communities. These reflect a common thread—the need to preserve the superior status of Islamic law and of Muslims over others. SEE SOURCEBOOK 7:1.

The various Mediterranean legal traditions took a similar approach, based on the notion of a hierarchy of religious status in which the politically dominant reli-

In 1105, at age nine, Roger II inherited the Counties of Sicily and Calabria, which his father, the Norman adventurer Roger Borsa and his uncle, Robert Guiscard, had conquered between 1061 and 1090. In 1127 he claimed Apulia, the rest of southern Italy, as his inheritance, and in 1130 the antipope Anacletus II (1130–1138) recognized him as king of Sicily.* In Sicily, Roger ruled over a population of Arabic-speaking Muslims and Greek-speaking Byzantine Orthodox Christians, together with a smattering of Latin colonists, and a cadre of Latin knights and clergy. In addition to waging war against Christian rivals in Italy, Roger launched attacks on Byzantium and Ifriqiya. Between 1135 and 1153 he conquered the coast of modern Tunisia, whose Muslim population he ruled over as "King of Africa." Roger's most steadfast political ally was Fatimid Egypt, and the Norman king imported Fatimid chancery practices for his realm, even adopting Arabic as a formal language of administration. His leading palace and military functionaries included Armenian adventurers, crypto-Muslim castrated ex-slaves, and former Byzantine officials. The king cultivated a rich and sophisticated court, the stylings of which blended Latin, Greek, and Arabo-Islamic influences, and he deliberately patronized and cultivated Arabo-Islamic learning and culture. His capital, Palermo, became one of the largest and wealthiest cities of its time.

* Divided cardinals elected both Anacletus II (1130–1138) and Innocent II (1130–1143) as pope. Innocent secured the support of Lothair II, the king of Germany (1125–1137) and, later, Holy Roman Emperor (1133–1137), while Anacletus supported Roger II.

A Latin Poem

The Book in Honor of the Emperor, or on Sicilian Affairs is an illuminated poem, written in Latin in 1196 by Petrus de Eboli, an Italian monk and courtier of the emperor, Henry VI. The book was meant to commemorate Henry's capture of the island kingdom in 1194 from Tancred of Lecce (1189–1194), an illegitimate grandson of Roger II. This excerpt shows Roger, first as count, then anointed king by Pope Anacletus, and finally marrying his first wife, Elvira of

FIGURE 7.1 The marriage of Roger II, from Petrus de Eboli's *The Book in Honor of the Emperor, or on Sicilian Affairs*, 1196 CE. © Historical Views / agefotostock.

FIGURE 7.2 Roger II receiving his crown. Gilt wall mosaic in the Church of La Martorana, Palermo, 1140s CE. Photograph by Matthias Süßen provided by Wikimedia Commons under the Creative Commons, Creative Commons CC-BY-SA-2.5.

FIGURE 7.3 A sultan, perhaps Roger II, depicted on painted ceiling panel in the Palatine Chapel, Palermo, 1132–1140 CE. Photograph The Yorck Project provided by Wikimedia Commons, Zenodot Verlagsgesellschaft mbH and licensed under the GNU Free Documentation License.

Castile (a daughter of Alfonso VI of Castile, possibly by Alfonso's lover, the Muslim princess Zayda).

Latin text: "Duke Roger—The Duke is anointed as king by Pope Calixtus—The king accepts Elvira as wife."

An Orthodox Church

The Matorana, or Church of St. Mary of the Admiral, in Palermo, was commissioned in 1143 by Roger's Byzantine-Armenian admiral and functionary, George of Antioch, who had previously served the Zirid kings of Ifriqiya. This Orthodox church was decorated in lavish Byzantine style, its floors and walls bedecked with marble inlay and gilded mosaics. The beginning of the nave is flanked by two mosaics: one depicting George prostrate before the Virgin Mary, and the other showing Roger II receiving his crown from Christ.

Latin text written in Greek characters: "King Roger—Jesus Christ"

A Painted Ceiling

The centerpiece of Roger's royal palace in Palermo was the "Palatine Chapel"—an audience chamber and sanctuary built between 1132 and 1140 that stunningly combined Latin, Byzantine, and Arabo-Islamic architectural and artistic elements. The chapel features a *muqarnas* (high-relief) ceiling interspersed with paintings of animal and human figures as well as ornamental designs. Among these is a Fatimid-style painting of a cross-legged ruler grasping a fly whisk (a symbol of power) and glass goblet of wine, thought to represent Roger II.

A Robe of Honor

This silk cape, measuring nearly twelve by five feet, was made to order in 1134 by the Muslim craftsmen of Roger's *tiraz*, or royal silk workshop. Inlaid with gold thread and set with precious stones and glass, it depicts a pair

FIGURE 7.4 The mantle of Roger II, Sicily, 1134 CE. © De Agostini Picture L / De Agostini Editore / agefotostock.

of lions pouncing on a pair of camels, each on either side of a palm tree or "tree of life"—an ancient Mediterranean motif. An inscription in square Kufic-style Arabic calligraphy is stitched into the lower edge.

Arabic text: "This belongs to the articles worked in the royal workshop, [which has] flourished with fortune and honor, with industry and perfection, with might and merit, with [his] sanction and [his] prosperity, with magnanimity and majesty, with renown and beauty and the felicitous days and nights without cease or change, with honor and solicitude, with protection and defense, with success and certainty, with triumph and industry. In the [capital] city of Sicily in the year 528 [1133/1134 CE]."[1]

A Multilingual Coin

This gold coin, approximately a half inch wide at the widest part, was minted in Sicily in 1136/1137 (531 AH). The coin is known as a *tarí*, the Christian version of a *ruba'i*, or quarter-*dinar*, which contained 0.037 ounces of gold. The coin had been popular in Islamic Sicily and was widely imitated by Italian trading cities. Roger II and his successors minted these coins bearing a Christian message on one side and honorifics or throne names of the type used by Muslim caliphs and kings on the other.

Obverse text: "Jesus Christ Conquers" [IC XC NIKA; Greek] with a crucifix; around the rim: In the name of God . . ." [partially cut off; Arabic]

Reverse text in Arabic: "He who is strengthened by God" [*al-Mu'tazz b-'illah*] / "King Roger" [*al-malik Rujjar*] / "He who seeks refuge [in God]" [*al-Mu'tasim*]; around the rim: ". . . the king . . ." [partially cut off; Arabic]

Discussion Questions

1. Why would Roger II not simply present himself as a Latin Crusader-king?
2. How might his different subjects view these various depictions of the king?
3. What do these artifacts tell us about the cultural, political. and economic world in which Roger moved?
4. Why were certain languages or styles chosen for certain inscriptions and representations?

FIGURE 7.5 A gold *tarí* of Roger II, 1136/37 CE. © Historical Views / agefotostock.

Further Reading

"Capella Palatina." *Archnet.org*. https://archnet.org/sites/3759.

Grierson, Philip, and Lucia Travaini. *Medieval European Coinage: With a Catalogue of the Coins in the Fitzwilliam Museum, Cambridge*. Vol. 14, *Italy (South Italy, Sicily, Sardinia)*. Cambridge: Cambridge University Press, 1986.

Hood, Gwenyth. *Book in Honor of Augustus (Liber Ad Honorem Augusti)*. Tempe: Arizona Center for Medieval and Renaissance Studies, 2011.

Mallette, Karla. *Kingdom of Sicily, 1100–1250: A Literary History*. Philadelphia: University of Pennsylvania Press, 2005.

Tronzo, William. *The Cultures of His Kingdom: Roger II and the Cappella Palatina in Palermo*. Princeton: Princeton University Press, 1997.

Note

1. "Mantle of Roger II of Sicily," in *TRC Needles: The TRC Digital Encyclopaedia of Decorative Needlework* (Textile Research Center, Leiden), https://www.trc-leiden.nl/trc-needles/individual-textiles-and-textile-types/secular-ceremonies-and-rituals/mantle-of-roger-ii-of-sicily.

gious community was acknowledged by all (minorities included) as holding prestige and power. Religious identity was not thought of primarily as what theology one followed, but rather what community one belonged to, and what law one was subject to. A Muslim, Christian, or Jew was one who was subject to the laws of that faith. And because law was anchored in religious belief, an infidel could not be bound by the law of the dominant group. Therefore, the rulers of diverse societies conceded legitimacy to other religious/legal traditions. Their religions might be erroneous, but unbelievers were seen as acting in "good faith." Thus, religious minorities were generally allowed to follow their own civil or personal laws as long as these did not contradict the laws of the dominant group, which had jurisdiction in most criminal matters.

Consequently, although late Roman law, the legal foundation across the Christian Mediterranean, was not amenable to religious diversity, and Christian law had no principle of *dhimma,* the status of minorities in Christian lands was functionally similar to that in the Dar al-Islam. It was the special status of Jews, as the biblical Chosen People, that led Roman jurists to grudgingly concede non-Christians a legal space. In the Byzantine "kingdom of God," where there was no fundamental distinction between loyalty to the emperor and loyalty to his church, this was the formal limit of toleration. Jews enjoyed a tenuous legitimacy, but practicing other faiths, including non-Greek Orthodox Christianities, was considered illicit (and punishable by death). But this applied only to Byzantine subjects. Christians and Muslims who presented themselves as subjects of foreign lords were exempt, allowing authorities to turn a blind eye when convenient. This encouraged a fluidity of identity, wherein, for example, Armenian or Turkic warlords who joined the Byzantine army might formally convert to Greek Orthodoxy and adopt Greek names while moving in imperial circles.

In the Latin West, Roman legal principles were revived in the church's canon law beginning in the eleventh century and the royal law codes promulgated in the thirteenth. There was little precedent for governing Muslims and Jews—particularly the former, given that Islam postdated not only those foundational Roman legal codes but the New Testament. In newly conquered Mediterranean lands, such as in the Iberian Peninsula, municipal legal statutes and town charters all but ignored non-Christian communities, granting them a near-par legal status and broad autonomy. This reflected the particularities of the frontier environment, where the economic need to maintain the Muslim population overrode the holy war ideology and Christian triumphalism.

In the thirteenth century, as Latin kings commissioned new law codes to cement their authority over the nobility, they were forced to grapple with the status of their minority communities in a systematic manner. The kings argued that because such groups were "new," and because minority groups were inherently vulnerable, Muslims and Jews should be subject to direct royal jurisdiction, rather than seigniorial authority. Taking Muslims and Jews out of the feudal equation gave kings a direct stream of income and deprived their perennially rebellious nobility of a source of power. Jewish communities, in particular, were often a lucrative source of direct taxation, given the outsized role Jews played in the credit sector. Direct royal protection provided minority communities with a counterbalance to seigniorial or municipal powers who would otherwise work to erode their rights. In contrast to the situation in Spain, in late eleventh-century Sicily, the mass enserfment of Muslim peasants to religious establishments provoked resistance and revolt, ultimately contributing to that community's expulsion in the early thirteenth century. In the Latin East, when authorities oppressed Muslim peasants, these sometimes withheld crops, abetted Muslim raiders, or simply emigrated to Islamic lands, leaving Latin lords without laborers.

Thus, monarchs became the special protectors of minority communities, preserving their rights and autonomy. The kings of Aragon qualified Muslim subjects as their "royal treasure," while Jews across the Latin Mediterranean were commonly referred to as *servi regis*—a term that could be interpreted as "slave," "client," or anything between, but signaled they belonged to the king's patrimony. This status embodied special protections, but also vulnerabilities. Many Muslims and Jews were immune from judicial mutilation or execution without the king's specific consent. On the other hand, rebels seeking to strike at royal power might strike against the king's Jews or Muslims, cloaking their rebelliousness in the robes of piety.

Lords, for their part, whether lay nobility, military orders, church chapters, bishops, monasteries, or convents, also treated their non-Christian dependents pragmatically, rarely proselytizing among them. To be sure, they tried to exploit them, but they viewed them as valuable assets and often discouraged their conversion. Muslim peasants in Spain were generally not subject to the tithes and other church taxes. This made them more valuable as tenants, given they could afford higher rents, and it encouraged their lords, even when these were ecclesiastical foundations, to defend Mudejar (free subject Muslim) communities. Many Mudejars were the tenants of military orders—as such they sometimes fought in their militias, and enjoyed the protection of these organizations. In general, the more Christian institutions there were that were competing for Mudejar or Jewish rents and taxes, the better off those communities were, as they could play the conflicting interests of Christian institutions against each other and recruit them as defenders against would-be exploiters.

Because non-Christians were not subject to canon law the church had little direct jurisdiction over them. The default legal position was that Muslims and Jews had the right to live in Christian lands as long as they were peaceable and did not harm Christians. It was not until the Fourth Lateran Council (1215) that non-Christians were officially required to wear special garments, cease building places of worship, and were forbidden from taking up positions in royal administrations. The call to prayer was not formally banned until the Council of Vienne in 1311/12. However, such statutes were not applied with any consistency by kings who ruled over substantial Muslim and Jewish populations and had an interest in cultivating them, and local church institutions showed little interest in enforcing such rules. Heretical Christians, on the other hand, did represent a grave threat to the Christian order and to the power of both kings and church, and were subject to uncompromising violence.

Papal lawyers justified the laws passed regarding Jews, Muslims, and pagans at Lateran IV on Old Testament principles that mandated the quarantine of the Children of Israel from their unclean and impious neighbors. The rationale was to prevent prohibited sexual contact between members of different faiths—particularly between infidel men and Christian women. Typical requirements might include wearing a particular article of clothing or colored patch of a special shape, a special hat, or a particular haircut. This was mirrored by similar mandates vis-à-vis Christians and Jews in the Islamic world. While the majority community rationalized the imposition of dress codes to protect the faithful against the temptations of other faiths, it was the minority groups that were most concerned with dangers of acculturation and the threat of conversion. Hence, minority authorities also endeavored to maintain social and legal boundaries. SEE SOURCEBOOK 7:2.

Intercommunal sexual activity was seen as particularly dangerous. Contemporary rabbinical *responsa*, for example, discouraged interfaith socializing and prescribed mutilation for women who had sex with non-Jews. In Christian and Muslim lands, death was the usual statutory penalty for interfaith sexual transgressions, although minority men might avoid punishment by converting to the majority faith. Because of the royal protections minority faiths enjoyed it was prohibited for these communities to impose capital punishment on their own members. In Christian Spain, Mudejar authorities could generally not carry out executions (which was a royal prerogative in the case of Jews and Muslims), so they handed over adulterous women to royal authorities, who enslaved them and could oblige them to work as prostitutes. To be sure, the punishments on the books for sex crimes within a given community tended to be no less harsh. Penalties for sodomy (which included any sex act considered non-normative) and adultery included mutilation (often nose removal for women and castration for men), torture, and death. That said, such gruesome punishments were not necessarily carried out even against Muslim and Jewish offenders, and especially when the accused was able to pay a hefty fine.

Integration and Segregation

Because religious identity determined one's legal and social status, the laws one was subject to and the taxes one paid, it was an ever-present factor in daily experience, and a near-constant reminder of the religio-social hierarchy. When one went to court, signed a contract, sold or bought property, or entered into a partnership, one was reminded of one's place in the ideal social hierarchy. However, this ideal did not reflect reality. While a humble Christian or Muslim felt a certain entitlement based on their status as members of the privileged community, in real life they were constantly encountering individual Jews, and subject Christian or Muslims, who as merchants, landholders, or royal functionaries were wealthier and more influential than themselves, and this could be seen as an affront to the divine order.

Consequently, opportunities to reaffirm the prestige of the ruling group and put minority subjects in their "place" were welcomed. This might take the form of ritual acts of humiliation (such as the symbolic strike on the neck *dhimmis* sometimes received when they paid their taxes), or acts of violence, such as Jews sometimes suffered in Latin lands during emotionally charged religious holidays, such as Holy Week and the Feast of Corpus Christi. Secular authorities and the institutional church endeavored to suppress such attacks, both to maintain social stability and because popular unrest posed a challenge to their authority, although many individual clerics fomented and participated in such violence. It has been suggested that occasional bouts of violence, whether ritualized or spontaneous, served to defuse intercommunal tensions and contributed to overall social stability. Indeed, in Christian Iberia these sometimes evolved into formal and choreographed public pageants, which Muslims and Jews took part in, often willingly, as musicians, dancers, actors, and extras. Here, the violence might be theatrical rather than actual, serving to reaffirm the superiority of the majority, and normalize the place of minorities in the larger community, subordinate as it may have been.

At times, members of minority communities lived in segregated neighborhoods, which were sometimes walled for protection. This might come at the behest of their own authorities or of their rulers, either as a means of control and preventing inappropriate social contact, or of better monitoring the collection of communal taxes. Self-segregation also played a role. Just as today, many preferred to live in close proximity to the places of worship, baths, butcher shops, and other communal facilities they patronized among social and legal equals who shared their religio-cultural orientation. They would be safer from surveillance by majority religious authorities, and there would be less opportunity for intercommunal transgressions that could lead to confrontation and violence.

Nor was there much interest in the conversion of infidel subjects. Generally, minorities were subject to higher taxes, and had little capacity to act politically, given their second-class status. Thus, rulers sometimes saw it as preferable to have them as subjects. Since they were in principle (if not in practice) prohibited from holding formal administrative office, were often formally barred from certain sensitive professions (such as medicine), and were subject to various other legal and social restrictions, they posed little competitive threat to ordinary members of the majority community. This did much to dampen enthusiasm for the conversion of one's infidel neighbors, who did not enjoy full legal or economic rights. Part of the reason that converts were commonly regarded with disdain even by the communities they converted into was that they were simply not welcome—members of the majority jealously guarded their position of privilege, and those who came to the "right faith" might be looked on as "turncoats" even by their new coreligionists.

That said, it was these very characteristics that made minority individuals attractive candidates to work in the fields they were formally excluded from. Muslim regimes employed Christians and Jews as tax collectors because rulers could keep them at arm's length, claiming that any excessive or uncanonical taxes they charged were the fault of these infidels. Thus, the financial administration in Fatimid and Ayyubid Egypt was dominated by Copts, the royal fiscal administration in the thirteenth-century Crown of Aragon was dominated by a handful of Jewish families, and Jews were prominent royal treasurers in fourteenth-century Castile.

This carried advantages for rulers. Wealthy financial officials could be coerced into giving forced loans. Rulers could dispose of these officials and confiscate their wealth at their will on charges that were genuine or trumped up, without exciting protest among their majority subjects. These officials could serve as scapegoats and deflect criticism from the monarch. Moreover, minority bureaucrats and officials could not hope to rebel against the ruler, because their religion disqualified them and they lacked popular support. This explains in part why, even when members of the majority community had acquired the necessary skills for these jobs, many rulers preferred to employ minority individuals in such positions. This at times provoked antiminority sentiments among the majority. The anti-Christian rhetoric of the *'ulama'* of thirteenth-century Egypt was a consequence of continuing Coptic dominance of financial offices that those members of the *'ulama'* increasingly aspired to themselves. In 1283 when the rebellious nobility of Aragon forced Pere the Great to grant them a charter of rights ("The General Privilege"), they demanded Jews be excluded from the royal administration.

Similarly, the reason why so many powerful individuals chose physicians from among their minority subjects was not necessarily because Jews, *mudéjares,* or *dhimmis* were more knowledgeable in medicine—although to be sure, medical science was more advanced in the Islamicate world at this time. Physicians enjoyed a deep intimacy with their patients, and the trust invested in doctors gave them tremendous power—including the ability to poison their charges. Hence, it was advantageous to choose a minority physician, someone who was not politically independent, and whose fate (and possibly that of their wider community) rested on the continuing good health and will of the king. Thus, we find Muslim physicians in the court of the eleventh-century Norman kings, Alfonso VI of Castile attended in his ailing dotage by the Andalusi Jew Yosef ibn Ferrusel, or Moses Maimonides as physician to the family of Salah al-Din and the Ayyubid court. The early Umayyads and 'Abbasids had patronized physicians from the Church of the East, and the Fatimids used Coptic doctors. The Bukhtishu' family were Persian Christians who served the caliphs in Baghdad for nearly three centuries beginning in the late 700s, while a fellow Christian, Hibit Allah ibn Tilmidh, was chief physician of Baghdad for decades until his death in 1165.

Whether tax collectors, financiers, or physicians, powerful minority individuals served as representatives and lobbyists for their religious communities, and the influence they enjoyed "trickled down" as protection for their coreligionists through the connections they held. Nachmanides, the rabbi called on by Jaume I of Aragon to debate the truth of Judaism against the Dominican order in 1263, also went by the name Bonastruc ça Porta; his brother, Benveniste ça Porta, was the king's bailiff. Conversely, if these individuals provoked the envy or betrayed the trust of the majority group, its wrath might fall on their religious community as a whole. Hence, when Yusuf ibn Naghrilla, the Jewish *wazir* of Zirid Granada, was revealed as a traitor in 1066, the Muslims of the city turned not only on him, but on the Jewish community in general. Nachmanides's effective defense of Judaism in the Barcelona Disputation provoked popular unrest and the Dominicans, stung by defeat, hounded him into exile—first in Mamluk Jerusalem, and ultimately in Crusader Acre.

In any event, the principle of segregation, and the notion that the socioeconomic hierarchy in these societies should reflect the hierarchy of religious communities, were ideals that were impossible to maintain. In both town and country, members of different communities were drawn into relations of economic interdependence, serving as each other's vendors, customers, suppliers, employees, partners, shipmates, tenants, landlords, agents, collaborators, and dependents. Men and women frequently made recourse to professionals of other faiths, even in intimate contexts, such as medicine, midwifery, wet-nursing, and magic. They were constantly making deals and forming partnerships with each other, lending and borrowing—rubbing shoulders around the village well, in the marketplace, the palace, the tavern, the brothel, and even in sacred sites of common worship. Public baths—a Roman institution adapted and disseminated within and beyond the Islamic world—were environments of social contact and flashpoints of tension, where the outward signs of privilege and inequality were literally stripped away. Thus, both religious and political authorities usually endeavored to segregate baths by both gender and faith. SEE SOURCEBOOK 7:3.

Given the propensity of minority communities to outwardly adopt the social mores of the majority, people of the various communities tended to look and dress the same, and speak in ways that were often indistinguishable. They enjoyed many of the same foods, stories, kinds of music, songs, dances, and pastimes. They often joined together in common public celebrations, whether these predated the Abrahamic faiths, such as processions and rituals meant to bring rain, or were religious holidays, such as the 'Id al-Fitr at the end of Ramadan and Christmas. People enjoy parties. But this provoked anxiety. A twelfth-century Islamic jurist worried that Muslim children were being tempted into apostasy by the sweets distributed by Christians at Epiphany; and a century later the celebration of the *mawlid* (birthday of Muhammad) was instituted as an Islamic rejoinder to Christmas. Sacred landscapes and common shrines, whether rooted in biblical, classical, or folkloric traditions, were shared by members of different faiths, and common religious and folk figures, such as Saint George/al-Khidr/Elijah and Alexander the Great, were popularly venerated among all of the major faith communities.

Maintaining fully segregated neighborhoods was all but impossible. Conversion, slavery, and intermarriage (whether open, clandestine, or informal) meant that not only neighborhoods, but households themselves, were often "blended," with Christians, Muslims, and Jews penetrating each other's most intimate domestic environments. Moreover, economic and social integration encouraged individuals to see themselves as members of formal and informal communities—some temporary, some permanent—that transcended ethno-religious community and were rooted in commonalities of economic class, vocation, trade, gender, spiritual inclination, or based on a myriad of other factors. Inhabitants of neighborhoods, towns, cities, and kingdoms would often band together in self-defense irrespective of religious identity, sharing a sense of local belonging—allegiance to what in Arabic was referred to as *watan* (homeland), as opposed to *umma* (religious community). Thus, Crusade and *jihad* waged against rival kingdoms rarely affected minority communities at home, who were seldom scapegoated as allies of their foreign coreligionists; indeed, some—including *mudéjares* in the Iberian Peninsula, Turkic clients of Byzantium, and native Christians in Egypt—readily supported their infidel rulers against aggressors of their own faith.

However, this image of collaboration and concord between members of different ethnic and religious communities should not be imagined in nostalgic terms. People got along to the extent they had to and were prepared to. In an age where wealth, power, and security within every stratum of society were accumulated through the expansion and entrenchment of family patrimony, as long as families identified with a single religious community, conflict and competition—whether it was at bottom ideological or mundane—could be framed as righteous and religious when the opposing party belonged to a different community. Permanent fusions of family patrimonies through marriage almost never took place across faiths without conversion. Thus, while in the short and medium term it was common for alliances and collaborations to cross communal boundaries, competition inevitably tended to shape up along religious lines over the long term, thus contributing to an appearance of *religious* conflict, even when the causes of conflict were economic or social.

Complex Societies

The cultivation of minority communities as subjects was not the result of some ideal of "toleration" or the value of diversity, but rather, because members of minority and majority communities felt that they needed and ben-

The Mengüjek clan were Turkmen vassals of the Seljuqs who perhaps arrived in Anatolia with Alp Arslan in 1071. One branch of the family established a small principality in the eastern highlands centered on the town of Divriği. In 1228–1229 the *amir* Ahmadshah (1227–1251) built a new congregational mosque (*ulu cami*) just outside the city walls, and his kinswoman and (presumed) wife, the "just queen" Turan Melek Sultan, constructed an adjoining *darüşşifa*, or teaching hospital. A mausoleum was also incorporated in the structure.

Divriği sits on a ridge above a fertile valley watered by a tributary of the northern Euphrates. Under the Mengüjeks the town prospered, and its overlords built a fortress, mosques, mausoleums, and hospitals. The surrounding countryside was populated by Muslims and (mostly Armenian) Christians. Local Muslim men often married Greek and Armenian Orthodox women, and it was common for Muslim children to receive baptism. At the time that Ahmadshah constructed the mosque-hospital, he was forced to become a client of the Seljuq Sultanate of Rum, which, with the fall of Constantinople to the Fourth Crusade, had become the dominant regional power. His dynasty would last only until the 1250s, apparently surviving the Mongol campaigns of the 1240s.[1]

The Dedication Inscription (Arabic)—North Portal (Mosque)

> This congregational mosque was ordered to be built for the sake of God Almighty by the servant in need

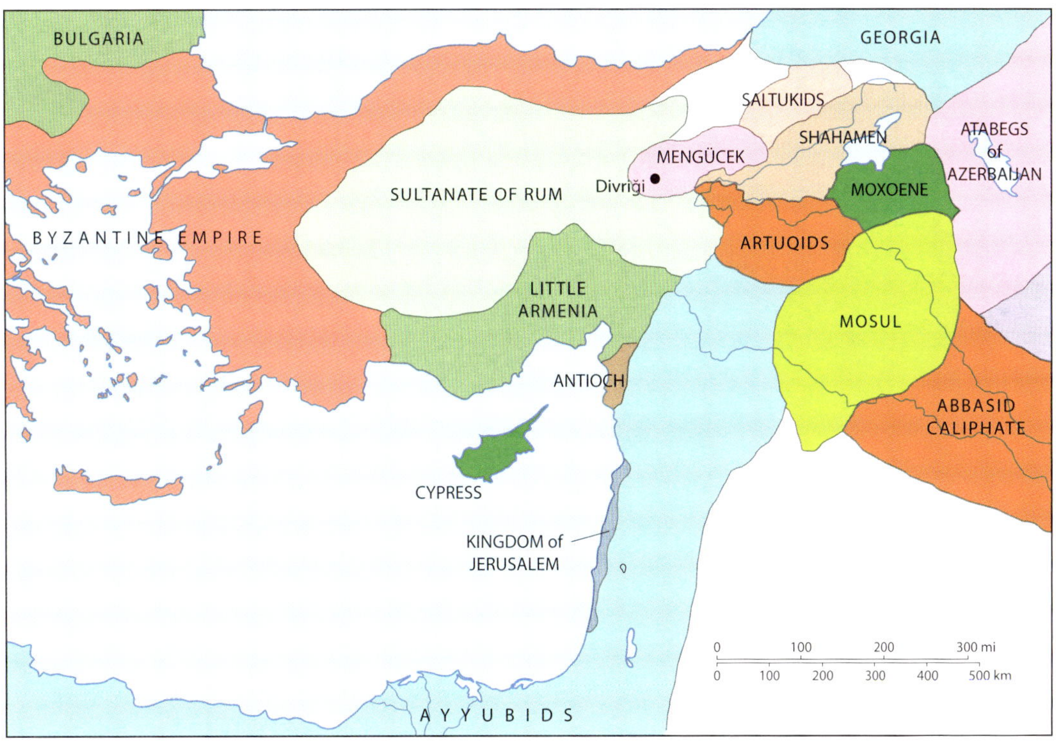

MAP 7.1 Anatolia, ca. 1200. From Gabagool, provided by Wikimedia Commons under the CC-BY-3.0 License.

FIGURE 7.6 The Great Mosque and Hospital of Divriği (Turkey). B.O.'Kane / Alamy Stock Photo.

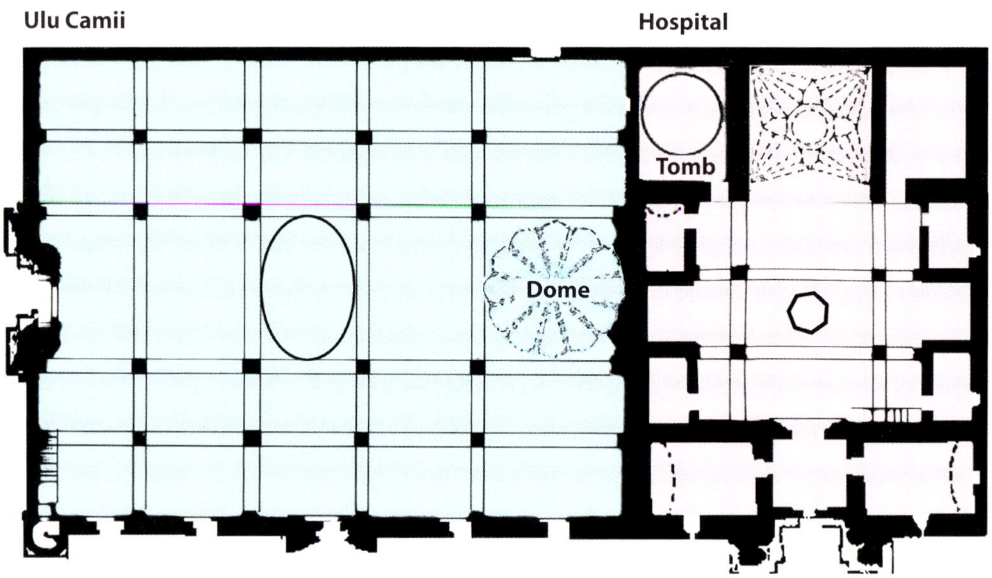

FIGURE 7.7 Floor plan of the mosque-hospital. © Historical Views / agefotostock.

of God's protection, Ahmêdşâh son of Süleymânşâh. May God perpetuate his sovereignty. On the date of the year six hundred and twenty-six [1228–1229].

[Added later, to acknowledge the Seljuq sultan]:

> In the days of the reign of the great sultan Alâeddünyâveddin Keykubâd, partner of the Commander of the Faithful.[2]

The Dedication Inscription (Arabic)—West Portal (Hospital)

> The just queen, in need of God Almighty's pardon, Tûrân Melik, daughter of the fortunate king, Fahreddin Behrâmşâh, ordering the building of this blessed house of healing, longing for God Almighty's benevolence May God accept it, Amen. In one of the months of six hundred and twenty-six [1228–1229].[3]

FIGURE 7.8 Detail of the main entrance of the Great Mosque. B.O.'Kane / Alamy Stock Photo.

The Great Mosque and Hospital

The mosque is completely covered and lacks a patio and outdoor ablution fountain (likely because of the cold climate). With five naves consisting of five bays each, the prayer hall evokes a basilica-style church and perhaps a caravanserai. A high dome is set in front of the *mihrab* (prayer niche) on the south wall, which adjoins the hospital. The interior of the hospital is arranged around four *iwans* (open-ended halls), which are typical of Iranian and Central Asian designs, as well as smaller rooms, but, unlike these, is also covered. The courtyard between them has a fountain at its center. Design and decoration were entrusted to the master craftsman, Khurramshah ibn Mughith al-Khilati, a Persian Muslim from Akhlat (near Lake Van, to the east), who is responsible for the exuberantly carved hospital and mosque portals, and interior vaulting. The monumental doorways are a singular example of high-relief Seljuq stone-carving, a complex synthesis incorporating diverse elements and motifs, from Anatolian, Armenian, Georgian, Byzantine, Iranian, and Central Asian cultures, including a tree of life and two anthropomorphic figures, which are likely allegories for the sun and moon. Ahmad ibn Ibrahim al-Tiflisi, a Georgian Muslim, carved the richly detailed alabastar *minbar* (pulpit inside the mosque). In 1985 the complex was added to the UNESCO World Heritage List.

The *darüşşifa* was a teaching hospital possibly founded to tempt the famous physician 'Abd al-Latif al-Baghdadi, who passed through Divriği as he was fleeing unrest in Anatolia and on his way to Iraq, to take up a position here. Such hospitals typically specialized in mental illnesses, eye-related conditions, and diseases requiring surgery. Patients were treated without regard to religion, ethnicity, or gender. Physicians who trained here received a diploma from the resident medical professors.

The mosque and hospital were independent foundations supported by pious endowments (*waqf*) established by the founders, perhaps as a strategy for sheltering their wealth in the face of rising Seljuq power, as a marker of status, and in exchange for their commemoration in prayers. These endowments of land and property provided income to support the staffing and maintenance of the mosque and hospital. Turan Melek Sultan also endowed a *madrasa* nearby, now gone. Both elite and nonelite women often donated property to such foundations.

Discussion Questions

1. Why might Turan Melek Sultan have endowed the hospital and Ahmadshah the mosque separately, and why would the buildings be conjoined?

2. What does the integration of diverse architectural and decorative elements suggest about Seljuq culture and Anatolian society?

3. How might this complex compare to analogous foundations in the Latin Mediterranean, and what conclusions can we draw from this?

Further Reading

Bakir, Betül. "How Medical Functions Shaped Architecture in Anatolian Seljuk Darüşşifas (Hospitals) and Especially in the Divriği Turan Malik Darüşşifa." *Journal of the International Society for the History of Islamic Medicine* 5 (2006): 64–82.

Canby, Sheila R., Deniz Beyazit, Martina Rugiadi, and A. C. S. Peacock. *Court and Cosmos: The Great Age of the Seljuqs*. New York: Metropolitan Museum of Art, 2016.

"Divrigi Ulu Camii ve Darüşşifası." *Archnet.org*. https://archnet.org/sites/1924.

Kuban, Doğan. *The Miracle of Divriği: An Essay on the Art of Islamic Ornamentation in Seljuk Times*. Istanbul: YKY, 2001.

Pancaroğlu, Oya. "Devotion, Hospitality, and Architecture in Medieval Anatolia." *Studia Islamica* 108 (2013): 48–81.

Ragab, Ahmed. *The Medieval Islamic Hospital: Medicine, Religion, and Charity*. Cambridge: Cambridge University Press, 2015.

Notes

1. After Martin Frishman and Hasan-Uddin Khan, *The Mosque: History, Architectural Development, and Regional Diversity* (London: Thames & Hudson, 2007), 143.

2. Oya Pancaroğlu, *Great Mosque and Hospital of Divriği: A Historical Approach* (Ankara: Republic of Turkey Ministry of Culture and Tourism, 2014), 158.

3. Pancaroğlu, 160.

efited from each other. Conquerors needed indigenous agricultural workers to maintain a tax base, merchants and craftsmen to sustain the economy, and functionaries to administrate complex economies and institutions. As for the colonized, as long as their communal rights were respected, they enjoyed the benefit of living under princes who had the capacity to maintain peace and guarantee security. If the price to be paid was to live as somewhat vulnerable, secondary subjects, many had no alternative, or saw this as a price worth paying, their own religious prohibitions against living under infidel rule notwithstanding. Conversely, rulers who justified their wars as pious paladins and champions of their own true faith were obliged also to present themselves as universal rulers and legitimate protectors of their infidel subjects.

Rulers and Rebels

Thus, like the Islamic regimes they sought to displace, the Latin-Christian warlords who swept into the Mediterranean in the late eleventh century came to present themselves as much as universal rulers as heralds of a new order. This is reflected in the policies of the Christian kings who conquered al-Andalus and the Norman warlords who came to dominate the central Mediterranean. Hence, Roger II of Sicily and his heirs were obliged to project distinct images of authority that resonated with their Latin-Christian, Greek-Christian, and Muslim subjects, posturing as Crusaders, affecting Byzantine regalia, and taking Arabo-Islamic throne names. Conquerors generally sought to convey continuity and stability by presenting themselves in a recognizable guise—thus, to their Syriac subjects, Hülegü Khan and his wife, Doquz Khatan, both members of the Church of the East, became the new "Constantine and Helena." The propensity for even the most zealous groups to quickly form long-term collaborations and alliances with their infidel neighbors and to accommodate their infidel subjects reflects the potency of Mediterranean social and economic norms, which newcomers were obliged to conform to. This can be seen in the Crusader East, where native-born Frankish settlers who had acculturated to local norms were viewed very differently than newcomers and visiting pilgrims, who treated indigenous peoples, whether Christian or Muslim, with violent disdain.

FIGURE 7.9 Hülegü Khan and Doquz Khatun as Constantine and Helena, Syriac Bible, 1270 CE. Niday Picture Library / Alamy Stock Photo.

In the western Mediterranean, Christian powers such as Castile and Aragon found themselves variably as allies or rivals not only of each other, but of Muslim powers like the Marinids of Morocco and the Nasrids of Granada. In the central Mediterranean the trading republics, the Normans, Angevins, Catalans, and the papacy fought among each other as they alternately cultivated and clashed with the Almohads, the Hafsids, and the Mamluks. In the eastern Mediterranean Venice, Genoa, Byzantium, the Crusader states, the Fatimids, and the Seljuq princes of Syria engaged in alliances of convenience that seldom aligned according to religious identity. The rise of the Mamluks, the splintering of Byzantium, the emergence of Armenian Cilicia, the continuing incursions of Turkic clans into Anatolia, and finally the arrival of the Mongols only served to further complicate the political-religious picture.

Occasionally, grand coalitions based on common religious orientation were proposed or launched—including the various Crusades against Egypt and the Holy Land, the Spanish Christian campaign against the Almohads in 1212, Saint Louis's Egyptian crusade of 1249, and the overtures made to the Mamluks in the 1280s by Hülekü's son, Tekuder, who had converted to Islam as Sultan Ahmed (1282–1284). But such religiously framed alliances were invariably short-lived and of limited effect. It was short- and mid-term goals that shaped alliances—rhetoric of holy war notwithstanding. But the rhetoric of holy war was useful for the advantages it brought both immediately and over the long term. Generally, cultivating a pious reputation brought prestige to kings, bolstering their legitimacy and their capacity to command reluctant subordinates. It inspired the rank and file to enlist in a cause that had a higher moral dimension, and would enhance their reputations, and perhaps contribute to their salvation. In the Latin West, qualifying campaigns as Crusades enabled kings to tap into the wealth of the church in order to fund their adventures. SEE SOURCEBOOK 7:4.

Vulnerable princes and generals seldom hesitated to call on infidel support against their coreligionists when it suited them. As Fatimid power collapsed in the 1160s, Shawar and Dirgham, two rival *wazir*s battling for control of this Shi'i caliphate, flip-flopped between courting the Christian Kingdom of Jerusalem and the Sunni Muslim Nur al-Din of Syria as allies, resulting in a brief Frankish occupation of the Cairo citadel. At the Battle of Las Navas de Tolosa in 1212, Christian León sided with the North African Almohad Caliphate against its Christian rivals. In 1213 Pere the Catholic of Aragon was forced by his obligations as overlord to aid his Cathar-supporting vassals in Languedoc against Innocent III's Crusaders, only to be deliberately killed at the Battle of Muret. In the south, the Sultanate of Granada—technically a vassal of Castile—repeatedly changed allegiance between Castile, Aragon, and the Marinids of Morocco through the thirteenth and fourteenth centuries.

The ever-shifting power dynamics of the region meant there was a steady stream of mercenaries, soldiers of fortune, rebels, and exiles willing to take up arms under infidel kings. Armenian forces, both Christian and Muslim, were instrumental to both the Byzantine and Fatimid militaries. Andronikos Komnenos, the dictatorial populist prince who murderously seized power in Constantinople in 1183, had served Frankish Jerusalem before fighting as a brigand for Turkic overlords. In the western Mediterranean Christian mercenaries sustained both the Almoravids and the Almohads, and Muslim princes fought as vassals and allies of Christian kings. Relationships of clientage and mercantile interests drew Christian forces to defend Muslim princes, while in Anatolia, particularly in the aftermath of the splintering and reconstitution of the empire of Constantinople in the 1260s, Turkic clans drifted in and out of Byzantine service with the winds of opportunity. Across the region, privateering warlords like Rodrigo Díaz de Vivar "El Cid" (d. 1099) and his Portuguese analogue, Geraldo Sem Pavor (d. 1173), posed as paladins when fighting infidels, while becoming popular heroes for Muslim populations they defended. From the late thirteenth century, exiled Muslim princes and warriors took refuge in Christian service, mirroring Christian mercenaries in the Maghrib. A pillar of Nasrid Granada's army were North African "Warriors of the Faith"; but these mujahidun and mercenaries were riven by their own family rivalries. They battled against each other as much as against Granada's enemies, and at any given moment the weaker faction could be found fighting in the service of Christian kings.

Thus, for noblemen and warriors, the Mediterranean was a region of permeable boundaries and shifting opportunities. And while Christian and Muslim societies embodied distinct aristocratic and military cultures that were rooted in particular religious, linguistic, and ethnic traditions, profound similarity in vocation, and analogous concepts of honor, virtue, and virility, united them, so that in many circumstances they conceived of themselves of sharing an identity that overrode their differences. They admired and respected each other, took part together in ceremonies and tournaments, gave each other gifts, appreciated similar styles of literature and luxury, appropriated each other's armor and tactics. Such affinities, did not, however, temper the violence with which these warriors faced each other once the tables had turned. In the second decade of the twelfth century, the Arabic-speaking Norman prince of Antioch, Roger of Salerno (1112–1119) cultivated a cordial alliance with Il-Ghazi ibn Artuq, the Seljuq lord of Mardin (1107–1122), helping him take control of Aleppo. Now a neighbor and ally, Il-Ghazi attacked Roger, slaughtering thousands of Crusader and Armenian troops at the "Field of Blood" in 1119. The prince himself was killed, although Il-Ghazi, in commemoration of their former friendship, had Roger's skull repurposed as a bejeweled goblet, which he used at his own table.

FIGURE 7.10 Crusaders expel the inhabitants from Carcassonne in 1209, from *Grandes Chroniques de Frances*, France, ca. 1415 CE. © British Library Board. All Rights Reserved / Bridgeman Images.

Sectarians and Heretics

Whatever tensions were manifested among the major Abrahamic faiths, conflict between those who considered themselves "orthodox" and those they branded "heretics" tended to be far more entrenched and bitter. In the Latin West, the greatest threat was posed by heretics, who by encouraging the denial of the rituals and authority of the church imperiled the souls of Christians and threatened the social and political order. Discontent at the church's failings among the increasingly literate urban populace, together with the regional nativism that accompanied the rise of vernacular cultures from the 1100s onward, spawned a whole series of antiestablishment populist heresies, beginning with the Waldensians of Lyon in the 1170s, and continuing with the Cathars in Languedoc and a whole succession of radical antiestablishmentarian Christian movements in the urban environments of the north of Italy and Germany's Rhone valley. The establishment of the Franciscan and Dominican orders in the early 1200s helped defuse these outbreaks and address some of the heretics' grievances, but ultimately, they could not be contained and would split the church apart in the Protestant Reformation of the 1500s.

In the Islamic world heterodoxy was less threatening because rulers did not stake their legitimacy on a specific doctrine. By the 1100s, Islamic regimes were dominated by military rulers who exercised *sultan* (secular power) in order to maintain order and guarantee the integrity of the *'ulama'*, who exercised legal and religious authority. As long as rulers fulfilled this function, their religious beliefs became almost irrelevant. This is why Egyptian Sunnis did not react against their Shi'i caliphs, and why some Muslims were even prepared to accept a Christian ruler, whether Roger II, Alfonso VI, or El Cid as *sultan*. This decoupling helped to depoliticize sectarian impulses within Sunni Islam, except in instances where Muslim rulers or their agents actively repressed believers. Hence, Almoravid suppression of Sufism and Almohad marginalization of Sunnis stirred popular revolts in which rebels were prepared even to ally with Christians in order to overthrow their Muslim oppressors.

While Shi'is supported the notion of a unique, divinely sanctioned, and messianic imam who embodied both spiritual and terrestrial authority, this was an abstract aspiration most did not pursue with the exception of the Isma'ili Fatimid Caliphate. This embodied the idea of the imam/caliph and actively promoted revolutionary Shi'ism abroad in an organized program that sent secret missionaries to foment revolt in Sunni lands. The corollary of the Fatimid position, however, was that each time there was a political controversy regarding who the legitimate successor to the caliphate was, the supporters of the unsuccessful claimant to the throne split off to comprise a distinct religious sect that denied the legitimacy of the new caliph and extolled the sanctity of their own candidate. With the esoteric and apocalyptic orientation of their faith, these claimants continued to be venerated as "divinely hidden" imams even after their deaths, and these sects took on a life of their own. This is the origin of the Druze religion, which venerates the caliph al-Hakim and took root on the Levantine coast; the Nizaris, or Assassins, who venerated

Nizar, the son of al-Mustansir, and established principalities in northern Iran and in Syria; and the Tayyibis, who took root in Yemen and venerated a son of the caliph al-ʾAmir.

The three major confessional groupings within Judaism—Rabbanite, Karaite, and Samaritan—were each recognized as constituting a legitimate *dhimmi* community within the Islamic world, but relations between them were often hostile. These divisions were not merely theological, but were also related to the political agendas of leading families. Rabbanite Jews worked aggressively to extinguish Karaism in the West by the twelfth century, whether through violence, or their influence with Latin or Muslim rulers. In the East, relations were more fluid, but by the thirteenth century Karaism was fading.

In the thirteenth-century West, Rabbanite elite families fell into deep conflict over the views of the great philosopher-physician Moses Maimonides (1135–1204), who reconfigured the Islamic Aristotelianism of Ibn Rushd and applied it to Judaism. But this religious controversy was also a conflict between rival elites for power within Christian Aragon. Indigenous Andalusi Jews tended to be more receptive to Maimonides's thought, while Jews from the South of France, who were coming into the Crown of Aragon in the aftermath of Louis IX's annexation of Languedoc and threatening the power of these native families, opposed it. As Maimonideans and the traditionalists who rejected his rationalism vied for control over their communities in Spain, they branded their rivals as "heretics," and in times of conflict, invited the intervention of Christian kings, demanding their opponents be deprived of religious appointments, ultimately undermining their own communities' autonomy. SEE SOURCEBOOK 7:5.

Formal heresies aside, the advocates of strictly defined orthodoxy within each of the three Abrahamic faiths had to contend with the rising tide of mystical and millenarian movements. Thanks in part to the work of the Persian scholar Abu Hamid al-Ghazali (d. 1111), the twelfth century saw the proliferation of Sufism in the Islamic Mediterranean, while in the thirteenth century Moses of León (d. 1305) composed the Zohar—the foundational text of Kabbalism—and the esoteric wing of the Franciscans, inspired by the twelfth-century Italian Joachim di Fiori, embraced mysticism. With a popular appeal that both scrupulous orthodoxy and rational philosophy often lacked, mysticism provided both an opportunity and a threat to the political and religious authorities. In its most extreme forms Abrahamic esotericism claimed to transcend doctrine, and threatened the scriptural foundations of the political order, not to mention the monopoly over religious authority held by a masculine, formally educated, and privileged elite. Sufi activists played a crucial role in bringing down the Almoravids and bringing the Almohads to power in al-Andalus.

Popular Christian preachers were responsible for mobilizing volatile masses in the Peasants' Crusade of 1096, the Children's Crusade of 1212, and the violent "Shepherds' Crusades" of 1251, 1309, and 1320. From the fourteenth century, mystics—often Franciscans—were frequently accused of heresy, and sometimes inspired organized anticlerical movements. Disruptive prophetic and messianic figures also appeared among Mediterranean Jewish communities, notably the controversial Abraham Abulafia (d. 1291), who in 1280 declared his intention to convert Pope Nicholas III to Judaism. Christian and Muslim rulers needed to tread carefully, seeking to temper and contain popular mystical movements without alienating their adherents, while attempting through patronage to obtain the approval and support of the charismatic, prophet-like figures who often led them.

Official Repression and Popular Aggression

Commonalities notwithstanding, the fact that the three Abrahamic faiths disagreed on how to venerate the same God brought their differences into higher relief and was used to justify both official repression and popular violence. However, it is difficult to isolate religion as the *cause* of such episodes because they were invariably rooted also in economic and political dynamics. Mass enslavements and expulsions of minority communities tended to take place when rulers believed there would be no negative consequences for them, whether at the time of conquest, or when the political loyalty of these communities became suspect.

Hence, in 1126 the Almoravids exiled a number of the Christian Mozarabs of southern al-Andalus to Morocco as punishment for collaborating with Alfonso I of Aragon, while Alfons the Liberal of Aragon enslaved the

Muslim population of Menorca in 1287 on charges of collaboration with the Hafsids. Jaume I of Aragon expelled the Muslims of Mallorca following the conquest of 1229 because he could resettle the island with Christians. On the other hand, when he conquered the region of Valencia in the following decade, Jaume was short of settlers and Muslims were encouraged to stay, although the capital was to be inhabited only by Christians and Jews. A Mudejar revolt in the 1260s prompted Castile to expel many Muslims from southern Spain, yet when the Muslims of the Kingdom of Valencia rebelled a few years later, the Aragonese kings—who needed them to maintain the kingdom's economy—were forced to grant them concessions. Frederick II of Sicily transported the island's increasingly restive and diminishing Muslim population to mainland Lucera in the 1220s but remained their patron and protector. When Charles II of Naples (1285–1309) finally enslaved and dispersed the community in 1300, it was for economic motives, although he justified it publicly on religious terms.

Likewise, when the Almohads took power in the Maghrib in the mid-1100s, by some reports they abolished the pact of *dhimma*, apparently justifying this on the grounds they did not need the taxes it generated. Although the extent of their persecution of Jews is debated, in this period many fled Almohad territories to relocate in Christian Spain or other Islamic lands. The family of Moses Maimonides is said to have escaped Córdoba and gone to Fez, having nominally converted to Islam, before continuing to Ayyubid Egypt, where they reassumed their faith. After the fall of Crusader Tyre in 1297 the Mamluks waged a campaign against the Maronite Christians of Lebanon; but this was a response to their political disloyalty—they had allied with the Frankish Crusaders—rather than for religious motives per se. The Christian Armenians of Cilicia would face similar retribution for their support of the Mongols.

It has been suggested that the development of canon law, together with the rise of rationalist approaches to the analysis of doctrine and scripture and the bureaucratization of the Catholic Church from the eleventh century forward, led to the "development of a persecuting society," in which any nonconformists, be they Muslims, Jews, lepers, homosexuals, or heretical Christians, were subject to systematic marginalization. While an institutional apparatus for repression within the church and the will on the part of some clergy to root out any dissenters certainly became hallmarks of Latin Christendom, such repression tended to occur only when the interests of reactionary clergy resonated strongly with popular anxieties or aligned with the political or economic agendas of rulers, nonreligious elites, or common folk.

This can be seen in the experience of Jews in the Latin Mediterranean, where they became the focus of aggressive clerical polemic thanks in part to increasing scrutiny of Hebrew religious works, especially Talmudic texts, by canon lawyers and theologians in the early 1200s. Moreover, their prominence as royal and noble administrators and moneylenders generated resentment on the part of members of the lower nobility and educated common classes who now aspired to administrative positions often held by Jews, as well as Christian subjects who found themselves indebted to them. The widespread Mediterranean Christian belief that Jews were inherently traitorous Christ-killers, together with the challenge to the claim that Jesus was the Old Testament Messiah that the continuing existence of Jewish communities posed, fed an increasingly hostile popular and clerical attitude. Beginning in the mid-1100s, "blood libel"—false charges that Jews committed ritual murder against Christian children—filtered southward from northern Europe, where anti-Jewish popular violence had first coincided with the launch of the Peoples' Crusade. In the mid-thirteenth century Jews were targeted with false accusations of host desecration—defiling the transubstantiated body of Christ. In the Iberian Peninsula, spontaneous or ritualized violence against Jews became increasingly common on holidays such as Easter and Corpus Christi by the late 1200s.

As early as the 1170s the French kings, with their sacred pretensions, drew on and sometimes encouraged popular and clerical anti-Jewish sentiment in order to reinforce their political and economic positions, formally expelling Jews from their realms and appropriating their outstanding loans, before eventually allowing them to resettle in the kingdom. After France's annexation of Languedoc following the Cathar Crusade, this dynamic began to affect the Jewish communities there. In 1306 the Jews of France (now including Languedoc) were expelled, and their properties confiscated. Readmitted in 1315, they were expelled again in 1323, and admitted back again in 1359. In 1320 the populist Shepherds' Crusade moved south into Languedoc and Catalonia, attacking Jewish communities and lepers, to the alarm of the kings and the papacy, and in 1321 Inquisitors claimed lepers were poisoning wells in southern France. The rising tide of anti-Jewish sentiment in Latin lands from the 1280s to 1350 was related to the contraction of the European economy, and the increasing interest of Christians in the credit and administration sectors, where Jews had sometimes held high position and were now seen as competitors. By contrast, there are almost no incidents of popular violence against subject Muslims in Latin Europe, the chief exception being the attacks suffered by the Muslims of Sicily in the late 1100s. However, this was political violence—a consequence of their defense of the unpopular Norman dynasty.

The Crusade movement set the stage for sectarian conflict in the Byzantine Empire. The schism of 1054 notwithstanding, the Greek and Latin worlds were drawn into ever-tighter political and economic interdependence. The settlement in Constantinople of Genoese and Venetians, seen as predatory and aggressive by Byzantines, and the incorporation of Latin noblemen in the imperial court aggravated ethnic and religious tensions among commoners, noblemen, and clergy. This culminated in the massacre of Consantinople's Latins under Andronikos Komnenos in 1183—the latest episode in long-simmering tensions between the two groups, fed by the papal claims to universal religious authority and Frankish coveting of the imperial title. Tensions and distrust had escalated with the Norman and Pisan campaigns against the empire in the mid-twelfth century and Alexios Komnenos's clandestine alliance with the Fatimids against the first Crusaders. The brutal sack and massacre of Constantinople in the Fourth Crusade in 1204 was, in many ways, the culmination of these tensions.

A similar alignment of ethnic, religious, regional, and political tensions can be seen in the Crusades launched against the Cathars of Languedoc soon after, which provided an opportunity first for the predatory northern French lay and clerical nobility and, subsequently, for the French crown to seize control of Languedoc under the pious banner of crusade. After 1229, when the region was brought under control of France, Gregory IX instituted the Inquisition, which soon came under control of the Dominican order, to root out the remaining heretics. Somewhat less successful was the Crusade Innocent III authorized Kálmán of Hungary to undertake against the Bogomils of Bosnia. Here, too, regional loyalties led local Catholics to defend their heretical countrymen against foreign invasion, while the Mongol invasion of Hungary and the Balkans in 1241 provided unexpected and crucial relief. Franciscans and Dominicans were dispatched to preach against the heretics—the former establishing an unsuccessful inquisition in 1291—and further Crusades would be launched in 1337 and 1367, but to little effect. Pragmatic rulers, such as Tvrtko of Bosnia (1353–1391), a Catholic, cultivated loyalty by turning a blind eye to their subjects' religious practices, just as the counts of Toulouse had done in Cathar Languedoc in the 1100s and 1200s.

In the Islamic Mediterranean ethno-linguistic, religious, and political/economic agendas sometimes aligned, manifesting themselves as sectarian conflicts, as can be seen in the violent irruption of Arab Bedouin tribes, the anti-Shi'i *jihad* championed by many of the Turkic peoples coming in from the East, the resistance of Andalusi Muslims (typically with the support of Spanish Christian rulers) against Muslim Berber invaders, and the various heterodox Berber movements that emerged in Ifriqiya and the Maghrib. The Almohad movement was the most successful of these, but lasted for less than a century and lost its nativist dimension almost immediately. Across the Islamic world Sunni and Shi'i rulers and religious elites worked to undermine each other: Shi'is through the medium of clandestine missionaries sent to infiltrate and subvert Sunni society, and Sunnis through purges of suspect functionaries and religious authorities. But the fact that Islamic societies remained so diverse and that most came to be dominated by foreign military elites meant that creed, language, religion, and ethnicity did not coalesce vertically as self-conscious and homogeneous regional "national" identities, as began to gradually occur in parts of the Christian Mediterranean in the thirteenth century.

Cosmopolitan Communities

By the mid-eleventh century Byzantium and much of the Islamic world (including Islamicate Jewish and Christian societies) had reached a high level of doctrinal and institutional development characterized by the establishment of systematic approaches to secular and religious law, the development of educational, charitable, and urban administrative institutions, and the establishment of vibrant and varied literary, intellectual, and religious cultures. Booming and ever-more interconnected economies spurred the emergence of urban and rural "middle classes" who had both increasing acquisitive power and growing political ambitions.

The chief beneficiaries of this process were those whom Muslims uniformly called the al-Ifranj (Franks): Latin Christians—whether peoples native to the Mediterranean, including Italian, Provençal, and Catalan merchants and Iberian and Occitan warrior elites, or outsiders from the north, notably Normans and Burgundians. Empowered by the boom of the Medieval Optimum, Latin elites were drawn into the Mediterranean political vacuum by the pull of commerce and a hunger for land and power. As Latin Christians (and Latinate Jews) established themselves here they readily adopted what they found, accelerating the development of civic and religious institutions and vernacular and learned culture in Western Christendom. The framework of "mutual intelligibility" among Muslims, Christians, and Jews around the Mediterranean lubricated acculturation, and Latins were soon active participants in these processes of innovation. They quickly developed an awareness of the larger Islamicate world and regions far beyond the Mediterranean in Africa and Asia, as they came to eclipse Byzantium and rival Dar al-Islam as the arbiters of culture and power in the Middle Sea.

Education, Language, and Identity

The increasing prosperity and complexity of Mediterranean economies and societies led to the extension of literacy and numeracy and the development of new educational and administrative institutions that would draw in broader sectors of the population, stimulate the development of vernacular and popular cultures, and shape the way people saw their own ethno-religious communities. In Latin lands, there had been schools attached to monasteries and cathedrals since the early Middle Ages, and Charlemagne had also established a palace school to promote learning at court. However, in the twelfth century the systematization of civil and canon law and the demand for competent administrators led to the development and dissemination of the university. The first law school, founded at Bologna in 1088, was a clear forerunner. The teaching masters at the cathedral school of Notre Dame and other schools in Paris received a charter to incorporate in 1200 as the University of Paris, and soon became the principal theological authority in Western Christendom. By the end of the century Latin rulers saw universities as an indispensable element of their power apparatus, and as incubators of local talent. With the exception of Frederick II's University of Naples (1224), all were founded as institutions of the church. Instruction was carried out in Latin, and students and faculty, by default, were considered clergy (most, especially among the students, of minor, nonpriestly rank)—making formal education subject to ecclesiastical control and limited to Catholic men.

Some sort of medical school had been in operation in Salerno since perhaps the tenth century; it was recognized by Frederick II in 1231. A similar school had coalesced in Montpellier by the 1130s; chartered in 1220, it was eventually incorporated into the university. Both were important points of transmission for Byzantine and Islamic medical knowledge to Latin Christendom, and for the professionalization of medicine. This professionalization would eventually spark laws that formally excluded all but male Christian practitioners, but these were disregarded in practice across the Latin Mediterranean.

By this time, Latin was no longer anyone's mother tongue, having evolved into the Romance languages: Occitan, Catalan, Castilian, Galician/Portuguese, Provençal, the various Italian languages, and Romanian. Latin was the universal language of higher learning, but universities became hothouses for the development of local nonseigniorial elites. These increasingly identified with the urban culture of their locale or region and its vernacular language and customs. The idea of nation (from *natio,* "birth") began to take root.

In the late eleventh century papermaking, by origin

By the fourteenth century the balance of power in the Iberian Peninsula had shifted toward the Christian principalities, and the only remaining independent Muslim kingdom was the Nasrid sultanate of Granada. Thanks to its silk industry and intensive agricultural output Granada was very wealthy and maintained a lively intellectual and artistic culture. Important innovations were made in architecture and decoration, not the least in plaster-casting, which allowed artisans to mass-produce elaborate, high-relief sculpted decorative elements, often incorporating Arabic calligraphy, which were then painted in vivid color. Nasrid palaces were typically arrayed around open-air courtyards, often incorporating a water feature, and sometimes plants.

The sultanate was deeply enmeshed politically and culturally with Christian Castile, which considered it a vassal state. Despite Nasrid political debility, the cultural capital embodied by Islam remained strong, Islamicate art and fashion continued to evoke sophistication and power, and Castilian elite culture was characterized by Maurophilia (the affectation of Arabo-Islamic styles of architecture, fashion, and popular culture). By the early fourteenth century noble palaces were being constructed in Nasrid style by Muslim craftsmen for the Muslim, Christian, and Jewish aristocratic elite of the peninsula not only in Granada but across Christian Castile.

The Alcázar of Seville

Originating as the palace of the eleventh-century *taifa* kings of Seville, the Alcázar (*al-qasr* or "fortress") was subsequently remodeled and expanded by the Almoravids and Almohads, and eventually by the Castilian kings, who ruled the city from 1248. Important Islamic-style additions were made by Alfonso XI (1312–1350), while his son, Pedro the Cruel (1350–1366), undertook a major remodeling in the latest Nasrid fashion. The so-called Patio of the Maidens was intended to be the main courtyard of the palace and was begun in 1356. Geometric designs in high relief are bounded by bands of Arabic calligraphy. The inscriptions include a series of typical invocations of the power of God, such as "Glory to God [Allah]," "To You, O Unique God, is all power," as well as evocations for good fortune, "Happiness and prosperity." King Pedro is recognized: "Glory to our lord, the Sultan Pedro, May God aid him and protect him." Other inscriptions strike an anti-Christian subversive tone, including "The kingdom for God" and "God is Unique. God is Eternal. He was not born nor was he born of, and he has no companion."[1]

The Synagogue of "el Tránsito," Toledo

Inaugurated in 1357, this compact, luxuriously appointed synagogue, known as "el Tránsito" was one of ten in Toledo. Built by the architect Meir Abdeil, it was commissioned by Samuel ha-Levi Abulafia, chamberlain, magistrate, and treasurer to Pedro the Cruel. A passageway connected Samuel's palace to the synagogue in emulation of the private chapels of Christian kings and magnates. In 1360 Samuel was accused of embezzlement. After confessing under torture, he was executed along with members of his family, and the synagogue was confiscated. The main section of the building is a prayer hall some seventy-five by forty feet with a height of thirty-one feet. While the exterior is plain, the interior is decorated with Nasrid-style painted stucco with geometric and floral motifs punctuated by coats of arms of the king of Castile and the Levi family, and features lobed windows and niches and a mujahidun *artesonado* (cabinetwork) ceiling. A women's gallery was on the second floor. The interior is notable for its inscriptions in Arabic and Hebrew, integrating verses from the Qur'an, Psalms, Chronicles, and the Book of Habbakuk, as well exhortations of praise and good fortune: "Happiness and Prosperity!" (in Arabic).[2] The Hebrew inscriptions around the niche for the Torah scrolls took a Messianic tone: "When there is no king in Israel, He has not left us without a Redeemer."[3]

The Alhambra Palace, Granada

Originally founded by the Jewish *wazir* Isma'il (Samuel) ibn Naghrilla, the Alhambra (Red Palace) sits on a hill above the Darro River, on the south side of the city of Granada. The present complex was begun in the 1230s by Muhammad ibn al-Ahmar, the founder of the Nasrid dynasty, as a fortress and palace, and was expanded by subsequent rulers. In the 1350s the sultans Yusuf I (1333–1354) and Muhammad V (1354–1359 and 1362–1391) carried out major expansions. Overthrown in 1354, Muhammad lived in exile in both Christian Castile and Marinid Morocco

FIGURE 7.11 The Patio of the Maidens. Paul Quayle / Design Pics / Bridgeman Images.

FIGURE 7.12 The interior of the Synagogue of "el Tránsito," ca. 1320–1360. Photo: Zev Radovan / BibleLandPictures.com / Alamy Stock Photo.

FIGURE 7.13 The "Courtyard of the Lions," in the Alhambra. iStock.com/Alxpin.

before returning to power. Most of the surviving decoration dates from Muhammad's second reign, and additions may have incorporated a *madrasa* (religious academy), a *zawiya* (Sufi convent), and royal mausoleum. The decorative style is similar to the *alcázar* —an interior of gravity-defying and graceful high-relief screens and stalactites, featuring brilliantly colored ceramic tiles, elaborately carved woodwork, and expanses of translucent marble. Dizzyingly complex geometric and vegetal patterns in stucco were interspersed with Qur'anic inscriptions and verses by the sultan's royal poets-laureate. Christian artists from Castile added paintings depicting scenes of chivalry and the hunt. The Courtyard of the Lions measures 115 by 66 feet; the alabaster fountain may be a relic of Ibn Naghrilla's palace, representing the Twelve Tribes. The patio featured orange trees and flowering plants.

Inscriptions cover virtually every wall surface, often duplicating those of the *alcázar*. Some are religious ("There is no victor but God," "Glory belongs to God"), others are exhortations ("Blessing!" "Happiness!"), and others praise the sultan ("Glory be to God the Sultan Abu 'Abd Allah"). The fountain is engraved with a poem by Muhammad's poet laureate, Ibn Zamrak, that begins:

> Blessed is He who gave the imam Muhammad
> the genius to beautify his mansions!
> In this garden aren't there marvels . . .
> the beauty of which God would not allow others to share?[34]

Discussion Questions

1. Why would a Christian royal palace and a Jewish synagogue feature Qur'anic inscriptions?

2. What do the common decorative styles of these three buildings suggest about how Christians, Muslims, and Jews saw each other or each other's cultures in the fourteenth century?

3. Were their practical reasons for Muslims, Christians, and Jews to patronize each other's artistic traditions? Or to avoid doing so?

Further Reading

"Alhambra," "Real Alcázar de Sevilla," and "Sinagoga del Tránsito." *Archnet.org.* https://archnet.org/sites/2547, https://archnet.org/sites/2852, https://archnet.org/sites/3756.

Dodds, Jerrilynn D. "Mudejar Tradition and the Synagogues of Medieval Spain: Cultural Identity and Cultural Hegemony." In *Convivencia: Jews, Muslims, and Christians in Medieval Spain*, ed. Vivian B. Mann, Thomas F. Glick, and Jerrilynn D. Dodds, 112–31. New York: Jewish Museum, 1992.

Goldman, Esther W. "Samuel Halevi Abulafia's Synagogue: El Tránsito in Toledo." *Jewish Art* 18 (1992): 58–69.

Puerta Vílchez, José Miguel, and Juan Agustín Núñez Guarde. *Reading the Alhambra: A Visual Guide to the Alhambra through Its Inscriptions.* Granada: Patronato de la Alhambra y Generalife, 2011.

Ruggles, D. Fairchild. "The Alcazar of Seville and Mudejar Architecture." *Gesta* 43 (2004): 87–98.

Notes

1. Rodrigo Amador de los Ríos and Fernández de Villalta, *Inscripciones Árabes De Sevilla* (1875; Mairena del Aljarafe (Sevilla): Extramuros Edición, 2008), 132–51.

2. Francisco Cantera Burgos, *Sinagogas españolas: Con especial estudio de la de Córdoba y la toledana de el Tránsito* (Madrid: Instituto "Benito Arias Montano," 1984), 30.

3. Cecil Roth and Federico Pérez Castro, *Las inscripciones históricas de la Sinagoga del Tránsito de Toledo* (Madrid: Instituto Arias Montano, 1948), 19.

4. Puerta Vílchez and Núñez Guarde, *Reading the Alhambra*, 169.

Chinese, was adopted from the Islamic world, notably in Iberia, before appearing in France and Italy. Access to cheap writing material stimulated administrative culture and vernacularization and served as a catalyst for the emergence of local identities. Rulers contributed to this process. The twelfth-century counts of Aquitaine and kings of Aragon wrote poetry in Occitan. In the 1200s, Frederick II wrote poetry in Sicilian, Alfonso X of Castile composed hymns in Galician, and Jaume I of Aragon dictated an autobiography in Catalan, each signaling the emerging prestige of these languages. By the 1300s vernaculars were beginning to displace Latin as the languages of law, diplomacy, and administration—coinciding with the rising power and prosperity of non-noble urban classes. In Italy, local urban elites would set the groundwork for a vernacular flowering in the fourteenth century, with authors such as Dante, Petrarch, and Boccaccio. The extension of literacy and education stimulated broader and more sophisticated engagement with scripture and religious doctrine. This energized popular piety and strengthened confessional identity, but also provoked popular criticism of doctrine, as well as dissent and heresy.

In addition to royal, aristocratic, and private libraries and centers of scholarship, institutions of formal education, typically attached to mosques, had existed in the Islamic Mediterranean for centuries. Al-Zaytuna in Kairouan (737), al-Qarawiyyin in Fez (859), and al-Azhar (970 or 972) in Cairo are often referred to as "universities" because of their public aspect and comprehensive and multidisciplinary curricula. Al-Qarawiyyin, it should be noted, was founded by a female aristocrat, Fatima al-Fihri, while al-Azhar was established in part to develop and disseminate Fatimid ideology.

The *madrasa*, a mid-eleventh-century innovation traditionally credited to the Persian-Seljuq statesman Nizam al-Mulk, was a residential religious college that provided free or subsidized education intended specifically to reinforce Seljuq legitimacy and Sunni doctrine. *Madrasas* were established across the Seljuq lands, thus nurturing a broad, popular class of literate jurists, administrators, and clerics who would be, in principle, loyal to the regime. Over the course of the next centuries the institution was adopted by later dynasties and spread westward, reaching Marinid Morocco and Nasrid al-Andalus in the mid-fourteenth century.

Among Muslims in this period the *madrasa* acted as a brake on the literary development of vernacular literatures (such as Berber, or Amazigh, and Turkic languages), which could not compete with the prestige and privilege that Arabic enjoyed as the language of scripture, culture, and business, dominating everyday speech across the urban Islamic Mediterranean. This, in turn, helped ensure that regional identities would not eclipse confessional community at this time, as began to happen in the Latin West, and maintained the legal and cultural integration of the Islamic world, even as political divisions became more acute. East of the Mediterranean the dominance of Arabic was reduced. Persian, which had been a literary language before Islam, reemerged in 'Abbasid lands in the ninth century, with the rise of native elites and the devolution of political power to the Persianate principalities of the East. By the thirteenth century, a rich and diverse literary tradition, strongly influenced by South Asia, and notable for its poetry, epic, and histories, was carried toward the Mediterranean through the medium of the Seljuqs. The great Persian-language poet, Sufi, and founder of the Mevlevi dervish order, Jalal al-Din al-Rumi (d. 1273)—one of the best-selling poets both in the US and around the world today—was born in Balkh (Afghanistan) but established his base in Konya, Anatolia. The Seljuqs brought their own mostly oral Turkic folk and poetic traditions west, but it was not until the rise of the Ottomans that Turkish literary culture gained the political patronage necessary for it to blossom.

Islamic thought exercised an enormous influence on the curricula of Latin universities, and there is some evidence of institutional influence as well—there are intriguing structural similarities between *madrasas* and the residential colleges that formed part of Latin universities, but both *madrasas* and universities flourished because they corresponded to the needs and capacities of the societies in which they evolved and the agendas of local rulers and elites. A similar dynamic can be seen in the development of urban medical and mental hospitals and charitable hospices. These developed first in the urban and urbane Dar al-Islam and Byzantium because hospitals here served a real need. Byzantine *xenodocheia* (hospice/charitable complexes) may have provided a model for the Islamic *bimaristan* (Persian for "place for the sick"), but the latter was distinguished by its "public" and "professional" (that is, staffed by trained physicians) character and its autonomy (as these were typically supported by *waqf* endowments). As the Christian West became more developed in the thirteenth century, analogous institutions evolved, sometimes influenced by earlier models that Latins had encountered in the eastern Mediterranean.

In the Christian East, including Byzantium, higher education was carried out in palace and monastic environments, with royal or church sponsorship, and under private tutelage. Greek was both the language of administration and liturgy, and—in most of the empire—the dominant language of daily speech and affairs. A palace school, the Pandidakterion (roughly, "university") had been established by Theodosius II in 425 to train administrators and survived until the early seventh century. In 855, the regent Bardas founded the short-lived Magnaura school, next to the palace, and some of the major provincial capitals also had schools. In 1047 Constantine IX briefly reestablished the Pandidakterion, but by now education was largely in the hands of private academies run by masters, such as the monk, historian, and philosopher Michael Psellos (d. 1078), although the Patriarchal School was also important. The destruction of the empire in 1204 had a catastrophic effect, but after the recovery of Constantinople in 1261, education resumed under clerical and royal initiative, and schools, such as that of the layman and polymath Maximus Planudes (d. ca. 1305), reenergized higher education.

The situation in Armenia and in the Slavic Balkans was similar. Education and literature here were church-oriented, except in those instances when autonomous local dynasties coalesced and supported court cultures. As Armenian Cilicia became increasingly linked politically to the Latin world in the twelfth and thirteenth centuries, high culture here took a corresponding turn. Because of their links to the Orthodox Church and Byzantine culture, literary culture in both the Serbian and Bulgarian Empires of the thirteenth and fourteenth centuries turned toward Kiev, and eventually Muscovy, which presented themselves as the successors of Byzantine authority. Among Coptic and Syriac Christian minorities, education was confined to monastic environments, and their languages (each with its own alphabet) were displaced as languages of common speech by Arabic. Neither was the "flagship" language of a kingdom, but the strong Coptic bureaucratic elite of Egypt provided patronage and support thanks to its influence. Rather than spark a decline, the increasing social repression and economic isolation of the Christian minority in the thirteenth century retrenched Coptic identity and was accompanied by a "renaissance" of its culture—but the literary dimension of this revival was all but exclusively in Arabic.

A similar dynamic can be observed among the Jews of Latin lands, who were increasingly marginalized economically and ideologically over the course of this period. Hebrew, having been deeply influenced by Arabic literary and grammatical models, had begun to emerge as a language of secular poetry. Although still not used in daily speech, by the eleventh century in al-Andalus under the *taifa* kings Hebrew letters flourished in a fondly remembered "golden age," sponsored by powerful Jewish officials, like the Banu Naghrilla of Granada. Through the 1200s, Hebrew literary culture was sustained in Latin lands by influential Jewish administrators and businessmen. Languedoc and the Crown of Aragon, where Islamicate Jewish families from the south and Latinate Jewish families from the north collaborated and clashed, became an epicenter for Hebrew language and Latinate Jewish learning. David Kimhi (d. 1235) of Narbonne compiled what are widely regarded as the first Hebrew grammar (*Miklol*) and dictionary (*Sefer ha-Shorashim*). Largely confined to theological and liturgical contexts, Hebrew was unevenly reestablished as a language of internal administration and secular literature, although local Romance languages dominated speech. Among Jews of the Islamic Mediterranean, Arabic remained the dominant literary and vernacular language, with Judeo-Arabic (often written in Hebrew characters) also used in popular and legal communications. The abundant quotidian documentation preserved in the Cairo *geniza* reveals the dizzying variety of languages and alphabets used by Jews of the Islamic Mediterranean. SEE SOURCEBOOK 7:6.

The crystallization of identities anchored in local customs and languages and the perception of humanity as composed of *gentes* (peoples) of distinct origins and faith are reflected in the historiographical traditions that developed in this era, particularly epic histories that sought to trace the origins of peoples back to either the flood narrative and the sons of Noah or the personalities and events of Virgil's epic poem, *The Aeneid*, or both. In Latin lands, this movement may have been stimulated by the Frankish experience in the East, where Archbishop William of Tyre (d. 1186) wrote works including a chronicle of the Kingdom of Jerusalem and a history of the Arabs. A half century later Archbishop Rodrigo Jiménez de Rada of Toledo (d. 1247) undertook similar projects focusing on the West. By the fourteenth century, protonational chronicles were common in Latin lands, and served to legitimize both the ruling houses and the local vernacular culture and local elites.

In al-Andalus chroniclers drew on the Arabic historiographical tradition and works composed in the tenth and eleventh centuries. Here, scholars had elaborated a distinct Andalusi/Umayyad historical identity in counterpoint to that of the Berbers, while in the Islamic East, the tenth-century verse epic, *Shahnameh*, sought to reclaim the prestige of Persian language and identity over that of the Arabs. A Jewish analogue can be seen in Ibn Dawwud's *Book of Tradition* (1160–1161), which charts the history of the Andalusi Jewish community from its purported foundation in the emperor Augustus's colony at Mérida through the Rabbanite authorities' triumph over Karaism in the peninsula. As part of their program of universal monarchy, in the late 1100s the Almohads invested heavily in official histories that charted their ascent and reinforced their legitimacy—a strategy that was appropriated by the Castilian king and would-be Holy Roman Emperor, Alfonso X, "the Learned," a century later.

Cosmopolitanism and Community

Counterintuitively, the forces that contributed to the development of ever-more clearly defined ethnic and religious identities across the Christian and Islamicate Mediterranean in the period from 1050 to 1350 were the result of the increasing economic, political, and intellectual integration of the region, and the processes of cultural syncretism and appropriation that accompanied this. This was a period during which both newcomers to the region and established communities engaged with one another confidently and optimistically, reinforcing a Mediterranean cultural and social dynamic that was remarkably cosmopolitan and pragmatic, in which the various communities borrowed from each other unabashedly. This is clearly seen in the evolution of intellectual culture in this era (the subject of the next two chapters), but can be observed across a gamut of cultural expressions.

Palatine and religious architecture reflects this complexity. Latin rulers frequently built churches and palaces dramatically combining Latin, Byzantine, and Islamicate design elements, as can be observed in the Norman royal palaces and churches in Sicily. In some instances, these were combined to produce new "hybrid" styles, but often elements of diverse provenance were simply placed together. By the mid-fourteenth century, the Castilian nobility (and the local Jewish elite) had fully embraced an Islamicate architectural aesthetic. Pedro the Cruel's remodeling of the Alcázar palace of Seville in the 1350s in flamboyant Islamic style predated Muhammad V's renovations of the Alhambra in Granada, which resembles it closely. Both were likely built by the same craftsmen. Across the Mediterranean, *spolia* (including recycled columns and sculptures from classical-era buildings) were incorporated into new palace and church constructions, including the enormous iron griffin, which likely originated in al-Andalus, perched on the cathedral of Pisa or the ceramic bowls (*bacini*) of North African provenance set into church exteriors as decorative elements. St. Mark's Square, the emblematic epicenter of the Venetian Empire, and home to the eponymous cathedral and the doge's palace, is a Latinate-Byzantine complex decorated with items either purchased or plundered from Constantinople. In the eastern Mediterranean Latinate and Persian architectural and decorative styles became increasingly fashionable as Latin and Turkic political influence grew in the region. Through much of the Iberian Peninsula, churches and palaces were built by Muslim craftsmen and engineers, who decorated these in the distinctive brickwork and ceramic patterns that typify this Mudejar architecture.

FIGURE 7.14 The Mudejar-style Church of San Salvador, Teruel, Aragon, thirteenth century CE. a-plus image bank / Alamy Stock Photo.

Churches, palaces, synagogues, and mosques often contained epigraphic inscriptions in combinations of Arabic, Latin, Hebrew, and Greek, while items such as oil lamps, ivory boxes, textiles and silk, and metal and wooden furnishings were incorporated, sometimes after having been repurposed and altered according to the tastes and needs of their new owners, in church and palace interiors. Such items were obtained as plunder, tribute, by purchase or as gifts. In addition to rock crystal ewers like the "Eleanor vase" (fig. 6.1), elaborately carved chests and cylindrical storage vessels made of ivory or gold or silver-plated wood and originating in al-Andalus or Fatimid lands were transformed by Christians into reliquaries or pyxides (containers for the Eucharist), while banners, flags, and lengths of embroidered silk were repurposed as church vestments. In addition to exotic items such as *olifants*, quotidien items of leather, ceramic, metal, glass, and woodworking items originating in the Islamic world soon proliferated and were imitated across the Mediterranean. This disseminated Islamicate tastes and motifs far beyond the Muslim world—for example, the decorative roundels, which came west from China via Central Asia in late antiquity and became so characteristic of textiles and carving of the Islamic world, were rapidly integrated into the standard repertoire of Latinate styles.

At times such appropriations and adaptations could be seen as demonstrations of the subjugation of rival communities; in other instances, they incorporated symbols or motifs that were universally associated with power and prestige or the sacred, such as the tree of life, or symbols

FIGURE 7.15 Arabic, Greek, and Latin scribes in the Norman court of Sicily, from the illuminated poem *The Book in Honor of the Emperor, or on Sicilian Affairs* by Petrus de Eboli, 1196 CE. Album / Alamy Stock Photo.

of the zodiac. In some cases, foreign objects and styles were simply regarded as more sophisticated or attractive, and at times styles were perpetuated because minority craftsmen continued to favor their own techniques and tastes, and these came to exercise an appeal among the majority group.

Both in Byzantium and the Latin West non-Muslim artists and craftsmen appropriated styles and motifs from the Islamic world. The Arabic language and alphabet exercised a fascination and aesthetic appeal such that non-Arabic-speaking Christian artists incorporated nonsensical Arabic-looking calligraphy into their artwork and objects from the 800s through the 1500s. Most common was "Pseudo-Kufic" (imitating the chunky Kufic script that was dominant in the Islamic world until the tenth century), although the more graceful and elaborate Naskh and Thuluth scripts were also imitated in later centuries.

In thirteenth-century Iberia Muslim *mudéjares* were often indistinguishable from Christians in speech and dress, while Christian noblemen sported Muslim-style weapons and costume. In the same era, Jews produced lavishly decorated *Haggadot* (Passover ceremonials) that were illustrated with scenes in contemporary Latinate styles likely by Christian artists, Jewish antipathy to human representation notwithstanding. Persian- and Central Asian–influenced art of the 'Abbasid lands also featured human representations in manuscripts, carving, and textiles, motifs that spread west to the Fatimid lands and al-Andalus.

Such acculturation can be seen across the gamut of cultural expression, including popular games and pastimes, notably chess and popular games of chance, both of which were adapted by Latins from the Arabs. In this era the cuisine of the Christian lands—most dramatically the Iberian Peninsula and Sicily—was transformed by an infusion of new crops, including asparagus, eggplant, rice, and new strains of wheat and legumes, as well as a great variety of fruits and nuts, not to mention spices, many of which originated in South Asia, and were now cultivated or imported to the Latin world. Once domesticated, the ingredients and recipes of the Islamic world became entrenched in European cuisine.

Similar processes of transmission and synthesis transformed literature and music, although here too the greatest impact can be seen in Latin culture. Near Eastern oral and written traditions of heroic epic poetry and folktales circulated and evolved among Slavs, Byzantines, Armenians, Turks, Persians, and Arabs from the Balkans to Mesopotamia, and were invigorated by Central and South Asian influences that were synthesized and then broadcast westward from the 'Abbasid East to Ifriqiya, Sicily, and al-Andalus. The chivalric "songs of deeds" (*chansons de gestes,* or *cantares de gesta*) that gained popularity in the 1100s were the Western echo of those Eastern heroic epics. Those, like the *History of Roderic* (and its later embellishment, the *Poem of the Cid*), which originated in the Mediterranean itself, tended to reflect a culture in which warrior ethos and vocation bridged confessional and ethnic divisions. On the other hand, those like the *Song of Roland,* which crystallized in the distant Latin north, tended to portray Muslims as monstrous personifications of evil. Muslims whose noble qualities could not be denied, such as Salah al-Din or Nur al-Din, were sometimes fictionalized in the Latin imagination as secret Christians or the offspring of captured Latin princesses. Conversely, a subgenre of Old French epic presented Charlemagne as being raised in boyhood in Umayyad al-Andalus and marrying a Muslim princess (who converts to Christianity).

Islamicate styles of verse and song (and, presumably, dance), together with a repertoire of new instruments—notably the oud (*al-'ud*; which became the lute, and in time the guitar) and violin—would transform Latin popular and high culture. The development of the troubadour tradition in Occitan lands in the eleventh century was heavily influenced by Arabic antecedents, thanks in part to the capture of Andalusi songstresses by William IX of Aquitaine at Barbastro in 1066. The evolution of the aesthetic of courtly love in the Latin West is also a product of this process. The Arabic poets patronized by the Norman kings of Sicily had an analogous impact on Italian literature.

Because of the common environment and cultural foundations of the Mediterranean, people appreciated foreign literatures, and the cohesiveness of a regional literary culture was reinforced by the broad multilingualism that characterized the area. In this diverse environment many people of all classes, even the most humble, spoke more than one language (although undoubtedly with varying proficiency). Greek, Hebrew, and Arabic all employed loanwords taken from each other, and it was Arabic that provided the basic vocabulary for medicine, science, and engineering in the vernaculars of Christian Europe. Even in distant Britain—the English language, which only evolved in its modern form in the late fifteenth century, has some 1,000 Arabic-derived words. But the impact of Arabic on the daily speech of the Latin Mediterranean was even more profound. Hundreds of quotidian and technical Arabic terms entered Portuguese, Catalan, and the Italian languages, while Castilian Spanish can be seen as the product of an Arabic vocabulary pressed into a Romance grammatical structure, like a medieval "Spanglish." At the farthest end of the spectrum, Maltese is essentially twelfth-century Sicilian Arabic, the lexicon of which was transformed by Latinate vernaculars. Some European words made their way into Arabic in this period, but these were related mostly to specific Latin military and technical innovations that were adopted by Muslims.

CHAPTER EIGHT

Reading Each Other's Books

Though crowned at a most auspicious moment, many things went badly for Alfonso X, Christian king of Castile-León (1252–1284). His father, Fernando III, had nearly doubled the size of his kingdom in a series of dramatic conquests of Muslim territory in southern Spain, including the great cities of Seville and Córdoba. His contemporary King Jaume I of Aragon, just to the east, had likewise conquered a great deal of Muslim territory, so that all modern Spain, other than the Sultanate of Granada in the far south, had come to be ruled over by Christian monarchs—and Alfonso X governed by far the largest territory. Yet as king, Alfonso frittered away enormous wealth in a decades-long, unsuccessful quest to become the Holy Roman Emperor, and by the 1270s his own son had rebelled against him. When Alfonso died in the middle of the following decade, he was nearly powerless.

Nevertheless, Alfonso X is remembered as a great Spanish king, for despite his political ineptitude, he was perhaps the most important patron of culture in Spanish history—indeed he became known to posterity as Alfonso El Sabio, "the Wise" or "the Learned," and modern scholars have dubbed him an "emperor of culture." Yet one of the most striking things about this cultural emperor's efforts is the degree to which they were rooted in Arabo-Islamic civilization. Not only were parts of the great law code that he commissioned derived directly from Arabic texts, but he underwrote the translation of a whole range of Arabic works into Spanish: sophisticated astronomical manuals, the *Lapidary* (a treatise on the properties of stones), the *Book about Animals That Hunt* (a guide to falconry), and the *Book of Chess*. Moreover, he put master craftsmen to work copying these originally Arabic texts into gorgeous, beautifully illustrated books.

While the Learned Alfonso, a pious Christian king, went to unprecedented lengths to embrace and domesticate Arabo-Muslim learning and ideas, there was nothing unusual about his fascination with the literature and ideas of a rival religious culture. Indeed, Mediterranean people read each other's books remarkably often, and while such reading across religious and linguistic boundaries happened throughout the Middle Ages, it was particularly intense in the period from 1050 to 1350. Translators insured that a wide variety of entertaining adventure stories jumped from one religious culture to the next, and even the foundational holy books of these civilizations found themselves in their rivals' languages. Naturally enough, furthermore, Jews, Christians, and Muslims living side by side and deeply aware of each other's sacred texts repeatedly fell to talking about them.

It is true that the educational systems of the medieval Mediterranean overwhelmingly focused students' attention, as we saw in chapter 4, on one holy book, studied in one holy language, but that did not keep Mediterranean people from reading across those boundaries. As we will see in the next chapter, moreover, this cross-boundary reading included seminal works of science and philosophy that profoundly shaped the civilizations surrounding the Sea in the Middle. But reading across religious and linguistic boundaries by no means erased them. Indeed, it tended to reinforce them: having acquired great cultural wealth from the outside and put it into its own language, each religious culture tended to become even more confident in its self-sufficiency.

FIGURE 8.1 Image of Alfonso X in thirteenth-century manuscript of the *Libro de los juegos*. Album / Alamy Stock Photo.

Translators and Terrific Stories

In medieval Arabic, a translator was called a *tarjuman,* and *tarjumans* were always in demand, what with Arabic, Syriac, Persian, Greek, Coptic, and Armenian speakers all living side by side. There was nothing new about this. In fact, *tarjuman* was already an ancient word by the time the Arabs adopted it: it had meant "translator" three millennia earlier in the ancient Semitic language, Akkadian. In different formulations, moreover, this word would pass from one language to the next around the Mediterranean—Jews called the Aramaic translations of the Bible *targums;* Persians and Turks followed Arabic practice in calling an interpreter a *tarjuman* or *terjüman* respectively; in Greek this came out as *dragoumanos,* which later became *dragamannus* in medieval Latin, and then *drugemen* in medieval French. By the late Middle Ages, English had turned the French version into *dragoman* (pl. *dragomen*). This Semitic word for "translator" sailed back and forth across the Sea in the Middle because translation was everywhere necessary, and the texts that *tarjumans/dragomen* translated journeyed just as far. Indeed, stories of great deeds and holy men appealed to people of all religions, and in translating and adapting them for new audiences, the countless, mostly anonymous medieval *dragomen* created a set of identifiably Mediterranean tales and literary conventions.

From India to Iberia: Stories That Crossed the Mediterranean

In about 300 CE, an Indian Brahmin composed a set of animal fables (something like Aesop's) in Sanskrit, the holy language of India. Called the *Panchatantra* and intended to impart wisdom to young princes, these Sanskrit stories—many of them featuring a pair of jackals named Kalilah and Dimnah—attracted one translator after the next. In the sixth century, a Persian king commissioned a Middle Persian version, and soon after a Syriac translation appeared. In the eighth century, Ibn al-Muqaffa', one of the creators of Arabic prose, translated it into that language, where it was known simply as *Kalilah and Dimna*. This Arabic version in turn became the origin of western European translations. By 1080 a Byzantine physician and courtier named Symeon Seth had created a Greek version—the jackals now called Stephanites and Ichnelates. Alfonso X, that Castilian emperor of culture, commissioned a Castilian translation (the *Libro de Calila e Digna*) in 1251, as did the queen of Navarre in the early fourteenth century. But a twelfth-century Hebrew translation of the Arabic also found its way into Europe: it was the source of a thirteenth-century Latin version, which in turn found its way into Italian and German in the early modern period. SEE SOURCEBOOK 8:1.

The countless tales of which the *Panchatantra/Kalilah and Dimna* consisted—often told as nested stories within

Everyone in the Mediterranean loved stories about Alexander the Great (356–323 BCE). The greatest general of antiquity, Alexander conquered all the Middle East including most of modern Egypt, Israel, Syria, Jordan, Lebanon, Iraq, Iran, Afghanistan, and significant portions of Pakistan. Soon after his death semilegendary accounts of his exploits began to circulate, and these were collected and written down—and usually referred to as the *Alexander Romance*—in Greek in the third century CE. Translations soon appeared in Latin, Syriac, Armenian, Arabic, and many other languages. Alexander even appears in the Qur'an (18:83–98), where he is called Dhu al-Qarnayn, "the possessor of two horns," because the passage is based on a Syriac version of the *Alexander Romance* in which Alexander has two horns growing from his head as a sign (common in ancient mythology) of his divinity. Stories about this great hero were entertaining of course, but they were told also because they were useful to the Mediterranean religious communities who embraced and adapted them. The following excerpts are drawn from, respectively, Latin, Hebrew, and Arabic accounts of Alexander from the central Middle Ages.

Otto of Freising (1114–1158)

Otto of Freising was a German scholar who wrote a history of the world called the *Chronicle or History of the Two Cities*. Meant to contrast the destinies of the Godly and ungodly (the "two cities" of his title), Otto's chronicle is the work of a Christian bishop deeply interested in upholding Christian belief and virtue, as this excerpt illustrates.

> After Alexander had won the victory over the entire East...he returned from India to Babylon.... Now Alexander, while tarrying at Babylon, died by poison through the treachery of an attendant, at the day, the hour and the place predetermined by the phases of the sun and the moon in India.
>
> How pitiful the lot of mortals! How blind, how wretched their minds! Is not this the Alexander who brought low the proud and glorious kingdom of the Persians and transferred their power to the Macedonians? Is he not the man before whom the whole world trembled though it had not seen him and, not daring to await his coming, voluntarily gave itself over to slavery? And yet so great and so fine a man is destroyed by draining a single cup, by the treachery of a single attendant, and the whole world is shaken by one man's death. The dominion of the Macedonian empire which had its beginning in him came to an end with him at his death....The City of Christ, however, founded upon a firm rock, is not shaken by the misfortunes and tempests of the world, but, continuing immovable and unshaken, gains an eternal kingdom and an eternal crown.[1]

A Hebrew *Alexander Romance* (Twelfth Century)

Probably translated in Spain, this version of the *Alexander Romance* has been attributed to an important Jewish translator and grammarian named Samuel ibn Tibbon (ca. 1150—1230). In this excerpt Alexander, while making his way to conquer Jerusalem, is about to encounter the people and Jewish priests of the city.

> When Alexander saw them, he recognized them. He ordered his troops to stop and he and some of his commanders who served him went up until he approached the hill mentioned before. When the High Priest saw his coming Alexander hurried, seeing him standing there with the golden diadem on his forehead and the Name [of God] engraved on it. He descended from his chariot and embraced him and he bowed down and prostrated himself before the Holy Name that was engraved on the diadem and he paid great honour to the priest. His servants who went with him were enraged and then Parmenius, the mightiest among them, said: "We have seen something from you, O lord our king, that astonishes your princes, commanders and dignitaries. You are the great king to whom kingdoms are subjected. Now you descend from your chariot for a man and you bow and prostrate yourself for this old person who is not even from your own people and who does not have the strength for a battle." Alexander answered him: "You must know, Parmenius, that I did not bow to this old man but to the Holy Name that is engraved on the diadem on his forehead." He turned his face to the crowd and said: "You must know that when I was still

in Macedon I beheld myself in a dream as the leader of an army, while I was standing in a desert, just like this one where we are now, before a great gathering of people who were dressed in white garments, and before them walked an old man just like him with precisely the same vestments and attributes. He associated himself with me and said: 'I am the king who will make you victorious in your warfare.' When I saw him <I knew> that God had sent him to me as a herald of help and goodness." <They changed their opinion> when he told this.

Afterwards, together with the High Priest he went up to Jerusalem and entered the Temple, and the Priest showed him the Holy of Holies.[2]

Abu 'Abd Allah Muhammad ibn 'Ali al-Shatibi (Mid-Thirteenth Century)

The following account of Alexander as Dhu al-Qarnayn appears in a historical work by Abu 'Abd Allah Muhammad ibn 'Ali al-Shatibi.

When God commanded (Alexander), he walked on water in the wake of his friend, the angel Zayaqil, with the power of the Almighty and Exalted One. Dhu al-Qarnayn followed each step Zayaqil took on water, and that is how he was able to walk on water. The Messenger of God, God bless him and grant him salvation, said: Each prophet that walked the earth had an angel from heaven who came to him with revelation from the Lord.

Gabriel, blessings and peace be upon him, was generally the beloved friend of the prophets. But God assigned the angel Zayaqil to inform and command Dhu al-Qarnayn. The young Rum king was a pious servant who loved God and who was loved by the Almighty and Exalted God. He obeyed God's word and religion in all matters, small and large. In turn, God made him strong and made him an example for the people of the earth so that they would not say, "Nobody came to us as a herald of good tidings or warning us that You are our Lord." God the Almighty and Exalted meant for Dhu al-Qarnayn to be evidence of Him among the people of the earth. God commanded him to go to the Children of Adam, by land and by sea, to the east and west, through level and rough terrain....

Dhu al-Qarnayn was able to do just what the angel explained much faster than it would have normally taken during that day and age. He moved quickly through the project because the time was right to begin the first raids of their military expeditions. He ordered twelve thousand craftsmen to come before him: three thousand were blacksmiths, three thousand were carpenters, and three thousand were craftsmen who made fittings for the horses. Beneath his command the carpenters and blacksmiths built his castle right away and drew it near to the other castle. Dhu al-Qarnayn was able to move his castle because it was carried on a bed mounted on wheels. The wheels were turned by mules which were driven by both slaves and men of distinction alike. When the slaves came near the castle, which was revolving quickly on a pivoting coil spring, it moved in a circle around them....The boards extending out from the walls of Dhu al-Qarnayn's castle jammed the revolving doors and they stopped. Dhu al-Qarnayn walked up to the castle and looked at the door and saw that on it was written, "I testify that there is no God but Allah and I testify that Muhammad is the Messenger of God." Then with the will of God Almighty, the castle opened up and Dhu al-Qarnayn stepped inside. Lo and behold, there was a locked chest made out of red gold and studded with different sorts of gems. On the lock there was written, "There is no power nor strength save in God, the Almighty One, the Greatest." Dhu al-Qarnayn said, "There is no power nor strength save in God, the Almighty One, the Greatest."[3]

Discussion Questions

1. What do all these very different accounts of Alexander agree on?
2. What uses was Alexander put to in these medieval accounts?
3. What about the historical figure of Alexander made him so useful?

Further Reading

Stoneman, Richard. *Alexander the Great: A Life in Legend*. New Haven: Yale University Press, 2008.

Zuwiyya, Z. David. *A Companion to Alexander Literature in the Middle Ages*. Leiden: E. J. Brill, 2011.

Notes

1. Charles Christopher Mierow, Austin P. Evans, and Charles Knapp, *The Two Cities: A Chronicle of Universal His-*

tory to the Year 1146 A.D.*, Records of Civilization, Sources and Studies 9 (New York: Octagon Books, 1966), 179–84.

2. Schmuel Tibbon, *A Hebrew Alexander Romance According to MS London, Jews' College No. 145*, trans. Wout Jac. Van Bekkum, Orientalia Lovaniensia Analecta 47 (Leuven: Peeters, 1992), 61–65.

3. Z. David Zuwiyya, *Islamic Legends Concerning Alexander the Great: Taken from Two Medieval Arabic Manuscripts in Madrid* (Binghamton, NY: Global Publications Services, 2001), 46–48.

FIGURE 8.2 The lion-king receives the ox, Shanzabeh, escorted by Dimna. Folio from a *Kalilah and Dimna*, second quarter of the sixteenth century. The Metropolitan Museum of Art, New York, The Alice and Nashli Heeramaneck Collection, Gift of Alice Heeramaneck, 1981, 1981.373.30, Open Access CC0.

stories—were immensely entertaining. The wily jackal Dimna, for example, always anxious to improve his position at court, attempted in one tale to gain favor with the lion (the king of the jungle in these tales, just as in Hollywood) by nurturing a friendship between him and a lonely bull, who, embarrassingly enough, actually frightened the king when he bellowed. But when his schemes succeeded and king and ox became fast friends (so much so that the lion "consulted him on every occasion, and his admiration of him continually increased"[1]), Dimna became jealous of their friendship. He then reversed course, sowing discord among them, knowing that once the lion-king became sufficiently angry, he would kill the bull. A good lesson, here, for young princes about how a crafty interloper can plant poisonous seeds of distrust, and this tale along with dozens of others became the common property of Jews, Christians, Muslims, Arabs, Greek, and Latin by the central Middle Ages.

It was probably traveling Buddhist monks who exported the *Panchatantra/Kalilah and Dimna* to the Mediterranean world where it enjoyed such popularity, and the same is true of another originally Indian text whose remarkable transformations illustrate the wide appeal not of animal fables, but of the stories of holy men and women. From early on Buddhists in India had told the tale of their religion's founder: how young Siddhartha Gautama (ca. 566–486 BCE), an Indian prince, abandoned his privileged life and experienced enlightenment under a sacred tree. As Buddhism moved west, so did different versions of this story. By way of a late Ancient Persian version, this story of the Buddha was reworked by the eighth century CE into a vaguely Islamic, Arabic tale, the *Book of Bilawhar and Yudasaf*, which even circulated in a specifically Shi'i reworking, and eventually Coptic and Hebrew versions followed. In a tenth-century translation, written in Georgian (a language spoken by Christians in the Caucasus), this Buddhist, then Islamic, tale was thoroughly Christianized as the epic *Balavariani*, and this version was reworked into medieval Greek by 1028, and just twenty years later into Latin. Now called

Barlaam and Josaphat, the tale then spread throughout western Europe in various vernacular versions (including Old Norse!). Now it was a story of an Indian king who hated the Christian religion and, "filled with wrath, and boiling over with indignation,"compelled "all Christians to renounce their religion,"[2] confining his son in the palace to keep him from converting. The son, Josaphat, nevertheless eventually shook off his confinement and met the saintly Christian monk Barlaam, and converted anyway. Inspired by his son's actions, the father eventually converts too, and at length hands over his throne to Josaphat, and becomes a desert hermit himself. Thus did Barlaam and Josaphat become widely venerated Christian saints. SEE SOURCEBOOK 8:2.

These stories traveled east from one *tarjuman*/translator to the next, but stories were perfectly capable of moving in other directions as well. After the Latin conquest of Byzantium in the Fourth Crusade, French knights and merchants lived side by side with Greeks, and, despite once being enemies, their literary cultures began to blend. One sign of this are Greek translations of contemporary French works. *Fleure et Blanchefleur,* the most popular of the thriving French genre of romance stories, and dating from about 1160, wound up in a Greek version by 1400. In the late 1350s, moreover, a French author of uncertain identity wrote a fictitious account of the travels of an English knight whom he called Sir John Mandeville. Full of stories of eccentric foreigners and monstrous races (and intriguingly accommodating of religious differences), the *Travels of Sir John Mandeville* became an instant bestseller, translated into English, Latin (four different times), German, Spanish, Italian, and even Czech. Sometimes, moreover, it is not clear which version of these mobile texts came first. The *Chonicle of Morea,* which tells how French knights imposed feudalism in Greece after the Fourth Crusade, survives in French, Greek, Italian, and Aragonese (a dialect of Spanish) versions. The latter two versions are clearly later than the former two, but scholars remain uncertain whether the French or the Greek is the original.

Certainly, the literary traditions of each Mediterranean language contained stories and themes that were unique to it—by no means do wandering texts such as *Kalilah and Dimna* or *Barlaam and Josaphat* represent the full scope of Mediterranean literary history—but the extent to which tales freely traveled across linguistic boundaries means that no medieval Mediterranean literature can be fully understood without recognizing the literary connectedness of the Sea in the Middle.

Translating Genres

But it was not just stories that crossed from one language to the next. So also did entire literary genres—sets of conventions, that is, about how to structure and organize works of literature. An early Arab writer named Badiʿ al-Zaman al-Hamadhani (969–1007), for example, created a genre called the *maqama* (pl. *maqamat*) at the beginning of this period. Told in alternating rhymed prose and poetry, his *maqamat* recounted fifty tales in which a sly trickster, named al-Iskandari, manages to fool the narrator, ʿIsa (i.e., "Jesus," in Arabic) ibn Hisham, who then marvels at al-Iskandari's clever use of rhetoric, despite having lost still more money to him. In one story, for example, al-Iskandari, disguised as a poor beggar with "little ones by his side" and "babes on his hips," fools Ibn Hisham into giving him a handful of coins, only to have the trickster reveal himself and crow about how he spends his "life in deceiving men and throwing dust in their eyes." The *maqama* quickly became a staple of medieval Arabic literature, especially after the eleventh-/twelfth-century writer al-Hariri (d. 1121) embraced the genre and made it widely popular. It then spread right across the Mediterranean, and by the mid-twelfth century, an Andalusi scholar named al-Saraqusti (the Zaragozan; d. 1143) was composing his own collection of *maqamat.*

It was not long, however, before the *maqama* genre vaulted linguistic and religious walls. Learned Jews of medieval al-Andalus had long since embraced Arabic as their daily spoken language and were typically deeply immersed in its literature, so we should not be surprised that Judah al-Harizi (1165–1225) translated al-Hariri's popular *maqamat* into Hebrew, and then, in about 1200, wrote his own set in Hebrew. At about the same time a Barcelonese Jew, Joseph ibn Zabara, composed the *Book of Delights,* a further collection of Hebrew *maqamat*—the genre thus moving into Christian Spain (Barcelona, in northeast Iberia, had only briefly been under Muslim rule), where it flourished among minority Jews. From the Jewish literati, the *maqama* then came to influence Christian authors as well. The *Book of Good Love,* written in Castilian in about 1330 by a priest named Juan Ruiz, is one of the great works of premodern Spanish literature, a rollicking, fictional autobiography, full of titillating stories and embarrassing incidents, alternating with apparently authentic piety. Though rooted in important Latin-Christian genres as well, the *Book of Good Love* embodies important aspects of the *maqama,* especially as it appears in the Ibn Zabara's Hebrew *Book of Delights.* Not only does Juan Ruiz's narrative voice remind us of the comic teller of the *Book of Delights,* but the works are similarly organized—not into the clearly divided chapters of similar length in the classical Arabic *maqamat,* but into more loosely connected episodes. Having entered Castilian, the *maqama* would evolve eventually into one of the standard genres of early modern Spanish literature—the picaresque novel, first appearing in the anonymous *Lazarillo de Tormes* of 1554.

But once again, the same process could work in the opposite direction. Beginning in the tenth century, Arab-Muslim poets in al-Andalus began to write in an entirely new genre called the *muwashshah.* This was a poem divided into stanzas of varying length with the first verse usually repeated as a refrain. Moreover, unlike other classical Arabic poetic genres, the *muwashshah* was sung to musical accompaniment, and, even more unusually, its final verses were a kind of punch line written, not in high-status, literary Arabic, but in street Arabic or the Romance vernacular still widespread in al-Andalus. In one of his poems, Ahmad al-'Utbi, known as the Blind Poet of Tudela (d. 1126) and one of the most famous *muwashshah* poets, lamented the pains of love: "Tears that are shed and a breast that is burned / Water and fire!... Sleep is taboo, visitation is far; / No peace and quiet!" But after fifteen verses in classical Arabic, he tied the poem off with three lines in early Castilian Romance: Meu l-habib enfermo de meu amar. / ¿Que no ha d'estar? / ¿Non ves a mibe s'ha de no llegar? (My beloved is sick for love of me. How can he not be so? Do you not see that he is not allowed near me?)[3]

The *muwashshah* form quickly spread east across North Africa, so that anthologies of the genre were being compiled in Cairo by the early thirteenth century, and Eastern poets were soon composing their own. But Jewish poets in al-Andalus learned to love these poems too, and began writing them in Hebrew. Samuel ibn Naghrella, the Jewish general and prime minister of the *taifa* court of Granada, was also one of the most famous Hebrew poets of the Middle Ages. He too laments the travails of love in a *muwashshah:* "Burnt by passion's flame— / How can I refrain? / Love has ruined me, / Lain in wait for me, / Ambushed, then gone free." Like the Blind Poet, moreover, he draws his lament to a close with a verse in a different language, this time an Arabic couplet: "Two lovers twain / never part again."[4]

Mediterranean Themes

That Andalusi poets—both Muslims and Jews—so often wrote bilingual poetry should not surprise us in the multilingual Mediterranean, where different ethnic, linguistic, and religious groups lived side by side. Indeed, crossing the boundaries between such groups actually became one of the common literary themes of Mediterranean literature as a whole. At the opposite end of the Sea in the Middle, for example, on the border between Byzantium and the 'Abbasid Caliphate, Greek poets began telling stories of a great warrior called Digenis Akritas. In these tales he and his equally warlike father—when they weren't wooing beautiful princesses—use their nearly superhero powers to save maidens from lions, defeat Amazons, and destroy vastly superior forces single-handedly. Strikingly enough, however, when versions of these stories were eventually written down (perhaps in the eleventh century) they make much of Digenis Akritas's mixed parentage. His name, in fact, means "The Two-Blood Border Lord." When we first meet his father, he is a Muslim *amir* from Syria and frequent raider on the Byzantine-Islamic border. On one expedition, however, he takes a Greek-Christian beauty captive and then falls hard for her—"A lovely woman," he remarks, "has conquered me"—and eventually converts to Christianity, marries her, and manages to persuade his own Muslim mother to convert as well: "For you, son, I'll believe in the Trinity... [and] be baptized for remission of my faults."[5] But though a Christian, the *amir* retains his Arab title (indeed he is called nothing but *amir* throughout the poem). His son Digenis, moreover, prefers to live his life right on the shifting border between Greek Christianity and Arab Islam, where, though a Greek-Christian hero,

FIGURE 8.3 Digenis Akritas saves a princess. Incised plate, twelfth century. © Historical Views / agefotostock.

he can easily cross over into Arab-Muslim territory, his paternal homeland. SEE SOURCEBOOK 8:3.

Though Digenis seems to have been a figment of literary imagination, such border-hopping warriors, willing to fight for anyone who would pay them, existed elsewhere in the Mediterranean world, as the case of Rodrigo Díaz de Vivar, El Cid (d. 1099), illustrates. A low-ranking aristocrat, Rodrigo rose to prominence as a loyal vassal of the Castilian monarchs. He ran afoul, though, of King Alfonso VI (1065–1109), who exiled him, forcing him to become a mercenary captain in the service of the Muslim kings of Zaragoza, and he later conquered the *taifa* kingdom of Valencia, ruling it as sultan. Like the Christian *amir* in *Digenis Akritas,* moreover, he bore an Arab title—El Cid, from the Arabic "Sayyidi," meaning "my lord"—given to him by the Muslim troops he commanded. His real-life exploits, furthermore, inspired a whole series of stories and songs, the most famous of which, *The Poem of the Cid,* written down in about 1200, became the national epic of Spain. On the one hand, the Cid of the poem happily fights Muslims in battles in which "the Muslims called on Muhammad and the Christians on St. James."[6] But on the other, he willingly fights for Muslim overlords, and one of his most loyal friends throughout the poem is the Muslim knight Abengalbón (*mio amigo el moro Abengalvón*),[7] to whom he entrusted his cherished daughters when they were traveling without his protection.

Both the fictional Two-Blood Border Lord and the semifictional El Cid are Christian heroes of Christian people, but they are fully entangled in a world of overlapping religions, languages, and ethnicities, and part of their prowess indeed derives from how they incarnate those entanglements. Border crossing shows up frequently in Mediterranean literature in other ways too. In Greek romances written in late antiquity, sea travel, shipwreck, piracy, and cross-border kidnapping were all popular themes, and they remain so even in Boccaccio's vast collection of Italian stories called the *Decameron* (ca. 1350). Here a merchant from Marseilles, just returned home after a business venture in Spain, finds that his three daughters have run off with their paramours to the Byzantine East (4.3); the Christian and Muslim kings of Sicily and Tunis strike up cordial relations (2.4); and Madonna Zinevra of Genoa flees her murderous husband, taking a Catalan ship to Muslim Alexandria, where, dressed as a man, she eventually becomes a market inspector in Baghdad (2.9). The plight of poor Alatiel (2.7) covers all the bases: a beautiful princess of Cairo, she is sent by her father to marry the king of Muslim Granada, but is shipwrecked near the end of her journey in Mallorca. There a young gentleman named Periocone de Visalgo espies her, is swept off his feet, gets her drunk ("though her [Muslim] law forbade it"), and seduces her. But male treachery and her stunning beauty make this only the first in a series of adventures that see her kidnapped by Pericone's besmitten brother, dragged back across the sea, desired by the prince of Morea who is killed in jealousy by the duke of Athens, married off to Osbech, king of the Turks, and eventually delivered once again to her father. Rather than offend him with the licentious details of her real travails, she concocts a story about how, after her initial shipwreck, she was forced into a Christian convent, from which she had only recently escaped to Cyprus and thence home. Overjoyed, her father marries her off happily to the king of Granada as originally intended. The Sea in the Middle overflowed with stories that traveled readily from one language and culture to the next, but it also ran deep with amazingly entertaining border-crossing plots and motifs.

FIGURE 8.4 Boccaccio sits outside a group of courtiers in fifteenth-century manuscript. *Decameron*, before 1467. © Historical Views / agefotostock.

Their Scripture, Our Language

The holy books of the medieval Mediterranean were each written in a different language and different script—Hebrew, Greek, Latin, Arabic—but that did not keep these books from winding up in outsiders' hands. For one thing, the already linguistically diverse Mediterranean—Aramaic-speaking Jew living next to Arabic-speaking Muslim living next to Greek-speaking Christian—witnessed huge shifts in linguistic hegemony in this period, especially as Arabic became the predominant language of learning and culture in the south. This meant that Jews and Christians living within the House of Islam almost necessarily began translating their own scriptures into

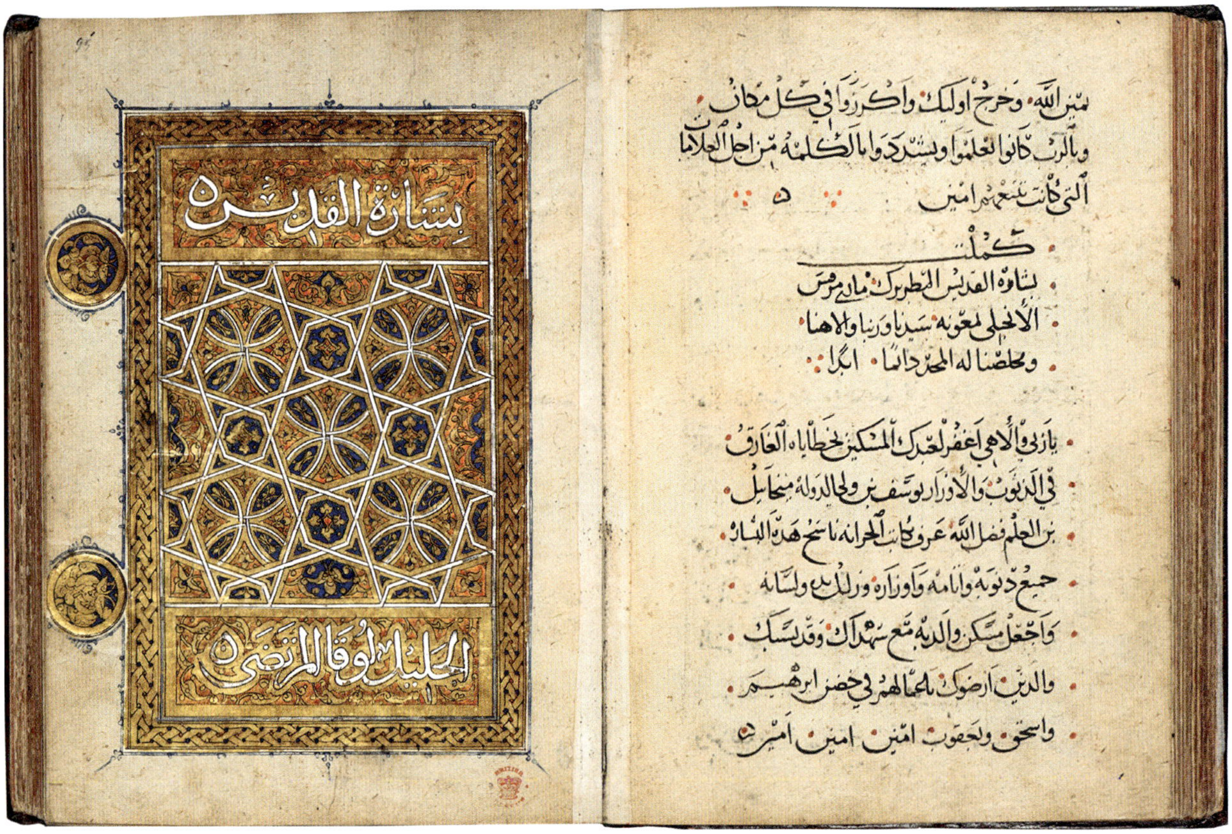

FIGURE 8.5 Carpet page of beginning of Gospel of Luke in Arabic, 1335. The British Library, MS 11856, ff. 94v–95.

the language of Islam as they themselves overwhelmingly became speakers of that language. Moreover, the universalistic ambitions of Christianity and Islam encouraged translation of their own scriptures as a tool of conversion, and, in the case of Christians at least, the translation of others' scriptures in order to refute them.

Arabic Bibles, Vernacular Qur'ans

While biblical stories clearly circulated orally among Jewish and Christian Arabs before the time of Muhammad, there is no evidence of written versions of the Bible in Arabic until the eighth century when Christian monks in Muslim Palestine began translating the Gospel readings. In the ninth century, Christian Arabic translation of individual biblical books became widespread (we have no evidence of connected Arabic translations of the whole Bible until the sixteenth century), and in the tenth century, Jews began translating the Hebrew Bible into Arabic as well. By far the most influential Jewish translator was the great rabbi and gaon whom we have met before, Sa'adyah ben Joseph (882–942), whose Arabic version of the Torah, copied normally in Hebrew characters for Jewish consumption (in what is usually called, therefore, Judeo-Arabic), became the standard version for Jews—and many Christians—for centuries afterward.

While the great age of Jewish and Christian Arabic biblical translation came before the period under consideration here, important new translations did appear after the mid-tenth century. In 946, for example, Ishaq ibn Balask (Isaac Son of Velasco) translated the Gospels from Latin into Arabic for Christians in Spain. A leading Baghdadi Christian intellectual named Ibn al-Tayyib (d. 1043), moreover, translated the ancient Gospel harmony called the *Diatessaron* (a version of the four Gospels that integrates them into a single text) into Arabic. Many other

FIGURE 8.6 The Arabic Qur'an with interlinear Persian translation, early sixteenth century. The British Library, MS 5551.

Arabic Bible translations by Jewish and Christian scholars appeared throughout the later Middle Ages, though the great majority of these have never been studied by modern scholars. SEE SOURCEBOOK 8:4.

Muslims, on the other hand, found themselves translating their holy scripture not into the languages of Jews or Christians, but into vernaculars spoken by Muslims on the edges or outside of the Arab world. In the tenth century the Persian language reemerged as an important written language in the Iranian world, and with it scores of Persian Qur'an translations. Many of these were word-for-word versions written between the lines of the Arabic Qur'an, meant, in other words, to help Persian speakers understand the Arabic original. The tendency, therefore, was for Persian versions to serve rather than replace the Arabic original. Some Persian versions, though, went far beyond this by attempting both to make the Qur'an beautiful on the Persian tongue and to make it more intelligible. Umar ibn Muhammad al-Nasafi (d. 1143), for example, created a Persian Qur'an written in compelling rhymed prose that amplified the original by incorporating explanatory information drawn from Arabic Qur'an commentaries. When he translated the first surah of the Qur'an, for example, he wrote: "Keep us on the path of righteousness . . . not the path of those who are the people of revenge, *and those are Jews,* nor the path of those who have lost the way, *and they are Christians*" (italics added).[8] The two clauses in italics are not in the Arabic Qur'an, but Arab-Muslim commentators normally made those identifications.

We see much the same thing happening from the fourteenth century on in Iberia, where Muslims began to translate the Qur'an into the Romance languages—Castilian, Aragonese, Portuguese—they spoke, writing these versions down in the Arabic alphabet (just as, of course, Persians such as al-Nasafi did with their vernacular). These translations also generally served, rather than replaced, the Arabic Qur'an, since in most manuscripts, sections of the Qur'an were given first in Arabic, and then translated into Romance written in smaller Arabic characters. Just as al-Nasafi's version amplified the Arabic Qur'an frequently in the interest of intelligibility, so also these so-called Aljamiado (derived from the Arabic *'ajamiya* = "vernacular") Qur'ans were meant to make the text easier to understand.

Our Beliefs in Their Language

Bearing in mind that Mediterranean intellectuals were so fond of writing commentaries on their holy texts, we will not be surprised to discover that these many Arabic versions of the Jewish and Christian scriptures inspired Arabic biblical commentators. The same Ibn al-Tayyib, the Christian who translated the ancient *Diatessaron* into Arabic, wrote a massive Arabic commentary on the whole Bible called *The Christian Paradise,* while two Arabic-speaking Coptic Christians of the thirteenth century, Bulus al-Bushi and Ibn Katib Qaysar, penned Arabic commentaries on the final book of the Christian Bible, the Apocalypse or Revelation. The same is true of Jewish scholars, beginning with Sa'adyah ben Joseph himself. But by expressing Jewish or Christian belief in Arabic, a language intimately connected with Islam, Jews and Christians almost necessarily found themselves speaking in intriguingly Islamic-sounding words and phrases.

In al-Andalus, for example, two Christians had translated the Psalms from Latin into Arabic by the mid-tenth century, and both translations circulated with a preface that instructed the faithful on the importance of praying these ancient prayers regularly. More than once, the preface's Christian author used the phrase "Praise be to God, the Lord of the Worlds." While this is a sentiment to which all Jews, Christians, and Muslims could ascribe, the Arabic words are drawn directly from the Qur'an's first surah (1:2). Even when speaking of Jesus's first followers, his disciples, this author used terminology with a strongly Qur'anic feel. They were *al-hawariyun,** just as they were in the Qur'an's many stories about Jesus and his mother. Far more written sources survive for Arab Christians in the eastern Mediterranean, and we find much the same practice there. Ibn al-Tayyib, for example, began his commentary on Genesis with the phrase "In the name of God, the Merciful, the Compassionate,"[9] with which almost all Qur'anic surahs begin. Ibn al-Tayyib called another of his works—a large treatise on canon law (the rules governing church life)—the *Fiqh al-Nasraniyah,* "the Fiqh of the Christians." *Fiqh* is the specifically Islamic term for "law," and the study of *fiqh* was the core discipline of advanced Islamic education. It was so central, in fact, that if one had managed to advance to the highest levels of Islamic learning, and had become an authority on Islamic belief and practice, one was called a *faqih*—a scholar of *fiqh*. But Christians also used that term from time to time. Indeed, at the beginning of his commentary on Genesis, the same Christian scholar is identified as "the Sublime Sheikh . . . , the Virtuous Priest, Abu al-Faraj 'Abd Allah ibn Tayyib, the Faqih."[10]

Often, when Christians adopted Islamic words and phrases, they aggressively Christianized them. While they frequently invoked God in the Qur'anic formula ("In the Name of God, the Merciful, the Compassionate"), just as frequently they used a quite different phrase, "In the name of the Father, Son, and Holy Spirit, One God." Up to the last two words, this invocation was a commonplace of all Christian writing in any language. Yet the firm "One God" at the end was a vivid affirmation in a culture dominated by Islam that the Trinitarian God of Christians was nevertheless the One God that Muslims followed. Where the Qur'an asserted multiple times that God "created the heavens, and the earth, and what was between them," the Andalusi-Christian preface to the Psalms pointedly described Jesus as "the Word who created the heavens and the earth and what was between them."[11]

Christians resorted, therefore, to a sort of balancing act while making use of the language of the Qur'an: they did often adopt its terminology and literary style, but did not hesitate to turn it directly to their Christian purposes. Over the course of the eleventh through fourteenth century, they produced a large library of Christian theology, prayers, and spiritual guide books in this carefully calibrated, Christianized Arabic—a body of materials that modern scholars are only just beginning to

* This Arabic word, probably of Ethiopic origin, refers only to Jesus's disciples in the Qur'an; its meaning was much debated by Qur'anic commentators without any consensus.

FIGURE 8.7 Manuscript fragment of Moses Maimonides's *Guide for the Perplexed* in Judeo-Arabic. © Historical Views / agefotostock.

study. The Coptic Christian Sim'an ("Simon") ibn Kalil (d. ca. 1240), for example, wrote not only a short treatise on God's triune nature, but also a substantial guidebook on Christian spirituality and ethics called *The Garden of the Hermit and the Consolation of the Solitary,* which was something of a bestseller in the Arab Christian world down to the modern period. Sim'an was part of a golden age of Coptic-Arabic literature in the thirteenth century whose greatest writer was probably Shams al-Ri'asa Abu al-Barakat (d. 1324), who wrote what amounts to an Arabic encyclopedia of Christian theology and practice called *A Lamp in the Darkness.*

While in the earlier Middle Ages, the great rabbi Sa'adyah ben Joseph had both translated the Torah into Arabic and written a commentary on many books of the Hebrew Bible in that language, in this central period Jewish scholars who wrote, as we will see later, many nonreligious works in Arabic were hesitant to discuss purely religious topics in Islam's (or Christianity's) sacred languages. The towering rabbi-physician-philosopher Moses Maimonides (d. 1204), for example, wrote his Aristotelian philosophical magnum opus, the charmingly named *Guide for the Perplexed,* in Arabic, though he composed his brilliant overview of Jewish law called the *Mishneh Torah,* a masterpiece of Talmudic interpretation and synthesis, entirely in Hebrew. Yet there were exceptions. In the late twelfth century two distinguished rabbis—one of them the head of a rabbinical academy in Baghdad—wrote treatises in Arabic on the nature of human resurrection. Since these works were critiques of Maimonides's own views as spelled out in the *Mishneh Torah,* he felt obliged to respond—likewise in Arabic—in a work called the *Treatise on Resurrection.*

Greek Qur'an, Latin Talmud

Sometime before about 870, someone produced a Byzantine Greek translation of the Qur'an that does not survive in its entirety, though numerous quotations of it appear in later Greek works. While it is possible a Muslim who knew Greek made this translation for the same purposes that Muslim missionaries translated the Qur'an into Persian, it is much more likely that this anonymous Greek Qur'an is the first of several translations into European languages made by medieval Christians for specifically Christian purposes—attacking Islam, that is, and defending Christian belief. In these cases, unlike those discussed just above, it was not insiders translating their holy text into a different language spoken by fellow believers, but outsiders translating a book that they saw as a fraudulent scripture.

While the earliest such version was Greek, and there is evidence of an early medieval Syriac Qur'an as well, the oldest Christian translations of the Qur'an that have come down to us intact are in Latin and date from the central Middle Ages. While Latin Christendom, poor and often disconnected from the Mediterranean in the early Middle Ages, had largely ignored Islam as a religion, the dramatic economic transformation of the period after 1000 brought with it a growing interest in the rest of the world. One of many signs of this new attitude was an initiative launched by one of the most powerful prelates in western Europe to provide information about Islam to his contemporaries. On a journey to visit daughter houses in Spain in the early 1140s Peter the Venerable (1092–1156), abbot of Cluny, put together a team of scholars to translate the Qur'an and other Islamic texts into Latin. This Latin Qur'an, made by an Englishman named Robert of Ketton and snidely entitled the *Law of Muhammad the Pseudo-Prophet*, would have enormous influence on European-Christian views of Islam. It was widely read in the medieval period, eventually printed in the middle of the sixteenth century, and still widely consulted until the end of the seventeenth century. But despite the success of Robert of Ketton's version, a second complete Latin Qur'an survives from less than a century later, this one done at the behest of another wealthy prelate—the archbishop of Toledo—by a Spanish native named Mark of Toledo.

Both these translations were made, we learn from prefaces attached to each, specifically to provide ammunition for Christians in their intellectual struggle against Islam. The same is true of another Latin translation of a non-Christian holy book. Almost exactly one hundred years after Robert of Ketton produced his Latin Qur'an, a group of scholars in Paris completed a work entitled *Extractiones de Talmut*, really an anthology, as that title suggests, of extracts from the Babylonian Talmud, the foundational text of rabbinical Judaism. The scholars who undertook this project were all Dominicans whose job was preaching the Gospel throughout the world. This collection of key Talmudic passages was meant, therefore, to assist missionary Dominicans in their contest with Judaism. SEE SOURCEBOOK 8:5.

These Greek Qur'ans and Latin Talmuds were made specifically for hostile purposes, therefore, and it is natural to wonder how accurately they captured the meaning of the Qur'an and Talmud as Muslims and Jews understood those texts. Certainly, these Christians translators made many mistakes as they worked through other peoples' holy books, but their mistakes were overwhelmingly a result not of intentional distortion but of inadequate knowledge in the face of a very difficult task. The way grammatical tense works in Indo-European languages such as Greek and Latin is strikingly different, for example, from how it does in Semitic languages such as Ara-

FIGURE 8.8 Muhammad as monstrous man-fish in the earliest manuscript of the Qur'an in Latin. © Historical Views / agefotostock.

bic and Hebrew (technically their verbs have no tense inherently, the time when an act happened or will happen being indicated by syntax and accompanying words). Repeatedly, therefore, we find Latin translators getting the tense of Arabic and Hebrew verbs wrong, putting past acts in the future or reading present acts as in the past. Moreover, both the Qur'an and the Talmud contain many rare words that even Muslims and Jews did not readily understand. As a result it is not surprising that Mark of Toledo (fl. 1193–1216), the second Latin Qur'an translator, had no idea what to do about the thoroughly peculiar word *ababil* that only appears once, in the Qur'an's surah 105, where it modifies the word for "birds." Muslim commentators (who also found it a puzzling word) usually said it meant something like "in flocks following one after the other." Poor Mark guessed, quite wrongly, that it must mean "Babylon."[12]

If their mistakes were mostly honest mistakes, moreover, it is even more striking to observe that these translators often went to some trouble to get across some of the specific literary qualities of the Qur'an and to translate its meaning as Muslims understood it. The anonymous translator of the ninth-century Greek Qur'an attempted in some cases to imitate the Arabic Qur'an's distinctive rhymed prose by adding Greek end rhyme. Robert of Ketton energetically translated the very high-status Arabic of the Qur'an into a quite different but equally high-status prose, the sort of ornate, complex Latin that contemporary scholars recommended for important texts. Moreover, it is evident that these translators turned either to Muslim scholars or to Arabic Qur'an commentaries to help them understand the book they were translating. Byzantine Christian translators, for example, clearly understood how medieval Muslims interpreted another unusual Qur'anic word, *samad* (supreme, everlasting), in the short surah 112, while Robert of Ketton often simply inserts—just as Muslim translators of the Qur'an into Persian or Castilian did—standard Muslim interpretations of rare words and unusual phrases into his Latin Qur'an rather than translate them word for word. When he confronted the vaguely suggestive term *kawthar* in surah 108—it means something like "abundance," but its concrete sense is not obvious in the context—he simply wrote "a river in Paradise"[13] because that is what Muslim Qur'anic commentators argued it referred to. We need not assume, though, that these Christian translators approached Islam's holy book so carefully out of some sort of impartial scholarly idealism. For one thing, turning to Muslim informants or commentaries for answers made pragmatic sense—translating is very hard work, after all. Moreover, combatting Islam, the purpose for which they were translating, required accurate translation to be effective. In the long run, seriously distorting the Qur'an was neither worth the effort nor particularly useful.

Talking Religion

What with Jews and Christians translating the Bible into Arabic, the Qur'an into Greek, Latin, and (probably) Syriac, and composing their own theological works in the language of Islam, it is scarcely surprising that people from all three religions fell to talking about their beliefs with each other. A Latin text called the *Disputation of Mallorca,* for example, recounts what appear to be real debates in 1286 between a Christian layman and merchant, Inghetto Contardo, and some rabbis on the island of Mallorca in the western Mediterranean. Generally, such religious debates involved highly educated scholars, and indeed, the rabbis in this disputation are dismissive of Inghetto, who, they say, "may have knowledge in the fashion of a merchant, but does not know anything about religion."[14] The Christians in this account, of course, see things differently. To them Inghetto is a hero whom rabbis can "neither contradict nor resist." Often, moreover, such debates took place at the courts of prominent secular rulers. While there is no doubt that such discussions occurred, the written accounts of them usually have been reworked to suit the intended audience—in Christian accounts the priests win; in Jewish versions the rabbis quash their rivals. But it is also clear that many accounts of such debates are actually literary fictions, and indeed there were a variety of genres of written texts in which such interreligious arguments occurred, especially exchanges of letters. Such debates, real or imagined, superficially appear to be attempts at conversion, but closer reading often reveals more complex motives—a desire simply to police the boundaries between religious communities, or to attack one's fellow believers who are straying from the path, by cleverly attacking another religion. Yet it is essential, amid all these loud critiques of other people's religion, to recognize as well that scholars were also borrowing religious ideas from each other, and benefiting from each other's spiritual techniques.

Debates, Rebuttals, Testy Letters

The Qur'an itself contains many passages that depict Muslims disputing with Christians and Jews about religion (see 2:135–42, for example), and some evidence indicates that actual debates between Christian bishops and Muslim leaders took place within thirty years of the death of Muhammad. Eventually a tradition of courtly debates about religion developed in the Islamic world. Caliphs and emirs hosted (and often participated in) debates among Jewish, Christian, and Muslim religious leaders about the merits of their faiths. While some of these powerful rulers seem to have had a truly religious interest in sponsoring such discussion, there was clearly also a political motive behind these events: the Muslim ruler projected a benign, but unchallengeable dominance over his subjects, Muslims and non-Muslims alike, as he amiably presided over polite religious conversation.

Perhaps the most famous courtly religious disputation in the early Middle Ages occurred in Baghdad in the early 780s when the caliph al-Mahdi (775–785) and Timothy, the leading bishop of the Church of the East, amicably discussed the Christian belief in Jesus as the Son of God, the Trinity, the mission of Muhammad, and many other points of contention. Soon after the event, Timothy wrote down an account of it in Syriac for a Christian

In the religiously plural world of the medieval Mediterranean people both frequently debated religious truth and frequently imagined such debates. We have many surviving accounts of both types—authentic reports of religious discussions that really did happen, and wholly imaginary descriptions of what might or should happen if Jews, Christians, and Muslims talked religion. In both of the following excerpts, one real, one imaginary, a key issue is the role of reason in making a case for one's religion.

Abu 'Abd Allah ibn Muhammad al-Humaydi (Eleventh Century)

Al-Humaydi (1029–1095), an Andalusi Muslim scholar who became an admired professor in Baghdad (where he died), compiled a collection of biographies of Arab scholars from al-Andalus. In that work he offered the following anecdote concerning one Ahmad ibn Muhammad ibn Sa'di who traveled to Baghdad in the late tenth century. While there he twice attended religious discussions that featured scholars from a whole range of religious persuasions. He was shocked.

> At the first session I attended I witnessed a meeting which included every kind of group: Sunni Muslims and heretics, and all kinds of infidels: Zoroastrians, materialists,* atheists, Jews and Christians. Each group had a leader who would speak on its doctrine and debate about it. Whenever one of these leaders arrived, from whichever of the groups he came, the assembly rose up for him, standing on their feet until he would sit down, then they would take their seats after he was seated. When the meeting was jammed with its participants, and they saw that no one else was expected, one of the infidels said, "You have all agreed to the debate, so the Muslims should not argue against us on the basis of their scripture, nor on the basis of the sayings of their prophet, since we put no credence in these things, and we do not acknowledge him. Let us dispute with one another only on the basis of arguments from reason, and what observation and deduction will support." Then they would all say, "Agreed." ... When I heard that, I did not return to that meeting. Later someone told me there was to be another meeting for discussion, so I went to it and I found them engaging in the same practices as their colleagues. So I stopped going to the meetings of the disputants, and I never went back.[1]

* People who do not believe that any nonmaterial, spiritual reality (including God) exists.

Ramon Llull's *The Book of the Gentile* (1274–1276)

The Mallorcan layman Ramon Llull (1232–1316) became convinced as a young man that God wanted him to write "the best book ever" to convert all unbelievers to Christianity. In order to accomplish this task, he not only learned Arabic, but devised a rationalist, philosophical-theological system—he called it his "Art"—that he believed would persuade all people to become Christians. Indeed, he believed strongly that, just as the spokesman in al-Humaydi's anecdote suggests, it was impossible to persuade people of anything on the basis of a scripture that they do not accept. A rationalist approach, therefore, was the only option. As it turned out, Llull did not write just one book to persuade unbelievers, but a small library (more than 260 books). The excerpt below comes from one of his most famous, *The Book of the Gentile and the Three Wise Men,* a charming fictional account of a thoroughly rationalist debate between and a Jew, a Christian, and a Muslim. The five trees in this passage exemplify and incorporate the rationalist principles of Llull's art of persuasion.

> Three wise men met upon leaving a city. One was a Jew, the other a Christian, and the third a Saracen. When they were outside the city and saw each other, they approached and greeted each other in friendly fashion, and they accompanied one another, each inquiring about the other's health and what he intended to do. And all three decided to enjoy themselves together, so as to gladden their spirits overtaxed by studying. The three wise men went on so long talking about their respective beliefs and about the things they taught their students.... And they came to a lovely meadow with a lovely spring watering five trees....
>
> Next to the spring there was a very beautiful lady, very nobly dressed, astride a handsome palfrey, which

FIGURE 8.9 Lady Intelligence explaining symbolism of Llull's trees. © Historical Views / agefotostock.

was drinking from the spring. The wise men, upon seeing the five trees, which were most pleasing to the eye, and upon seeing the lady, who was of agreeable countenance, went up to the spring and greeted the lady most humbly and devoutly, and she most politely returned their greetings.

The wise men asked the lady her name, to which she replied that she was *Intelligence*. And the wise men asked her to explain to them the nature and properties of the five trees, and what was the meaning of the writing on each of their flowers.

. . .

"These conditions govern the flowers, which are principles and doctrine to rectify the error of those who have no knowledge of God nor of His works, nor even of their own beliefs. Through a knowledge of these trees, one can console the disconsolate and calm those in anguish. And by these trees one can subdue temptation and purify the soul of guilt and sin; and by the use of these trees—for someone who knows how to pick their fruit—a person can escape infinite pain and achieve everlasting peace."

When the lady had spoken these words to the three wise men, she took leave of them and went on her way; and the three wise men remained by the spring, beneath the five trees; and one of the wise men began to sigh and to say: "Ah! What a great good fortune it would be if, by means of these trees, we could all—every man on earth—be under one religion and belief, so that there would be no more rancor or ill will among men, who hate each other because of diversity and contrariness of beliefs and sects! And just as there is only one God, Father, Creator, and Lord of everything that exists, so all peoples could unite and become one people, and that people be on the path to salvation, under one faith and one religion, giving glory and praise to our Lord God.

"Think, gentlemen," the wise man said to his

companions, "of the harm that comes from men not belonging to a single sect, and of the good that would come from everyone beneath one faith and one religion. This being the case, do you not think it would be a good idea for us to sit beneath these trees, beside this lovely fountain, and discuss what we believe, according to what the flowers and conditions of these trees signify? And since we cannot agree by means of [scriptural] authorities, let us try to come to some agreement by means of demonstrative and necessary reasons."

The other two agreed to what this wise man had said. And they sat down and began to study the flowers on the trees and to recall the conditions and the words the lady had spoken to them; and they decided to hold their discussion according to the manner the lady indicated to them.[2]

Discussion Questions

1. Though attempts like these real and imagined religious debates using reason did occur from time to time, most scholars were critical of this approach. Why do you suppose this is?

2. What do you make of the fact that later in his career, Llull became an outspoken advocate of crusade?

3. Would such debates likely succeed or fail? Why?

Further Reading

Bertaina, David. *Christian and Muslim Dialogues: The Religious Uses of a Literary Form in the Early Islamic Middle East.* Piscataway, NJ: Gorgias Press, 2011.

Szpiech, Ryan, ed. *Medieval Exegesis and Religious Difference: Commentary, Conflict, and Community in the Premodern Mediterranean.* New York: Fordham University Press, 2015.

Tolan, John. *Saracens: Islam in the Medieval European Imagination.* New York: Columbia University Press, 2002.

Notes

1. Sidney Griffith, *The Church in the Shadow of the Mosque: Christians and Muslims in the World of Islam* (Princeton: Princeton University Press, 2008), 64.

2. Ramon Llull, *Selected Works of Ramon Lull (1232–1316)*, trans. Anthony Bonner (Princeton: Princeton University Press, 1985), 113–16.

audience, and that account was translated several times into Arabic as well and circulated widely in the Islamic world. Such sophisticated discussions, in which both sides were (or were depicted later as) infallibly polite to each other continued throughout the Middle Ages. Sometime in the early eleventh century, for example, Elias, the Church of the East's bishop of Nisibis (modern Nusaybin in eastern Turkey), and a powerful Muslim courtier, Ibn 'Ali al-Maghribi, debated the full range of Christian-Muslim theological differences, over the course of seven different meetings. At session one they discussed God's unity, which they agreed on, and Bishop Elias defended the Christian doctrine of the Trinity; in session two they debated the Incarnation; in session three, Christian monotheism as presented in the Qur'an; in session four, miraculous and rational proofs of Christianity; and so on. Both parties paraded their great learning as they discoursed on such subtle philosophical issues as whether one could refer to God as a substance (*jawhar*) as Christians did, or not (as Muslim philosophers universally preferred). In the surviving account, moreover, written down in Arabic by Elias, both bishop and *amir* go out of their way to be friendly—the *amir* is anxious to hear all about the bishop's recent activities, the bishop asks God's favor upon the *amir* at the first mentioning of his name ("May God's mercy be upon him!"), and at one point, after mentioning the whole Muslim community, this Christian bishop invoked God's blessing on them all ("May God protect them!").[15]

In the cases of both al-Mahdi's debate with Timothy and Bishop Elias's debate with Ibn 'Ali al-Maghribi it is certain that the surviving written accounts are the result of careful editing and reworking—one cannot help but notice that in each case the Christian bishop who wrote down the debate happened also to have maintained the upper hand throughout. In many cases, however, what seem to be written accounts of religious disputations are entirely fictional. In the late thirteenth century the deeply, if eccentrically, learned Mallorcan-Christian layman Ramon Llull (d. 1316) penned a treatise called

The Book of the Gentile and Three Wise Men, in which a pagan, nonmonotheist (the "gentile") happens across three scholars—a Jew, a Christian, and a Muslim—in a glade where they are greeting each other amicably as they each stretch their backs after hours of sitting with their learned codices. A debate ensues after the gentile asks the three scholars to defend their beliefs. They do so just as amicably, and there is no clear winner by the conversation's end (at least on the surface: just underneath one easily detects the author's own unusual Christian philosophy quietly winning the day).

Such real or imagined religious debates were by no means the only form of religious discussion. Throughout the Middle Ages, scholars wrote countless works with titles like *Rebuttal of the Christians* or *Silencing the Jews* (both by Muslim authors), *Against the Religion of Islam* or *Against the Sect of Muhammad* (both by Christian authors), and *Refutation of Christian Principles* (by a Jewish author). Here the opposite religion was directly attacked: Muslims and Jews decried the "irrational" doctrine of the Trinity (it would make just as much sense, they often pointed out, for God to have four or five persons—a Quarternity or Quintinity!); Christians vehemently attacked both Muhammad's life (he was a warlike polygamist, they uniformly asserted) and the Qur'an (an incomprehensible mishmash of stolen biblical passages and invented fables); Jews denied against Christians and Muslims alike that any further revelation beyond the Torah was necessary at all.

The same range of arguments appeared in still another genre of religious debate: the (often) fictitious exchange of letters between representatives of two of the faiths. The bestseller in this category was surely the ninth-century work called the *Apology of al-Kindi,* which consisted of two letters: one written by a Muslim (al-Hashimi) inviting his Christian friend (al-Kindi) to become a Muslim, and the second written by the Christian rejecting the Muslim's appeal and inviting him to become a Christian. The whole is almost certainly a Christian fabrication, the Christian's book-length letter in response attacking Islam with unusual hostility, but also demonstrating great learning in Muslim thought. This text circulated widely throughout the period, and was even translated into Latin in the twelfth century by the same team that created the first Latin Qur'an. But other exchanges of letters were authentic. A Melkite-Christian bishop of Antioch named Paul composed in Arabic a *Letter to a Muslim Friend* in about 1200. Relatively brief—just twenty-four pages—this work, and a longer revision of it, provoked a huge response. No fewer than three Muslim intellectuals, including Ibn Taymiyya (d. 1328), one of the most influential thinkers in Islamic history, refuted it in much longer letters (Ibn Taymiyya's is, in fact, seven thick volumes long in one modern printing!).

Convert, Defend, Attack Enemies Within?

Christianity and Islam are avowedly conversionary religions, so when their faithful engage in religious debate in any of the above forms, it is natural to conclude that their goal is to convert. Surely the point of all this arguing—whether amicable or hostile—is to get the nonbelievers to join up. In some cases this is absolutely true. Ramon Llull who wrote, as we have seen, about the gentile and three wise men, also wrote 260 other works, all of them intended, he tells us in his short autobiography, either to reform the beliefs and behavior of Christians, or to convert everyone else to Christianity. Indeed, he invented a philosophical method—an intellectual forebear, as it turns out, to the modern, mechanized methods of thought that gave us computers—that he believed would convince the whole world of the truth of Christianity, and he tirelessly tried both to convince other Christian intellectuals to adopt it (very few did) and to persuade unbelievers using it (who remained overwhelmingly unconvinced).

But it is also certain that many such works, while overtly attacking another religion, were meant primarily to comfort their author's coreligionists. Jews had for the most part refrained from attacking the religions of the kingdoms and principalities in which they lived—whether Christian, Muslim, or otherwise. This was in part because medieval Judaism was not a proselytizing religion. But Jews also knew that they were a tiny religious minority wherever they lived, and were thus reluctant to rock the boat. Yet sometime in the first decade of the twelfth century a southern Occitan rabbi named Joseph Kimhi wrote the *Book of the Covenant,* which attacked the beliefs and behavior of the Latin Christians among whom he lived. That it is written in Hebrew—a

FIGURE 8.10 Beginning of the Letter of 'Umar II to Emperor Leo III in Aljamiado (Spanish written in Arabic letters). © Historical Views / agefotostock.

language that only a tiny minority of Christian scholars could then read—is the first sign that his goal was to firm up the faith of his fellow Jews. Kimhi's focus, moreover, was to discredit the basic Christian approach to reading the Hebrew Bible. Where Christians allegorically interpreted passages such passages as Isaiah 9:6 ("For unto us a child is born, to us a son is given, and the government will be upon his shoulder . . .") as referring to the birth of Jesus, the divine Son of God, Kimhi insisted that they be interpreted absolutely literally and within the historical context in which they were first written. Such an argument was never going to convince Christians, so central was such allegorical interpretation to all of Christian belief, but Kimhi's attack would help keep Jews from being seduced into Christian belief. SEE SOURCEBOOK 8:6.

But sometimes such works defended something else: the social hierarchy of Mediterranean religious communities. Everywhere one religion—Islam or Christianity—governed subordinate groups of other Peoples of the Book. Much of the time, all parties involved recognized that living with this unequal, but mostly peaceful, religious diversity, was preferable to the explosively dangerous consequences of upending it. Better that everyone knew, and more or less accepted, the boundaries between Jew, Christian, and Muslim than that wild-eyed evangelists or seekers of martyrdom should call down violent rebellion or murderous repression by flagrantly crossing them. In the ninth century a fictitious correspondence between the eighth-century caliph 'Umar II (717–720) and his contemporary the Byzantine emperor Leo III (717–741) began to circulate among both Christians and Muslims, first in Greek, then in Arabic, Armenian,

Aljamiado (Castilian in Arabic characters), and Latin versions. The fact that the same text could be reworked and retranslated sometimes for Christian readership, sometimes for Muslim, suggests that its real function was to carefully sketch out the religious boundaries between those groups, lest anyone on either side, dangerously destabilize them.

In still other cases, attacks on another religion were actually campaigns against coreligionists with whom one disagreed. The great Sunni sheikh Ibn Taymiyya's fat, multivolume *Sound Answer* putatively refutes Christianity, but not so far under the surface actually attacks Shi'is, Sufis, and many other Muslim groups with whom he disagreed (and there were many!), whose beliefs, he argues, are not so different from those of Christians. When attacking Christian belief in the Trinity, for example, Ibn Taymiyya pointedly argues that "the wayward among those who associate themselves with Islam resemble the Christians in this matter and can be likened to them." At other times, hostile polemic wound up, intentionally or not, engaging issues that were mostly of interest to scholars of one's own religion. The brilliant Catalan Dominican and linguist Ramon Martí (fl. 1250–1284) wrote a huge book called the *Dagger of Faith* in which, he said, he meant "to cut the jugular of Jewish infidelity."[16] Yet he did not address standard objections that medieval Jews leveled at Christian teaching (why not a Quaternity or Quintinity, for example, rather than a Trinity), focusing instead largely on questions that only Christian scholars in the new universities north of the Pyrenees asked. Perhaps the most important of these was whether one could demonstrate, *using the Old Testament alone,* that the Messiah had come in the person of Jesus, thereby disproving Judaism. And indeed this very question was at the center of one of the most notorious public religious disputes of the Middle Ages, the so-called Disputation of Barcelona in July 1263, convened by Jaume I, king of Aragon. He ordered one of the leading rabbis of Spain, Nahmanides (d. 1270), to appear at his court to debate a Jewish convert to Christianity on this very topic. While the Christian disputants at Barcelona do seem to have wanted to convert Jews, the theological questions that they demanded Nahmanides answer were principally of interest to Christians. SEE SOURCEBOOK 8:7.

Interreligious Edification

Sometime in the fourteenth or fifteenth century, a Christian scholar somewhere in France read carefully through a manuscript copy of the Qur'an in Latin translation, jotting notes in the margin as he did so. While most of these comments simply pointed out important biblical figures mentioned also in Islam's holy book or complained about passages that seemed un-Christian, when he came to Qur'an 2:115, he did something surprising: he wrote *bene,* "well said!" or "eloquently spoken!"[17] beside a verse that struck him as profoundly true ("To God belongs the East and the West. Wherever you turn, there is the face of God"). In addition, therefore, to responding to each other's holy books with hostility, in addition to writing treatises against other people's religion, it was entirely possible for Jews, Christians, and Muslims to find edification in their rivals' religious texts.

A fifteenth-century Muslim scholar from Cairo named al-Biqa'i is the best example. In general Muslim scholars in the later Middle Ages believed that while the Hebrew Bible and Christian New Testament had originally been valid, if limited, revelations from God, Jews and Christians had so fully "corrupted" them by changing or removing verses or adding extra material that in their surviving form they were largely useless—and anyway the Qur'an, the final and fullest revelation, had made them superfluous. Muslims did not, therefore, use the Bible for worship or theology in the way that Christians used the Hebrew Bible. But al-Biqa'i was an iconoclast. After reading the Bible in Arabic he became convinced that it was essential for understanding the Qur'an, and proceeded to write a vast commentary on the Qur'an in which he quoted it repeatedly. Yet the Bible was not just useful, as al-Biqa'i saw it. It was beautiful and edifying. After quoting a long passage from the biblical prophet Jeremiah, al-Biqa'i exulted that his "speech is sublime in its style, exquisite in its tenderness, such that it . . . rends the hearts, and makes the eyes swell with tears."[18] *Bene* indeed.

Most of the time such cross-religious scriptural readers were not so forthright, however, since explicit admiration for someone else's holy book could bring down condemnation from religious authorities (as it did in al-Biqa'i's case). But it went on nonetheless, often indirectly or furtively. Muslim Sufi ascetics, for example, saw the wandering prophet Jesus as the model for their way of life. Though their veneration of him was based on the many Qur'anic passages in which he figures, from an early period they clearly began to encounter biblical stories of Jesus as well, many of them drawn from the Gospel of Matthew. Throughout the Middle Ages and well beyond, then, Sufis have told, retold, and elaborated on these ultimately biblical stories. Indeed, al-Ghazali's spiritual and theological masterpiece called *Bringing Religious Studies Back to Life* (see chapter 4 above) contains the largest number of sayings and stories of Jesus of any work of Arabic literature.

It was nonscriptural religious texts, however, that most easily came to inspire unbelievers. We met Yahya ibn 'Adi (d. 974) earlier as a Christian philosopher and theologian in Islamic Baghdad, but he also wrote a guide to living an ethical life in Arabic called the *Reformation of Morals*. This work became widely read in Islamic circles, and in the surviving manuscripts from this period is often wrongly attributed to Muslim authors. Similarly, in the sixteenth century, a Spanish Muslim author called El Mancebo de Arevelo (the Young Man of Arevelo) wrote a treatise called the *Summary of the Account and Spiritual Exercise,* which borrowed heavily from perhaps the most influential guide to Christian spirituality ever written, Thomas à Kempis's fifteenth-century *Imitation of Christ,* written originally in Latin.

FIGURE 8.11 Image of Abraham Abulafia in manuscript of his *Light of the Intellect*. The Picture Art Collection / Alamy Stock Photo.

Much the same thing could happen in reverse. The Mallorcan Christian Ramon Llull (d. 1316) was passionately dedicated to converting Jews and Muslims to Christianity, but he also had deep admiration for Sufi spiritual practices, clearly read Sufi works in Arabic, and modeled some of his own works on them. But perhaps no one exemplifies how religious edification could operate across religious boundaries better than Llull's contemporary the Spanish Jewish spiritual master Abraham Abulafia (d. 1291). A deeply learned scholar who had read the rationalist works of the great Aristotelian Jewish philosopher Maimonides (d. 1204), Abulafia's own intellectual and spiritual development went off in a very different direction—toward the same mystical practices that fascinated Llull. Indeed, he was one of the central creators of the Kabbalah, an enormously influential strand of Jewish mystical thought and practice. While scarcely identical to it, Abulafia's brand of Kabbalah has many similarities with the Muslim mystical thought of another Andalusi, the great Sufi sheikh Ibn 'Arabi (d. 1240). Both saw themselves in messianic terms—Ibn 'Arabi proclaiming himself the Seal of the Saints, and Abulafia actually declaring himself the Messiah who would be recognized by both Jews and Christians. Both also emphasized the knowledge of God's names in their spiritual practice, and especially the mystical awareness of what they both called the "greatest name" (Allah for Ibn 'Arabi, Yahweh for Abulafia). Indeed, it seems likely that Abulafia, like Ibn 'Arabi, practiced "recitation" or "remembrance" (*dhikr*) of God's names, a commonplace of Sufi spirituality. Certainly, some of his Jewish followers did. But Abulafia, who traveled throughout the Mediterranean, also had close contacts with Christians. Not only did he frequently preach to groups of Christians and Jews, but he even spent a month living at a Franciscan convent in Rome in 1280 (where he had come to try to convert the pope to Judaism!). Indeed, Abulafia's belief that he was the Messiah who would usher in the last day (after converting the pope) was shaped deeply by his knowledge of a strain of apocalyptic ("end-time") thought that flourished within the same Franciscan order.

Notes

1. *Kalila and Dimna, or, The Fables of Bidpai,* trans. Wyndham Knatchbull (Oxford: J. Parker, Messrs. Longman, Hurst, Rees, Orme, and Brown, 1819), 103.

2. *Barlaam and Ioasaph* (Cambridge, MA: Harvard University Press; London: W. Heinemann, 1914), 13.

3. James T. Monroe, *Hispano-Arabic Poetry: A Student Anthology* (Berkeley: University of California Press, 1974), 250.

4. Raymond P. Scheindlin, *Wine, Women, and Death: Medieval Hebrew Poems on the Good Life* (New York: Oxford University Press, 1986), 107.

5. *Digenis Akritas: The Two-Blood Border Lord, The Grottaferraa Version,* trans., with introduction and notes, Denison B. Hull (Athens: Ohio University Press, 1972), 11, 29.

6. *The Poem of the Cid,* trans. Rita Hamilton and Janet Perry, with introduction and notes by Ian Michael (London: Penguin Books, 1984), 61 (l. 731).

7. *Poem of the Cid,* 160 (l. 2636).

8. Travis Zadeh, *The Vernacular Qur'an: Translation and the Rise of Persian Exegesis* (Oxford: Oxford University Press in association with the Institute for Ismaili Studies, 2012), 284.

9. Ibn al-Tayyib, *Commentaire sur la Genèse,* ed. J.C.J. Sanders (Leuven: Peeters, 1967), 1.

10. Ibn al-Tayyib, 1.

11. *Le psautier mozarabe de Hafs le Goth,* ed. and trans. Marie-Thérèse Urvoy (Toulouse: Presses Universitaires du Mirail, 1994), 11, 13.

12. Thomas E. Burman, "*Tafsīr* and Translation: Traditional Arabic Qurʾān Exegesis and the Latin Qurʾāns of Robert of Ketton and Mark of Toledo," *Speculum* 73:3 (1998): 703–32, at 723.

13. Burman, 724.

14. Inghetto Contardo, *Disputatio contra iudeos: Controverse avec les juifs,* intro., ed., and trans. Gilbert Dahan (Paris: Les Belles Lettres, 1993), 88.

15. Khalil Samir, "Entretien d'Élie de Nisibe avec le Vizir ʿAlī al-Maġribī sur l'unité et la trinité," *Islamochristiana* 5 (1979): 31–117, at 49, 68.

16. Ramon Martí, *Pugio fidei adversus Mauros et Iudaeos* (Leipzig, 1687; repr. Farnborough, Eng.: Gregg, 1967), 2.

17. Thomas E. Burman, *Reading the Qur'an in Latin Christendom, 1140–1560* (Philadelphia: University of Pennsylvania Press, 2007), 192.

18. Walid Saleh, "'Sublime in Its Style, Exquisite in Its Tenderness': The Bible Quotations in al-Biqā'ī's Qur'ān Commentary," in *Adaptations and Innovations: Studies in the Interaction between Jewish and Islamic Thought and Literature from the Early Middle Ages to the Late Twentieth Century, Dedicated to Professor Joel L. Kraemer,* ed. Y. Tzvi Langermann and Josef Stern (Paris: Peeters, 2007), 331–48, at 331.

CHAPTER NINE

A Sea of Technology, Science, and Philosophy

Sometime in the 1250s Nasir al-Din al-Tusi (1201–1274), a brilliant Shi'i polymath and opportunist, persuaded Hülegü, the Mongol conqueror of Baghdad, to build the most advanced astronomical observatory in the world in northeastern Iran in the city of Maragha. Researchers invited from all over and beyond the Islamic world (including China) lived in lodgings provided by the observatory's generous endowment. Al-Tusi and his colleagues spent twelve years making careful observations at Maragha, and then collectively produced the most accurate tables for calculating the positions of planets and stars then available. Al-Tusi himself, moreover, invented what scholars now call the "Tusi couple," an elegant theory that explained one of the most troubling problems that medieval astronomers inherited from the ancients—how to explain the apparent backward ("retrograde") motion of the planets. From Maragha the "Tusi couple" eventually made its way to Copernicus, who adopted an identical approach in his groundbreaking *On the Revolutions of the Heavenly Spheres*, and so it was that medieval Islamic astronomy directly influenced the work that kicked off the European Scientific Revolution. But al-Tusi was much more than an astronomer and mathematician. One of the most prolific scholars in the medieval Islamic world, he was the author of more than 150 works, including important philosophical treatises. In these he cultivated with great nuance a revived Aristotelian system of thought devised in the eleventh century by the most influential medieval philosopher, the Persian Muslim Ibn Sina (980–1037; Avicenna, in the Latin world).

These are exceptional accomplishments, but al-Tusi is, nevertheless, profoundly representative of a central strand of Mediterranean culture in the eleventh through fourteenth century: its enduring commitment to rationalism. Al-Tusi and his team could make their calculations because the observatory at Maragha possessed remarkable technology, such as a massive quadrant—one-quarter of a circle forty meters in diameter fixed to a wall—by means of which the elevations of stars and planets could be calculated with great precision. But the wall quadrant is only one of many amazing new or amazingly improved pieces of technology that spread throughout the medieval Mediterranean. The library at Maragha is said to have possessed 400,000 volumes, some composed in Arabic, many translated into that language from Greek or Persian, all of them bearing witness to intensive scientific study throughout the region—many of them, moreover, having already been translated into Latin at the other end of the Mediterranean, where they became the foundation of the Scientific Revolution. As an institution of rational thought, the observatory at Maragha was itself an innovation, but not the only one in this period. Far west in contemporary Latin Christendom, the distinctive European universities were enjoying their first century of efflorescence. By the time al-Tusi was making his calculations, the basic curriculum of the university bachelor's degree course had become an extended tour through the rationalist scientific and philosophical system of Aristotle as interpreted and developed by the great Arab philosophers, such as the same Ibn Sina whom al-Tusi so admired. It is true that there was plenty of mysticism and nonrationality in medieval culture, just as there are in nearly all cultures and ages in world history (and we will examine some of this in chapter 13), but we would seriously misunderstand the civilizations surrounding the Sea in the Middle, if we did not recognize how regularly their approach to life and its problem was a strictly rational affair, assisted by rationally designed tools, informed by rational scientific observation and theory, and sustained by sophisticated and thoroughly rational reflection on the nature of God, humans, and the cosmos.

Technology

Technological innovations had flowed around the Mediterranean—and indeed across Eurasia—since antiquity, and indeed the earlier Middle Ages had continued this trend. The military culture of much of the Mediterranean, for example, had been transformed by the adoption of the stirrup, which allowed warriors to stay firmly mounted on their horses in combat. Thus was born the central medieval military unit: the heavily armed knight, replacing the foot soldier of antiquity. Likewise, the borrowing of the horse collar and the invention of the heavy wheeled plow in Germanic Europe allowed for its heavy clay soils to be cultivated much more efficiently, this leading in part to the transformation of the poor economy of Latin Europe into the productive powerhouse of the later Middle Ages. But the period of the eleventh through fourteenth century presents us with remarkable examples of the capacity of Mediterranean civilization to adopt, adapt, or invent powerful new technologies.

Paper

When Mediterranean sultans and kings conquered lands, they often conquered flourishing new industries and technologies as well. Pragmatists at heart, they usually embraced and expanded them. So it was with paper. Invented originally in China, perhaps as early as the first century BCE, the technology of papermaking gradually spread throughout Asia. As they traveled along the Silk Roads, Buddhist monks—like the ones who had brought the story *Barlaam and Josephat* west—brought paper technology with them to the central-Asian regions of modern Uzbekistan, Pakistan, and Iran by the time of the Arab-Muslim conquests of the early eighth century. Under Muslim control, this paper industry flourished, especially after the 'Abbasid dynasty took power, and then spread quite quickly throughout the vast Islamic empire. The oldest complete Arabic book manuscript dates from about 900, and by the year 1000, paper was being used for written texts of every kind—including the Qur'an itself.

Some regions were a little slower to adopt this new medium. Ironically, Iran and Central Asia, where Muslims first came across paper, are a case in point, but so also were western North Africa and al-Andalus, where a thriving sheep industry kept parchment prices lower. As a consequence, the first entirely paper Qur'an from these regions dates to about 1140. Yet papermaking eventually flourished in the far West as well, including in al-Andalus, especially in the city of Játiva near the Mediterranean coast, whose paper was considered without equal, according to how the Muslim geographer, al-Idrisi, put it in 1144. Indeed, paper from Islamic Spain began to trickle into Latin Europe at an early date: a Christian liturgical book copied in the second half of the tenth century, though written mostly on parchment, contained thirty-eight leaves (sixty-four pages) of text copied on paper, presumably because the supply of animal hide had run out.

Conquest also played a big role in introducing intensive papermaking to Latin Christendom. King Jaume I of Aragon's conquest of the Muslim kingdom of Valencia in 1232–1245 brought Játiva and other important papermaking centers under Christian rule. Indeed, Játiva became a crown city, and its paper industry the ward of King Jaume himself. Crown bureaucrats, therefore, began to copy official royal documents on paper soon afterward, and the resulting vast cache of charters and records represents the first large-scale use of paper for administrative purposes in Latin Europe. Since, moreover, the great majority of the population of Valencia after the Christian conquest remained Muslim for generations, it is not surprising that papermaking remained overwhelmingly a Muslim trade in Christian Valencia until the fifteenth century.

But papermaking arrived in other parts of the Christian Mediterranean without any antecedent conqueror. We find evidence of it in many towns in central and northern Italy in the last decade of the thirteenth century and the early years of the fourteenth. Indeed, Tuscan and Lombard paper soon spread to markets across Latin Europe. By the mid-fourteenth century paper was being made in France, and in 1389, Nuremberg became the first German center. Though scribes continued to

Though there is a sea in the middle of them, the lands surrounding the Mediterranean are, with some notable exceptions, quite arid. Finding enough water to farm effectively was, therefore, a constant challenge. In response, medieval Mediterranean people adopted, invented, and exported ingenious technologies to bring water to needy crops and thirsty mouths. Up until the late Middle Ages, technology and scientific innovation tended overwhelmingly to travel from the Islamic East across North Africa and thence to western Europe, and so it was with methods for moving and lifting water.

In many dry climates there is water available in aquifers deep beneath adjoining foothills and mountains, and it could be used for irrigation and drinking water except that much of it would evaporate if transferred toward lowlands in open-air canals. Though expensive to build, qanats were an amazingly effective solution to this problem. *Qanat* meant "canal" in ancient Persia, where this technology was invented sometime in the first millennium BCE, and a qanat consisted of a well (or sometimes multiple wells) dug upland from arable land, in combination with a slightly sloping underground channel running from the well toward the arable land. At regular intervals, vertical maintenance shafts were dug connecting the underground canal to the surface. By this means, water could be transported at considerable distance with almost no loss to evaporation, and the system could be regularly maintained for centuries. Indeed, the vast qanats of Gonabad in Iran, a system of some 427 wells and qanats (whose total length is 108,638 feet), have been in use for more than two millennia.

During the medieval period, qanat technology followed the expansion of Islam right across the southern Mediterranean into Spain and Sicily. Called *galarías* in Spanish, many examples still survive (though few currently function) throughout the Iberian Peninsula. So successful were qanats in Iberia, that they continued to be built well after the Middle Ages. Though Madrid, for example, had

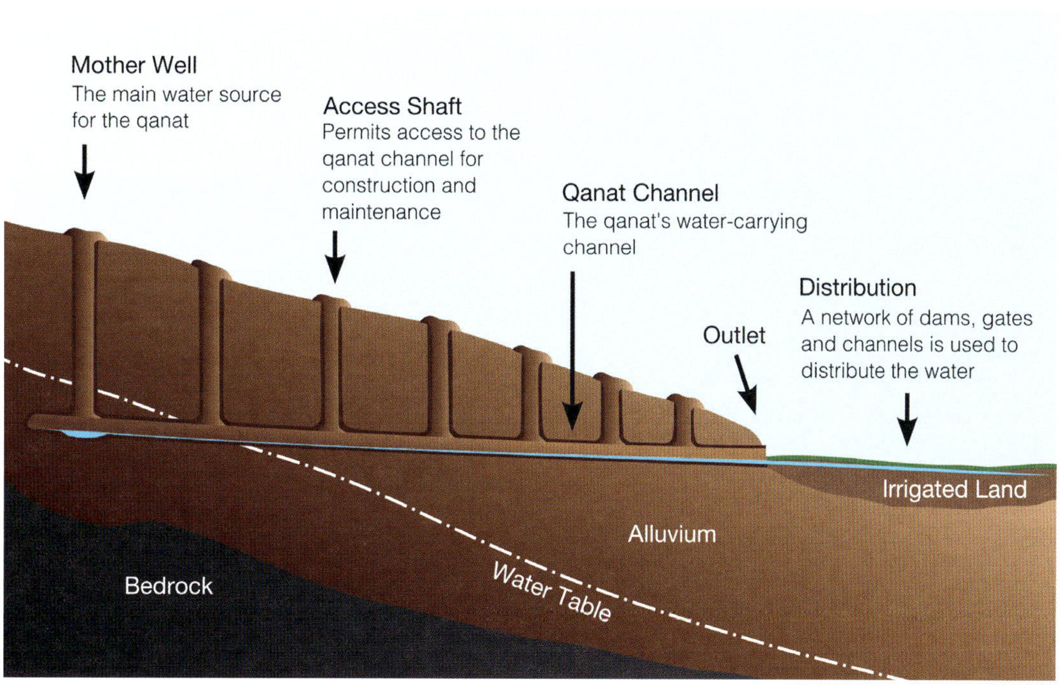

FIGURE 9.1 *Qanat.* Image by Samuel Bailey provided by Wikimedia Commons under the CC-BY-3.0 license.

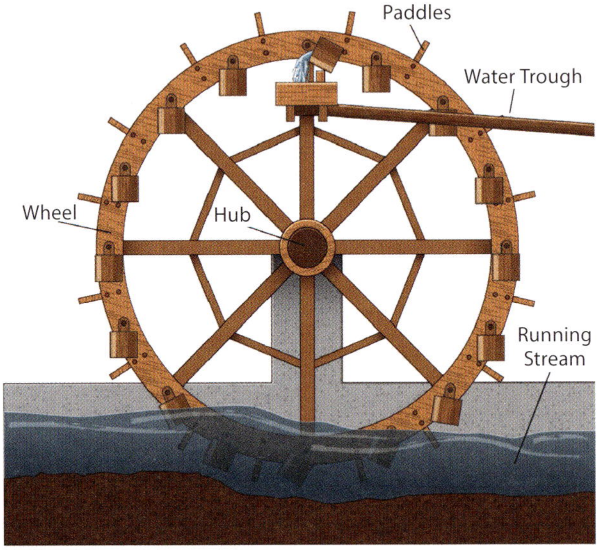

FIGURE 9.2 *(left) Qanat* of Palermo, Sicily. Photo: Archipenzolo provided by Wikimedia Commons under Creative Commons CC0 license.

FIGURE 9.3 *(above)* Parts of the Noria. © Noria Corporation, Image courtesy of Noria Corporation.

FIGURE 9.4 Norias of Hama, Syria. Chronicle / Alamy Stock Photo.

a relatively small qanat dating to the Islamic period, it was totally insufficient to the needs of the large city it became in the sixteenth and seventeenth centuries, so a vast, multiwell system was built in that period and continued to be used well into the nineteenth century. The Muslim rulers of Sicily likewise imported the technology, creating a large system that supplied water to Palermo. Though not in use, substantial portions of it can be toured today.

The Noria

But what if one wanted to lift water out of a river or well to higher levels for irrigation or human consumption? In a world without electricity or internal combustion engines, pumping water was not easy. By the fourth century BCE, however, an effective mechanism had been invented that was apparently first used in Egypt.

The noria was an undershot waterwheel with buckets or compartments built-in that, using the energy of a stream or river, raised water to a higher level, as in the diagram in figure 9.2. With the coming of Islam, these wheels, which the Arabs called *na'urat* (sing. *na'ura*, from a verb meaning "to groan"), spread throughout the Mediterranean. The town of Hama in modern Syria, for example, became famous for its many water-lifting norias, some as much as sixty-five feet in diameter.

But if one wanted to raise standing water from a well or reservoir, a different kind of noria, sometimes called a *sania*, was necessary. This was a short-shafted wheel with gears that was moved by an animal as in the diagram in figure 9.5.

FIGURE 9.5 *Sania*. Drawing from *A Descriptive and Historical Account of Hydraulic and Other Machines for Raising Water, Ancient and Modern: Including the Progressive Development of the Steam Engine*, by Thomas Ewbank, page 126. Hathi Trust Digital Library, digitized by Google, original in the collection of Harvard University.

This kind of noria likewise spread throughout the medieval Islamic Mediterranean basin and allowed a single family farm to produce enough surplus crops to supply markets. As one historian put it, "The cultivated belts around many towns from Spain to India owed their prosperity to [the] introduction [of the noria]."[1] After the conquest of Spain by Christian monarchs in the High Middle Ages, moreover, many norias continued to be used throughout Iberia for centuries.

Discussion Questions

1. What does the spread of the noria and qanat tell us about the place of engineering and technology in medieval Islamic civilization?

2. What kinds of interactions between regions and between peoples would have been necessary for the diffusion of these technologies?

Further Reading

Glick, Thomas F. *Irrigation and Society in Medieval Valencia*. Cambridge, MA: Harvard University Press, 1979.

Glick, Thomas F., and Helena Kirchner. "Hydraulic Systems and Technologies of Islamic Spain: History and Archeology." In *Working with Water in Medieval Europe: Technology and Resource-Use*, ed. P. Squatriti, 267–329. Leiden: E. J. Brill, 2000.

Kirchner, Helena. "Water Management and Irrigation in Medieval Mediterranean Societies: An Overview." In *Convivencia and Medieval Spain: Essays in Honor of Thomas F. Glick*, ed. Mark T. Abate, 65–98. Cham: Palgrave Macmillan, 2019.

Note

1. Thomas F. Glick, "Noria," in *Medieval Science, Technology, and Medicine: An Encyclopedia*, ed. Thomas Glick, Steven J. Livesey, and Faith Wallis (New York: Routledge, 2005), 369–71, at 370.

copy books on parchment well into the sixteenth century, increasingly Latin manuscripts, like contemporary Arabic ones, were made of paper in the later Middle Ages. Byzantine bureaucrats began using paper intermittently from the mid-eleventh century on, and paper became common for administrative purposes in the Greek world from the mid-twelfth century on. Byzantium, though, never had its own paper industry, preferring to import its supplies from Syria and then, in the thirteenth century, from Italy and Spain. It was only in the aftermath of the Ottoman-Muslim conquest in 1453 that the first paper mill was set up in the suburb of Istanbul still called "Paper Mill" (Kagithane).

That the techniques of papermaking could cross linguistic and religious borders without conquest is especially interesting if we bear in mind how complicated this process was. The basic ingredient was used rags made of linen (flax) or cordage made of hemp. These had to be unraveled first, and then softened by combing, after which they were soaked in lime water. The resulting pulpy mass was then kneaded by hand and bleached in the sun—a process repeated several times. After the remaining fibers in the pulp were cut up with scissors, the whole was rinsed in fresh water and then pounded with a mortar or ground by mill wheels. Once all this was done, the processed pulp was placed on a mold consisting of a wooden frame with a screen stretched across—something like a flat, rectilinear sieve. The maker smoothed the pulp out over the mold to an even thickness, and then laid the layer of pulp on a flat board, and afterward transferred it to a wall where, still moist, it stuck. Once it dried, however, it fell off. The process was still not complete, though: the sheets, which were ribbed by the pattern of the mold screen, were then rubbed with meal and wheat starch, after which water was sprinkled on them, this filling out any unevenness and whitening the paper.

For Muslims to learn these elaborate steps from Buddhists, or, later, Christians from Muslims, required a great deal of side-by-side work across religious lines, and the widespread cross-cultural commerce in paper meant constant interactions between Jewish, Christian, and Muslim merchants. Sometimes this led to problems: Christian producers began putting paper watermarks on each sheet—images or patterns visible if the sheet is held up to the light, and meant to identify the papermaker. Not uncommonly, such marks contained Christian symbols or human images that were controversial in Islamic law. Eventually Muslim jurists were called upon to comment on the legality of using such paper (usually they found ways to justify it). What is certain, however, is that the spread of paper and papermaking technology had a huge cultural impact on the whole Mediterranean. Since paper was so much cheaper than parchment (in 1280 it was as much as six times cheaper), the costs of producing books declined precipitously. Not surprisingly, a lot more books were made. This helps account for the fact that largest libraries in the Islamic world around the year 1000 were far bigger than the best libraries in Latin Europe, but it also helps us understand why Muslim scholars wrote such enormous books in this period and well into the later Middle Ages. As we have seen, Qur'anic commentaries twelve volumes long in modern printings were not uncommon, and some were far longer.

The Astrolabe

An astrolabe was the medieval equivalent of a smartphone: a beautifully crafted tool with many amazing uses, a piece of technology that put on display the great scientific sophistication of the society that built it. Made of metal, usually brass, the key parts of the astrolabe were the *tympanum,* a round plate upon which a map of the coordinate lines of the three-dimensional dome of the heavens was projected in two dimensions, and a *rete* or "web," a stylized overlay that maps out the path of the sun and the locations of the brightest stars. The center of this "web" was attached to the center of the *tympanum* by a pin in such a way that it could rotate on top of it. On the other side, finally, a sight called an *alidade,* held in place by the same pin, allowed the user to measure the angle above the horizon of celestial objects, whether sun, stars, or planets.

The basic use of an astrolabe was to tell local time by the altitude of the sun during the day or the stars at night. To do this, one held up the astrolabe, by a ring connected to the top, in the direction of, say, a star, and then used the alidade to measure the angle of the elevation of that heavenly body. This was done by rotating the alidade from pointing at the horizon up to the position at which the star could be seen through its sights. Taking the angle of elevation (these were indicated by degree on a scale along the outer edge of the astrolabe), one then turned over the astrolabe and turned the rete until its marker for that star aligned with those degrees of elevation as indicated on the tympanum. By doing so, one had a full map of the heavens as they appeared at that moment. Assuming one knew the day of the year, the local time could then be worked out by several different means, drawing on tables of information usually etched onto the back of the astrolabe.

But the astrolabe had many other applications as well. The same assemblage of tympanum, rete, and alidade could be used to estimate the height of towers or the depth of wells or the distance of an approaching enemy. It was essential for calculating the dates of religious festivals such as Easter or Ramadan or determining the direction to Mecca. A court astrologer necessarily used it to cast horoscopes in order to determine propitious days for launching invasions or marrying off a daughter (rulers everywhere in the Mediterranean were enthralled with astrology). Builders and city planners used it for surveying—the great 'Abbasid city of Baghdad was laid out along the Tigris River by surveyors using astrolabes. By the tenth century, this remarkable computer—the astrolabe—was already an age-old technology. In using it century after century, scientists and engineers throughout the Mediterranean were, in fact, perpetuating and indeed improving perhaps the most remarkable scientific instrument of the ancient world.

The great Greek astronomer Ptolemy described something very like it around 150 CE, but the first whole treatise on its uses survives in a sixth-century Syriac version, and actual astrolabes from around the Mediterranean survive from the tenth century on. They were used everywhere. While only one astrolabe inscribed in Byzantine Greek survives (dated 1062), Byzantine scholars, beginning with the late antique philosopher and mathematician John Philoponus (d. 574) and ending with Nikephoros Gregoras (d. 1360) wrote countless treatises on its use. At just about the time Islam was expanding north from Arabia, a Christian bishop, Severus Sebokht, composed a treatise on the astrolabe in Syriac, and in 815, a Jew from Basra in southern Iraq composed the first such work in Arabic. For the next several centuries, the most sophisticated astrolabes and the most advanced treatises about them were produced in the Islamic world. Muhammad ibn Ahmad al-Biruni (973–1048), an astounding Persian polymath (he learned Sanskrit in order to write the world's first study of Indian thought and religion by an outsider), wrote the single most important work on constructing astrolabes, while North African astronomers made the most significant improvement to this ancient tool. Since an astrolabe's tympanum works for only one latitude, it had to be swapped out for a different tympanum if one traveled just a few miles north or south. But by the eleventh century, the greatest Islamic astronomer in the West, al-Zarqalluh (d. 1087) of Toledo, wrote treatises describing a universal astrolabe—one that works at any latitude—and in the early fourteenth century, an astronomer from Aleppo in Syria named Ahmad ibn al-Sarraj built one that still survives.

It was from North Africa and al-Andalus that astrolabes arrived in Latin Europe, beginning in the tenth century. By the early eleventh century, a monk at the German monastery of Reichenau was writing a treatise on the uses of the astrolabe, and no less than Geoffrey Chaucer, author of the *Canterbury* Tales, composed a guidebook for his son in the 1390s. Up through the thirteenth century, Latin Europeans typically used astrolabes made in al-Andalus—which is why we have surviving examples with Latin words etched into the brass above the Arabic. Eventually, however, European craftsmen began producing exceptional instruments themselves. Indeed, some 150 European astrolabes from before 1500 survive to this day.

When Peter Abelard, the brilliant bad boy of twelfth-century Latin philosophy and theology, had an illegitimate son with Heloise, the beautiful French woman whom he was supposed to be tutoring, they named the boy Astrolabe (this romance, by the way, inspired Heloise's uncle and guardian to have Abelard castrated against his will, and both lovers to join monastic orders!). This curious episode makes clear how attractive Mediterranean technology was far to the north, beyond the Alps and Pyrenees in damp, cold Paris. For the very terminology connected to the astrolabe enunciated its Mediterranean origins. *Astrolabe* (*astrolabius,* in Latin) is from the Greek roots *astron,* "star," and *lambanein,* "to take," but the *alidade* on the back of this "star-taker," the thing that made it possible to measure the elevation of heavenly

FIGURE 9.6 Bilingual (Arabic/Latin) astrolabe from Spain. The Aga Khan Museum, Toronto, Canada. Photograph provided by Wikimedia Commons under Creative Commons CC0 1.0 Universal Public Domain Dedication license.

bodies, is etymologically Arabic (*al-duddiyah* = "ruler"), and each circle of equal altitude on the tympanum was called an *almucantar,* likewise from Arabic (*al-muqantarah* = "sundial"). *Tympanum* and *rete* are perfectly ordinary Latin (meaning "drum" and "net" respectively). Here then was a remarkable computing machine, the common property of all the lands surrounding the Sea in the Middle, the learned languages of its constituent civilizations adhering to it across dozens of generations. SEE SOURCEBOOK 9:1.

The Mechanical Clock

Arguably the most significant medieval invention was the mechanical clock—a clock that accurately measures time by capturing the energy of a falling weight, using it to drive a mechanism of gears that in turn operate a display system such as the one still familiar to us: hands that mark out the time in even intervals on a dial. While other kinds of clocks had been long in use, such as sundials and water clocks, mechanical clocks were an engineering achievement on a remarkable scale. For a mechanical clock was (and is), in reality, a machine that combined a handful of other simpler mechanisms that had existed in the Mediterranean for centuries, to which was added a newly invented but essential component, the mechanical escapement (on which more below), all of which were joined together in a limited space. The result was a highly accurate timekeeping instrument.

The ancient Greeks had, of course, invented remarkable machines—the screw-driven pump attributed to Archimedes (d. 212 BCE) is the most famous example. But Arab engineers, building on this Greek legacy, had far surpassed them, as we can see in a treatise called *The Book of Knowledge of Ingenious Mechanical Devices* written in 1206 by the Muslim scholar Ibn al-Razzaz al-Jazari. Supplying instructions that are so detailed that modern craftsmen are able to recreate working versions of the machines he discusses, al-Jazari describes a range of ingenious mechanisms including water clocks and candle clocks, musical automata, and water-raising devices. Among them, for example, is a water-driven assembly that accurately marked out the hours by forcing a metal ball into the mouth of a mechanical falcon, which caused it to rotate downward, dropping the ball into the mouth of a mechanical serpent, which, weighted with the ball, then rotated downward as well, dropping the ball on a cymbal to mark the time. As long as balls were regularly inserted into a magazine at the top, the clock would accurately chime out the time, hour after hour.

Now most of the simpler mechanisms that make up the mechanical clock appear in one form or another in sophisticated medieval Arabic treatises such as al-Jazari's. Arab engineers had much to say about the core principle—capturing the power of a freely suspended weight as it fell—and had experimented with methods of regulating its speed. A mechanical clock transfers the energy from the falling weight to gearing systems that drive the visual and audible indicators of the hour—whether hands on a dial, the chiming of bells, or the crowing of a mechanical rooster. Ancient Greek and Muslim engineers were quite familiar with such complex gear systems, and the Muslims had put them to work in hand-driven mechanical calendars and mechanized astrolabes, and even used them to transfer hydraulic power, as we find in an eleventh-century treatise by the Andalusi Muslim Ibn Khalaf al-Muradi. As we have seen already, moreover, engineers such as al-Jazari had invented complex signaling devices such as the mechanical falcon/serpent described just above. Finally, there is a great deal of evidence of the ability of Arab craftsmen to assemble complex mechanisms like these in a tight space—something that the falcon/serpent device attests as well.

What Muslim engineers had not solved, however, was the problem of regulating the speed at which a suspended weight falls. Left to itself such a weight would, as the laws of physics demand, fall at an accelerating, rather than constant, speed, making the mechanism by itself quite useless in keeping regular time. An unknown clockmaker in Europe, however, did hit upon a solution sometime in the later thirteenth century, inventing what is known as the verge escapement. This device—which, by the way, gives to mechanical clocks and watches their ticktock sound—controls the descent of the weight (or, later, the uncoiling of a spring) by forcing a gear to advance only at a fixed rate, and, in so doing, introduces an oscillating motion to the timekeeping mechanism that is inherently conducive to regular timekeeping. Soon after the verge escapement was invented, we begin to find large mechanical tower clocks being built all over Europe that combine all the early machines known to Greeks and Arabs with the verge escapement, thereby creating the basic timekeeping machine of the next half millennium, whether in the form of large clocks or pocket watches.

It is probably impossible to trace how the various elements of the mechanical clock came to be joined together in Latin Europe with the verge escapement in the form of a clock. While many of those elements appear in Greek and Arabic texts far earlier than in Latin treatises, it is not even certain that the weight drive, for example, was not used in western Europe for some task far earlier than the thirteenth century. It is the nature of such transference of mechanical ideas that much of it happens not by way

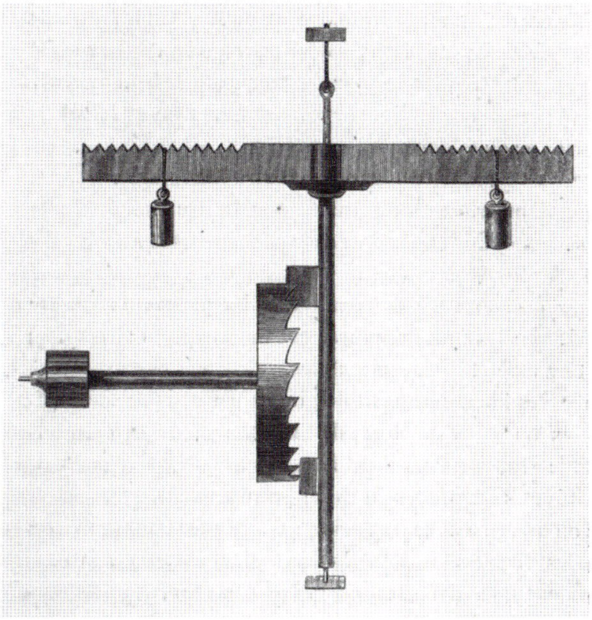

FIGURE 9.7 *(Top right)* Verge escapement. Drawing from *History of Watchmaking from its Origin to Present Day: preceded by research on the measurement of time in antiquity and followed by the biography of the most famous watchmakers in Europe,* by Pierre Dubois, page 221. Original scanned from University of Michigan, Digitized by Google. HathiTrust.

FIGURE 9.8 *(Bottom right)* Medieval clock (1386) in Salisbury Cathedral, England. Photograph by Rwendland provided by Wikimedia Commons under CC-BY-SA-3.0 license.

of texts, but through direct imitation or the accounts of travelers. What is clear, however, is that the invention of the mechanical clock exemplifies both the technical creativity of the medieval Mediterranean and its cumulative nature. Around the rapidly crossable sea in the middle, machines could move as quickly as people.

Science

If medieval Mediterranean scholars were alike in being peoples of the book who recognized the transcendent authority of a sacred text, they were similar as well in being peoples of reason who believed that the unaided human mind could arrive at true knowledge of the cosmos. While they quibbled a great deal about exactly how far human reason could go in that venture, virtually no one thought it was impossible to understand nature, at least in part, by unaided reason, and everyone lived and thought in a cultural world that was informed by science (what they would have called "natural philosophy"). The basic contours of that rationalistic, scientific view of the cosmos had been inherited from Persian and Hellenistic thinkers, and while it was partly based on deduction from first principles that themselves were not rooted in observation, nevertheless an impressive amount of real observation was involved in its development. But Mediterranean scientists also built in important ways on their inherited scientific Perso-Hellenism, something that shows up in striking ways in perhaps the two most important scientific disciplines in the premodern world: medicine and astronomy.

A Common Cosmos

While linguistic, cultural, and religious differences divided the medieval Mediterranean world, and meant that scholars and religious leaders had much to argue about with each other, when educated people throughout the region looked up at the sky at night, or looked down at the ground beneath them, or reckoned with the place of humans in the natural order, they had almost identical views—identical because their origins were the same. Like Greeks and Romans before them they understood that the Earth, in the first place, was round (no scholar anywhere thought it was flat!), a great ball at the center of the cosmos. Around this "ball of the lands," as it was called in Latin (*orbis terrarum*), a series of celestial bodies orbited—the moon, Mercury, Venus, the Sun, Mars, Jupiter, and Saturn. Each planet was a point of brilliant light affixed in a giant, transparent, crystalline sphere, one nested inside of the other, each rotating permanently, having been set in motion by a first cause, whom Mediterranean scholars considered to be God. From the sphere of the moon upward, all the way to stars, all of which were fixed in the outermost sphere, all was made of an eternal, weightless substance.

Below the moon, however, things were quite different. Rocks, trees, animals—everything in the sublunary world—was comprised of four basic elements: earth, water, fire, and air. This was the realm of change, decay, and death. The celestial realm did, though, influence the sublunary world. Not only did the light of the sun feed the plants, which in turn fed the animals, but the planets and stars, weightless and eternal beings, were considered intelligent powers that also, though less forcefully, influenced the Earth. Just as the moon caused tides, so, for example, each planet influenced a different region of the globe, and the alignment of stars and planets shaped historical events.

Uniquely, each human occupied a middling position in this celestial and terrestrial system: a microcosmos, the one entity in the whole created order who recapitulated all the rest. Like a flower or fish, humans consisted of the four sublunary elements, and would eventually decay back into them upon death. Like them, humans were subject to the sublunary laws of motion (downward toward the center of the Earth, unless impelled forcibly and then only in a straight line). Unlike flora and fauna in the sublunary realm, however, humans participated at the same time in the celestial realm because they had the faculty of reason. Through reason, humans had access to eternal truths, making them somehow like the celestial intelligences, and this was the proof, moreover, of something else: that humans, despite being corruptible compounds of earth, water, fire, and air, had eternal souls with a celestial, eternal destiny.

Jew, Christian, Muslim, Greek, Syrian, Arab, Latin, Slav—educated people everywhere—agreed on this basic image of the cosmos, though almost none of it derives from their holy scriptures. It does not conflict notably

Wherever they lived in the medieval Mediterranean, Jews, Christians, and Muslims all thought that the planet Earth was surrounded by seven concentric heavens, each identified with one of the moving bodies that appeared in the sky: the moon, Mercury, Venus, the sun, Mars, Jupiter, and Saturn. One of many intellectual carry-overs from the ancient world, the outlines of this notion can be found, for example, in the *Timaeus,* Plato's dialogue about the nature of the cosmos.

Plato, *Timaeus*

> Time, then, and the heaven came into being at the same instant in order that, having been created together, if ever there was to be a dissolution of them, they might be dissolved together. It was framed after the pattern of the eternal nature, that it might resemble this as far as was possible; for the pattern exists from eternity, and the created heaven has been, and is, and will be, in all time. Such was the mind and thought of God in the creation of time. The sun and moon and five other stars, which are called the planets, were created by him in order to distinguish and preserve the numbers of time; and when he had made their several bodies, he placed them in the orbits in which the circle of the other was revolving—in seven orbits of seven stars. First, there was the moon in the orbit nearest the earth, and next the sun, in the second orbit above the earth; then came the morning star [Venus] and the star sacred to Hermes [Mercury], moving in orbits which have an equal swiftness with the sun, but in an opposite direction; and this is the reason why the sun and Hermes and [Venus] overtake and are overtaken by each other.[1]

By the Middle Ages, most scholars believed that each of the moving lights mentioned here by Plato—the planets, sun, and moon—was, in fact, a point of brilliant light affixed in a giant, transparent, crystalline sphere, one nested inside of the other, each rotating permanently. Artists frequently depicted these concentric heavens.

Various versions of this heavenly architecture passed over into literary and religious texts in which medieval people imagined the hereafter. The following short text circulated in Latin, Old English, and Irish in the early Middle Ages.

The Apocalypse of the Seven Heavens

> Abottem [is] the third heaven: in the midst of it [there is] a burning furnace. The height of the flame is fixed thus: 12,000 cubits. The souls of saints and sinners are carried through it. The souls of the saints pass through it in a moment, but the souls of sinners dwell twelve years in the midst of the burning furnace. Then the angel comes, and carries him up to the fourth heaven, which is called Jothiam, where dwells a fiery river and the wall of the river. The height of the river is 12,000 cubits, and its wave is raised up to the fifth heaven. There sinners remain for twelve years in the midst of the river. Then the angel takes him up to the sixth heaven, which is called Seloth. In the midst of it [there is] a wheel, and an angel of Tartarus [i.e., of hell] striking the wheel with iron rods.... The person who is a sinner is put on the wheel and is tormented for twelve years. A hundred sparks come from the wheel and a hundred pounds in each splinter, and a hundred souls are burnt up. Then the person who is a sinner is handed over to the seventh heaven, which is called Theruch, where the Lord dwells on a precious stone, whence comes light, and fire comes from the stone. The Lord judges concerning that person who is a sinner and hands him over to an angel of Tartarus. And the angel plunges him into hell, an iron city... [with] twelve towers and twelve dragons in each tower and twelve punishments and twelve burning whips.[2]

Though Jews and Christians universally believed in this basic understanding of the cosmos, there is no reference to it in the Hebrew Bible and only a faint suggestion of it in the New Testament (see 2 Corinthians 12:2–4). The Qur'an, however, is quite explicit about the seven heavens: "Then [God] ordained seven heavens in two days, and inspired each heaven with its disposition. And [God] adorned the lowest heaven with lanterns, and for protection. Such was the devising of the Almighty, All-knowing" (41:12). References to this cosmology, therefore, are abundant in medieval Islamic literature, including in a whole series of Arabic traditions concerning the Prophet

FIGURE 9.9 Diagram of seven heavens in manuscript of *De sphere mundi* by Sacrobosco. Photo: Historical Views / agefotostock / Alamy Stock Photo.

Muhammad's ascent through each of the sevens heavens culminating with a meeting (and negotiation with) God himself.

Muhammad's Ascent through the Heavens

> One whom I have no reason to doubt told me on the authority of Abu Sa'id al-Khudri: I heard the prophet say, "After the completion of my business in Jerusalem a ladder was brought to me finer than any I have ever seen. It was that to which the dying man looks when death approaches. My companion mounted it with me until we came to one of the gates of heaven called the Gate of the Watchers. An angel called Isma'il was in charge of it, and under his command were twelve thousand angels each of them having twelve thousand angels under his command." As he told the story, the apostle used to say, "and none knows the armies of God but He." When Gabriel brought me in, Isma'il asked who I was, and when

he was told that I was Muhammad he asked if I had been given a mission, and on being assured of this he wished me well. . . .

Then I was taken up to the second heaven and there were the two maternal cousins, Jesus, son of Mary, and John, son of Zakariah. Then to the third heaven and there was a man whose face was as the moon at the full. This was my brother Joseph, son of Jacob. Then to the fourth heaven and there was a man called Idris. "And we have exalted him to a lofty place." Then to the fifth heaven and there was a man with white hair and a long beard, never have I seen a more handsome man than he. This was the beloved among his people, Aaron son of 'Imran. Then to the sixth heaven, and there was a dark man with a hooked nose like the Shanu'a. This was my brother Moses, son of 'Imran. Then to the seventh heaven and there was a man sitting on a throne at the gate of the immortal mansion. Every day seventy thousand angels went in not to come back until the resurrection day. Never have I seen a man more like myself. This was my father Abraham. Then he took me into paradise. . . .

From a tradition of 'Abdullah ibn Mas'ud from the prophet there has reached me the following: When Gabriel took him up to each of the heavens and asked permission to enter he had to say whom he had brought and whether he had received a mission and they would say "God grant him life, brother and friend!" until they reached the seventh heaven and his Lord. There [God laid] the duty of fifty prayers a day upon him.

The prophet said: "On my return I passed by Moses and what a fine friend of yours he was! He asked me how many prayers had been laid upon me and when I told him fifty he said, 'Prayer is a weighty matter and your people are weak, so go back to your Lord and ask him to reduce the number for you and your community.' I did so and He took off ten. Again, I passed by Moses and he said that same again; and so it went on until only five prayers for the whole day and night were left. Moses again gave me the same advice. I replied that I had been back to my Lord and asked him to reduce the number until I was ashamed, and I would not do it again. He of you who performs them in faith and trust will have the reward of fifty prayers."[3]

Discussion Questions

1. In light of what we know of the solar system and universe thanks to modern science and technology, this universally shared view of the cosmos seems a bit silly perhaps. To what extent, though, was it based on careful observation—all speculation about angels of hell and divine bartering aside? To what extent, indeed, is it a rational view of the cosmos?

2. How would you explain the Jewish and Christian adoption of it, even though it is not really mentioned in their holy books? How would you explain the Qur'an's specific references to it?

Further Reading

Edson, Evelyn, and Emilie Savage-Smith. *Medieval Views of the Cosmos*. Oxford: Bodleian Library, 2004.

Simek, Rudolf. *Heaven and Earth in the Middle Ages: The Physical World before Columbus*. Woodbridge: Boydell Press, 1996.

Notes

1. Plato, *Timaeus*, trans. Benjamin Jowett, http://classics.mit.edu/Plato/timaeus.html.

2. Richard Bauckham, *The Fate of the Dead: Studies on the Jewish and Christian Apocalypses* (Leiden: E. J. Brill, 1998), 315–16 with adaptations.

3. *The Life of Muhammad: A Translation of Isḥāq's Sīrat Rasūl Allāh*, trans. A. Guillaume (Oxford: Oxford University Press, 1982), 184–87 with adaptations.

with their scriptures either, though, and, indeed, generally complements them. Just as they nurtured Hellenistic Neoplatonism, therefore, they perpetuated and elaborated upon this Perso-Hellenistic cosmology. While some of it seems fanciful in light of Galileo's much later demonstration that the Earth is not the center of the solar system, let alone the whole cosmos, much of it made vivid, rational sense to premodern thinkers. Observation of change in nature, for example, seemed readily to demonstrate that all things were composites of a very small number of basic elements, as examples from across the region (and across time) make clear. Theodore Abu Qurra

(d. 823), the first Christian philosopher to write in Arabic, pointed out that if one burns a stick, part of its substance is converted to flame (fire), part to vapor (water), and part to ash (earth). The Franciscan priest, Roger Bacon (d. 1292), writing in Latin in England, drew the same conclusion from observing the distillation of milk, during which a clear liquid rises to the top, then a yellowish liquid emerges in the middle, and at the bottom, a black residue is left in the flask. The yellow water represents air, the black substance, earth, and the smoky vapors, fire. Joseph ibn Saddiq (d. 1149), an Andalusi Jew writing in Hebrew, argued that we can see the same thing in the life stages of a plant:

> We can see, by sense-perception, that when the seed falls to the *ground* it cannot grow without *water*… Nor will it grow without the *sun* shining upon it and a *wind* blowing upon it. For the single seed does not grow without nourishment and nourishment comes from the four elements (italics added).[1]

All other scientific disciplines assumed and built on this basic understanding of the cosmos, as we will see below in the case of astronomy and medicine, but it also worked its way into the literature and art of all the Mediterranean cultures.

Latinizing Arab Science

Sometime in the mid-twelfth century, a learned Italian from northern Italy named Gerard of Cremona (ca. 1114–1187) had become deeply dissatisfied with how few useful books on astronomy, mathematics, and philosophy were available in the libraries of Latin Christendom—and with good reason. Since Latin thinkers in the ancient world such as Cicero (106–43 BCE) had normally known Greek, and could thus keep current in the best Greek science and philosophy, no one bothered to translate the works of Plato, Aristotle, and other Greek systematic thinkers into Latin. Early medieval Latin Europe, therefore, only had access to much simplified Latin textbooks and popularized versions of the great works of Greek science and philosophy. Gerard, however, decided to change that. Because he knew (we don't know how precisely) that much of that legacy had been translated into Arabic centuries earlier and then had been built on extensively by Arab scholars, he left Italy and traveled to Toledo in central Spain where Arabic speakers and Arabic books were plentiful, learned Arabic, and set himself to translate dozens of scientific texts into Latin, including the *Almagest*, the foundational text of late antique astronomy by Ptolemy (ca. 100–170). SEE SOURCEBOOK 9:2.

And Gerard of Cremona was not the only one. As one contemporary scholar put it, many Latin scholars in this period were willing "to traverse distant provinces and exile themselves in remote regions in order to acquire a fuller knowledge of astronomy"[2] and other sciences from the Arabs and Greeks. As early as the tenth century, the French monk Gerard of Aurillac (ca. 946–1003)—who would later become Pope Sylvester II—spent time in northeastern Spain studying Arab mathematics. But during the twelfth and thirteenth centuries a remarkable collection of Latin intellectuals undertook such scholarly adventures: Robert of Ketton (fl. 1141–1157) from England, James of Venice (fl. 1125–1150) from Italy, Herman of Carinthia (ca. 1100 –1160) from Austria. The focus of this movement was—as Gerard's interests indicate—primarily astronomy and mathematics. The twelfth-century translator, Robert of Chester, while residing in Spain, produced a Latin version of the most up-to-date and comprehensive book on algebra by the Muslim Persian mathematician Muhammad ibn Musa al-Khwarizmi (ca. 780–850), thereby introducing this branch of mathematics to the Latin world, and giving it the name it still has—"algebra"—derived from the Arabic title of al-Khwarazmi's book, *Kitab al-jabr wa-al-muqabalah* (*Book of Calculation by Completion and Balancing*). It is true that, as Gerard of Cremona's translation of Ptolemy's *Almagest* indicates, many Greek works found their way into Latin, therefore, through an intermediate Arabic version, but Latin European philosophers and scientists knew quite well that Latin translations based on Greek would be better. As a result, some of these science-hungry traveling scholars made their way to Constantinople, such as James of Venice, who translated key works of Aristotle directly from the Greek originals that were easily available there.

James of Venice translated Aristotle's *Physics*, perhaps the most influential work on what we would call science in the medieval and early modern periods, but he also translated Aristotle's *On the Soul* and *Metaphysics*, two difficult treatises that are much more philosophical in character. By late in the twelfth century this shift from natural philosophy to other areas of philosophy became more pronounced. By the middle of the thirteenth century the full range of Aristotle's works together with an equally broad range of innovative works by the great Arab scientists and philosophers working in the Aristotelian tradition had flooded into Latin libraries, revolutionizing all aspects of Latin education, as we will see below. Indeed, the names of Arab scientists—in Latinized versions of various degrees of accuracy—became commonplace in Latin texts and required no explanation. A mid-thirteenth-century Latin treatise on medicines cites the opinion of Avicenna, the brilliant Persian-Muslim physician and philosopher, that "the dried brains of the camel, when mixed with oil and drunk treats epilepsy," and that its "blood, dried and roasted, staunches the flow of blood."[3] In addition to Avicenna, Averroes (Ibn Rushd, 1126–1198, commentator on Aristotle), Rhazes (al-Razi, ca. 854–935, physician), Albumashar (Abu Ma'shar, 787–886, astrologer) and many other Latinized Arabic names littered the pages of hundreds of scientific and philosophical treatises written in Latin. SEE SOURCEBOOK 9:2.

Medicine

There were learned, professional physicians in the medieval Mediterranean, and every language had its word for such a healer—*tabib* in Arabic, *medicus* in Latin, *iatros* in Greek. But the range of people who provided health care was much broader than the narrow strata of (almost entirely) men who had claim to that title, and the healing arts included many techniques that seem supernatural or indeed superstitious to us, though they made thorough sense within the Hellenistic, scriptural monotheism that everywhere dominated. For people living in rural settlements, the only healer was often an illiterate man or woman who nevertheless knew a great deal about the healing properties of plants and minerals. A priest, nun, or imam who was literate and had learned a smattering of the theory and practice of medicine as originally developed by the Greeks was often the closest thing to a professional physician that most medieval people ever encountered. Powerful and wealthy people living in urban centers, on the other hand, often had access to fully trained doctors, though at all levels of society a great deal of strictly medical practice occurred side-by-side, and indeed in open alliance with, faith healing. In Latin Europe, for example, a well-to-do woman might be attended by a physician during her pregnancy, but during labor itself draped a "birth-girdle"—a parchment sash with pious images and biblical verses inscribed on it—across her womb to insure a safe delivery. In the same way, a prosperous Muslim might drink water from a bowl decorated with magical symbols and Qur'anic verses to heal stomachaches, nosebleeds, or snakebites, or for protection during childbirth as well.

If a healer was a well-educated *tabib* or *iatros*, the medical theories and practices he had learned were deeply rooted in the thought of ancient Greek physicians, especially Galen (129–216 CE), who had deepened and systematized centuries of earlier Greek medicine. A few key principles informed this approach. Humans, microcosms of the whole universe, contained four key liquids, or "humors," that paralleled the four elements of which the sublunary cosmos consisted: black bile, yellow bile, phlegm, and blood. Ill health and disease were for Galen and his medieval followers the result of imbalance among these humors, which each had their characteristic qualities. Since an excess or deficiency of any humor led to ill health, the job of a physician was to prescribe therapies that would maintain humoral balance. Too much phlegm, physicians learned, could cause scrofula (a kind of tuberculosis). One should prescribe a substance such as mustard associated with warmth and dryness to counterbalance the excessive moistness and wetness typical of excessive phlegm. The long lists of medicines that medieval doctors could prescribe were likewise meant to adjust the humors—an emetic such as a large dose of salt caused vomiting, while a diuretic such as sneezewort (*chamaemelum ptarmica*) increased urination, bodily events that rebalanced the four humors. Of course, physicians, or more likely barber-surgeons who had much less education but a great deal of practical experience, dealt with nonhumoral medical issues such as broken bones or combat wounds, but the healing process in the aftermath of surgery was likewise understood through and guided by humoral theory: a physician would prescribe the proper diet and humoral therapies to insure recovery.

Galenic medicine spread throughout the Mediterranean through the scientific translation movements

FIGURE 9.10 Muslim magic medicinal bowl, Syria, ca. 1200. © Historical Views / agefotostock.

described above so that Syriac, Arabic, Hebrew, and Latin scholar-physicians not only perpetuated but elaborated extensively on it. The greatest medical systematizers were Arab-Muslim physicians such as Ibn Sina and Ibn al-Nafis (d. 1288). The former wrote *The Canon of Medicine*, a lengthy synthesis of Galenic medicine that became the basic textbook for physicians in both the Muslim and Latin-Christian worlds up through the eighteenth century. Its dependence on Greek thought is evident even in the title: *canon* is a Greek word that Ibn Sina adopted directly into Arabic (*qanun*), meaning here "measuring stick" or "fundamental principle." When translated into Latin, the same Greek term was the core of the title (*Canon Avicennae*). Ibn al-Nafis went much further than this, compiling a vast encyclopedia fully eighty volumes long called *The Complete Book of the Medical Art*.

Not only did academic medical thought cross religious boundaries, but so did medical practice. The powerful and wealthy often consulted physicians of another faith because of their perceived expertise. The Christian Hunayn ibn Ishaq (d. 873), best known today because of his many translations of Greek scientific works into Arabic, was also personal physician to Caliph al-Mutawakkil (822–861). The great Jewish philosopher Maimonides (d. 1204) was court physician in Cairo to a Fatimid grand vizier and later to Saladin himself—scourge of the Crusader states and founder of the Ayyubid dynasty. But out-faith physicians treated patients of humbler status as well. In early fifteenth-century Iberia, one Samuel of Granada, a Jewish doctor, for example, treated a Christian carpenter named Gil Blay for impotence. Indeed, sometimes both religiously other practitioners and their therapies were actually preferred, precisely because of the exotic, perhaps occult, powers associated with them. Christian women in fourteenth-century Aragon sometimes wore Jewish birth amulets while in labor. SEE SOURCEBOOK 9:3.

Astronomy/Astrology

Nasir al-Din al-Tusi, the great Shi'i deviser of the "Tusi couple," with whom we began this chapter, was able to persuade Hülegü, the Mongol conqueror of much of the Islamic Middle East, to build the great observatory at Maragha not so much because the khan loved science, but because he was frequently disturbed, like all rulers everywhere, by horrifying uncertainty. A close relative, Berke Khan, for example, launched a bloody civil war against him in 1262. Like countless Mediterranean rulers since antiquity, therefore, Hülegü turned to the science of the stars because, in the shared cosmological understanding of the whole region, the stars affected events on earth, not least because they necessarily influenced the characters and fortunes of humans. The leaders of the early 'Abbasid period had likewise wanted to know what the stars predicted about contemporary events, and this was one of the main reasons they so adamantly commissioned the translation of astronomical and other scientific works into Arabic. Maragha, and a series of later Islamic observatories in Iran and India, were, then, outgrowths of a courtly culture that especially valued the practical advantages of studying the stars, and such courtly cultures existed throughout the Mediterranean lands.

Etymologically the originally Greek words *astronomy* and *astrology* meant virtually the same thing and were often used interchangeably in the medieval world. While it is true that medieval scholars well understood the differences between observing and modeling the movements of heavens (what we now call *astronomy*) and deriving guidance about how to act from those movements (what we now call *astrology*), as a normal matter, both pursuits were undertaken at the same time by the same people. Not surprisingly, the same Islamic culture that produced the most advanced astrolabes also produced the most advanced work in this area as well. Ninth-century scholars in Baghdad and Damascus had already reconciled the complicated and differing astronomical models and observations of the ancient Greek, Persian, and Indian traditions, and by the eleventh century, the Andalusi Muslim astronomer al-Zarqalluh had adapted the eastern Islamic astronomical tables—by which the first day of each month could be correctly calculated, the positions of all the planets could be accurately pinpointed, and even eclipses could be predicted—in the form of his influential *Toledan Tables*. Astrology, the predictive branch of star study, flourished just as much in the Islamic lands—as much among Jews and Christians as among Muslims. By the ninth century, the long-lived

FIGURE 9.11 Manuscript image of al-Tusi and his colleagues working at Maragha. Science History Images / Alamy Stock Photo.

court astrologer in Baghdad Abu Ma'shar (787–886) had already compiled an enormous body of Greek and early Islamic astrological lore into such voluminous guidebooks as *The Book of the Great Introduction*.

In the early medieval Latin West, the study of the stars on the Greek model had nearly died out, though some knowledge of astronomy had always been necessary to calculate the date of Easter. But when in the late eleventh century, Latin scholars began hungrily to translate Arabic works into Latin, treatises on the stars were among the first works they sought out. Gerard of Cremona (1114–1187), as we have seen, produced a Latin version of the Arabic translation of Ptolemy's *Almagest*, the Hellenistic foundational text of the discipline, and in the thirteenth century, Alfonso X, another ruler harassed by political problems, commissioned the translation of al-Zarqalluh's astronomical tables into Castilian. Moreover, seventy Arabic treatises on astrology proper were also translated into Latin, including Abu Ma'shar's *Great Introduction*. On the basis of this flood of new material a thriving Arabo-Latin astronomical/astrological tradition flourished, with Latin astronomical works such as John of Sacrobosco's thirteenth-century *Sphere* becoming textbooks in Latin universities, and astrological works such as Guido of Bonatti's roughly contemporary *Introductory Book on the Judgments of the Stars* guiding countless practitioners as they sought astral guidance.

While historians have long known that Arab astronomy/astrology became the core of the medieval Latin study of the stars, only recently has it become clear that Byzantine scholars were receptive to Arab learning as well. In about 1032 an anonymous Greek reader wrote comments on a copy of Ptolemy's *Almagest* that refer to Arabic astronomical tables, and later in the same century a Byzantine astronomer wrote a manual that likewise drew heavily on Arabic sources. In the fourteenth century, alongside vigorous study of the ancient Greek sources of astronomy, we find Byzantine scholars intentionally turning east for scientific input. In about 1350, George Chrysococces wrote a Greek astronomical text based directly on Nasir al-Din al-Tusi's *Ilkhanic Tables*, originally written in Persian, a seminal treatise based on the observations of al-Tusi and his scientific team at Maragha. We will not be surprised to learn that Abu Ma'shar's guide to astrology was already available in Greek versions by the year 1000.

It is true that, on the whole, Mediterranean monotheisms were leery of determinism—the view that humans were fated to make decisions, and thus lacked free will—making astrology proper a frequent target of theological attack throughout the Middle Ages. Moses Maimonides (d. 1204), for example, the greatest medieval Jewish philosopher, born in al-Andalus, harshly attacked the practice of consulting astrologers ("Know... that all things concerning... astrology... are far from being scientific; they are stupidity"),[4] and Christian and Muslim scholars sometimes advanced similar views. Nevertheless, learned Jews often practiced astrology quite happily: the Andalusi rabbi Abraham ibn Ezra (d. 1167), famed to this day as a great biblical commentator, wrote numerous Hebrew treatises on topics such as how astral cycles govern history. Despite the views of critics such as Maimonides, most Jewish, Christian, and Muslim counterparts agreed that the practice of astrology, in some form or another, was a respectable occupation.

In the meantime, extensive research on the motions of the heavens, such as occurred at Maragha, and the sophisticated reflection on the basic physical theories that lay behind medieval star study, as undertaken in European universities, eventually paved the way for the revolutionary new theories of the Scientific Revolution of the sixteenth and seventeenth centuries. University scholars such as Thomas Bradwardine (d. 1349) and Jean Buridan (d. 1363), in Oxford and Paris respectively, demonstrated that key elements of Aristotle's theories on motion were deeply flawed, thereby laying the groundwork for Newtonian theories of motion. We have already seen that Copernicus incorporated al-Tusi's couple in his *On the Revolution of the Heavenly Spheres*, which not only argued for a heliocentric universe, but used complex mathematics to make its case.

Aristotle: The Master of All Who Know

These technological and scientific achievements of the twelfth through fourteenth century tended, furthermore, to be connected to a broader, highly rationalist, intellectual movement: the enthusiastic embrace of Aristotle (384–322 BCE), rather than Plato, as the "master of all who know,"[5] as the Italian poet Dante (1265–1321) put it. Though Aristotle was, in fact, Plato's most famous student, he created his own immensely powerful and wide-ranging system of thought that, while drawing in important ways on Platonism, departed notably from it in some key ways that Jewish, Christian, and Muslim intellectuals found deeply attractive in this period. First, where Plato and his followers had taught that the best path to truth about the self, the world, and God was through an inner, ascetic journey to discover the foundational "ideas" already available in the human mind, Aristotle insisted that we only come to true knowledge by examination of the world around us, there being no universal "ideas" residing from birth in our brains at all. As his later medieval Latin followers put it, "What is in our mind was first in our senses."[6] Second, Aristotle had created a powerful descriptive vocabulary that allowed the world around us, and available to us first only through sensation, to be described and analyzed systematically. All things, he taught, were combinations of *form* and *matter*; changes in them are a result of their *potentiality* (dictated by their specific forms) coming into *actuality*; occurrences in the world around us derive from a dense web of causality: the *material cause* (what a thing is made of), the *formal cause* (the structure or essence that makes a thing one thing rather than another), the *efficient cause* (the moving "causer" or maker of what happens), and the *final cause* (the reason or goal for which something happens).

Aristotle developed this analytical vocabulary primarily to describe the natural world—he was biologist, chemist, physicist, and astronomer all in one, so his system was naturally appealing to medieval physicians and astronomers. But, as Aristotle had also shown, his approach could apply powerfully to broader philosophical issues such as ethics and metaphysics (the rational study of nonphysical realities). Jewish, Christian, and Muslim scholars in the High Middle Ages would, therefore, apply his system of thought to nearly every branch of knowledge from zoology to theology in this age of brilliant scientific and philosophical achievement. But if Aristotle was read everywhere in the shared culture of the medieval Mediterranean, there are notable differences in the kinds of Aristotelianism that flourished around the sea, reminding us once again that while ideas and texts and technologies traveled easily across linguistic and religious boundaries, those boundaries separated cultures and civilizations that were scarcely identical.

Aristotle and Ibn Sina in the East

We have met Ibn Sina (980–1037) above as the Muslim author of the most important medical textbook of the medieval and early modern periods, but he was also the most important philosopher as well. Indeed, he was the only systematic, rationalist thinker to shape the thought of the whole Mediterranean basin—that of Jews, Christians, and Muslims writing in Hebrew, Latin, and Arabic. Growing up at the far east end of the Islamic world in Bukhara, Ibn Sina nevertheless read and absorbed the whole range of Hellenistic-Arabic philosophy, immersing himself especially in the works of Aristotle. A man of great ambition, moreover, he tells us that he set out as a young man "to gather the loose ends [Aristotle] left, repair any breach [he found] in what he constructed, and supply corollaries to fundamental principles he presented."[7] To this end he compiled a vast body of outstanding works, such as his multivolume *The Cure*, a systematic presentation and reevaluation of all of Aristotle's thought, and *Pointers and Reminders*, a brilliant teaching text that set out philosophical problems that students then had to complete on their own as they mastered the thought of the master of all who know.

But Ibn Sina was no mere imitator of Aristotle. In repairing the breaches and supplying corollaries, he developed a distinctive school of thought. For one thing, he held on to key Neoplatonic notions: God did not so much create the cosmos; rather it emanated or flowed from him just as the Divine Mind, World Soul, and cosmos emanated from the One in Plotinus's thought. Furthermore, Ibn Sina went into great and lucid detail about matters upon which Aristotle had been largely silent. He carefully analyzed, for example, the process of human thought, arguing that on its own the human soul is only capable of receiving knowledge imprinted on it by a universal divine mind called the Active Intellect. Muslim scholar that he was, moreover, he devised a theory of prophecy rooted deeply in his revised Aristotelianism: a prophet such as Muhammad, he taught, is a philosopher who is able to translate knowledge gained from the Active Intellect into images capable of moving ordinary people.

Philosophers and theologians in the eastern Islamic world recognized almost immediately that Ibn Sina was *al-sheikh al-ra'is*, "the chief master," second only to Aristo-

FIGURE 9.12 Aristotle teaching in Arabic manuscript miniature. Photo: British Library, London, UK © British Library Board. All Rights Reserved / Bridgeman Images.

tle himself. His version of Aristotelianism set the terms of philosophical study for centuries to come, not just among Muslims, but also among Jews and Christians in the eastern Mediterranean. The thirteenth-century Syrian Orthodox bishop, Gregory Barhebraeus (1226–1286), for example, adopted most of Ibn Sina's positions in his own Syriac philosophical summa entitled *The Cream of Science*. Moreover, while Ibn Sina certainly did not consider himself a theologian—a practitioner, that is, of Islamic *kalam*—Muslim theologians readily adopted much of his philosophy into the kalamic tradition.

While earlier Arab philosophers, therefore, had focused much of their work on commenting on Aristotle's own works, the norm going forward was to comment on Ibn Sina's oeuvre, whether elaborating on his ideas, revising them, or critiquing them. Some, indeed, were highly critical. Fakhr al-Din al-Razi (1149–1209), a brilliantly contentious sort ("as to the city of Bukhara," he once wrote, "when I arrived there, I argued with a lot of people"!),[8] took issue with Ibn Sina over and over in his massive commentary on the chief master's *Pointers and Reminders*. One of Ibn Sina's most celebrated and influential positions was that what separates God from everything else is that He is the Necessary Existent, the only thing, that is, that by its very essence must exist. Al-Razi wasn't buying it. Such a view, he insisted, undermined the absolute unity of God, since it assumed that God's essence and His existence were two different things. But others doughtily defended the great Ibn Sina. Nasir al-Din al-Tusi, the astounding astronomer, took on al-Razi in his own commentary on the *Pointers and Reminders*. What al-Razi did not understand about the Necessary Existent, al-Tusi pointed out, is that God's existence is fundamentally the same as his essence. Whether for him or against him, therefore, one could only undertake systematic philosophical thought in the later medieval Islamic East by carefully engaging Ibn Sina and his works.

Aristotle, Ibn Sina—and Especially Ibn Rushd—in the West

To travel overland from Valencia on the coast of al-Andalus to Bukhara, where Ibn Sina philosophized and al-Razi later debated his conclusions, is a journey of some 4,000 miles. We should not be surprised to discover, therefore, that the Aristotelianism that flourished in the other great theater of rationalism in the High Middle Ages—Islamic Spain and Latin Christendom—was in some ways rather different from the Ibn Sina–dominated currents of the East. Systematic philosophy had, in fact, come late to these regions, and when it did so, it was shaped in part by the rather peculiar ethos of the Almohad movement, which was both rigorist in its interpretation of Islam (and even attempted to forcibly convert Jews and Christians) and intriguingly rationalist at the same time. Abu Bakr Muhammad ibn Tufayl (1110–1185), an Ibn Sina–influenced courtier and physician at the Almohad court, for example, wrote the entertaining, Robinson Crusoe–like philosophical novel called *Alive Son of Awake* within this rationalist atmosphere.

But the most remarkable example of the flowering of philosophy in the West was a second towering, Muslim interpreter of Aristotle, Abu al-Walid Muhammad ibn Ahmad ibn Rushd (1126–1198), or Averroes, in European languages. We have seen that Ibn Sina thought through and revised the whole of Aristotle's thought, but maintained certain key Neoplatonic ideas quite foreign to it as he did so. Ibn Rushd's goal was rather different. The great majority of his works are lucid commentaries on all of Aristotle's works—indeed in most cases he wrote two or even three such commentaries of different lengths. In these he attempted to clarify what Aristotle himself had taught, and only that, and in doing so rejected all Neoplatonic additions. The emergence of the cosmos by emanation—a Neoplatonic idea of great importance in Ibn Sina's system—was, Ibn Rushd complained, "something which [Aristotle and his followers] knew nothing about!"[9]

In the long run Ibn Rushd's influence was nearly as great as Ibn Sina's, but, intriguingly, more among Christians and Jews than among Muslims. Indeed, Latin-Christian and European-Jewish philosophers learned their Aristotle at Ibn Rushd's knee, for his works were translated into Latin and Hebrew almost as soon as he had completed them. His erudite commentaries found few readers, on the other hand, among Muslim scholars in the East—some of the Arabic versions of his commentaries have actually been lost over the centuries, and are only preserved in Latin or Hebrew translations. In the Latin world, Ibn Rushd's commentaries—along with Aristotle's own works—were at the heart of what historians call "scholasticism," the learned culture of the new universities that were flourishing in Europe. By the middle of the thirteenth century the curriculum of the bachelor of arts degree (which had to be mastered first before one went on to study theology or law or medicine) was essentially a survey of Aristotle's works as interpreted by Ibn Rushd, who was regularly referred to not by name, but simply as "the commentator" on the thought of the master of all who know. This meant that all university-educated Latin Christians were intimately familiar with Aristotle, and attempted to apply his thought, in varying degrees, to all the subjects they studied, including theology.

But while this was a heady, thrilling intellectual movement, it was also chock-full of inherent controversies. Aristotle's views in some ways fit easily into Christian theology, but in some key ways, especially as interpreted by Ibn Rushd, there were serious conflicts that worried the theologians. Aristotle and his interpreter, for example, argued that the cosmos was eternal, but Catholic teaching insisted that God created all things at a definite point in the past. This led to a plethora of debates and treatises about the eternity of the world, with some scholars arguing that Aristotle's views on this point had to be utterly rejected, others that from a philosophical point of view he was correct, but that Christian theology trumped philosophy on this point, and still others that, in fact, Aristotle's arguments about this issue were not conclusive, and therefore there was no conflict.

Eventually, some prominent churchmen and theologians became so concerned about the excessive influence of Aristotle and Ibn Rushd on theology that the bishop of Paris (at the pope's urging) issued in 1277 a list of 219 teachings, heavily associated with teaching masters in the bachelor of arts faculty, that were condemned in the eyes of the church, the eternity of the world among them. This is but one sign of how fraught the scholastic reception of Aristotle, his commentator, and other Arab and Jewish thinkers was. In fact, there was a whole range of positions on this vast, newly available library of Aristotelian thought. Some leading scholastics, such as the Franciscan Bonaventure (1221–1274), while fully educated in these works, were very cautious about applying Aristotelian ideas to theology, whereas the Dominican Thomas Aquinas (1225–1274)—about whom more below—brilliantly and daringly attempted to show how Aristotle's system could be wed harmoniously to Catholic doctrine.

So widely were Aristotle and Ibn Rushd admired, in fact, that in Dante's vision of the underworld in *The Divine Comedy*, Aristotle, a pagan philosopher, and Ibn Rushd, a pious Muslim religious judge, are not in hell; rather Aristotle and "Averroes who," Dante observed, "wrote the commentary"[10] pass eternity without punishment in Limbo, alongside Plato and many other non-Christian worthies. That Dante imagined the same fate, though, for Ibn Sina makes clear that if that great Persian philosopher did not have quite the same stature in the West as in the East, he was nevertheless well known in al-

Andalus and Latin Europe too, as we can see if we ponder the two most important Jewish and Christian thinkers in the western Mediterranean.

Ibn Rushd's near contemporary and fellow native of Córdoba in southern Spain, Moses Maimonides (1135–1204), left Iberia when he was a teenager because of Almohad persecution of Jews, but nevertheless was influenced throughout his life by the Almohad, rationalist ethos. He would go on to become the greatest philosopher in medieval Jewish history (in addition to being a distinguished doctor and Talmudist), most famous for his delightfully titled *Guide for the Perplexed* in which he attempted to demonstrate the coherence of Jewish religion with Aristotelian philosophy. It is true that like all other high medieval thinkers in the Islamic world, he had learned a great deal from Ibn Sina, and put it to use while guiding the perplexed. We find, for example, Ibn Sina's conception of God as that thing that is necessarily existent. But he had great respect for his Western contemporary Ibn Rushd, and he clearly knew at least some of his works, even though he was living far away in Cairo by the time Ibn Rushd was writing his commentaries. This explains, for example, distinct similarities in their views on how God can foresee and intervene in the events of the future.

While only some of Ibn Sina's works made it into Latin—the *Pointers and Reminders* that inspired so many Eastern commentaries was entirely unknown in Latin universities, for example—the massive *Cure* did, and its importance was readily recognized. The Latin translator of its first major portion, the treatise *On the Soul*, exulted that "by my labors the Latins will have firm knowledge of something hitherto unknown, namely of whether the soul exists, and what it is and what kind of thing it is… corroborated with true reasons!"[11] As a young man, Thomas Aquinas entered the new and highly educated Dominican order, and was sent to university to study with the best Christian philosophers and theologians in thirteenth-century Latin Europe. He not only devoured the Ibn Rushd–inflected Aristotelianism of the arts course, but consumed Ibn Sina's works as well. Having essentially memorized vast portions not only of the Bible and the writings of Saint Augustine and other Christian thinkers, but also of the works of Aristotle, Ibn Rushd, Ibn Sina, and many others, he went on to write (usually by dictation) some of the most influential works in Christian thought, most notably his *Summa of Theology*, a profound argument for the harmony of Arab-Aristotelian philosophy and Christian theology. Even in his commentary on the basic university textbook of Christian theology, the twelfth-century *Four Books of Sentences* by Peter Lombard (1100–1160), he quotes these Muslim philosophers dozens of times. Like Maimonides (from whom he also learned a great deal), moreover, Aquinas borrowed Ibn Sina's distinction between essence and existence, and made it a centerpiece of his own philosophical-theological system: God is the only thing whose very essence is to exist. But like "the commentator" Ibn Rushd, Aquinas was intent on understanding Aristotle's original positions, purified as much as possible of Neoplatonic additions. Though his positions were often seen as radical in his day (and some were even condemned for a time), his very Arab-Aristotelian philosophical-theology would go on to become the quasi-official theology of the Catholic Church. SEE SOURCEBOOK 9:4.

Aristotelianism in Byzantium

While Greek versions of some Arabic scientific works survive from the later Middle Ages, Byzantine scholars made no attempt to translate the works of Ibn Sina, Ibn Rushd, and the other leading Arab followers of Aristotle into Greek. Moreover, modern historians of philosophy have barely begun sustained research on philosophy in Byzantium. Yet it seems clear that something of an Aristotelian revival began there in the twelfth and thirteenth centuries as well and became a major movement from the mid-fifteenth century on. In part this was the result of geopolitics: when the Fourth Crusade established the Latin Empire in Constantinople (1204–1261), an influx of Latin culture followed. A Latin-to-Greek translation movement was one result. Though far more modest in its scope, this movement saw not only classic works of Latin thought such as *The Consolation of Philosophy* by the Neoplatonist Boethius (477–524) but also contemporary masterpieces such as Thomas Aquinas's *Summa of Theology* become available to Greek readers for the first time.

A theological conflict within Byzantium, on the other hand, provided the context in which these Aristotelian tools could be applied. Monks on Mount Athos had been

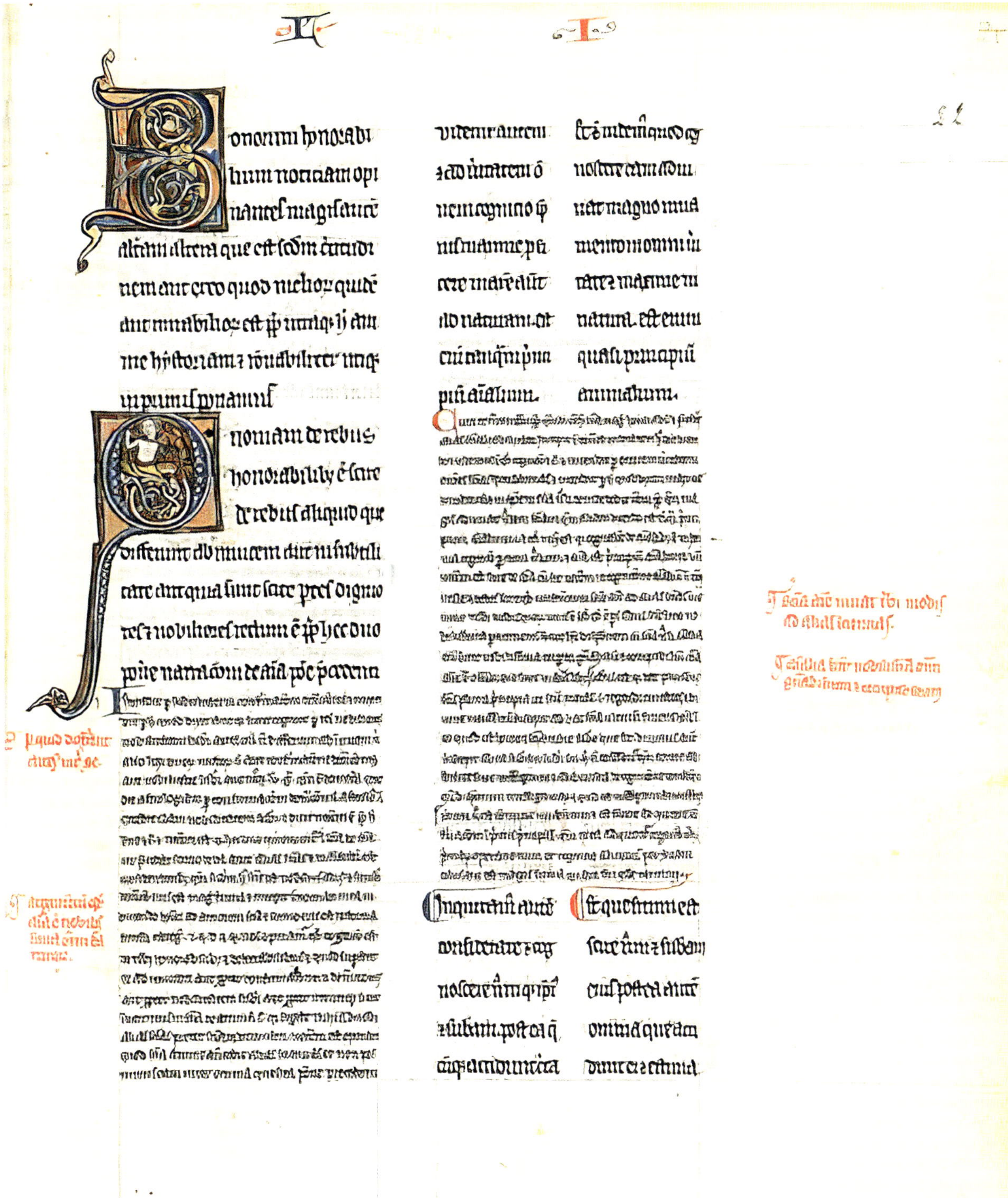

FIGURE 9.13 Ibn Rushd's long commentary on Aristotle's *De anima* in Latin. Historical Views / agefotostock.

FIGURE 9.14 Fifteenth-century painting of Gregory Palamas. Photograph provided by Wikimedia Commons under CC0 license.

using a method of prayer called Hesychasm through which the individual monk, by controlling his breathing and repeating the so-called Jesus prayer ("Jesus Christ, Son of God, have mercy on me, a sinner") over and over, came to have ecstatic visions of the light of God, filling them, it was said, with loving joy. But a Greek-speaking monk-scholar originally from southern Italy named Barlaam (1290–1348, named, yes, after the monkish figure in the Christian-Latin version of the Buddha story) came to Mount Athos, found the Hesychast movement in full swing, and was shocked. To claim that a mere human can see the uncreated light of God was the height, he thought, of arrogance. So Barlaam went on the attack, and when he did so he adapted the thought of Thomas

Aquinas, who argued that humans only behold God through his created manifestations. The light of God, therefore, is merely a creation of God. There is no way then that Hesychast monks had been granted a vision of God as He is. Indeed, as one of Barlaam's followers put it, "No one has seen the divine light, even those who have thought that they have seen it."[12]

It is true that Barlaam's position lost out in the long run. He was condemned by the Ecumenical Council of 1341 and returned to Italy, while his main opponent, the brilliant theologian Gregory Palamas (1296–1359), became archbishop of Thessaloniki and was declared a saint soon after he died. Palamas's argument that while we can know nothing of God's essence, we can—especially in Hesychast meditation—have direct experience of God's activities built on and reaffirmed the strongly mystical character of Byzantine theology. Yet even Palamas was deeply influenced by Aristotelian thought, especially Aristotelian logic. The so-called Hesychast Controversy, moreover, continued well into the fifteenth century, and most of the anti-Hesychast followers of Barlaam were influenced by Latin Aristotelianism, and it was by this means—as quoted in the works of Aquinas and others—that the names of Avicenna and Averroes became somewhat familiar to Greek philosophers. By this means also, at least some Byzantine philosophers came, finally, to admire the thought of the Latin world, which traditionally Greek Christians had dismissed as crude and unsophisticated. By the later fourteenth century, the philosopher Demetrios Kydones admitted that while "we used to classify Latins as barbarians," Aquinas was clearly "a man who had eclipsed everyone else in the science of theology."[13] Eventually Thomist thought would spread even farther east when Armenian Christian scholars embraced it as well. SEE SOURCEBOOK 9:5.

The Limits of Aristotelianism

But the surge of Aristotelianism did not sweep away everything in its path. Trends of thought quite different from, or even hostile to, Aristotle's system thrived throughout the Mediterranean. As we have already seen, Avicenna's hugely influential reworking of Aristotle's preserved key Neoplatonic features such as cosmic emanation. But even in more thoroughgoing Aristotelians, Neoplatonism survived. For one thing, while the master of all who know had powerful tools for describing the concrete world, they became ever less effective the closer one approached the Prime Mover. So it is that when Thomas Aquinas writes about the nature of God in Himself, his philosophical theology becomes Neoplatonic. Some systematic thinkers, moreover, rejected Aristotle almost entirely. The Iberian layman Ramon Llull (1232–1316), whom we met earlier as Christian apologist deeply learned in Jewish and Muslim thought, elaborated a philosophical system that he believed could guide one to truth about all aspects of reality. He called this system "the Art" or "the Technique," and constructed it on thoroughly Neoplatonic principles that he inserted into an original, highly mechanistic approach to inquiry. This made his thought seem utterly bizarre to contemporary, university-trained philosophers. Llull frankly (and rather good-naturedly) admitted near the end of his long life that many churchmen and philosophers thought him a "fantacist" (*fantasticus*),[14] though in the eighteenth century Leibniz would revive Llull's approach, creating thereby the foundations for the modern computational methods of computers.

Moreover, systems of thought that verged on magic or the occult, or that focused on divining the future, were far more popular among the educated than recent scholarship has suggested. Ahmad ibn 'Ali al-Buni (d. 1225), for example, was born in North Africa but came to prominence in Egypt for a work called *The Sun of Esoteric Knowledge and the Subtleties of the Experts*. Here he showed Muslims how to devise magic squares based on God's divine names, though he intermixed such occult teachings with traditional Islamic prayers and pious texts from the Qur'an and Hadith. Though little studied until recently, it is clear that works such as *The Sun of Esoteric Knowledge* were actually widely read in the Islamic world, and similar esoteric works flourished among Christians and Jews. Furthermore, scholars in all three traditions often devoted great intellectual effort to determining when the end-time would arrive. An Italian abbot named Joachim of Fiore (ca. 1135–1202) propounded one of the most influential of such theories, asserting that the history of the world is divided into three ages corresponding to the members of the Trinity, with the Age of the Holy Spirit to begin with a cataclysm in 1260. Though 1260 saw no outbreak of universal love, as Joachim had calculated, his thought continued to be enormously attractive, especially among Franciscan friars, and was probably much more influential in thirteenth-century Europe than Aristotelian scholasticism. SEE SOURCEBOOK 9:6.

Such occult or apocalyptic thought was not so much opposed to Aristotelianism as utterly uninterested in it. But some related intellectual currents became quite hostile to it. In twelfth- and thirteenth-century Provence and Iberia, for example, visionary Jewish scholars came to view God as comprising ten attributes, or *sefirot*, such as "understanding," "wisdom," "majesty," "beauty," and "presence." In the beginning, there was perfect harmony among these "cups of being," as they are sometimes described, but when Adam sinned, not only did all creation fall, but so did the harmonious relationship among the *sefirot*. This view of God, put forth in Moses de Leon's thirteenth-century *Book of Splendor*, was not based primarily on philosophy, but on an esoteric reading of the Bible. The elite scholars initiated into this mystical tradition—called Kabbalah, "tradition," in Hebrew ever since—had the duty, moreover, of doing good works, especially the study of the Talmud, through which, they taught, this disharmony in God could be restored. Not only did Kabbalah circulate around the Mediterranean, but Kabbalist rabbis, such as Nahmanides (1194–1270), became impassioned critics of the great Maimonides himself, viewing his attempt at reconciling Jewish thought with Aristotle as dangerously arrogant, setting off a widespread debate known as the Maimonidean Controversy.

Notes

1. *The Microcosm of Joseph ibn Saddiq*, ed. and trans. Jacob Haberman (Madison, NJ: Fairleigh Dickinson University Press; London: Associated University Presses, 2003), 6.
2. Petrus Alfonsi, *Epistola ad peripateticos* 2, trans. John Tolan, in *Petrus Alfonsi and His Medieval Readers* (Gainesville: University Press of Florida, 1993), 172–80, at 175.
3. Vincent of Beauvais, *Speculum naturale*, Brussels, Bibliothèque Royale MS 18466, fol. 44r.
4. Moses Maimonides, "Letter on Astrology," in *A Maimondes Reader*, ed., with introductions and notes, Isadore Twersky (New York: Behrman House, 1972), 463–73, at 465.
5. Dante, *Inferno* 4.31 (consulted at https://digitaldante.columbia.edu/dante/divine-comedy/inferno/inferno-4/).
6. Thomas Aquinas, *De veritate*, q. 2, a. 3, arg. 19, at Corpus Thomisticum, https://www.corpusthomisticum.org/qdv02.html.
7. As quoted in Dimitri Gutas, "Ibn Sina [Avicenna]," section 2, in *Stanford Encyclopedia of Philosophy*, https://plato.stanford.edu/entries/ibn-sina/.
8. As quoted in Peter Adamson, *Philosophy in the Islamic World* (Oxford: Oxford University Press, 2016), 310.
9. As quoted in Majid Fakhry, *Ibn Rushd: His Life, Works, and Influence* (Oxford: Oneworld Publications, 2001), 7.
10. Dante, *Inferno* 4.144 (consulted at https://digitaldante.columbia.edu/dante/divine-comedy/inferno/inferno-4/).
11. As quoted in Dag Nikolaus Hasse, *Avicenna's "De Anima" in the Latin West: The Formation of a Peripatetic Philosophy of the Soul, 1160–1300* (London: The Warburg Institute; Turin: Nino Aragno Editore, 2000), 5.
12. As quoted in Basil Tatakis, *Byzantine Philosophy*, trans., with introduction, Nicholas J. Moutafakis (Indianapolis: Hackett Publishing Company, 2003), 221.
13. As quoted in Tatakis, 222.
14. As quoted in J. N. Hillgarth, *Readers and Books in Majorca, 1229–1550* (Paris: CNRS, 1991), 1:199.

PART III

THE CONTEST FOR THE MEDITERRANEAN (1350–1650 CE)

New Empires, New Sects, New Worlds

Over the course of 1610 more than 18,000 Moriscos, the descendants of forcibly baptized Muslims, departed Spain through Seville, an inland port on the Guadalquivir River and the Spanish empire's commercial capital—a boom town that Spain's acquisition of American lands in the previous century had utterly transformed. These Moriscos joined some 300,000 of their brethren who by royal decree were sent into exile through other Spanish ports for their alleged refusal to abandon their Islamic faith and embrace Catholicism. As they floated away on ships headed for North Africa, they would have seen the Torre de Oro, the "Golden Tower" that the Almohad caliph Abu Ya'qub Yusuf had in the thirteenth century ordered built along the river, one of several monuments of Islamic architecture in Seville that would evermore stand in mute testimony to 900 years of Muslim life on the Iberian Peninsula.

Yet in the mid-fourteenth century Islamic architecture in Seville was not vestigial but vital and rooted in a markedly different social and religious landscape. In the 1360s the Castilian king Pedro I remodeled the royal Alcázar palace, originally a Muslim foundation, in the Iberian-Islamic style, complete with Arabic inscriptions and luxuriant stucco work. For Pedro this was a natural expression of his Andalusian upbringing and was inspired by his friendship with Muhammad V, the sultan of Granada and patron of the Alhambra who had taken refuge in the Alcázar from 1359 to 1362. Pedro's Jewish treasurer, Samuel ha-Levi Abulafia, had already built synagogues in Seville and Toledo in the Iberian-Islamic style, with walls displaying Castilian coats of arms interwoven with Hebrew and Arabic inscriptions. Though Seville had fallen under Castilian rule back in 1248, it still housed a Muslim community and a large and prosperous Jewish one. In the coming centuries, however, Seville, like the rest of the Iberian Peninsula, would, little by little, become uniformly Catholic.

Seville was the site of the first act in a wave of anti-Jewish violence that swept Christian Spain in 1391, resulting in the murder of many Jews and in the forced baptism of thousands more. In 1480 the new Spanish Inquisition first set up shop in Seville for the purpose of prosecuting Conversos, descendants of the converts of 1391, who clung to their Jewish ways. The port city was also the point of exit for thousands of Jews who hastily left Spain in early August 1492 in accordance with a royal order issued just four months before. Their departure prevented Christopher Columbus from embarking from Seville on his first voyage to America. At the beginning of this momentous year, Muhammad XII, the sultan of Granada, the last Muslim state on Iberian soil, had surrendered to Isabel of Castile and Fernando of Aragon. A decade later these rulers presented all Muslims in Castile with the choice of baptism or exile. Most opted for baptism.

In its transition to Catholic homogeneity, Spain seemingly followed the rest of western Europe. Muslims were long gone from Sicily and southern Italy; Jews had been expelled from England, France, and parts of Germany, and were migrating in growing numbers to Poland and Lithuania; and Jews in Italian cities were under pressure to convert and pushed into ghettos in the latter half of the sixteenth century. By this time, however, Martin Luther and other Protestant reformers had demolished any semblance of Catholic unity in Europe. From the 1520s until the mid-seventeenth century Europe was shaken by wars of religion that pitted Catholic dynasties like the Habsburgs of Spain and Austria against Protestant enemies in Germany, England, and the Netherlands. Meanwhile, the Habsburgs contended with their bitter Catholic rivals, the Valois of France. The latter feared that their realm would be enveloped by a Habsburg empire which by the mid-sixteenth century included not just Spain and America but large parts of Germany, Austria, the Netherlands, and Italy. The Valois therefore did not hesitate to seek alliances with the Ottoman empire, even though many Christians in Europe regarded the Ottomans as the gravest threat.

The Ottomans had indeed put an end to the Byzantine Empire by capturing Constantinople in 1453 and

FIGURE P3.1 Almohad Torre de Oro, Seville. Photograph provided by Wikimedia Commons under the CC-BY-SA-3.0.

had brought the Balkans under their dominion by the mid-sixteenth century. Mirroring the image that the Habsburgs projected of themselves as Catholic champions against Muslim and Protestant foes, the Ottoman sultans portrayed themselves as upholders of Sunni orthodoxy engaged in holy struggles against Christian states in the West and the Shi'i Safavid state in the East. For all this, they had little compunction about expanding their empire at the expense of the Sunni Mamluk rulers of Syria and Egypt and Sunni princes across much of North Africa. Another manifestation of their religious scruples was their maintenance of the *dhimma* with Christian and Jewish minorities, though here too practical concerns moved them to welcome, promote, and sometimes convert Jewish and Christian immigrants and subjects for their commercial connections, technological know-how, and loyalty.

Such pragmatism, then, was not necessarily inconsistent with religious ideals but often enough it overshadowed them. War between Christian and Muslim states frequently alternated with long truces when commercial treaties could be negotiated and political alliances, whether with coreligionists or infidels, reconfigured. For less powerful imperial players like the Venetians, hanging on to their dominions and keeping commercial arteries open required astute, culturally sensitive diplomacy at the Ottoman court. The Ottomans' integration into the European diplomatic system built on centuries of Venetian, Genoese, and Catalan diplomacy and trade in ports controlled by Mamluks, Hafsids, and Marinids. Yet the period of intense conflict between Ottomans and Habsburgs paradoxically saw the opening of more channels of communication and more cultural exchange among Christians, Muslims, and Jews, which was itself partly the result of another paradox: that the growing number of religious converts, exiles, and captives—the victims of imperial aggression—often functioned as the most effective intermediaries.

Commerce in food, cloth, and slaves continued to link the peoples of the Mediterranean. Even though piracy and captive-taking among Christians and Muslims, which rose to new heights in the sixteenth and seventeenth centuries, were disruptive and antagonizing, they were forms of interfaith business in which stolen cargoes were resold to all comers and captives exchanged for ransom. Meanwhile, the intertwined Mediterranean economies increasingly felt the impact of Iberian expansion into the Atlantic world. From the mid-fifteenth century enslaved Blacks acquired by Portuguese traders in West Africa and redistributed through Lisbon and Seville were a growing presence in Christian Mediterranean cities, as they had long been in Muslim cities, though most of the Africans whom Christians enslaved were sent across the Atlantic to labor on plantations where Mediterranean crops like sugar were harvested. In the sixteenth century the precious metals, especially silver, carried by Spanish galleons from America to Seville ultimately circulated throughout the Mediterranean, so that Turks as well as Spaniards experienced the resultant monetary inflation. Attracted by the wealth generated by the fusion of Atlan-

FIGURE P3.2 View of the port of Seville, late sixteenth century, with the Cathedral and Giralda Tower and Torre de Oro; attributed to Alonso Sanchez de Coello (d. 1588). Photograph provided by Wikimedia Commons under the CC-PD-Mark | PD-Art.

tic and Mediterranean economies, English and Dutch merchants, often carrying northern European products that undercut higher-priced Mediterranean goods, came to be major, even dominant players in the changing Mediterranean economy by the mid-seventeenth century.

In addition to the man-made misfortunes of war and captivity that sometimes afflicted them, Mediterranean folk suffered from environmental calamities such as plague, drought, and poor harvests. The Black Death of 1346–1353 and the "little ice age" of the seventeenth century were devastating, Mediterranean-wide events that brought economic crises and social rebellions in their wake. Even in less dire circumstances the relative scarcity of material resources contributed to making the intangible moral commodity of honor an essential element of social status for individuals and their families jockeying for power and position within their own faith communities. In Christian, Muslim, and Jewish societies, anxieties about honor and shame shaped and perpetuated specific gender roles and behaviors both within families and in feuds between them. If violent social competition was one response to the uncertainties of life, a deeper, sometimes ecstatic spirituality was another. To events of great triumph or tragedy members of all three faiths reacted with millenarian hopes and messianic longing; the end-time was at hand, they believed, and Ottoman sultans, Christian emperors, or Jews migrating to the Holy Land might be the ones to usher it in. Some found inspiration in a new faith, even if it had been forced upon them or their parents. In an age when hitherto unknown worlds were discovered and when so many people found themselves in places and faiths far from those of their birth, anything seemed possible, everything changeable. In 1650 a native of Seville could only shake her head at God's mysterious ways: the Giralda Tower, the grand minaret converted into the cathedral's bell tower, was a reminder of the Spanish monarchy's victory over Islam in the Old World just as the urban palaces built with American wealth reflected its dominion in the New World. Yet already the Guadalquivir River was silting up and Seville, the linchpin between the Mediterranean and the Atlantic, was starting to fade, as was the Spanish empire it served. The rise of France, England, and the Netherlands at the expense of Spain was the most noticeable aspect of the shift in the balance of global political and economic power from the Mediterranean to the Atlantic world.

CHAPTER TEN

Imperial Rivalry and Sectarian Strife

Ahmad al-Mansur, "the Victorious," the Sa'did sultan of Morocco (1578–1603), struggled to survive in a tough neighborhood: to the north were the Spanish Habsburgs who possessed outposts on the Moroccan coast at Melilla as well as at Ceuta, which they acquired in 1580 along with dominion over the rest of Portugal's maritime empire; to the east lay the Maghribi provinces of the Ottoman sultanate. To secure his authority against such formidable opponents, Ahmad combined the charismatic religious leadership cultivated by his Sa'did predecessors with shrewd diplomacy, military aggression, and bold propaganda. The Sa'dids had emerged as important political players in southern Morocco in 1510, bolstering their power with claims to be *sharifs*, or descendants of the Prophet Muhammad, and through conducting holy war against the Portuguese, whom they drove out of Agadir in 1541 with the help of gunpowder weapons purchased from European merchants. By 1554 they had conquered Fez, eliminated the rival Wattasid dynasty, and brought the entire country under their leadership. Ahmad earned his sobriquet and the throne in 1578 by crushing an invading Portuguese army led by its rash crusading king Sebastian at the Battle of Alcázar during which the reigning sultan, his brother 'Abd al-Malik, died, along with Sebastian. Aware that the Spanish and the Ottomans outmatched him militarily, Ahmad expanded his realm in the only direction he could, toward the south, where in 1591 his army, composed of Morisco, renegade Christian, and Arab troops, conquered the Sunni Muslim West African kingdom of Songhay. West African salt and gold had kindled Ahmad's ambition, but he was especially driven by a vision of himself as the rightful caliph who would establish a caliphate in the West to rival that of the Ottomans. Ahmad nonetheless dealt cautiously with the Ottomans: placating them with tribute or making overtures to their great enemy Felipe II of Spain (1556–1598), when necessary, but at the same time disseminating propaganda in which he claimed that his sharifian lineage made him, not the Turkish Ottoman, the true caliph. The Ottomans' preoccupation with the Shi'i Safavids in Iran prevented them from silencing him. The Spanish, however, were much closer and more menacing. Ahmad kept these Catholic foes off-balance by negotiating an alliance with their Protestant enemy Elizabeth I of England (1558–1603). English trade with Morocco consequently increased even if joint military action against Spain never came to pass.

The rise of the Sa'dids and the career of Ahmad al-Mansur illustrate patterns of political conduct that appear consistently in the period covered by this chapter. Military success against infidel states enabled Muslim and Christian rulers to lay or strengthen the spiritual foundations of their political power and then to draw upon this source of legitimacy to compete more effectively with rival monarchs of their own faith, even if such rivalry occasionally pushed them into tactical alliances with unbelievers.

The two great empires that worried Ahmad al-Mansur, the Ottoman and the Spanish Habsburg, had originally been insecure frontier polities that only gradually built on their military victories, over coreligionists but especially over infidels, to become the bulwarks of their respective faiths. For the Ottomans, the signal moments were the capture of Constantinople in 1453, which seemingly confirmed their destiny as heirs to the Roman Empire, and the defeat of the Mamluks in 1516–1517, which made the Ottomans the preeminent power among Sunni Muslims. The achievements of the Spanish rulers Fernando and Isabel in conquering Muslim Granada in 1492 and in eradicating Jews and Judaizing heretics from their realms moved the pope in 1496 to confer on them the title of "Catholic Monarchs," a title that became especially significant for their Habsburg successors in the next century when they led the fight against Protestant states and the Ottoman menace.

MAP 10.1 The Mediterranean, ca. 1350.

Each step along the way of the rise of the Ottoman and Spanish empires saw the rulers of other Mediterranean states, both Muslim and Christian, making the unavoidable adjustments. Much like the Sa'dids, they drew upon all the ideological, political, and economic resources at their disposal in order to govern and maintain the loyalty of their subjects, and to survive or, as in the case of the Venetians, even prosper as the empires expanded and clashed. Few contemporaries were shocked when avowedly righteous rulers compromised their religious principles out of political or economic necessity, for such had long been the way of pursuing and clinging to power in the Mediterranean arena.

Even so, on account of the sheer size, military might, and propaganda of the Ottoman and Habsburg empires, the Mediterranean world had by the 1520s apparently entered upon a new era of polarization into Sunni Muslim and Catholic blocs. Yet what was new in the sixteenth century was less the battling of Muslim and Christian potentates than the emergence of Protestant states in Catholic Europe and of a Shi'i Safavid state challenging the Ottomans on their eastern frontier, which provided Mediterranean rulers with a wider array of potential allies and commercial partners. The chessboard had expanded and some of the pieces on it were new, but, as Ahmad al-Mansur's reign evinced, the rules of the game had not changed all that much.

The Rise of Frontier Empires, ca. 1350–1500

In the fourteenth century the Ottomans were among the newest players in the Mediterranean arena. Rulers of a small Turkish emirate on the eastern perimeter of a weakening Byzantium, they made the most of the fluid frontier conditions, not only rapidly expanding their domain at the expense of Christian states but also allying

and intermarrying with Greek and Slavic Christian aristocrats from across the frontier, making them key functionaries in their growing hybrid empire. Even though the Ottomans would by the fifteenth century increasingly represent themselves as warriors for the Islamic faith, their openness to other traditions and pragmatic flexibility enabled them to develop institutions for effectively governing and exploiting an empire the majority of whose subjects were, until 1517, Christian. Mehmed the Conqueror's deep interest in Constantinople's classical and Christian past was therefore not incongruous with his position as its new Muslim ruler, for he aimed to build on and surpass the achievements of his Roman predecessors.

At the western end of the Mediterranean, Castile, which in 1516 would become the heart of the Spanish Habsburg empire, was in the fourteenth century already a much older polity than the Ottoman state, one that was firmly rooted in the Catholic faith but that still accommodated its Muslim and Jewish subjects. Castile's location on the frontier with Muslim Granada had long made campaigning against the Muslim enemy a source of legitimacy for its kings. Even so, conflict with neighboring Aragon and civil war prevented them from making much progress until after the princess and heir Isabel married Fernando, the heir to Aragon and king of Sicily, in 1469. This dynastic union set the stage for the conquest of Granada, and enabled Aragon to pursue territorial claims in southern Italy with the backing of Castile's prodigious military resources. It was in the Italian Peninsula that Spain would give notice to Europeans that it had arrived as an imperial power.

Although the contentious Italian Renaissance city-states were no match for the Ottoman, Spanish, and French powers that invaded in the late fifteenth century, the northern states of Milan, Venice, and Florence were formidable, having gained dominion over their smaller neighbors in previous decades. Together with the other major states to the south, the Papal States and the kingdom of Naples, they engaged in risky balance-of-power politics. The Genoese, long the Venetians' rivals for commercial dominance in the eastern Mediterranean, had by this time been compelled by both Venetians and Ottomans to shift much of their trade and investment farther west.

The Ottomans did not become a significant naval power until their capture of Constantinople demanded it; even then, they were not ready to challenge the existing

When Martin V (1417–1431) returned to Rome in 1420, three years after the Council of Constance ended the Great Schism by electing him pope, the authority of the papacy within the church was weak. A "conciliar movement" had emerged among the clergy assembled in Constance that attempted to change the governance of the church by requiring regular meetings of a general council of the church and asserting the supreme power of the council on certain key matters such as reform. Martin accordingly convened a council at Basel just before his death, but his successor Eugenius IV (1431–1447) frustrated the aims of the conciliarists by transferring the council to Ferrara and Florence, where, in 1439, he presided over the union of the Latin and Greek Churches, thereby enhancing papal prestige. Constitutional issues, however, were not laid to rest. Also, papal income remained greatly diminished, for during the schism European rulers had limited the amount of church taxes that flowed from their realms to Rome, which, as a result, had fallen into a dilapidated state. Popes therefore had to rely increasingly on revenue from the Papal States—nearly 60 percent of Sixtus IV's budget in 1480–1481—and to devote substantial resources to defending or expanding them.

A crucial part of the popes' efforts to restore the authority of their office involved the projection of an ideology of papal supremacy through various mediums, such as architecture, painting, and the treatises of humanists. Humanists studied classical texts in order to gain insight into how best to live a virtuous life as a citizen in the service of one's state. Based on their studies of Roman history, humanists in Rome increasingly articulated an "imperial humanism," which viewed the church, with its capital in Rome, as a continuation of the Roman Empire, and the popes as princes or Caesars.

Pope Nicholas V (1447–1455) considered the architectural renovation of Rome to be essential for reviving papal authority. He reportedly stated on his deathbed, "Noble edifices combining taste and beauty with imposing proportions would immensely conduce to the exaltation of the chair of St. Peter."[1] To this end, he laid plans to tear down and rebuild St. Peter's Basilica (which was not achieved until over a century later) and to enlarge the Vatican palace, which he made the permanent papal residence, instead of the Lateran palace. Nicholas believed that the popes, as successors to the priestly power of the keys that Christ had bestowed on Saint Peter, should perform their duties from the precinct of Peter's tomb. He also significantly expanded the Vatican's collection of classical manuscripts, laying the foundation of the Vatican Library and fostering a Roman renaissance.

Following Nicholas's lead, Pope Sixtus IV (1471–1484) sponsored the construction of the Sistine Chapel in the Vatican palace. It became the main papal chapel and the setting for ceremonies associated with the papal court. It was decorated with frescoes (wall paintings) with scenes from the lives of Moses and Christ. According to the principles of typology, in which Old Testament (Torah) events foreshadowed those in the New, Moses, in his roles as lawgiver, ruler, and priest, was a "type" or model for Christ. Furthermore, as humanist defenders of the papacy argued, Moses was a model for the popes, his authority to judge all matters relating to the worship of God among the ancient Hebrews foreshadowing the even greater powers of the popes among Christians.

Two of the frescoes that powerfully conveyed these typological messages were Sandro Botticelli's *Punishment of Korah* and, on the wall directly opposite it, Pietro Perugino's *Delivery of the Keys*. Botticelli's painting illustrates the revolt of Korah and other rebels against the authority of Moses and the high priest Aaron in the Old Testament (Numbers 16), which was understood to refer to the conciliarists' challenge to papal primacy. In the center of the painting the bearded Moses raises a rod to call down God's power against the rebels while Aaron, wearing a crown behind him, waves a censer at the altar. In the left foreground, Moses stands over a chasm where the earth has swallowed up the Korists. In the background rises the accurately rendered Roman Arch of Constantine, except that Botticelli replaced the original inscription on it with a text from the New Testament Epistle to the Hebrews: "Nobody arrogates the honor [of the high priesthood] to himself unless he is called by God, as was Aaron."

Perugino's fresco depicts Christ handing the keys to the kneeling Saint Peter, symbolizing the transmission of supreme power within the church to Peter and his rightful successors, the popes. The building behind them signifies the church and alludes to Christ's words "Thou art Peter and upon this rock I will build my church" (Matthew 16:18). The inscription on the arch on the left—"You, Sixtus IV, unequal in riches but superior in religion to [King] Solomon, have consecrated this vast temple"—not

FIGURE 10.1 Sandro Botticelli, *The Punishment of Korah and the Stoning of Moses and Aaron*, 1481–1482. Photo: Web Gallery of Art provided by Wikimedia Commons under the CC-PD-Mark | PD-Art.

FIGURE 10.2 Pietro Perugino, *Delivery of the Keys*, 1481–1482. Photograph provided by Wikimedia Commons under the CC-PD-Mark | PD-Art.

only commemorates Sixtus as the builder of the chapel but also suggests that the Roman Church, founded by Christ's delivery of the keys, has surpassed the Jewish Temple of Solomon that foreshadowed it. In the middle ground on the right is a scene of the stoning of Christ teaching in the Temple (John 8:59 and 10:31), which parallels the threatened stoning of Moses in the right foreground of Botticelli's painting. Both frescoes, then, depict challengers to the lawgivers Moses and Christ and indicate their ultimate defeat by God. The message to all who might question the supreme authority of the papacy was clear.

As rulers of the Papal States, Sixtus and his successors could not confine themselves to countering the claims of conciliarists; they had to conduct wars against other Italian states. Alexander VI (1492–1503), of the Spanish Borgia (Borja) family, directed his general and son, Cesare Borgia, to subjugate princes and towns within the Papal States that were resistant to papal control. Cesare earned Machiavelli's praise for his ruthless efficiency. But the pope who most embodied the humanists' vision of a papal Caesar was Julius II (1503–1513). He expanded the Papal States by conquering towns such as Perugia, Bologna, and Parma, and he was more effective than Alexander at employing art and architecture to publicize his successes and promote his imperial image. Julius, for instance, issued a medal in 1507 commemorating his victory over Bologna the previous year. One side, with a portrait of the pope in profile, includes an inscription linking him to his Roman imperial namesake, Julius Caesar. The reverse side, with the crossed keys of the papal insignia, has the legend "Blessed is he who comes in the name of the Lord," which refers to Christ's triumphant entry into Jerusalem. The medal combined representations of Pope Julius's spiritual and secular power; he was at once the successor of Caesar and the vicar of Christ.

Moses also served as a model or "type," for Julius's dual roles, his freeing of the Hebrews from slavery foreshadowing the pope's military leadership. A huge statue of Moses, sculpted by Michelangelo Buonarroti around 1515—after he painted the ceiling of the Sistine Chapel—thus occupied a prominent place in the tomb of Pope Julius, which Michelangelo had designed at the pope's behest. In his *Moses*, Michelangelo was attempting to capture, scholars think, the forceful personality of the warrior pope.

The military power of the Spanish Habsburgs in Italy and the sack of Rome in 1527 inhibited later popes from styling themselves as papal Caesars. But the popes persisted in their efforts to make Rome the magnificent holy city Nicholas V had imagined, and they secured their spiritual authority within the church.

FIGURE 10.3 Medal of Pope Julius II, issued for the triumphal celebration of Palm Sunday, 1507. National Gallery of Art, Samuel H. Kress Collection, 1957.14.832.a+b. Images: Courtesy National Gallery of Art, Washington.

Discussion Questions

1. What were the historical factors that enabled the conciliarists to challenge the supreme authority of the popes?

2. How did magnificent architecture and art contribute to the revival of papal authority within the church?

3. Who was intellectually equipped to comprehend the messages conveyed in the paintings of Botticelli and Perugino, and who was the intended audience of these paintings?

4. How did Christian interpretations of Jewish history and the Torah (Old Testament) enable artists and their papal patrons to make use of the figure of Moses?

Further Reading

Ettlinger, L. D. *The Sistine Chapel before Michelangelo: Religious Imagery and Papal Primacy.* Oxford: Clarendon Press, 1965.
Hibbard, Howard. *Michelangelo.* 2nd ed. Harmondsworth: Penguin Books, 1985.
Oakley, Francis. *The Western Church in the Later Middle Ages.* Ithaca: Cornell University Press, 1979.
Stinger, Charles L. *The Renaissance in Rome.* Bloomington: Indiana University Press, 1985.

Note

1. Peter Partner, *Renaissance Rome, 1500–1559: A Portrait of a Society* (Berkeley: University of California Press, 1976), 16.

FIGURE 10.4 Michelangelo Buonarroti, statue of Moses for the tomb of Pope Julius II, San Pietro in Vincoli (Rome), 1505–1545. Photograph by Jörg Bittner Unna provided by Wikimedia Commons under the CC-BY-3.0.

alignment of political and economic power across North Africa. The Mamluk rulers of Egypt and Syria were therefore content to maintain a defensive posture, prospering from trade and confident in their military prowess and in the prestige that came from their custodianship of Islam's holy places. Farther west, the Hafsids in Tunis, the Zayyanids in Tlemsen, and the Marinids in Fez pursued debilitating territorial wars that rendered them vulnerable to the encroachments of Spain and Portugal.

Ottoman Rise and Byzantine Demise in the East

The Ottoman state emerged in the early fourteenth century in the former Byzantine province of Bithynia, one of several Turkic emirates in western Anatolia whose establishment was enabled by the collapse of the Seljuq and Mongol Ilkhanid empires and by the Byzantine emperors' inattention to their eastern frontier. Through their success as raiders, the early Ottoman leaders Osman, the founder of the dynasty, and his son Orhan attracted a growing number of ambitious fighters, among whom were Turkic immigrants and Christian nobles: first Byzantine Greeks, later Balkan Slavs. The Ottomans' Muslim identity lent their raiding a religious aspect, but their knowledge of orthodox Islam was minimal and their spiritual guides were Sufi dervishes whose heterodox Islam integrated shamanistic and Christian customs. This syncretic Islam facilitated the conversion of the Ottomans' Christian followers, who established leading Ottoman warrior families and served as officials in the expanding state. Some remained Christian, though by the mid-fifteenth century conversion was a requirement for holding a post in Ottoman government.

The Ottomans' raiding led to their conquest of Byzantine cities as well as rival Turkic emirates in Anatolia. Civil war between the rival emperors John V Palaeologus and John VI Kantakouzenos moved the latter in 1346 to ally with Orhan, marrying his daughter Theodora to the sultan. In 1352 Kantakouzenos granted Orhan access to a fortress on the Gallipoli peninsula and thus a foothold in Europe and a springboard for Ottoman incursions in the Balkans. Here, they captured strategic Adrianople (Edirne) in 1369, Sofia in 1385, and Thessaloniki in 1387. In 1389 Murad I (1362–1389) defeated the Serbian king Lazar (1373–1389) at Kosovo, though both died in the battle. Murad's successor Bayezid I (1389–1402) married Olivera, the sister of Lazar's successor Stephen, who became Bayezid's vassal. King Sigismund of Hungary attempted to check Ottoman expansion, first by allying with the Byzantine emperor Manuel II, and then by organizing a Crusade of eastern and western Christian forces that Bayezid crushed in 1396 at Nicopolis, Bulgaria, with the help of a Serbian contingent led by Stephen. After this, Bayezid worked to extend Ottoman rule in Anatolia until he came up against Timur-Lenk (Tamerlane), the Turkic restorer of the Mongol Empire, who defeated and captured him at Ankara in 1402.

MAP 10.2 The Mediterranean, ca. 1450.

Timur-Lenk's victory gave Byzantium a fifty-year respite. In the years before his death in 1405, he dismantled much of Ottoman Anatolia, and a decade of civil war between Bayezid's sons allowed Christian leaders in the Balkans to recoup some losses and put the Ottomans on the defensive. The sultans Mehmed I (1413–1420) and Murad II (1420–1444, 1446–1451) therefore devoted their reigns to reestablishing Ottoman suzerainty in Anatolia and the Balkans. Murad's most signal triumph occurred in 1444 at Varna, on Bulgaria's Black Sea coast, over a crusading army led by Vladislav I of Hungary and John Hunyadi, Lord of Transylvania. Pope Eugenius IV had helped to mobilize this Crusade in an effort to assist the Byzantine emperor John VIII (1425–1448), who, in exchange, had agreed in 1439 to the Union of the Greek and Latin Churches. The Union left many Byzantine Greeks disgruntled, while the failed Crusade left the Balkan Peninsula firmly in Ottoman hands. SEE SOURCEBOOK 10:1.

By this time most institutions of the Ottoman state were in place, the products of a creative fusion of central Asian, Islamic, and Byzantine ways. The system of dynastic succession ensured that the state remained uni-

fied under very capable rulers. All Ottoman territories were transferred undivided to one of the sultan's sons, the one who managed to eliminate his brothers after their father's death. Each son was raised by his mother in a separate household and acquired governmental experience in the provinces. The mothers were usually enslaved concubines from the palace harem. Prior to 1450 the Ottomans did contract marriages with Byzantine and Serbian princesses, for example, but such marriages were more for political than for reproductive purposes. Their abandonment of political marriages after 1450 reflected their confidence in their control over their Balkan Christian subjects. As in other Muslim states, the Ottomans' Christian and Jewish subjects enjoyed the status of protected minorities and the freedom to practice their respective faiths.

The sultans governed the provinces of the empire at first through local princes and nobles who had become their vassals and then, from the fifteenth century, through governors they appointed. A key provincial institution was the *timar*, a species of the fief that was allocated to a cavalryman who, in return for military service, collected taxes from the peasants residing on it. Cavalry formed an important part of the sultan's armies, as did the Janissaries, an infantry corps who also served as the sultan's bodyguard. The Janissaries were recruited through the *devşirme,* or "collection," of a certain number of boys, mostly Christians from the Balkans, who were enslaved, educated in Islam, and given military or, in some cases, administrative training.

The Byzantine Empire in the fifteenth century was essentially the city-state of Constantinople, governed by the emperor and Greek aristocrats. Having lost their landed possessions to the Ottomans, many nobles invested in trade, sometimes with the Turkic merchants who visited the city but mostly with the Genoese and Venetians, the dominant players. Some Greek aristocrats used these connections to win grants of citizenship from Genoa and Venice. They unsurprisingly supported the 1439 Union of the Greek and Latin Churches, a strategy that Emperor John VIII pursued in order to win western aid against the Ottomans. The anti-Latin Greek lower classes and many members of the Orthodox clergy opposed this policy.

But when Mehmed II (1444–1446, 1451–1481) laid siege to Constantinople in spring 1453, most western kingdoms were too mired in conflict to send relief forces. They probably underestimated the threat, believing the city's great walls would save it from a Muslim siege, as they had so many times in the past. Constantinople, however, had only around 5,000 men to defend it, compared to Mehmed's army of some 50,000. Ottoman artillery, especially a huge cannon made by a Hungarian cannon-founder, proved crucial for breaching the walls and enabling Mehmed's troops to enter the city on May 29.

The fall of Constantinople resonated throughout the Mediterranean world, signifying the passing of the old Roman Christian order and disheartening Christians. For Muslims, it was the fulfillment of a dream that began with the first Umayyad siege of the city in 674–678. For the Ottomans, the conquest symbolized their inheritance of the mantle of the Roman emperors. The city's location between the Ottomans' European and Asian territories made it the ideal place for their imperial capital. Mehmed and his successors architecturally transformed Constantinople into a Muslim capital, Istanbul, and in encouraging the settlement of Muslims, Greek and Armenian Christians, and Jews, they made the city a microcosm of their diverse, inclusive empire. SEE SOURCEBOOK 10:2.

FIGURE 10.5 Woodcut of Ottoman Sipahis (Cavalry) and Janissaries, 1683. Antiqua Print Gallery / Alamy Stock Photo.

Castilian and Aragonese Expansion in the West

When Alfonso XI of Castile died of the plague in 1350 while besieging Gibraltar his kingdom was poised for the conquest of Granada. With Catalan and Portuguese assistance, Castile had recently overcome the combined forces of Granada and the Moroccan Marinids in the contest for the Straits of Gibraltar. Yet Alfonso's son Pedro I, the Cruel (1350–1369), set his sights not on Granada, a vassal and tributary of Castile, but on the Crown of Aragon. Unresolved territorial disputes and Castile's alliance with the Catalans' maritime rivals, the Genoese, led to a long war, 1356–1366, in which the much larger and militarily superior Castile occupied territory in Aragon. Civil war in Castile saved Aragon's king, Pere III, the Ceremonious (1356–1387), from total defeat. This struggle, which pitted Pedro against his bastard half-brother Enrique de Trastámara, drew the Iberian Peninsula into the Hundred Years' War between England and France (1337–1453). In 1369 with the backing of France and Aragon, Enrique (II, 1369–1379) wrested the Castilian crown from Pedro, who had enjoyed English support. The English would take revenge on Enrique's successor Juan I (1379–1390) in 1385, when they assisted the Portuguese in foiling Juan's attempt to conquer Portugal.

Meanwhile the Crown of Aragon worked, with the encouragement of the Catalan merchant classes, to extend its western Mediterranean domains. Pere the Ceremonious returned Mallorca to the Crown's dominion in 1343, while his successors Joan I (1387–1396) and Martí I (1396–1410) reannexed Sicily to the Crown and suppressed much of the Sardinian resistance to Catalan rule that the Genoese had long been inciting.

Castile's growing influence over Iberian affairs became clearer in 1412 in the Compromise of Caspe: following Martí's death without heirs, a board of Catalan and Aragonese electors chose Fernando, the younger son of Juan I of Castile, as his successor. The new Castilian rulers of the Crown of Aragon, Fernando I (1412–1416) and his ambitious son Alfonso V (1416–1458), nonetheless pursued the Crown's traditional goals in Italy. Notably, Alfonso conquered the kingdom of Naples in 1443 after defeating an Angevin rival for its vacant throne. His efforts to dominate Italy failed, however, and distracted him from containing Ottoman expansion and attempting to save Constantinople. Upon his death in 1458, Naples passed to his illegitimate son, Ferrante (1458–1494), and out of Aragonese control.

Political elites in the Crown of Aragon, especially in Catalonia, had resented Alfonso's long absences in Italy and his frequent demands for financial support. Their indignation was symptomatic of a fundamental disagreement between a Castilian dynasty imbued with Castilian traditions of authoritarian monarchy and their Catalan-Aragonese subjects accustomed to a contractual relationship with the monarchy in which the parliament (Cortes) controlled legislation and taxation and monarchs were bound to observe their subjects' constitutional liberties. During the reign of Juan II (1458–1479) these tensions exploded in Catalonia in a devastating civil war (1460–1472). Though ultimately victorious, Juan preserved Catalonia's constitutions.

The marriage in 1469 of the future Fernando II of Aragon (1479–1516) to the future Isabel I of Castile (1474–1504) established a union in which Castile became the dominant partner while Aragon retained its distinct institutions. The couple's first task was taming Castile's ever-rebellious nobility. They channeled the nobles' bellicose energies into a final Crusade against Granada, an enterprise now more feasible since Granada could no longer play Aragon against Castile. Conquering the sultanate nonetheless entailed ten years of grueling campaigning—from February 1482 to Fernando and Isabel's triumphal entry into Granada on January 6, 1492—in which Castile's armies and artillery, papal support in the form of crusading indulgences, and infighting among Granada's Nasrid dynasty all proved decisive. Although the victorious monarchs guaranteed the surrendering Muslims the same religious freedoms and protections that Christian kings had granted to Iberian Muslims in past centuries, Granada, now a possession of Castile, would be forcibly Christianized, along with the rest of Castile, by 1502. Only the Muslims of the Crown of Aragon and Navarre would remain unbaptized.

With papal support, Spain's "Catholic Monarchs" extended their Crusades into North Africa, capturing the ports of Melilla in 1497, Marsa al-Kabir in 1505, Oran in 1509, and Bijaya and Tripoli in 1510. Strategic concerns to protect Castile's recently acquired Granadan coastline and Spanish shipping from Muslim corsairs motivated these conquests at least as much as religious zeal. Between 1494 and 1504 Fernando was just as busy outfoxing and outfighting the French kings Charles VIII and Louis XII in the contest for the kingdom of Naples after the death of Ferrante. In claiming Naples, Fernando trumpeted his crusading credentials, asserting that he could better defend it, and all of Italy, against an Ottoman invasion. Fernando hoped to expand eastward into Egypt and the Holy Land from Spain's bases in southern Italy and the Maghrib, but his death in 1516 and the Ottoman conquest of Egypt the following year extinguished such Spanish dreams.

Spain's treaties with Portugal before and after Columbus's voyages to America ensured that most of Morocco and West Africa would continue to be areas for Portuguese expansion. Portugal had seized Ceuta by 1415, and Tangier fell in 1471, followed by other cities on Morocco's Atlantic coast. Initially encouraged by Prince Henry the Navigator (d. 1460), the Portuguese gradually moved down the West African coast establishing outposts where they acquired gold and slaves. After Vasco da Gama sailed into the Indian Ocean in 1498, they began to encroach on the lucrative trade in eastern spices that Muslim merchants carried to Mamluk-controlled Mediterranean ports, often for resale to Italian and other European merchants. SEE SOURCEBOOK 10:3.

Italian Renaissance States in the Shadow of Empires

The Italian city-states had grown prosperous from commerce, banking, and textile production, wealth their elites used to display their piety and power through the art for which the Italian Renaissance is justly famed. But they also employed it to manipulate local politics and hire mercenaries to fight their internecine wars.

Through the fourteenth and fifteenth centuries most Italian cities experienced a transition from "republican" government, in which citizens from a broader range of social classes participated, to government by an oligarchy of wealthy families, often of mercantile origin, or by one princely family. The process was by no means painless. In Florence, for example, strong oligarchic rule emerged partly in reaction to the proletarian Ciompi (Companions) revolt of 1378. The circle of power narrowed further as Cosimo de Medici (1434–1464) and his grandson Lorenzo the Magnificent (1469–1492) controlled Florentine government through their influence over elections to public office. Milan was ruled by one ducal family, either the Viscontis (ca. 1354–1447) or the Sforzas (ca. 1450–1500). From around 1323 the offices of the famously stable government of Venice were in the hands of a closed aristocracy.

Between these leading northern city-states and the kingdom of Naples, which changed hands between Angevin and Aragonese dynasties, lay the extensive Papal States. The popes' sojourn in Avignon from 1309 to 1378 had weakened their authority in Italy while depressing Rome economically. This situation was aggravated by the ensuing schism (1378–1417), when the western church was divided between one pope in Avignon and another in Rome, and the states pledged allegiance to either one. The persistent disunity of the Papal States encouraged attempts by Milan and Naples to appropriate papal lands. Only after the Council of Constance healed the schism by electing one pope, Martin V (1417–1431), could the papacy begin to assert its authority over the towns and baronies comprising the Papal States. In waging war, disciplining barons, levying taxes, and engaging in nepotism, the popes behaved like secular rulers. Between 1417 and 1521 almost all the popes were Italian (except the Spanish Borgias Calixtus III and Alexander VI) and thus more capable players in peninsular politics. Like other Renaissance princes, the popes invested heavily in their capital's architecture and art, patronizing artists such as Michelangelo Buonarroti (1475–1564). They made Rome magnificent again.

The devastating effects of the Black Death (1347–1349) had left smaller cities easier prey for Florence, Milan, and Venice, which could afford larger mercenary armies. Florence expanded its territory in Tuscany; taking Pisa in 1406, it gained access to the sea. The duchy of Milan conquered much of Lombardy. In the fifteenth century Venice added to its modest maritime empire in the Adriatic and Aegean by subjugating Verona and Bergamo on the Italian mainland, thereby securing Alpine trade routes to northern Europe. Commercial interests in the Aegean and Black Seas had caused Venice's ultimately victorious wars with Genoa in 1350–1355 and 1378–1381. Though often hampered by discord among its leading families, Genoa continued to be a power at sea with merchant colonies on the Aegean island of Chios, at Pera near Constantinople, and at Kaffa on the Black Sea.

By 1454 the five major powers in Italy were Venice, Milan, Florence, the kingdom of Naples under Alfonso V of Aragon, and the Papal States. They distrusted each other, but they worried more about intervention from outside Italy, whether by the revitalized French monarchy, which had finally succeeded in driving the English out of France and retained dynastic claims to Naples and Milan, or by the Ottomans, who had captured Constantinople. These five powers therefore formed the Italian League in 1455 for the purpose of fostering internal peace and unity. For nearly forty years they strove, through a dizzying array of alliances and treaties among themselves and weaker Italian polities, to maintain a balance of power. The intense diplomatic activity led by 1480 to the regular use of resident ambassadors, the foundation of an international diplomatic system in which foreign powers, including the Ottomans, eventually participated.

Unfortunately for the Italian states, Mehmed II did not rest on his laurels after taking Constantinople. He completed the conquest of Serbia and Bosnia by 1464. Italian disunity and the failure of Pope Pius II (1458–1464) to mobilize a Crusade against the Ottomans left the Genoese and the Venetians to face them each on their own. Genoa lost most of its Aegean and Black Sea colonies, while Venice surrendered Negroponte in the Aegean and Scutari in Albania at the end of a long war (1463–1479). In 1480 Mehmed seized Otranto, in the kingdom of Naples, kindling fears that Rome was next. His death in 1481, however, prompted an Ottoman withdrawal. Venice fought another costly war against Bayezid II (1481–1512) in 1499–1502 and relinquished more of its possessions in Greece. A long peace ensued as the Venetians opted to cultivate commercial relations with the Ottomans, with whom they shared a concern regarding the Portuguese threat to the Indian Ocean spice trade from which they both profited.

By this time French and Spanish armies were carving up Italy, often with the connivance of self-interested Italians. Encouraged by Neapolitan exiles and the duke of Milan, Charles VIII of France (1483–1498) occupied Naples in 1495 following the death of its ruler, Ferrante I, only to be driven back home as a consequence of an anti-French alliance of Venice, the duplicitous duke of Milan, Maximilian Habsburg of Austria, the papacy, and Fernando of Aragon, its mastermind. It was maneuvering like this that led the Florentine political theorist Niccolo Machiavelli to grudgingly describe Fernando as "the first king in Christendom." Charles's successor Louis XII (1498–1515) avenged him by seizing Milan in 1499, but in 1503–1504 Fernando defeated Louis to win the Neapolitan crown.

Reverberations of the French invasions resulted in other Italian casualties. The Medicis of Florence fell in 1494, replaced by a republican regime inspired by the fiery Dominican preacher Girolamo Savonarola, who supported Charles VIII. Even after patrician families hostile to Savonarola's reformist agenda brought about his execution in 1498, the republican government survived until 1512 as a vassal of the French king. Venice, the remaining great power, lost many mainland possessions in 1508–1509 to Pope Julius II's (1503–1513) League of Cambrai, which included France, Spain, and Austria. In 1511 the pope reversed course, organizing a "Holy League" of the papacy, Spain, Venice, Austria, and England against France, forcing Louis XII to withdraw from Milan. Next, League forces overthrew the republican regime in Florence and restored the Medicis to power, and the Medici popes Leo X (1513–1521) and Clement VII (1523–1534) exercised great influence there through relatives and allies. SEE SOURCEBOOK 10:4.

Mamluk Stagnation and Maghribi Division

Religious war had been crucial for establishing the authority of the sultans of the older North African emirates. The Mamluks had gained Islamic legitimacy in the thirteenth century by defeating pagan Mongols and western Crusaders, and through their custodianship of the 'Abbasid caliphs and the holy cities of Mecca and Medina. They enhanced their pious image by appointing judges and founding *madrasas* and Sufi lodges in their capital, Cairo, which superseded Baghdad as the center of Sunni Islam. Yet the political situation in the fourteenth and fifteenth centuries that propelled Ottoman expansion encouraged Mamluk complacency, until it was too late. In the Maghrib religious charisma had long bolstered the authority of the leaders of tribal confederations and sanctified their imperial ambitions, and dynasties continued to cultivate the support of the *'ulama'*. The Marinids in Morocco, like their off-and-on Nasrid allies in Granada, had justified their rule partly through conducting *jihad* against Christian Spain, but no Maghribi Muslim polity would prove capable of halting Iberian Christian aggression.

The solidarity and discipline that had enabled the Mamluk military caste to establish dominion over Egypt and Syria waned in the fourteenth century in the absence of serious external threats, since the Ilkhanid Mongols had made peace in 1322. Internal instability increased after 1340 as rival Mamluk factions competed for power under ever-weaker sultans. Recurring outbreaks of plague after 1347 devastated Egyptian agriculture and industry, reducing the revenue of the Mamluks, whose own ranks were decimated by disease. This state of affairs likely emboldened Peter I of Cyprus to attack Alexandria in 1365.

In 1382 the sultan Barquq (1382–1389) instituted a new, more stable regime of Circassian Mamluks, mostly recruited in the Caucasus instead of in Turkic Central Asia. After surviving the onslaught of Timur-Lenk, who had sacked Aleppo and Damascus, the Circassian sultans consolidated their authority. Barsbay's (1422–1438) campaigns against Genoese and Catalan pirates and his subjection of Cyprus to vassalage in 1425–1426 signaled the Mamluk recovery. Seeking more revenue to fund such expensive projects, Barsbay established a state monopoly over the eastern spices trade, particularly their sale to European merchants.

By the late fifteenth century, however, the revenues from the spice monopoly and Egypt's deteriorating agricultural sector were insufficient to meet the new challenges the Mamluk sultanate faced. Internally, Mamluk troops desirous of higher stipends grew restive, occasionally rebellious. Externally, the Ottomans in Istanbul had become at least the political equals of the Mamluks in the Sunni world. The Mamluks' fundamentally defensive strategy, which entailed maintaining profitable trade relations with Europe while paying lip service to *jihad*, was ill-suited to match Ottoman sultans inclined to wage war against Christians and weaker Muslim principalities in the pursuit of universal empire. Although the Mamluk forces of Qaytbay (1468–1496) held their own in a frontier war with the Ottomans in eastern Anatolia in 1485–1491, the naval assistance that the Ottoman Bayezid II began providing in 1505 to the Mamluk Qansuh al-Ghawri (1501–1516) to combat Portuguese aggression in the Indian Ocean reflected the true extent of Ottoman power.

The mid-fourteenth-century Maghrib was dominated by the Marinids of Morocco. After 1344, when the sultan Abu al-Hasan (1331–1348) and his Granadan allies suffered a final defeat in their war with Castile over the Straits of Gibraltar, he and his son Abu Inan (1348–1358) turned to incorporating Zayyanid domains in the central Maghrib and Hafsid Ifriqiya into their realm, with the goal of dominating the trans-Saharan trade routes that extended from Mali to Zayyanid Tlemsen and Hafsid Tunis. Their empire, however, was transitory. After Abu Inan, Marinid sultans were ineffective, enabling the Portuguese to capture Ceuta in 1415.

The Marinids' failure to stop the Portuguese heightened popular discontent and enflamed religious sentiment. The Wattasids, a family of *wazirs* who became the power behind the throne in 1420, saved the regime through their military success against the Portuguese. In 1465, after the sultan 'Abd al-Haqq (1437–1465) replaced his Wattasid *wazir* with an unpopular Jewish one and the Portuguese renewed their attacks, a revolt in the Marinid capital, Fez, brought down the regime. Religious figures, both Sufi shaykhs and individuals of sharifian descent, played a key role. The Wattasid Muhammad al-Shaykh (1472–1505) nonetheless seized power from the *sharifs* in Fez in 1472, once he appeased the Portuguese by surrendering Asila and Larache to them. He made other such tactical agreements with the advancing Portuguese. The Sa'dids, a family of sharifian lineage, were able to play on the growing popular disgruntlement with the Wattasids, whose authority was limited mainly to northern Morocco, to build a politico-religious movement in the south.

The Marinid decline permitted the Hafsid sultans to unify Ifriqiya. Ruling from Tunis, Abu al-'Abbas (1370–1394) and his successors reined in the Arab tribes that had been dominant in the countryside and imposed their authority on the cities. Hafsid-sponsored corsairs operating out of Bijaya and Mahdiyya preyed on Italian, Catalan, and French ships. Christians retaliated with piracy and organized expeditions. The sultans, however, also concluded treaties with Venice, Genoa, and Aragon, so that periods of war alternated with years of trade. Usually Christian merchants visited the Hafsids' ports. The sultans increasingly depended on the revenue generated by this commerce to finance their government, while collaboration with urban elites became a key basis of their authority.

During the fifteenth century the Hafsids became perhaps the most influential of the Maghribi dynasties. Zayyanid Tlemsen fell under their suzerainty from 1424 until the end of the century, whereas previously it had often been subordinate to the Marinids. By the end of the century, however, Hafsid authority over the rural Arab tribes had weakened. Despite the growing importance of cities in the Maghrib, they could not provide the Hafsids or any other dynasty with the fiscal and military resources sufficient to resist the Spanish, and Hafsid and Zayyanid ports soon came under Christian domination.

The Duel of Empires and the Web of Alliances, ca. 1500–1650

The year 1517 was momentous. In April, the Ottomans completed the conquest of Mamluk realms, making them supreme among Sunni Muslims and giving their empire a Muslim majority population for the first time. Yet all was not well, for the "heresy" of Shi'ism propagated by followers of the Safavid shah of Iran, Isma'il I (1501–1524), was spreading into Ottoman Anatolia. In October, the monk and university professor Martin Luther published his Ninety-Five Theses against the papacy's sale of indulgences in Wittenberg (Germany), igniting a series of religious and political controversies that soon led to the emergence of Protestant churches and principalities in Catholic Europe. The first arose in the German lands of the young Habsburg Holy Roman Emperor Charles V (1516–1556), whose vast empire included Spain and its New World possessions.

Hence, from the 1520s, the duel between Muslim Ottomans and Christian Habsburgs for domination of the Mediterranean intersected with sectarian conflicts

ARTIFACT DUELING CAESARS: REPRESENTATIONS OF OTTOMAN AND HABSBURG IMPERIAL POWER

The Arabic inscription on the Imperial Gate of the New Palace (today known as the Topkapi Palace) built in Constantinople between 1459 and 1478 by the Ottoman sultan Mehmed II read: "By the grace of God... the foundations of this auspicious castle were laid... by the command of the Sultan of the two Continents and the Emperor of the two Seas..., the Favorite of God on the Two Horizons, the Monarch of the Terraqueous Orb, the Conqueror of the Castle of Constantinople... Sultan Mehmed Khan."[1] The conqueror of the Byzantine capital who ruled lands that extended from Asia Minor to southeastern Europe, Mehmed was doing more than stating a simple geopolitical fact in the inscription; he was laying claim to the dominion that the ancient Roman emperors had possessed in the East and the West. This was a claim that nervous European Christians took seriously, but until the election of the Habsburg Charles V as Holy Roman Emperor in 1520 it seemed as if there were no Christian monarchs who could contest it. Among the weapons that the would-be Caesars—Muslim Ottoman and Catholic Habsburg—deployed in their struggle for supremacy were symbolic expressions of sovereign power that were directed at foreign observers as well as at their own subjects.

Seeing himself as the successor to the Roman emperors, Mehmed II set about transforming Constantinople into the capital of a world empire that combined older Roman-Byzantine traditions with newer Turco-Islamic ones. Through monumental architecture the sultan proclaimed the establishment of a new imperial order. His New Palace was built where the ancient Byzantine acropolis once stood, on the tip of a peninsula where the Mediterranean and Black Seas met. The site of the palace between two seas and two continents was symbolic of the world dominion to which Mehmed aspired. His employment of both Muslim and European Christian architects and decorators reflected his broad vision as well as Europeans' acknowledgment of the emergence of a new Caesar.

The construction of the New Mosque complex, 1463–1470, on the site of the Church of the Holy Apostles—originally built by the emperor Constantine, rebuilt by Justinian, and torn down by Mehmed—signaled that the new

FIGURE 10.6 Panoramic view of Istanbul, showing the Topkapi Palace, from the Golden Horn, ca. 1590. © Historical Views / agefotostock.

FIGURE 10.7 Melchior Lorck, Mosque of Mehmed II, the Conqueror. *Prospect of Constantinople,* part 13, 1526/27–1583. Leiden University Libraries, Digital Collections, CC-BY License.

FIGURE 10.8 Gentile Bellini, Medal of Mehmed II, 1480. © Historical Views / agefotostock.

FIGURE 10.9 Jacopo Ligozzi, *Charles V and Pope Clement VII at His Imperial Coronation*, ca. 1518. Photo by Discasto provided by Wikimedia Commons under the CC-PD-Mark | PD-Art.

imperial order was accompanied by a new religious dispensation. The clear resemblance of the New Mosque to the Church of Hagia Sophia accentuated this point, as did the conversion of the great church into a mosque.

Mehmed was keenly aware that there was a European audience for his momentous deeds. He therefore employed the Italian artist Gentile Bellini to paint his portrait and to engrave it on bronze medals, which were disseminated in European courts as representations of his power. Mehmed's profile on one side of the medal was encircled by the legend "Of the Great Emperor and Sultan Mohamet [Mehmed]"; on the obverse side were the three crowns of Byzantium, Trabzon, and Asia.

For Europeans engaged in the perennial contest with Muslim powers, there were few encouraging developments until Fernando and Isabel captured Granada in 1492. Yet the "Catholic Monarchs" alone lacked the resources to halt the Ottoman advance. Hope came in the person of their grandson Charles, heir to Spanish and Habsburg possessions in Europe, North Africa, and America. After his election as Holy Roman Emperor in 1520, Charles V explained to his Castilian subjects that the "enemy" of the Catholic faith could not be defeated "unless I shall link Spain with Germany and add the name of Caesar to Spanish king."[2] Although Charles was first crowned emperor in Aachen that year, the most symbolically resonant coronation ceremonies took place in Bologna in February 1530, just a few months after imperial armies turned back the Ottomans at Vienna. There Charles received from Pope Clement VII the iron crown of the Lombard kings and the golden imperial crown, which the pope described as "the principal crown of the empire of the world."[3] The emperor promised to wage war against the Turks.

News of the coronation ceremonies and Charles's claim to universal sovereignty angered the Ottoman court. For was not Sultan Suleyman, ruler of a growing empire that now incorporated Mamluk domains and victor over Christian forces at Rhodes, Belgrade, and Mohács in Hungary, the true Caesarian world emperor? Grand Vizier Ibrahim Pasha, who had already supervised the expansion of the New Palace following Suleyman's military triumphs, responded to Charles's pretensions by commissioning Venetian goldsmiths and jewelers to produce a magnificent helmet-crown for the sultan. It was designed as one of the ceremonial accessories that Suleyman used on his triumphal march to Vienna in 1532, which included various spectacular parades like the one in Belgrade, where the streets were decorated with classical triumphal arches "in the manner of ancient Roman triumphs." Even though the armies of Suleyman and Charles never met at Vienna, Habsburg ambassadors witnessed the sultan's parades and saw his Venetian-made helmet-crown. Indeed, the helmet-crown was mainly intended for a European audience; it bore little resemblance to the turbans that Ottoman sultans normally wore.

Suleyman's helmet-crown was designed to resemble a combination of the imperial crown worn by Charles at Bologna, Habsburg ceremonial helmets, and the papal tiara with its three tiers of crowns. Yet by adding a fourth tier to his helmet-crown Suleyman was proclaiming his superiority to both the pope and the emperor whose lands he intended to incorporate into his world empire. The plume on the helmet-crown made it reminiscent of crowns worn by Near Eastern kings and by Alexander the Great, at least as he was portrayed in Ottoman paintings. Like Mehmed II, Suleyman was inspired by histories of Alexander, the conqueror who had united East and West.

In the West, far from the Austro-Hungarian frontier, Charles made his own statement in stone. In 1533 he ordered the construction of a new imperial palace within the precinct of the Alhambra in Granada. (It was largely completed by 1550.) By building a new residence that dominated the old palace of the vanquished Muslim enemy, Charles sent a signal to Spaniards and other Europeans that he would defend the territory his grandparents had recovered from Islam and then lead a united Christendom in a Crusade against the current Muslim foe, the Ottomans. In signifying the institution of a new regime, political and religious, Charles's palace paralleled Mehmed II's New Palace in Constantinople. Granada, however, could not be the center of Charles's empire, since he was very much an itinerant monarch. The symbolism of Charles's palace was nonetheless potent and pointed, conveying the message that the emperor would equal and even surpass the achievements of the Roman emperors. The palace's classical style, particularly its Doric columns, immediately linked it to the Roman Empire.

But there was more. Engraved at the base of the palace's columns was Charles's device, which included a Roman imperial eagle with its talons spread over the top of a globe of the world, and two columns that denoted the pillars of Hercules at the Straits of Gibraltar, which once marked the end of the known world. The banner above the eagle was inscribed with Charles's motto, in French, "Plus Oultre" (Further Beyond) , which signified that Charles's empire extended beyond the pillars to America, where the

FIGURE 10.10 Anonymous Venetian artist, *Sultan Suleyman the Magnificent Wearing the Jewel-Studded Helmet*. The Metropolitan Museum of Art, New York, Harris Brisbane Dick Fund, 1942, 42.411, Open Access CC0.

Ottomans could not challenge him. Charles could look westward and Suleyman eastward, but both wanted to be Caesar of the Sea in the Middle.

Discussion Questions

1. Why was the title Caesar so symbolically powerful, and what different meanings did it have for Christian and Muslim rulers?

2. Why were European architects and artists, especially Italian ones such as Gentile Bellini, so willing to work for the Ottoman sultan?

FIGURE 10.11 South façade of Palace of Charles V, Granada. Photo by Alberto-g-rovi provided by Wikimedia Commons under the CC-BY-3.0 License.

FIGURE 10.12 Charles V's device on columnar base of the south façade. Photo by Jebulon provided by Wikimedia Commons under the CC0–1.0 | CC-SA License.

3. Why were Ottoman sultans such as Mehmed II and Suleyman I concerned to reach a European audience and get the favorable opinion of Europeans?

Further Reading

Dandelet, Thomas James. *The Renaissance of Empire in Early Modern Europe.* Cambridge: Cambridge University Press, 2014.

Kafescioglu, Çigdem. *Constantinopolis/Istanbul: Cultural Encounter, Imperial Vision, and the Construction of the Ottoman Capital.* University Park: Pennsylvania State University Press, 2009.

Necipoglu, Gulru. "Suleyman the Magnificent and the Representation of Power in the Context of Ottoman-Hapsburg-Papal Rivalry." *Art Bulletin* 71 (1989): 401–27.

Rosenthal, Earl E. *The Palace of Charles V in Granada.* Princeton: Princeton University Press, 1985.

Notes

1. Gulru Necipoglu, *Architecture, Ceremonial, and Power: The Topkapi Palace in the Fifteenth and Sixteenth Centuries* (Cambridge, MA: MIT Press, 1991), 34.
2. Dandelet, 83.
3. Dandelet, 97.

between Sunnis and Shi'is in the Middle East and Catholics and Protestants in Europe. Ottoman and Habsburg monarchs not only engaged in external warfare against each other and against their respective Shi'i and Protestant enemies; they also endeavored to eliminate heretics in the lands they ruled lest the souls of their orthodox subjects be endangered and their righteous government subverted. Their incessant struggles against unbelievers and heretics at home and abroad fueled each other, sharpening the Sunni and Catholic character of their empires. Policy-makers in both empires were well aware of the economic benefits that might result from attacking religious adversaries, such as access to trade routes or the produce of fertile provinces. Still, they believed that wars for the faith brought special rewards and they were willing to deplete their treasuries pursuing them.

The rulers of weaker Sunni and Catholic Mediterranean states usually did not have the luxury of conducting foreign policies guided largely by religious concerns. Indeed, they sometimes viewed the great empire spearheading the struggles for their own faith as their worst enemy. Thus the Catholic Valois of France allied with Ottomans or Protestants against the Habsburgs, and the Sunni Sa'dids of Morocco with England or Spain against the Ottomans. Even the popes were ambivalent about the Spanish Habsburgs, since these Catholic champions also dominated Italy. The Catholic Holy League whose ships vanquished the Ottoman fleet at Lepanto in 1571 did not last long, partly because one of its members, Venice, quickly made its own peace with the sultan. By 1650 domestic problems and commitments on other fronts had compelled the Ottoman and Habsburg empires to disengage in the Mediterranean and to accept the political and religious status quo.

MAP 10.3 The Mediterranean, ca. 1550.

The Ottomans' Sunni Empire

In the sixteenth century the Ottoman empire assumed a markedly orthodox Sunni character, the result of its acquisition of Mamluk and Maghribi territories whose populations were almost entirely Sunni, and its wars against the Shi'i Safavids, in opposition to whom the Ottomans increasingly defined themselves. Ottoman authorities no longer tolerated the activities of heterodox Sufi dervishes, who in their realm's early years had helped make it so welcoming to new followers of diverse backgrounds.

Under Shah Isma'il, the Safavids had by 1510 constructed a powerful empire encompassing Iran, parts of Iraq, and northern Syria. In Anatolia they had attracted fervent Shi'i supporters, the *kızılbaş* ("redheads," for their headgear), who rebelled against Ottoman rule in 1511–1513. Sultan Selim I (1512–1520) harshly quashed the rebellion and then in 1514, at Chaldiran, defeated "the heretic" Shah Isma'il in battle—the first of many Ottoman-Safavid wars over the next 150 years. The Ottoman chief mufti, or main religious-judicial official, of Sultan Suleyman I, the Magnificent (1520–1566), would declare in 1548 that fighting the Safavids "is more important than fighting the infidels [Christians]."[1] By then Suleyman had already taken Baghdad (1534) from them and

other areas of Iraq with large Shi'i populations, thus potentially compounding the internal danger that Safavid sympathizers in Anatolia continued to present.

Selim invaded Mamluk Syria in 1516 in order to forestall a Safavid-Mamluk alliance, though economic interests likely also figured into his calculations. Artillery, which had been crucial for his victory at Chaldiran, helped Selim at Marj Dabiq to beat the redoubtable Mamluks, who had been slow to adopt gunpowder weapons. In 1517 he conquered Egypt, before moving farther west to counter Spanish expansion into Zayyanid and Hafsid territories. Owing to the initiative of Khayr al-Din Barbarossa, a corsair of Greek-Muslim background, Algiers fell under Ottoman suzerainty in 1525 and became the main base for the Ottoman battle with Spain for the central Mediterranean.

Selim's conquest of Mamluk domains made the Ottoman sultans the guardians of the holy cities of Mecca, Medina, and Jerusalem; his successors' continuing leadership of holy wars against Christians and Shi'i Safavids confirmed their authority in the Sunni world. Sulyeman the Magnificent, under whom Ottoman power peaked, claimed the title of caliph. Aware, however, that the Ottoman sultans could not claim descent from the family of the Prophet—a discrepancy on which the sharifian Sa'dids capitalized—court propagandists insisted that they were nonetheless caliphs by divine right. Arab-Muslim subjects who would not acknowledge the Ottomans' caliphal status gave them their loyalty as long as they defended Sunni Islam and upheld Islamic law.

By Suleyman's reign the Ottomans had made great progress in their understanding of Islamic law, thanks in part to their acquisition of great centers of learning, such as Cairo and Damascus. The empire had a system of colleges for the study of *shari'a*, especially the Hanafi school, which trained future teachers, scribes, and judges. Judges played a key role in Ottoman society and government, administering *shari'a* and executing the sultan's orders at the local level. At the top of the legal system were the chief mufti, the sultan's legal adviser, and the "military judges" of the Imperial Council, who handled appeals. While *shari'a* regulated most aspects of daily life, the Ottomans supplemented it with secular laws (*kanun*) in areas such as criminal law and taxation. The flexibility and efficacy of the legal system were increased through the compilation of provincial law codes that incorporated local customs.

Sultans ruled the empire through their household in the capital, Istanbul. In theory, all decisions were theirs;

in practice, they received advice from the Imperial Council, which dealt mainly with political and military affairs. The council was headed by the grand vizier (*wazir*) and included ministers (*viziers*), treasurers, judges, and the chancellor. Prior to 1453 most viziers were Turkic Muslims; subsequently many were Muslims of noble Christian descent, an effective means of accommodating Byzantine and Balkan elites to Ottoman rule. After 1521, however, most were peasant *devşirme* recruits, slaves entirely dependent on the sultan and symbols of his absolute power.

The provinces of the empire—thirty-two in 1609—were administered by governors responsible for commanding the provincial military, maintaining order, and collecting taxes, which financed, among other things, the Ottoman army and navy. These appointees of the sultan had short terms of office, lest they develop local ties and interests. Since Ottoman Turkish was the language of government, there was a linguistic divide between the governors of Arab provinces, who usually did not speak Arabic, and the local populace. Local elite families, often of Mamluk origin in Egypt, and Arabic-speaking *'ulama'* mediated between the government and provincial society. Although Ottoman government cannot be described as a smoothly running machine—no premodern government was—its relative institutional uniformity made it more efficient at amassing taxes and other resources than its Habsburg counterpart.

The Spanish Habsburgs' Catholic Empire

Charles V (I of Spain, 1516–1556) inherited a huge, global empire—Castile and Aragon and their Italian, Maghribi, and American possessions from his maternal grandparents, Fernando and Isabel; Austria and the Netherlands from his paternal grandparents, Maximilian Habsburg and Mary of Burgundy; and then Germany in 1519, when the German electors chose him to succeed Maximilian as Holy Roman Emperor. This empire, however, was weaker than it appeared; it was a "composite monarchy" within which each constituent polity had its own institutions and laws. There was no administrative structure uniting the empire as a whole, just a common allegiance to Charles. Even this was questioned in Castile in 1520–1521 by rebelling Comuneros, urban folk who objected to the Flemish advisers and foreign commitments of the young, Netherlands-born emperor who could not speak Spanish.

The rebellion failed, but Charles learned Spanish and ruled increasingly through Castilian officials. Castile became the heart of his empire, and under his Spanish son Felipe II (1556–1598) Madrid became the imperial capital. The monarchs governed through an array of councils staffed by nobles and university-trained lawyers. The council of state, the most important, handled foreign affairs; others dealt with particular concerns, such as finance and Inquisition, or regions outside Castile, such as Aragon, Italy, and America.

Defending this vast inheritance required Charles to fight against the Ottomans and the French, who threatened it from the outside, and against Protestants, who were subverting it from within. Charles's wars were consequential in geopolitical terms, but when he struggled against Muslims and Protestants the Catholic cause weighed heavily on his mind. Anxiety over the spread of Lutheranism moved him to introduce an Inquisition in the Netherlands in 1522 and to demand severe punishment of heretics. In this respect he was like his Spanish grandparents who had established the Spanish Inquisition in 1478 for the purpose of eradicating Judaizing Conversos. During Charles's reign the Spanish Inquisition also prosecuted Moriscos, who clung to Islam, and Illuminists, mystics with alleged Protestant leanings. In Charles's empire non-Catholics were all potential enemies of the state.

Yet Charles's bitterest foes were the Catholic Valois kings of France, François I (1515–1547) and Henri II (1547–1559), who fought and schemed to prevent the encirclement of their realm by Habsburg territories. Though fundamentally secular, this conflict complicated Charles's relationship with the papacy and his efforts to stem the Protestant tide in Germany. Charles won the renewed contest with France over the strategic duchy of Milan, which had been sparked when François reoccupied it in 1515. In a decisive battle outside Pavia in 1525, the emperor's army defeated French forces and captured François. François, however, refused to fulfill the terms of the treaty to which he had agreed as a condition for his release and organized an alliance against Charles that included Pope Clement VII (1523–1534), Venice, and Florence. Vengeful and unpaid imperial troops responded in 1527 by sacking Rome, an act that horrified Christendom. News of Rome's calamities inspired republican opponents to overthrow the Medici regime in Florence. Charles and Pope Clement, however, reconciled in 1529, forcing François to acknowledge Charles's lordship over Milan, which the Sforzas then held from Charles as an imperial fief. The following year at Bologna the pope formally crowned Charles as Holy Roman Emperor and enjoined him "to take up . . . arms, against the infidel [Turks] and others who are against the Holy Mother Church."[2] Shortly thereafter Charles restored the Medicis in Florence as the dukes of Tuscany. With Genoa having already joined the imperial camp, all the Italian states, except Venice, were under the control or clients of the Spanish Habsburg empire.

Charles, however, enjoyed much less success in the German Holy Roman Empire, where support for the reformer Luther spread rapidly in the 1520s. The empire's fragmentation into many autonomous princedoms, duchies, and city-states limited the emperor's authority, inhibiting him from acting decisively against the princes who, for religious and political reasons, espoused the Lutheran cause. Yet Charles was sympathetic to the idea of church reform; moreover, he needed and got the military backing of Protestant princes to counter an Ottoman invasion of Austria in 1532. He finally resorted to force against the Protestants after attempting fruitlessly to reconcile them with the Catholic Church, which condemned Protestant teachings outright at the first meeting of the Council of Trent in 1545. He smashed Protestant armies in 1547 at Muhlberg. At this point, however, Henri II of France took his revenge on Charles by supporting the Lutheran princes, which was enough to turn the tide in the Protestants' favor in 1552–1553. Already on the defensive against the Ottomans in the Mediterranean, the demoralized emperor handed German affairs over to his brother Ferdinand. In 1555's Peace of Augsburg, Ferdinand achieved a settlement that allowed the ruler of each German state to determine whether it would be Catholic or Protestant. Charles abdicated in 1556 and retired to Castile, leaving all of his realms, except the Habsburgs' German and Austrian possessions, to his son Felipe .

Felipe II (1556–1598) was determined to preserve the territories bequeathed to him by his father and to combat the enemies of the Catholic faith. Like Charles, Felipe controlled the appointment of all important ecclesiastical officials in Spain, and he was an earnest promoter of church reform. Political tensions with the papacy did not stop him from championing its anti-Protestant agenda. Felipe thus inherited Charles's adversaries and a foreign policy in which political and religious interests were usually intertwined. He disposed of the troublesome French early with decisive military victories over Henri II in 1557–1558, which led to the peace of Cateau-Cambresis the next year. The French were afterward too embroiled in Catholic-Protestant civil wars to challenge Spain. Within Spain the Inquisition efficiently extinguished Protestant cells between 1559 and 1562. The problem of heresy, however, shifted to the Netherlands, where Dutch discontent with Spanish government combined in the mid-1560s with Protestant dissent, now in the form of Calvinism, to detonate a revolt that proved to be interminable and, like Felipe's Mediterranean wars against the Ottomans, tremendously expensive.

Acquiring the funds for so many wars was difficult for monarchs who had to contend with the institutional peculiarities of each of their realms. Castile, where royal authority was more absolute, carried by far the heaviest tax burden; Aragon, on account of effective parliamentary resistance, a much lighter one. The church in Spain and the Italian states rendered important contributions. But all of this was never enough, and Felipe declared bankruptcy four times so that the Crown could renegotiate its debts with its creditors. The principal creditors were Genoese financiers whom Felipe repaid with American silver that was transported from Seville through Barcelona to Genoa—a financial system linking the Atlantic to the Mediterranean that oiled the gears of the Habsburg war machine.

The War for the Mediterranean

On the accession of Suleyman I in 1520, the Ottomans dominated the eastern Mediterranean, and Spain under Charles V the west. Neither was satisfied with the status quo, if only because protecting their own subjects on land and sea required taking from the infidel strategic coastal towns or islands whose corsairs posed a persistent menace. The economic dividends from securing trade routes and seizing merchandise and captives from the enemy also drove aggression. Military success, moreover, enhanced imperial prestige, earning rulers the loyalty of their subjects, the cooperation of client states and allies, and the respect, if not fear, of their foes. Conscious of their image, both Suleyman and Charles styled themselves heirs of the ancient Roman emperors who, as contemporaries knew, had ruled over the entire Mediterranean.

During the 1520s, however, the Danube frontier was the main theater of imperial conflict. Suleyman conquered Belgrade in 1521; in 1526 he crushed Hungarian forces at Mohács, killing King Lajos, and seized Buda. The claim of Charles's brother Ferdinand to the empty Hungarian throne brought the Habsburgs into conflict with Suleyman, who attempted unsuccessfully to capture Habsburg Vienna in 1529. The Danube region remained volatile for decades to come.

The Mediterranean, however, was far from calm. In 1522–1523 the Ottomans took the island of Rhodes from the Knights of St. John, who had imperiled Muslims sailing from Istanbul to Egypt with their piracy. Under Charles's sponsorship, the Knights relocated in 1530 to Malta from where they continued to harry Muslim shipping. Charles's ally the Genoese admiral Andrea Doria attacked Ottoman possessions in Greece in 1532–1533.

Suleyman responded by placing the Ottoman fleet under the command of Khayr al-Din Barbarossa, whose corsairs had been raiding Spanish coasts from their base in Algiers. Barbarossa's objective was to establish control over the southern side of the crucial narrows between Tunis and Sicily, which would enable the Ottomans to move more easily from the eastern into the western Mediterranean. In 1534 he captured Tunis, the Hafsid capital. Determined to halt the Ottoman advance, Charles mounted a massive expedition in 1535 that forced Barbarossa out of Tunis and restored the Hafsid sultan, who became Charles's vassal.

Charles's victory persuaded Suleyman to accept a French alliance in 1536. Rumors of the allies' plans to attack Habsburg domains in Italy and the Ottomans' siege of Venetian Corfu brought about a counter-alliance uniting Charles, the papacy, and a reluctant Venice, which since 1503 had been negotiating trade agreements with the Ottomans. It was also the biggest loser in the war, for after Barbarossa's fleet defeated allied forces led by Doria off Preveza (Greece) in 1538, the Ottomans seized Venetian strongholds on the Dalmatian coast and put the city's commerce at risk. In 1540 Venice sued for peace. Charles, however, was intent on capturing Barbarossa's headquarters of Algiers, which would put an end to the corsairs' depredations and make Spain dominant in the Maghrib. For Charles, the expedition against Algiers in 1541 was a disaster.

Habsburg defeat encouraged more corsair raiding as the Ottomans renewed their alliance with France. In the winter of 1543–1544 Barbarossa anchored his fleet in the French port of Toulon, which threatened Spain's vital silver route between Barcelona and Genoa. Barbarossa died in 1546, but in 1551 the Ottomans took Tripoli from Spain, and in 1555, Bijaya. Spain was thus losing the network of North African strongholds that served to limit the attacks of Muslim corsairs on its own coasts. On top of Charles's failure in Germany, these Mediterranean setbacks persuaded him to abdicate in 1556.

As the Ottomans deepened their penetration of the Maghrib, they had come up against the ambitious Sa'dids, who had ejected the Portuguese from Agadir in 1541 and put an end to the Wattasid regime in Fez in 1549. Both powers could claim to be Muslim champions against Christian foes, but the Sa'did Muhammad al-Shaykh (1540–1557) was also a *sharif.* Their conflict over Tlemsen in 1550–1551 went in the Ottomans' favor, but when the Ottomans occupied Fez in 1554, Muhammad al-Shaykh quickly reconquered it and entered into an alliance with Spain. The Ottomans therefore engineered the assassination of Muhammad al-Shaykh in 1557. His successors moved the Sa'did capital to Marrakesh, farther from the Ottoman sphere of influence, and continued an informal alliance with Spain.

The peace of Cateau-Cambresis in 1559, which detached France from the Ottoman alliance, emboldened Felipe II to take the offensive in the Mediterranean. The results were mixed: a calamitous expedition to recapture Tripoli in 1560, and the successful defense of Spanish Oran against an Ottoman attack in 1563. Felipe also sent a relief force in 1565 to help the Knights of St. John on Malta withstand an Ottoman siege; hence the Knights remained an obstacle to the Ottomans' maritime progress in the central Mediterranean.

The death of Suleyman in 1566 while campaigning in Transylvania did not give Felipe much of a respite. Unrest in the Netherlands took a violent turn, requiring Felipe to dispatch an army there. In 1568 the Moriscos of Granada rebelled in reaction to the Spanish government's efforts to suppress all vestiges of their Islamic culture. The new Ottoman sultan Selim II (1566–1574) sent a small force in 1569 to assist the Moriscos, but it was not enough to save them from defeat in 1570. Taking advantage of Felipe's various distractions, the Ottoman governor of Algiers wrested Tunis from Spain's Hafsid vassals in 1569.

Like Felipe, Selim had commitments outside the Mediterranean, among them suppressing a revolt in Yemen, where the Ottomans had established themselves as part of their endeavor, since the 1530s, to contain Portuguese aggression in the Indian Ocean and Red Sea. Though they could not defeat the Portuguese, the Ottomans saw to it that eastern spices continued flowing through their domains to eastern Mediterranean markets.

In order to consolidate their domination of the eastern Mediterranean, in 1570–1571 the Ottomans conquered Cyprus, a valuable Venetian possession since 1489. Even if the Greek inhabitants of the island did not mind being relieved of their Catholic overlords, Venice was sufficiently antagonized to join the papacy and Spain in a Holy League. The League organized a huge fleet under the command of Don Juan of Austria, Philip II's illegitimate half brother, which met the Ottoman fleet off Lepanto, Greece, on October 7, 1571. It was a great Christian victory: much of the Ottoman fleet was destroyed with around 30,000 men lost, compared to 8,000 Christian dead.

The Aftermath of Lepanto

Despite the Ottomans' losses, the Battle of Lepanto did not significantly alter the balance of power in the Mediterranean. Instead of pressing its advantage, the Holy League dissolved. Venice made peace with the Ottomans in 1573 in order to protect its commerce in the East. Spain went on the offensive alone later the same year and seized Ottoman Tunis. In the meantime Selim had ordered the Ottoman fleet rebuilt, a remarkable and expensive display of imperial power and efficiency. This fleet took Tunis back from Spain in 1574 and restored the empire's prestige.

Ottoman policy-makers, however, realized that sending such naval expeditions from Istanbul to the central Mediterranean or beyond was too difficult. Murad III (1574–1595) therefore chose to pursue an ultimately successful war on land in the East against the Safavids in 1578–1590. At the same time, the rapid reversal in Tunis, the successes of Calvinist rebels in the Netherlands, and the necessity of declaring bankruptcy in 1576 convinced Felipe II of the impossibility of fighting wars on two fronts. In 1577 his ambassador in Istanbul put out peace feelers to Murad.

Developments in Morocco had been arousing the interest of both monarchs, though without causing a clash between them. Murad made the most of dissension within Morocco's ruling Sa'did family and backed 'Abd al-Malik (1576–1578) in overthrowing his nephew al-Mutawakkil (1574–1576), thereby placing an Ottoman client on the Moroccan throne. The deposed sultan sought aid from the crusading king of Portugal, Sebastian, who obliged him with an invasion of Morocco in 1578. In the Battle of Alcázar, both sultans and Sebastian were killed. Ahmad al-Mansur (1578–1603), the triumphant brother of 'Abd al-Malik, succeeded him. Ahmad solidified his authority by emphasizing his credentials as a *sharif* and holy warrior. He also wisely sent tribute money to Murad, who was content to have a Sa'did buffer-state between his Maghribi provinces and the Iberian Peninsula. Felipe was also content with the outcome of the Battle of Alcázar, since Sebastian's death positioned him, the son of a Portuguese princess, to win the inheritance of Portugal and its maritime empire in Brazil and Asia.

In 1580 Murad and Felipe agreed to a truce, which turned into a long-term disengagement from the contest for the Mediterranean. The Portuguese inheritance increased the Atlantic orientation of the Spanish empire, while logistical realities limited the Ottomans' western ambitions to maintaining their sway in the Maghrib through semiautonomous governors in Algiers, Tunis, and Tripoli. Neither Murad nor Felipe had the stomach to renew large-scale warfare in the Mediterranean. Both rulers had major military commitments on other fronts that would consume them and their successors for many years, leaving both empires wracked by internal problems.

On the Ottomans' western front, thirteen years of war with the Austrian Habsburgs ended in a stalemate and the Peace of Zsivtatorok in 1606, while in the East, intermittent war with the Safavids resulted in 1639 in a treaty that only reestablished imperial boundaries set nearly a century earlier. The Ottomans' invasion of Venetian Crete in 1645, seemingly another manifestation of their supremacy in the eastern Mediterranean, was actually only the start of a conquest that took twenty-five years to complete and revealed their waning naval power.

These wars greatly increased the recruitment of Janissaries and other infantry equipped with firearms. As a consequence of the monetary inflation caused by the influx of American silver into the eastern Mediterranean, the government paid these troops in debased coinage. Janissaries reacted by rioting several times from 1585 on. Also, the *timar* system was gradually abandoned, partly because of the diminishing role of cavalry in Ottoman armies. In order to more rapidly acquire funds to pay the Janissaries and for other needs, the government converted *timars* into tax-farms. The holders were not military men and often lacked administrative experience. This reduced Istanbul's authority in the provinces, where underpaid soldiers were turning to banditry or joining the retinues of rebellious local notables. Seventeenth-century sultans, finally, were not as effective as their forebears; an oligarchy of viziers wielded real power.

The truce with the Ottomans in 1580 freed Spanish monarchs to spend what would be another sixty-eight years trying to prevent Dutch Calvinists from establishing an independent state. The assistance that Protestant England was providing the Dutch rebels provoked Felipe II in 1588 to send the famous "Spanish Armada" to invade England. The costliness of this disastrous mission did not stop Felipe from launching two other armadas in 1596 and 1597 and sending more armies to the Netherlands. Religious and dynastic concerns also pushed Felipe III (1598–1621) to side with the Catholic Holy Roman Emperor Ferdinand Habsburg in the Thirty Years' War (1618–1648) between Catholics and Protestants that engulfed central Europe. The difficulty of paying for this perpetual warfare moved the chief minister of Felipe IV (1621–1665), the Count-Duke of Olivares, to devise the "Union of Arms," an ambitious plan for more justly allocating fiscal responsibilities among the various realms of the empire while relieving overburdened Castilian taxpayers. Imperial subjects violently rejected the

MAP 10.4 The Mediterranean, ca. 1650.

plan. The Catalans revolted from 1640 to 1652, putting themselves under French rule for some years. The Portuguese also rebelled in 1640, partly in frustration over Spain's inability to protect their Brazilian and Asian possessions from the Dutch, who were creating their own maritime empire. Portugal would finally achieve independence in 1668 with English and French aid. Rebellions broke out in Naples and Sicily as well in 1647–1648. With too many enemies and too few resources, a crippled Spanish monarchy finally recognized Dutch independence in 1648, when the Thirty Years' War, the last of the great bloodlettings between Catholics and Protestant in Europe, drew to a close. SEE SOURCEBOOK 10:5.

With the withdrawal of the Ottoman and Spanish empires from their decades-long struggle, the nature of Mediterranean warfare changed. Large-scale naval campaigns became a thing of the past, and there was little territorial conquest. Corsairs became more active and the seas more dangerous. Motivated by some combination of religious animosity and greed, corsairs preyed on the commerce and coastlines of religious enemies and sometimes of coreligionists. No longer the instruments of Ottoman sultans, corsair captains operating out of Algiers and other Maghribi ports—the so-called Barbary corsairs—commanded crews consisting of Turks, Maghribi Muslims, expelled Moriscos, and renegade Christians, increasingly of English and Dutch origin. Spain and Italy were their principal but not only targets. From Malta, the Knights of St. John and independent corsair captains harried Muslims traveling and trading in the eastern and central Mediterranean as well as Greek Christian merchants, especially if they were subjects of the Ottoman sultan. The Uskoks of Senj, an ethnically diverse band of Christian pirates who sailed out of a base on the northern Dalmatian coast, attacked Turkish ships in the Adriatic but they also victimized Venetians because they were so often at peace with the Ottomans.

During the seventeenth century northern Europeans—the English, the Dutch, and, to a lesser degree, the French—played an increasingly influential role in Mediterranean commerce and politics. As their victories over Spanish and Portuguese fleets in the Atlantic and Indian Oceans demonstrated, England and the Netherlands were in aggressive pursuit of maritime empire. With their faster, more maneuverable, and better-armed ships, northern Europeans came to dominate long-distance trade while the Venetians and the Genoese, long the major players in the commerce linking the wider Mediterranean world to Europe, invested more in industry and finance. Keen to access eastern goods, the northerners negotiated commercial agreements with the Ottomans, who wanted to obtain northern products such as gunpowder, tin, and ships. English and Dutch merchants, each organized in their own Levant Company, were particularly effective operators in the eastern Mediterranean. They and the French joined and then surpassed Venetian merchants trading in Muslim ports.

Yet political and religious concerns often guided the actions of northern Europeans in the Mediterranean as much as the desire for profit. For instance, Elizabeth I, the Protestant queen of England, considered allying with the Ottoman sultan against their great enemy, Felipe II of Spain. Commercial and political interests were similarly intertwined in English dealings with Morocco. The English Barbary Company purchased products such as sugar and saltpeter, an ingredient of gunpowder, from Moroccans and sold armaments to them that could be employed against the Spanish and Portuguese. Motivated by their common fear of Felipe II, Elizabeth and the Sa'did sultan Ahmad al-Mansur negotiated an anti-Spanish pact in 1589, which Felipe subsequently managed to undo. It was not coincidental that growing numbers of English and Dutch renegades joined the Barbary corsairs when Catholic Spaniards were among their main victims. Aiming to uphold Spain's reputation as a Catholic power, Felipe III's response was an aggressive, anti-Islamic policy that involved the expulsion of the Moriscos and the occupation of Larache in Morocco in 1610. Growing instability in Morocco following the death of Ahmad al-Mansur in 1603 facilitated this action. But Spain achieved little else in Morocco, nor did the Ottomans in the eastern Mediterranean, except for finally conquering Venetian Crete with the acquiescence of northern European powers who hoped to profit from Ottoman possession of it.

By 1650 the great struggle for the Mediterranean between the Ottoman and Spanish empires was over. The massive resources at their disposal, acquired through conquest or inheritance, had allowed them to pursue wars on many fronts in defense of both faith and empire, goals that went hand in hand. But by 1650 these wars had left both empires financially and militarily depleted, their sheer fatigue an indication of how much the cause of their respective faiths had meant to them. Ottoman and Spanish policy-makers began asking how much treasure could be spent and how much blood shed for this cause. From their empires' exhaustion came enlightenment and their acceptance of the division of the Mediterranean into its Muslim and Christian parts. And the northern European states that had come to surpass the Ottoman and Spanish empires commercially and militarily did not focus on stripping them of their Mediterranean possessions. The Mediterranean was no longer the center of the universe. There were other worlds to conquer.

Notes

1. Colin Imber, *The Ottoman Empire, 1300–1650: The Structure of Power* (Houndmills, Eng.: Palgrave Macmillan, 2002), 121.
2. Dandelet, 96.

CHAPTER ELEVEN

Minorities and Diasporas

In the spring of 1553, the party of the affluent Portuguese Jewish widow Doña Gracia Mendes (ca. 1510–1569) entered Istanbul to the enthusiastic reception of local Jews and with the assent of the Ottoman authorities, who were keenly interested in her commercial connections. Gracia and her late husband Francisco Mendes (d. 1536) had come from prominent families of Portuguese Conversos (baptized Jews and their descendants, also called New Christians), who were descended from Jews expelled from Spain in 1492. The Mendes family's commercial banking business had profited greatly from Portugal's expansion of its trading empire to the Indian Ocean and had established a branch in Antwerp (in modern Belgium), a major commercial center and Habsburg possession. Because of their Jewish leanings and wealth, Gracia and her relatives became prime targets of Catholic inquisitors whose investigations pressured them to move in 1536 from Lisbon to Antwerp, and next, in 1544, to Italy, first to Venice and then, in 1550, to Ferrara, where the liberal duke Ercole II d'Este (1534–1559) permitted the New Christian family to practice Judaism openly. Nevertheless, the Ottoman empire, widely known among European Jews and Conversos as a safe haven, was Gracia's intended final destination. All the while Gracia had been employing the Mendes fortune to assist Conversos fleeing Europe, such that the Portuguese Jewish writer Samuel Usque described her as "the heart in the body of our people." Once in Istanbul, Gracia supported synagogues, Talmudic academies, and hospitals with her philanthropy while managing a commercial network that extended through the Balkans to Italy and farther west. Her nephew João Migues soon joined her in Istanbul, converting to Judaism and taking the name Joseph Nasi. With his commercial clout and knowledge of European politics furnished by his business agents, Joseph became a key adviser of Sultan Selim II (1566–1574). Gracia and Joseph made their influence at the Ottoman court felt as early as 1556, when Pope Paul IV (1555–1559) ordered the burning of twenty-four Conversos for practicing Judaism in Ancona, the papal port on the Adriatic. Not only did they persuade Sultan Suleyman the Magnificent to send a letter of protest to the pope, they also organized an ultimately unsuccessful boycott of Ancona by Jewish merchants. With the sultan's permission, the pair later sponsored the building of a Jewish settlement on the ancient ruins of Tiberias in Palestine, the concrete expression of the Jewish identity of individuals born and baptized as Catholics across the Mediterranean in Portugal.

Though their careers were unusually stellar, Gracia and Joseph followed a path toward the east and the south taken by many Jews and Conversos during the period covered in this chapter. This new phase in the history of the Jewish diaspora began in the later fourteenth century with the migration of persecuted Jews from Germany and southern France to Italy, to Poland and Lithuania, which by the late sixteenth century would become a major center for European Jewry, and to Ottoman domains. The slow trickle of migrants became a flood in 1492, when all Jews were expelled from Spain; thousands of Spanish and Portuguese Conversos hounded by their countries' Inquisitions also took flight. The ethnic cleansing of Spain continued in 1609–1614 with the expulsion of its entire Morisco population, the descendants of Muslims coercively baptized between 1499 and 1526. Muslim rulers in the Maghrib as well as Ottoman sultans admitted many of these Iberian exiles of Jewish and Muslim background, hoping that the immigrants would benefit their economies. Indeed, economic pragmatism increasingly shaped the policies of some Mediterranean states toward religious minorities. Hence the Ottomans tended to treat their Christian and Jewish subjects more benignly than had the Mamluks. Even in Italy, despite the papacy's harshening Jewish policies, the economic concerns of city-states such as Venice enabled Jewish communities to take root and survive, if not thrive. Still, there was a marked contrast between Mediterranean Muslim states expanding and usually protecting their minority populations, in keeping with the tradition of *dhimma*, and Catholic states, anxious about "heresies" of all sorts, forcibly converting, expelling, or isolating minority communities in ghettos. The religious refugees who were mostly the victims of Catholic state policies had a profound impact on the societies and cultures of the coreligionists among whom they settled. From the tragedy of exile came regeneration and creativity.

FIGURE 11.1 Bronze medal portrait of Doña Gracia Mendes, nineteenth-century recast of sixteenth-century original. © RMN-Grand Palais / Art Resource, NY.

Toward Religious Uniformity in the Catholic Mediterranean

The deteriorating position of religious minorities in the Iberian Peninsula and Italy, though it might be viewed as indicative of a long-term pattern of Western Christian intolerance of non-Christians, is best explained as resulting specifically from the efforts of lay and ecclesiastical authorities to combat new threats to the Catholic Church coming from baptized Christians with "heretical" beliefs and practices—Judaizing Conversos, Islamizing Moriscos, and Protestants. In Spain, the forced conversions of Jews in 1391 and of Muslims in the decades following the conquest of Granada in 1492 created an unprecedented socioreligious crisis of masses of New Christians clinging to their Jewish and Islamic ways and thus dangerously blurring the once-clear boundaries separating the three faiths. The monarchy responded to the potential corruption of the Catholic faith of its subjects by Judaizers and Islamizers with inquisition and expulsion, measures adopted in neighboring Portugal and in some parts of Italy. Italy's political fragmentation, however, impeded the formulation of one consistent "Italian" policy toward native Jews and northern European and Iberian Jewish and Converso immigrants. The one more unifying voice came from the papacy in Rome, and its tone was increasingly harsh. From the mid-sixteenth century, popes spearheading the "Counter-Reformation" took measures to prevent any harmful or heretical influences from infecting the Catholic laity, which meant prosecuting alleged Protestants and Judaizers but also isolating Jewish communities in "ghettos," partly in the hope of encouraging the Jews' conversion and demonstrating the truth of a triumphant Catholic faith. Fortunately for the Jews, not all urban governments subscribed to the papacy's more severe interpretation of Saint Augustine's injunction to put the Jews in a position of servitude to Christians.

Jewish Conversion, Inquisition, and Expulsion in the Iberian Peninsula

The Castilian civil war of 1359–1369 between Pedro I the Cruel, and the usurper Enrique de Trastámara, during which Enrique's partisans propagandized against Pedro for his reliance on Jewish advisers and attacked Jewish communities, initiated a pattern of virulent anti-Judaism that had disastrous consequences for Iberian Jewry. The failure of Enrique II (1368–1379) and his son Juan I (1369–1390) to fulfill their promises to remove Jews from government made resentful Castilian Christians suffering from the economic effects of plague susceptible to the anti-Jewish preaching of the

On March 19, 1588, laborers involved in demolishing the minaret of Granada's main mosque to allow for more work on the new cathedral found a lead box containing relics and a parchment. Among the relics were part of a handkerchief that the Virgin Mary had used to dry her tears during Christ's crucifixion and a bone of Saint Stephen. Written on the parchment were a Latin text identifying the relics, which had been given in Athens to Saint Cecilio, the first bishop of Granada, in the mid-first century CE; a Castilian Spanish translation by Cecilio of a previously unknown work of Saint John the Evangelist that prophesied the coming of the Prophet Muhammad and Martin Luther, and the end-time; and an Arabic text written and signed by Cecilio himself in which he described his journey from Jerusalem to Athens and how he had translated Saint John's prophecy "into the common Spanish tongue" and "made on it a full commentary . . . in Arabic—both being languages used in the land of Spain . . . —so that Arabic Christians would not be without it."[1] The archbishop of Granada, Juan Méndez de Salvatierra, entrusted the translation of the Arabic texts to two learned Morisco physicians, Alonso del Castillo and Miguel de Luna. The contents of the parchment were stunning, for they provided historical evidence of a first-century bishop of Granada—Cecilio—and showed that many of Granada's earliest Christians were Arabic speakers.

In February 1595, treasure hunters discovered on a hill Granadans soon called Sacromonte (Holy Mountain) the first of nineteen "lead books" that would be found over the next five years. The books' sheets were covered with an unusual Arabic script accompanied by six-pointed stars. Human remains were also uncovered near the books. The new archbishop, Pedro de Castro, appointed a team, which included the Moriscos Castillo and Luna, to translate the lead books. Startling new details of the early Christian history of Granada and Spain emerged. Cecilio, the future bishop, and his brother Tesifón were Arabs whom Jesus himself had converted to Christianity in the East. One lead book included the assertion that "the Arabs are among the most excellent of peoples, and their language is among the most excellent of languages." The brothers had then accompanied Saint James ("Santiago") on his first mission to Spain and were with him when he performed the first Mass in Europe, on Sacromonte. Later, in 56 CE, while Cecilio was serving as Granada's bishop, Roman authorities executed him, Tesifón, and ten other martyrs on Sacromonte.

The discovery of the lead books and the remains of early Christian martyrs generated great excitement in Granada. People flocked to Sacromonte and miraculous cures occurred there. Archbishop Castro enthusiastically and sincerely affirmed the authenticity of the lead books

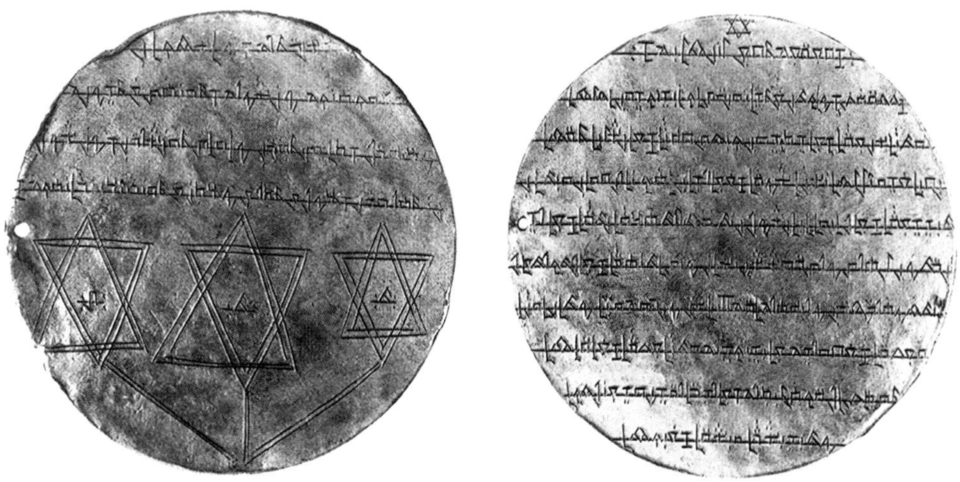

FIGURE 11.2 Sheets from the lead books of Granada. © Historical Views / agefotostock.

and the relics. Unfortunately, they were all part of an elaborate hoax, though it was not until 1682 that Pope Innocent XI finally condemned the contents of the lead books and the parchment from the minaret.

Scholars have concluded, on the basis of painstaking philological analysis, that the translator Miguel de Luna (d. 1615) was almost certainly the forger of both the parchment and the lead books. Born in Granada in 1550 into a Morisco family of *hidalgo* (lower noble) status, Luna learned Arabic as a child and earned a medical degree from the University of Granada. He married an Old Christian woman and was well integrated into Granadan Christian society. In 1571 Luna was one of the 3,000–4,000 Moriscos remaining in the city of Granada from a population of more than 15,000 Moriscos who had been recorded along with 30,000–35,000 Old Christian immigrants in a census of 1561. The intervening decade had seen the enactment of harsh royal legislation in 1566–1567 prohibiting the Moriscos' use of Arabic, traditional dress, music, and baths, ownership of slaves, and bearing of arms; the ensuing Morisco rebellion throughout the kingdom of Granada in 1568–1570; and the expulsion and dispersion throughout northern Castile of most Granadan Moriscos, after royal armies subdued the rebels.

Luna was one of the highly acculturated Moriscos permitted to stay in the city after the mass deportations, among whom were noble families descended from the old Nasrid aristocracy. These Morisco nobles led a life similar to that of the Old Christian nobles with whom they sometimes intermarried. Their public religious observances were scrupulously Catholic, even if they still clung to some Islamic beliefs. Some noble Moriscos held office in municipal government and could boast of relatives who had honorably served Charles V in suppressing the Comunero rebellion and in his North African wars. Some had openly sided with the monarchy during the Morisco rebellion. Yet most Morisco noble families had since 1492 maintained their connections with the wider Morisco community, often acting as intermediaries between their own people and the royal authorities. Occupying such an ambiguous position in Granadan society became increasingly difficult in the years following the rebellion, as steps were taken to restrict the privileges of Morisco nobles, and more institutions adopted exclusionary "purity of blood" laws that discriminated against Conversos and Moriscos regardless of their religious beliefs. In this environment it is unsurprising that an aristocratic Morisco family—the Granada Venegas—produced a false genealogy that traced the family's origins back to Spain's Visigothic kings, while Luna wrote the fictitious *True History of King Rodrigo*, which praised the Muslim conquerors of the Iberian Peninsula for saving it from the corrupt Visigoths and urged current rulers to evaluate their subjects on the basis of their merits, not their ancestors' faith.

Precisely what Luna hoped to achieve with forgeries that so many Old Christians and Moriscos regarded as genuine is difficult to say. The parchment and lead books promoted the acceptance of Moriscos by Spanish society by showing that Arabic speakers could be devout Christians and that there was no essential connection between the Arabic language and the Islamic faith. After all, had not Granada's first bishop been an Arab and members of its first Christian community Arabic speakers? The implication was that the Moriscos were the descendants of these early Christians and therefore had much deeper roots in Granada than Old Christians, who had only settled there after 1492. Moriscos surely should not be denied access to Spanish institutions because of their blood and social customs.

Luna's amazing texts at the same time presented a syncretic version of Christianity that Moriscos, particularly those adhering to Islam, would have found easier to accept. The lead books referred to Jesus as the "Spirit of God," but never as "God" or the "Son of God." Yet Luna may well have meant his lead books to be a polemic against Christianity. An anonymous Morisco witness testifying in the Inquisition trial of a Morisco merchant described Luna telling a group of Moriscos in Toledo "how, on the lead sheets that have been found on the Sacromonte in Granada, it is written in the hand of Jesus Christ himself that he was neither God nor the son of God, and that God has no son." Luna went on to say that "on the Day of Judgment, the poor deceived Christians" will be "damned" because the church distorted the true Revelation with its Latin and councils.[2]

Granada's Old Christians, however, interpreted the forgeries in ways that Luna had not anticipated. The discovery of new relics and saints deepened their Catholic devotion and identity, and their archbishop was thrilled by the evidence that he was the successor of Saint Cecilio, the convert of Jesus and companion of Saint James. With "historical" evidence of the existence of a Christian community in Granada as early as the first century, they could more easily regard the centuries of Muslim rule and the city's Islamic architecture as historical aberrations. Few of the Old Christians would protest the final expulsion of all Moriscos from Spain within fifteen years of the discovery of the first lead book.

Discussion Questions

1. Why were so many Old Christians and Moriscos so willing to believe in the authenticity of the minaret parchment and the lead books?

2. Would Miguel de Luna's forgeries have persuaded many Old Christians that Moriscos who used Arabic were not necessarily believers in Islam?

3. Why was it so difficult for Morisco nobles to tread on the fine line between fealty to the monarchy and loyalty to their people and the Islamic faith many of them harbored?

4. Did the seemingly syncretic theology suggested by Luna in the lead books offer a path to effective Morisco-Old Christian reconciliation?

Further Reading

Coleman, David. *Creating Christian Granada: Society and Religious Culture in an Old-World Frontier City, 1492–1600*. Ithaca: Cornell University Press, 2003.

García-Arenal, Mercedes, and Fernando Rodríguez Mediano. *The Orient in Spain: Converted Muslims, the Forged Lead Books of Granada, and the Rise of Orientalism*. Trans. Consuelo López-Morillas. Leiden: Brill, 2013.

Wiegers, Gerard. "The Granada Lead Books Translator Miguel De Luna as a Model for Both the Toledan Morisco Translator and the Arab Historian Cidi Hamete Benengeli in Cervantes' *Don Quixote*." In *The Conversos and Moriscos in Late Medieval Spain and Beyond*, vol. 3, *Displaced Persons*, ed. Kevin Ingram, 150–163. Leiden: Brill, 2016.

Notes

1. García-Arenal and Rodríguez Mediano, 16.
2. García-Arenal and Rodríguez Mediano, 187–88.

archdeacon Ferrán Martínez. Martínez blamed Jews for being the source of their difficulties, and finally in June 1391, when the child Enrique III (1379–1406) was on the throne, incited Christian mob violence against the Jews of Seville. The violence spread rapidly throughout Castile and much of the Crown of Aragon, where Christians were inspired by rumors of happenings in the neighboring kingdom. Almost everywhere Christians murdered numerous Jews, but they compelled many more to seek baptism with the threat of death. With the aim of achieving the conversion of all Spanish Jews, the charismatic Dominican friar Vicent Ferrer (1350–1419) first traveled around preaching to traumatized Jewish audiences while fomenting more Christian aggression against them with his inflammatory sermons. He then inspired the kings of Castile and Aragon in 1412 and 1415, respectively, to pass tough anti-Jewish legislation, and Pope Benedict XIII (1394–1423) to organize a formal "disputation" at Tortosa (Catalonia) in 1413–1414, in which Aragonese rabbis were subjected for two years to harangues about Christian "truth" by one of Ferrer's converts, Jerónimo de Santa Fé. Many more demoralized Jews converted. By 1416 not much more than a third of Spain's pre-1391 Jewish population remained.

After this tumultuous quarter century, the rulers of Castile and Aragon returned to more traditional, protective Jewish policies, which helped many, now smaller, Jewish communities to recover and their economic and social relations with local Christians to stabilize. There were also instances of intellectual collaboration, such as Rabbi Moses Arragel's translation of the Old Testament from Hebrew into Spanish at the request of a Castilian noble; this "Alba Bible" was accompanied by a commentary written in 1422–1433 by the rabbi with the assistance of two friars.

The Jews, however, could not remain unaffected by the grave religious and social controversies involving their baptized brethren, the Conversos, who numbered in the tens of thousands. Despite the church's position that baptism, even when coerced, was indelible and that any New Christians who returned to their former faith were therefore heretics, most of the converts of 1391 continued to practice Judaism in some way. The number of Judaizers diminished in succeeding generations as a result of the Conversos' gradual assimilation, but not sufficiently to silence the clergy who worried that New Christians were infecting Spanish Catholic society with their Judaism from the inside. This supposed religious threat was compounded by the social and political success of many

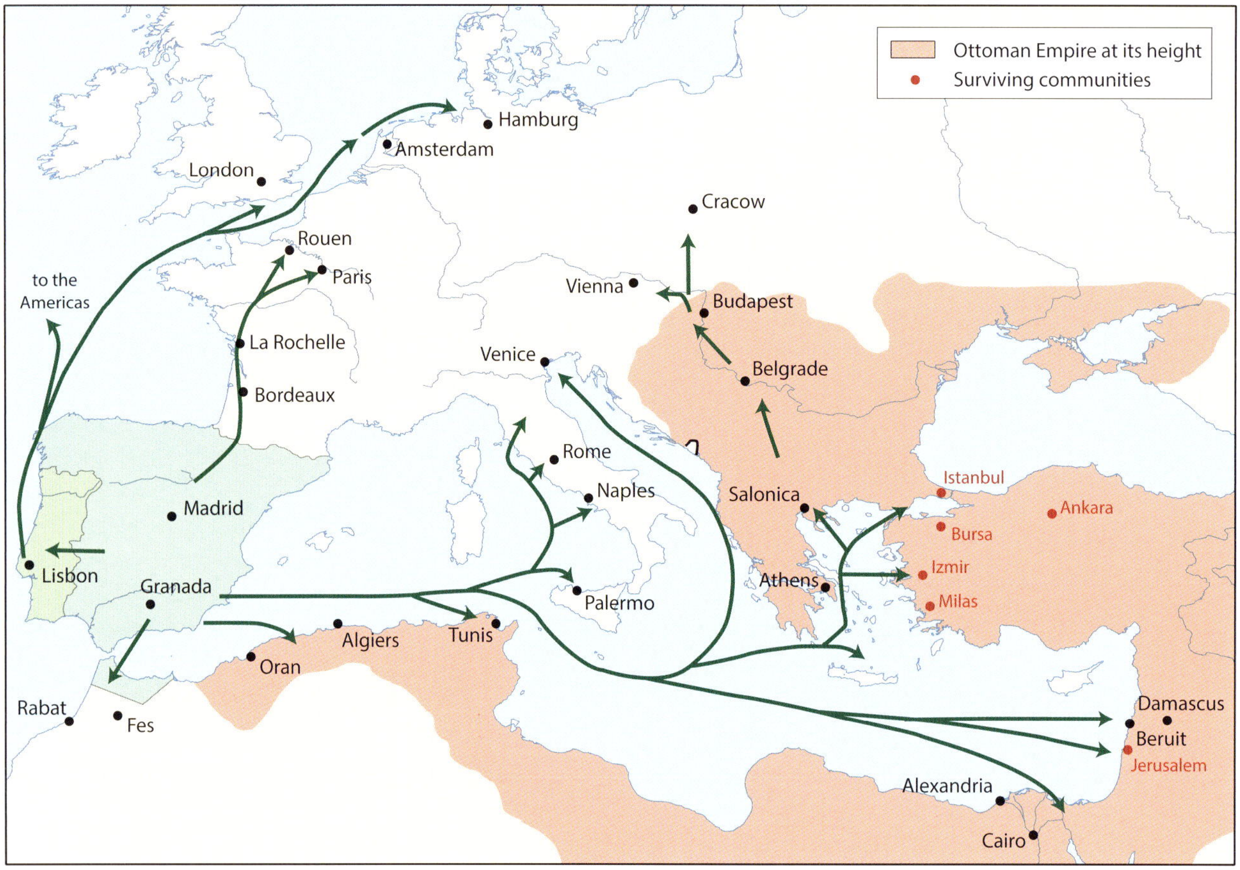

MAP 11.1 Map of Sephardi Migration. Original source unknown.

Conversos who by the mid-fifteenth century had attained important positions in municipal and royal government and even in the church. In Castile, for example, Pablo de Santa María, formerly the rabbi Solomon Halevi, became the bishop of Cartagena in 1403 and of Burgos in 1416. He was also the tutor and chancellor of King Juan II. His brother, Alvar García de Santa María, served as Juan's official chronicler, while his son, Alonso de Cartagena, succeeded him in the see of Burgos (1435–1456). Many Old Christians resented the progress of such Converso upstarts and harbored suspicions about their true religious allegiances. They clashed violently with Conversos in a number of Castilian cities and, from 1449 on, passed "purity of blood" laws to exclude anyone of Jewish lineage from governmental and church institutions as well as from universities.

As part of their effort to promote Catholic reform and quell social unrest, in the 1480s Fernando and Isabel established, with papal approval, a new Spanish Inquisition with tribunals in both Castile and Aragon. Its main task was to eradicate the Judaizers from among the Converso population. Remarkably efficient, the Inquisition prosecuted thousands of Conversos, forcing them to renounce their Jewish "heresies" in public *autos de fé* (acts of faith) and punishing them with varying degrees of severity. Conversos who refused to abandon Judaism or who later relapsed were burned—at least 2,000 by 1530. Through their thorough investigations, the inquisitors revealed that in many towns Jews had been helping Conversos to practice Judaism by offering them religious instruction, kosher food, and fellowship. In 1490–1491 the Inquisition tried and burned a group of Jews and Conversos on trumped-up charges of having profaned a Host and ritually murdered a Christian child whose body was never found, the so-called Holy Child of La Guardia. This widely publicized trial further mobilized popular opinion against the Jews. Advised by the inquisitors, the monarchs concluded that the Converso population would never completely and sincerely embrace the Catholic faith as long as it was exposed to the influence of unbaptized Jews. They therefore decreed on March 31, 1492, shortly after their conquest of Granada, that by July 31 all Jews must either leave Spain or convert. A few thousand converted, and some 100,000 went into exile.

Some exiles simply moved next door to the peninsular kingdoms of Portugal and Navarre, which had their own Jewish communities. João II of Portugal (1481–1495) permitted the Spanish refugees to remain temporarily but sent most, save for a few thousand, on their way. His successor Manuel I (1495–1521) was keen to curry favor with Spain's powerful monarchs, who did not want any professing Jews on the Iberian Peninsula who might communicate with Conversos. Thus, after marrying Fernando and Isabel's widowed daughter Isabel in 1496, he ordered the expulsion of Portugal's 30,000 Jews. Manuel, however, did not want to lose this enterprising population, and so persuaded most of them to convert by forbidding them to take their children with them into exile. The rulers of tiny Navarre had little choice but to command the expulsion of their 3,550 Jewish subjects in 1498; most converted.

The elimination of Jews, however, did not result in the elimination of Judaism. True, the Spanish Inquisition had by 1530 decimated the country's crypto-Jewish community, and most remaining Conversos assimilated into Catholic society. Some of the learned among them became humanist intellectuals and Catholic reformers, like Saint Teresa of Ávila (1515–1589), mystic and founder of the Order of Discalced Carmelite nuns. However, once the new Portuguese Inquisition started prosecuting Judaizers in the 1530s, Portuguese Conversos began moving to Spain, immigration that increased after 1580, when Portugal became a Spanish possession. A good number of these immigrants retained some attachment to Judaism, a result of the minimal scrutiny that the Portuguese authorities had given to the New Christians' religious practices between 1497 and the 1530s. Spain's inquisitors were therefore busy prosecuting and sometimes burning Judaizers as late as the 1720s. SEE SOURCEBOOK II:1.

The End of Islam in Spain

Prior to the conquest of Granada in 1492, relations between the Muslim minorities (Mudejars) and Christians in Castile and the Crown of Aragon were stable and often economically beneficial. The demographic toll taken by the Black Death in 1348–1349 had if anything made Mudejar labor more valuable to Christian nobles and kings, especially in the Crown of Aragon, where the Muslim population was very large. Unusual violent outbursts, such as a Christian mob's sacking of Valencia's Mudejar neighborhood in 1455 in response to the papacy's call for a Crusade against the Ottomans after their capture of Constantinople, did not have lasting effects. In Granada in 1492 Fernando and Isabel thus unhesitatingly granted the surrendering Muslims Mudejar status, with the usual religious freedoms and royal protection.

In 1499, however, the zealous archbishop of Toledo, Francisco Jiménez de Cisneros, shattered the arrangement with the Granadan Mudejars by forcibly converting Muslims and burning Islamic texts in the city of Granada. Rebellions erupted throughout the former sultanate in 1500–1501; as Fernando and Isabel suppressed them, they offered the defeated Muslim rebels baptism as a condition of pardon. Using the logic that had guided them in their treatment of Conversos and Jews, the monarchs decided that unbaptized Muslims had to be prevented from contaminating the faith of these newly converted Moriscos. They therefore completed the Christianization of Granada, which had already been annexed to Castile, and in 1502 pressured most of Castile's relatively small Muslim population to convert.

Fernando nevertheless protected the Mudejars of *his* Crown of Aragon from forced conversion until his death in 1516. His foreign grandson Charles V had other ideas, for he wanted to be seen by Europeans as a Crusader who would defend Christendom against Islam. Thus, after an army of radical Christian artisans in Valencia—the Germania or Brotherhood— forcibly baptized thousands of Muslims in 1521 in the course of an ultimately unsuccessful rebellion against the nobility and monarchy, Charles, with the backing of inquisitors and theologians, insisted on the legitimacy of the baptisms and then, in 1525–1526, required all Muslims in the Crown of Aragon to become Christian. Exile was intentionally made so difficult for the

FIGURE 11.3 Vicente Mostre, *Expulsion of the Moriscos at the Port of Denia*, 1613. The Picture Art Collection / Alamy Stock Photo.

Muslims that it was not really an option. Consequently, in Aragon as in Granada, the labor force remained in place, freshly baptized.

Officially, Islam no longer existed in Spain; actually, like Judaism, it had only been driven underground. An even higher proportion of Moriscos than Conversos continued to adhere to their ancestral faith. Maghribi religious scholars encouraged them in this, citing the doctrine of *taqiyya*, or "prudent dissimulation," according to which persecuted Muslims could conceal their true belief in Islam while outwardly practicing another faith. Furthermore, compared to the smaller Converso communities, which were scattered in cities and usually more affluent, educated, and exposed to Christian high culture, the large Morisco populations of the kingdoms of Granada, Valencia, and Aragon were more insular, composed mostly of peasants and artisans living in rural villages on the estates of Christian nobles. There, Moriscos could more easily evade the Catholic clergy's inconsistent efforts to indoctrinate them, while their noble lords often turned a blind eye to their Islamic observances, as long as they tilled the soil and paid rent.

Among the Moriscos there were also wealthy merchants and, in Granada, descendants of old noble families who advocated for their people at the royal court. Some Moriscos sincerely embraced the Catholic faith, and in some Castilian towns there was a fully assimilated and well educated Morisco elite. Nevertheless, most Moriscos identified with Islam, however rudimentary their knowledge, and received guidance from a class of religious scholars. Since so many of their people outside of Granada and Valencia had lost knowledge of the Arabic language, these learned Moriscos composed and circulated religious texts written in *aljamiado*, that is, Romance vernacular language in Arabic script. Some of these texts were apocalyptic and predicted an Ottoman or Moroccan reconquest of Spain.

The Inquisition prosecuted and punished Moriscos, especially in the later sixteenth century, as frustration with their persistent Islamizing mounted. "Purity of blood" laws also targeted Moriscos, whose religious dissidence and alleged political disloyalty were seen to inhere in their supposed "racial" difference. In 1567 Felipe II passed legislation outlawing all aspects of the Muslim culture of the Granadan Moriscos, who responded in 1568 with a massive, bloody insurrection. After defeating the rebels in 1570, Philip had approximately 84,000 Granadans deported northward and dispersed around Castile where they would hopefully assimilate into Catholic society. The result, however, was often a strengthening of the Islamic identity of the Castilian Moriscos with whom the Granadans came into contact.

In addition to being perceived as incorrigible heretics, the Moriscos were also feared, even before the Granadan revolt, as threats to the Spanish state who were conspiring with its Ottoman, Maghribi, and Protestant enemies. These fears had some substance, for the oppressive policies of the Spanish state and church had pushed Moriscos to resort to desperate measures. Finally, Felipe III and his advisers decided on the expulsion of all Moriscos, regardless of the Catholic faith of some of them. Removing the Morisco menace, they concluded, was worth the risk of angering the Moriscos' noble lords, damaging regional economies, and losing baptized souls to Islam. Between 1609 and 1614 over 300,000 Moriscos were sent into exile, mostly to Muslim lands. SEE SOURCEBOOK II:2.

Jewish Survival and Segregation in Renaissance Italy

Italy became a refuge for Jews and Conversos ejected from other parts of Europe mainly because of the economic interests of individual city-states; Renaissance "enlightenment" had little to do with it. The religious intolerance of Spanish rulers in southern Italy and of antagonistic friars and popes farther north often made the position of Jews, native and immigrant, unpredictable and insecure.

Spanish possession of Sicily and the kingdom of Naples led to the elimination of Jews in the south. The Sicilian Jewish community dated back to when the island was under Muslim rule and some Jews still used a Judeo-Arabic dialect. The community was economically diversified and numbered some 30,000 in 1492, almost equaling the entire peninsular Jewish population. Nevertheless, King Fernando implemented the same policies in Sicily as he had in Spain: expulsion of the Jews in 1492–1493, followed by the establishment of a branch of the Spanish Inquisition in 1500 to root out Judaizers from among the many Jews who had chosen to remain as converts. Though Spain captured Naples in 1504, local resistance helped the kingdom's Jews avoid exile until 1541 and its influential Converso families to escape inquisitorial prosecution until 1569.

Prior to the sixteenth century Jewish communities in northern Italy were mostly small and dispersed, even with the addition of French and German Jewish refugees. Though not the Jews' only livelihood, their moneylending activities gained them entry to towns, since lower-class Christians needed credit that Christian bankers were unable or unwilling to provide. Urban governments granted Jewish communities temporary charters of residence that specified the terms of their business and other essential matters. Sometimes the charters were not renewed, usually because Franciscan preachers had agitated against the Jews for allegedly exploiting Christians and had persuaded the civic authorities to set up loan banks offering lower interest rates. Consequently, by the end of the fifteenth century scattered Jewish communities were coalescing in fewer places and Jews were abandoning the lending business.

This somewhat insecure existence, however, did not mean social and cultural isolation for the Jews. The small size of Jewish communities actually made mixing with local Christians unavoidable and occasionally stimulating. As a result of their exposure to Christian intellectuals and their texts, some Jews became enthusiastic students of Renaissance humanism.

The complexion of northern Italian Jewry changed again with the influx of Jewish exiles from Spain after 1492 and Portuguese Conversos fleeing their homeland's Inquisition after the 1530s. Some immigrants went to Rome but many settled in ports whose rulers were ever more intent on developing their trade. The Venetian government, which had previously excluded Jews from the city, created the first segregated ghetto for Jews in 1516, and established a second adjacent one in 1541 to house Ottoman Jewish merchants, some of Converso origin who had returned to Judaism in the sultan's domains. At the same time, Portuguese Conversos with suspect religious allegiances lived outside the ghetto. In 1589 the government boldly responded to the Venetian Inquisition's concerns about Converso Judaizing by granting Conversos the freedom to revert to Judaism as long as they lived as Jews in the ghetto. The city's rulers were willing to defy the church in order to attract Portuguese Conversos whose familial ties, ethnic solidarity, and religious flexibility enabled them to manage trade networks that extended from the Ottoman empire to America.

With similar liberal religious policies, the Medici dukes of Tuscany attracted Jews and Conversos to their port of Livorno; by the mid-seventeenth century its trade was flourishing and 20 percent of its population was Jewish. The Venetian and Medici governments were both sufficiently powerful to limit the activities of the Inquisition in their states. Even Popes Paul III (1534–1549) and Julius III (1549–1555) were willing to accord Converso merchants such protection in the interest of developing Ancona, the Papal States' Adriatic port. Paul IV (1555–1559), however, abruptly ended such lenience and insisted that the Inquisition prosecute and execute Conversos for practicing Judaism in Ancona.

More damaging to Italian Jews overall was Paul IV's bull of 1555. It required all Jews in Rome and throughout the Papal States to reside in ghettos that were purposely more confining and more degrading than Venice's. Jews, moreover, were forced to wear a humiliating badge, and their economic activities were strictly limited. While this stark segregation of Jews from Christians with walls and gates was part of a general papal campaign of shielding Catholics from all heretical, especially Protestant, influences, the Jewish policies of Paul and his successors were also aggressive, aimed at demoralizing and proselytizing Jews. The popes thus periodically commanded the burning of copies of the Talmud so that its "false" doctrines would not blind the Jews to Christian "truth," and they compelled Jews to attend missionary sermons. As a consequence of papal influence, over the course of the next 200 years the authorities in other regions of Italy forced Jews into urban ghettos. A house of catechumens for the instruction of Jewish converts was built next to the ghetto in some cities. The number of converts indeed increased, partly the result of impoverishment and isolation in the ghetto.

Yet ghettos did give Jewish communities a fixed place in Christian society, though, as Saint Augustine had preferred, one unambiguously subordinate to Christians'. Furthermore, confinement in the ghettos enhanced Jewish solidarity, strengthened the institutions of Jewish self-government, and moved Jews to creatively draw upon spiritual resources like Kabbalah. SEE SOURCEBOOK 11:3.

Religious Pluralism in the Muslim Mediterranean

Although Muslim rulers across the Mediterranean continued to uphold the scripturally sanctioned system of *dhimma*, within its legal framework there was considerable variability from one state to another in the actual conditions of religious minorities. In the domains of Mamluk and Maghribi sultans the position of Christians and Jews tended to worsen after 1350, partly because the economic crises that came in the wake of the Black Death heightened the hostility of the Muslim populace toward the minorities, particularly their elite, office-holding families. In these realms *dhimmis* survived because of the strength of centuries-old traditions. The Ottoman empire, however, was a new polity whose expansion—rather like that of the Arabs in the seventh century—entailed bringing large numbers of Christians under Muslim rule for the first time. The pragmatic Ottoman sultans governed Balkan Christian and Jewish communities with policies that met the needs of both the state and the minority populations and mostly complied with Islamic law. Christians and Jews in Egypt saw their circumstances improve after the Ottoman conquest of 1517. The sheer expanse of the Ottoman empire, moreover, brought previously disconnected Jewish and Orthodox Christian communities into fruitful contact with their coreligionists.

Minorities under Mamluk and Maghribi Sultans

Life for the Coptic Christians of Egypt did not significantly improve after the Mamluks destroyed the Cru-

At the time of Ottoman expansion into the Balkans in the fourteenth century, one of the most important spiritual centers of Orthodox Christianity was Mount Athos, often referred to as the Holy Mountain. Actually a narrow Greek peninsula some sixty kilometers long, Athos was (and is) inhabited mostly by monks organized in dozens of communities. Saint Athanasios (ca. 920–1003) founded the first Athonite monastery—the Great Lavra—in 963, taking the spiritual program of the Byzantine monastic reformer Saint Theodore the Stoudite (d. 826) as his model. This and other monastic foundations in Athos enjoyed the patronage of Byzantine emperors. By the twelfth century Slavic monks were establishing monasteries there—Chilandar by Serbs and Zographou by Bulgarians—where Greek texts were translated into Slavonic and diffused to southeastern Europe. The Athonite monasteries experienced hardship in the thirteenth century under the Latin rulers of Greece but revived in the fourteenth century, due in no small part to the donations of the reinstalled Byzantine emperors and the rulers of Serbia, espe-

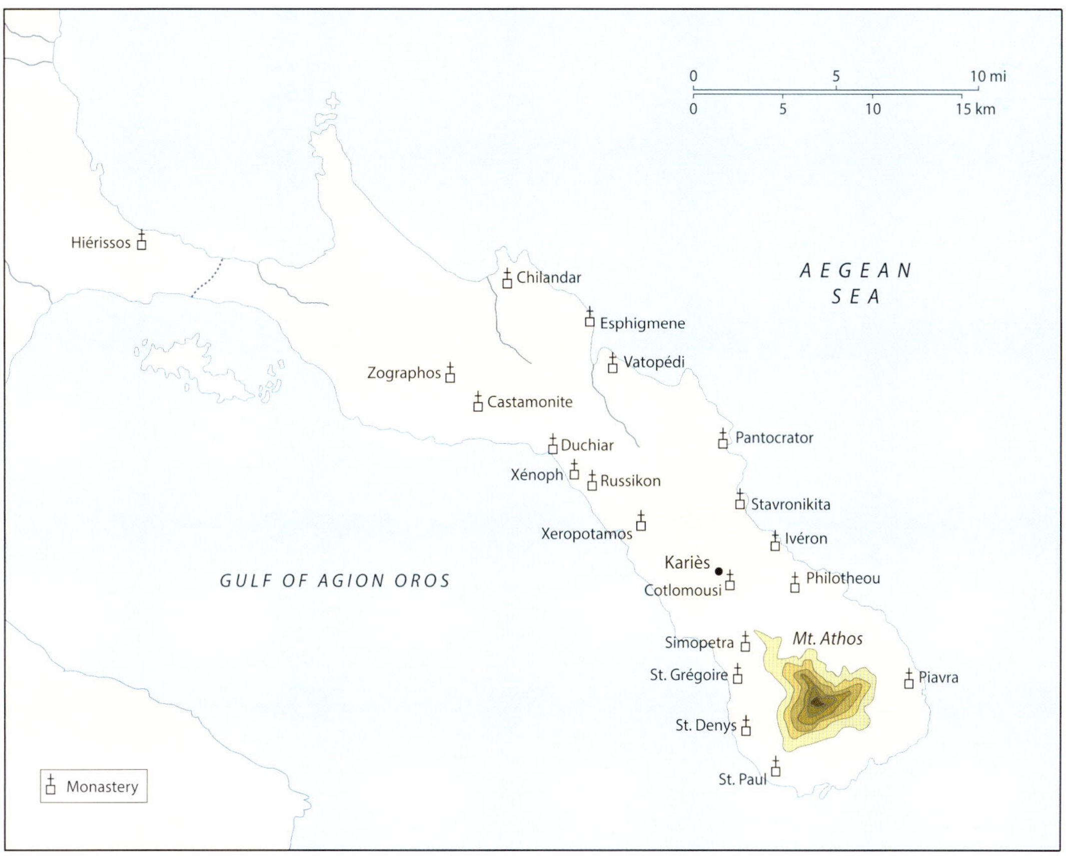

MAP 11.2 Map of Mount Athos. From "Mont Athos, 1866," in V. Langlois, *Le Mont Athos et ses monastéres* (Paris: Firmin Didot frères, fils et cie, 1867). Hathi Trust Digital Library, digitized by Google, original from Princeton University.

FIGURE 11.4 Chilandar Monastery on Mount Athos. Photo provided by OrthodoxWiki under the CC-SA License.

cially Stefan Dushan (1331–1355), and Wallachia (in modern Romania, just north and technically not part of the Balkans). The Holy Mountain had become a focus for the devotion of Orthodox Christians throughout the Balkans and beyond.

Like other monasteries in Byzantine Thessaly, the Athonite monasteries negotiated arrangements with the conquering Ottoman sultans long before the fall of Constantinople, perhaps as early as the reign of Orhan (d. 1362). The sultans could appreciate that their new Orthodox subjects, whom they did not want to alienate, held the monks in high esteem. They therefore brought the monasteries under their protection, confirmed them in the possession of their extensive properties, and granted them other privileges, such as exemption from certain state taxes. Mount Athos nonetheless maintained close relations with the emperor and patriarch in Constantinople until 1453. The monks, however, opposed the Union of the Greek and Latin Churches that Emperor John VIII pursued in 1439 and seem to have preferred Ottoman lordship to that of the Venetians or any other Latin power. It is possible, too, that the Athonite monks' firm embrace of Hesychasm, an inner, more mystical spirituality, made them more politically cooperative and less inclined to overtly oppose the rule of the Ottomans.

In any case, Mount Athos flourished under Ottoman dominion through the fifteenth and much of the sixteenth century. Ottoman hegemony in Anatolia eliminated the naval raids that other Anatolian Turkic emirates had once made on its monasteries. Suleyman the Magnificent granted monasteries permission to build fortifications for defense against the attacks of other pirates, who became increasingly troublesome in the sixteenth century.

The size of the monastic population in Athos increased as monks, many of them Slavic speakers, moved there from other parts of the Balkans in order to escape, ironically, the upheaval in their own homelands associated with the sultans' incessant wars of conquest. Since the Holy Mountain was, in contrast, so secure, faithful Orthodox Christians, including members of the old Byzantine and Serbian aristocracies, continued to make donations of land and money to the Athonite monasteries; some even retired there. Rulers of the Danubian principalities of Moldavia and Wallachia, who from the end of the fourteenth century were sometimes compelled to render tribute to the sultans, were also generous benefactors. The monasteries' prosperity in the sixteenth century enabled them to fund new decorative programs, especially wall paintings executed by the Cretan school of artists.

FIGURE 11.5 Jesus feeding the 5,000. Fresco, Stavronikita Monastery, fifteenth century. © Historical Views / agefotostock.

One prominent patron of Athonite monasteries was Stefan III the Great, of Moldavia (1457–1504). Through his lavish support Stefan emulated the deeds of Byzantine emperors and hoped, in the wake of the fall of Constantinople, to attain the authority that the emperors had held among Orthodox Christians under Ottoman rule. Espousing the Orthodox cause also bolstered his efforts to maintain Moldavia's independence in the face of aggression from the rulers of Catholic Hungary and Poland, on the one hand, and the Ottoman sultans, on the other. Through building churches and monasteries modeled on Athonite communities Stefan strengthened Moldavia's Orthodox identity. He countered the ambitions of the Hungarians and the Poles, but the Ottomans were a greater challenge. Though he paid them tribute when necessary, he also defeated their invading armies in several campaigns. Still, disgust with the policies of his Catholic neighbors moved Stefan to advise his son and successor Bogdan III (1504–1517) to comply with the Ottomans and become their tributary.

Petru Raresh (1527–1538, 1541–1546), however, was less cooperative than Bogdan. His political maneuvering antagonized Sultan Suleyman, who invaded Moldavia in 1538 and deposed Raresh. The sultan allowed Raresh to return to the throne in 1541 but forced him to pay a much heavier tribute and accept the presence of a Janissary guard at his court. After 1538 Moldavia joined Wallachia in becoming a vassal state of the Ottoman empire. Unlike Christian states south of the Danube, such as Serbia, these principalities were not fully incorporated into the Ottoman political system and retained their autonomy.

Prior to 1538 Raresh had, like Stefan, patronized the construction, renovation, and decoration of Orthodox churches and monasteries. The frescoes decorating some of the monasteries, both on the interior and, remarkably, on the exterior, had an unmistakably anti-Ottoman message. In this sense they differed from the frescoes painted at around the same time in the monasteries of Mount Athos, which had mostly been thriving under Ottoman rule.

For example, the fresco on the exterior of the church of Moldovita monastery, built by Raresh in 1532, includes a large scene of the siege of Constantinople by the Persians in 626. The Byzantine emperor Heraclius had, according to legend, defeated the Persians with the help of the Virgin Mary. The Moldovita artists painted the 'Persians' in the turbans and uniforms of contemporary Turkish soldiers. The fresco conveyed a message of hope to Moldavian viewers—that the Ottomans would one day be vanquished and Moldavia freed from their yoke.

FIGURE 11.6 The siege of Constantinople. Fresco, Moldovita Monastery, ca. 1532. Photo: Gavriel Jecan / Danita Delimont / Alamy Stock Photo.

Benign Ottoman lordship over Mount Athos ended in 1568, when Selim II decided, on the advice of his chief mufti, to confiscate the landed properties of monasteries throughout the empire. The mufti argued that all rural land in the empire belonged to the sultan and that the profits from it should not be used for the benefit of Christian monasteries. Whatever the legal argument, the sultan needed more revenue for his military campaigns. He therefore allowed the Athonite monasteries to buy back their properties. They managed to do this with generous financial support from the princes of Moldavia and Wallachia.

Discussion Questions

1. Why were Ottoman sultans so inclined to offer their protection to Mount Athos, and why were its monasteries so willing to accept the lordship of a Muslim monarch?

2. Why did Mount Athos, a tiny peninsula in northern Greece, persist in being such a focus for the piety of Orthodox Christians throughout the Balkans and beyond? Was this partly a result of the Ottoman protectorate?

3. What was the relationship between the Moldavian princes' patronage of the construction and decoration of churches at home and their patronage of monasteries on Mount Athos? Were they both forms of Orthodox resistance to Ottoman domination?

Further Reading

Angold, Michael, ed. *The Cambridge History of Christianity*. Vol. 5, *Eastern Christianity*. Cambridge: Cambridge University Press, 2006.

Grabar, André. *Rumania: Painted Churches of Moldavia*. Greenwich: New York Graphic Society, 1962.

Hitchins, Keith. *A Concise History of Romania*. Cambridge: Cambridge University Press, 2014.

Speake, Graham. *Mount Athos: Renewal in Paradise*. New Haven: Yale University Press, 2002.

Sullivan, Alice Isabella. "The Athonite Patronage of Stephen III of Moldavia, 1457–1504." *Speculum* 94:1 (2019): 1–46.

sader states, the potential threat of which had caused Muslims to be suspicious of the Copts, the Crusaders' coreligionists. After 1350 there were new sources of discontent for the Muslim populace, who suffered—as did Christians and Jews—from the deteriorating living conditions brought on by famine, plague, and the imposition of higher taxes by struggling Mamluk rulers. In order to curry favor with the Muslim masses and with the *'ulama'* who exercised great influence over them, Mamluk sultans purposely humiliated *dhimmis* through enforcing discriminatory laws. In 1448, for instance, Sultan Jaqmaq (1438–1453) prohibited Christian and Jewish physicians from treating Muslim patients, a dramatic break from Muslim rulers' customary practice of employing *dhimmi* doctors. Coptic Christian and Jewish officials nonetheless continued to serve in the Mamluk government, especially in the financial administration. In such hard times, these officials and their communities became the targets of popular Muslim resentment and, occasionally, violence. In response to pressure from Muslim commoners and the *'ulama'*, sultans sometimes dismissed *dhimmi* officials and even those who had converted to Islam, for they too were mistrusted. Systematic degradation caused the conversion of Copts and Jews, especially from among the elite who had felt the humiliations most acutely. Christians, who suffered more from Muslim hostility than Jews, abandoned their faith in greater numbers. Still, Mamluk sultans never tried to dismantle the *dhimma* and so did not turn away the Spanish Jewish exiles arriving in Egypt, Palestine, and Syria after 1492.

In the Maghribi sultanates the Jews were the only minority group. Their experience after 1350 did not differ appreciably from that of their brethren in Egypt, in that they generally benefited from the protection of the *dhimma* but sometimes endured hardship in times of political instability or economic crisis. Jewish life was calmest in Hafsid Tunisia and Zayyanid Algeria, which is probably why Jews from mainland Aragon and Mallorca fleeing the violence of 1391, as well as Jews expelled from southern France in 1394, settled in their cities. Leading Spanish rabbis like Isaac ben Sheshet Perfet (1326–1408) contributed to making Algeria an important religious center in the fifteenth century.

The history of Morocco's Jews was more tumultuous. The religious militancy and political infighting that Portuguese and Spanish invaders inspired among Moroccan Muslims affected their attitudes toward the Jewish population. The conspicuous role that a few Jews played in the government of the Marinid sultans particularly outraged some Muslims. An outburst of anti-Jewish violence in 1438 moved the sultan to establish a special quarter for the protection of the Jews in Fez. Unfortunately, in 1465 most of its inhabitants fell victim to a Muslim mob angered by Sultan 'Abd al-Haqq's appointment of a Jew, Aaron ibn Batash, as his chief minister. This did not stop Wattasid and Sa'did sultans from later employing Jews or permitting the settlement of Iberian Jewish refugees. Some Iberian immigrants served the Wattasids as intermediaries in their negotiations with the Portuguese and soon assumed leading roles in the Moroccan Jewish community as merchants and scholars. Yet at the same time the sultans enforced humiliating sumptuary laws meant to display the Jews' inferior status. It was what many of their Muslim subjects demanded and was a price the Jews were willing to pay.

Christians in the Ottoman Empire

From their state's earliest days, the Ottomans dealt with Christians practically, forming alliances with Christian rulers while admitting Christian nobles into their own warrior elite. When they conquered the Christian Balkans over the course of the fourteenth and fifteenth centuries, a similar pragmatism, and the Islamic law of *dhimma*, guided the sultans in their treatment of their new subjects. Thus taxing Christians—at higher rates than Muslims—and utilizing their talents for the benefit of the state were usually more important than converting them. Despite the voluntary conversion of many Christians and the compulsory—though un-Islamic—recruitment of some 200,000 Christian boys through *devşirme*, the Balkans remained largely Christian.

Mehmed II's conquest of Constantinople was a key moment in the organization of Orthodox Christian life under Ottoman rule. Prior to 1453, the sultans had viewed the Orthodox patriarch and bishops as their enemies and allies of the Byzantine emperor. However, as the self-proclaimed heirs of the Byzantine emperors, Mehmed and his successors supervised the appointment of the Orthodox patriarch and made use of the church's hierarchical structure to centralize the governance of the autonomous Orthodox communities. The patriarchs in Istanbul now exercised jurisdiction over civil cases between Christian litigants in addition to their traditional jurisdiction over cases involving canon law; and while bishops collected ecclesiastical taxes, they also helped in the assessment and collection of taxes that the Christian laity owed to the Ottoman state.

The Orthodox patriarchate in Istanbul benefited from the Ottomans' expansion into the Greek Aegean world, much of which had been under Latin rule since 1204. Not only did the Ottoman conquest of islands such as Rhodes in 1522–1523 and Cyprus in 1570 free Greek Orthodox peasants from Latin lordship, it extended the patriarch's authority at the expense of the Roman Catholic Church. The empire's acquisition of Mamluk Syria in 1516 also brought its Arabic-speaking Orthodox Christians, who still used the Greek liturgy, under the patriarch's jurisdiction. Istanbul became the center of the Orthodox and Greek worlds.

Among the Ottomans' Orthodox subjects in the Balkans, there was great ethnic and linguistic diversity; in fact, the majority were Bulgarians and Serbs, not Greeks. The sultans allowed the archbishopric of Ohrid, Bulgaria, and that of Pec, Serbia, which they granted patriarchal status in 1557, to continue functioning with considerable autonomy. Church Slavonic instead of Greek was the liturgical language used in their churches. Furthermore, not all of the Ottomans' Christian subjects were Orthodox. The sultans put these Christians—Armenians, Syrian and Egyptian (Coptic) Miaphysites, and Bosnian Bogomils—under the loose authority of the patriarch of the Armenian community in Istanbul, although the true head of the Armenian Church resided outside Ottoman territory in Erivan. For the Copts, in any case, Ottoman government was an improvement on that of the Mamluks.

The Ottomans, however, sometimes treated their Christian subjects with a heavier hand. They practiced *sürgün*, or the forced relocation of populations, for political and economic purposes. For instance, they sent potentially troublesome Christian warriors from the Balkans to Anatolia in exchange for Turkic Muslims, and they repopulated Istanbul after the conquest with transplanted Greeks, Armenians, Serbs, and Jews. Even if deported populations benefited economically in the long term, initially the process could be wrenching. *Devşirme* was doubtless painful for Christian peasant families whose sons were "collected," enslaved, and converted to Islam. Yet these boys were given the opportunity to rise in the sultan's service as Janissaries or ministers. Some at least did not forget their Christian families back home. Mehmed Sokollu, a grand vizier of Serbian Christian origin, advocated for the restoration of the Serbian patriarchate, and he helped his brother Makarius become the patriarch.

The conversion of most other Balkan Christians was voluntary. Before the sixteenth century most converts were Greek and Slavic nobles serving in the Ottoman military; proximity to political power and exposure to the more syncretic Islam of Sufi dervishes encouraged their conversion. Bosnia, where large numbers of Christians converted in 1463 after the conquest, was an exception. Conversion accelerated over the course of the sixteenth and seventeenth centuries. With the empire's achievement of a Muslim majority in 1516–1517 and with the government placing ever more emphasis on Sunni orthodoxy, embracing Islam probably seemed a prudent choice to some Christians, especially the ambitious. Most conversion took place in urban centers where Muslims had settled. Social interaction with Muslims led to intermarriage and then to a widening of the web of contacts between Christians and Muslims, developments similar to those seen in the Muslim Mediterranean many centuries earlier.

Abandoning Christianity of course meant escaping payment of the *jizya* tax, which could be onerous for some families, and not having to worry about how strictly the Ottoman authorities would enforce the discriminatory *dhimma* laws forbidding them, for instance, to build their houses higher than those of Muslims or to ride horses. Conversion peaked during the reign of Mehmed IV (1648–1687), a period of Islamic religious revival when the *dhimma* restrictions were more harshly enforced.

Peasants formed the bulk of the Balkan Christian population. Ottoman conquest had often improved their lot, removing them from under the thumb of Christian lords who owned the lands on which they labored and whose ability to tax or abuse them was uncontrolled. In the centralized Ottoman *timar* system, the land belonged to the

FIGURE 11.7 Illustration of the *devşirme*, sixteenth century. Photograph provided by Wikimedia Commons under the CC0 License.

sultan, the cavalryman who temporarily held the *timar* was answerable to the sultan, and taxation was more consistent and predictable, even if burdensome. In the seventeenth century, however, the peasants' conditions deteriorated as a result of the decline of the *timar* system, itself a consequence of the diminishing importance of cavalry in the Ottoman army. *Timar* estates were sold to private owners or tax-farmers who exploited peasant production as much as was feasible. Peasant discontent mounted. Some migrated to cities, or to Christian realms; others fled to the mountains, becoming bandits who preyed on Turks and merchants.

Ottoman expansion had a more consistently positive impact on the fortunes of Greek Christian merchants and intellectuals. The Ottomans' displacement of the Genoese from the Black Sea region and the pressure they exerted on the Venetians created commercial opportunities in the eastern Balkans and Mediterranean that Greeks readily seized. The Greeks' connections with the wider Christian world enabled them in the seventeenth century to study medicine at the University of Padua, and then to displace Jews as the main physicians at the Ottoman court. SEE SOURCEBOOK II:4.

Jews in the Ottoman Empire

The Ottomans' readiness to take advantage of the skills and experience of non-Muslim subjects, new and old, made their empire a haven for Jewish and Converso refugees from France and Germany and especially the Iberian Peninsula. In the sixteenth century the Portuguese Jew Samuel Usque exclaimed: "As He [God] opened the Red Sea at the time of the Exodus... here [Turkey] the gates of liberty are always open for the observance of Judaism."[1] Jewish migration there had started long before 1492. Jews and Conversos, for instance, began leaving Spain for Ottoman lands after Mehmed II captured Constantinople, believing that the conquest foreshadowed the coming of the Jewish Messiah in the East. Jews with such a messianic or mystical orientation were particularly drawn to Jerusalem and other towns in the Holy Land after the Ottomans began to rule them in 1516. Most Jews, however, settled in the empire's commercial centers, or wherever the sultans wanted them.

As a consequence of conquest and immigration, the Ottoman Jewish population was ethnically diverse, composed of Greek-speaking "Romaniot" Jews from Anatolia and the Balkans; Ashkenazi immigrants from France and Germany; Iberian Jews and Conversos returning to Judaism; and Arabic-speaking Jews of Syria, Palestine, Egypt, and the Maghrib. Iberian Jewish immigrants put down roots throughout the empire, adding economically and culturally dynamic strata to existing Jewish populations. Jewish self-government under the sultans was not centralized and hierarchical like that of Orthodox Christians. It was instead organized around autonomous synagogue congregations formed on the basis of their members' place of origin. In some towns there was an overarching community organization, the *kehillah*, which included the various local synagogues and administered institutions such as the courts of Jewish law. Since the *kehillah* was more efficient for purposes of tax collection, it became more important in the hard times of the seventeenth century, when the Ottoman government was seeking more revenue from all of its subjects.

Jews engaged in a wide range of occupations from physician to fisherman, and tax registers show that a significant percentage of the families in many communities was poor. Still, it was the Jews' potential contributions to the empire's trade and industry and to fields such as medicine that most attracted the Ottomans' attention. They especially welcomed Jewish immigrants from Europe on account of their familiarity with European technologies and politics and their European medical education, which now surpassed what the Muslim world had to offer. Many Jewish physicians served at the Ottoman court in the sixteenth century. Some of the refugee doctors translated European medical works from Latin into Turkish. Jews also introduced printing from Europe, though their presses only printed books in Hebrew or Latin characters, since the Ottomans prohibited the printing of books in Arabic.

Through *sürgün* sultans transferred Jews to cities such as Istanbul and Thessaloniki. Thessaloniki changed from having no Jewish inhabitants in 1478 to housing over 3,000 Jewish families in 1519. The Jews there developed a major textile industry with technology imported from Italy and Spain. Safed in Palestine became another center of Jewish textile production. In the sixteenth century Jews, especially those of Iberian origin, played an important part in the empire's international commerce. They settled in cities along trade routes linking the empire to Christian markets in the eastern Mediterranean, central Europe, and farther afield. Their linguistic and cultural diversity—including, in some cases, their former Christian status—their knowledge of European markets and languages, and their maintenance of extensive trading networks composed of relatives and business partners of Jewish and Converso background made them effective competitors. Some Jews used the resources obtained through trade and manufacturing to win tax-farming contracts from the Ottoman government and became influential at the Ottoman court. None rose higher than the merchant and financier Joseph Nasi (ca. 1505–1579), who served as the sultan's adviser on European affairs. Selim II rewarded him by appointing him as the governor of Naxos, a group of Aegean islands that he administered through an agent.

The seventeenth century saw a gradual deterioration of the Jews' economic and social position. This was partly the result of global economic changes, particularly the impact of northern European merchants and manufacturers on the Mediterranean and Ottoman economies. The textile industries in Thessaloniki and Safed, for instance, declined when faced with northern European competition. At the same time, Jewish immigration from Europe began to peter out so that fewer Jews had the skills and education that had made them such useful intermediaries between Ottomans and Europeans. Ottoman Christians, Greek and Armenian, who were sending their children to European schools and universities, started replacing Jews as physicians at the sultan's court and as middlemen with western Christian merchants with whom they had religious and cultural affinity. Rebellion and banditry in the empire's provinces also affected Jewish communities. In Palestine, Bedouin and Druze attacks sometimes forced Jews to leave Safed; the community in Tiberias, whose foundation Gracia Mendes and Joseph Nasi had sponsored, was entirely dispersed in 1656. Most communities in the empire, however, survived and experienced only a slow decline.

Diasporas

Imperial conquests, sectarian wars, and ethnic cleansings produced large numbers of refugees whose migrations were mostly guided by their sense of religious identity. Some departed their homelands voluntarily because of fear of conquerors of a different faith or sect, or to escape inquisitions and other forms of religious persecution. Others had no choice and were forcibly expelled or relocated in the interests of the state or church. Christian Europe in this period saw a dramatic expansion in the number of religious refugees, not just through the removal of Jewish and Morisco populations but especially as a result of wars between Catholics and Protestants. The devastation of Catholic Ireland by the English Protestant ruler Oliver Cromwell in 1649–1653, which entailed the deportation of 50,000 Catholics and the flight of many others, was as brutal as anything witnessed in the Mediterranean world.

No matter how traumatic their departure from home, exiles managed to make new lives for themselves, often in or near communities of their coreligionists. Such dispersion—or diaspora—created new connections between once distant coreligionists, and new economic opportunities, as in the cases of Orthodox Greeks moving within and between Ottoman and Venetian domains, and Moriscos settling in Muslim states. A new dynamism in Jewish culture resulted from the Mediterranean-wide dispersion of Iberian Jews and Conversos. For some Moriscos, dispersion created the desire and the opportunity to take revenge on the country that had expelled them. SEE SOURCEBOOK II:5.

Orthodox Greeks between Ottoman and Venetian Empires

The reaction of Orthodox Greeks to Ottoman expansion in the eastern Mediterranean varied. Many welcomed or at least chose not to flee the Ottoman conquerors. Greeks living under Venetian dominion—still 480,000 of them in the late sixteenth century—were not sorry to see their Latin overlords go. Even in Constantinople before the Ottomans captured it, there were many, especially among the lower classes and Orthodox clergy, who fiercely opposed the Union of the Greek and Latin

In 1608 the English traveler Thomas Coryat remarked on the diverse population and headwear he encountered in the Jewish ghetto in Venice: "Some of them do wear hats and those red, only those Jews who are born in western parts of the world, as in Italy... but the eastern Jews being otherwise called Levantine Jews, who are born in Jerusalem, Alexandria, Constantinople... wear turbans upon their heads, as the Turks do." He also observed that there were "at the least seven" synagogues, which were needed to accommodate the various western and eastern communities with their distinct customs.[1] Long a port for merchants of many nations, Venice had since the sixteenth century been a magnet for Jews driven out of their homelands in western Europe and for those who wanted to expand the trade they had been developing further east.

In 1516 the Venetian government for the first time permitted Jews to establish a segregated community in the city, on the island of the New Ghetto (Ghetto Nuovo) or "new foundry." All Jews had to reside there, and gates were erected at both entrances to prevent them from exiting the ghetto at night. Its inhabitants were Ashkenazi Jews who had been pressured to leave Germany and France, and Italian Jews whose families had migrated from southern and central Italy. Identified by the yellow (or later red) hats they were required to wear, most were moneylenders whom the government intended to serve the needs of the Venetian poor. In order to revive Venice's declining commerce, the government sought the business of Levantine Jewish merchants from Ottoman lands. In 1541 it created the Old Ghetto (Ghetto Vecchio), on the site of the old copper foundry, to house them, though only temporarily. A wooden footbridge connected the two ghettos. The government was reluctant to allow these "eastern" Jews to reside in Venice permanently because some of them were actually Conversos of Iberian origin whose Judaizing and contacts with the ghettos' Jews were upsetting the papal authorities. Finally, in 1589, as a result of the petitions of Daniel Rodriga, a Jewish merchant from a Portuguese Converso family who effectively played on Venice's economic interests, the government granted formal residence privileges to Levantine Jews and "Ponentine Jews," Rodriga's euphemism for "western" Iberian Conversos who were henceforth allowed to revert to Judaism with impunity upon their arrival in Venice. Hoping to attract still more Jewish merchants, in 1633 the government allocated twenty more buildings for Jews across from the New Ghetto—the Newest Ghetto (Ghetto Nuovissimo).

The lack of adequate space was a consistent problem for Venice's Jews, whose numbers ranged from around 2,000 to over 3,000 in the late sixteenth and seventeenth centuries. Jews tried to solve the problem by adding stories to buildings or by subdividing apartments and creating additional floors with low ceilings inside buildings. In his autobiography, the rabbi Leon Modena complained of the "high rent" he paid for a "dark and poorly lit dwelling, because it is low."[2] He described how the cramped quarters in his building facilitated the rapid spread of the pestilence in 1631: "Above and below me and on all sides... people have taken ill and died from the plague."[3] Because of the high death toll, the Newest Ghetto was not really needed in 1633.

FIGURE 11.8 Entrance to the Ghetto of Venice. Photo courtesy of Bogdan Smarandache.

FIGURE 11.9 Scuola Grande Tedesca, or Great German Synagogue. Photo courtesy of Bogdan Smarandache.

FIGURE 11.10 Scuola Levantina, or Levantine Synagogue. Photo courtesy of Bogdan Smarandache.

Despite the enforced proximity of the different Jewish communities to one another, each one maintained its ethnic identity, which was expressed through the construction of separate synagogues and through the division of power in communal government. In the New Ghetto Ashkenazi Jews had the "Great German Synagogue" (Scuola Grande Tedesca) built in 1528–1529 (probably by local Christian artisans who controlled the guilds). Its five arched windows signified the five books of the Torah, and its large hall served as the meeting place for the Jewish government's Great Assembly.

Two other smaller synagogues in the same ghetto were the Scuola Canton, founded in 1532, probably by French Ashkenazi Jews whose liturgy differed slightly from the Germans', and the Scuola Italiana, established by 1575 by Italian Jews, who were officially categorized as "German" Jews, even though they had their own confraternities and ritual customs. Leon Modena felt compelled to urge fellow rabbis to defend the Italians' custom of not covering their head, except during prayers, "so that the Levantine and German Jews would have no basis for looking upon us as heretics and upon themselves as pious Jews."[4]

In the Old Ghetto the Levantine and the Ponentine Jews established separate synagogues in the late sixteenth century, which they had refurbished or rebuilt in the following century. The Ponentines' Spanish Synagogue (Scuola Grande Spagnola) was the largest one in Venice and a reflection of the growing numbers, wealth, and influence of the Sephardim. There were cultural differences between the Ponentines and the Levantines. Because they were the descendants of former Conversos or themselves former Conversos with a weaker understanding of Hebrew, the Ponentines kept most of their records in Portuguese or Spanish. The Levantines were more firmly grounded in Jewish traditions, for they were either Ottoman Jews of "Romaniot" (Byzantine) ancestry or Jews of Iberian origin whose families had emigrated to the Ottoman lands earlier in the sixteenth century. The Jewish community's sumptuary laws from 1616 indicate that Levantine women dressed splendidly in silk garments. Perhaps these were the Jewish women who caught Coryat's eye: "Some were as beautiful as ever I saw, and so gorgeous in their apparel."[5]

There was one communal government for the diverse population of the ghettos. Like other Jewish governments in the Mediterranean, it was oligarchic, but it also required ethnic power-sharing. For purposes of political representation, three ethnic groups were counted: the German (including the Italians), the Spanish (including the Portuguese), and the Levantine. All Jews who met certain criteria of age and wealth belonged to the Large Assembly. Its main function was to elect members of the executive Small Assembly, which managed most of the community's affairs, and to supervise the banking committee and the assessment committee, which determined each family's tax contribution. At the beginning of the seventeenth century the Germans were the dominant political force, which was counterbalanced by an alliance of Spanish and Levantine representatives on the Small Assembly and other committees. By the 1620s, however, the Spanish group had grown large and powerful enough alone to counter the Germans, who continued to dominate only the banking committee, since lending was their principal activity. Most of the Spanish (or Sephardim), by contrast, were merchants and often wealthier than the Germans. In 1636 they contributed over half of the communal government's budget.

The Jews of Venice overcame ethnic division to work for larger Jewish causes, such as organizing relief for the poor Jews of Palestine and ransoming Jews who had been captured by pirates. Venice also played a key role in shaping a transnational Jewish culture. It was a major center of printing Hebrew, Ladino (Judeo-Spanish), and Yiddish (Judeo-German) texts. One of the main publishers of Hebrew books was Daniel Bomberg, a Christian from Antwerp who employed Jewish editors, proofreaders, and typesetters. He published, for instance, the first complete edition of the Babylonian Talmud with commentaries in 1520–1523 as well as works of Maimonides. Such printed works linked the communities of the Jewish diaspora together. Venice's mainland empire, moreover, included Padua, whose university and medical school admitted and granted medical degrees to hundreds of Jewish students from all over Europe. The Padua-trained physicians came to form an intellectual elite in the Jewish world and functioned as crucial intermediaries with non-Jewish culture. Some lived in the Venetian ghetto and practiced in Venice. Only they were permitted to leave the ghetto at night, without wearing yellow or red hats.

The fortunes of the Jewish community of Venice declined over the course of the seventeenth century along with the fortunes of the city. Not only was there competition from the growing Jewish community in Mediterranean Livorno, but Sephardim were also settling in northern European centers such as Amsterdam, Hamburg, and London.

Discussion Questions

1. How would you explain the seemingly contradictory impulses of the Venetian government to attract Jews and to segregate Jews?

2. Even though the Jews of the ghetto—or ghettos—were forced to reside in cramped, sometimes unhealthy quarters, how might they have benefited from their segregated existence?

3. What factors would have counterbalanced the government's segregationist measures and fostered interaction between the ghetto's inhabitants and the city's Christian population?

4. How and why did the Jews from different backgrounds maintain their distinctive ethnic identities?

Further Reading

Curiel, Roberta, and Bernard Cooperman, eds. *The Ghetto of Venice*. London: Tauris Parke Books, 1990.

Malkiel, David. *A Separate Republic: The Mechanics and Dynamics of Venetian Jewish Self-Government, 1607–1624*. Jerusalem: Magnes Press, 1991.

Modena, Leon. *The Autobiography of a Seventeenth-Century Venetian Rabbi: Leon Modena's "Life of Judah."* Trans. and ed. Mark R. Cohen. Princeton: Princeton University Press, 1988.

Ravid, Benjamin, and Robert C. Davis, eds. *The Jews of Early Modern Venice*. Baltimore: Johns Hopkins University Press, 2001.

Notes

1. Thomas Coryat, *Coryat's Crudities: hastily gobled up in five moneths travells in France, Savoy, Italy, Rhetia commonly called the Grisons country, Helvetia alias Switzerland, some parts of high Germany and the Netherlands* (Glasgow: J. MacLehose and Sons, 1905), 1:370–71.
2. Modena, 156.
3. Modena, 135.
4. Malkiel, 112.
5. Coryat, 1:372.

Churches in 1439 and who thought that the Ottomans would give them more religious freedom than the hated Latins.

Yet many Greeks fled west to Christian states either because they disliked the prospect of living under Muslim rule or because they feared the brutalities that conquest usually entailed. Greeks from Thessaloniki took refuge in Venetian Crete before the Turks seized their city in 1430, but it was the Ottoman conquest of Constantinople in 1453 that generated the largest stream of refugees. Greeks migrated throughout western Europe, some only temporarily, begging for alms or for funds to ransom their loved ones from Muslim captivity. Others settled permanently in cities as far afield as London, where they formed a small community of merchants and manufacturers of gold thread for luxury fabrics. The large majority put down roots in the eastern Mediterranean. Latin-ruled Cyprus, whose queen, Helena Palaiologina, was the niece of Constantine XI, the last Byzantine emperor, took in many refugees. Italy, however, was the Greek migrants' main destination. Many settled in the kingdoms of Naples and Sicily, attracted partly by the existence of older Greek communities there. Venice housed the largest Greek community. Numbering some 4,000 in 1478, it was permitted in 1514 to have its own Orthodox Church of St. George, which was finished in 1573. By this time the community had tripled in size, though many of its members were not refugees from Ottoman rule.

FIGURE 11.11 Greek Orthodox Church of St. George in Venice. Photo by Jakub Halun provided by Wikimedia Commons under the CC-BY-SA 4.0 License.

Greeks encountered a fair amount of prejudice in Latin Europe, but there was also much sympathy for them as fellow Christians. Byzantine clergy who had supported the Union of the Churches were welcomed by the papacy. Some defected to the Roman Church, like Cardinal Basilios Bessarion (ca. 1403–1472), who nonetheless worked to aid Greek refugees and to preserve Byzantine culture. Greeks were esteemed as bearers of the Hellenic legacy. Prior to 1453 Italian humanists had studied Greek in Constantinople, while Byzantine scholars like Manuel Chrysoloras, professor of Greek in Florence from 1397, had taught in Italy. After 1453 many Greek scholars relocated to Italian cities where they taught and copied or translated Greek manuscripts into Latin. Venice became an important Greek cultural center; a Greek printing press was set up there in 1494, and at the nearby University of Padua Greeks were professors and, later, medical students.

Many of the Greeks who moved to Venice, however, were not refugees; rather, they, like their fellows who chose to settle in Istanbul, were pursuing economic opportunities that the new alignment of power in the eastern Mediterranean presented. These immigrants came from Venice's colonial possessions, Crete and other Aegean islands. The merchants among them, who became Venetian "citizens," assumed during the sixteenth century the commercial role once played by native Venetians whom Ottoman expansion had discouraged from investing in trade. Other Greek merchants, especially Cretans, preferred to settle in and conduct their business from Istanbul. Some families had branches in both cities. Istanbul also attracted to its shipbuilding and textile industries needier Greeks from Venice's colonies escaping grinding poverty, unpaid debts, or criminal convictions. Such immigrants nonetheless sometimes provided intelligence to the Venetian diplomatic mission resident in Istanbul. They added to the Greek population that the Ottomans had transplanted to Istanbul in their effort to revitalize the city after the conquest. With communities in both the Ottoman and Venetian empires as well as in other western European cities, Greeks, rather like Jews, were well positioned to act as intermediaries between the Ottoman and European Christian worlds.

The Sephardi Diaspora

Many Jews were on the move in the post-1350 period, but none had as significant a cultural and political impact as the exiled Jews and Conversos from Spain and Portugal, the "Sephardim" (from the Hebrew for "Spain," *Sefarad*). Their apparent political neutrality in a world frequently riven by wars between Muslim and Christian or Catholic and Protestant states, their familiarity with Muslim and Christian intellectual traditions, and the willingness of many Conversos to change their outward religious allegiance for political and economic convenience made them useful to Christian and Muslim rulers and enabled them to establish family and commercial networks extending from Ottoman lands to America. In northern Europe, Conversos first settled in Antwerp; by 1600 there were sizable Converso communities in Amsterdam (modern Netherlands), Hamburg (Germany), several French cities, and London. Rulers hoping to attract and retain these immigrants out of economic interest often permitted them to return to Judaism quietly. In 1656 Cromwell's government in England formally readmitted Jews, mostly Sephardim. Olivares (d. 1645), the chief minister of Philip IV of Spain, had already seriously considered readmitting unbaptized Jews after Portuguese Converso financiers proved to be so effective at using their international connections to amass loans for the Spanish government.

Sephardi exiles became a dominant cultural force among Mediterranean Jews. Their sense of Sephardi identity and group cohesion emerged gradually from the experience of exile and migration, and from an awareness of what distinguished them from the native Jews among whom they settled. Initially settling in foreign cities as distinct Castilian, Aragonese, and Catalan congregations, they eventually unified into one Sephardi whole, joined by a shared nostalgia for life in Iberia, by the common use of a Judeo-Spanish language (Ladino or *judezmo*), and by a sense of family honor and cultural superiority rooted in the vibrant intellectual tradition their ancestors had cultivated in Iberia since the days of the Umayyad caliphate.

Leading Iberian Jewish families, whose status had been based on a combination of learning and affluence, often retained their status in the diaspora. International networks of Sephardi intellectuals and rabbis developed that mirrored those of Sephardi merchants. Intermarriage as well as interpersonal and intertextual communication among these mobile scholars perpetuated their sense of cultural and ethnic distinctiveness. Elite Sephardi immigrants sometimes forged marital and other ties with native Jewish families, but it was the latter who usually adopted Sephardi cultural and religious norms. By virtue of their learning, nomadic Sephardi scholars were able to attain positions of religious leadership in non-Sephardi communities, further spreading the influence of Sephardi culture.

The Sephardim were also influenced by the customs of other Mediterranean Jews, who sometimes resisted their predominance and disagreed with their views. Non-Sephardi Jews, for instance, were less willing to acknowledge the Jewishness of Conversos, whose religious adaptability aroused their suspicions. Such discrepancies, however, did not counteract the larger cultural trend. Joseph Karo (ca. 1488–1575), an Iberian exile raised in Istanbul whose rabbinic appointments and studies took him to Edirne, Thessaloniki, and Safed, wrote a code of Jewish law, *The Prepared Table*, that proved to be so authoritative among Jews in and beyond the Mediterranean world that a Polish rabbi, Moses Isserles (1525–1572), felt compelled to write a work to go along with it that highlighted the distinctions between Sephardi and his own Ashkenazi law: the *Tablecloth*. Many of the scholars studying Kabbalah in Safed were Sephardim and disciples of the mystical teacher Isaac Luria (1534–1572), himself the son of an Ashkenazi family who was raised in Egypt and who married into a Sephardi family. As a result of the contacts between Italian rabbis and Sephardi scholars in Safed, Lurianic Kabbalah had a great impact on the religious life of many Italian Jewish communities. Printing presses in Venice, Istanbul, and Amsterdam—also home to a major Sephardi community—disseminated the works of Sephardi scholars, medieval "classics" as well as more current works. They also printed religious works in Spanish and Portuguese meant for the edification of Conversos returning to the Jewish faith. Some of these works were polemical attacks on Christianity.

The Morisco Diaspora

The Moriscos expelled from Spain in 1609–1614 almost all settled in Muslim lands under Ottoman dominion: especially in Algeria and Tunisia but also in Egypt, Syria, and the Turkish heartland. Morocco was an important exception. For most Moriscos, Christian realms were not a desired destination. Although Henri IV of France (1589–1610) offered asylum to Moriscos who would sincerely embrace Catholicism, the negative reaction of his subjects to Morisco immigration ensured that France was only a place of embarkation for North Africa for all but a few. Duke Cosimo II of Tuscany (1609–1621) tried to attract Moriscos to his port of Livorno, but it served mostly as a way station for those heading to Istanbul.

Substantial numbers of Moriscos had been emigrating to North Africa throughout the sixteenth century. Though Morisco departures peaked following the forced conversions early in the century and the monarchy's harsh suppression of the Granadan rebellion in 1570, inquisitorial prosecution and other forms of oppression kept the flow of emigrants steady. Thus when masses of exiles arrived in the Maghrib in 1609–1614, there were already Morisco communities in a number of places who could facilitate their settlement.

While Moriscos felt a deep attachment to their Spanish homeland, many also desired revenge against the Spanish government that had persecuted or expelled them and against the Christian faith that had been forced on them. Both before and after 1609–1614 Morisco exiles joined the ranks of Maghribi corsairs. Piracy was a livelihood, but it was also a form of holy war against Christians. Morisco corsairs operated out of both Mediterranean and Atlantic ports in Morocco. They established a particularly important community in Rabat-Sala; from this fortified Atlantic port they harried Spanish and Portuguese ships sailing to and from America as well as any Christian vessel traversing the Straits of Gibraltar. Moriscos also served in Sa'did armies, especially as musketeers and artillerymen. They played a key role in Ahmad al-Mansur's conquest of the West African Songhay state in 1591. Al-Mansur did not always trust these ambitious Moriscos, and in the decades of upheaval following his death in 1603 the Morisco community in Sala achieved autonomous status for a time.

Algiers, the corsair capital that had become the symbol of Muslim resistance to Habsburg Spain in the western Mediterranean, attracted many bitter Moriscos to man its ships. By the end of the sixteenth century, 30 percent of the city's population was Morisco. Morisco immigrants in Istanbul employed more diplomatic means to make trouble for Spain: in 1612 they helped the Dutch, Spain's great Protestant enemies, negotiate a treaty with the Ottoman government.

The majority of Morisco immigrants labored as farmers and artisans. With the encouragement of Muslim governments, they established prosperous agricultural communities across North Africa and in Anatolia. In the cities Moriscos were involved in the armaments industry and shipbuilding, and they also manufactured textiles, clothing, and ceramics, often using the "Andalusi" techniques and styles developed by their ancestors.

Morisco assimilation into North African Muslim societies, however, was usually a gradual and in some places a difficult process. Fitting into the host society was often easier for Morisco immigrants who had voluntarily departed Spain prior to 1609, since they often possessed the economic resources to settle elsewhere, a stronger commitment to and deeper knowledge of Islam, and the ability to speak if not read Arabic. The exiles who had been forced out in 1609–1614 were a more diverse group. Many were impoverished and could not speak Arabic, and even though most saw themselves as faithful Muslims, they had at best a rudimentary knowledge of the Islamic faith. Some exiles, however, were sincere Catholics; in Morocco they died for their faith. Even if they did not see themselves as Christians, many Moriscos were highly acculturated to Spanish Christian ways, particularly in language and dress. The immigrants therefore seemed "Christian" to some native Muslims and encountered prejudice as a result. Assimilation was slowest in Tunisia. Because of Spanish rule over Tunis from 1535 to 1574, the region had seen minimal Morisco immigration. Suddenly, in 1610–1611, Tunisian Muslims were faced with the arrival of some 80,000 mostly Spanish-speaking Morisco exiles. The Moriscos needed time to learn Arabic and Tunisian ways.

In order to foster the full Islamization and integration of their people into North African societies, Morisco scholars across the region composed in Spanish works that provided instruction in Islamic religion and law, such as the anonymous *Treatise of the Two Paths*, which told Morisco readers about the rewards that living a righteous Islamic life would bring. Scholars like Juan Pérez from Toledo, who took the name Ibrahim Taybili in Tunis, also wrote polemics against Christianity, deeming it essential to eradicate all vestiges of this faith from the Morisco community. Such works nonetheless contained quotes from or references to the works of Spanish Catholic writers such as the playwright Lope de Vega and Miguel de Cervantes, the author of *Don Quixote*. Morisco authors could not so quickly reject the culture of the country that had rejected them.

Only the first generation of Morisco immigrants required such Spanish-language education in Islam. Their children grew up speaking Arabic and with the freedom to practice Islam without fear; they integrated more rapidly into their family's new Muslim homeland. Like the Greeks and Jews scattered in their own diasporas, the Morisco exiles clung to some of the customs and ways of their ancestors. Yet, no matter how much they cherished such memories, they could not undo the work of kings, conquerors, and inquisitors and recover the world that had been lost.

Note

1. Samuel Usque, *Consolation for the Tribulations of Israel*, trans. Martin A. Cohen (Philadelphia: Jewish Publication Society of America, 1965), 231.

CHAPTER TWELVE

Slavery and Captivity, ca. 650–1650

In the summer of 1518 Spanish pirates captured a ship from Ragusa (or Dubrovnik), a Catholic port and Ottoman protectorate, that was sailing from Cairo to Morocco. Among the sixty Muslims on board was a valuable prize: al-Hasan ibn Muhammad al-Wazzan, an ambassador for the Wattasid sultan Muhammad al-Burtughali (1505–1524, known as "the Portuguese" for his fluency in the language he had learned as a child captive). Born in Granada around 1487 and raised in Fez, where he received an advanced *madrasa* education, al-Wazzan had served the sultan on diplomatic missions across the Mediterranean. The pirate captain made a gift of al-Wazzan to Pope Leo X (1513–1521), a declared enemy of Islam who was intrigued by what this captive might know of Muslim political affairs. Although al-Wazzan's imprisonment was not harsh, he accepted baptism in January 1520 in order to avoid a future of confinement and slavery. Al-Wazzan was given the Christian name Joannes Leo, after his papal master, but is known to history as Leo Africanus for his great work, the *Cosmography and Geography of Africa*. Written in Italian and finished in 1526, it was a work of geography and history peppered with the author's accounts of his extensive travels. Valued for his knowledge of Arabic, Leo was involved in various intellectual projects, such as transcribing an Arabic translation of Saint Paul's Epistles, correcting a Latin translation of the Qur'an, and collaborating with the Jewish scholar Jacob Mantino on an Arabic-Hebrew-Latin dictionary. After imperial troops sacked Rome in 1527, he returned to the Maghrib and to the Islamic faith he had never truly abandoned. Al-Wazzan is last known to have been living in Tunis in 1532.

Al-Wazzan was unusual and lucky. More typical was al-Wazzan's capture at sea by pirates of an enemy faith, for most captives were victims of such piracy or of warfare and raiding across the land frontiers separating Christian and Muslim states. Indeed, it was the Mediterranean's location as the principal zone of contact between the Christian and Muslim worlds that made it a center of the international slave trade. In al-Wazzan's day the Mediterranean was on the verge of its "golden age" of piracy, when corsairs operating out of Muslim Algiers, Christian Malta, and many other ports fed on the sea's growing commercial traffic. Ransoming captives, long a lucrative enterprise for pirates, thus became a booming business in the early modern period. Al-Wazzan, because he had been carried off to Rome, probably despaired of ever being found and ransomed by the Wattasids in distant Fez. He converted to Christianity lest he endure the fate of other captives who were not ransomed: being sold as a slave. The learned Moroccan was doubly fortunate. Not only did the pope liberate him upon his conversion—a step which, as we will see, was by no means automatic in either Christian or Muslim lands—but the intellectual labor that he performed both as a captive and as a dependent freedman was milder than that with which most other captives and freed clients were tasked.

Yet there were other captives who were never meant to be ransomed and who were captured for the sole purpose of being sold and used as slaves. They usually came from among pagan peoples inhabiting regions far beyond the Mediterranean whom slave traders transported to slave markets around the Middle Sea: Slavs from eastern Europe, Turkic and other ethnic groups from Central Asia, and Black people from sub-Saharan Africa. Most of them were sold in the Muslim world, where the males served as slave soldiers or eunuchs for caliphs and sultans and the females as concubines in their harems. White female Tatars labored in the households of elite Italian families whose men often sexually exploited them. Sub-Saharan enslaved Blacks did not become a significant presence in southern European cities until the late fifteenth century, though they had been imported into the Muslim world as early as the seventh century.

In his *Geography of Africa*, al-Wazzan expressed a view of Black Africans that many Muslims shared: their religion was the factor that determined their status, not their skin color. Pagan Blacks, then, could be enslaved because they were not Muslims, like the White Circassian slave-soldiers al-Wazzan encountered in Egypt. Yet, as a result of the Islamic world's enslavement of millions of pagan sub-Saharan Africans, some White Muslims had come to equate the enslaved people's Blackness with their supposed natural suitability for servitude. By 1650 Christian Europeans were also making this fateful association.

Medieval Transformations of an Ancient Institution

Dating back to as early as 2000 BCE in Mesopotamia, the institution of slavery was deeply rooted in the societies of the wider Mediterranean world when Arab Muslims embarked on their seventh-century conquests. Ancient Greece and Rome had both been what historians call "slave societies," societies that depended primarily on slave labor for agricultural and industrial production. Although neither the Christian nor the Muslim states that emerged in the post-Roman Mediterranean ever challenged the legitimacy of slavery, they were not slave societies. Religious leaders of all three monotheistic faiths accepted their followers' possession of slaves but, with the backing of secular rulers, discouraged their enslavement of coreligionists or sale of them to unbelievers. "Infidels" adhering to rival monotheisms and pagans thus became the preferred targets of enslavement. Slavery and the slave trade persisted in the Mediterranean world because of its religious diversity. The patterns of the commerce in human commodities shifted over the centuries in accordance with the relative political and economic strength of the states involved and with the ability of authorities to prohibit dealers from selling some peoples while legitimizing their marketing of others. Nothing quite captures the mixture of seemingly contradictory religious, political, and economic motives shaping Christian-Muslim relations in the Mediterranean as much as the slave trade.

Ideological and Social Rationales for Slavery

The holy scriptures of Judaism, Christianity, and Islam all assumed the existence of slavery and implicitly accepted it. They all also encouraged believers to treat their slaves decently. The Hebrew Bible, significantly, distinguished between Hebrew slaves, whose servitude the ancient Hebrews were urged to limit, and outsiders, particularly the Canaanites inhabiting the Promised Land, whom Hebrews could enslave perpetually as chattels (movable possessions). Medieval Jews' statelessness and lack of military power, however, meant that the ownership of slaves was not a major concern of theirs, except in a few cases. Neither the New Testament nor the Church Fathers challenged the institution of slavery; it was part of the Roman world in which Christianity emerged. Slaves were supposed to accept their lot in this sinful world since true freedom for the individual was internal and spiritual. The church's position did not change with the Christianization of the Roman Empire. In their use of slaves, the adherents of the new religion of Islam were perpetuating an institution that was well established both in the Arabian Peninsula and in the Roman and Persian territories they conquered. The Prophet Muhammad himself owned slaves, and Qur'anic revelations recommended that masters show kindness to their slaves and eventually free them.

Even though medieval Mediterranean states were not slave societies and owners did not employ their slaves in capitalist plantation systems like those later established on Atlantic islands, slaves did contribute to the economies of Muslim and Christian households as domestic servants, farmhands, assistants in artisan workshops, and business agents. Household slaves also functioned as symbols of their master's power and wealth, enhancing the master's honor in local society. None fulfilled this role more than the military slaves who served 'Abbasid caliphs and later Muslim rulers, their systematic use a

FIGURE 12.1 Muslim captives brought before Byzantine emperor Romanos III (1028–1034). The Picture Art Collection / Alamy Stock Photo.

new development in the history of Mediterranean slavery. SEE SOURCEBOOK 12:1.

Mediterranean Christian states saw both the gradual disappearance of Christian slaves, especially those belonging to the ruler's sect, and the growing presence of foreign, non-Christian slaves. The slavery of indigenous Christians diminished more rapidly in Byzantium because early on Greek Christians could obtain infidel slaves on land and sea from among Muslims and pagan Slavs and Bulghars. Although the early Germanic kingdoms enslaved Christians in their internecine wars, once the Carolingians established their Christian empire, they took slaves from among the pagan Saxons and Slavs on the empire's borders, selling many Slavs on the Mediterranean market.

A number of complex economic factors contributed to the disappearance of Christian slaves from most rural areas in the Latin West by the tenth century, causing them to merge gradually into the rest of the free peasant population. Yet in the tenth and eleventh centuries some lords took advantage of free peasants' need for land and protection—from predatory local knights or foreign raiders—and tied them perpetually to their estates as serfs through legal arrangements and imposed more taxes on them. Serfs, though unfree, could not be sold as chattel slaves.

After 1000, slaves, mostly non-Christian in origin, appeared increasingly in the households of Mediterranean Christian cities. Some were victims of Latin crusade, conquest, and piracy, and were kept or sold by their captors; others, like many of the slaves found in Muslim households, could be purchased from professional slave traders.

The Trade in Human Merchandise

Like other merchants, slave-dealers sold their merchandise where the demand and the prices for it were highest. By the ninth century, the richest market was the 'Abbasid Caliphate; having reached the limits of its expansion, it needed to import non-Muslims and non-*dhimmis* from the outside. The great toll taken by bubonic plague in Muslim lands in 743–752 had increased their need for labor. Traders conveyed slaves to the Muslims from three regions. One was Central Asia, the source of Turkic slave-soldiers. Another was sub-Saharan Africa, from which merchants transported enslaved Blacks eastward to the Nile valley and Muslim Egypt or to Red Sea ports for export to Muslim domains farther east, and northward across the Sahara to the Muslim Maghrib.

From the late eighth through the tenth century, Europe was a third major source of slaves. Traders could sell the slaves in Muslim lands for two or three times the price they could get in the West, where the economy was poorer and the labor supply adequate. In exchange, the traders brought back to Europe luxury goods for resale—silks, spices, and drugs—and 'Abbasid gold and silver coinage. The majority of the slaves sold to the Muslims were eastern European pagans, mainly Slavs. In fact, our word "slave" derives from the medieval Latin term, *sclavus*, for Slav. Most of these enslaved Slavs—*saqaliba* in Arabic—were male and young, and served as soldiers and eunuchs throughout the Muslim world.

Among the slave-dealers were pagan Scandinavians, who carried the slaves down the Volga River to the port of Itil on the Caspian Sea; from here Muslim merchants took them to Persia and Iraq. Pagan Slavs also sold their fellows to the Muslims or to Christian and Jewish traders. Jews conveyed slaves to Itil and also joined Christians in transporting slaves across Frankish territories to Verdun (modern France), a castration center, and then on to Muslim Spain. Another main route crossed the Alps to Venice—also a center for creating eunuchs—whose merchants were middlemen in the slave trade between Europe and Muslim domains to the south. Both Venetians and Byzantine Greeks sold Christians of sects or ethnicities different from their own as well as pagans to Muslim buyers. The profits, after all, were substantial. The slave trade with the Muslim world helped fuel the expansion of the western European commercial economy. SEE SOURCEBOOK 12:2.

Although the traffic in slaves remained profitable for Latin merchants after 1000, their trade routes and the ethnicity of their cargoes changed. As a result of the conversion of Slavic and Scandinavian peoples to Christianity by the twelfth century and the growing power of European monarchies to prevent the enslavement of their subjects, northern Europe ceased being a zone where Latin dealers procured slaves. The dealers instead looked to the south and east, for Latin domination of Mediterranean sea-lanes and territorial conquest had created new opportunities. After the dismemberment of the Byzantine Empire in the early thirteenth century, Catalan and especially Venetian and Genoese traders sold Greeks to Christian and Muslim buyers in the markets of the eastern Mediterranean and Black Sea. Northern Italian cities also began importing Muslim slaves from Spain. Later in the century, the Genoese regularly supplied the Egyptian Mamluks with Turkic slaves they had purchased north of the Black Sea. They and the Venetians also sent Central Asian slaves to northern Italian markets. Most of these slaves were young and female and worked as domestic servants. In the late fourteenth century the import of these slaves accelerated in order to supplement urban labor forces depleted by the Black Death. Ottoman expansion into the Black Sea region cut off this commercial route in 1475, forcing Italians to import more Maghribi Muslim and sub-Saharan African slaves.

The sale or ransoming of captives taken at sea by Muslim and Christian pirates had long supplemented the large-scale commerce in mostly pagan slaves acquired by dealers far beyond the shores of the Mediterranean. After 1500, however, piracy escalated dramatically, transforming the Mediterranean itself into a central slaving zone. The slave trade—or, perhaps better said, the ransoming business—became integral to the war at sea between the Ottoman and Habsburg empires and their corsair surrogates.

The commerce in pagan enslaved Blacks between sub-Saharan Africa and the Muslim world increased after 1000 with the spread of Islam south of the Sahara and the foundation there of Muslim states such as Mali and Songhay. The rulers of these states had a religious justification for warring against and enslaving non-Muslims and an economic motive for sending them to the north and the east for sale. White Muslim purchasers, including the Ottomans, especially sought women and boys, many of whom were castrated and sold as eunuchs at a high price. Portuguese expansion into West Africa after 1448 created a new Atlantic route for the transport of pagan enslaved Blacks to Christian buyers in the Mediterranean. Merchants sold them in Iberian cities such as Lisbon, Seville, and Valencia, in Sicily, and in northern Italian cities. The number of these slaves in southern Europe was tiny in comparison to the millions sold in the Muslim world and America.

Life of the Enslaved

Enslaved people could never entirely escape the brutality and indignities inherent in the institution of slavery or the bald reality, enshrined in Christian and Muslim

The personnel, architectural setting, and functions of the harem of the Ottoman sultans in Istanbul changed significantly between Mehmed II's conquest of the city in 1453 and the late sixteenth century. The harem in the New Palace (known today as the Topkapi Palace) eventually became the chief residence of the sultan's family, while its enslaved and manumitted female inhabitants came to exert considerable political influence. The harem bore little resemblance to European images of it as a pleasure palace where degenerate sultans indulged their sexual appetites. Europeans were left to fantasize because the harem—a word signifying both the inviolable domestic space and the imperial family it guarded—was purposely inaccessible and difficult to learn about. Historians have nonetheless

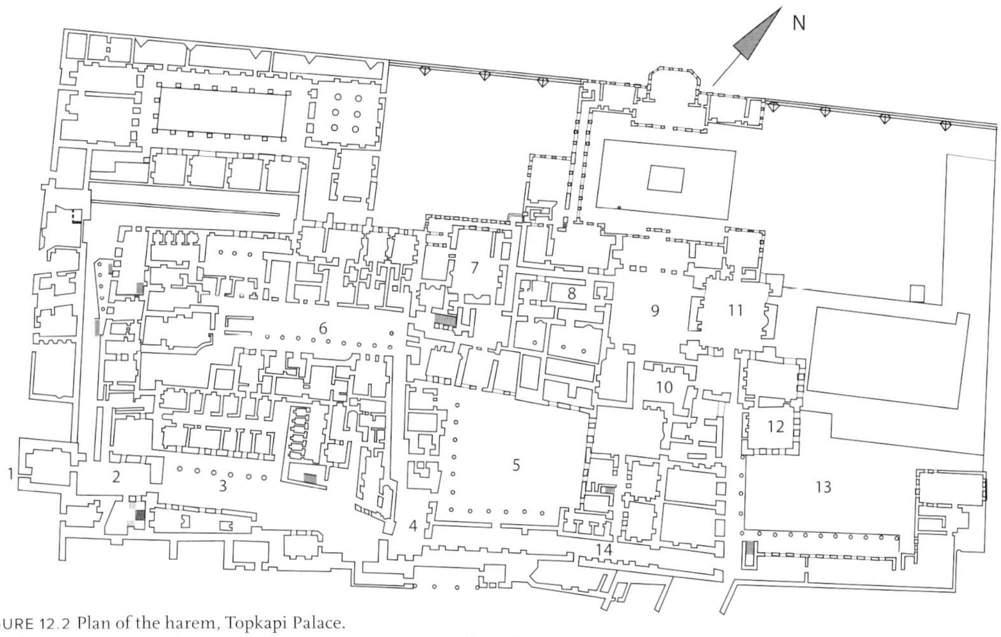

FIGURE 12.2 Plan of the harem, Topkapi Palace.
Drawing by Gothika provided by Wikimedia Commons under the CC-BY-SA 3.0 License.

PLAN OF THE HAREM OF TOPKAPI PALACE

1. Gate of Carriages and Haremeyn Treasury/Dome with Cupboards.
2. Sofa with Fountain—Tower of Justice—Mosque of Harem Eunuchs.
3. Courtyard and Dormitories of the Harem Eunuchs—Chief Harem Eunuch's Quarters and School of Princes—Door of Aviary (Harem Exit).
4. Main Gate of Harem and Sentry Post.
5. Courtyard of Queen Mother—Quarters of Queen Mother, Sultan's Consorts, Princes, Senior Maid, Superintendent of Servants.
6. Passage and Courtyard of Concubines—Quarters of Consorts of the Sultan—Dormitories and Baths.
7. Queen Mother's Quarters.
8. Baths—Bath of Sultan and Bath of Queen Mother.

THE SULTAN'S PRIVATE APARTMENTS

9. Imperial Hall—Apartments of Abdühamid I, Selim III, and Osman III.
10. Hall with Fountain—Hall with Fireplace.
11. Privy Chamber of Murad III—Privy Chambers of Ahmed I and Ahmed III (Dining Room/Fruit Room).
12. Twin Kiosks (Apartments of Crown Prince).
13. Terrace and Apartments of Favorites/Anteroom between Men's and Women's Quarters.
14. Golden Road/Passage.

managed to reconstruct the evolution and inner life of the imperial harem from Ottoman archival sources and the soberer accounts of European ambassadors and travelers.

When Mehmed II created a centralized administration in Istanbul staffed by male household slaves—the most talented and highly trained *devşirme* recruits—he based it in his New Palace (built 1458–1479). The sultan's family, however, lived in the Old Palace (built 1454–1458) in the center of the city. This family included the enslaved concubines with whom the sultan had conceived children, who were the future of the Ottoman dynasty. Most of the other concubines also resided in the Old Palace and received the training suitable for a potential companion of the sultan. The sultan selected some of these enslaved women to join him in the New Palace; they were lodged in its smaller harem quarters. According to a Genoese merchant serving at the Ottoman court in 1475, 250 women lived in the Old Palace, while 150 of "the most splendid, well-kept, and beautiful women that could be found in the world" might enjoy the sultan's attentions in the New.[1] If impregnated, they transferred back to the Old Palace where they raised their offspring. Once the princes came of age, the sultan sent them, accompanied by their mothers, to govern provinces. After their father's death, the princes would contend for the throne. The victor, having killed all his brothers, would return to Istanbul and establish his mother—now the Queen Mother (*valide sultan*)—as mistress of the Old Palace. She could never marry again. Concubines who did not bear a prince were married off to one of the household slaves, some of whom became high imperial officials.

This system began to change when Hurrem, Suleyman the Magnificent's favorite concubine, moved into the New Palace after the sultan, unusually, married her. The couple, however, did not share the same quarters, but resided in distinct parts of the palace's third court: the sultan in the privy chamber where he was attended by male pages under the supervision of White eunuchs, and Hurrem, along with 100 ladies-in-waiting, in the harem, where Black eunuchs guarded her and the concubines. Suleyman could visit Hurrem by passing through a small walled garden that led to her rooms.

The most dramatic changes to the harem in the New Palace occurred when Murad III (1574–1595) rebuilt and enlarged it, making it an important center of political power. The expanded harem now included quarters for the sultan himself, an imperial hall where the sultan and other inhabitants of the harem could be entertained by female musicians and singers, new quarters for the Queen Mother, and apartments for the sultan's consorts and their children. With the days when the sultans were frontier warriors long past, Murad and his successors withdrew into the inaccessible harem and were only occasionally seen by their subjects. Furthermore, Ottoman princes were no longer assigned to govern provinces as part of their education; instead, they were confined to the harem and educated in a school within. The princes fell increasingly under the influence of women and eunuchs. Of the over 1,000 eunuchs serving in the palace during Murad's reign, the Black eunuchs, as protectors of the harem that now housed the sultan, acquired more political clout than their White counterparts.

Aside from the sultan, the most powerful figure in the harem, and therefore one of the most influential in the realm, was the Queen Mother. Originally an enslaved concubine who had been freed upon the death of her master (the current sultan's father), she was responsible for the administration of the harem household and functioned as guardian of the royal family. The central location and great size of her suite, which included a large salon and a courtyard, were the architectural expression of her authority. The Queen Mother extended her influence beyond the walls of the palace through manumitting household slaves who then served as her political agents, and through playing a central role in arranging the marriages of princesses, both her own daughters and the daughters of her son and his concubines, to men from elite Ottoman families. Such marriages crucially strengthened the loyalty of these families to the Ottoman dynasty in a time when sultans interacted far less with their chief subjects.

Below the Queen Mother in the hierarchy of the harem was the sultan's favorite concubine. Though a slave, she enjoyed higher status than the sultan's sisters and aunts, and she was given her own quarters and female attendants. Other, less-favored concubines lived in more modest apartments with their entourages. There was a large, two-story dormitory for the young enslaved women. More senior women taught them Islam, to speak and read Turkish, to sew and embroider, and to sing and play musical instruments. Their education paralleled that received by the enslaved male pages. The most accomplished and attractive of these young women acquired more polish in the service of the Queen Mother. According to Albert Bobovius, a royal page of Polish origin, the sultan usually chose his concubines from among this group: "[The Queen Mother] takes care to keep them splendidly outfitted and to have them instructed in all that they can learn so that they might be capable of inspiring in the Grand Seigneur [the sultan] the love which might allow them to become concubines, and perhaps one among them the

FIGURE 12.3 The Queen Mother (*Valide Sultan*) in the harem, 1720. © Historical Views / agefotostock

favorite and honored mother of his eldest son, or else be married to persons of quality outside the palace."[2]

When a sultan died, the women of his harem—his mother (if she were still alive), concubines, the many other slaves, and unmarried princesses—were moved to the Old Palace. As Bobovius noted, marriages were arranged for many of the enslaved women, often to manumitted officials who had been trained in the New Palace. The women were normally freed at the time of their marriage and granted a dowry. As a result, an important segment of the Ottoman elite was formed in the harem and the school for pages in the New Palace's third court. This world of slaves set the tone for elite Ottoman society.

Discussion Questions

1. How did apparently powerless enslaved women attain so much influence in Ottoman state and society?

2. Did the influence acquired by enslaved women, such as the Queen Mother, make Ottoman society less patriarchal? What effect did the slavery of women have on gender relations in Ottoman society, or in any of the Mediterranean societies studied in this book?

3. How did slavery in the Ottoman empire contribute to the strength and efficacy of its government? Did it ultimately weaken the empire?

Further Reading

Necipoglu, Gulru. *Architecture, Ceremonial, and Power: The Topkapi Palace in the Fifteenth and Sixteenth Centuries.* Cambridge, MA: MIT Press, 1991.

Peirce, Leslie P. *The Imperial Harem: Women and Sovereignty in the Ottoman Empire.* Oxford: Oxford University Press, 1993.

Notes

1. Peirce, 120.
2. Peirce, 142.

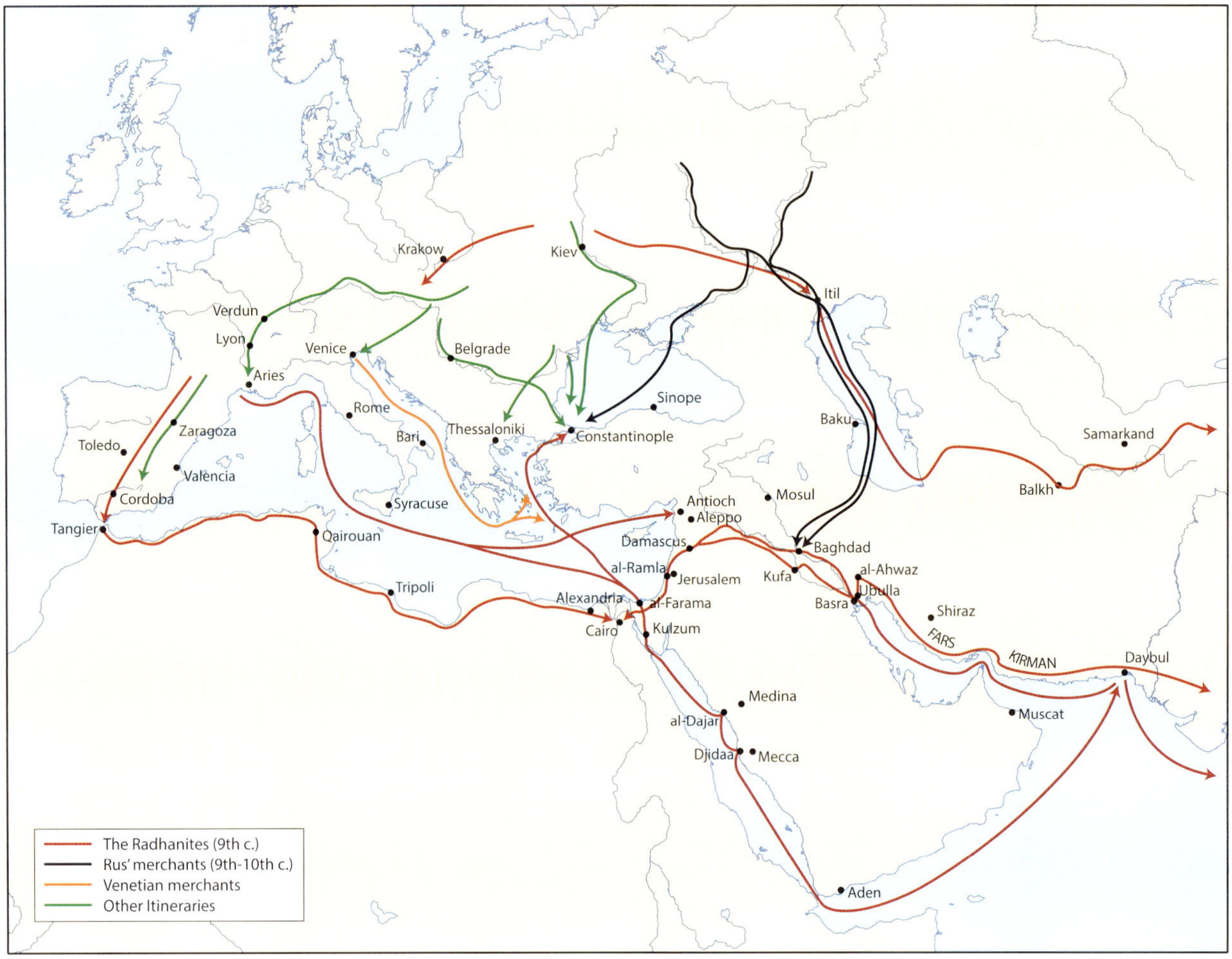

MAP 12.1 Map of Slave Trade in the Central Middle Ages. Youval Rotman from © "The Map of the Medieval Slave Trade, 9th–11th c.," *Human Trafficking in the Central Middle Ages: Map and Data*. Map excludes African, Cross-Saharan, and North-European itineraries. Reproduced with permission of Youval Rotman.

laws, that they were their master's property. Yet within this universal legal framework various factors shaped the lives of slaves, sometimes making for quite different experiences. The slaves' religion, ethnicity, color, and gender were all crucial variables, as was the nature of the work that masters commanded slaves to perform. Moreover, since Mediterranean slavery was largely domestic and most slaves resided in the master's household, familiar, even intimate relations might develop between slaves and masters. In such circumstances masters could hardly avoid recognizing their slaves' humanity, as religious scriptures urged them to do. Some masters came to feel almost parental or familial responsibility for their slaves, a sentiment that having a child with an enslaved woman often enhanced. Both the timing and the terms of the liberation of slaves depended on their origin and religion as well as on the nature of their relationship with their master. Though some slaves managed to return home through ransoming or captive exchanges, many, if not most, freed slaves remained in their new homeland, often still dependent on their former masters. SEE SOURCEBOOK 12:3.

Legal and Religious Status

No matter where in the Mediterranean they found themselves, enslaved people, as the property of their master, could be commanded to perform any task, hired out, bequeathed in a will, and sold, though Islamic law forbade masters thereby to separate a slave mother from her child of less than seven years. Slaves lacked the legal capacity to own, inherit, or bequeath property, nor could they act as witnesses in court. Masters had the right to harshly punish their slaves, though they could not kill them with impunity. Anyone who killed, wounded, or impregnated a slave belonging to another owner was liable to pay compensation to the owner for having damaged his property. The slave received nothing.

Slaves were usually outsiders, infidels a long way from home. Possessing them not only enhanced the master's honor but also symbolized the triumph of the master's faith. The institution of slavery reinforced Christian and Muslim ideals of religious and social hierarchy. Thus in Latin Christian states adherents of the ruling faith could own Muslim or even Greek Christian slaves, but the latter could not own Catholics. Islamic law similarly prohibited non-Muslims from possessing Muslim slaves.

The master's religion was also promoted through the conversion of slaves to it. Patterns of conversion, however, varied in accordance with slaves' origins. Pagans, White and Black, were almost always converted by Muslim and Christian masters, or even prior to being sold to them. Muslim slaves of Christian masters and Christian slaves of Muslims converted far less frequently, since they hoped to be ransomed by coreligionists; masters, moreover, expected to profit from the ransom payments. Because masters in Christian Spain identified unbaptized Muslim slaves with the foreign Muslim enemy, they tended to trust them less than their Christianized enslaved Blacks who were bereft of all possible connections with their homeland. Muslim and Christian slaves who lost hope of ever being redeemed and returning home often abandoned their ancestral faith.

Conversion did not necessarily lead to manumission. Both Christian and Islamic traditions encouraged masters to emancipate converted slaves eventually, and in the twelfth century freeing baptized slaves was customary in the Latin Kingdom of Jerusalem and Catalonia. Yet, in response to friction between missionizing friars seeking to convert Muslim slaves and the slaves' Christian masters trying to protect their investments, Pope Gregory IX (1227–1241) ruled in 1237 that baptism did not change the legal status of a slave. Civil law codes followed the pope's decision. Slaves' souls could be saved, but when their bodies would be released from bondage was left to the master's discretion.

Conversion helped slaves fit into their master's household. For reasons of ritual purity, Jewish masters in Fatimid Cairo obliged their (non-Muslim) slaves to participate in some Jewish observances and encouraged them to convert, a practice the Fatimids permitted despite its violation of Islamic laws forbidding conversion to any faith other than Islam. Consistent with scriptural exhortations to treat their slaves humanely, masters assumed responsibility for properly feeding and clothing their slaves. In Valencia some Christian masters provided slaves with their own rooms furnished with beds and linens. Not all masters had the resources or the inclination to treat their slaves so well, though few saw any sense in starving the sources of labor in which they had invested.

Slaves could marry other slaves, but only after their conversion to their master's faith. Slaves also needed the consent of their master to wed. According to Islamic and Christian law, the offspring of slave marriages were, like their parents, still slaves and the property of the master, a stark reminder of the fact that, ultimately, slaves had no legitimate status in the master's society and were powerless to ameliorate the condition of their children. This was in the master's hands.

Slave Labor

In the Mediterranean economy slaves were mainly a source of supplementary labor that masters employed in their homes, workshops, or fields. Gangs of slaves were rarely used on a large scale in agriculture. The 'Abbasids' employment of large numbers of enslaved Black Zanj from eastern Africa to drain marshes in southern Iraq is the most famous early instance, but it ended disastrously. In 868 the Zanj rebelled and established a small state; caliphal armies could not defeat them until 883. In contemporary Byzantium, aristocrats, monasteries, and small landowners had individual slaves laboring in their fields. In the Latin West the use of slaves for this purpose was diminishing. Some later medieval conquests, however, resulted in the victors' drafting of gangs of enslaved defeated infidels to labor on their estates. Such was the fate of some conquered Muslims in Catalan Mallorca in the thirteenth century and of some conquered Christians in Ottoman Anatolia in the late fifteenth century, but only for a few decades. After 1200 Mediterranean masters did not utilize slaves extensively in the agricultural sector.

Female slaves usually worked in their master's home, doing daily chores such as cooking, cleaning, and laundering. Some nursed the master's children and served as their nannies. Others served their master sexually, though in Christian lands the church authorities censured such activity. Both Islamic and Christian laws prohibited masters from prostituting their female slaves, but not always successfully. Innkeepers in Valencia's famous brothel district purchased slaves with prostitution in mind.

Male slaves labored more often outside the home in the workshops of their artisan masters. In early medieval Byzantium slaves worked in the silk industry and in imperial workshops as goldsmiths and gold embroiderers. In late medieval Christian cities artisans employed their slaves in carpentry, baking, metalwork, and textile manufacturing. Muslim slaves knowledgeable about silk production were highly valued. Female slaves spun yarn and worked at dressmaking, usually in the master's home. Some masters hired out their slaves to fellow artisans. Free salaried laborers occasionally complained about the competition that slaves posed, which moved guilds in Barcelona, Valencia, and Genoa to pass statutes limiting the number of slaves a master artisan could employ. Some guilds expressed additional concern that the "honor" of their profession might be sullied if slaves were associated with it.

Although sources from Muslim lands do not yield as much information on slaves engaged in industrial activities, they do show that Muslim and Jewish merchants in Fatimid Egypt empowered trusted slaves to act as their commercial agents in long-distance trade or to take charge of their business when they were out of town. In Mamluk times, *karimi* merchants employed enslaved Blacks as their agents. The medieval biography of one such merchant reports that one of his slaves "was even gone for twenty years but he returned and died in his master's house."[1]

Male slaves performed less artisanal work in Muslim lands because so many of them were employed as soldiers and eunuchs. While Western Christian and Byzantine rulers seem to have followed the example of the Romans who had prohibited slaves from serving in their armies, slave soldiers in the Muslim world had great political importance. Called *ghulams* (young men, slaves) or *mamluks* (possessions, slaves), these crack troops played key roles, for instance, in the Seljuqs' crushing victory over Byzantine forces at Manzikert in 1071, in the Egyptian Mamluks' defeat of both Mongols and Crusaders in the thirteenth century, and in the Ottomans' conquest and defense of their great empire.

The 'Abbasid caliphs al-Ma'mun (813–833) and al-Mu'tasim (833–842) established military slavery as an institution, procuring slaves from among pagan Turks living beyond the borders of Islamdom in Central Asia. Brought in as children, converted to Islam, given rigorous military training, and finally manumitted, these enslaved recruits, so far from their homeland, became the "children" of the caliph, dependent on him and instruments of his will. Caliphs believed that their *mamluks* were more reliable than Arab or Persian troops with suspect political allegiances, though at times they were proved wrong. Umayyad emirs and caliphs in al-Andalus engaged in similar practices, though they manned their slave regiments with European Slavs and Black Africans.

The most comprehensive and effective system of military slavery was the Mamluk sultanate (ca. 1250–1517) in Egypt and Syria. Established by *mamluk* soldiers who overthrew Salah al-Din's Ayyubid dynasty, the regime perpetuated itself through importing enslaved pagan, Turkic (and later Circassian) children who were placed in military schools where they received an Islamic education and the martial training that made them, for a long time, an unbeatable cavalry force. After graduation and manumission, the young adult *mamluks* staffed the army and government, becoming, in effect, the Egyptian and Syrian nobility. Yet they were a one-generation nobility. Their sons, the offspring of marriages to slave women or the daughters of local families, could not become *mamluks*, since the children of Muslims could not be enslaved.

The *mamluks* distinguished themselves from their children and the rest of Arabic-speaking society by keeping Turkish names and speaking Turkish among themselves. Despite being a foreign military elite, the Mamluk regime earned the acceptance of the local population through defending the lands of Islam and patronizing Islamic religious institutions.

The Ottoman Janissaries, who finally vanquished the Mamluks, were the most accomplished slave soldiers of all. Yet, because of the difficulty in finding large numbers of pagans or Christian enemies to capture, convert, and train, the Ottomans had resorted to enslaving Christian *dhimmis* in the Balkans through the *devşirme,* which technically violated Islamic law. In addition to forming an elite infantry corps, these slaves were groomed to administer the empire as viziers. The great effectiveness of this system of recruitment outweighed any questions religious scholars raised about its legality.

Concubines and Eunuchs

Throughout the Mediterranean masters exploited female slaves as concubines. The Qur'an gave the master the right to have sexual intercourse with his female slaves. Yet in Muhammad's Arabia slaves were not held in large numbers. It was the Muslim conquerors' acquisition of thousands of slaves in the seventh and eighth centuries that prompted the formulators of *shari'a* to make laws that eased the absorption of slaves into the family. Thus the child born from the union of an owner with his female slave was regarded as free and legitimate, a member of the father's kinship group enjoying the same legal and social status as the offspring of his free wife. The slave mother earned the status of *umm walad* (mother of the child); she could not be sold by the master and was automatically freed upon his death. The master could marry her, but he first had to manumit her. The resulting integration of slave concubines and their children into free Muslim society increased the demand for new slaves.

The possession of large numbers of slaves increasingly became a measure of the power and wealth of caliphs and elite families. In the eighth century, Umayyad caliphs, emulating Sasanian Persian practices, began secluding their wives and creating large harems of wives and concubines. The term *harem* (from Arabic *harim,* meaning "sacred, inviolable") designated the women's private quarters and the women of the family. Only some affluent urban households could afford to have concubines and harems. Still, slave concubinage became so normalized among the 'Abbasid caliphs that all but three of them had slave mothers. Although monarchs from the 'Abbasid and later dynasties had legal wives as well as concubines, the Ottoman sultans from the mid-fifteenth century reproduced only through concubines, while their resort to marriage declined.

Some concubines acquired considerable power through their relationships with rulers. Shaghab, the freed slave mother of the 'Abbasid caliph al-Muqtadir (908–932), exercised great influence over her son and was famed for her philanthropic activities. The concubine Hurrem (d. 1558), the mother of all six of Suleyman the Magnificent's children, was his favorite as well as his political counselor. Suleyman broke Ottoman custom by freeing and marrying her. After Hurrem, the enslaved mothers of sultans—"queen mothers"—became especially influential figures. Other concubines were prized in Mediterranean court circles as singers, composers of music, and poets.

Eunuchs performed important functions in Muslim societies where concubinage, harems, and military slavery were practically institutionalized. In resorting to eunuchs, Muslims followed the examples of Persia and especially Byzantium. Eunuchs served Greek emperors as palace officials; they were recruited from among enslaved ethnic outsiders and free, even prominent, Byzantine families. Umayyad caliphs began using eunuchs to guard their women and harems. Valued for their trustworthiness, eunuchs were expensive because of the high mortality rates from castration. There were reportedly 11,000 eunuchs at the court of the 'Abbasid al-Muqtadir—7,000 Black and 4,000 White—to watch over 4,000 free and enslaved women. By this time, however, eunuchs had been filling a number of other roles, such as army commanders on the Byzantine frontier and administrators of caliphal estates. Under the Mamluk regime eunuchs supervised the education and training of the young slave soldiers. Rulers often regarded Black eunuchs as highly as their White counterparts.

Jewish communities condemned sexual relations between masters and their female slaves. Transgressors, who were not unusual, were forced to sell their slave and to distribute the proceeds from the sale among the poor; sometimes they incurred excommunication. In Fatimid Egypt a number of Jewish masters married slaves whom they had converted and emancipated.

Even though the church held a dim view of slave concubinage, the practice was widespread in late medieval Italian and Spanish cities. Masters' sexual relationships with their slaves sometimes sparked marital discord in Christian homes; wives felt especially threatened when a concubine gave birth to her husband's child. With so many female slaves serving as domestics, lawmakers were compelled to address the question of their children's status. Roman law had ruled that the child of a free father and a slave mother was a slave. Though Italian cities initially followed the Roman ruling, in the later fourteenth century many cities changed their laws, stipulating that the offspring from such unions were free. The toll taken by plague and fears of family extinction as well as pangs of conscience moved masters to formally acknowledge and adopt their children by slave women. While Italian masters were not legally obligated to manumit the child's mother, in Valencia masters were supposed to free both the concubine and her offspring. In order for his slave's child to be freed, the master first had to acknowledge that the child was his. Many masters did but many did not, which led some slave concubines in Valencia to file what were basically paternity suits against their masters. The babies of slave mothers whose fathers had rejected them were often left at foundling hospitals. The logbook of Florence's hospital from 1451 described two abandoned twins who "came from the house of Agostino Capponi, born of Polonia his slave; they were brought by...the midwife . . . wrapped in two linen rags . . . half dead; if they had been two dogs, they would have been better cared for."[2] Like many foundlings, one of the twins soon died. Those who survived were considered free and legitimate.

Paths to Freedom

Although slaves' conversion to their master's faith did not automatically result in their emancipation, it was a crucial step on the path to freedom, for, once freed, they could more easily integrate into their former master's society. All three faiths encouraged masters to manumit their slaves as an act of piety, and masters often complied, even if only—and tellingly—on their deathbed. Since Mediterranean economies did not depend on slave labor and the breeding of slaves, slaves could be freed with minimal impact on local productivity. Indeed, the frequency and scale of manumission, especially in the Muslim world, helped fuel the lucrative slave trade. Purchasing, possessing, and freeing slaves allowed Mediterranean masters to enhance their honor in society and display their religiosity.

Manumission was a legal and a religious act, often one of the stipulations in a master's will. Christian wills normally included the formula that the slave was being freed on the master's death "for cure of my soul" or "for remission of sins." There were other contractual arrangements for slaves' liberation. In conformity with a Qur'anic recommendation, a Muslim master could grant freedom to a slave in exchange for the slave's payment of a specified sum of money. The slave was thereby given the right to retain his own earnings. In Italy and Spain Christian masters issued charters of manumission with the condition that the slave continue to serve them or their heirs for a set number of years. Sometimes the slave was required to pay the master a redemption fee, which was usually equivalent to the slave's original purchase price. The slave slowly earned the money through additional labor. In Valencia Muslim slaves could obtain a license to beg for alms from Mudejars for this purpose.

Manumission did not end the relationship between masters and slaves. Because of the strong ties that had developed between them during the slaves' years of service, masters often still felt responsible for their freed slaves, while the latter, who were usually poor, still depended on their former masters. Islamic law formalized the persisting bond between the emancipator and the freedperson as "clientage" (*wala'*), which became, as legal scholars explained, "like the relationship between father and son." Thus in Mamluk Egypt, for instance, freedperson adopted their patron's profession, so that the former slaves of *'ulama'* also became scholars. In Byzantium freedperson often remained among the economically dependent "people" of their former masters, still working in their homes or on their farms. Freed Muslim slaves, who had been baptized and married to a Christian woman, were settled in frontier areas where they served the Byzantine state. Italian and Spanish masters took special care to provide for their freedwomen, often leaving them money for their dowry so that they could marry well. Through the act of manumission, then, the slave's utter powerlessness changed into a kind of dependence on the former master that continued to bolster the latter's prestige. Far from endangering the social hierarchy, freeing slaves strengthened it.

The process of manumission was not always smooth. Sometimes the heirs of masters refused to execute clauses in their parent's will that called for a slave's liberation, or masters did not honor the terms of the conditional grants of freedom they had conceded to their slaves. In Valencia and Istanbul at least slaves responded by suing their masters or the heirs in court for breach of contract.

Some slaves were not inclined to wait until their master felt a pious impulse or died to win their freedom, so they ran away. Fugitive slaves were a persistent problem wherever there were slaves, though most extant evidence comes from the archives of Christian realms. Since slaves were expensive, masters exerted considerable effort in recovering their property, with the assistance of state authorities. Italian cities established mutual agreements to extradite any runaways they apprehended. Enslaved Blacks in Europe had a harder time escaping because they could not easily blend into the free population. This was less of a problem for fugitive Muslim slaves in the Crown of Aragon with its large free Mudejar population. Valencian Mudejars ran an "underground railroad," hiding escaping Muslim slaves in their communities and then spiriting them away to Granada by land or to the Maghrib by sea.

Captives and Ransoming

Many slaves originated as prisoners of war or as victims of frontier raiding or piracy. Yet their captors did not necessarily intend to keep or sell them as slaves, since liberating them in exchange for a hefty ransom was an option, one that over the centuries became ever more attractive and viable. Institutions and conventions for the redemption and exchange of captives—what we might call "laws of war"—emerged first on the terrestrial and maritime frontiers of Byzantium, taking firm root throughout the Mediterranean by the fourteenth century. Ransoming institutions were continually needed because even peaceful, trading relations between states created opportunities for Muslim and Christian pirates (who acted without the consent of their rulers) to seize the passengers and crews of ships along with their cargoes. The elaboration of an institutional framework for the redemption of captives only encouraged the depredations of corsairs (who acted with the license of their rulers) and pirates, since they could count on receiving ransom payments. The ransoming enterprise became most lucrative in the decades following the Battle of Lepanto (1571), when the Ottoman and Habsburg empires disengaged from their Mediterranean struggle and allowed corsairs freer rein. Muslim Algiers and Christian Malta rose as thriving corsair capitals.

The Evolution of Ransoming

From the days of their first political community in Medina, Muslims dealt with the matter of captive enemies. The Qur'an urged freeing them or permitting their ransom. Frequent warfare on land and sea with Byzantium afforded Muslims many opportunities to obey this injunction as well as to work for the redemption of coreligionists captured by the Greeks. In the eighth and ninth centuries caliphs and emperors dispatched envoys to each other's courts to negotiate the exchange or ransoming of captives. Subjects of both empires donated money for ransoming efforts, which they regarded as charitable and meritorious. The occasional public humiliation or execution of prisoners of war alerted them to the bleak alternatives to ransoming.

Thus when the Crusaders first arrived in the eastern Mediterranean, Muslim and Byzantine conventions for ransoming captives were well established. Conscious of their vulnerability, Jews too had long encouraged the redemption of coreligionists as a form of charity. During the tumultuous era of the Crusades, Egyptian Jewish communities collectively raised funds to redeem captives, and in Palestine most Jewish marriage contracts included a ransom clause in which the groom promised his bride: "If you are taken captive, I will ransom you with my possessions... and I will take you back."

The Crusaders, however, did not come east with such customs. They were initially disinclined to take Muslims

ARTIFACT MALTA TRANSFORMED: THE IMPACT OF THE ORDER OF THE KNIGHTS OF ST. JOHN

The arrival of the Order of the Knights of St. John, or Hospitallers, in Malta in 1530 set in motion architectural, institutional, and demographic changes that transformed the island, by the late sixteenth century, into a bulwark of the Catholic faith in its struggle against Islam in the Mediterranean. The island's strategic location and excellent harbor made it seem promising as a base from which to conduct naval warfare, but its small size—seventeen miles long and nine miles wide—weak fortifications, and poor soil initially discouraged the Hospitallers, who assumed that their stay would only be temporary. Furthermore, though the Maltese were mostly devout Catholics, some the descendants of Muslims who had converted when Frederick II of Sicily removed their coreligionists from the island, they were largely peasants, not soldiers, and were unprepared for the new role in which the emperor Charles V had cast their island home. Malta suddenly became the headquarters of an international military order whose mari-

FIGURE 12.4 Matteo Perez d'Aleccio, *The Siege of Malta in 1565*, Grand Hall of the Palace of the Grand Masters, Valletta, detail. © Fine Art Images / Heritage Image Partnership Ltd / Alamy Stock Photo.

FIGURE 12.5 The Grand Harbor, Valletta. Photo by John Haslam provided by Wikimedia Commons under the CC-BY-2.0 | CC-SA License.

time crusading, or corsairing, was promoted by popes and Catholic princes. As the vassals of Charles V, who included Malta among his Italian possessions, the Knights also participated in Spain's naval campaigns against its Muslim foes. Their anti-Muslim aggression eventually made Malta a prime Ottoman target.

The Hospitallers, however, did not move rapidly to improve Malta's fortifications. First settling in the port town of Birgu and its Fort Saint Angelo, they concentrated just on strengthening their own defenses. But in 1551, after the Ottomans and their Algerian surrogates devastated the neighboring tiny island of Gozo and captured Tripoli, both part of the domains Charles had granted the order, the Knights set about building Forts Saint Elmo and Saint Michael to protect Malta's harbor. These forts, though helpful, proved to be inadequate when the forces of Sultan Suleyman the Magnificent, whom the Hospitallers had angered by attacking Muslim merchants and pilgrims, besieged Malta for four months in 1565. The Ottomans captured Saint Elmo and rained much destruction upon Saint Michael before the arrival of a relief force under the command of Don García de Toledo, the Spanish viceroy of Sicily, compelled them to raise the siege.

The order reacted to this near disaster by executing an earlier plan to build a new fortified city on the heights of the Sciberras Peninsula commanding the harbor. Completed in 1575 and named after the Hospitaller Grand Master Jean de la Valette, who had heroically led the defense in 1565, Valletta was encircled by high ramparts and bastions and had within its walls the grand master's palace, which was decorated with frescoes of the great siege, the churches of St. John and Our Lady of Victory, and residences for each of the seven "nations" comprising the order (Aragon, Castile and Portugal, Italy, Germany, and the three French ones of France, Provence, and Auvergne). Valletta's construction was financed by revenue from the order's European estates and contributions from popes and kings who were convinced of the essential role the Knights played in defending the coasts of southern Europe. The harrowing siege that had brought Valletta into being had also deepened the identification of the Maltese people with their Hospitaller lords; many subsequently served as soldiers on the order's galleys. The new city became a symbol of a militant and triumphant Catholic Church on the Mediterranean frontier with Islam and rooted the order permanently in Malta. But the frontier outpost also served as a commercial entrepôt, attracting foreign merchants and corsairs hoping to profit from the trade in stolen goods and captives or in locally grown cotton. Malta rapidly urbanized as its population expanded; by 1617, 42 percent of its once heavily rural population lived in Valletta or other towns.

While the fortress city of Valletta and additional fortifications protected Malta from military threats, Malta's bishops and inquisitors labored to shield the island's Catholic inhabitants from the Islamic, Jewish, and Protestant influences to which the activities of Hospitallers, other corsairs, and merchants potentially exposed them. Yet it was not until the Hospitallers were installed in Malta that its bishops even resided on the island. The king of Spain chose the bishop from among candidates presented by the grand master, and the pope confirmed the appointment. In 1561 the papacy invested the bishop with inquisitorial powers; in 1574 a separate papal Inquisition was established in Malta. The spread of Lutheran ideas from a few Knights and priests associated with the order was a grave concern. Inquisitors persuaded some of these "heretics" to abjure their errors and to return to the Catholic faith; those who refused or who relapsed into heresy were imprisoned and even burned. Inquisitors also prosecuted English and Dutch Protestant sailors and merchants who came into the port as the Hospitallers' captives or for commerce. Such inquisitorial activity ended, however, in 1604, when Spain made peace with the Dutch. Henceforth Protestant merchants could trade in Malta, but under strict regulations.

A more persistent problem was the large population of Muslim captives, a product of the Knights' naval campaigns. (There were also some Jewish captives who had been seized on Muslim ships.) Although there had been a few Muslim slaves in Malta in the fifteenth century, by 1600 they numbered around 3,000 and mostly belonged to the order. The Muslims presented a security risk. In 1531 and 1596 the order had to suppress slave uprisings; it also foiled many attempted escapes. For this reason, Muslim captives were required to wear shackles on their ankles and to spend nights in a largely underground prison—by 1629 there were three such prisons.

The bishop and the inquisitors, however, were more worried about the possible spread of the captives' religion on the island. The order allowed the Muslims to have mosque facilities of a sort and prayer leaders in the prisons, and the Muslims were evidently mixing with the Catholic laity when on the outside. The bishop thus issued legislation in 1620 commanding Christians to refrain as much as possible from sharing meals or otherwise mingling with the Muslims lest their own customs be corrupted. In 1658 the Inquisition threatened to heavily penalize sexual relations between Muslim men and Christian women.

The Maltese Church's anxiety about losing the faithful to Islam was heightened by the large number of renegade Christians the Knights brought to Malta among their other captives—921 between 1577 and 1670. Most of the renegades were Christians who had converted to Islam after their capture by Muslim corsairs; some were *devşirme* recruits and former Moriscos. Many willingly returned to Christianity in Malta, but the inquisitors had to persuade, even coerce, others to reject their Islamic faith and be "reconciled" to the Catholic Church. The Jesuits, who came to Malta in 1593, played a special role in catechizing renegades who returned to the faith. As for the renegades who refused to abandon Islam, the inquisitors sentenced the men to the galleys and the women to domestic slavery; relapsed "Islamizers" were burned. The renegades' rejection of Islam and return to the Catholic faith, or their penalization, took place in public *autos de fé* (acts of faith) orchestrated by the Inquisition and attended by the bishop and the grand master. Like the crusading Knights of St. John and the ramparts of Valletta, the Inquisition helped transform Malta into a Catholic fortress.

Discussion Questions

1. How did the presence of the Order of St. John in Malta affect the lives of the indigenous Maltese population?
2. How did the activities associated with Malta's role as the Christian corsair capital sometimes work against the endeavor to transform the island into a fortress of the Catholic faith?
3. Why did the popes think that an Inquisition in Malta was so necessary?
4. Why was Christian Europe so concerned with the exploits and survival of the Knights of St. John in Malta?

Further Reading

Mallia-Milanes, Victor, ed. *Hospitaller Malta, 1530–1798: Studies on Early Modern Malta and the Order of St John of Jerusalem*. Msida: Mireva Publications, 1993.

Wettinger, Godfrey. *Slavery in the Islands of Malta and Gozo, ca. 1000–1812*. San Gwann: Publishers Enterprises Group, 2002.

captive, preferring to slaughter them instead; nor were they keen to ransom their comrades, whose captivity they thought to be shameful. Over the course of the twelfth century the Franks' views and practices changed, so that by its end they also regarded ransoming as one of the laws of war. The Franks quickly realized that there was money to be made from taking Muslim adversaries alive and holding them for ransom. Once the rulers of the Crusader states established diplomatic relations with Muslim princes, arranging for the redemption or exchange of captives became part of their negotiations. The Crusaders learned from the example of Byzantine emperors, who sometimes played a role in ransoming Frankish nobles, and from the conventions of their Muslim foes. Even so, the Latin kings of Jerusalem did not create public funds to assist captives in dealing with the cost of their ransom; this was the private responsibility of the captives and their families.

Latin Christians East and West came to the realization that collective, institutional measures were needed to address the problem of ransoming after thousands of Christians were captured by Salah al-Din in the Battle of Hattin in 1187 and by the Almohads in their triumph at Alarcos, Spain, in 1195. Two religious orders were therefore founded in Europe for the purpose of collecting funds to ransom Christian captives: the Trinitarians in Burgundy in 1198 and the Mercedarians in Catalonia in the 1220s. Upon authorizing the Trinitarian Order, Pope Innocent III encouraged all Christians to contribute to the redemption of Christian captives as an act of charity. Both orders were especially active in Spain, and the Trinitarians established a house in Acre. But in the East the Hospitallers and Templars took the lead in ransoming. As the embattled Crusader states diminished to the point of extinction over the course of the thirteenth century, their endeavors were all the more necessary.

Muslims across the Mediterranean had by this time adopted a range of measures for redeeming Muslim captives, in addition to the funds the captives' families were able to muster. Rulers such as Nur al-Din and Salah al-Din granted large sums from the state treasury for ransoms. Most important were the pious endowments (*waqf*s) established by individual Muslims specifically for this purpose. When contemplating the plight of captives, Muslims and Christians experienced similar anxieties: that despairing captives might convert to the religion of their captors, and that female captives might suffer sexual abuse.

On the Spanish frontier institutions for ransoming captives had been operative since at least the early twelfth century. First towns and then rulers on both sides appointed special officials to negotiate the exchange of prisoners and redemption of captives. Jewish envoys first filled this role, but it was increasingly taken on by Christian and Muslim merchants accustomed to dealing with state authorities on the other side. The services of such agents were required along the maritime frontier as well, especially from the mid-fourteenth century, when the western Mediterranean saw an explosion of activity by Muslim and Christian corsairs. During the war over the Straits of Gibraltar corsairs functioned as the naval arm of the Marinid *jihad* against Christian Spain. After the Marinids' defeat in the 1350s, Hafsid sultans began sponsoring corsairs operating out of Tunis and Bijaya. The one-fifth of the booty seized by corsairs that the sultans received helped compensate for the customs revenue they were losing with the decline of maritime commerce in the decades following the Black Death. Christian corsairs and their royal patrons had similar motives, though they were more likely than Muslim corsairs to attack the ships of coreligionists from rival states. Genoese corsairs, for instance, captured Catalans and sold them to the Muslims.

However, it was not a free-for-all in the western Mediterranean. The frequent truces and commercial treaties between Muslim and Christian states prohibited corsairs from preying on the subjects of realms with which their monarchs had made peace. Offending corsairs were liable to punishment and their royal patrons to paying reparations to the corsairs' victims. Consistent communication between states facilitated the resolution of such problems when they were at peace as well as the ransoming of captives when the truces expired.

It has been estimated that in any given year in the fourteenth and fifteenth centuries there were 2,300 subjects of the Crown of Aragon held captive by Maghribi and Granadan Muslims. Of these, roughly 10 percent returned home, through a variety of means. Peace treaties normally entailed the release of captives by both signatories. Mercedarian and Trinitarian friars, who tended to act on behalf of poor families, ransomed dozens annually. Town governments worked to raise funds for their captured citizens, while monarchs and bishops licensed the relatives of captives to beg for ransom money. Families with means hired merchants to travel to Muslim ports to negotiate the liberation of their loved ones. Ransoming captives had become a community responsibility, involving all social ranks and lay and religious institutions. It was equally the case in Muslim societies. Even Valencian Mudejars, who were mostly peasants and artisans, managed to ransom hundreds of Granadan Muslims captured during Fernando and Isabel's conquest of the sultanate, giving what little they possessed, they said, "for the love of God."

Algiers, the "Barbary Corsair" Capital

For much of the sixteenth century the campaigns of Ottoman and Habsburg imperial fleets limited the activities of corsairs. Maghribi ("Barbary") corsairs like Khayr al-Din Barbarossa even served as Ottoman admirals. The withdrawal of imperial navies after Lepanto opened up the Mediterranean to corsairs and pirates. The profitability of corsairing—an index of the vibrant commerce on which it preyed—fueled the demographic expansion of the two corsair capitals from the end of the sixteenth century. Malta's population doubled, from 22,000 to around 50,000, by 1632, while that of Algiers increased from 60,000 to 100,000 by 1650.

Algiers remained under the authority of an Ottoman governor and exercised suzerainty over the corsair nests of Tunis and Tripoli. After the 1570s Istanbul's control loosened, freeing corsairs from Algiers to capture ships from countries with which the sultan had made peace, such as France. The spirit of *jihad* motivated some corsairs, perhaps especially the vengeful Moriscos who had joined their ranks and the Janissaries who did much of the fighting once an enemy ship was engaged. Yet for the growing number of renegade Christians who flocked to Algiers from southern and northern Europe, the motives were more mercenary and monetary. Some renegades commanded corsair ships. The Flemish captain Simon Danzas apparently never even converted to Islam, though he did capture at least forty Christian ships before settling down in 1609 in Marseille, where he had a Christian wife and children. Of course, when the targets were the ships and coastal towns of Spain and Spanish Italy, both the religious and the economic aims of many corsairs would have been satisfied. After 1600 Algerian corsairs were sailing beyond the Straits of Gibraltar into the Atlantic where they seized hundreds of English and French ships, and plundered coasts as far north as Iceland. One result of such exploits was a large and diverse population of captives in Algiers.

The corsairs' ships were owned by either private individuals or the state. The corsairing enterprise attracted many investors in Algiers who jointly owned ships as shareholders. The booty seized by corsairs—ship cargoes, the ships themselves, and captives—was systematically shared out among state officials, the corsair crew, and private investors in proportion to their initial investment. Algiers functioned as a market for the plundered goods of Christian ships. Merchants from Livorno and Marseille traveled there, and to Tunis and Tripoli as well, to purchase the stolen goods, which they would then resell for a handsome profit back home. The rise of Livorno as a major Mediterranean entrepôt in the seventeenth century owed much to its merchants' participation in this illicit corsair economy.

Christian captives were the most valuable merchandise the corsairs brought to Algiers. The corsairs initially sold most captives as slaves to local Muslim buyers who usually later freed them in exchange for substantial ransom payments. In the meantime the masters put their slaves to work. The harshest task was rowing corsair galleys, which had high mortality rates. Other slaves performed heavy labor as stevedores or carrying stones to build local fortifications. Many worked as household servants or in shops. In the seventeenth century European captives constituted roughly one-quarter of the population of Algiers.

The methods and institutions for ransoming Christian captives that existed in the fifteenth century continued to operate after 1571, but more efficiently, resulting in the redemption of most captives. The greater sophistication of government and finance in this period smoothed the ransoming process by, for instance, making it easier for the families of captives to obtain loans. The ransoming orders were more effective, too. The Spanish government offered financial support to the Mercedarians and Trinitarians, who, between 1575 and 1769, ransomed approximately 15,500 Spanish captives. One was Miguel de Cervantes, author of *Don Quixote* and prisoner in Algiers from 1575 to 1580. Various Italian states, such as Naples and the Papal States, established new ransoming associations over the course of the sixteenth century. The effectiveness of such ransoming institutions both encouraged and was made possible by the profit motives of Algerian corsairs and slave-owners. Muslim masters even permitted captives to finance their own ransoms by running businesses the earnings of which were split between the captive and the master. The growing number of renegade Christians in the corsairs' ranks enhanced this entrepreneurial outlook, as did the mounting cynicism, on all sides, regarding wars for religious causes. Considering that between 1530 and 1780 at least one million European Christians were taken captive, it is clear that ransoming was a big business and that the Barbary corsairs were among its most accomplished practitioners.

Malta, the Christian Corsair Capital

Strategically located in the center of the Mediterranean in the narrows between Sicily and North Africa, the small island of Malta was an ideal spot from which to conduct a maritime crusade against Islam. Emperor Charles V therefore granted Malta in 1530 to the Knights of St. John (Hospitallers) after the Ottomans ejected the order from Rhodes. Because the Knights' galleys had become a danger to Muslim commerce and to Muslim pilgrims traveling to Mecca, the Ottomans laid siege to Malta in 1565. The failure of the siege and the Ottoman defeat at Lepanto five years later further encouraged the Knights' aggression against Ottoman shipping in the eastern Mediterranean and against North African corsairs and coastlines. In this fight "for the faith of Christ," they were joined by the Knights of St. Stephen, a new order founded in Livorno by Duke Cosimo I in 1561. Yet, rather like in Livorno, where Christian merchants sold both the Muslims captured by the local order and the stolen Christian goods they had purchased from Barbary corsairs, on Malta the Knights' well-publicized crusading did not exclude profit-oriented corsairing.

The naval expeditions of the Knights of Malta were not geared toward making a profit, and the order simply paid the crews of sailors and soldiers a salary. However, there were growing numbers of "private" corsairs on Malta with their own ships, Christians from across the Mediterranean as well as Maltese. The order attempted to regulate the private operators; between 1605 and 1635 it issued them nearly 400 licenses. Private corsairing was more of a business venture that attracted investors from among Maltese and foreign merchants, the community of corsairs, and enterprising knights. The licensed corsairs' spoils were divided between the order and affiliated religious institutions, the captain and crew, and the investors. Corsairs sailing out of Malta preyed not only on Muslim ships but also on those of the Ottomans' Greek Christian subjects who, in the seventeenth century, conducted much of the short-distance trade in the eastern Mediterranean. Some Greek victims appealed to Rome for reparations, since the papacy was the order's superior and had been sponsoring Catholic missions to Ottoman Orthodox Christians; their petitions were occasionally successful. Venice also had reason to complain since the Knights sometimes targeted its ships after it made peace with the Ottomans in 1573.

The corsairs of Malta disposed of captured merchandise in a manner that mirrored the activities of the Barbary corsairs. They sold captured cargoes in public auction to merchants, many of them French and Greek, who then distributed the goods for resale in various ports, such as Marseille, Livorno, Istanbul, and Izmir. Ransoming Muslim captives was a lucrative business on Malta. The island had a large Muslim slave population of around 3,000. There were also some Jewish captives. The order owned most of the slaves and had more than half of them rowing in its galleys, while assigning others to do heavy labor maintaining the fortresses. Private corsairs also used galley slaves. Domestic service and toiling in workshops were the lot of more fortunate Muslim captives. Most captives were eventually ransomed. Christian merchants of different backgrounds—Greek, French, southern Italian, and Maltese—as well as Jews functioned as intermediaries between the families and home governments of the Muslim captives and the order and other Maltese owners. They escorted the Muslim captives back home, collected the ransoms from their families, and delivered the ransom money to the order, receiving a commission for their efforts. The merchants also arranged captive exchanges with Muslim governments. The Maltese authorities frequently allowed Muslim captives to return home to obtain ransom money for themselves and for other captives. Such permits reflected the trust that sometimes developed between masters and slaves, and, most importantly, the acknowledgement of all parties involved that captivity and ransoming constituted an extended and difficult business transaction. Still, even if many corsairs, Christian and Muslim, had wholly economic motives, and even if most of their captives were finally redeemed, the depredations of corsairs and pirates created a climate of fear across the Middle Sea, fostering mutual religious hostility on its Muslim and Christian shores. SEE SOURCEBOOK 12:4.

Slavery and Racism

The history of enslaved and freed Blacks in the Mediterranean substantiates the assertion of Eric Williams, an eminent historian of the Caribbean: "Slavery was not born of racism; rather, racism was the consequence of slavery."[3] Arab Muslims initially enslaved Black Africans because they were unbelievers, not because of their skin color. After 1000, Black Muslim rulers in sub-Saharan Africa also began enslaving pagan Blacks, a new rationale for slavery in a region where monarchs had long reduced defeated political enemies to servitude, using them in domestic service, agriculture, and mining, and as symbols of their wealth and power. Black Muslims also sold their pagan slaves in the well-established trans-Saharan trade, which between 700 and 1500 saw Muslim slave-dealers transporting more than four million enslaved Blacks to the wider Muslim world. The scale of this commerce led some White Muslims to associate Blackness with servility and unbelief. With the import of enslaved Black pagans and Muslims into Mediterranean Christian cities from the mid-fifteenth century, similar associations started forming in the minds of their White inhabitants. However, neither the Christian and Muslim Mediterranean nor sub-Saharan Africa had plantation-based "slave societies" like the Caribbean societies studied by Williams in his classic work *Capitalism and Slavery*. Nevertheless, the emergence of racism among White Europeans, itself a legacy of the enslavement of Black people in the Mediterranean, provided a justification for the sending of what would come to be millions of Black Africans across the Atlantic to the Americas. White colonists and other Europeans complicit in this "new world" of plantation slavery would also develop assumptions about the supposed natural suitability of Black people for slavery, but with a conviction exceeding that of their Mediterranean ancestors. SEE SOURCEBOOK 12:5.

Black Africans in the Muslim Mediterranean

The Qur'an did not advocate prejudice on the basis of skin color or "race." In it, the main distinction was between believers in the Prophet's revelation and unbelievers. As pagan inhabitants of the Abode of War, Black Africans were legitimate targets of *jihad* and enslavement. Although they formed only part of a large and diverse slave population in the Muslim world, enslaved Blacks, especially males, tended to be assigned more menial tasks, such as laboring in salt and gold mines or draining swamps. Muslims used the Arabic word *'abd* (slave) to refer to enslaved Blacks, who, except for the many Black eunuchs, were cheaper and of lower status than enslaved Whites, who were called *mamluk*s. Blacks also served as slave-soldiers, especially in the Maghrib and Egypt, but they rarely attained the prominence and power of White *mamluk*s. Writing in the fourteenth century, Ibn Khaldun distinguished between enslaved Whites and Blacks, suggesting that the latter were naturally servile. Blacks, he observed, "are, as a rule, submissive to slavery, because they have little (that is essentially) human and have attributes that are quite similar to those of dumb animals." In contrast, "are those who by accepting slavery hope to obtain high rank or to get money or power. This was the case with the Turks in the East." Yet, in making such a statement, Ibn Khaldun ignored, for instance, Rasad (d. ca. 1078), the Black concubine of the Fatimid caliph al-Zahir (1021–1036) and de facto regent for her son al-Mustansir (1036–1094), as well as the Black eunuchs who staffed the Fatimid administration or who served as the honor guard at the Tomb of the Prophet in Medina.[4]

Ibn Khaldun's views in any case were not universally shared but were based on negative stereotypes of enslaved Blacks as dishonest, frivolous, and overly sexual, and on cosmologies that linked Blackness to sin, unbelief, and the devil. Neither the conversion of enslaved Blacks to

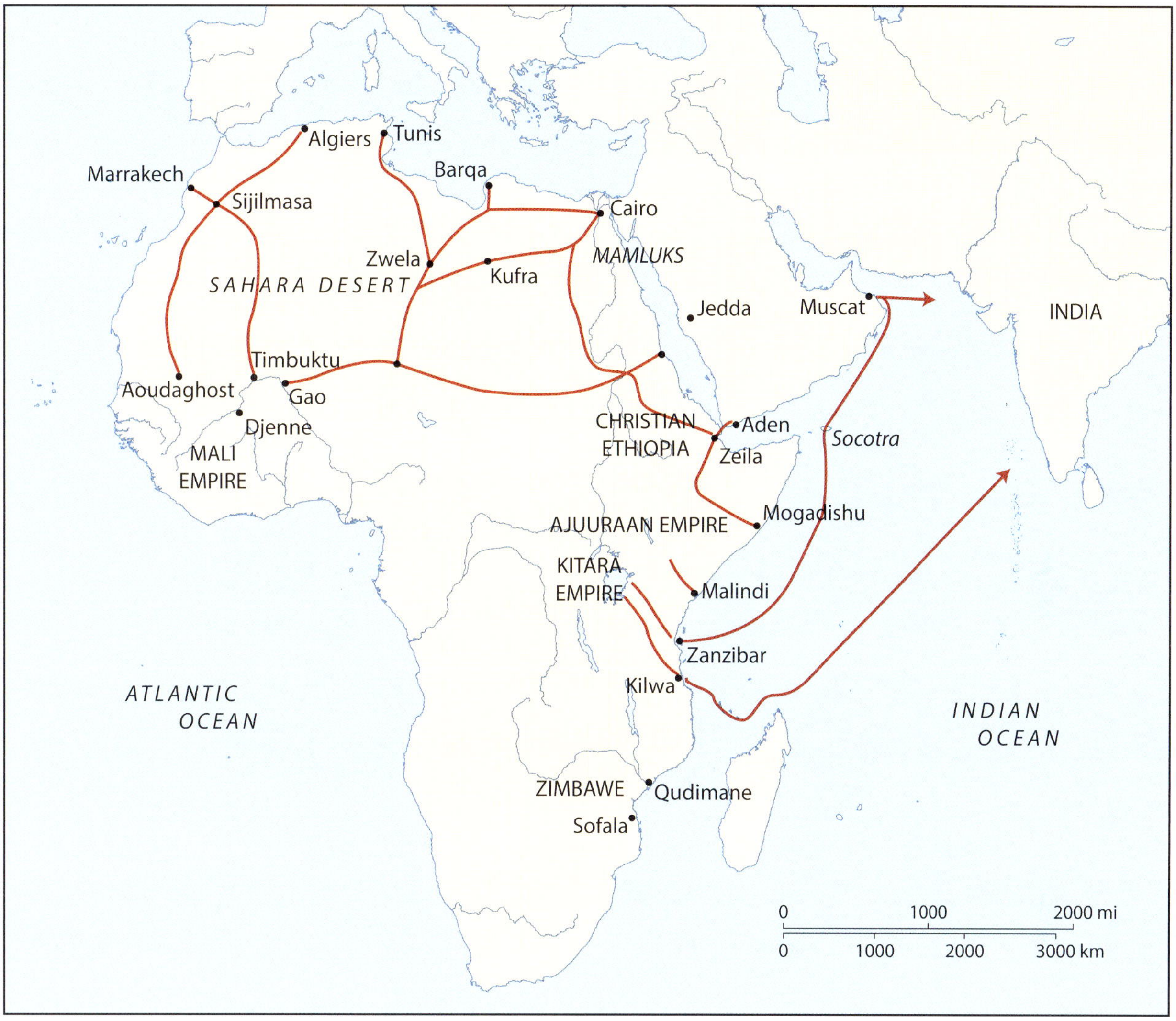

MAP 12.2 Map of Muslim Slave Trade Routes. Drawn from "Medieval Muslim Slave Trade Routes," Crossing the Ocean Sea. Reproduced by permission of illustrator Mary Ames Mitchell.

Islam nor their manumission changed such perceptions, which some Black freedpersons' continuing performance of degrading labor helped perpetuate. That Blacks would have been the targets of such bias in the early Islamic centuries is not surprising in light of the fact that Arab Muslims sometimes discriminated against any convert to Islam who did not have an Arab lineage. A Black poet from the Umayyad era, al-Hayqutan, responded to anti-Black prejudice with the verse "Though my hair is wooly and my skin coal-black, / My hand is open and my honor bright."[5]

The *'ulama'*, however, insisted on the fundamental equality of all believers before God. Regardless of their color, manumitted Black Muslims were supposed to be, according to manumission documents, "one with the free Muslims, partaking both of their privileges and their responsibilities." *Hadith* collections included traditions emphasizing that piety and meritorious deeds were more important than lineage or race. The first muezzin was a freed Black of Ethiopian descent and a Companion of the Prophet, Bilal ibn Rabah. Later, other Black

FIGURE 12.6 Black Africans in the slave market of Zabid in Yemen, 1237. Photo: Pictures From History / CPA Media Pte Ltd / Alamy Stock Photo.

Muslims were esteemed for their piety and religious knowledge. The opinions of the *'ulama'* and like-minded Muslims existed in tension with those of Muslims who continued to view their Black coreligionists as inferior. *'Ulama'*, for instance, condemned Muslims who tried to prohibit intermarriage between Black men and White women, since Islamic marriage laws did not permit such discrimination among believers. A pernicious, persistent problem in the Maghrib was the tendency of White Muslims to ignore the religious difference between pagan and Muslim Blacks, and to enslave both on the basis of their skin color. In the late fifteenth century, for instance, White Maghribi Muslims sold free Black coreligionists to Spanish Christian merchants.

Yet, despite the persistence of such attitudes through the seventeenth century and Muslims' enslavement of

ARTIFACT BLACK AFRICANS IN THE ART OF WESTERN MEDITERRANEAN CHRISTIANS

Artwork produced in Mediterranean Europe offers some evidence of when and where Western Christians would have encountered Black Africans and how they perceived them. Although such artistic representations of Black people cannot be taken as wholly accurate renderings of contemporary social realities, and indeed are often more revealing of White Christian ideologies than of Black lived experience, the far more frequent appearance of Blacks in painting and sculpture beginning in the later fifteenth century reflects a new social and economic phenomenon: the importation of large numbers of enslaved Blacks into Mediterranean Europe from West Africa. Artwork from this period sheds precious light on the lives of enslaved and freed Blacks in Europe at a time when the transatlantic slave trade was first developing and beginning to create a distorted image of Black Africans that obscured not just this chapter of their history but also the history of their sub-Saharan homelands.

Prior to the late eleventh century and the wave of Christian expansion into the Muslim Near East, southern Italy, and Spain, Western Christians had rarely, if ever, encountered Black Africans. Campaigning in and colonizing Muslim lands, however, brought them into physical contact with Black soldiers and servants, both enslaved and free, and with free Blacks in various occupations. Yet such contact did not necessarily alter the portrayal of Blacks or Blackness in Christian art, where the color black had often been employed to signify sin. For example, a late twelfth-century *Exultet* roll, which was used for Easter celebrations, from Troia in southern Italy shows the light of Christ illuminating and dispelling the blackness of Night, symbolizing sin.

FIGURE 12.7 Detail from *Exultet* roll, Troia, southern Italy, late twelfth century. © Historical Views / agefotostock.

FIGURE 12.8 Alfonso X, *Book of Games*, 1283. Photo: Juan García Aunion / Agefotostock / Alamy Stock Photo.

FIGURE 12.9 Lorenzo Cosmati, mosaic in Church of San Tommaso in Formis, Rome. Photo by Roundtheworld provided by Wikimedia Commons under the CC-BY-3.0 License.

FIGURE 12.10 Andrea Mantegna, *Adoration of the Magi*, ca. 1497–1500. Photograph provided by WikiArt under the CC-PD License.

Manuscript painters from Christian Spain, however, transcended such symbolism to portray Black people in Muslim Spain in a matter-of-fact manner that corresponded to the knowledge of Muslim society that Christians had acquired over the centuries. It is not surprising that these more accurate representations of Blacks were produced in the later thirteenth century, an era of supreme Christian confidence and military success against Andalusi Muslims. Works sponsored by the Castilian king Alfonso X the Learned contain illustrations of Black Muslims of varied social ranks in Andalusi society. Alfonso's *Book of Games*, for example, shows turbaned Black aristocrats playing chess while being served by Black attendants and entertained by a Black musician.

Other thirteenth-century works of art demonstrate that Mediterranean Christians identified Black Africans with slavery, though in a complicated way. A mosaic, completed around 1210, on the façade of San Tommaso in Formis in Rome, the convent of the new ransoming Order of the Trinitarians, illustrates a vision of the order's founder, the Provençal Jean de Matha, in which an enthroned Christ appeared holding two shackled captives, one White and one Black. For some scholars, the mosaic's message is straightforward: the Black man as well as the White could be ransomed and saved. Others, however, have noted that whereas Christ has unlocked the shackles on the ankles of the cross-bearing White man, those binding the Black man remain in place, suggesting his continued enslavement to infidelity. They have also observed that the Black man appears to be carrying a whip, which identifies him as one of the White captive's Muslim captors.

Because of the association of Black Africans with Islam—as "Black Moors"—the new Dominican and Franciscan orders saw them as objects of their missionary endeavors, along with other (White) Muslims and Jews. The missionaries' influence emerges clearly in Spanish

FIGURE 12.11 Titian, *Portrait of Laura de Dianti*, ca. 1520–1525. Photo: The Yorck Project provided by Wikimedia Commons under the CC-PD | GNU Free Documentation License.

FIGURE 12.12 Cristóvão de Morais, *Portrait of Joanna of Austria 1535–1573, daughter of Emperor Charles V.*, 1551. Royal Museums of Fine Arts of Belgium, Brussels. Art Collection 4 / Alamy Stock Photo.

art. Alfonso X's *Songs of Holy Mary*, for instance, illustrates the story of a captive Black Moor who seeks baptism with the encouragement of Mary.

The idea of Christian universalism, that the message of Christ could reach all peoples, gained greater impetus in the fifteenth century, when the Portuguese moved down the Atlantic coast of sub-Saharan Africa and Columbus reached America. Many southern and northern European artists elaborated on this idea in paintings of "The Adoration of the Magi," based on the story in the Gospel of Matthew in which three "wise men" gather in Bethlehem to venerate the newborn Christ. These paintings, like that of the Italian Andrea Mantegna, often include a Black wise man, who is meant to represent the peoples of Africa, supposedly eager to hear the teachings of Christ.

Unlike their northern counterparts, painters in Mediterranean Europe had growing numbers of living models for a Black African "wise man" in their own societies. Painters, however, did more than translate their experience of Black Africans into representations of biblical figures; they depicted the diverse roles that Blacks, enslaved and free, played in contemporary Christian society. By the sixteenth century many princely and aristocratic families in Italy and the Iberian Peninsula were employing enslaved Blacks as household servants. These families increasingly commissioned painters to include the Black servants in their portraits as symbols of their wealth and power. The precise meaning of a Black servant's presence in a painting, however, could vary in accordance with the status of the master being portrayed. The first portrait of this sort, of Laura Dianti, the lowborn mistress of Duke Alfonso d'Este of Ferrara, was painted in the 1520s by Titian. It includes a Black child to show that Laura shared the fashionable tastes of the Estes and was thus "aristocratic." The enslaved Black girl in Cristóvão de Morais's 1553 portrait of Juana of Austria, the daughter of Emperor Charles V and Isabella of Portugal and wife of Prince João Manuel of Portugal, signifies something more than Juana's princely rank; she also, along with the Japanese folding fan in her right hand, functions as a symbol of Portugal's empire.

The status—slave or free—of Blacks in some paintings is difficult to determine. The presence of Black gondoliers in the Venetian lagoon in a Carpaccio painting from the

1490s confirms what contemporary written sources reveal regarding the large number of Black men employed in this job. Many were free, but they would have first come to Venice as slaves. The great seventeenth-century Spanish painter Diego Velázquez immortalized his mulatto (half-African) slave Juan de Pareja in a painting of 1650 and manumitted him shortly afterward. Velázquez also taught his art to Pareja, who became a painter in his own right and painted seventeen known works.

Despite the success of individuals like Pareja, people of African descent in Mediterranean Europe could not easily escape the prejudice of a White society that had always associated Black Africans with the Muslim enemy and increasingly linked Blackness to servitude. Most artwork only strengthened such associations. For instance, in 1617, Duke Cosimo II of Tuscany commissioned Pietro Tacca to sculpt the *Monument of the Four Moors* in Livorno, which

FIGURE 12.13 Diego Velázquez, *Portrait of Juan de Pareja*, 1650, detail. The Metropolitan Museum of Art, New York, Purchase, Fletcher and Rogers Funds, and Bequest of Miss Adelaide Milton de Groot (1876–1967), by exchange, supplemented by gifts from friends of the Museum, 1971, 1971.86, Open Access CC0.

FIGURE 12.14 Pietro Tacca, *The Quattro Mori (Four Moors)*, Livorno, Italy, ca. 1623–1626. Photo: Nico Tondini / REDA & CO srl / Alamy Stock Photo.

was intended to symbolize the victory of his father Ferdinand over Muslims in North Africa. One of the four "Moors" in chains clearly has a physiognomy thought to be typical of Black Africans. This sculpture was based on the reality that all Black Africans brought into Europe had originally been Muslim or animist—that is, non-Christian—which is what had legitimized their enslavement in the first place.

Discussion Questions

1. How did Christian ideology shape the ways in which Black Africans were represented in the art of Mediterranean Europe?

2. Did more "realistic" portraits of Black Africans in European art ever serve to improve European perceptions of them?

3. The patrons of the artwork depicting Black Africans were all members of the Christian elite. Can you imagine lower-class White Christians having experiences of Black Africans that differed from those depicted in art?

4. Do these premodern representations of Black Africans correlate with modern understandings of the development of racial categories and racism?

Further Reading

Bindman, David, and Henry Louis Gates Jr., eds. *The Image of the Black in Western Art*. Vol. 3, *From the "Age of Discovery" to the Age of Abolition*; pt. 1, *Artists of the Renaissance and Baroque*. Cambridge, MA: Belknap Press of Harvard University Press, 2010.

Devisse, Jean. *The Image of the Black in Western Art*. Vol. 2, *From the Early Christian Era to the "Age of Discovery"*; pt. 1, *From the Demonic Threat to the Incarnation of Sainthood*. Trans. William Granger Ryan. Lausanne: Office du Livre, 1979.

Earle, T. F., and K. J. P. Lowe. *Black Africans in Renaissance Europe*. Cambridge: Cambridge University Press, 2005.

some seven million more Black Africans between 1500 and 1900, the Islamic world did not develop the rigid racial barriers and institutionalized discrimination that became standard in European colonies. The Muslims' enslavement of much larger numbers of Black females—by a ratio of 2 to 1—and Islamic laws encouraging the manumission of these women and their children, particularly any mixed-race children they had with their master, resulted in the gradual assimilation of the Black population. The castration of many enslaved Black men, who did not reproduce, contributed to this. Since economies in the Islamic world did not depend on slave labor, Muslims did not establish laws and institutions to keep enslaved Blacks or any enslaved peoples perpetually in bondage.

Black Africans in the Christian Mediterranean

In the 1450s, a decade after the first Portuguese forays along the coast of West Africa, the papacy issued several bulls authorizing the Portuguese monarchy to conquer and enslave the peoples of the Maghrib, particularly Morocco, and sub-Saharan Africa. The Portuguese sometimes confused Black Muslims with Black pagans, labeling all of them "Black Moors": they were all enemies of Christianity. Reducing them to servitude and baptizing them would save their souls and serve the church. This sense of religious mission legitimized the Portuguese quest for sub-Saharan gold and trafficking in enslaved Blacks.

Some Portuguese argued that by enslaving Black Africans they were exposing them not only to Christianity but also to more "civilized" ways. Most Portuguese merchants conducting business in West Africa, however, knew better. They encountered monarchs with sophisticated courts and with militaries formidable enough to prevent them from penetrating the African interior. West African political elites controlled the internal slave trade and dealt with the Portuguese as equals, exchanging gold and slaves for European textiles and iron, not because they lacked their own high-quality cloth and ironware but because they valued the European versions as luxury items that would add to their prestige. The Portuguese nonetheless benefited from the absence of any "Pan-African" solidarity among West Africans and were therefore able to pit one African state against another in order to procure slaves. The ruler of the kingdom of Kongo, Nzinga Mbemba (1509–1543), for instance, allied with the Portuguese, converted to Christianity—taking the name Afonso I—and supplied the Portuguese with slaves through warring against neighboring polities.

Yet White Christians in Portuguese, Spanish, and Italian cities had a markedly different experience of Black Africans. They first encountered uprooted, disoriented, terrified people speaking unknown languages, often in a state of relative undress, partly by custom but also for purposes of sale on the auction block. Europeans came away with a lasting impression that these enslaved Blacks were "barbaric." The slaves, however, quickly learned the languages and customs of their masters and adopted, often sincerely, their masters' Catholic faith. At the same time, they had to abandon their former ethnic or tribal affiliations and religions, which had no place or meaning in Europe. Freed and enslaved Blacks in many cities established confraternities, dedicated, like those of White citizens, to different Catholic saints. The members provided alms, food, and shelter to needy Blacks, and, most importantly, strove to redeem their fellows from slavery. These institutions fostered Black solidarity.

Enslaved Blacks usually did menial labor as porters, stable boys, rowers in galleys, artisans' assistants, field hands, and domestic servants. Some performed as musicians and entertainers to "amuse" their masters. For Italian masters in Renaissance city-states, enslaved Blacks were exotic possessions and tokens of their wealth, while at the Portuguese court enslaved Blacks symbolized the expanding Portuguese empire. Even oppressed Spanish Moriscos asserted to the royal authorities in the 1560s that they should be permitted to continue enjoying the esteem that came from owning Black slaves. As the Morisco notable Francisco Núñez Muley put it, "Don't these blacks deserve their wretched state? Must everyone be seen as equals? Let them bring the water pitcher on their backs, or carry burdens, or handle the plow."[6]

Once they were manumitted or even if they were born to free parents, Blacks and mulattoes (people of mixed African and European descent) could never escape the taint of slavery that, in the eyes of White Europeans, their dark skin carried. Many freed slaves were mistaken for runaways, seized, and thrust back into servitude; some successfully appealed in court for their freedom. Recognizing that most people identified Blackness with slavery, in 1566 a widow in Granada bequeathing property to two free Blacks emphasized in her will: "The color of their faces gives rise to the suspicion that they are slaves, but... they have never been but free people."[7]

The economic necessity of continuing in the menial jobs they had labored in as slaves made it difficult for freedpersons and their descendants to improve their position in European society. Some, however, found employment as soldiers, and others were ordained as Catholic priests. A Black Franciscan in Sicily, Bendetto "il moro" (ca. 1524–1589), was so renowned for his humility and piety that the church eventually made him a saint. Juan Latino (d. 1590), a Black professor of Latin at the University of Granada, was born a slave and freed by his master—and possibly father—the Duke of Sessa, who saw to it that he received a fine education.

While it was highly unusual for a Black man to be given the educational opportunities and to achieve the position of a Juan Latino, some economic and social mobility among the population of free Blacks and mulattoes was probably inevitable. In Spain and Portugal, the growing "racial" consciousness in regard to the supposedly polluted blood of Conversos and Moriscos moved White Old Christians to lump free Blacks together with these impure races and to include them in exclusionary "purity of blood" laws. In Spain, where there were approximately 100,000 slaves in the mid-sixteenth century, mostly in southern cities, and in Portugal, where at the same time slaves comprised one-tenth of the population of cities like Lisbon and Evora, Blacks, enslaved and free, were becoming, like Conversos and Moriscos, a source of economic competition. In 1589 a Portuguese bishop complained that slaves were taking jobs from native White Christians. By the seventeenth century Portuguese institutions of all sorts were prohibiting the admission of Black people. In 1640 the Archdiocese of Lisbon forbade entrance to holy orders to anyone having "any Hebrew blood, or any other that is impure, or mulatto, or black." For Blacks in Mediterranean Europe, being Christian and free was rarely enough to be regarded as an equal, no more than it was sufficient for Blacks to be Muslim and free on the other side of the Mediterranean. They could not completely break the chains of slavery.

Notes

1. Shaun Marmon, "Domestic Slavery in the Mamluk Empire: A Preliminary Sketch," in *Slavery in the Islamic Middle East*, ed. Shaun Marmon (Princeton, NJ: Markus Wiener Publications, 1999), 13.

2. Iris Origo, "The Domestic Enemy: The Eastern Slaves in Tuscany in the Fourteenth and Fifteenth Centuries," *Speculum* 30:3 (1955): 347.

3. Eric Williams, *Capitalism and Slavery* (Chapel Hill: University of North Carolina Press, 1944), 7.

4. Ibn Khaldun, *The Muqaddimah: An Introduction to History*, trans. Franz Rosenthal (London: Routledge and Kegan Paul, 1958), 1:301–2.

5. Bernard Lewis, *Race and Slavery in the Middle East: An Historical Enquiry* (New York: Oxford University Press, 1992), 29.

6. *A Memorandum for the President of the Royal Audiencia and Chancery Court of the City and Kingdom of Granada*, ed. and trans. Vincent Barletta (Chicago: University of Chicago Press, 2007), 91.

7. Aurelia Martín Casares, "Free and Freed Black Africans in Granada in the Time of the Spanish Renaissance," in Earle and Lowe, 252.

CHAPTER THIRTEEN

Mystical Messiahs and Converts, Humanists and Armorers

Pico della Mirandola (1463–1494), a wealthy Italian count and brilliantly precocious Christian philosopher, collected fascinating friends. While mastering an immense range of philosophical and theological thought—Aristotle, Plato, Neoplatonism, Thomas Aquinas, ancient and medieval esotericism—he had studied Kabbalah, the medieval Jewish mystical tradition of Spanish origin, with a learned opportunist who grandiosely called himself Flavius Mithridates. This Mithridates's birth name was Samuel ben Nissim, and he had been born a Jew in Sicily. After converting to Christianity as an adult, Mithridates became known in Italy as a teacher of and translator of Semitic languages. After learning Kabbalah from him, Pico della Mirandola put Mithridates to work on a huge translation project: putting thousands of pages of Hebrew and Aramaic Kabbalistic works into Latin (his handwritten copies still survive in Rome), so that Pico could read them and incorporate their ideas into his syncretistic Christian philosophy. But Pico was also friends with Marsilio Ficino (1433–1499), Catholic priest, Renaissance scholar, translator of Plato into Latin, and sophisticated philosopher—the most important exponent of a revived Neoplatonism that flourished in this period overwhelmingly outside the Aristotelian-dominated thought of the universities.

FIGURE 13.1 Pico della Mirandola, portrait by Christafano dell'Altissimo (1525–1605). The Picture Art Collection / Alamy Stock Photo.

Pico's connections with the likes of Mithridates and Ficino help explain how he was able to assemble by the age of twenty-three his *900 Theses*, an eclectic collection of theological and philosophical propositions over which he planned in 1486 to hold a debate with any scholar who cared to come to Rome (he even offered to pay their travel expenses). This initiative ended badly. A papal commission charged with examining Pico's theses found a few of them objectionable, and eventually the pope, annoyed at the count's arrogance, condemned them all in a fit of pique, and caused most of the copies to be burned. Pico was imprisoned, and set free only through the intercession of the French king.

But Pico, this hotheaded and sometime reckless

scholar-count (at one point he carried on a notorious love affair with a married aristocrat in Arezzo and nearly lost his life over it) had still another surprising friend: Girolamo Savonarola (1452–1498), a Dominican priest of Florence known far and wide as an unstinting moralist and impassioned prophet. In the early 1490s Savonarola began preaching apocalyptic sermons calling on the Medici family, who controlled Florence, to end their corrupt ways and cease exploiting the poor. Alluding to mystical journeys to heaven, he is said to have predicted the arrival of a "new Cyrus"[1] from the north who would reform the church. When King Charles VIII of France did, in fact, invade in 1494, many saw Savonarola as a divinely appointed messenger. Eventually, with the Medici family pushed aside, this stern Dominican came himself to dominate Florentine politics, transforming the city for a time into a theocratic republic. Yet eventually Savonarola ran afoul of Pope Alexander VI (1492–1503) who excommunicated him and had him burned at the stake. Though Pico never renounced his rather unorthodox Christian philosophy, he remained a close friend of the rigorist Christian prophet Savonarola to the end of his life.

Pico della Mirandola's range of acquaintance was broader than most, but the dizzying array of religious tendencies, philosophical schools, and theological positions represented by his circle of friends is actually quite characteristic of Mediterranean culture in the age of the Ottoman and Spanish empires. Savonarola was but one of many Jews, Christians, and Muslims to claim prophetic authority or messiahship in this period, and Pico's interest in Kabbalah—and creation of a specifically Christian version of it—exemplifies the widespread mystical preoccupations that crossed all religious boundaries in this period as well. Many other converts from one monotheism to another, moreover, played, like Flavius Mithridates, important cultural roles in this period. But while messianic mystics loudly attracted enormous followings and inspired angry denunciations, systematic, rational approaches to complex problems flourished too. Like Ficino and Pico, many other Mediterranean intellectuals turned energetically back to Plato and Neoplatonism for inspiration, as the vogue for Aristotle slowly receded, and as it did so, the first key works of the Scientific Revolution appeared. As in earlier periods, ideas and technologies continued to travel with ease around the Sea in the Middle, but now, for the first time, Latin Europe served as a point of origin. The brutal technology of firearms, for example, while invented in China, first thrived on a large scale in the western Europe and from there traveled back east to the Islamic world. These cannons and sidearms, of course, paved the way for both the European conquest of the Western Hemisphere and the Muslim "gunpowder empires"—Ottoman, Safavid, and Mughal—of the eastern Mediterranean and beyond. Where Mediterranean culture spread around the globe, furthermore, the complex web of interests exemplified by Pico and his fascinating friends traveled as well.

Mediterranean Mystics

At least some Jews, Christians, and Muslims had sought a direct, mystical experience of the divine in almost all periods of medieval Mediterranean history—whether the Brethren of Purity in tenth-century Baghdad, Saint Symeon the New Theologian in eleventh-century Constantinople, or Abraham Abulafia in thirteenth-century Iberia. Yet the trauma and dislocation caused by such events as the Jewish expulsion from and Muslim forced conversion in Christian Spain, and the Ottoman advance into the Balkans and central Europe, helped sow mystical ideas across vast distances, and intensify them in the fifteenth and sixteenth centuries. Sufi mysticism—an already venerable tradition in the Islamic world—flourished in the Ottoman lands in such novel forms as the whirling followers of the great Persian mystic and poet Jalal al-Din Rumi. The originally Iberian Kabbalah put down deep roots among Spanish-Jewish exiles in Italy and the Ottoman empire, and from Italy spread even among Christians in Latin Europe. Making sense of being a Muslim when it was no longer legal to be one generated mystical insights among Iberia's Moriscos.

Ascetic Virtuosi and Whirling Dervishes

Ascetic and mystical movements go back to the early Islamic centuries, and are most strongly associated with Sufis, pious men and women who apparently wore simple woolen garments—hence their name, Arabic *suf* meaning "wool." What had originally been an ascetic move-

If many Jews, Christians, and Muslims claimed to have mystical experiences of God in the fifteenth, sixteenth, and seventeenth centuries, as the following section will show, one artist who migrated by steps across the whole of the Sea in the Middle earned permanent renown for depicting such experiences on canvas. Born of Greek parentage, Domenikos Theotokopoulos (1541–1614), known today by his later Italian-Spanish nickname, El Greco (The Greek), grew up on the island of Crete in the eastern Mediterranean, then a possession of the Republic of Venice. Though governed by Latin Christians, much of the population, like El Greco, were Greek Orthodox Christians whose Byzantine culture continued to flourish, including one of its most distinctive features: icon painting. Though suppressed during the iconoclast movement in the eighth and ninth centuries, the production and devotional use of

FIGURE 13.2 El Greco, *The Dormition of the Virgin*, 1565. Art Heritage / Alamy Stock Photo.

icons continued unbroken throughout Byzantine history and lived on despite the Ottoman conquests in much of Orthodox Christendom. El Greco's first artistic works were in this tradition.

While he would later gain fame for his paintings of Christian mystics in spiritual ecstasy, his icons—like all Orthodox icons—had a different but related purpose: to assist the faithful in a kind of mystical experience of their own. Indeed, as Orthodox theologians had argued since John of Damascus (675–749), Christ, the second person of the Trinity, had taken on human flesh in Jesus, and therefore depictions of Jesus and his saints are not merely images of humans, but are images of the incarnate Word of God through which believers may contemplate visually the central mysteries of Christian faith. El Greco's earliest surviving painting, *The Dormition of the Virgin*, depicts a standard event in Orthodox iconography: the death of Mary, the mother of Jesus, without suffering, with Jesus at her side receiving her soul in the form of swaddled baby. Here the believer could contemplate in color some of the central mysteries of Christian faith: Christ's incarnation in the womb of Mary, and Mary's perpetual virginity and status as the Theotokos, or "mother of God."

While much about this depiction is typical of icon painting—the figures are mostly two-dimensional and elongated, with no attempt to suggest three-dimensional space—art historians point out that Christ's posture here, bending solicitously over his mother, departs from Byzantine tradition, and appears to reflect Italian influences that were readily present in Venetian Crete. What is certain is that some years after completing this work, El Greco had, in fact, moved to Venice in 1567, there to immerse himself for three years in those Italian influences. In Venice, he mastered perspective and Italian Renaissance methods of using color in oil painting, and came deeply under the sway of the great masters Titian (1488–1576) and Tintoretto (1518–1594). From there he traveled to Rome in 1570 where he would spend six years seeking patronage (mostly unsuccessfully) and continuing to mature as a painter.

Among the many paintings he produced in his Italian period is a depiction of one of the most famous mystical experiences of Latin Christendom: Saint Francis of Assisi (1182–1226) receiving the stigmata, the miraculous piercing of his hands and feet that he was granted, in imitation of the crucified Christ, during a vision of the seraphic angels in the last year of his life. This painting in tempura on a wooden panel is partially Byzantine in technique with its glossy, enamel-like finish. Yet the brushwork, use of color and perspectival technique, and naturalistic detail

FIGURE 13.3 El Greco, *St. Francis Receiving the Stigmata*, ca. 1571. Art Heritage / Alamy Stock Photo.

exemplify how thoroughly El Greco had learned from the Italian masters. Here Saint Francis's encounter with the divine is given physical form not just in the dark wounds in his hands, but in the filaments of light that seem to connect them directly to heaven.

Though he would finally secure lasting fame and success only after he moved still farther west across the Mediterranean to Spain in 1576, this Cretan painter would continue to be referred to by the Italian adjective "Greco" (rather than the Spanish "Griego") there as well, now in some ways doubly an outsider. He seems to have traveled to Madrid in that year in hopes of artistic employment during the construction of Felipe II's (1556–1598) massive palace-monastery at El Escorial. This hope came to nothing as well, but he soon found favor with ecclesiastical patrons in Toledo, and it was there that he would live the rest of his life and produce the brilliant paintings of his maturity. Mystical encounters of one kind or another figure prominently in these works. In the late 1580s, for example, he painted another version of Saint Francis receiving the

FIGURE 13.4 El Greco, *St. Francis Receiving the Stigmata*, 1585–1590. The Walters Art Museum, Creative Commons license.

FIGURE 13.5 El Greco, *The Vision of Saint John*, ca. 1608–1614. The Metropolitan Museum of Art, New York, Rogers Fund, 1956, 56.48, Open Access CC0.

stigmata, the miraculous piercings plainly visible in his hands, his eyes fixed on heaven.

El Greco communicates the otherworldliness of Saint Francis's encounter through nonrealistic lengthening of his body—his wounded hands are unnaturally long and slender, for example, giving us a sense that his physical being was somehow being spiritually transformed—a technique he employed frequently in his Toledan period. His large painting of the opening of the fifth seal, from the last years of his life, exemplifies this method in its most advanced form. It depicts an even more central Christian mystical experience than Saint Francis's stigmata: one of the visions of Saint John the Divine that make up part of the New Testament book of Revelation. In this vision, recounted in Revelation 6:9–11, Saint John gazes upon the elongated bodies of the martyred saints in heaven, some of whom are reaching upward toward pure white garments (which will mark their sanctity) being delivered by a flying cherub. El Greco places Saint John himself, though, directly in the foreground in looming, elongated ecstasy, making the painting more about Saint John's mystical experience than the heavenly events it depicts. Here, caught up in divine vision, the writer of Revelation seems to be dematerializing before our eyes in mystical ecstasy.

Though he traveled far from the Greek island of Crete, making an artistic life for himself on the high, dry plains of Catholic Castile, El Greco continued to sign all his paintings in his Greek name, Domenikos Theotokopoulos, in the Greek letters of his Orthodox youth. His Greek origins clung to him in other ways too. We cannot help notice that in stretching out the bodies of his mystical subjects, El Greco, having learned Renaissance realist methods, had reincorporated an artistic technique he first learned as a painter of Byzantine icons. In an age when, as we will see below, Kabbalistic mysticism flourished among Mediterranean Jews, Muslim dervishes took up mystical dance in the Ottoman empire, and, in Castile itself, the great doctors of the Catholic Church, Santa Teresa de Ávila (1515–1582) and San Juan de la Cruz (1542–91), described mystical encounters with God in searching prose and poetry, one wandering artist—migrating slowly, like so many Mediterranean people before him, from island to peninsula to mainland, from one language and religious confession to another—brought his whole experience to the canvas, putting mystical ecstasy into living color.

Discussion Questions

1. What features do all these El Greco paintings have in common? What are the most important differences?

2. As far as we know El Greco was not himself a mystic. What does his fascination with mystical experience tell us about his religious views? Why did he paint such images so frequently?

Further Reading

Bray, Xavier, et al. *El Greco London: National Gallery*. New Haven: Yale University Press, 2004.

Bronstein, Léo. *El Greco (Domenicos Theotocopoulos)*. New York: H.N. Abrams, 1990.

Denysenko, Nicholas E., ed. *Icons and the Liturgy, East and West: History, Theology, and Culture*. Notre Dame: University of Notre Dame Press, 2017.

ment emphasizing self-denial and intense devotion, however, developed a strong mystical emphasis as well, with Sufi masters such as the Andalusi Ibn 'Arabi (1165–1240) creating vast theosophical systems that explained the transformative experience of personal "annihilation" (*fana'*), the result, Sufis claimed, of the direct experience of God. Often referred to in this period by the Persian term "dervishes," Sufis had begun organizing themselves into formal orders called *tariqat* ("ways," sing. *tariqa*) named usually after a charismatic founder.

This institutionalizing of Sufism into orders did have its detractors, though. Beginning in the thirteenth century, many Sufis rejected such domestication by embracing extreme asceticism and aggressive social deviancy. Such Sufis as the Qalandars took inspiration from an intriguing *hadith* in which Muhammad called on his followers to "die before you die."[2] To them it meant that they should, out of devotion to God, reject all worldly duties—gainful employment, marriage, socially acceptable clothing, polite behavior. Rather, they preferred, having shaved all the hair on their bodies, to live in graveyards, clothed with leaves. The Haydari dervishes, on the other hand, wore iron collars and belts, with heavy rings suspended from their ears and genitals. These radical ascetics, moreover, often flaunted Islamic law through sexual promiscuity, wine drinking, and devotional music and dancing. To more mainstream Muslims, such as the great scholar-astronomer Nasir al-Din al-Tusi, these wild ascetics were mere "rabble,"[3] but they had a presence in much of the Islamic world from Egypt and Syria to Iran and Asia Minor.

While the early Ottoman sultans had great fondness for Sufis, they worried about the socially deviant dervishes, and gradually forced them to adopt the more mainstream ways of the respectable Sufi orders. Many of the wilder sort wound up in the Bektashi order, who themselves had extreme practices: they wore white conical caps, carried drums and banners, chanted hymns and prayers in public, and shaved all their hair as well. Yet the Bektashis were closely allied with the Janissaries of the Ottoman army, who considered Hajji Bektash, the order's founder, to be their patron saint. As a result, the Ottomans allowed them to survive in a moderated form, having absorbed the remaining Qalandars and Haydaris.

But even Sufi orders that had always had an air of respectability cultivated suspect practices. Indeed, the most famous Sufi order is the Mevleviye, founded by the brilliant poet Jalal al-Din Rumi (1207–1273). Though of Persian origin, his family moved to Anatolia when he was young, and he would spend most of his life in Turkish Konya. While his father had raised him in traditional Sufi piety, and he had studied with mainstream Sufi teachers, his religiosity changed profoundly after he met a wandering dervish named Shams al-Din Tabrizi (1185–1248). Under his influence, Rumi founded an order in which whirling and dancing were primary ways of achieving mystical experience. The Mevleviye were not, though, the first Sufis to embrace mystical music and dances. Indeed, they could point back to the works of the twelfth-century mystic Ahmad al-Ghazali (ca. 1061–1123), who had recommended such practices:

> The dancing is a reference to the circling of the spirit round the cycle of existing things. . . . The whirling is a reference to the spirit's standing with Allah in its inner nature and being, the circling of its look and thought, and its penetrating the ranks of existing things. . . . And his leaping up is a reference to

his being drawn from the human station to the state of unity [with God].[4]

But Rumi's order codified these practices and made them socially acceptable, joining them to the profound body of Persian mystical poetry of which he himself was a master. Translated into many languages, and very popular in modern Europe and North America, Rumi's poems often alluded directly to deviant practices:

> God has given us a dark wine so potent that,
> drinking it, we leave the two worlds.
> God has put into the form of hashish a power
> to deliver the taster from self-consciousness....
> Be a connoisseur,
> and taste with caution.
> Any wine will get you high.
> judge like a king, and choose the purest....
> Drink the wine that moves you
> as a camel moves when it's been untied.[5]

While in a less radical form the Mevleviye had close connections to the Ottoman court, and many members of the order were held in high regard in the fourteenth through sixteenth century, the order nevertheless harbored many wilder dervishes. Rumi's grandson, Ulu ʿArif Çelebi (d. 1320), publicly drank wine, for example, and the notorious Divane Mehmed Çelebi (fl. 1550–1600) openly flouted Islamic law and ritual.

FIGURE 13.6 Contemporary image of a Qalandar. The Picture Art Collection / Alamy Stock Photo.

The Kabbalah of Exile

After his victory over the Mamluks in the early sixteenth century, the Ottoman sultan Selim I made it attractive for Jews to immigrate to Palestine, and many—including Jewish exiles from Spain—did. This influx turned the originally small town of Safed, perched in the Galilean hills, into one of the most dynamic centers of Jewish thought in the world. Not only did great Talmudists, such as the Spanish-born Joseph Karo (1488–1575), work there, but Safed became the headquarters of a widespread Kabbalist mystical movement that spanned the Mediterranean. In thirteenth-century Iberia, Kabbalistic thought and practice had been the preserve of small circles of self-consciously elite scholars, but the trauma of expulsion changed all that. As one prominent rabbi put it, from that moment on "the most important commandment will be for all to study [Kabbalah] in public, both old and young, since this, and nothing else, will bring about the coming of the Messiah."[6] Moses Cordovero (1522–1570), of Spanish origin too, as his name suggests, provided a systematic theological framework for this popular mysticism in a series of lengthy works written in Safed. While Kabbalists had long believed that disharmony among the *sefirot*—those ten aspects of God's being—resulted particularly from the estrangement between the male and female aspects of God, Cordovero and his Safed colleagues focused their spirituality especially on the latter. By identifying personally with the divine feminine, whom they referred to as Shekhinah (divine presence), and going even to the extent of wandering intentionally through the Galilean wilds to imitate her wandering, they believed that they could help restore the harmony among the *sefirot*. Of course, the best way to restore that balance was, as Cordovero made clear, to meditate "upon words of Torah and holiness," filling the heart with "reflection on the commandments," and so "become a dwelling place for the *Shekhinah*."[6] Intriguingly, the Safed Kabbalists, like the Sufis and dervishes of the Ottoman empire in which they also lived, organized themselves into brotherhoods that identified with particular spiritual masters.

Though he spent only a few years there before he died, Isaac Luria (1534–1572), born of German and Polish ancestry in Jerusalem, was ultimately the most influential voice among Safed Kabbalists. Immensely charismatic—his followers considered him a divinely appointed Messiah—he insisted that pious commitment would bring about harmony among the divine *sefirot*, and *tiqqun olam*, or "repair of the world," would be the result. "Before an individual begins to pray in the synagogue," he wrote, "he should concentrate upon loving every member of the house of Israel... by this means his soul will be able to rise above and effect the *Tiqqun Olam*."[7] Stories of his supernatural acts traveled rapidly as Safed's popular mysticism quickly spread throughout the Jewish world, as far away even as the Jewish communities in Poland and Lithuania. By the early seventeenth century stories about the great Safed masters were the talk along the canals of Venice, for example, where Safed-trained theologians such as Israel Saruq (d. 1610) were making this popular Kabbalism the dominant intellectual and religious movement among Venetian Jews. There were detractors, of course, such as Leon of Modena (1571–1648), who wrote a lengthy attack on the outlandish accounts of Luria's miracles, but even he was deeply influenced by other aspects of Luria's thought. SEE SOURCEBOOK 13:1.

Christian Kabbalists

Christian scholars as early as the thirteenth century had become aware of Kabbalah—indeed, Ramon Llull (1232–1316), the philosopher-missionary from Iberia, had almost certainly drawn on Kabbalistic ideas as he formulated his rationalist method of conversion. But it was in the early sixteenth century that Christian mystics and theologians embraced Kabbalism wholeheartedly, beginning with Pico della Mirandola—the learned Italian count with whom this chapter began. In his ambitious *900 Theses*, Pico was attempting to show that the core Christian teachings accorded with all other religious and mystical knowledge, including Kabbalah. Indeed, like Jewish Kabbalists he came to believe that the doctrine of the ten divine *serifot*, together with methods for mystically interpreting the letters of the Hebrew alphabet and the words of the Hebrew Bible, had been orally transmitted to Moses at Mount Sinai. Christians were entirely justified, Pico argued, in adopting them, therefore, as their own. Indeed, he saw in them a powerful confirmation of Christian belief. The concluding seventy-two of his 900 theses are titled "Kabbalistic Conclusions Confirming the Christian Religion," and here he proclaimed that "every Hebrew Kabbalist, following the principles and sayings of the science of Kabbalah, is inevitably forced to concede... precisely what the Catholic faith of Christians maintains concerning the Trinity and every divine person, Father, Son and Holy Spirit."[8]

But if Italy with its learned and dynamic Jewish population was the birthplace of Christian Kabbalah, it soon spread elsewhere, through the work especially of a German linguist and scholar named Johann Reuchlin (1455–1522). Born in the Black Forest in southern Germany, Reuchlin quickly demonstrated academic aptitude, entering the University of Freiburg at the age of fifteen, eventually studying as well at the Universities of Paris and Basel, where he excelled particularly in Greek. He spent much of his career working as an interpreter, lawyer, and judge, but found time to cultivate a deep interest in Hebrew. Indeed, he eventually wrote the first Hebrew grammar and lexicon for Christians, entitled *De rudimentis Hebraicis* (1506). In 1490, however, he had met Pico della Mirandola in Italy, and under his influence became fascinated with Jewish mysticism, and this bore fruit in two seminal works of Christian Kabbalah, *On the Wonder-Working Word* (1494) and *On the Kabbalistic Art* (1517). In these he drew on a vast range of Kabbalistic and other Hebrew writings to demonstrate, much as Pico had done, the underlying harmonies of religious thought—whether Jewish, Christian, Muslim, or otherwise. Indeed, the latter work takes the form of a dialogue between a Christian and a Muslim who journey together to study Kabbalah with a Jew. Of course, Reuchlin's underlying harmonies happen to match Christian teaching quite closely. Yet his works nevertheless introduced Christian readers not only to a vast amount of Hebrew mystical theology, but also to specific Jewish techniques for mystically interpreting the Bible, such as *gematria*—a method of assigning numerical value to each Hebrew letter or word on the assumption that words or phrases with the same numerical value have a mystical connection to each other, and these connections reveal layers of hidden meaning in God's revelation.

As a result of the efforts of Pico and Reuchlin, Kabbalah became an important—if controversial—aspect of Christian thought in Europe well into the eighteenth century. In 1677–1678, for example, a German Christian Hebraist named Christian Knorr von Rosenroth (1636–1689) published a multivolume work called *The Kabbalah Unveiled*, in which he argued, among other things, that the three highest *sefirot* are equivalent to the Christian Trinity. His work was very widely read. Indeed, the great scientist Isaac Newton (1642–1727) was fascinated with the mystical interpretation of the Hebrew Bible and had at least one volume of *The Kabbalah Unveiled* in his library.

Converso and Morisco Mystics

The late fifteenth-century Jewish expulsions from Iberia and the early sixteenth-century forced conversion of its Muslims deeply influenced religious thought and experience for those who remained. Two of the most admired spiritual writers in all of Christian history, Santa Teresa de Ávila (1515–1582) and San Juan de la Cruz (1542–1591), were Iberian members of the Carmelite mendicant order. While they both worked tirelessly in reforming their order to bring it in line with the high standards of devotion that characterized its thirteenth-century founders, they were inspiring mystics as well. Santa Teresa's *Interior Castle* offered profound guidance to those wanting to experience God. Believers, she wrote, should enter the "interior castle" of their souls, moving from one of the seven interior courts within it to another—the first ones focused on living the ascetic life, the later ones on contemplation of and union with the divine. In the final interior court, "God removes the scales from the eyes of the soul," which sees Him as He is: "The most holy Trinity reveals itself, in all three persons... and yet, by a wonderful kind of knowledge... the soul realizes that most certainly and truly all these three persons are one substance."[9] San Juan de la Cruz, on the other hand, wrote a series of mystical poems, universally considered among the best poetry in the Spanish language. In the incomparable "On a Dark Night" he tells of the journey of his soul, in utter darkness, to unity with God. The darkness guided him, he said, *más cierto que la luz del mediodia* (more certainly than the light of mid-day), and joined his soul (*la amada*, "the beloved") to God (*el amado*, "the Lover"), so that ultimately, *la amada en el amado transformada* (the beloved was transformed by the Lover).[10] Yet these two devoted, visionary Christian saints—both of whom were later proclaimed as among the thirty-six official Doctors (official teachers) of the Catholic Church alongside Augustine and Aquinas—were direct descendants of converted Jews. Indeed, Santa Teresa's father was condemned by the Inquisition for Judaizing (and she herself was investigated by the Inquisition late in her life, though for reasons other than Judaizing). It is not easy to say precisely how the Jewish ancestry of Santa Teresa and San Juan de la Cruz shaped their mystical experience, but it is striking nonetheless.

But converts, willing or otherwise, showed up elsewhere among mystics in the western Mediterranean. Sidi Ridwan al-Januwi (d. 1583) was a Moroccan Sufi, referred to in his lifetime as the "imam of the ascetics and the scrupulous,"[11] whose father was a Christian convert to Islam and mother a Jewish convert. Rather than hide this background, moreover, he put it to effective use, for Sidi Ridwan embraced an influential strand of Sufi thought—the asceticism of blame—that emphasized that anyone attached only to God would inevitably attract condemnation or blame from the world, which has, of course, strayed far from God. The fact that he was derided as the child of converts, he said, was merely a sign of how close he was to God. Meanwhile in Spain itself, mystical insight lived on among Moriscos, the forcibly converted Muslims, who generally continued to practice Islam. Though only one Sufi text, al-Ghazali's *Path of the Worshipful Servants to the Garden of the Lord of the Worlds*, is known to have circulated among the Moriscos, Sufi spirituality clearly lived on, as the case of a Valencian Morisco baptized as Joan ("John") Crespo makes clear. Known to other crypto-Muslims as Abrahim al-Fatimi, he was brought before the Inquisition in Valencia in 1575 for stirring up rebellion among that region's enormous population of Moriscos. The testimony before the inquisitorial tribunal as well as later chronicles makes clear that he was considered a wonder-working saint rather like the Kabbalist Isaac Luria. One witness believed that he must "be from another world," while another asserted that, like notorious Sufis from the past, he considered himself divine. Others insisted that he had miraculous knowledge of everything, past, present, and future, and that he could levitate, make himself invisible, and—like Luria—converse frequently with angels.

Mediterranean Messiahs

If the Sea in the Middle was ringed by powerful mystical movements shaped by the calamities of the age, those same cataclysms also nurtured the belief among many that they were living in the end-time. For many Jews, the expulsion from Spain, which had been a stable homeland for so many centuries, portended the coming of the Messiah to restore justice to God's Chosen People. For Muslims, the powerful rise of the Ottoman empire could begin to look like God had sent the Mahdi, the Islamic Messiah who would restore proper Islam. For Christians, the shock of the Protestant Reformation and the titanic struggle against the Ottomans likewise fueled a sense that the Day of Judgment was nigh. In fact, the powerful mystical currents in Safed, Istanbul, and Iberia were often closely related to this apocalyptic sense. Of course, like mysticism, apocalypticism was scarcely new to the Mediterranean monotheisms in the fifteenth and sixteenth centuries. It was already present in the Christian Bible in the Book of the Apocalypse or Revelation, for example, and the twelfth-century founder of the Almohad dynasty in the Maghrib, Ibn Tumart, had claimed the status of Islamic Messiah, or Mahdi, in 1121, while the Latin-Christian followers of Joachim of Fiore, as we have seen, expected the beginning of the Age of the Holy Spirit in 1260. But apocalyptic musings were particularly intense in this period, as visions of the end raced round the Mediterranean.

Muslim Mahdis

Apocalyptic thought could be useful to rulers, or so it seemed to Suleyman (Solomon) the Magnificent (1520–1566), the conquering Ottoman sultan, and it was certainly alive during his reign. A compilation of prophecies called *The Key to Comprehensive Divination*, composed in Arabic in the fifteenth century, circulated widely at his court, for example. This text foretold the final conquest of Egypt (which had happened under Suleyman's father, Selim), the return of Jesus, the destruction of Antichrist, and the establishment of a universal empire, united in purified Islamic religion, and ruled over by Jesus and the Mahdi. Threatened in the early decades of his reign by violent factionalism, Suleyman happily sought ruling legitimacy by allowing seers and scholars to depict him as precisely this foretold, reforming sultan who would purify Islam. The shadowy figure known as Haydar the Geomancer, for example, a ubiquitous presence at Suleyman's court for decades, produced annual prophecies that proclaimed Suleyman as both *sahib-kiran* (the divinely ordained world conqueror) and *sahib-zaman* (the spiritual ruler of the age) who would prepare the way for the return of Jesus.

It is true that later in his reign, when he was in a stronger position, Suleyman abandoned these claims, but Islamic apocalypticism continued to flourish nonetheless, as we can see at the other end of the Mediterranean. Moriscos dwelling under Christian rule had high hopes for deliverance as well. Prophecies circulated breathlessly among them. One proclaimed that "the Turk will come and disembark in Barcelona . . . and the Lutherans will come from the other side," both to fight with Moriscos against their Catholic oppressors and so "ruin Christendom."[12] Another promised that "the prophecy of the Prophet Daniel would be fulfilled, which stated that [Granada] would be freed after its fall to a tyrant king."[13] Other prophetic traditions spoke not of Ottoman deliverance but of a conqueror called *El moro Alfatimí* (Alfatimi the Moor) who would appear at the end of time, riding his green horse, and triumph in an apocalyptic battle against the Spanish Catholic armies. The trial records of Abrahim al-Fatimi, whom we met above as a levitating mystic, make clear that many believed that he was indeed the

In the midst of huge geopolitical, economic, and social changes around the Sea in the Middle from the mid-fifteenth to mid-seventeenth century, many Jews, Christians, and Muslims saw God's hand at work. The end—of religious oppression or worldly iniquity and corruption or Godless rule—seemed close at hand, and could be read in both the cataclysmic events of the age and in their ancient holy books. What follows are three examples from across the period.

1. Excerpts from the *Minor Order of Elijah*, a history of the Ottoman Turks written by Rabbi Elijah Capsali (ca. 1483-1555), who was born in Crete but later lived in Padua and Venice, Italy.

> [In order] that man may learn wisdom and understanding in hearing the stories...we will tell of the kings and gentiles and the Turks (Togarmim), and especially of the wisdom of the great king, Sultan Selim, whose like has never been among the kings of the gentiles. Certainly, "The wise man, hearing them, will gain more wisdom; the discerning man will learn to be adroit" (Proverbs 1:5).
>
> The second reason [we will do so] is that "all the peoples of the earth shall know" (Joshua 4:24) "that the Lord alone is God" (Deuteronomy 4:35.39) and "that there is divine justice on earth" (Psalm 58:12). For whoever will read my stories, my words and my deliberations, will fear (God) and will accept the yoke of heaven on himself. Then all this (Jewish) people will know that "the eyes of the Lord are scanning the whole earth" (Zachariah 4:10), "observing the bad and the good" (Proverbs 15:3), "so as to repay every man according to his ways, and with the proper fruit of his deeds" (Jeremiah 32:19), and that He watches over the nations to overthrow one people and to raise another one.
>
> Peruse [therefore] the chapters of this book...have a look at its stories, pay attention and see that in His wisdom and understanding the Lord...has made these Turks a strong and mighty people, "He blessed their efforts and spread their possessions in the land" (cf. Job 1:10). The Lord brought them from a distant land and blessed them exceptionally. The Turk is the "rod of" His "anger," and the "staff of" His "fury" is in [the Turks'] "hand" (cf. Isaiah 10:5), so that he may strike with his hand the nations, people, and noble states, whose measure has been filled. "For the Lord is an all-knowing God; by Him actions are measured" (1 Samuel 2:3).
>
> ...
>
> On the 19th day of April of the year 1453 of the Christian calendar..."came the days of punishment, came the days of requital" (Hosea 9:7), and peace departed from him [the Byzantine emperor]; since the Lord inspired Sultan Mehmet to succeed him. For, the measure of the wicked kingdom of Greece was full, because of all the evil they had inflicted on Judah and Israel since they [the Greeks] had become a people. Then the Lord spoke to Himself:..."I will blow upon" Constantinople, "with the fire of my wrath" (Ezekiel 21:36) and consume it. "I will march against it and set it on fire" (Isaiah 27:4). Because of the evil that the Greeks inflicted on my people, on my nation, I will give [Constantinople] into the hand of the executor of my ban and will pour out my wrath over them.[1]

2. Excerpt from "Unusual Prophecies Prophesied by the Old Master Wilhelm Friess of Maastricht...extending from 1558 to 1563, In Which Very Unusual and Horrible Changes are Prophesied." This brief Christian text circulated in several different versions in both German and Latin in sixteenth-century Europe. In the following passage we are told how, after a period of terror brought about by an "un-Christian emperor," a good emperor and good bishop will rise.

> Afterwards, in the year 1564, there will be one religion and faith, and it will no longer be necessary to carry any kind of weapons. The bishop and emperor will make a law that no one should bear any kind of weapon that can be used for killing, and whoever violates it will be killed with the same weapons that are found with him without a lengthy trial or appeal.
>
> The entire world will strive for unity, for people will remain in proper order and in harmony forever after. Indeed, it will be such a unity as has not existed since the creation of the world.

After that the emperor will travel over the ocean, conquer the Promised Land, and have the Christian faith proclaimed there. After that has been done, he will return and take leave of the world and his empire and lead a holy life. He will leave someone after him who will rule the land wisely, but it will not last long. His rule will last five years. The highest bishop will not survive the emperor by five years, which will trouble the holy apostolic church greatly. Then after that the entire world will enjoy wonderful peace and joy without any discord or contention. People will live forever after in true and sincere love for one another. Every person will be filled with virtue, and everyone will have understanding and wisdom like the apostles at the beginning of the apostolic church. They will be illuminated by the Spirit of God in holy scripture, which had previously long been dark. They will also understand all prophecies and predictions that the prophets have prophesied and foretold. There will also be many who will not only understand the prophets but will themselves also proclaim future things by the Holy Spirit.[2]

3. An account of prophetic awakening. In the following passage from the introduction to a mystical treatise by Rabbi Nathan of Gaza (1643–1680), he describes the dramatic moment when he realized that he was a prophet meant to proclaim the arrival of the self-proclaimed Jewish Messiah, Sabbatai Zevi (1626–1676).

These things [I write] to make known unto you in faithfulness the certainty of the words of truth, the great cause and reason of the tidings which I have announced to the assembly of the congregation of Israel concerning our deliverance and the redemption of our souls. Whosoever knoweth me can truthfully testify that from my childhood unto this day not the slightest fault [of sin] could be found with me. I observed the Law in poverty, and meditated on it day and night. I never followed after the lusts of the flesh, but always added new mortifications and forms of penance with all my strength, nor did I ever derive any worldly benefit from my message. Praise be to God that there are many faithful witnesses to testify to this and to much more. I studied the Torah in purity until I was twenty years of age, and I performed the great tiqqun which Isaac Luria prescribes for everyone who has committed great sins. Although, praise be to God, I have not advertently committed any sins, nevertheless I performed it in case my soul be sullied from an earlier transmigration. When I had attained the age of twenty, I began to study the book Zohar and some of the Lurianic writings. [According to the Talmud] he who wants to purify himself receives the aid of Heaven; and thus He sent me some of His holy angels and blessed spirits who revealed to me many of the mysteries of the Torah. In that same year, my force having been stimulated by the visions of the angels and the blessed souls, I was undergoing a prolonged fast in the week before the feast of Purim. Having locked myself in a separate room in holiness and purity, and reciting the penitential prayers of the morning service with many tears, the spirit came over me, my hair stood on end and my knees shook and I beheld [Ezekiel's Chariot], and I saw visions of God all day long and all night, and I was vouchsafed true prophecy like any other prophet, as the voice spoke to me and began with the words: "Thus speaks the Lord." And with the utmost clarity my heart perceived toward whom my prophecy was directed [that is, toward Sabbatai Ṣevi], even as Maimonides has stated that the prophets perceived in their hearts the correct interpretation of their prophecy so that they could not doubt its meaning. Until this day I never yet had so great a vision, but it remained hidden in my heart until the redeemer revealed himself in Gaza and proclaimed himself the messiah; only then did the angel permit me to proclaim what I had seen. I recognized that he was [the] true [messiah] by the signs which Isaac Luria had taught, for he [Luria] has revealed profound mysteries in the Torah and not one that faileth of all that he has taught. And also the angel that revealed himself to me in a waking vision was a truthful one, and he revealed to me awesome mysteries.[3]

Discussion Questions

1. What assumptions about God and history do these Jewish and Christian prophecies share?

2. Which is more important as a source for these prophecies—scriptural texts or direct divine inspiration?

3. What are the political and social contexts of the Mediterranean that help us understand the emotional resonance of these passages?

Further Reading

Fleischer, Cornell H. "Shadows of Shadows: Prophecy in Politics in 1530's Istanbul." *International Journal of Turkish Studies* 13:1–2 (2007): 51–62.

Green, Jonathan. *Printing and Prophecy: Prognostication and Media Change, 1450–1550*. Ann Arbor: University of Michigan Press, 2011.
Scholem, Gershom. *Sabbatai Ṣevi: The Mystical Messiah, 1626–76*. Princeton: Princeton University Press, 1973.

Notes

1. Martin Jacobs, "Exposed to All the Currents of the Mediterranean—A Sixteenth-Century Venetian Rabbi on Muslim History," *AJS Review* 29:1 (2005): 33–60, at 39–41.
2. Jonathan Green, *The Strange and Terrible Visions of Wilhelm Friess: The Paths of Prophecy in Reformation Europe* (Ann Arbor: University of Michigan Press, 2014), 33–34.
3. Scholem, 840–41.

long-awaited *moro Alfatimí*, restorer of Islamic rule and justice. SEE SOURCEBOOK 13:2.

Jewish Deliverers

As conditions for Spain's Jews declined in the fifteenth century, some Jewish scholars began to suggest that the Ottoman triumph over Christian Constantinople in 1453 must be the harbinger of a messianic age of Jewish deliverance—and indeed a significant number of Jews and Conversos immigrated to the Ottoman East in the 1450s and 1460s to await the advent of the Jewish Messiah. Abraham ben Eliezer ha-Levi (ca. 1460–1530), for example, a learned Kabbalist who had been born and educated in Spain, but finished his days in Jerusalem, boldly claimed in a commentary on the book of Daniel that deliverance would begin in 1524 and the Messiah himself would appear in 1530. Such ideas were widely popular among the far-flung Jewish communities of the Mediterranean, including in Safed itself, where an anonymous commentary on the Psalms also circulated, teaching that these age-old prayers were to be the battle hymns of the upcoming final messianic war.

The Messiah did not arrive in 1530, though, and as result, Kabbalists in Safed and elsewhere largely abandoned messianic visions. Yet messianic longings showed up in other ways. The expulsions from Spain also inspired historical writing among Jews on a scale not seen since the biblical period, and such reflections on the past—as often happened in the medieval Mediterranean—inspired a sense that the Day of Judgment must be drawing near. Joseph Ha-Kohen (1496–1578), for example, wrote a history of Jewish sufferings entitled the *Vale of Tears* in which he hinted often that the end was near: "The expulsions from France as well as this exceedingly bitter exile [from Spain] have aroused me to compose this book, so that the Children of Israel may know what [the gentiles] have done to us in their lands, their courts, and their castles, *for behold the days approach*" (italics added).[14] In a history of the Ottoman Turks by Elijah Capsali (ca. 1483–1555) called *The Minor Order of Elijah*, on the other hand, messianism is the central theme. Capsali turned for inspiration (like Savonarola in Florence) to the Hebrew Bible account of the ancient Persian King, Cyrus the Great, who, though not a Jew, had delivered the Jews from their captivity in Babylon (see Ezra 1:1–11). Two thousand years later, Capsali claimed, the Turkish sultans were the new Cyruses, restoring the exiled Jews to the land of Israel and ushering in the messianic age.

So Jewish longing for the Messiah did not go away. Indeed, it reached its zenith in the middle of the following century. In 1648 news of horrible massacres against Jews in Poland and Ukraine began to spread among the Jewish diaspora, at just the point when an eccentric, though exceedingly charismatic, young rabbi from Ottoman lands convinced himself that he was, in fact, the destined deliverer of the Jewish people.

FIGURE 13.7 *Sabbatai Zevi Enthroned*, Amsterdam, 1666. Photo: Lebrecht Authors, Lebrecht Music & Arts / Alamy Stock Photo.

Sabbatai Zevi (1626–1676) had been precocious: he was an ordained rabbi and admired Kabbalist by the age of twenty. Yet he had a genius for the grand, indeed outrageous, gesture. In the very year of the massacres, he proclaimed himself Messiah, basing his claim in part on a passage of the Kabbalistic *Book of Splendor* that he said predicted 1648 as the messianic year. As a sign of his status, moreover, he boldly pronounced the Tetragrammaton (the four-consonant biblical name of God never uttered by Jews), and immediately began attracting followers, though the rabbinical establishment of his hometown of Izmir eventually banished him and his devotees. He wandered then from Constantinople to Thessaloniki and beyond, inspiring more followers, and meeting rabbis who vociferously supported his claim. He eventually settled in Cairo and then Jerusalem. Along the way he managed to marry a beautiful young girl who had escaped the massacres in Poland, and met a Jewish prophet named Nathan of Gaza, who immediately became his strongest supporter—bosom companion, valued adviser, and public relations guru all in one.

By 1665 he had returned to Izmir in considerable triumph, loudly proclaiming himself King and Messiah. Through Nathan's publicity, moreover, his story had spread throughout the Jewish world, with rabbis and whole congregations throughout Europe proclaiming loyalty to him, and even selling their homes in anticipation of the messianic age. From there, though, things went very badly indeed. Not only did he offend many Jews by seeming to abolish important Jewish rituals, but the Ottoman sultan, Mehmed IV, began to worry about the uproar he was causing. Eventually imprisoned by the sultan and given the choice of death or conversion to Islam, he shocked everyone by choosing the latter. A few hundred of his followers, including his wife, converted as well (and their descendants still form an identifiable Muslim community in Istanbul—the *domneh* (converts)—complete with their own mosque). "Now let me alone," he later wrote, "for God has made me a Turk."[15] Vast disillusionment was the result in much of the Jewish world, Sabbatai Zevi's excesses giving a very bad name to messianism for generations thereafter.

Christian Last World Emperors

Breathless speculation about the end-time was just as common in the Christian world, especially in the form of prophecies announcing the coming of a figure called the Last World Emperor, who, like Charlemagne back in the ninth century, would unite Christendom, reform the church, and bring about an age of tranquility and peace. In Aragon, for example, there had been a lively tradition of such prophecy since the fourteenth century. Arnau de Villanova (1240–1311), for example, a learned physician and mystic, had foretold that the Last World Emperor would rise up in Spain, expel unbelievers, defeat Antichrist in Jerusalem, and unite the whole world in Christian unity. By the late fifteenth century, a Converso astrologer and doctor called Jeroni Torrella was compiling prophecies that depicted King Fernando as the deliverer who would defeat Christendom's Muslim enemies and recapture Jerusalem. Farther north German scholars assembled prophecies that proclaimed this or that Holy Roman Emperor as the expected Last World Emperor. In 1488 Johannes Lichtenberger (d. 1503) had penned a prophetic text called the *Prognosticatio* that one modern scholar described as a multigenerational bestseller—it was printed in more than sixty editions in both German and Latin over the next few generations. In this work, Lichtenberger variously identified both the reigning emperor, Frederick III (1452–1493), and his son, Maximilian I (1508–1519), as the culminating ruler of history, and these prophecies were widely influential—even translated into verse and reworked into drama performed on stage in Basel.

FIGURE 13.8 Antonio Arias Fernández, Charles V, Holy Roman Emperor and King of Spain.

Not surprisingly, with the accession of the king of Spain, Carlos I, to the throne of the Holy Roman Empire (as Charles V) in 1519, uniting thereby the vast new Spanish empire with the older European empire, such prophecies—drawing on both the Spanish and the German traditions—reached a fevered pitch. The town council of Barcelona, for example, issued a proclamation in 1520, upon hearing news of Carlos/Charles's imperial coronation, that lauded him as a second Charlemagne who would defeat the Turks, make peace between Catholic and Orthodox Christians, reestablish the Christian Roman Empire, and usher in a new age of peace in which the lion would lie down with the lamb. This was an image, moreover, that Emperor Charles's grand chancellor, Mercurino di Gattinara (1465–1530), worked energetically both to spread throughout his vast realms and to inculcate in Charles himself. The latter he did in confidential memoranda that instructed the young ruler that, as a second Charlemagne, he would bring the whole world to the single shepherd, Jesus Christ.

Yet, just as in the Islamic and Jewish worlds, prophecy was by no means the sole preserve of ruling elites in Latin Christendom, but had appeal across wide swaths of society. Indeed, prophetic rhetoric—sometimes originating among Jews—could be used by oppressed European Christians to oppose powerful rulers, as the case of one Augustin Bader (d. 1530) makes clear. A humble weaver from Augsburg in Germany, Bader adhered to the movement called Anabaptism, the most radical arm of the Protestant Reformation, a group that was brutally persecuted not only by Catholics, but by the other main Protestant groups, the Lutherans and Calvinists. Under the influence of a former Catholic priest and scholar of the Hebrew Bible named Oswald Leber, Bader eventually came under the influence of German-Jewish followers of Abraham ben Eliezer ha-Levi, whom we met above proclaiming that 1530 would be the year of Jewish deliverance. Combining this Jewish strand of millenarianism with Christian ideas, the Augsburg weaver came to believe that a deliverer would arise who would free both the Jews and the Anabaptists from the oppression of German-Christian rulers such as Emperor Charles. Indeed, Bader eventually concluded that he himself was the expected Last Emperor who would accomplish all this, and even had his own set of imperial robes and vestments made. Once word of all this reached the authorities, Bader and his handful of followers were arrested in 1530 and executed, but not before demonstrating that prophecy in the wrong hands scared those in powerful positions.

Converts

As the case of Sabbatai Zevi, Jewish Messiah who converted to Islam, indicates, conversion was a living reality in the fifteenth and sixteenth centuries. Such had been the case, of course, throughout much of the earlier period as well, with vast populations of Christians (and smaller numbers of Jews) converting to Islam, for example, in the centuries after Muhammad first preached. One of the Prophet's first followers was the Persian-Jewish convert Salman al-Farisi, while the author of one of the most influential early Muslim refutations of Christianity, 'Ali al-Tabari (ca. 780–860), was a Christian convert to Islam, likewise of Persian origins. Of course, people had changed religions in other directions over the centuries as well. The Frankish Christian cleric Bodo (814–876) made his way to Islamic Spain to convert to Judaism, changing his name to Eleazar after doing so, while a Spanish-Jewish convert to Christianity who took the name Paul Christian became an unstinting Dominican opponent of Judaism who debated theological questions with Rabbi Nahmanides at Barcelona in 1263. In general, though, we know little about such converts—other than their names and their works, if they wrote any—until we reach this later period, when some left behind accounts of their conversions and others drew the attention of onlookers who recorded what they saw. These sources make clear that against the backdrop of mystical messianism and imperial conflict, changing from one monotheism to another was an attractive option for some. They also indicate that even among converts who eventually embraced their new religion wholeheartedly, captivity or force had sometimes played a role, but also that, having converted from one religion to another, some wound up adhering in some ways to both. Such converts, moreover, could rise to the highest levels of the societies that embraced them.

Friar Anselm Turmeda Becomes 'Abd Allah al-Tarjuman

Born sometime between 1350 and 1355, Anselm Turmeda (d. 1423) was from a Mallorcan family in Iberia, and was sent off at a young age to study with a priest. This led to formal education in the universities of Lleida in Catalonia and Bologna in Italy as well as entrance into the Franciscan order and ordination as a Christian priest. Yet by 1420 Turmeda had moved across the Mediterranean to Tunis, where he had accepted Islam and taken the new name of 'Abd Allah al-Tarjuman—literally, "'Abd Allah the Translator," for he earned his keep in the age-old Mediterranean profession of interpretation between languages. More strikingly, he completed in that year an Arabic treatise called *The Gift for the Cultivated Person in Rebuttal of the People of the Cross*, a lengthy attack on Christianity that outlines the errors of the Christian Gospels, argues that Muhammad was foretold in the Bible, and attacks core Christian doctrines such as the Trinity and Incarnation.

Scholars know little about what actually happened in between Turmeda's university education and his publication of *The Gift*, other than what he tells us in the curious autobiography that forms the first part of that work. Here he tells us that his conversion began when his Bolognese professor of theology admitted to him that the Paraclete described by Jesus in John 14:16, 26, and usually understood by Christians as the Holy Spirit whom Jesus would send to comfort them, referred in fact to Muhammad. These verses, then, as Muslims had long argued, were actually a prophecy of the coming of Islam. When Turmeda asked his venerable professor why he had not formally converted to Islam, he answered that his love of status and prestige kept him from abandoning a faith he knew to be wrong. However true this account might be, it is certain that Turmeda himself formally converted to Islam in Tunis, spending the rest of his life there in service of the local sultan. Eventually he became one of the mostly widely read Muslim polemicists against Christianity, especially after *The Gift* was translated into Ottoman Turkish in 1603.

Yet 'Abd Allah al-Tarjuman, having apparently left Christianity behind, nevertheless continued, in something of a parallel life, to be a Franciscan friar, for he continued to write moralizing Christian works in Catalan under the name Fra Anselm—Friar Anselm. In 1398 he reworked an Italian treatise called *The Book of Good Precepts* into a rhyming text on living the good life, and this work went on to be widely beloved among Christians in Catalan-speaking lands. In 1417 he wrote the *Dispute of the Ass*, a Catalan dialogue between a donkey and a Christian friar about the superiority of humans to all other animals. Though eventually placed on the index of forbidden texts by the pope (because it concluded, surprisingly, that humans were, in fact, not at all superior to animals!), it also was widely read in Europe in a variety of vernacular translations. There is no way to know whether Anselm/'Abd Allah maintained this double religious life cynically or was somehow not troubled by being both pious anti-Christian polemicist and Christian moralist at the same time, but there are figures in this period whom we know to have shifted comfortably from one religious guise to another.

Rabbi Solomon ha-Levi Becomes Bishop Pablo de Burgos

Anselm Turmeda/'Abd Allah al-Tarjuman's double identity suggests, as does a fair amount of other evidence, that conversion was often messy and incomplete. Other cases, though, like that of another learned Iberian convert, appear much more clear-cut. A near contemporary of Turmeda, Solomon ha-Levi (ca. 1351–1435) was born into an elite Jewish family and became a rabbi. Like so many of his Iberian coreligionists, however, he found himself a Christian after the pogroms of 1391. While he himself says that he was convinced to abandon his ancestral faith by the works of Thomas Aquinas, we do not know the exact circumstances of his conversion—whether forced or free or some combination. What is clear is that he soon embraced Christianity vigorously, having taken the name Pablo. He eventually earned a doctorate in Christian theology at Paris, served the pope as counselor, and rose through the Spanish ecclesiastical hierarchy, first as bishop of Cartagena in 1403 and then as bishop of Burgos from 1406 until his death (after which he was succeeded by his convert son Alfonso!).

Moreover, like Anselm Turmeda/'Abd Allah al-Tarjuman, Pablo de Burgos (as he is usually known) was

FIGURE 13.9 Nineteenth-century image of Pablo de Burgos. The Picture Art Collection / Alamy Stock Photo.

an influential author, composing two rhyming Castilian historical chronicles, and two erudite treatises in Latin. He certainly made use of his sophisticated, preconversion education as a Jewish rabbi. His most widely read work was his *Additions*, a supplement to the seminal fourteenth-century biblical commentary of the Franciscan Nicholas of Lyra (ca. 1270–1349), who had drawn extensively on Jewish commentaries as he presented the Christian interpretation of the Hebrew Bible. Though Pablos's *Additions* was often critical of Lyra's conclusions, the value of his learned observations was quickly recognized. Indeed, they often were copied (and eventually printed) right alongside Lyra's commentary and were read throughout Christian Europe (including by the reformer, Martin Luther, who studied them avidly). Yet we do not find evidence of anything like Anselm/'Abd Allah's religious ambivalence. Pablo's *Six Ages of the World* advanced a view of history drawn almost entirely from Saint Augustine of Hippo, and he appears utterly convinced by the core Christian theological positions. He certainly never wrote seemingly Jewish works for Jewish readers under his former name while he presided as Catholic bishop.

Turning Turk

In 1658 an English cleric named Thomas Warmstry published a sensational pamphlet entitled *The Baptized Turk*, telling the story of one Rigep Dandalo, "who, a Turke borne," had nevertheless "converted to the true Christian faith,"[16] and there had been other publicly celebrated converts in London as well, such as a certain "Chinano a Turke," who had converted in 1586. Such figures were naturally fascinating, but especially so because it was clear to everyone that there were far more Christians becoming Muslims—"turning Turk" in the parlance of the day—than the other way round. With the expansion of the Ottoman empire, and its gradual integration into the economic and diplomatic networks of Europe, numerous Europeans embraced Islam. Their motives were varied and complex. A certain Niccolo de Bello, for example, an Italian from Crete who traveled with an embassy from the Holy Roman Empire to Istanbul in 1591, very publicly converted to Islam. No force appears to have been involved, though he may have converted in order to help free a brother in captivity in Ottoman lands. Another member of the same embassy, an aristocrat named Ladislaus Mörth, converted in 1593, and it seems likely in his case that he did so to escape the consequences of a sexual affair with a kitchen boy on the embassy's staff.

In other cases, we are much better informed. In 1526, a Hungarian named Balázs Somlyai was captured by the Ottoman army at the Battle of Mohács, after which, perhaps as a recruit for the Janissary corps, he acquired a basic education in Islam and Ottoman Turkish, and then converted to Islam, taking the name Murad ibn 'Abd Allah. Eventually, like Anselm/'Abd Allah, he became a translator, in his case in the imperial service. Moreover, like Pablo of Burgos, in whose conversion force may well have played a part, Murad ibn 'Abd Allah nevertheless became a devoted follower of his new religion. Indeed, he eventually wrote a polemical treatise against Christianity entitled *The Guide for One's Turning toward Truth* that makes clear that embracing Islam had been for him the natural consequence of intellectual and religious trends in Christian Europe itself—which he called Firengistan, by the way, "the land of the Franks."[17] Like the Christian humanists in Latin Europe to be discussed just below, Murad was anxious to get back to the original sources of religion and culture, and his study of the Qur'an convinced him that, unlike the Bible—which he argued had been changed and distorted through frequent translation—Islam's holy book survived unchanged in the Arabic language of God. Furthermore, it is likely that he had been aware of the thought of Christian Unitarians (Protestants who, in opposition to all other Christians, opposed the traditional Christian doctrine of the Trinity) and saw converting to Islam as the natural consequence. It is, at any rate, certain that some Christian anti-Trinitarians did in fact "turn Turk," as the case of Adam Neuser (d. 1576) makes clear. A Christian minister in Heidelberg, he became a convinced opponent of Trinitarianism, and eventually moved to Istanbul where he converted to Islam, studied Murad's *Guide*, and often tried to persuade other Christian Unitarians visiting Istanbul to become Muslims. SEE SOURCEBOOK 13:3.

Humanists and Philosophers, Scientists and Engineers

But just as the transformative philosophical and scientific thinkers of the twelfth- and thirteenth-century Mediterranean lived in an intellectual world that was also rich with belief in natural magic and Kabbalist theosophy, so the mystical messianism and fraught conversions of the age of Catholic-Ottoman conflict existed side by side with hardheaded scholarship, rational inquiry, and well-engineered tools. Indeed, in some cases they coexisted in the same person. In the wealthy Italian city-states, the dynamic commercial hubs of the later medieval Mediterranean, scholars in the mid-fourteenth century embraced a new vision of education based not so much on the Bible and Aristotle, as on the secular culture of ancient Rome

Scientific theory and practical technology did influence each other in the medieval Mediterranean, but it is often difficult to piece together how. A good example is another of the great Mediterranean inventions: eyeglasses. These now ubiquitous devices first appeared in Italy in the 1280s. We do not know who invented them, but a number of texts mention their use, including a 1306 sermon by the Dominican theologian Giordano da Pisa (ca. 1255–1311), who commented that "it is not twenty years since there was discovered the art of making spectacles which help you to see well." Intriguingly enough, however, the dominant scientific theory of how sight worked in the medieval Mediterranean was completely out of step with this new technology. Indeed, according to this theory, eyeglasses should have made eyesight *less* accurate. Often called the theory of *extramission* (casting out), it went back to Greek antiquity.

> And so in the vessel of the head, they first of all put a face in which they inserted organs to minister in all things to the providence of the soul, and they appointed this part, which has authority, to be by nature the part which is in front. And of the organs they first contrived the eyes to give light, and the principle according to which they were inserted was as follows: So much of fire as would not burn, but gave a gentle light, they formed into a substance akin to the light of every-day life; and the pure fire which is within us and related thereto they made to flow through the eyes in a stream smooth and dense, compressing the whole eye, and especially the center part, so that it kept out everything of a coarser nature, and allowed to pass only this pure element. When the light of day surrounds the stream of vision, then like falls upon like, and they coalesce, and one body is formed by natural affinity in the line of vision, wherever the light that falls from within meets with an external object. And the whole stream of vision, being similarly affected in virtue of similarity, diffuses the motions of what it touches or what touches it over the whole body, until they reach the soul, causing that perception which we call sight.[1]

According to this theory, whereby the eye sees by sending out rays that bump into things in front of them, eyeglasses would distort the direction of these rays, therefore causing worse eyesight. Strikingly enough, however, at just about the same time as eyeglasses were invented, several important Latin scientists, including the Englishman Roger Bacon, were writing extensively about optics—the science of light and sight—and Bacon, in particular, directly denied the extramission theory. As was so often the case with Latin thought in this period, Bacon's theorizing here had been deeply influenced by an earlier Arab-Muslim scholar, Hasan ibn al-Haytham (ca. 965–1040), from Basra in modern Iraq, who had argued with great sophistication that extramission was impossible.

> If sight is due to something issuing from the eye to the visible object, that thing is either corporeal or incorporeal. If it is corporeal, it follows that when we look at the sky and see the stars in it, corporeal substance issues from our eye in that time and fills the whole space between heaven and earth, and [yet] the eye is in no way destroyed; and this is [obviously] false. Therefore, sight does not occur through the passage of corporeal substance from the eye to the visible object. But if that which issues from the eye is incorporeal, it will not perceive the object, since there is no perception except in corporeal things. Therefore, nothing issues from the eye to the visible object to perceive that object.[2]

According to Bacon, following Ibn al-Haytham, eyesight must work by rays of light coming into the eyes—what scholars call the theory of intromission—a view that made perfect sense of eyeglasses that focused light rays properly on the retina. But we have no evidence that the inventor of eyeglasses had any knowledge of scientific theories of optics—whether of extramission or intromission—and thus no way to know whether the new theory helped bring about the technological change or vice versa.

What is certain is that the use of eyeglasses spread like wildfire. Less than a century later, Petrarch, the founder of the humanist movement, lamented his need for glasses.

> In my prime I was blessed with a quick and active body, although not exceptionally strong; and while I do not lay claim to remarkable personal beauty, I was comely enough in my best days. I was possessed of a clear complexion, between light and dark, lively

FIGURE 13.10 The Dance of Death, La Chaise-Dieu Abbey, France, fifteenth century. JAUBERT French Collection / Alamy Stock Photo.

> eyes, and for long years a keen vision, which however deserted me, contrary to my hopes after I reached my sixtieth birthday, and forced me, to my annoyance, to resort to glasses. Although I had previously enjoyed perfect health, old age brought with it the usual arrays of discomforts.[3]

Eyeglasses show up in countless later medieval paintings as well, as in the depiction of a student with glasses in a fresco of the Dance of Death from La Chaise-Dieu Abbey, France.

Because they quickly became associated with learning—scholars then as now often needed them to read their old books—glasses soon adorned people who never could have worn them, such as the great translator of the Vulgate Bible, Jerome (347–420), whose eyeglasses, in the painting in figure 13.11, rest just below his right hand.

Eyeglasses spread quickly not only within Latin Europe, but, in opposite movement to the theory of intromission, into the Islamic world as well. By the fourteenth century, a Muslim schoolteacher named Muhammad, like his contemporary Petrarch, lamented his need for them.

> He [Muḥammad] recited to me literally from his own poem [the following verses] concerning the eyeglasses from which he suffered, since his eyesight was too weak to see small handwriting, and he [had to] put them [the glasses] on his nose: "[Not only] the sorrow I feel for the elapse of my youth / I was destined that my sorrow would grow. I used to have eyes upon my cheeks / and today they have come to be upon my nose."[4]

In the fifteenth century an anecdote told about Sultan Qaytbay (ca. 1468–1496) of Mamluk Egypt indicates that eyeglasses were well known in the Arab world, still associated with European manufacture, and, oddly, could become issues of state.

> In this [month] the chief judges and the Islamic dignitaries ascended to greet the sultan [Qaytbay] for the [new] month as usual. . . . They greeted him in the new canopied platform at the edge of the Sultanic Hawsh. The chief Hanafi judge requested from the sultan [Qaytbay] spectacles that were produced by the Franks

FIGURE 13.11 Domenico Ghirlandaio, *Saint Jerome in His Study*. Darling Archive / Alamy Stock Photo.

> [i.e., Europeans] so that he might see the writing with them. A number of them [= these glasses] were imported [lit. brought] to him. [The sultan] replied: "[The spectacles] which you have asked for, [have] silver frames, which you are not allowed to use." He [the Qadi] had no choice but to remain silent. He frowned since he could not answer him [the sultan] in the presence of his company [the other Qadis and dignitaries]. I wish I knew what made him [the Qadi] do that [to ask for the silver-framed spectacles]. God is the Governor and the Ruler.[5]

Discussion Questions

1. What are the possible relationships between the invention of eyeglasses and the circulation of Ibn al-Haytham's theory of intromission?
2. What kind of interactions between scientists and artisans would those possible relationships require?
3. Would there be any reason why Muslim scholars might feel uncomfortable using a Christian invention?

Further Reading

Lindberg, David C. *Theories of Vision from Al-Kindi to Kepler.* Chicago: University of Chicago Press, 1981.

Mazor, Amir, and Keren Abbou Hershkovits. "Spectacles in the Muslim World: New Evidence from the Mid-Fourteenth Century." *Early Science and Medicine* 18:3 (2013): 291–305.

Rosen, Edward. "The Invention of Eyeglasses." *Journal of the History of Medicine and Allied Sciences* 11:1 (1956): 13–46, and 11:2 (1956): 183–218.

Notes

1. Plato, *Timaeus* 45b-d, trans. Benjamin Jowett, http://classics.mit.edu/Plato/timaeus.html.
2. Alhazen, *De aspectibus*, bk. 1, ch. 5, sec. 23, as quoted in Lindberg, 64.
3. Petrarch, *Letter to Posterity*, https://sourcebooks.fordham.edu/source/petrarch1.asp.
4. Khalil ibn Aybak al-Safadi, *A'yan al-'Asr fi A'wan al-Nasr*, as quoted and translated in Mazor and Hershkovits, 301.
5. Ali b. Dawud al-Jawhari al-Sayrafi, *Inba' al-Hasr bi-Abna' al-'Asr*, as quoted in Mazor and Hershkovits, 298.

and Athens. In searching out the best ancient guidebooks for their curriculum, they vigorously revived Latin and Greek classical texts that modeled this urban culture. We find the same urge among Jewish rabbis, and the broader concern to examine the strictly human role in history has direct analogues in the Islamic world as well. Rationalist philosophy and science also thrived in both the Islamic and Christian worlds, with the Scientific Revolution beginning in the early sixteenth century. Skilled technicians, moreover, created amazing tools, many of them meant to give military advantage to one side or another in this age's enormous battles.

Humanists

By the fourteenth century, Italy's trading cities were home to prosperous merchants and artisans whose lives were shaped by commerce and politics: they administered complex business partnerships through sophisticated accounting procedures and international correspondence; they participated vigorously in government as elected officials and judges or as secretaries and advisers. For them the education of European universities, where theology was the queen of sciences and Aristotelian methods predominated, was not so much wrong (they were, for the most part, pious Christians after all) as unhelpful. Instead, Italian scholars after 1350, such as Petrarch (1304–1374), increasingly advocated a return, they said, *ad fontes*, "to the sources," of Latin culture in the works of ancient Roman scholar-statesmen such as Cicero (106–43 BCE). Like Italian burghers, Cicero had been both a man of affairs and a scholar—a brilliant defense attorney and politician as well as a philosopher and rhetorician—and he had written works that give unsurpassed advice on all those pursuits. Moreover, his treatises, such as *On Duties*, a guide book for statesmen, were written, they found, in artful, ornate Latin, unlike the dry, logic-heavy summas of the scholastics. In place of the university curriculum focused on divine things—logic, metaphysics, theology, canon law—Petrarch and his ilk advocated the *studia humanitatis*, the "studies of humanity," what we now call the humanities: rhetoric, languages (especially Latin and Greek), literature, history, and ethics. This new educational program, they argued, was far more useful in training the worldly leaders of urban Italy.

Moreover, to this new curriculum they joined zealous historical and linguistic research. While some of the works of Cicero and other ancient luminaries had been studied and recopied throughout the Middle Ages, these humanist scholars were dedicated to finding every last surviving work of antiquity, and hunted through dusty monastic and aristocratic libraries to do so, copying what they found. In this way humanists such as the papal secretary Poggio Bracciolini (1380–1459) made available to Latin readers for the first time in centuries ancient texts such as long-lost orations of Cicero and the daring philosophical poem *De rerum natura* by Lucretius (99–55 BCE). Though initially focused on Latin literature, the humanists soon turned their interests to Greek texts as well, often learning Greek from Byzantine scholars who fled Constantinople after its fall to the Ottomans, such as Cardinal Basilios Bessarion (1403–1472), a Byzantine churchman who eventually rose to prominence in the West after converting to Catholicism.

Both the humanist curriculum and its method spread widely, first in Italy, and then in the fifteenth century to the rest of Latin Europe. So it was that in the early sixteenth century, the Dutch Catholic scholar Erasmus (1466–1536) wrote works not on philosophical theology, but on practical Christian ethics, such as his *Handbook of a Christian Knight* and *In Praise of Folly*. Moreover, using his brilliant command of Greek, he published the first edition of the New Testament to be based on the oldest Greek manuscripts then available. His contemporary, the Reformer Martin Luther (1483–1546), was similarly educated in the new humanist curriculum (alongside having a theological, scholastic education). He not only applied the *ad fontes* principle to religion—the ancient Bible by itself, without the supplement of medieval commentaries or theology, was sufficient for the salvation of Christians—but put humanist scholarly tools to work in his new German translation of the Bible, which he made directly from the Greek and Hebrew originals. Indeed, all three streams of Reformed Christianity (Lutheranism, Calvinism, and Anabaptism) put great emphasis on the sufficiency of the Bible alone as a source of Christian belief and practice, a doctrine usually summed up in the phrase *sola scriptura* (by scripture alone). Moreover, there was nothing in scripture, they argued, to justify the pope's supreme position in ecclesiastical affairs, nor was there any warrant for what they saw as the Catholic Church's emphasis on doing good works to gain salvation. Resolutely, on the contrary, they asserted that Christians are saved *sola fide* (by faith alone).

Especially in Italy, these humanist urges took root among Jews too, as the father and son rabbis Judah (ca. 1420–1498) and David Messer Leon (ca. 1470–1535) make clear. The former, a prolific philosopher and physician, is best known today for a treatise entitled *The Honeycomb's Flow*, an educational handbook in Hebrew for Jewish readers. Like Christian humanists, Judah Messer Leon turned to ancient Roman scholars, especially Cicero and Quintilian, for guidance, arguing that to produce the properly educated Jewish scholar— what both father and son...called a *hakham kolel* or "comprehensive scholar"[18]—a classical, rhetorical education was essential, and it must include broad familiarity with both Jewish and non-Jewish literary traditions. His son David lived out this Jewish humanism thoroughly, even after moving to the Ottoman empire in 1495. Having imbibed the *studia humanitatis* as a child from his father, he then sojourned in his youth in Florence where he read widely in the works of Cicero, Seneca, Virgil, and Ovid. Later, when exiled in Istanbul, he drew on Augustine of Hippo's famous Christian defense of the study of the pagan classics in *On Christian Teaching* to formulate his own arguments in favor of Jewish humanism, which he presented in a commentary on Proverbs 31.

But the *studia humanitatis*—in slightly different forms—were thriving as well in the Islamic world. For centuries, learned Arab scholars had immersed themselves in a set of studies called *adab*, including rhetoric, grammar, and ancient and pre-Islamic Arab poetry, that likewise cultivated an urbane ability to thrive at court and in positions of influence, and its great masters, such as the Iraqi al-Jahiz (776–869), had been widely admired. While *adab* was alive and well in this later period—the Granadan Ibn Hudhayl al-Fazari (d. 1409), for example, published a guidebook called the *Well of Adab and Administration*—a concern with the human dimension of life in the world shows up in a different way in the sophisticated historical works of Ibn Khaldun (1322–1406). Like many Italian humanists, Ibn Khaldun was active in public affairs—serving as secretary and even prime minister for various Muslim courts ranging from Granada to Tunis to Cairo. Yet he was also an astute observer of human affairs and fascinated by the lessons of history. As part of a massive Arabic history of the world, moreover, he wrote a preliminary study called the *Muqaddimah* (Introduction), which laid down his explanatory principles. While giving God his due, Ibn Khaldun, like the Italian humanists, emphasized especially the social forces that shaped history, and he is thus often seen as the ancestor of the modern social sciences. While he had little direct influence among Arab thinkers, Turkish scholars embraced his ideas. Though he may not have read Ibn Khaldun directly, Mustafa 'Ali (1541–1600), the greatest Ottoman historian, interpreted history in a similarly social way, as a panoply of interconnected events shaped by human choice—a historical humanism like that of his North African predecessor.

Philosophers

The strongly Aristotelian strand of philosophy that had developed from the eleventh century on remained powerfully influential well into the seventeenth century. Averroes's deeply Aristotelian works, for example, were printed in Latin in 114 different editions before 1700. Yet the rational probing of the cosmos, God, and humankind scarcely stood still. We saw above that Pico della Mirandola, Renaissance prince and Christian Kabbalist, was also a philosopher, but Neoplatonic, rather than Aristotelian, in approach. In that also he was representative of his age. There was a notable tendency as well in this period for Mediterranean philosophy to move far away from the Sea in the Middle, as Islamic civilization moved ever east, and Latin European civilization traveled to the Western Hemisphere.

Though the Ottomans dominated the Islamic Mediterranean, Islamic philosophy thrived primarily in Iran under the Ottoman's enemies to the east, the Shi'i Safavids, who generously cultivated learned scholars and recruited them to their courts. Here in the Iranian heartlands, Ibn Sina's revised Aristotelianism still dominated philosophical education, but an interesting fondness for other parts of the Greek philosophical tradition developed too, especially for the oldest Neoplatonic texts available in Arabic—a kind of Arab philosophical return *ad fontes*. Such works as the remarkably misnamed *Theology of Aristotle*—a misattributed and thoroughly Neoplatonic work—had been available in Arabic since the tenth century, but scholars had long ignored them. Safavid philosophers rediscovered them and began putting their ideas to work. These tendencies culminated in the stunning achievement of Sadr al-Din Muhammad Shirazi (ca. 1571/72–1640), usually known as Mulla Sadra. In scores of works, but most especially in his massive *Transcendent Theosophy in Four Intellectual Journeys*, he advanced a synthesis of Ibn Sina, Neoplatonism, and Sufism that still dominates Shi'i thought. His highly original account of divine and human existence manages to preserve Ibn Sina's emphasis on God's radical difference from creation while at the same time incorporating the Sufi mystic's experience of God in all things. He achieved this by arguing that existence comes in gradations or degrees—what is known as the doctrine of "intensification." God, of course, is true existence, but the existence of everything else flows from Him in ever less complete or intense forms the farther they are from God. This view obviously derives from the Neoplatonic notion that being emanates from the One, but Mulla Sadra expressed it in a fusion of Ibn Sina, Qur'an, and Sufism. "Thus," as one scholar put it recently, "does Sadra have his cake and eat it too, able to enjoy the sublime taste offered by Sufis' [doctrine of the] unity of existence, without giving up Ibn Sina's fundamental contrast between divine necessary existence and created contingent existence."[19]

But far away at the northwestern edge of Eurasia, Neoplatonism was flourishing as well in the newly wealthy Atlantic trading states. In England the so-called Cambridge Neoplatonists followed Pico della Mirandola in arguing for a perennial philosophy steeped in the *prisca sapientia*, the "ancient wisdom" preserved variously in the thought of Pythagoras and Plato, but also in highly Neoplatonizing Jewish and Christian Kabbalah. Such currents flowed especially strongly, moreover, among Iberian Conversos who reverted to Judaism in the Netherlands. Abraham Cohen de Herrera (ca. 1562–1635/39), for example, was born Alonzo Nuñez de Herrera in Florence, the child of a Spanish Converso family. As a young man he read deeply in the Neoplatonic thought of Pico, but also studied Lurianic Kabbalah. After eventually settling in Amsterdam, he wrote a treatise called *The Door of Heaven* that interprets Kabbalah through the Renaissance Neoplatonism that he learned from the likes of Pico in Florence. We find a surprisingly similar strand of Neoplatonism in a slightly later contemporary Portuguese/Dutch Jew of Converso background, Baruch de Spinoza (1632–1677). One of the most important philosophers of early modern Europe, Spinoza is famous for radical innovations that outraged Jewish and Christians theologians then and now: he argued for a pantheistic view of God and nature, seeing them both as one, and was an unstinting critic of all organized forms of religion with their rituals and irrational laws. Yet some of his contemporaries saw him as a veiled Kabbalist, his pantheism being just a reworking of the Lurianic view that every human had a spark of divinity within. Indeed, there are many portions of Herrera's *Door of Heaven* and Spinoza's *Ethics* that are surprisingly similar, not least because their conceptions of being draw from the same mystical Neoplatonic well as Mulla Sadra's. As Mediterranean culture expanded east and west around the globe, the close, fifteenth- and sixteenth-century connection between philosophy and mysticism expanded with it.

Scientists and Engineers

What historians call the Scientific Revolution is usually thought to have begun with the publication of Copernicus's *On the Revolutions of the Heavenly Spheres* in 1543, which argued daringly for a heliocentric, rather than geocentric, cosmos, and to have culminated in 1687 in Isaac Newton's *Mathematical Principles of Natural Philosophy*, which brilliantly advanced a series of basic laws of motion—whether of the orbiting planets or of a ball thrown by a child—that were far better at explaining movement in the natural world than any previous theory. Yet, like all revolutions, this one was deeply rooted in the rich soil of historical context, in this case in the Mediterranean scientific tradition.

As had been the case for centuries, astronomy, the breakout science of this revolution, was widely practiced in the sixteenth century because it was necessary for astrology. Johannes Kepler (1571–1630), who showed that the planetary orbits in Copernicus's heliocentric cosmos were not circular, but elliptical, spent a good deal of his career as the official astrologer to the Holy Roman Emperor, for whom he was required to cast regular horoscopes. Moreover, astronomy itself was still a thriving enterprise throughout the region. Indeed, before the invention of the telescope in Europe in 1608, the best astronomical observations were being done in Islamic observatories. The Turkish scientist Takiyuddin (1526–1585), another court astronomer-astrologer (for Murad II), made systematic astronomical observations every bit as precise as the best available in contemporary Europe—and using many of the same tools. Furthermore, Arab science remained deeply admired throughout Europe. While Avicenna and Averroes (the Latin spellings of Ibn Sina and Ibn Rushd) had long been read by Latin intellectuals, only in the sixteenth century did it become common to include their biographies, and those of many other Arab luminaries, alongside those of the great Greek and Latin thinkers, something we find, for example, in the *Treasury of Celebrated Astronomers* by Simon Phares (ca. 1445–1500). SEE SOURCEBOOK 13:4.

Yet real change is obvious in this period too. Just as in philosophy, it is impossible to ignore how far Mediterranean astronomy had moved beyond its shores. The telescope was invented in the Netherlands, where Spinoza philosophized (and earned his living as a lens grinder), while Copernicus, Kepler, and Newton were, respectively, Polish, German, and English. The best Islamic observatory of the period was in Samarkand (modern Uzbekistan), more than 200 miles farther to the east than Ibn Sina's hometown of Bukhara, itself more than 2,000 miles from the Mediterranean.

Moreover, though books, ideas, and technologies had been traveling across and around the Sea in the Middle for centuries, for the first time western Europe—what Murad ibn 'Abd Allah had called Firengistan —became intellectually influential in the Islamic world. Mehmed II's great library contained many texts in Christian languages, for example, and Takiyuddin probably made use of a European spherical globe. Certainly traditional Arab science was energetically cultivated in the Ottoman world—the vast thirty-volume medical summa of the Andalusi Muslim Abu al-Qasim al-Zahrawi (936–1013), for example, appeared in full Turkish translation. Yet increasingly Turkish physicians drew on Latin European methods. The Iranian-born and educated Ottoman physician Shemseddin Itaqi (b. 1570) merged fourteenth-century Persian anatomical knowledge with the insights of the Flemish physician Andreas Vesalius (1514–1564), the most influential European anatomist of his age, in his Turkish *Treatise on the Anatomy of the Human Body*. Furthermore, while Ottoman sultans turned to many Muslim (especially Iranian) doctors to serve as court physicians, in the sixteenth century Bayezid recruited Joseph Hamon (d. 1517/18), an exiled Spanish Jew for this post, and Suleyman engaged Joseph's son, Moses (ca. 1490–1565), as his personal physician. Like Shemseddin Itaqi, both father and son combined extensive knowledge of Arab medicine with awareness of the new European breakthroughs in the healing arts. In the seventeenth century Greek-Christian physicians, who had attended European universities, increasingly replaced Jewish physicians at the Ottoman court.

But Firengistan's scientific and technical influences in the Ottoman world were not always so benign, for it was from Europe that the armies of the sultans learned the murderous chemistry of gunpowder. Though Latin Europe did not invent this explosive mixture of sulfur, charcoal, and potassium nitrate (it was Chinese alchemists centuries earlier who had done that), nor were European soldiers the first to put it to killing use (the Mongol invaders did that in the 1230s), it was warriors and rulers in Latin Europe who, starting in the late thirteenth century, most aggressively embraced this technology and developed the tactics for its use. By the 1320s European armies used guns on campaign, and by a century later cannons were a naval commonplace. While gunpowder weapons may have been used in this period elsewhere in the Islamic world, it is clear that the Ottomans adopted firearms from Europe after having had these weapons fired at them in the Balkan wars in the late fourteenth century. By early in the following century, the Ottomans were producing enormous cannons—often called "bombards"—that their engineers frequently manufactured on site during sieges, and were imitating European tactics for their use, such the *wagenburg*, a sort of mobile fortress consisting of wagons chained together with cannons mounted on them, that collectively served as a defensive wall behind which soldiers carrying handguns could walk. Just as the sultans recruited physicians with knowledge of Latin medicine, so did their foundries recruit European gunsmiths.

Yet, just as early medieval Arabs had learned their science and philosophy from the Greeks, but then developed their own distinctive tradition of rational inquiry, and Latin Europeans borrowed the astrolabe from the Arabs, but became master makers and users of that technology, so the Ottoman firearms industry quickly became self-sustaining and sophisticated. Indeed, in the manufacture of musket barrels, using flat sheets of steel in a manner reminiscent of how swords had been forged in earlier centuries in Damascus, the Ottomans clearly outclassed European arms makers—Ottoman gun barrels were far stronger and much less likely to burst. From the Ottomans, moreover, the Safavids (1501–1722), their Shi'i rivals in Iran, learned to use and make cannons—

FIGURE 13.12 The Dardanelles Gun, a Turkish bombard. Photo: Historical Views / agefotostock / Alamy Stock Photo.

primarily to defend themselves from the Ottomans—and from both the Muslim Mughal (1526–1857) rulers of India likewise adopted gunpowder weapons. At the beginning of the sixteenth century, Islam and Muslim rule continued to spread far to the east, and Europeans had begun exporting Christianity to the Americas in the far West. In both ventures, key Mediterranean cultural practices went with them, gunpowder weaponry not by any means least among them. SEE SOURCEBOOK 13:5.

Notes

1. Donald Weinstein, *Savonarola: The Rise and Fall of a Renaissance Prophet* (New Haven: Yale University Press, 2011), 90.

2. Ahmet T. Karamustafa, *God's Unruly Friends: Dervish Groups in the Islamic Later Middle Period, 1200–1550* (Oxford: Oneworld Publications, 2006), 41.

3. Karamustafa, 5.

4. J. Spencer Trimingham, *The Sufi Orders in Islam,* with a new foreword by John O. Voll (1971; Oxford: Oxford University Press, 1998), 195.

5. Coleman Barks, *The Essential Rumi: New Expanded Edition,* trans. Coleman Barks with Reynold Nicholson, A. J. Arberry, and John Moyne (New York: Harper Collins, 2004), 5–6.

6. "Pious Customs of Moses C.," trans. Lawrence Fine, in Fine, *Safed Spirituality: Rules of Mystical Piety, The Beginning of Wisdom* (Mahwah, NJ: Paulist Press, 1984), 34.

7. "Pious Customs of Isaac Luria," in Fine, *Safed Spirituality,* 66.

8. S.A. Farmer, *Syncretism in the West: Pico's 900 Theses (1486); The Evolution of Traditional, Religious, and Philosophical Systems; with Text, Translation, and Commentary* (Tempe, AZ: Medieval & Renaissance Texts and Studies, 1998), 523.

9. Teresa of Ávila, *The Interior Castle* 7.1.8–9, trans. The Benedictines of Stanbrook, rev., with notes and introduction, Fr. Benedict Zimmerman, OCD, 3rd ed. (London: Thomas Baker, 1921), 265–66.

10. San Juan de la Cruz, *La noche oscura,* 4, 5 (consulted at https://onemorelibrary.com/index.php/es/?option=com_djclassifieds&format=raw&view=download&task=download&fid=13863).

11. Adapted slightly from Manuella Ceballos, "Theology from the Margins: Sīdī Riḍwān Al-Januwī and His Community of Ousiders," *Medieval Encounters* 24 (2018): 581–612, at 583.

12. Mayte T. Green-Mercado, "The Mahdī in Valencia: Messianism, Apocalypticism, and Morisco Rebellions in Late Sixteenth-Century Spain," *Medieval Encounters* 19 (2013): 193–220, at 204.

13. Green-Mercado, 200.

14. Yosef Hayim Yerushalmi, *Zakhor: Jewish History and Jewish Memory* (1982; Seattle: University of Washington Press, 1996), 14.

15. Scholem, 686.

16. Palmira Brummett, "The Early Modern Convert as 'Public Property': A Typology of Turning," in *Conversion and Islam in the Early Modern Mediterranean: The Lure of the Other,* ed. Claire Norton (London: Routledge, 2017), 103–28, at 103.

17. Tijana Krstic, *Contested Conversions to Islam: Narratives of Religious Change in the Early Modern Ottoman Empire* (Stanford: Stanford University Press, 2011), 98.

18. Hava Tirosh-Rothschild, *Between Worlds: The Life and Thought of Rabbi David ben Judah Messer-Leon* (Albany: State University of New York Press, 1991), 105.

19. Peter Adamson, *Philosophy in the Islamic World* (Oxford: Oxford University Press, 2016), 392.

CHAPTER FOURTEEN

Family, Gender, and Honor, ca. 650–1650

One night in Rome in 1608, Adriano Pardo and his friends appeared before the house of Giovanni de Bassi whistling, blowing horns, shouting that Giovanni's wife, Margarita, was a "slut" who pimped for her sister Caterina, and proclaiming "we want to put horns on the door of your [Giovanni's] house."[1] Horns were the sign of the cuckold, the humiliated husband of an adulterous woman. Adriano had tried to court Caterina, who lived with Margarita and Giovanni, but she had rejected him. Loudly and publicly defaming the de Bassi household was the spurned suitor's way of taking revenge. In early modern Rome, such rituals of "house-scorning" were common, part of the day-to-day politics of honor.

Christian neighbors in the kingdom of Valencia's towns ritually assaulted each other's houses in contests for prestige and status. Practiced since the late thirteenth century, these household assaults involved a series of aggressive acts: men or women chanting insults—usually sexual ones like "whore" and "cuckold"—outside an adversary's house; armed men invading the house and beating up or wounding the male owner of the house in order to demonstrate his inability to defend his house and the female relatives it was supposed to protect; and men roughing up one of the women of the house in the course of the invasion, suggesting to the neighborhood audience that they could have raped her. Sometimes household invaders slashed the face of a woman with a dagger, a form of symbolic rape that left a lasting mark of dishonor. In the course of their own family feuds, the kingdom's Muslim men abducted the daughters of enemies from their homes; it was popularly understood that they then sexually abused them. Even though some abductions were actually elopements, fathers who could not guard and control their daughters still endured a loss of face in the eyes of the Muslim community.

Abducting women was commonly practiced by both Christians and Muslims in many areas of the eastern Mediterranean, such as Byzantium, the Venetian colony of Istria in the north Adriatic, and Ottoman Anatolia. The women's families suffered dishonor, a public wound that could be at least partly healed if the abductors married their victims. As in Valencia, the precise aims of the abductors were not always clear, though there was no mistaking the intentions of the Turk Huseyin when, in 1630, he lashed out at an Ottoman judge to whom he was in debt by carrying off his wife from a town near Bursa and giving her to one of his henchmen "to use."[2] One of the ways early Ottoman sultans enhanced their power and honor at the expense of their political rivals was through abducting their women. No Mediterranean man, whether monarch or peasant, could uphold his reputation if he could not protect his female relatives and keep his house in order.

The aggressive actions described above, which involved the symbolic or real violation of women, served to accentuate and perpetuate the high value that families and communities placed on the virginity of unmarried women and the chastity of wives. Throughout the Mediterranean, a family's honor—that is, the respect granted it by social peers—was partly based on the sexual propriety of its women. The family's house stood at the center of this moral universe and structured ideal gender roles. The domain of women lay inside the inviolable house, where they cared for children, performed domestic tasks, and remained chaste. The world of men was outside the house, where they provided for the family and defended its reputation by responding violently to any insult or attack against it. The failure of women and men to live up to these gendered behavioral standards might bring shame on them and their families; their disgrace benefited their rivals in the local struggle for social status. In this intensely competitive social environment different family structures and marriage strategies arose for the purpose of advancing the interests of the family.

Yet no matter how much gender ideals shaped the outlook of women and men, they did not always determine their economic and social behavior. By necessity lower-class women often worked outside the home. Upper-class women who could afford to stay inside frequently did not and sometimes exercised considerable influence in economic, political, and cultural affairs. The material assets that women brought to a marriage strengthened their voice in the family's economic planning. Women also played roles in the feuds that erupted in Mediterranean communities, not only as passive victims but as conspirators who incited their menfolk to behave in accordance with widespread notions of masculinity and attack the family's enemies. Maintaining the honor and prosperity of the family from one generation to the next required its members to be mutually supportive and careful of their conduct.

Honorable Families

Anthropologists have questioned the supposed distinctiveness of the Mediterranean as a region of "honor cultures" and they have rightly cautioned against making sweeping generalizations about Mediterranean societies. It is nonetheless clear that in premodern times honor was a special concern of Mediterranean families. Explorations of the history of marriage, however, reveal important differences between Christian, Muslim, and Jewish societies and thus provide a sense of the variety of Mediterranean honor cultures. Within the framework of their religious traditions and laws, families organized their human and economic resources in ways that enabled them to compete most effectively with their coreligionists and social peers. Marriages were critical moments for individual families, linking past, present, and future generations in the endeavor to preserve the honor of the family name while involving them in the exchange of property and the formation of political alliances with other families in the community.

Family Structures and Marriage Patterns

Throughout the Mediterranean world families were patriarchal and patrilineal; that is, men were dominant and families were organized around the father's line, tracing their ancestry back to a male founder. Ideally, male kin from the paternal line—agnates—would cooperate economically and politically, and jointly compete with other families for power in the community. Wives, who came from another patrilineal family, played an important role, at least for the potential allies and economic assets they brought to a marriage and the children they bore. Within this general Mediterranean framework, however, there was variation, most significantly between Muslim and Christian marriage patterns and conceptions of family organization.

In Muslim societies, and among the Jewish and Christian communities they incorporated, a man's preferred marriage partner was his paternal cousin, or the daughter of his father's brother. The preference for such marriages made Muslim families more patrilineal in orientation than those in Christian Europe. Cousin-marriages enhanced the solidarity of the agnatic clan—a group of lineages descended from a common male ancestor—and maximized its economic and political potential. Instead of the agnatic kin of the bride and the groom enduring the economic losses that normally resulted from exogamous marriages (out-marriages) between unrelated families, in endogamous cousin-marriages (in-marriages) the bridewealth the groom customarily gave to the bride and whatever property she inherited from her parents remained within the clan. Furthermore, the natural political alliance between brothers and their families was reinforced through the marriage of their children, thus contributing to the "group feeling" rooted in shared paternal blood that Ibn Khaldun regarded as fundamental to the political success of nomadic Arab and Berber tribes. The wife who was the daughter of her husband's paternal uncle, moreover, could be relied on to conduct herself virtuously and uphold the honor of her husband's lineage and clan, which were also her own. Many marriages, however, were exogamous, not only because marriage to a cousin often

ARTIFACT MARRIAGE ISSUES IN THE JEWISH DIASPORA: THE CASE OF THE OTTOMAN NEAR EAST

Like their counterparts in other minority communities, Jewish communal and religious leaders faced the challenge of defending their authority and the legal autonomy of their communities against the encroachments of majority governments with their own secular and religious laws and courts. This common jurisdictional concern sometimes coincided with legal complications that were especially characteristic of the Jewish diaspora and resulted from the frequent migration, both coerced and voluntary, of Jewish populations: the convergence and even clash of distinct rabbinical legal traditions. In the sixteenth century, these two problems noticeably overlapped in Ottoman Syria-Palestine and Egypt, where Sephardi, Ashkenazi (French and German), Italian, and Maghribi Jews immigrated, often with the encouragement of the Ottoman authorities, and settled among their indigenous Arabic-speaking (*musta'rab*) brethren. The influx of immigrants caused the Jewish population in Palestine, for example, to quadruple by the middle of the century. Rabbis from different backgrounds found themselves grappling with pressing legal questions surrounding the institution of marriage, some of them stemming from the forced conversions and expulsions of Iberian Jews.

Among the myriad marital questions that the rabbis addressed—everything from how parents negotiated and celebrated the engagement of their children to divorce—the issue of whether a man could take a second wife was consistently controversial. Talmudic law (*halakhah*) did not forbid polygamy, but the extent to which it was actually practiced varied in accordance with the origins and traditions of the couple involved. In *musta'rab* communities, long exposed to the influence of Muslim society, couples were more likely to have polygamous marriages (with rare exceptions, it was always bigamy), though even here wives sometimes included clauses in the marriage contract (*ketubah*) forbidding their husband to marry a second wife, on pain of divorce. Couples of European origin, on the other hand, normally followed the ban against polygamy attributed to the great Ashkenazi rabbi Gershom ben Judah (ca. 960–1040), known as "the light of the Exile." Although polygamy had never been completely prohibited among the Jews in Christian Spain, they had been influenced by Rabbi Gershom's ban. Jewish husbands, moreover, had been required to obtain authorization from their Christian king to take a second wife, usually in the case of the infertility of their first wife. In the Ottoman East, the coexistence of rabbis holding different views on this issue was conducive to intense legal debates, particularly when Ashkenazi husbands sought the rabbis' permission to take an additional wife. While Ashkenazi rabbis condemning such violations of Rabbi Gershom's prohibition received the support of some Sephardi sages, other Sephardim, such as the great rabbi Joseph Karo in Safed, argued that Gershom's ban had expired and was no longer binding. With the lack of rabbinical unanimity, bigamy became more common in Ashkenazi and Sephardi marriages—and for various reasons, such as the first wife's insanity, severe illness, or "rebelliousness" as well as the couple's childlessness.

Another area in which the customs of indigenous Jewish couples differed from those of European immigrants pertained to the rights of wives to dispose of their marital gifts as they saw fit and to control the earnings from their labor in, say, embroidery or moneylending. Whereas the immigrants' *ketubahs* commonly stipulated "[the proceeds from] her handiwork belongs to *him*," *musta'rab* marriage contracts stated that "her handiwork belongs to *her*."[1] The Muslims' example most likely inspired this *musta'rab* custom, which lent women greater economic independence, and, like Muslim wives, *musta'rab* Jewish wives were willing to sue their husbands or parents in court—in the Muslims' *shari'a* court—to gain control of their bridal gifts.

Jewish leaders throughout the diaspora worried that such resort to gentile (non-Jewish) courts would lead to the excessive intrusion of gentile officials into the Jewish community's internal affairs and to the erosion of individual Jews' obedience to Jewish law. Despite their leaders' protests, Jews in Ottoman lands frequently appealed to the gentile authorities, much as Jews had in Christian Spain. Yet there was a significant difference. In Spain, when Jewish litigants had brought disputes involving family matters, such as inheritance and divorce, before Christian kings, the kings had ensured that such cases were adjudicated in accordance with *halakhah* either by assigning them to rabbis who were known halakhic experts or by ordering Christian judges to consult with rabbis and make decisions in conformity with Jewish law. Ottoman judges, however, treated Jewish litigants like Muslim litigants and decided Jewish family disputes in accordance with Islamic law. And this was precisely why Jewish women turned to them: they knew that in certain areas, such as inheritance rights, *shari'a* treated women more favorably than did *halakhah*. Whereas Islamic law granted daughters half the share their brothers received of their father's inheritance, Jewish law excluded daughters from inheriting any of their father's estate if they had brothers, a provision that many Jewish fathers and communities devised legal strategies to circumvent. Jewish wives also sometimes appealed to the Ottoman authorities to compel their abusive or negligent husbands to grant them a bill of divorce when rabbis, perhaps especially intent on keeping couples together in the tumultuous conditions of the time, proved reluctant to allow for such compulsory divorces. In certain cases, however, rabbis seconded the decisions of Muslim magistrates. Moses Trani (1500–1580), a Thessaloniki-born rabbi who had immigrated to Safed, agreed when a Muslim court in Beirut forced a Jewish man to divorce the wife with whom he neither lived nor supported. Trani described the husband as "a man who defaulted on the biblical commandments of maintenance and cohabitation. He has left his wife . . . while he wanders from city to city. Wherever he goes, he takes a new wife. He has never sent his wife anything . . . and has never come near the home. There is no way of compelling this man to pay maintenance to his wife, for one of the reasons he is constantly on the go is in order to avoid being traced by creditors."[2]

Rabbis resident in Ottoman domains had to deal with serious legal dilemmas in the wake of the expulsion of the Jews from Spain in 1492, which had torn Jewish families apart. Some spouses—usually the husband—had converted and remained in Spain while their partners went into exile. Other couples had gotten separated during the exile and were never reunited. As a result, as one Sephardi preacher put it when describing Spanish refugees in Palestine, "men arrived without women, and women without men."[3] The situation was particularly dire for the women. Jewish law prohibited the wife of a convert from remarrying until she received a valid writ of divorce from him; it also stipulated that an *agunah*, a wife whose husband had disappeared or deserted her, could not remarry unless she provided conclusive proof of his death or of a divorce. When their husband's whereabouts were unknown or when their husband lived across the sea and proved uncooperative, the refugee women—who sometimes had their children in tow—were left in desperate straits. In Safed, one rabbi reported, "the marketplace and the streets are full of wailing women . . . who have been abandoned by their husbands."[4] Extant letters from Jerusalem tell of the efforts of its Jewish community and of the relatives of the deserted women to track down their husbands. One letter beseeched the leaders of an unnamed Jewish community to assist an *agunah* and her daughter: "May you succeed in persuading him [the husband] to return to his wife forthwith and live with her as man and wife, as is the custom of Jewish men. Do not rest until you see him setting out on his way. . . . Make him vow not to stray from the path, but to make his way directly home."[5]

The rabbis whose decisions determined the fate of these women mostly responded with leniency, searching for almost any legal loophole that would allow them to remarry. In more than 78 percent of the known cases, the rabbis freed them from their legal predicaments. While the rabbis had the women's best interests at heart, they also feared that the women might simply ignore Jewish law and remarry anyway, engage in promiscuous behavior, or convert to Islam. Through their leniency the rabbis endeavored to strengthen the social and legal foundations of new Sephardi communities in the Ottoman Near East.

Discussion Questions

1. In what ways did settlement in the Ottoman Near East potentially change the marriage customs and married life of European Jewish immigrants?
2. How did the presence of rabbis from communities with different legal traditions and the presence of Ottoman *shari'a* courts sometimes benefit Jewish wives? How did this complicated legal situation sometimes work against women's interests?
3. How did the rabbis' legal interpretations and decisions in cases of family law help to preserve Jewish marriages, families, and communities in the particularly difficult conditions of the sixteenth century?

Further Reading

Assis, Yom Tov. *The Golden Age of Aragonese Jewry: Community and Society in the Crown of Aragon, 1213–1327*. London: Vallentine Mitchell, 1997.

Falk, Ze'ev. *Jewish Matrimonial Law in the Middle Ages*. Oxford: Oxford University Press, 1966.

Lamdan, Ruth. *A Separate People: Jewish Women in Palestine, Syria, and Egypt in the Sixteenth Century*. Leiden: Brill, 2000.

Notes

1. Lamdan, 123.
2. Lamdan, 179.
3. Lamdan, 203.
4. Lamdan, 205.
5. Lamdan, 204.

proved to be impossible but because marital alliances with unrelated lineages were politically advantageous. Cousin-marriages nevertheless remained a cultural ideal in much of the Muslim world. Thus, even though, as Ibn Khaldun observed, the agnatic solidarity that had motivated larger tribal groups tended to peter out once tribes settled down in cities and towns, related patrilineal families continued to reside in particular urban quarters and to unite in defense of their blood kin in local feuds.

In permitting marriage between cousins Islamic law was simply legitimizing pre-Islamic Arab practices. Neither Jewish law nor Roman law forbade this marriage pattern, which had been widespread in the Roman world. It was the church that effected a major change in both Latin Christendom and Byzantium over the course of the early Middle Ages. Church councils prohibited "incestuous" marriages, that is, marriage between kin related by blood or through marriage. The ban even extended to "spiritual kin" or godparents. The church also insisted on monogamous marriage and tried to suppress concubinage. Even though canon law had no bearing on Jewish practices, the marriage patterns of Jews in Christian realms tended to be more exogamous, probably influenced by the changing behavior of their Christian neighbors.

The reasons for the church's new rulings on marriage are not entirely clear, but the prohibitions against polygyny and cousin-marriage certainly prevented wealthy and powerful men from taking too many wives and concubines and kept more marriageable women circulating more widely in society. Consequently, fewer frustrated men resorted to abducting women, just as leading Carolingian churchmen had hoped. The problem of abduction, however, did not completely disappear. Because of the shortage of Christian women on the Spanish frontier in the eleventh and twelfth centuries, town governments were compelled to pass laws against the abduction of nubile women.

In any case, the church's rules gradually took effect throughout the Christian world. Adjusting to them was most difficult for peasant families in small, isolated villages and for noble and royal families with property and power at stake. In 997, the Orthodox patriarch issued a decree against cousin-marriages in Byzantium with the encouragement of Emperor Basil II, who aimed thereby to weaken his aristocratic opponents. In the Latin West, the issue continued periodically to spark confrontations between popes and monarchs trying to arrange politically convenient cousin-marriages for themselves or their children.

After 1000 Christian Europe also experienced a shift toward the organization of lineages around the male line, especially among rural nobles and elite families in the growing cities. During the Carolingian era, when the aristocracy was in formation and there was land for the taking, ambitious noble families had drawn on both male and female lines for their property and pedigree. The stabilization of feudal principalities by 1000, however, limited opportunities for aristocratic families, forcing them to adopt strategies that tightened their grip on the estates they possessed while enhancing their ability to contend with noble rivals. Rather than ruinously dividing their property among all their heirs, noble fathers transmitted most of their inheritance undivided through the male line, increasingly to the elder son (primogeniture). Younger sons might go on Crusade and seek their fortune or wed the daughter of a noble family with a rich dowry. The emerging dynastic lineages developed pride in their ancestry and an esprit de corps that made them formidable political players. In the expanding urban centers, where society was initially more fluid and opportunities greater, families attained power and influence through the economic and political cooperation of agnates commonly identifying with the paternal line. In northern Italian cities such as Genoa and Florence, agnatic lineage groups and their allies dominated entire neighborhoods where they built fortified towers for defense against other lineages. The patrilineal family continued to be prevalent in town and country in subsequent centuries because of its effectiveness as a means of economic and political organization. Yet, since European patrilineal families were necessarily formed through the marital union of unrelated lineages, they gave more recognition to the maternal line than did Muslim families, allowing wives' relatives to exert more influence in family affairs.

Marriage Contracts

Marriages were not only or even primarily matters of the heart. Rather, premodern folk viewed them pragmatically as alliances between two families with significant social, economic, and political implications. While marriages were made in conformity with religious laws, they were also based on contracts with a marked secular orientation. Contracting a marriage entailed negotiations between the parents of the bride and groom, with both families making often substantial investments in the newlyweds' household.

Parents, especially fathers, normally arranged the marriages of their children, for there was a lot at stake. Fathers tried to ensure that their child's spouse belonged to a family of at least the same social class. Islamic and Jewish laws both gave the father the right to contract marriage for a minor (prepubescent) daughter to whomever he wished, without her consent. Once daughters reached the age of majority, or puberty—around age twelve—they had more of a voice and parental consultation with them was recommended. Jewish daughters were, in theory, free to choose their husband; in practice, their parents were still in control, though evidence from late medieval Spain and Renaissance Italy suggests parents were growing more attentive to their children's wishes. "Mature" virgin Muslim daughters did not escape paternal control either and they were legally required to be married off by a "guardian," normally a member of their agnatic clan. The Hanafi school of law, however, did not insist on the role of the guardian, which led the Ottoman sultan Suleyman I in 1544 to prohibit such women from marrying without a guardian's permission so that their families would not be "ruined."

The Catholic Church had by the twelfth century arrived at the view of marriage as a sacrament, a physical and spiritual union between man and wife that was analogous to the relationship between Christ and the church. According to canon law, the couple's mutual exchange of words of consent before witnesses and preferably a priest (though his role was not indispensable prior to the Council of Trent in 1563) sufficed to make a valid marriage, which was later perfected through sexual relations. Yet the church, with its emphasis on spirituality, also praised married couples who pledged themselves to a life of sexual abstinence. The church's position that parental approval was not essential for a marriage existed in tension with secular law codes that insisted that it was and that punished children who married against their parents' wishes with disinheritance. Ideally, as in Muslim and Jewish families, children and parents would agree on the choice of a spouse.

In Mediterranean societies brides were usually young, marrying before the age of twenty, often at around sixteen or even earlier. The brides' youth made them more attractive partners: they could more easily adjust to the demands of their husband and his family, and would hopefully bear more children. Fathers, moreover, could ensure their daughter's virginity at the time of marriage and preserve the honor of their house. The Florentine Catasto of 1427—a tax census that is an unrivaled source for the history of the premodern family—confirms this pattern for women and shows that men from elite merchant and professional families tended to delay marriage until their late twenties, by which time they would have acquired enough resources to establish a household suitable for their social station. Artisans married a bit earlier, since they required less wealth to settle down, and farmers earlier still, because they needed a wife and children to help them run a farm. Among the Jews of medieval Egypt and Renaissance Italy, however, there was less of an age gap between bride and groom. All men and women were supposed to marry and procreate, and men were encouraged to marry young. The celibate life was not an option for Jews or Muslims, as it was for Christians, who could enter a religious order.

Contracting marriage involved both spouses and their families contributing material assets that had economic and symbolic value. Jewish and Muslim grooms were legally obligated to pay bridewealth (or dower) to their brides, in exchange for which they gained control over their brides' sexual and reproductive capacity. The payment was often made in two stages: the first at the outset of the marriage and the second at the time of the dissolution of the marriage through the husband's death or divorce. The amount of the bridewealth accorded with the status of the bride's family. In early medieval Germanic kingdoms, husbands customarily paid a "morning gift" to their brides on the morning after the consummation of the marriage. As an expression of the husband's claim of exclusive sexual access to his wife, it was similar to the Jews' and Muslims' bridewealth, and it also gave the wife rights to a portion of her husband's property.

From the twelfth century, however, Christian Europeans increasingly reverted to the dowry as defined in Roman law: the donation granted by the bride's family to the groom to help him handle the economic "burdens of matrimony." Husbands continued to render gifts or counter-gifts to their wives, which became part of the couple's assets, but these amounted to no more than half the size of the dowry. The reemergence of the dowry was linked to the shift toward patrilineal family organization. Parents transmitted their main landed property to their sons while granting their daughters cash dowries as their inheritance. Dowries came to symbolize the honor and status of the bride and her paternal family, and large dowries became essential for catching a husband from a respectable family. Because of the resulting "dowry inflation," poor families often had to rely partly on charity to put together decent dowries for their daughters. Even wealthy families could not always afford to marry off all of their daughters, and so sent some to convents. Families, however, could hope that their sons would wed well-dowered daughters-in-law. The circulation of dowries among elite urban families furnished capital that helped fuel the commercial economy.

The significant contribution the dowry made to a Christian family's resources enhanced wives' influence in economic decision-making. Husbands, however, possessed the legal authority to manage the dowry and collect the income earned from investing it. Wives still retained ultimate ownership of the dowry and could—and sometimes did—sue their husbands for restitution of their dowry if they squandered or mismanaged it. Dowries were meant to support wives after the death of their husband. When wives predeceased their husband, the dowry usually either passed to their children or, if they had died childless, it reverted to their father's family. Since dowries represented a substantial investment on the part of fathers, they maintained great interest in their daughter's marriage, interfering when they thought it necessary. Marriage was as much a union of two lineages as it was of husband and wife.

In Jewish marriages in both Christian and Muslim lands, brides' parents also provided their daughters with dowries, in accordance with long-standing Jewish custom. As among Christians, dowries often constituted the daughter's inheritance, were larger than the marital gifts granted by husbands, and ultimately passed into the possession of the widow. Muslim brides, too, brought substantial assets to the marriage in the form of trousseaus (clothes, linen, household items, jewelry) furnished by their fathers—essentially dowries amounting to their inheritance—which often exceeded their husband's marriage gifts. However, unlike Christian and Jewish wives, whose marital property fell under the legal control of their husbands, Muslim wives retained the authority to manage and dispose of their property, including the bridewealth. While the greater legal competence of Muslim wives did not create equality in their marriages, it did give them more room to maneuver within the framework of a patriarchal order.

FIGURE 14.1 Jewish marriage contract between Jacob ben Nathan and Durra bat Kisan, in Aramaic, 1065. © Historical Views / agefotostock.

Divorce

One pillar of patriarchy in Muslim and Jewish societies was the laws empowering husbands to unilaterally divorce their wives. Husbands could use the law to threaten disobedient spouses or, if necessary, finally repudiate them.

Regulations in both faiths, however, required husbands to pay the remainder of the bridewealth to wives they divorced in this fashion, which discouraged husbands from acting rashly.

Muslim and Jewish wives, on the other hand, could include clauses in their marriage contracts that enabled them, without loss of marital assets, to opt for a divorce under specific conditions, such as the husband's abusive behavior. One common condition that could trigger divorce was the husband's taking a second wife or concubine. These contractual stipulations overrode religious laws that permitted Jewish men to take a second wife and Muslim men to marry as many as four wives, provided that they treated them all equitably. Polygyny was only a concern of affluent men who could afford to maintain more than one wife.

Jewish sources from twelfth-century Cairo and later Muslim sources from Mamluk domains show that women often sued for divorce. In order to be released from an unhappy marriage, however, they usually had to relinquish rights to their bridewealth and other marriage gifts from their husband. The economic independence that Muslim wives were authorized to exercise in marriage perhaps lent them greater confidence to leave their husbands, especially when the women were well-to-do. Divorce rates were rather high: around 30 percent for Muslim couples and around 20 percent for Jewish ones. Among the reasons for divorce were the husband's impotence, sexual incompatibility, infidelity, the husband's inability to support his wife in the manner to which she had grown accustomed, the husband's lengthy absences from home, and spousal abuse. Many divorcées remarried.

Catholic canon law did not permit divorce, though it did allow for the annulment of marriage in cases of impotence, bigamy, and marriage within the prohibited degrees of kinship. Couples could also separate on grounds of one spouse's adultery, heresy, apostasy, and excessive violence; the marital bond, however, remained intact. Since the Orthodox Church also viewed marriage as a sacrament, it was very strict about granting divorces. According to its canon law, grounds for divorce included the attempted murder of a spouse, a wife's adultery, and the impotence of the husband for three years. The Orthodox Church, however, gradually became more flexible after 1453 in an effort to discourage Christian couples from applying to Ottoman *shari'a* courts for divorce. Ottoman judges treated Christian women much as they treated Muslim women, and they determined the economic responsibilities of divorcing Christian couples in conformity with Islamic law. In order to attract Christian couples to its own courts, the church acknowledged more grounds for divorce.

The recourse of unhappy Christian couples to Ottoman courts was not unlike Jewish and Muslim couples and their families in Christian Spain appealing to Christian kings as a last resort to ensure that the terms of their marriage and divorce agreements were upheld. Women and men of all faiths would do whatever they could to see to it that these turning points in their and their children's lives were handled properly. SEE SOURCEBOOK 14:1.

Women Inside, Women Outside

Patriarchy in the premodern Mediterranean world was sustained through mutually reinforcing social and religious ideologies: a social rationale requiring the control of women and their sexuality for the honor of the family; and Jewish, Christian, and Islamic traditions considering women as inferior and subordinate to men. While all three religions portrayed women and men as equal before God in a spiritual sense, they all conveyed the message that women's righteous conduct in this world entailed fulfilling prescribed roles as subservient, chaste daughters and wives.

In medieval Judaism and Christianity the negative image of women was in part founded on the biblical stories of creation and of Adam and Eve in the Garden of Eden. Eve was created from Adam's rib and was therefore inferior to him. Eve, moreover, was responsible for provoking God to expel her and Adam from the Garden, and thus for bringing sin and death into the world, by succumbing to the temptation of the serpent (or devil) and then tempting Adam. Although the Qur'an does not portray Eve as the seducer of Adam, later Muslim interpretations were influenced by Judeo-Christian views, and traditions (*hadiths*) ascribed to the Prophet describe women as a harmful temptation for men. Celibate Christian clergymen, especially in the Latin West, felt threatened by female sexuality and in their writings they described

The duty of Catholic inquisitors in Spain and Italy to investigate, prosecute, and punish Catholics who propagated heretical beliefs or engaged in heretical rituals—be they Protestant, Jewish, Islamic, or inspired by the devil—did not necessarily lead them to focus on women. A heretic, after all, was a heretic, regardless of her or his gender. Inquisitors, for instance, did not treat heretical Converso and Morisco women differently from their menfolk. Yet, like much of the male church leadership, most inquisitors held views that made them more suspicious of women: that women were intellectually incapable of understanding complex theological ideas and were therefore more likely to fall into religious error, and that women were inherently more susceptible to diabolical temptation and, as witches, to becoming the devil's accomplices.

In early sixteenth-century Spain, inquisitors anxious to prevent the spread of Lutheran ideas began prosecuting the members of a new mystical movement known as "illuminists" (*alumbrados*). Many were Conversos, as were two of the group's three female leaders, the *beata* Isabel de la Cruz and María la Cazalla, a married woman. The third, the *beata* Francisca Hernández, was of Old Christian lineage. Emphasizing the "abandonment" of their souls to union with God, these women and their followers, who included clergymen, rejected external Catholic rituals, such as praying to saints, as well as the role of priests as mediators between the human and the divine. Although the illuminists' beliefs and practices were probably not Lutheran in inspiration, they were certainly unorthodox. Between 1524 and 1534 the Inquisition tried the three women. Isabel publicly abjured her heretical errors in an *auto de fé* in Toledo in 1529 and was imprisoned for a few years. Unlike Francisca, who incriminated her accomplices and whose sentence is unknown, María refused to confess under torture and so was sentenced only to perform public penance in church for a "light" suspicion of heresy.

Inquisitors punished real Protestants much more harshly. In a series of trials and *autos de fé* conducted in Valladolid and Seville in 1559–1560, the Inquisition extinguished Protestantism in Spain, condemning both women and men to death. In Valladolid, the bones of the deceased matriarch of the Cazalla family were exhumed and burned, and four nuns were burned alive. In Seville, a mother, Leonor Gómez, and her three daughters suffered the same fate. None of these women were leaders of the local Protestant cells. Mystical *beatas* still attracted numerous followers eager to learn about their visions and hear their prophetic utterances. One Catalina de Jesús had nearly 700 followers in Seville and environs in the 1610s. Alarmed by the challenges posed by such *beatas* to clerical authority and by their illuminist or other unorthodox views, inquisitors continued to prosecute them—eleven in Seville alone between 1609 and 1645. Penalties for these *beatas*, however, were relatively light, usually involving public penance or several years of reclusion. While the inquisitors cast their net widely in their campaign to uphold Catholic orthodoxy in Spain, they did not punish women or men indiscriminately. They could usually distinguish between verifiably Protestant and other less dangerous beliefs.

Despite the inquisitors' distrust of female visionaries and of "little women" who presumed to read and interpret religious texts for themselves, Teresa of Ávila, the influential mystic and monastic reformer of Converso lineage, managed to avoid prosecution by the Inquisition. She did this through cooperating with her male confessors and through disarming potential male critics by employing in her writings a self-deprecating rhetoric that conformed to clerical stereotypes of female weakness and ignorance. In her *Book of Her Life*, written on her confessors' orders and examined by the Inquisition, Teresa explained that God had bestowed mystical visions as a gift on "a poor little woman like myself" because she, like other women, lacked the "learning and high intelligence" of men.[1] In her mystical masterpiece, *Interior Castle*, Teresa suggested that she was amenable to the correction of superior clergymen: "In difficult matters even though it seems to me that I understand and that I speak the truth . . . I'm very much prepared to believe what those who have a great deal of learning say."[2] Teresa did not persuade all inquisitors of her orthodoxy. After her death in 1589, one, Alonso de la Fuente, campaigned to have her books banned, insisting that they had "heretical" elements and were "diabolical" because no woman had the ability to write them. The church nevertheless canonized Teresa as a saint in 1622.

In Italy until the 1580s inquisitors were mainly concerned with combatting the Protestant threat, and they mostly prosecuted men. Women, however, constituted the great majority of those they suspected of diabolical witch-

FIGURE 14.2 Peter Paul Rubens, *Teresa of Avila,* 1615. The Picture Art Collection / Alamy Stock Photo.

craft. Inquisitors in both Italy and Spain had been sporadically investigating the phenomenon since the late fifteenth century, encouraged by a 1484 papal bull that recognized it as a real problem. In 1487 the German Dominicans Heinrich Kramer and Jakob Sprenger published their influential handbook for prosecutors of witchcraft, the *Hammer of [Female] Witches,* which consolidated the image of witches selling their souls to the devil, flying to nocturnal reunions or "sabbaths" where they worshipped and copulated with him, and employing their magical powers to cause illness and other natural calamities. This image was rooted in learned and popular belief in the intervention of the supernatural, whether holy or demonic, in the natural world and in the widespread resort to magic among common folk, especially women, to deal with life's difficulties, such as sickness or romantic problems.

In northern Europe these accusations resulted in the death of thousands of women in the sixteenth and seventeenth centuries. In Spain and Italy, in contrast, far fewer alleged witches were executed, due, perhaps surprisingly, to the actions of inquisitors who mostly refused to be swayed by or to contribute to the frenzy of the laity and local secular officials. Initially some Spanish and Italian inquisitors proved to be as credulous as northern European authorities and in the early sixteenth century prosecuted and sentenced witches to the stake, but skepticism regarding the reality of phenomena like the witches' sabbath and doubts about the delusions of hysterical local people soon set in. In 1526 the central authority of the Spanish Inquisition, the Suprema, instructed inquisitors to handle witchcraft accusations with the utmost caution and urged them to educate the so-called witches instead of punishing them. The Suprema could not always prevent secular officials from persecuting alleged witches, but in 1550, after the inquisitor in Barcelona presided over the burning of seven women, the Suprema dismissed him. In 1610 a witch scare gripped the province of Navarre because of a massive and bloody witch hunt that had occurred across the border in France the previous year. The local inquisitors' involvement in the trial and execution of six witches prompted the Suprema to send the one critical inquisitor, Alonso de Salazar Frías, to investigate the supposed proliferation of witches. After questioning some 1,800 people, a good number of whom believed themselves to be satanic witches, Salazar concluded: "I have not found a single proof, not even the slightest indication, from which to infer that an act of witchcraft has actually taken place."[3] Influenced by Salazar's report, the Suprema issued instructions in 1614 that strengthened the cautionary policy of 1526. An institution staffed largely by trained canon lawyers, the Spanish Inquisition insisted on very high standards of evidence when evaluating accusations of diabolical witchcraft.

Italy saw a similar evolution in the views and practices of inquisitors. The centralization of the various regional inquisitions under papal control in 1542 helped to enforce rigorous procedural standards; in 1620 Rome sent out an *Instruction,* which was analogous to the Suprema's policies. Many women, especially poor spinsters and widows, were investigated for diabolical witchcraft but convictions were rare and executions rarer still. Some, the inquisitors concluded, were just simple-minded women prone to delusions.

Spanish and Italian inquisitors nonetheless continued to prosecute many female practitioners of magic, particularly after the Council of Trent promoted a campaign to stamp out "superstition" and to assert an ecclesiastical monopoly over all aspects of the supernatural. Inquisitors therefore tried women healers who used Catholic prayers to enhance the efficacy of their herbal remedies, or those who invoked supernatural forces to win a lover for themselves or others. But punishment normally only took the form of penance, since inquisitors knew that the devil had not been involved.

Discussion Questions

1. How did negative clerical stereotypes of women encourage inquisitors to prosecute women, and how did such stereotypes sometimes help female defendants?

2. How did feminine spirituality and the social and professional roles of women expose them particularly to inquisitorial suspicion and investigation?

3. How did the institutional regulations and procedures of the Spanish and Italian Inquisitions cause the inquisitors to treat alleged witches far less harshly than officials in northern Europe did?

Further Reading

Duni, Matteo. *Under the Devil's Spell: Witches, Sorcerers, and the Inquisition in Renaissance Italy*. Syracuse: Syracuse University Press, 2007.

Giles, Mary, ed. *Women in the Inquisition: Spain and the New World*. Baltimore: Johns Hopkins University Press, 1999.

Henningsen, Gustav. *The Witches' Advocate: Basque Witchcraft and the Spanish Inquisition*. Reno: University of Nevada Press, 1980.

Seitz, Jonathan. *Witchcraft and Inquisition in Early Modern Venice*. Cambridge: Cambridge University Press, 2011.

Weber, Alison. *Teresa of Avila and the Rhetoric of Femininity*. Princeton: Princeton University Press, 1990.

Notes

1. *The Life of Saint Teresa of Ávila by Herself*, trans. J.M. Cohen (New York: Penguin Books, 1957), 81.

2. Teresa of Ávila, *Interior Castle*, trans. E. Allison Peers (New York: Doubleday, 1961), Fifth Mansion, chapter 1, p. 43.

3. Gustav Henningsen, ed., *The Salazar Documents: Inquisitor Alonso de Salazar Frías and Others on the Basque Witch Persecution* (Leiden: Brill, 2004), 340.

women as lustful beings who needed to be subjected to the guidance of men. Through their encouragement of devotion to the Virgin Mary, the clergy propounded a feminine ideal combining motherhood and virginity that no earthly woman could possibly meet.

While the male authorities of all three religions extolled the institution of marriage and the role of women in it as their husband's "helpmate," they also contributed to universal social anxieties surrounding female sexuality and family honor. Throughout the Mediterranean social practices emerged that were meant to control and protect women. Some women were kept inside the house as much as possible in order to minimize their exposure to men who were not their relatives. Other women circulated more freely outside the house but they remained at least under the legal supervision of male heads of household. In order to engage in economic pursuits outside the domestic sphere, women had to operate within the confines of patriarchal law and social custom or devise strategies that enabled them to evade legal strictures. With men holding the reins of political and religious authority, the political power that women had was mostly informal and was exercised through their influence on their kinsmen. Even queens possessing formal political power were expected to act in accordance with ideal gender roles. Women potentially had more autonomy in spiritual matters, but their limited access to the education that men had meant that their achievement of religious authority was exceptional and likely to arouse the male authorities' suspicion.

Guarding Women

With Mediterranean cultures placing such a high value on the chastity of women, families, communities, and states adopted various means of preserving it. The extent to which families could protect their women depended on their economic status. Affluent fathers tried to marry off their virgin daughters at a young age and transfer them to the custody of a husband by offering rich dowries to suitors whose families would not allow their sons to take a bride who was poor or impure. Christian parents had the option of dedicating their daughters to a religious life, though residence in a convent did not guarantee their celibacy and thereby shield family honor. Some Italian and Spanish nuns lacking a spiritual vocation had amorous affairs. For elite families in Christian cities whose young daughters usually wed older men, prostitutes performed

FIGURE 14.3 Byzantine empress Theodora and court ladies, ca. 547. Mosaic, Church of San Vitale, Ravenna, Italy. Photo by Petar Milošević provided by Wikimedia Commons under the CC-BY-SA-4.0 License.

a crucial function by providing a sexual outlet for unmarried young men who might otherwise prey on their daughters. Municipal governments therefore licensed and regulated prostitution, usually the profession of poor girls without a dowry or means of support. Yet even such indigent women were considerate of their family's honor and so often left their hometowns to ply their trade in cities where they were unknown.

Throughout the Mediterranean upper- and even middle-class families secluded and covered their daughters and wives to varying degrees. In Byzantium until the twelfth century unmarried daughters of these classes were ideally confined to the home away from the world of men. Within imperial and aristocratic households eunuchs served to segregate women. When daughters or their mothers left the house, they donned a veil. In the fifteenth century, Greek families in Constantinople again sequestered their women, perhaps an instinctive response to the empire's vulnerability in the face of the mounting Ottoman threat.

When Muslim caliphs began in the eighth century to seclude their women in harems, they were, as has been noted, following the example of Byzantine and Persian rulers. Among Muslims the seclusion of women was also mainly a practice of the urban elite and middle class. Only the wealthiest families had harems populated by multiple wives and concubines; most harems contained one wife and her daughters. Over the course of the premodern era the appearance of upper- and middle-class women in public was increasingly restricted. *'Ulama'* interpreted Qur'anic verses to assert that women should be veiled, and their writings from the Seljuq, Mamluk, and Ottoman periods emphasized the desirability of feminine seclusion. If respectable women ventured outdoors, they were supposed to be covered and accompanied by attendants. Yet women did not always comply. Jewish families in the Muslim world also sequestered and veiled their women. Maimonides's view, that "it is shameful for a woman to be constantly going out . . . in the streets," would have been applauded by the *'ulama'*.

Elite Christian families in Mediterranean Europe were no less concerned to protect the honor of their women, even if their customs were somewhat less restrictive. In Iberia modest Christian dress might include the veil, a garment that evoked comment from northern European visitors to the peninsula in the seventeenth century. Immigrant Sephardi Jewish women in Amsterdam at this time were noticeably kept indoors much more than Dutch women, and so were more like their sisters in, say, Padua, Italy.

Lower-class Mediterranean families could not afford the luxury of having their daughters and wives sequestered, veiled, and chaperoned. Their women had to work. The necessarily "immodest" behavior of women laboring in fields, marketplaces, and elite households implied that only the daughters of the wealthy were assuredly pure, a quality that bolstered their families' prestige. In Christian cities such as Venice and Seville, males from elite families regarded humbler women as fair game whom they could seduce at little cost to themselves. Poor men, on the other hand, dared not mix with aristocratic women.

Yet, regardless of the presumption of their social superiors, nonelite families throughout the Mediterranean were anxious to defend the sexual honor of their women and thereby uphold the family's reputation. Rival families' customary "scorning" or invasion of each other's houses or abduction of each other's daughters served to remind common people of the necessity of guarding the household and its female members. Religious writers and preachers added their voices, for feminine virtue was a universal concern. Miquel Agustín, a Catalan friar, thus advised peasants in his influential 1617 manual that they should keep their unmarried daughters upstairs, and that if the daughters went out, they should "stay close beside their mother [and] wear their shawl a little down over their face."[3] State authorities, too, got increasingly involved in regulating the sexual conduct of their subjects, since in their view women's unchaste behavior not only shamed them and their families but could also cause social and political crises or provoke God to punish the country with plague. Spanish Habsburg law codes, for instance, prohibited married men and priests from taking concubines and put adulterous wives and their lovers at the mercy of their vengeful husbands. The statutes of Ottoman sultans imposed fines for cuckoldry on husbands who did not immediately divorce their adulterous wives. Men, the laws signaled, must guard their wives and the honor of their households. Disorder in the domestic sphere would corrupt society and weaken the empire.

Women in the Economy

The widespread concern of Mediterranean families to preserve the honor of their women suggests that women could not have had much of a role in the economy beyond the considerable contribution they made through the performance of essential household tasks. Yet extant sources for Muslim societies—which are generally far less abundant than sources for Christian societies—record a good deal of female economic activity oriented outside the domestic sphere. Veils and cloaks perhaps facilitated the work of Muslim women by shielding them from the unwanted attention of unrelated men. Poorer women of course had little choice but to supplement their family's income through additional labor, as was the case for lower-class Christian and Jewish women. Wealthier women often stayed at home and engaged with the economy indirectly through male representatives.

The legal power of Muslim wives to control and dispose of their marital assets and inheritances enabled them to participate in the wider economy at least as much as their Christian and Jewish counterparts. Many Muslim women, however, first had to defeat the efforts of male relatives to deprive them of their property. Granadan, Mamluk, and Ottoman sources record Muslim women going to court to claim inheritances, negotiate divorce settlements, and free themselves from economic restrictions fathers and husbands attempted to impose. Once they secured control of their assets, wealthier women invested funds in local and regional commerce, in lending money at interest, and in backing the male administrators of taxfarms. As an expression of their piety, they also endowed local mosques or larger *waqf* institutions that provided charitable assistance to the poor, and they were active on the real estate market. Poorer Ottoman women labored in vineyards processing grapes, which they then sold on the market. They were busy, too, as peddlers selling goods to upper-class women. Throughout the Muslim world women worked at home as spinners, weavers, and embroiderers. Women either sold their manufactures on the market or worked for wages. Though women could independently manage their assets and earnings, they normally collaborated with their husbands in supporting the family and sometimes made joint investments.

The economic activities of Jewish women in Muslim lands mostly paralleled those of Muslim women. Cairo Geniza evidence shows them selling and leasing real estate or spinning silk and flax for sale on the market through the mediation of female brokers. Some poor women labored as domestic servants, usually for widowed rabbis, while others cleaned synagogues and schools. Women also worked in professions that met the needs of other women, such as midwife or dresser of brides. Like their male coreligionists, Jewish women in Christian Spain and Italy lent money. Widows were the most active lenders and dealers in real estate, since in Jewish families, just as in Christian ones, the husband's legal authority to manage the couple's assets left wives with little economic autonomy.

The economic role of European Christian women was apparently more varied than that of Muslim women, though this may be an impression created by the wider range of extant European sources. The occupations of European women in any case became more restricted in the later Middle Ages. The control that husbands exercised over their wives' dowries and other family assets was also a limiting factor, though wives acted without their spouse's authorization far more frequently than the law would suggest. Furthermore, husbands could not alienate assets from their wives' dowries without their consent, and wives could sue their husbands if they invested such assets irresponsibly. Christian couples, in other words, had to cooperate.

FIGURE 14.4 Manuscript illustration of Naamah, the daughter of Lamech and Stella, working at her loom, ca. 1360. British Library, London, UK © British Library Board. All Rights Reserved / Bridgeman Images.

In addition to buying and selling property and making loans, well-to-do women invested in long-distance trade, noticeably during periods of western European commercial expansion. Prior to 1348, women in cities such as Genoa and Montpellier invested in the cloth trade with Muslim ports; in the early modern period, women in Seville participated in commerce with America, usually as the sedentary partners. Wives also represented their merchant husbands when they were away on business. Widows were the most prominent investors, though they sometimes appointed their sons as their agents. As long as they remained single, widows could make use of assets from their dowry and deceased husband's property. Therefore, unlike Muslim widows, they had incentives not to remarry.

In Mediterranean cities women lower on the social ladder had a wide range of occupations, such as food-sellers, bakers, shopkeepers, midwives, innkeepers, and artisans. A great number were domestic servants; many had migrated from the countryside as young girls with the hope of earning enough for a decent dowry after years of service in the home of their employer. Some girls were apprenticed to master artisans, as in early fourteenth-century Montpellier, where they learned skills such as spinning gold thread, making silk and linen fabrics, and tailoring. During the centuries of urban and industrial expansion before the Black Death, women were members of artisan guilds in cities like Florence, Toulouse (France), and Barcelona, especially in branches of the all-important textile industry. In the fifteenth century, however, women began to be systematically excluded from guilds, which were becoming more specialized and professionalized organizations for "men's work." For wives burdened with the responsibilities of child-rearing and food preparation, acquiring the necessary artisanal training grew more difficult. However, since much artisanal labor was done in workshops attached to the home, wives could assist their husbands and their male apprentices by performing auxiliary tasks. Women also supplemented the family income through spinning and weaving at home. Male silk and woolen manufacturers in seventeenth-century Florence were therefore able to employ an army of poorly paid, low-skilled female weavers. Men monopolized the high-level work in the textile industry. Economic organization mirrored the patriarchal family. SEE SOURCEBOOK 14:2.

Women and Political Power

Women gained access to and exercised political power through the patriarchal family. Families were political entities, whether they were peasant families feuding with their peers over land, honor, and power in the village or royal families running governments and fighting wars. Within the households of lower- and middle-class feuding families, women plotted with their husbands and sons and roused them to defend the family's honor through acts of violence. Outside the house, women often shouted the insults that publicly initiated hostilities between families or circulated the gossip that functioned as a form of political propaganda against their local enemies.

Because the institution of monarchy was built around the family, royal women were able to exert considerable political influence through the various roles they played in relation to the men of their family: as the wives and counselors of kings and caliphs, as the mothers of heirs to the throne, and as the guardians of underage royal heirs who were sometimes left governing the realm after the death of their husband. In the Mediterranean lands of Islam, female political power only rarely acquired a formal, public dimension, and very few Muslim women ruled independently. In Christian domains, the position and power of queens and empresses were manifested more publicly, and a number of Christian queens in the Latin West did rule in their own right. These distinctions between Muslim and Christian royal women and their relation to political power were rooted in different family structures and forms of royal household organization.

Byzantine empresses overcame the restrictions excluding other aristocratic women from public life through their status as the emperor's wife and "hostess of the court." In the imperial court at Constantinople empresses participated in all court ceremonies and sometimes influenced foreign policy. They were also patrons of the religious institutions that helped transform the imperial capital into a Christian fortress. Their greatest opportunity to wield political power publicly came during widowhood, if their husband's heir was underage, as in the case of Empress Irene, the restorer of icon veneration in 787.

In the Latin West the changes to marriage practices encouraged by the church had a significant bearing on the evolution of queenly power. Through its promotion of monogamy, the church enhanced the status of the queen in the royal family as *the* wife of the king and as the only source of the king's heir. The queen thus ensured the legitimacy and continuity of the ruling dynasty. Her partnership with the king therefore needed to be publicly displayed, which accustomed subjects to her role in governing the realm. Furthermore, the church's outlawing of cousin-marriage often forced kings to forge marital alliances with foreign royal houses, which increased the prestige of the king's dynasty as well as the political influence of his foreign queen.

On the other hand, the growing practice in Europe of having the oldest surviving son of the king succeed him on the throne usually prevented women from inheriting kingdoms and ruling in their own right. Political instability and violence along the Christian-Muslim frontier, however, created opportunities for Mediterranean princesses. Queen Melisende succeeded her father Baldwin II as ruler of the kingdom of Jerusalem from 1131 to 1153, despite the efforts of her husband Fulk V of Anjou to limit her authority. Queen Urraca (1109–1126), the daughter of Alfonso VI, outlived her brothers and inherited the kingdom of Castile-León. Neither of her husbands, including the redoubtable Alfonso I the Battler, of Aragon, loosened her firm grip on its government. Yet Urraca was the last Iberian queen to rule in her own right until Isabel I (1474–1504) seized the throne of Castile with the help of her husband, Fernando of Aragon. While Isabel and Fernando were famously cooperative, Isabel governed her realm as its sole monarch and Fernando his. Queens played a crucial and uniquely institutionalized role in the government of the Crown of Aragon and its empire. In the early fourteenth century kings began appointing their spouses as lieutenant general, an office that had been created to help the king govern the diverse territories of the empire in his absence. Maria of Castile (d. 1458), the queen of Alfonso V (d. 1458), served in this capacity for more than twenty years in the Crown's Iberian lands while her husband was away conquering and ruling Naples.

FIGURE 14.5 The tomb of Isabel I of Castile and Fernando II of Aragon in the Royal Chapel, Granada. Album / Alamy Stock Photo.

The public exercise of political authority by women was more unusual in Mediterranean Muslim states. In the earliest days of Islam, A'isha, the favorite wife of the Prophet, played such a public role, but this decisively changed when the Umayyad caliphs began sequestering their wives and creating large harems with slave concubines. The continuing practices of polygyny, extensive concubinage, and reproduction of royal heirs through multiple wives or enslaved women meant that the legitimacy and survival of Muslim dynasties did not depend on the maternity of any one woman. The mothers of heirs to the thrones of caliphs and sultans therefore did not publicly represent or embody the dynasty. Women rarely ascended to the throne and only in unusual circumstances, as when Shajar al-Durr, the widow of the last Ayyubid sultan, al-Salih Najm al-Din (d. 1249), briefly ruled Egypt in 1250 as "queen of the Muslims" until the establishment of the Mamluk regime.

The more usual pattern was for Muslim women to exert political influence behind the scenes, informally and unofficially. Among the Mamluks the wives and mothers of sultans functioned as intermediaries between competing factions of troops, and mothers guided their sons in statecraft. 'Abbasid, Andalusi, and Ottoman harems, moreover, became political arenas where, as has been seen, favorite concubines or the mothers of caliphs acquired considerable political clout as advisers. Politics, normally associated with the public sphere, was linked to the private domain of the harem. Women wielded power from the inside. SEE SOURCEBOOK 14:3.

Women and Religion

From defining orthodox theologies to serving as judges in religious courts, men dominated religious affairs in all Mediterranean societies. Men upheld their authority partly through excluding women from the main institutions of religious education—Jewish *yeshivas*, Muslim *madrasas*, and Christian cathedral schools and universities. Male religious leaders regarded women to be intellectually unsuited for complex theological and legal studies. Women, in their view, needed only to learn such rituals and basic doctrines as would enable them to properly raise their children as good Christians, Muslims, or Jews. The male authorities took great care to supervise those women who managed to attain a high level of religious learning or who cultivated a mystical spirituality that attracted public attention.

Jewish women were exempted from the obligation to study Torah (Hebrew Bible), the fundamental text of Jewish learning, and they were not permitted to enter the house of study, the province of men. The lack of an understanding of Hebrew was an educational barrier for many women, who therefore had to learn about Jewish laws and traditions in the vernacular. Yet some women acquired at least a rudimentary knowledge of Hebrew, enough to enable them to read Hebrew prayers on the Sabbath and during the synagogue service. (Not all men were well versed in the biblical language either.) In the women's section of the synagogue female cantors led less educated women in chanting the prayers. There were scholarly families who prepared their daughters to study the Torah or, even more unusually, the Talmud. The daughter of a certain Rabbi Samuel in twelfth-century Baghdad was "expert in Scripture and Talmud," and in her father's *yeshiva* she taught Torah to male youths through a window in a separate room where they could not see her. In Renaissance Italy, where Jewish women seem to have received a fuller education, two sisters, Fioretta Modena and Diana Rieti, reportedly mastered Torah, Talmud, and Kabbalah. Fioretta moved to the mystical center of Safed after her husband's death. The Italian translations of Hebrew liturgical poetry by another woman, Debora Ascarelli of Rome, were published in 1601. But women did not need Hebrew literacy to manifest devotion to the Jewish faith. In 1492, some Jewish wives departed Spain alone with their young children, leaving behind husbands who had converted when Fernando and Isabel gave Jews the choice of baptism or exile. Among Spanish Conversos, for whom synagogue attendance was no longer possible, the home became the center of Jewish life and learning, and women emerged as key guardians of Jewish traditions.

For Muslim women in Arabic-speaking lands, there were no linguistic barriers to their study of the Qur'an and related religious and legal texts. Even though women could not pursue the most advanced legal or theological studies available in *madrasas*, in the Mamluk empire at least women did take advantage of the wider informal system of education to advance well beyond the elementary level. This system depended on the relationship between the individual student and the teacher, who issued the successful student an *ijaza*, which certified that the student was qualified to teach a certain subject or book. The daughters of scholarly families normally began their education at home with a male relative, and then, on the initiative of their family, studied with teachers in other venues. Women participated in study circles usually led by male scholars in mosques or in private homes, despite the warnings of conservative thinkers worried about the mixing of the sexes during study. Sometimes their teachers were learned women who had earned *ijazas*. In sixteenth-century Spain, where all Islamic institutions had been uprooted, Morisco women proved to be just as committed as their menfolk to Islam, and, like Conversas, they helped to keep their ancestral faith alive among their people.

Sufi mysticism offered Muslim women a way to cultivate their spirituality beyond the confines of orthodox legalism. Early mystics engaged in ascetic practices and some were celibate, especially the women, who sought to achieve the same spiritual capacity as men through denial of their sexuality. Rabi'a al-'Adawiyya (d. 801), from Basra, inspired other mystics with her poetry stressing the absolute love of God. Throughout the Muslim world women participated in the life of the Sufi orders. Affluent women endowed Sufi convents (*khanaqahs*) for men or women as well as mosques and schools for renowned mystics. Though most female Sufis were disciples, some were teachers who achieved a saintly status in the eyes of their contemporaries. The great Andalusi mystic Ibn 'Arabi (d. 1240) studied with two women teachers. In Ottoman lands, women like Mihri Khatun (d. 1506) gained fame as mystical poets.

Acknowledging the spiritual needs of women, the hierarchical Orthodox and Catholic Churches allowed for the foundation of convents, institutional spaces where women could express their Christian devotion in prayer, contemplation, and study and yet remain under the ultimate supervision of male clergy. Some women sought to become nuns in order to escape marriage to earthly husbands. In eleventh-century Byzantium, the church ruled that married women who fled to convents had first to serve a six-month trial period before taking monastic vows. Most Orthodox nuns came from well-to-do families, since nuns were required to give a substantial dowry to the convent. But all Byzantine women, poor or rich, could express their faith through the veneration of icons. Many found it particularly appealing, since they could engage in this form of worship at home without the intervention of male priests.

In the Latin West women manifested their deepening piety by entering nunneries in growing numbers or by engaging in welfare work and mystical practices outside a convent's walls. The enthusiasm for religious and social reform that generated new orders of monks and friars engulfed women as well. Thousands of women joined convents associated with the new Premonstratensian and Cistercian orders, despite the male leadership's reluctance to admit women, whom they regarded as undisciplined and therefore warranting strict regulation and enclosure. Women were also attracted to Franciscan and Dominican ideals of poverty and active service in imitation of Christ. Clare of Assisi (d. 1253), Francis's companion, founded the first female Franciscan house around 1212. The papacy, however, insisted that Franciscan and Dominican nuns be enclosed and served by male priests.

The life of poverty, celibacy, and prayer inside the convent was nonetheless spiritually rewarding for nuns with a vocation. Though prayers were read in Latin, many nuns could not understand Latin well. They therefore read devotional texts and Bibles in vernacular languages and composed their own works in them. As in Byzantium, the necessity of providing convents with a dowry limited this form of religious life mostly to women from well-off families. Poorer women became lay sisters of convents and performed much of the manual labor.

Many women expressed their religious ardor outside the framework of monastic institutions, sometimes because convents were inaccessible to them. Beginning in the thirteenth century, groups of women—often called Beguines or, in Spain, *beatas*—worshipped together, pledged themselves to a life of poverty and celibacy, and dedicated themselves to charitable work. Uncomfortable with the independence of these women, the church in the early fourteenth century began suppressing some Beguine communities and persuaded other pious women to become members of the "third orders" of friars and to live under a rule. In 1535 Angela Merici founded in Brescia, Italy, the Company of St. Ursula, an association of celibate laywomen dedicated to serving the poor and sick and to educating young girls. The papacy approved of the Company but eventually saw to it that all Ursuline communities were enclosed, which was consistent with the Council of Trent's ruling that all women religious needed to be cloistered.

FIGURE 14.6 Altar screen of Clare of Assisi with scenes from her life, ca. 1280, monastery of Santa Chiara. INTERFOTO / Alamy Stoc Photo.

The period between the thirteenth and seventeenth

centuries saw a growing number of Christian women channeling their religious feeling into mysticism, perhaps because they were denied spiritual fulfillment in the priesthood. Some female mystics, like Teresa of Ávila (1515–1582), were nuns; others, like Catherine of Siena (1347–1380), were members of mendicant third orders. Identifying with the suffering of Jesus Christ, they engaged in extreme asceticism, especially rigorous fasting. Through rejection of the body they endeavored to achieve a state of holiness and mystical communion with God. They also, like Jesus, ministered to the poor and sick. Some women mystics were charismatic and attracted a following from among women and men, their visionary experiences lending them spiritual authority. The church hierarchy took care to supervise female mystics, appointing male confessors and spiritual directors to guide them and inspecting the orthodoxy of their visions and utterances. Those women whose views were regarded as heretical were usually imprisoned or enclosed. SEE SOURCEBOOK 14:4.

Men and Violence

In the competitive social environment of Mediterranean communities, the women and men of families striving to earn and retain the respect of others had to behave as much as possible in conformity with ideal gender roles. Femininity, as has been seen, primarily meant chastity. Standards of masculinity required men to provide for their families and defend them, with arms if necessary. One of the bases of a family's power and prestige in the community was the willingness and ability of its men to avenge any harm done to another member of the family. Feelings of mutual responsibility uniting male kin were usually strong, inspiring acts of retaliatory vengeance that could keep family or tribal feuds alive for many years. This same sense of duty bound men to guard the sexual honor and reputation of their female relatives or sometimes to dispose of kinswomen when they shamed the family through extramarital sexuality. Such obligations of manhood were a heavy burden that not all men were willing to shoulder; yet, because most did, lay and religious authorities were kept busy preventing or limiting the bloodshed of feuds.

Conflict and Feuding

Men performed on a public stage under the scrutiny of other families in the community, all potential rivals who either awarded them and their family honor for virtuous behavior or readily degraded them for failing to live up to social norms. Men were therefore sensitive to any perceived slights to themselves or their kin, especially those that questioned the purity of their women or their own trustworthiness or courage. They often responded to insults, or any act of physical aggression, with fists or daggers, sparking still more violent encounters in which male relatives from both sides, moved by sentiments of family solidarity, quickly became involved. Yet, as antagonistic families tested each other in the public arena of honor, they took care not to allow the violence to escalate too rapidly, avoiding homicide and the detonation of a destructive feud as long as possible. Acts of retaliatory violence were therefore usually measured—"a tooth for a tooth"—and were intended more to repair a dishonored family's reputation than to eliminate its rivals. Christian, Muslim, and Jewish sources from across the Mediterranean record the efforts of state officials to prevent or at least delay the perpetration of violence by threatening or exacting fines for insults, blows, and wounds. Officials sometimes supervised public truces between contending families and factions; respected local religious figures also functioned as mediators. As judicial institutions developed, state authorities gradually became more effective at resolving disputes or discouraging acts of private vengeance by penalizing violent offenders themselves. Furthermore, since feuds were disruptive and often costly for local communities, neighbors frequently intervened to pacify and arrange compromises between adversaries outside of court. Effectiveness as a peacemaker was one of the qualities of an honorable man in Mediterranean societies.

In the violent strife that punctuated the life of Mediterranean communities, individuals and families fighting over economic resources or political office often rationalized and talked about their conflicts in terms of family honor, which raised them to a higher moral plane and galvanized the support of kinsmen. Material goals were nonetheless very real. It was thus frequently the case in many cities that artisans practicing the same craft vio-

FIGURE 14.7 Skyline of San Gimignano, Italy, showing towers of family compounds of feuding families. Photo: iStock.com/Bisla.

lently clashed, with the victor winning not only more esteem for himself and his family but also more customers for his goods. The statutes of artisan guilds therefore often included provisions for resolving disputes and inhibiting violence between members. The internal legislation of minority communities similarly aimed at preventing the violence that might arise, for instance, between contenders for communal office and the prestige that came with it, and minority religious leaders often served as peacemakers among their people. The perhaps surprising phenomenon of peasants, artisans, and religious minorities speaking in the language of honor was a manifestation of the intense social competition within these groups. Caught up in the struggle to win honor among their fellows, they paid less attention to and directed less aggression at their social superiors or other religious groups, which probably had the unintended effect of reducing lower-class rebellion and interfaith violence within Mediterranean societies.

When elite families clashed, the rewards were potentially much greater: not only the respect of peers and deference of social inferiors but also landed estates, high office, noble titles, even kingdoms. A family's political success depended on the cooperative action of its male kin whose ancestral pride and solidarity had been forged and repeatedly tested through violent confrontations with enemies. The solidarity of particular noble families, clans, or tribes and their effective employment of violence enabled them to dominate others, attract followers, and lay the foundations of states. In the Muslim world, the combination of tribal solidarity and charismatic religious leadership propelled the conquests of Arabs in the seventh century, for instance, and those of Berber Almoravids and Almohads in the eleventh and twelfth centuries. In Christian Europe many successful royal dynasties originated as aristocratic houses that were more cohesive and aggressive than their noble competitors. Persisting rivalries between potent patrilineal groups contributed to instability in most Mediterranean states. With the rise of centralized monarchies in Muslim and Christian lands, and of powerful city-state governments in Italy, unruly nobles and tribal leaders either were tamed and transformed into servants of the state or were marginalized and excluded from the centers of power.

Yet, because of the fundamental connection between masculine honor and violence, even the most powerful rulers could not prevent or completely suppress feuding among their subjects, especially the aristocrats. Rulers strove to maintain law and order and to monopolize the administration of justice, but they recognized the great difficulty of stopping the male relatives of a murder victim from taking private revenge on the perpetrator or one of his kinsmen. Ottoman sultans, for instance, worked within the framework of Islamic law, which viewed homicide as a private matter, leaving it to the victim's kinsmen either to retaliate, on the principle of "an eye for an eye," or to accept "blood money" as compensation from the culprit or his family. Ottoman *kanuns* permitted such retaliation, but, if it was not carried out, the killer was required to pay a heavy fine. Imperial officials at the same time tried to persuade feuding factions to settle their differences in court.

Mediterranean Christian rulers increasingly made similar efforts to curb and even prohibit feuding while recognizing that there was only so much they could do to restrain families motivated by deeply rooted codes of male honor. Shakespeare's vivid portrayal of the animosity between Verona's Montague and Capulet families that led to the tragic deaths of Romeo and Juliet is a fictionalized version of the aristocratic vendettas that governments in northern Italian cities had long worked to suppress. With their limited manpower resources, urban officials in Italy and elsewhere often did not try pursuing fugitive murderers beyond city limits and left it to the kinsmen of the victim to hunt and slay them. Not even imperial governments could exert much control over feuding in more peripheral regions, such as the highlands of the Crown of Aragon and the islands of Corsica, Sardinia, and Sicily. In the sixteenth century nobles started resorting to dueling to resolve questions of honor. Because duels were formalized and limited to two or a few combatants (with equal numbers on either side), they were less destructive than noble feuds, which produced far more casualties. Both state and church nonetheless condemned dueling. Restraining men from fighting to preserve their honor, whether in duels or in feuds, continually challenged authorities.

Crimes of Honor

Men felt obligated to act when the chastity of their female relatives, a foundation of their family's honor, was violated through rape or adultery. They either turned to state officials to punish the offenders or they worked to repair family honor themselves, sometimes violently. SEE SOURCEBOOK 14:5.

While jurists and laypersons of all three faiths viewed rape as a violent crime, they generally placed greater emphasis on the damage done to the honor of the victim's family than on the physical and psychological harm inflicted on the victim. Rape was often perceived as a crime against the property of the victim's father or husband, the legal guardians of her sexual honor, and tended to be categorized with abduction, the theft of a daughter from her father's house. The meaning of abduction was itself ambiguous, though whether it involved the sexual abuse of the victim or her willing elopement with the abductor, it dishonored her father and his family.

Rape and abduction sometimes provoked the retaliatory violence of the victimized woman's kinsmen, though there is not much extant evidence of this form of private vengeance. Legal commentaries and judicial records reveal a range of measures taken by the state against the perpetrators of sexual violence. Most Muslim *'ulama'* viewed rape as coercive *zina* (unlawful sexual intercourse), for which the convicted rapist should incur *hadd* (divinely sanctioned) penalties: death by stoning for married offenders and flogging with 100 lashes for the unmarried. While Ottoman *kanuns* called for the castration of abductors, presumably those not simply eloping with their beloved, Ottoman courts administered various penalties for rape— banishment, flogging, or fines— depending on the details of the case. In Christian Europe some law codes demanded the death penalty for rapists, though judges' actual sentences were as variable as those handed down by Ottoman magistrates. In Renaissance Italy, rapists usually incurred fines, their size determined by the social status of the victim and her attacker.

Rape was almost certainly underreported in premodern Mediterranean societies, for it was extremely difficult to prove. Islamic law, for instance, required four witnesses to any *zina* crime, though in practice judges made more of an allowance for circumstantial evidence. Nevertheless, because of the premium society placed on the sexual purity of women, women everywhere were reluctant to face the public shame that they and their families would experience if they brought charges against their assailants. If the assault had not yet been publicized, many victimized women preferred to keep it that way. This was especially the case of married women, who jeopardized their husband's honor if their charges could not be proven. Some families of unmarried daughters also avoided making their rape a matter of public knowledge because they feared it would make them unmarriageable, but others restored the reputation of their daughters and the honor of the family by persuading the rapist to marry their daughter. This solution to the problem of rape was widely practiced in eastern and western Christian societies. Upper-class rapists who refused to marry their lower-class victims often paid them compensation so that they would have enough money for a dowry and be able to marry honorably. The ruling of most schools of Islamic law that the rapist, in addition to incurring *hadd* penalties, should pay bridewealth to the victim, indicates that the marriage of the victim—though probably not to the rapist—was integral to repairing the damage done to the honor of a daughter and her father's family.

The most serious crime of honor, and the cause of many honor killings, was a wife's adultery. It gravely dishonored her husband, who proved himself unable to control his wife's sexuality; in more strictly patrilineal Muslim societies, the adulterous woman's father and brothers were also affected. Although both canon law and *shari'a* deemed adulterous husbands to be as blameworthy as unfaithful wives, a husband's marital infidelities normally resulted in significantly less judicial or private violence, unless the husband's lover was a married woman. This double standard arose and persisted because a wife's adultery raised questions about the legitimacy of her offspring, thus complicating inheritance practices and potentially subverting family solidarity.

Secular law codes in Christian realms called for harsh punishments of adulterers, such as publicly flogging them after shaving their heads, and sometimes, at least in theory, executing them. Their public humiliation was intended to send a warning to the community. By the later Middle Ages, however, corporal penalties were often commuted to fines. Husbands were encouraged to deal with their adulterous wives in court, but in doing so they potentially exposed themselves to public humiliation as cuckolds. Many men therefore resorted to murdering their wives or their lovers or both. Canon law did not approve of such homicide for the sake of honor, but secular codes sometimes legitimized it. Even when laws did not explicitly permit such honor killings, rulers normally pardoned aggrieved husbands who committed them. Just like their subjects, kings understood both the compulsion and the social pressure that men felt to regain their honor in this fashion.

Considering the potential of adultery to disrupt a community's social harmony, the codifiers of Islamic law required *hadd* punishments for it: 100 lashes for women and men who had never been married and death by stoning for those who had consummated marriage. Yet, because of the high standards of evidence for conviction—the testimony of four witnesses or the confession of the offenders—Muslim judges proceeded cautiously before imposing these penalties. Mudejar judges in the Crown of Aragon condemned adulterous wives to *hadd* punishments, but they did it knowing that the royal authorities would commute these penalties to enslavement, which rendered the women socially dead to the families of their husbands and fathers while removing them from the community. The Ottoman government discouraged judges from imposing *shari'a* penalties, preferring that adulterers be fined. It also encouraged husbands to divorce their adulterous wives, who would lose their bridewealth and related assets, as a nonviolent means of restoring their honor. Honor killings, committed by husbands or fathers or brothers of adulterous women, were nonetheless a customary practice. Although this ancient tradition was not formally sanctioned in Islamic law, most jurists condoned the killing of an adulterous woman and her lover. Suleyman the Magnificent upheld the legitimacy of such honor killings, and his chief mufti ruled that the killers need not pay blood money to compensate the family of their victims. In the Mediterranean, customary codes of honor were uniformly unforgiving in cases of a woman's adultery: the wife and her lover had to pay in some way.

Notes

1. Elizabeth S. Cohen, "Honor and Gender in the Streets of Early Modern Rome," *Journal of Interdisciplinary History* 22:4 (1992): 597–625, at 604–5.
2. Leslie Peirce, "Honor, Reputation, and Reciprocity," *European Journal of Turkish Studies* 18 (2014). http://ejts.revues.org/4850.
3. James Casey, *Early Modern Spain: A Social History* (London: Routledge, 1999), 204.

CHAPTER FIFTEEN

Mediterranean Economies and Societies in a Widening World

The Black Death came to Siena, Italy, in May 1348. "It was a cruel and horrible thing," wrote the local chronicler Agnolo di Tura. "The victims died almost immediately. They would swell beneath the armpits and in their groins, and fall over while talking.... And in many places in Siena great pits were dug and piled deep with the multitude of dead.... And I... buried my five children with my own hands. And so many died that all believed it was the end of the world."[1] The description of the Muslim historian Ibn Khaldun (1332–1406), whose parents perished when the epidemic struck Tunis that spring, was equally apocalyptic: "Civilization both in the East and the West was visited by a destructive plague which devastated nations and caused populations to vanish.... Civilization decreased with the decrease of mankind."[2]

Black Death is the name coined for the plague that swept across Eurasia between 1346 and 1353. Caused by the bacillus *Yersinia pestis*, the plague was transmitted to humans through the bites of fleas carried by black rats. The symptoms of the plague in its more common "bubonic" form were swellings of the lymph nodes (buboes), massive hemorrhaging, and dark blotches on the skin. It killed the majority of its victims, perhaps 60 percent, in around a week. "Pneumonic" plague developed when the bacilli infected the lungs; transmitted between people through coughing, it was almost always fatal.

In 1347, Genoese and Venetian sailors brought the plague to the Mediterranean from their merchant colonies at Kaffa and Tana on the Black Sea, the result of trade with the Mongols of the Golden Horde, through whose major cities the disease had already spread. An invented contemporary Latin account depicting the leaders of a besieging Mongol army catapulting corpses of their plague dead over the walls of the Genoese fortress at Kaffa was more compelling than the mundane truth: that the Italians shipped contaminated cargoes of Black Sea grain, along with plague-infested rats and fleas, to Constantinople. From there the Black Death spread to eastern and then western Mediterranean port cities. While it moved overland, maritime traders disseminated it most rapidly. By 1350 the epidemic had reached as far north as Norway and as far south as the Arabian Peninsula.

Over the course of the next century there were further outbreaks of plague, which afflicted different places with variable frequency and lethality. Altogether the plagues wiped out up to half of Europe's population of around 80 million. Despite the lack of comparable demographic data for most Muslim lands, we know that Egypt suffered similar losses. Between the late fifteenth and late sixteenth centuries, most regions recovered their pre-1347 populations. Toward the end of the sixteenth century, however, the onset of a "little ice age" with its droughts and famines caused a sharp setback, which the ravages of war and disease compounded. In 1650 many people in the Mediterranean were suffering.

These dramatic changes in the size of populations had a great impact on local and regional economies throughout the Mediterranean world, as individuals, social groups, and states adjusted their economic strategies in response to the shifting supplies of labor and fluctuating levels of production of and demand for goods. Relations between social classes were also affected, often negatively. The efforts of social and political elites to protect their position in changing circumstances at the expense of peasants and artisans exacerbated preexisting tensions

FIGURE 15.1 Burial of plague victims at Tournai (Belgium) in 1349; from *Chronicle* of Abbot Gilles de Muisis. The Picture Art Collection / Alamy Stock Photo.

and sparked rural and urban revolts. Governments developed institutions to meet the basic needs of the poor and hungry in the hope of preventing social disorder.

More transformative than the Black Death in the long term were the European conquest and colonization of America and charting of an Atlantic route to the spices of South Asia. Though the emergence of an expansive Atlantic economy after 1492 benefited some Mediterranean entrepreneurs and farmers, by the seventeenth century the naval, commercial, and industrial might of Atlantic states, especially England and the Netherlands, was beginning to reduce the standing of Mediterranean polities in the global economic and political order.

Economy and Society after the Black Death

Medieval people did not understand how the plague was caused and spread. A common explanation was that the disease was transmitted through contaminated air, or miasma. Urban officials therefore attempted to quarantine infected individuals and later, when the plague periodically returned, to clean up unsanitary, malodorous quarters. Many believed that the plague was God's punishment for their sins. Christian and Muslim governments took steps to isolate supposed sources of sin, such as prostitutes. In towns in the Crown of Aragon and Italy Christians immediately channeled their fear of the Black Death into violence against Jews. The economic hardships caused by plague formed part of the context for Muslim rioting against Copts in Egypt in 1354 and Christian attacks on Jews throughout Spain in 1391. Nothing in the Mediterranean matched the carnage that ensued in northern Europe on the coming of the Black Death. Sometimes incited by rumors that Jews had poisoned the wells, Christians slaughtered thousands of Jews in over a hundred communities. In German lands, between 1348 and 1351 probably more than half of the Jewish population

"The eighth miracle of the world" was what the Marquis of Guasto, Emperor Charles V's general in Italy, called the Arsenal, Venice's public industrial complex of shipyards and armories.[1] In the early seventeenth century, an English visitor, Thomas Coryat, described it as "the richest and best furnished storehouse for all manner of munition... not only of all Christendom, but also of all the world."[2] Covering at least sixty acres and employing around 2,000 workers at its peak of activity in the 1560s, the Arsenal built and outfitted the galleys that were crucial for Venice's position as a major commercial and naval power. Galleys necessarily fulfilled the dual role of merchantman and warship, for Venice's trade could not prosper if it was not well protected.

First established in 1104 to store naval supplies and to repair galleys built in private shipyards, the Arsenal in the 1320s quadrupled in size—to approximately thirty-two acres—so that the Venetian government could have all the galleys it needed for the city's expanding trade built in its own shipyards. The Arsenal's most notable product was the great galley or merchant galley, "more than almost any other a distinctly Venetian ship."[3] Different from the smaller and speedier one-masted "light galley," which was built for war, the great galley was originally designed to carry merchandise, but with the military capacity to deter pirates. In the fifteenth century, the largest great galleys could carry 250 to 300 tons in their cargo holds and more weight on deck. They had two or three masts with lateen sails and were "triremes," that is, each of the twenty rowers' benches on either side of the ship was manned by three oarsmen. The great galleys relied on the wind to move them from one port to the next; oars enhanced their maneuverability when entering and leaving port and increased their speed in emergency situations. These ships had crews of around 200: in addition to the oarsmen, who were free men recruited from throughout Venice's empire, there were twenty specialized crossbowmen—and gunners after 1486—equipped with weaponry stored in the Arsenal, a dozen expert sailors, and an officer in charge of navigation.

The great galleys were state-owned. Each year the Venetian Senate leased them for specific voyages to groups of investors, usually members of patrician families, who were responsible for paying the rent of the ship as well as the crew's wages. The "galley master" who then commanded the ship was at least nominally the head of the partnership. The investors divided the profits earned from the freight that the galleys carried from and to Venice.

FIGURE 15.2 Jacopo de' Barbari, *View of Venice*, 1500. Minneapolis Institute of Art, The John R. Van Derlip Fund, 2010.88.

FIGURE 15.4 Venetian war galley, 1571. Illustrated by David Bocquelet, *Naval Encyclopedia*. Image courtesy of the artist.

FIGURE 15.3 The Main Gate to the Arsenal. Photo courtesy of Bogdan Smarandache.

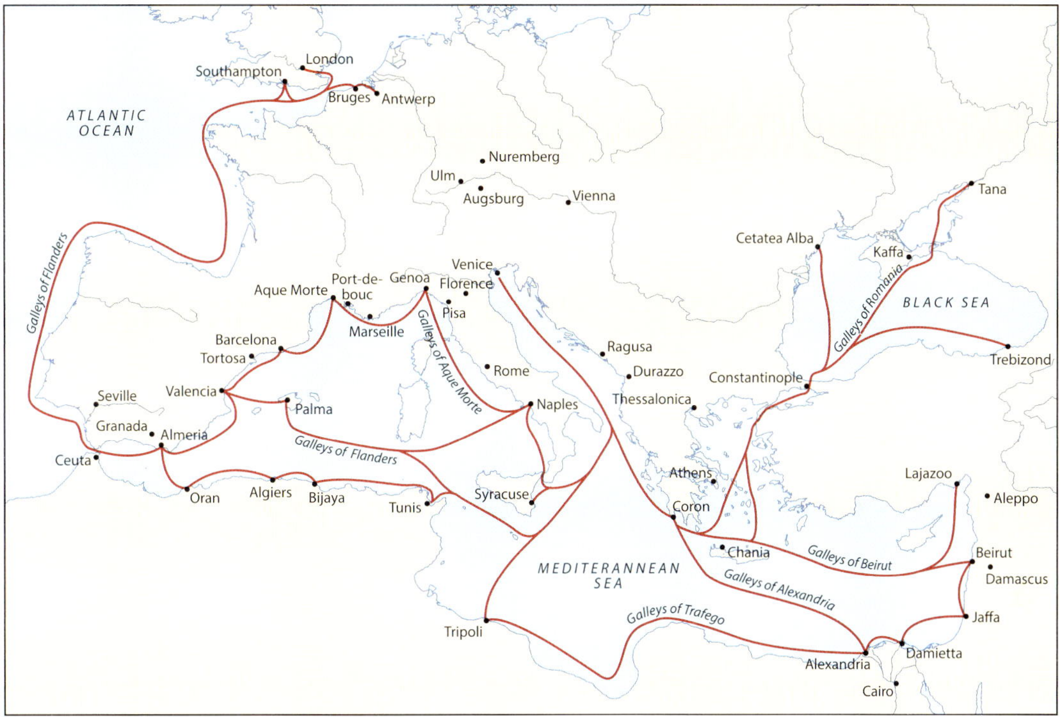

MAP 15.1 Venetian Convoy Lanes. From Aliesin, provided by Wikimedia Commons under the CC-BY-SA-3.0 License.

Great galleys carried the most precious cargoes, such as spices and fine fabrics, while cogs and other round ships transported other commodities like grain and salt. Not only did the government supervise the construction of the galleys; it also regulated the timing and route of their voyages. For security, the great galleys sailed in convoys of three to five vessels, which meant a fighting force of from 600 to 1,000 men; they were often escorted by light galleys. One "captain" commanded the fleet. By the mid–fifteenth century there were galley convoys traveling annually on set routes to Flanders (Bruges); to Constantinople and Black Sea ports; to Alexandria and Beirut; to ports along the Italian, French, and Spanish Mediterranean coasts; and to North African ports.

The emergence of Ottoman naval power in the final decades of the fifteenth century was the first of several political and technological developments that brought about changes to the Arsenal and to the role of the great galleys. In 1470 the Ottomans sent a fleet of 300 vessels to capture Venetian Negroponte; it appeared to a Venetian galley commander like "a forest on the sea."[4] Venice responded to this defeat in 1473 by doubling the size of the Arsenal. The aim was to build and equip under the cover of the shipyards' sheds a reserve fleet of galleys, great and light, that could be rapidly manned and set to sea in the event of future Ottoman challenges. The goal at first was a reserve of fifty galleys; after 1540 it was 100, though this was rarely attained. However, in 1570, as part of a failed effort to prevent the Ottomans from taking Cyprus, the Arsenal produced more than 100 galleys in two months. The next year at Lepanto, at least half of the victorious Holy League's ships were Venetian-built.

During the sixteenth century great galleys functioned primarily as warships. The Arsenal produced larger galleys that combined the ordinary galley's speed and mobility with the firepower provided by bronze cannons mounted on the bow. Some war galleys were quadriremes, a few were even quinquiremes. At the same time, the great galleys' role in commerce diminished and the established routes of the galley convoys were shut down or abandoned. The Ottomans had closed the Black Sea to Venice in 1479, and the navies of western European enemies and Barbary corsairs were making the western routes increasingly perilous. Portuguese intrusion in the Indian Ocean reduced the flow of spices to Alexandria, which finally led the Venetian government in 1564 to stop sending galley convoys there. By this time the merchant galleys had already lost their monopoly in the spice trade to another kind of ship, the carrack. This tall round ship had greater carrying capacity than the galleys, was more stable in storms, and was armed with more cannons. Even in naval warfare, the galley would be eclipsed in the seventeenth century by the northern European "ship–of–the–line," a faster vessel equipped with yet more artillery. But at midcentury galleys still played a role in the Venetian–Ottoman struggle over Crete; and the Knights of Malta continued to use them.

The Arsenal that amazed Thomas Coryat in the early 1600s had long been unique in Christian Europe for its scale and extent of governmental control, though this too would change over the course of the century as national shipyards like the one in Chatham, England, arose. The Arsenal was divided into three manufacturing centers: the main one for the building and repair of ships, and two subsidiary ones that produced cables and ropes, and arms and gunpowder. The workers, called *arsenalotti* or "sons of the Arsenal," had considerable group pride and identified strongly with their place of work. At least three–quarters of the workforce was composed of master craftsmen and their apprentices from the shipyards' three major guilds of shipwrights, caulkers, and oarsmakers. They saw to the actual shipbuilding and were supplemented by hundreds of porters, blacksmiths, and sawyers. In order to meet the needs of an efficient and standardized system of production, the shipbuilders were transformed from independent craftsmen with guild traditions into *arsenalotti* working under the management of the Venetian state. A board of patricians appointed by the Venetian Senate supervised production in the Arsenal, though it had to rely on intermediaries among the laborers to maintain control. The *arsenalotti* all lived in neighborhoods near the Arsenal, where the government made sure they and their families were adequately provisioned with bread, cheese, dried fish, and wine. Although their wages often did not keep up with the rate of inflation, there were other compensating factors: guaranteed lifetime employment and the right of their children to inherit their position. The *arsenalotti* neighborhoods were not as cosmopolitan as the rest of Venice, because their inhabitants built the galleys, a sensitive task that was fundamental to Venice's security. The thirty–foot-high brick walls and watchtowers that surrounded the Arsenal symbolized its great importance. The ultimate decline of this massive industrial center mirrored the commercial and political decline of the city it had served.

Discussion Questions

1. What role did the Arsenal and galleys play in the creation and defense of Venice's maritime empire?
2. Compared to the organization, working conditions, and lifestyle of other workers in post-1350 Europe, what was unusual about the workforce of the Arsenal?
3. Why were Venice and its Arsenal ultimately unable to compete effectively with the Ottoman empire or the northern European powers?

Further Reading

Davis, Robert C. *Shipbuilders of the Venetian Arsenal: Workers and Workplace in the Preindustrial City.* Baltimore: Johns Hopkins University Press, 1991.

Guilmartin, John F., Jr. *Gunpowder and Galleys: Changing Technology and Mediterranean Warfare at Sea in the 16th Century.* Cambridge: Cambridge University Press, 1974.

Lane, Frederic C. *Venetian Ships and Shipbuilders of the Renaissance.* Baltimore: Johns Hopkins University Press, 1934.

Notes

1. Davis, 3.
2. Coryat, 1:358.
3. Lane, 13.
4. Frederic C. Lane, *Venice: A Maritime Republic* (Baltimore: Johns Hopkins University Press, 1973), 358.

was wiped out. Ashkenazi Jews therefore later migrated toward the south and east.

Christian and Muslim peasants also migrated, to cities, where they hoped to replace a decimated workforce or to escape oppressive landlords, who, like them, were reacting to radically altered economic conditions. The unprecedented population decline affected each social group and class differently; their distinct responses to calamity frequently put them at odds. Laborers answered elite intransigence with resistance and rebellion. Crisis also spurred resourcefulness, moving merchants, artisans, and farmers to seek new markets for their products and more profitable ways of investing their labor and capital. The policies of Christian and Muslim rulers and the fortunes of war at the same time contributed to the reshaping of commercial networks in and around the Mediterranean.

Demographic Catastrophe and Economic Turmoil

Even before the Black Death struck the Mediterranean there were signs of economic difficulty. In some regions the growth of the population was beginning to exceed the amount of arable land and the supply of food. As a result, food prices rose while the wages of plentiful laborers declined. Conditions remained favorable for the landlords of peasants, who were able to extract the labor and rent that they wanted from peasants, who had few options. Though occasional poor harvests were a cause for worry, nothing could have prepared Mediterranean folk for the devastation of the Black Death and subsequent epidemics. SEE SOURCEBOOK 15:1.

Across the Mediterranean the populations of agricultural villages declined precipitously. In Byzantine Macedonia villages were abandoned. In Egypt some areas of the Nile valley were nearly deserted and the intricate and enormously productive irrigation system—the economic foundation of the Mamluk state—fell into decay. Absentee Mamluk landlords, whose possession of tracts of land was temporary and nonhereditary, did not undertake needed repairs, and Bedouin tribes from the desert fringes occupied some rural areas. Agricultural productivity therefore remained low and food prices high while peasants grew poorer. The more general pattern in the Mediterranean and farther north, however, was a gradual improvement in the standard of living for peasants and urban workers. Because the decline in population decreased the demand for food, agricultural prices fell; with the scarcity of labor, wages rose. As the value of land collapsed, enterprising peasants acquired and cultivated more land. Peasants were in a stronger bargaining position and some negotiated lower rents and higher wages with noble lords who needed their labor. Even Muslim peasant families in the Crown of Aragon thereby raised their economic status. Christian nobles in the kingdom of Valencia valued the Mudejars' labor so highly that they persuaded King Martí in 1403 to pass legislation forbidding their emigration to Muslim lands.

For noble landlords, on the other hand, the reduced productivity of their estates, the lower prices that crops fetched, and the higher cost of labor and manufactured goods meant diminishing incomes. Many nobles had few economic options, especially when the amount of rent they could collect from their peasant tenants was set by custom or prior contractual agreement. The limitations imposed by such fixed rents, however, did not stop nobles from purchasing at inflated prices the luxury goods they deemed appropriate to their status and lifestyle, such as silk garments, high-quality furnishings, and spices. Some nobles consequently fell into serious debt. The contraction of revenue flowing into their treasuries from peasant villages similarly troubled the rulers of Italian city-states and Mamluk emirs resident in Cairo and Syrian cities.

Landlords had to contend, moreover, with the flight of peasants to nearby urban centers. Plagues repeatedly hit Mediterranean cities hard, seriously depleting their labor force. Male peasants moved to cities with the expectation of receiving good wages in urban industries. Young women migrated there to gain employment as maidservants in the households of affluent families and hoped eventually to find an artisan husband. Rural immigration at least partly replenished urban populations.

Thus, while the bulk of the Mediterranean population continued to be rural, many regions saw a redistribution of the population that favored cities and expanded their industrial capacity. Craft guilds grew in number and became more specialized, responding to the increasingly diverse tastes and needs of Mediterranean consumers. With the encouragement of urban entrepreneurs, farmers cultivated industrial crops, such as cotton in Syria and mulberry trees, for the leaves that fed silkworms, in Lombardy (Italy). Each city found its niche in the wider Mediterranean economy, which, though depressed by the Black Death's toll, was becoming more commercially integrated.

A Plague of Rebellions

Economic variables after the Black Death mostly favored peasants and artisans. Nevertheless, they often encountered resistance from their social and political superiors when they tried to take advantage of the changed circumstances and better their lives. Rural lords attempted to restrict peasant mobility and reimpose forms of peasant servitude. In order to recoup their losses, governing classes everywhere taxed the lower orders more heavily. As a result, peasant and artisan revolts erupted from Egypt to England until the early sixteenth century. A sense of frustrated expectations drove many rebels who understood that their labor was now worth more. SEE SOURCEBOOK 15:2.

Rebellious peasants unfortunately had to confront the military opposition of the ruling elite, which was toughest in the more centralized states. Between the late fourteenth and mid-fifteenth centuries Mamluk troops harshly suppressed numerous peasant uprisings against increasing taxation and systematically disarmed rural villages. Escaping to the city became the only feasible option for overburdened Egyptian peasants. The governments of Italian city-states, which viewed villagers in their respective rural districts as their exploitable subjects, also resorted to force when peasants protested against their heavy fiscal demands. Sometimes, however, recalcitrant Italian peasants achieved their objectives. The revolt of over 200 villages under the dominion of Florence between 1401 and 1404 compelled the government to grant the peasants some tax exemptions, cancel or reduce their debts, and allow them to carry weapons.

The most successful peasant rebellion took place in Catalonia, where peasant serfs began agitating in the 1380s for liberation from their servile status. Despite royal expressions of sympathy for the peasants' cause, Catalan lords managed for decades to resist the forces of economic change and to maintain control over their serfs while exacting from them the "bad customs," which included high "redemption" fees for being freed from the land, taxes on inheritance and marriage, and fines for adultery. The Catalan civil war (1460–1472), however, turned the tide in the peasants' favor, since Juan II depended on the support of peasant armies for his triumph over a coalition of Catalan nobles and urban patricians intent on preserving the traditional social and constitutional order. In 1486 Fernando II abolished serfdom.

Peasant movements in the Balkans achieved much less. In Ottoman Bulgaria and western Anatolia, Shaykh Bedreddin (1358–1416) inspired rebellions against the more centralized and orthodox Sunni government that Sultan Mehmed I (1413–1420) was establishing after years of civil war. Bedreddin, the son of a Christian mother and a Muslim father, was a charismatic mystic who preached the common ownership of property and the equality of Muslims and Christians. Reminiscent of the more syncretic religious stance of the early Turkic dervishes, his message particularly appealed to Christian peasants, whom the Ottoman government was taxing more heavily because of their religious affiliation. The sultan quelled the revolts, and Bedreddin was hanged in 1416. In Christian Hungary, a peasants' crusade against the Ottomans encouraged by Franciscan preachers turned into a peasants' revolt against the Hungarian aristocracy in 1514. The peasants' leader, Gyorgy Dozsa, blamed the nobles for not protecting the realm from the Turks and for instead exploiting the peasantry. The nobles eventually defeated the peasant army and sternly warned other potential rebels by roasting Dozsa alive on a hot iron throne and forcing some of his followers to eat his flesh. Legislation then strengthened the regime of serfdom.

The revolts of urban laborers were less organized and less revolutionary in Muslim cities than they were in Christian cities, either because workers lacked guilds through which to mobilize and pursue their goals, which was the case in Mamluk domains, or because, as in the Ottoman empire, the state created the guilds to suit its own economic needs. Mamluk cities nonetheless saw frequent popular riots against excessive taxation and the high price or shortage of grain. Rioters sometimes attacked corrupt local officials or, with the support of the *'ulama'*, persuaded the sultan to replace them, but they did not seek to change the government. The most serious unrest occurred after 1485 in Damascus, where the *zu'ar*, organized youth gangs, periodically resisted state taxation with violence. In 1502, after the gangs battled with Mamluk soldiers, the government abolished some taxes and then neutralized the *zu'ar* by enlisting gang members in the army as auxiliary infantry.

In Christian cities guilds provided the organizational

FIGURE 15.5 Woodcut of execution of Gyorgy Dozsa, from Stephanus Taurinus, *Stauromachia* (Vienna, 1519). Photograph provided by Wikimedia Commons under the CC-PD | PD-Art License.

basis for workers' revolutionary movements, though rigid guild structures were sometimes a source of workers' frustrations. Workers believed that change could only come about if they had a voice in or, better yet, command of local government. In Florence, where the cloth industry was fundamental to the city's prosperity, wool workers excluded from the guild system—the Ciompi—rebelled in 1378, temporarily gained control of the government, and created guilds for disenfranchised workers. An oligarchic reaction undid their achievements in 1382. In Barcelona, the Busca, a party of merchants and artisans demanding municipal policies that would benefit the local textile industry, rose to power in 1453 at the expense of the patrician oligarchy, the Biga, which was then embroiled in conflict with the monarchy. The Biga's return to government in 1460 unfortunately led to civil war with Juan II and the ruination of the city. Partly as a consequence of Barcelona's troubles, industry and commerce expanded greatly in Valencia. There, in 1520, the Germania, a "Brotherhood" of armed artisans, overthrew the government dominated by urban patricians and nobles, and tried to reform a guild system that had limited the upward mobility of many artisans. The movement quickly radicalized, rejected Emperor Charles V's authority, and spread to other towns. Royalist forces finally crushed it in 1522. The artisans' one lasting achievement was their forced baptism of thousands of Muslims living on the lands of their noble enemies.

Continuity and Change in Mediterranean Trade

Although the Black Death reduced the number of consumers and the volume of Mediterranean commerce, there was considerable consistency in how states pursued their economic interests because their established political elites usually remained in charge. The mercantile oligarchies governing Venice and Genoa and the rulers of the Crown of Aragon who were so responsive to their cities' concerns continued formulating policies for expanding their states' commerce and industry. With Italians and Catalans dominating maritime trade routes, Mamluk and Maghribi sultans persisted in employing their power on land to control access to, respectively, South Asian spices and Saharan gold, commodities that kept European merchants coming to their ports. Changes to patterns of international commerce often resulted from war and related political developments.

Ottoman expansion had a major impact on trade in the eastern Mediterranean, where the Venetians and Genoese had long been the leading players. Primarily concerned with the conquest and exploitation of new territories, the sultans were keen to attract western merchants to their cities for the customs revenue trade generated and for obtaining essential commodities. Italian traders, then, could earn handsome profits, but only as long as it suited Ottoman imperial interests. Thus in the later fourteenth century the Ottomans encouraged the activities of Genoese merchants and tax-farmers in their domains, but after they captured Constantinople in 1453 they deprived the Genoese of their monopoly over the mining and production of alum (a key chemical for cloth industries) in Anatolia, they replaced the Genoese as the farmers of customs duties in their ports with their Greek and Jewish subjects, and they took control of the slave trade and occupied Genoese outposts in the Black Sea region, the resources of which—grain, meat, and salt—were crucial for provisioning their growing capital. Genoese merchants, however, were still welcome to trade in

FIGURE 15.6 Ragusa/Dubrovnik, showing port and medieval walls. Photo by GFDL provided by Wikimedia Commons under CC-BY-SA-3.0 License.

Bursa, a major Ottoman emporium in Anatolia, where they joined Florentines in purchasing Iranian raw silk for Italian industries and Indian pepper.

In 1458 Mehmed II acquired Ragusa (Dubrovnik), a Catholic Slavic port on the eastern Adriatic coast, as an Ottoman protectorate and made it a rival of Italian cities in regional trade. In exchange for paying the sultan an annual tribute, Ragusan merchants gained a privileged role in the commerce between the Balkans and western Europe, exporting Balkan goods such as hides, wool, and wax to Italy and importing to the Balkans manufactures such as textiles, glass, and paper.

Venice continued trading with the Ottomans, despite losing some Aegean possessions to them, but the city's most important commercial relationship was with the Mamluks. As a result of the closing of the overland trade route to East Asia with the breakup of the Mongol Empire, Mamluk Alexandria emerged in the 1340s as the main hub through which western merchants purchased eastern spices for distribution in Europe. From 1345 the Venetians concluded several commercial treaties with the Mamluks and by the early fifteenth century they dominated the lucrative spice trade. Defeated militarily by Venice in 1381, the Genoese had a much smaller share, as did Catalan and French merchants.

Muslim *karimi* merchants operating in the Indian Ocean and Red Sea conveyed the spices to Egypt for sale to European merchants. The Mamluk regime, which protected and taxed this transit trade, profited immensely. *Karimi* activity came to an end when Sultan Barsbay (1422–1438) established a state monopoly over the spice trade, requiring Europeans to purchase fixed amounts of spices at set prices. The trade still thrived, such was the demand for spices.

Once flourishing industries in Egypt and Syria, however, declined in the fifteenth century. Their textile industries could not compete with the high quality and cheaper woolen, cotton, and silk fabrics that Venetian and other merchants were importing from Europe. Whereas municipal governments in northern Italy and Catalonia promoted local textile manufacturing, the Mamluk military elite, hit hard by declining agricultural revenue, gave less patronage to local industries. Timur-Lenk's deportation of skilled artisans from the Syrian cities he sacked in 1400–1401 did additional damage. It became more profitable for the Mamluks to allow European merchants in Syrian ports to purchase large quantities of raw Syrian cotton and Iranian silk for industries back in Europe than to retain these materials for native artisans. Other Egyptian industries declined in the face of European, especially Italian, competition: sugar refining and confection, paper, soap, and glass. The Venetians, the leading producers and exporters of glass, even crafted mosque lamps for the Muslim market. Cloth manufacturers in Byzantine territories also suffered from the competition of the industries of Italian cities whose merchants bought up the raw materials they needed. SEE SOURCEBOOK 15:3.

The Crown of Aragon's main sphere of economic activity still lay in the western Mediterranean. It exported Catalan and Valencian cloth to its southern Italian possessions—Sardinia, Sicily (reacquired in the 1390s), and Naples (conquered in 1443)—and imported their wheat, sugar, and salt. To the more industrial cities of northern Italy, however, it exported primary products such as wool, dyestuffs, raisins, and rice. Genoa remained an important commercial partner, despite its clashes with Aragon over Sardinia, and its merchants joined Catalans and Valencians in the North African ports of Tunis and Bijaya and in the Granadan ports of Almería and Málaga. Not only did these Christian merchants trade European cloth for African gold and Granadan silk and sugar, they also redistributed to these western Muslim cities spices and other eastern commodities that they had originally purchased in Mamluk Alexandria or Beirut.

Pressured by Ottomans and Venetians to look westward, Genoese merchants and financiers were increasingly active in the Iberian Peninsula, making the most of the growing maritime commerce between the Mediterranean and the Atlantic that Castile's securing of the Straits of Gibraltar in 1344 facilitated. Genoese settled in and invested in the commerce of Cádiz and Seville, Castilian ports from which Andalusian wool, grain, wine, and olive oil were exported to northern Europe. In the later fifteenth century they played a crucial role in the economic development of the Atlantic islands: Portugal's Azores, Madeira, and Cape Verdes, and Castile's Canaries. Having gained experience with sugar production in Sicily, Genoese entrepreneurs financed the sugar industry in Madeira, and in the Cape Verdes they helped introduce a sugar plantation economy based on the labor of slaves acquired by the Portuguese in nearby West Africa. Genoese merchants earned additional profits by distributing this Atlantic sugar in the eastern Mediterranean through their colony on the Aegean island of Chios. The Portuguese in West Africa were at the same time siphoning off Saharan gold, which Europeans had until then only been able to access through trading in Maghribi ports. The appearance of a Genoese seaman named Cristoforo Colombo—Columbus—in the Portuguese and Spanish courts in the 1480s seeking backing for Atlantic voyages to "the Indies" was not at all unusual.

Economic and Social Problems in an Age of Empire

By the time Columbus set sail the populations of most Mediterranean regions were growing; by the 1570s they would reach their pre–Black Death levels, amounting to some 60 or 70 million people altogether. Such demographic expansion boosted economic productivity but also increased pressure on available resources, leaving some workers without land or employment. At the same time, the Ottoman and Spanish Habsburg empires and other Mediterranean states were becoming ever more efficient at taxing their subjects in order to support their military endeavors. Growing numbers of taxpayers consequently experienced hardship. Elite classes in town and country, on the other hand, benefited from the abundant supply of labor and from exemption from paying many taxes, one of the perquisites of cooperating with their rulers. Concerns about the unrest of the needy, however, did move governments to develop institutions of social welfare, though these were never adequate. Governments in any case could not have been prepared for the natural disasters of the "little ice age," which caused a worldwide crisis in the seventeenth century. In the resulting disorders and rebellions, lower-class discontent sometimes combined dangerously with the disgruntlement of regional notables who felt threatened by the encroachments of highly centralized monarchies. Banditry also plagued Mediterranean societies as both nobles and commoners resorted to illegal means to survive in hard times.

From Recovery to Crisis

Rapid demographic recovery in the sixteenth century spurred economic growth. Rising demand for food and clothing encouraged farmers to bring more land under the plow and stimulated textile manufacturing, most notably in northern Italian cities and Ottoman Thessaloniki. Master artisans and merchant-industrialists employing cheaper wage labor earned significant profits, while western European nobles and Ottoman *timar*-holders collected more rent from the larger populations of peasants on their lands. Some peasants also did well because of high grain prices or through producing specialized crops for industries and the market, such as mulberry trees, cotton, wine, and wool. Since agriculture was so profitable, urban merchants and industrialists in Spain and Italy started investing more of their capital in landownership, which enabled them to live in the style of noble lords and even to win noble titles. As the economy expanded, more revenue flowed into state treasuries.

By midcentury, however, the negative effects of population growth were becoming apparent, especially in rural areas across the Mediterranean. Villages experienced increasing polarization between a few middling or well-to-do peasant families with substantial landholdings and the majority of families possessing small farms that were barely adequate for subsistence or no land at all. In many areas, such as the French Languedoc, the practice of parceling out the family's property among heirs shrunk the size of individual farms; at the same time, expanding populations made it difficult to find new land available to purchase or cultivate. When peasants farmed new land it tended to be of marginal quality with poor soils that produced diminishing harvests. The cultivation of profitable specialized crops instead of grain also left families more vulnerable in times of scarcity. Some peasants borrowed money from affluent urban folk in order to make improvements on their farms or to survive after a poor harvest; when they could not pay their debts their creditors expropriated their land. Other struggling peasants sold their land to urban investors and became wage laborers or sharecroppers subject to the growing demands of their landlords. By the late sixteenth century few independent peasant farmers remained in the countryside near Italian cities such as Florence, Siena, and Milan. In Ottoman Boeotia (Greece), only a quarter of the families still had a full farm; in the area around Mosul (Iraq) half of the peasants were landless.

Many indebted and landless peasants abandoned their villages and migrated to cities where they joined a growing proletariat. Urban populations thus expanded dramatically. Seville and Venice, for instance, had more than 100,000 inhabitants, Naples more than 200,000, and Istanbul around half a million. With such an abundance of labor, the bargaining position of workers deteriorated and real wages declined in city and countryside. Heightening demand meanwhile pushed up the prices of essential foodstuffs. Poverty and hunger tormented growing numbers of people.

Mounting state taxation compounded these difficulties. The Ottomans and Habsburgs required the funds to support their imperial war machines. In the Castilian heart of the Habsburg empire the tax burden probably quadrupled between 1570 and 1670. Lesser states also needed the wherewithal to defend themselves against predatory neighbors. The middle and lower classes—those who could least afford to pay—paid the bulk of the taxes. When the elite of military nobles, state officials, and urban patricians paid taxes, it was usually sales taxes that they could afford far more easily than the poor. Nobles nonetheless fell into debt through their conspicuous consumption of luxury goods. The elite classes maintained their privileged position through serving monarchs whose power and political objectives were thought to be divinely sanctioned.

Although economic and social conditions were dire for many people, they were not moving inexorably toward what historians call "the crisis of the seventeenth century." The crisis, rather, was precipitated by a series of extreme weather events—the "little ice age"—that began in the final decades of the sixteenth century and afflicted much of the known world. In the Mediterranean there was some variation in the precise nature and timing of the climatic disasters, but all regions experienced from at least the 1590s and often earlier bouts of extreme weather that involved severely cold winters, sometimes with heavy precipitation and flooding, and droughts followed by famine. Such spells of awful weather occurred throughout the seventeenth century. Plague also struck Mediterranean populations periodically and would continue to do so (in Mediterranean Europe at least) until 1721. The plague's impact on overcrowded cities could be devastating: Barcelona, for instance, lost nearly a third of its people in 1589 and 45 percent in 1651; one half of Milan's inhabitants died in 1630. Other diseases such as smallpox and typhus also took their toll. Famine conditions made people more susceptible to them. Climate change, disease, and war brought the demographic expansion of the sixteenth century to a grinding halt. Populations stagnated, or even declined, in the seventeenth century.

They would not return to their sixteenth-century peak until sometime in the eighteenth century.

Poverty and Welfare

Even when economic and environmental conditions were favorable, poor farmers and urban workers eked out meager livings. The increasing scarcity of land and employment and the more frequent destruction of crops through inclement weather or war pushed many poor families into the street or onto the road in search of work and food. The signs of crisis were most manifest in cities where masses of poor, hungry immigrants fleeing starvation in their home villages joined indigent locals needing assistance.

Governments exerted considerable effort to ensure that there was enough bread to distribute to the needy, hoping to prevent the rioting of the hungry or their death by starvation. The Ottoman authorities managed to deliver food to famine-stricken areas in a number of cases. In the Italian city of Modena and its district, however, 5,000 perished during the famine of 1590–1593. In times of dearth governments therefore strove to control the price of grain and prohibited suppliers within the state from exporting grain or engaging in speculation. Replenishing urban storehouses with imported grain was a crucial task for municipal leaders, who endeavored to maintain commercial relations with major wheat-producing regions such as Sicily and the Nile valley. States competed for access to sources of grain; war with the Ottomans caused difficulties for Venice in this regard. Toward the end of the sixteenth century the supply of grain in the Mediterranean was simply insufficient to meet the demands of all its peoples. Importing grain from northern Europe became necessary for some states.

Charitable institutions developed further in the sixteenth century on account of both the needs of burgeoning populations and the enhanced capacity of centralized states to organize poor relief. Yet in their initiatives Christian and Muslim governments were building on foundations laid by religious institutions. The Catholic Church, first of all, had long used the tithes (one-tenth of the harvest) it collected from the laity for almsgiving. Christian cities also had numerous confraternities, voluntary associations of well-off pious laypersons that founded and administered small hospitals for the sick and homeless,

FIGURE 15.7 Bartolomé Esteban Murillo, *The Young Beggar*, ca. 1645–1650. Photograph provided by Wikimedia Commons under the CC-PD-Mark | PD-Art License.

or provided charity to indigent families in their homes as well as burial services for their deceased members. Such confraternal activities helped alleviate social tensions between the wealthy, who earned spiritual benefits through their compassionate acts, and the poor recipients of their charity.

Because of the growing numbers of vagrants and beggars, however, elite views of the poor began to change. Those once seen as "Christ's poor" were regarded by many as indolent beggars in need of moral improvement or as possible carriers of disease. During the sixteenth century city governments—seconded by the royal government in Spain—began to distinguish between "native" paupers from their own city or urban district, who were candidates for assistance, and the "foreign" ones whom they attempted to eject and send back to their home districts. They made efforts to regulate begging, licensing only the "deserving poor," especially widows, children, and the aged. They centralized the administration of

FIGURE 15.8 Children carrying the Qur'an, collecting alms. © Historical Views / agefotostock.

charity and sometimes consolidated smaller hospitals to create larger "beggars' hospitals" that provided the unemployed with food, a bed, and the chance of learning a trade. Foundling hospitals were established to care for the large numbers of infants abandoned by their impoverished, desperate mothers—hundreds annually in large cities like Milan and Seville. Many of these children did not survive their first year. Florence's foundling home, the Hospital of the Innocents, which opened in 1445, had 1,220 residents in 1579. Yet because the city fathers were so keen to protect the virtue of the girls who survived infancy, they kept them in the Hospital until they married. Thus, 60 percent of the female inmates in 1579 were of marriageable age and some were over forty years old. Urban orphanages took in older children who, in contrast to many foundlings, were usually of legitimate birth. The orphanages apprenticed most of the boys to artisans, though gifted boys might get a Latin education. Orphaned girls received a small dowry to help them find a husband. Confraternities continued to supplement the welfare provided by governmental institutions.

In Muslim states the central institution of welfare had long been the *waqf* (*hubus* in al-Andalus and the Maghrib), or "pious endowment," usually of urban properties such as shops or rural agricultural land, the revenue from which was used for charitable purposes. Donors, it was believed, gained God's blessings in the afterlife through performing such acts that benefited the community after their death. In the Ottoman empire, sultans, viziers, and their wives endowed *waqf*s, especially in Istanbul, as did governors and local notables in provincial towns. Even individuals of modest means contributed to poor relief in this manner. With its huge population, native and migrant, Istanbul had the greatest needs. Sultans such as Mehmed the Conqueror and Suleyman the Magnificent responded by establishing imperial *waqf* complexes that were centered around a mosque and included primary schools, hospitals, soup kitchens, and medical schools as well as the shops and markets that generated the income to subsidize the provision of charity. The soup kitchen of the Fatih mosque complex founded by Mehmed in 1470 fed 2,500 to 3,000 people per day in 1545—and this was but one of many such *waqf*s operating in the city. Poor Muslims were not the only beneficiaries of the free food and medicine; poor Christian and Jewish subjects of the sultan could receive this assistance. Minority communities of course had their own internal institutions of social welfare, which in Ottoman lands included *waqf*s. In Renaissance Italy, where Jews were influenced by the traditions of Spanish and southern French Jews as well as by Christian institutions, Jewish communities established confraternities whose members cared for the poor and sick and saw to it that they received a proper burial.

The resources at the disposal of Christian, Muslim, and Jewish welfare institutions, however, often proved to be inadequate. State governments were certainly not equipped to deal with the calamities of the "little ice age." Through their continual prosecution of war and exaction of taxes they probably exacerbated social distress as much as they relieved it. SEE SOURCEBOOK 15:4.

Rebels and Bandits

Rebellion and banditry were manifestations of resistance, popular as well as elite, against the growing power of states to systematically tax their subjects and to punish lawbreakers. They became widespread in the straitened circumstances of the "little ice age." SEE SOURCEBOOK 15:5.

Southwestern France (Aquitaine) saw a series of agrarian "Croquant" revolts against the monarchy's fiscal demands in 1594, 1624, and 1636–1637. The region was a center of Protestant (Calvinist Huguenot) activity, and its peasant communities felt the impact of the wars between

FIGURE 15.9 *(above)* The Piazza Santissima Annunziata, facing an orphanage for foundlings, the Hospital of the Innocents. Photo by Warburg provided by Wikimedia Commons under the CC-BY-SA-3.0 License.

FIGURE 15.10 *(left)* Hospital of the Innocents. Detail of ornamentation depicting foundlings. Photo by Sailko provided by Wikimedia Commons under the CC-BY-PD-3.0

Huguenots and Catholics. Not only did the productivity of their farms decline, but they also faced the extortionate taxation of military leaders from both sides. The peasants first organized and took up arms in 1594 to defend themselves amid the political disorder and to resist additional taxation. The last Croquant revolt, however, was the most serious. Despite famines and plague epidemics in 1630–1631, Louis XIII (1610–1643) and his chief minister, Cardinal Richelieu, did not abandon their costly foreign policy and declared war on Spain in 1635. When the Crown then increased the land tax, insisted on the payment of tax arrears, and requisitioned grain for French troops, the Croquant peasants rose in rebellion. Minor nobles in the region joined and led the peasants, for royal centralization had eroded their traditional privileges and they resented the actions of the king's lowborn officials. Royal forces defeated the Croquant army in June 1637. Some of the Croquant nobles escaped to become bandit leaders.

The Spanish Habsburgs' "composite empire" similarly endured a sequence of dangerous revolts caused by a combination of natural catastrophes with exorbitant wartime taxation. Rebellion spread to different states within the empire because of their common disgruntlement with the "Union of Arms," the plan of Felipe IV's chief minister Olivares requiring each state to contribute more money and men to the imperial war effort in northern Europe. In Catalonia a series of droughts and poor harvests between 1627 and 1640 darkened the mood of Catalans of all classes, heightening their discontent with the government in Madrid, which, they argued, was violating their constitutional privileges with its demands. In 1640 the billeting of Castilian troops in Catalan towns sparked uprisings throughout the principality. In June rebels rioted in Barcelona and murdered Felipe's viceroy on the beach; in January 1641 they transferred Catalonia's allegiance from King Felipe to Louis XIII of France. Felipe would not recover Catalonia until 1652.

Revolts also erupted in 1647–1648 in Spanish Sicily and Naples, which bore a heavier tax burden than the Crown of Aragon. The high price of food following poor harvests caused rebellion in Palermo. In Naples a new tax on fruit provoked the people to rally around a charismatic fisherman, Masaniello, in an uprising against the Spanish government and its local noble collaborators. Although these rebellions were all suppressed by April 1648, they convinced King Felipe to reduce taxes. Castile, the kingdom that paid more taxes than any other to the imperial government, unsurprisingly experienced rebellion. In Andalusia, widespread hunger in the wake of extreme weather events moved the people of around twenty towns to revolt between 1648 and 1652. The king quieted some of the insurrections by dispatching supplies of grain to suffering towns.

The calamitous triad of bad weather, war, and taxation lay at the root of grave disorder and rebellion in the Ottoman empire. The Celali Rebellion that convulsed Anatolia broke out in 1596 after five years of drought and continued until 1610 through years of extreme cold, drought, and famine. Oppressive taxation to pay for the sultans' long war against the Habsburgs in Hungary (1593–1606) increased popular disaffection for the government, while the departure of troops to the Hungarian front left Anatolia vulnerable to the depredations of bandits. The bandits were a mix of cavalrymen, Janissaries, and state officials, who, instead of fulfilling their duties, tried to make the best of the dire conditions through plundering peasant villages. Desperate peasants, townsfolk, and unemployed *madrasa* graduates joined bandit bands, some of which had hundreds of members. The mercenary commander Karayazıcı (d. 1602) organized the bandits into an army in 1598. Under his command and that of other bandits, the Celalis fought several campaigns against the sultan's forces until their final defeat in 1610. The suppression of the Celalis reduced but did not extinguish banditry in the provinces, since some of the conditions originally responsible for it persisted.

The most serious upheavals next occurred, remarkably, in Istanbul, leading to the killing of two sultans, Osman II (1618–1622) and Ibrahim I (1640–1648). After leading Ottoman armies in an expensive and fruitless campaign in Poland, Osman returned in January 1622 to a capital facing famine because severe cold had frozen the Bosphorus and prevented the passage of grain shipments. Continuing famine conditions and rumors that the sultan was plotting against them moved elite Janissaries in Istanbul to do away with both the grand vizier and the sultan. Another response to the natural and man-made disasters afflicting the city and the empire was a puritanical movement led by the preacher Kadizade Mehmed (1582–1635), who demanded the strict enforcement of

Islamic law in an effort to appease God. Eradicating sin, however, could not prevent drought, food shortages, and earthquakes in 1647–1648 or the erratic behavior of Sultan Ibrahim, whose deposition and execution Janissaries engineered in 1648.

If in Ottoman Anatolia the temporary breakdown of government contributed to the proliferation of bandits, in Mediterranean Christian states it was the development of more effective judicial institutions that helped to create bandits. Feuding nobles and their retinues who had once killed their enemies with relative impunity as an acceptable form of "popular justice" were now labeled as "criminals" by the state and liable to prosecution. Many such noble outlaws, however, managed to evade state justice and fled to mountainous or wooded areas beyond the state's effective reach. Men from lower-class families, embroiled in their own blood feuds, also became bandits with a price on their head. Since competition for limited resources usually lay at the root of feuds, the number of bandits rose as economic conditions worsened. The same conditions drove other poor peasants and townspeople to join bandit bands as a means of subsistence. In Italy during the famines of the 1590s the bands grew.

Bandits preyed on wealthy landowners, lay and clerical, and on merchants; they made travel perilous. Some operated with the complicity and protection of powerful nobles and unscrupulous state officials. Villagers supported bandits, though often out of fear. Some bandits, however, robbed from the rich and gave to the poor in the style of "Robin Hood." The nobleman Marco Sciarra, a bandit since 1585, won the love of the poor of Naples. Pursued by both the viceroy and papal armies, Sciarra was eventually murdered by a lieutenant who betrayed him for gold and a pardon. No more tolerant of bandits than of Judaizers, Pope Paul IV and his successors were perhaps their most determined opponents and executed a good number of both. Spanish and French kings sometimes pardoned bandits in exchange for their service in their armies.

Morisco banditry was a problem specific to sixteenth-century Spain. Deep animosity for the Spanish church and government that systematically persecuted their people motivated some Morisco bandits to target Catholic clergy and state officials. From the perspective of the latter, the Granadan *monfies* (from Arabic *munfi*, or "outlaw") were the most notorious and dangerous, though many members of their own ethnic group saw them as heroes. Worsening economic conditions, however, drove other Moriscos into a life of crime, and, like Old Christian bandits, they did not discriminate between Old and New Christians when they assaulted and robbed people on the highways. Regardless of the Morisco bandits' motives, the royal authorities lumped them together with other perceived Muslim threats to Catholic Spain, heightening the fear that contributed to their decision to expel the Moriscos.

The Mediterranean and the Atlantic

Mediterranean states were not the only ones to be devastated by war and extreme weather or shaken by rebellion. The "little ice age" was a global phenomenon, and the Thirty Years' War between Protestant and Catholic states (1618–1648) ravaged northern continental Europe, while a Calvinist revolution and civil war rocked England (1642–1649). Nevertheless, by 1650 the balance of political and economic power was noticeably shifting in favor of northern European states, especially the Atlantic powers. The Austrian Habsburgs had fought the Ottomans to a stalemate, and the English and the Dutch were dominating international commerce in the Mediterranean. These same naval powers had been successfully challenging Spanish hegemony in the Atlantic world, while the armies of Louis XIV of France (1643–1715) were besting Spanish forces in Europe. The establishment of new trade routes in the Atlantic world and the continuous development of its colonial economies generated economic forces that enabled English, Dutch, and French entrepreneurs to outdo Mediterranean competitors. The shift in the locus of power, however, was gradual. The Spanish and Ottoman empires remained formidable and for much of the post-1500 period it was their policies, their conquests, and their financial needs that created the framework within which many economic actors in the Mediterranean operated. In the face of the invasion of northern European merchants and manufactured goods, moreover, local Mediterranean economies were resilient and adaptable. In 1650 the Mediterranean was by no means a backwater, for the rising North Atlantic

ARTIFACT PROFIT, FEAR, AND FASCINATION: ELIZABETHAN ENGLAND AND THE MUSLIM WORLD

The reign of Elizabeth I (1558–1603) saw England develop commercial and political relations with Muslim states for the first time since the heyday of the crusading movement. Aiming to obtain the luxury commodities so in demand in England and northern Europe, English merchants began in the 1550s to trade in Morocco, exchanging English cloth for Moroccan sugar. From Ottoman domains they imported Aegean currants and sweet wines, cotton, Persian silk, and Anatolian carpets, which a trade agreement with Sultan Murad III in 1580 facilitated. Elizabeth supported the merchants' ventures by granting charters to the Turkey Company in 1581 (renamed the Levant Company in 1592) and to the Barbary Company in 1585. The Protestant queen hoped that commercial ties would lay a foundation for separate military alliances with Ahmad al-Mansur, the Sa'did sultan of Morocco, and with his Ottoman rival against Felipe II of Spain. In their various negotiations, all three monarchs acknowledged that Muslims and Protestants shared an abhorrence for what they regarded as the Catholics' "idolatrous" religious iconography and ritual. In 1587, for example, Elizabeth's ambassador praised the Ottoman Murad as having been sent by God "for the destruction of the idol-worshippers."[1] Although Murad proved reluctant to return to war with Spain, England's defeat of the Spanish Armada in 1588 piqued al-Mansur's interest in allying with the "sultana Isabel [Elizabeth]" against Felipe, "the pillar of polytheism."[2] Felipe's acquisition of Portugal in 1580 had made him more of a threat to Morocco, and gaining English naval support would be an asset.

FIGURE 15.11 'Abd al-Wahid al-Annuri, Moroccan ambassador to Elizabeth I. © Fine Arts Images / Heritage Image Partnership Ltd / Alamy Stock Photo.

Al-Mansur therefore sent two embassies to London, in 1589 and 1600, to discuss a possible military alliance. Even though Elizabeth ultimately did not accept the sultan's proposals for a joint invasion of Spain or for a joint naval campaign to intercept Spanish silver galleons returning from America, the exotic appearance of the Moroccan delegations, dressed in long robes and turbans, generated considerable excitement among her subjects. In 1600 an anonymous English painter captured al-Mansur's chief ambassador, the Morisco 'Abd al-Wahid al-Annuri.

By this time, the importation of luxury goods from the Ottoman East and Morocco had already heightened English fascination with what they perceived as the opulent and mysterious Muslim world. Aristocrats furnished their homes with "Turkey carpets," tapestries, and cushions, such conspicuous consumption being a sign of their wealth and supposed cosmopolitan connections. They also enjoyed dressing in eastern costume with turbans. English manufacturers began using imported Persian silk to produce clothes "in the Turkish manner" for the middle classes as well. Many people developed a taste for eastern spices, currants, wines, and the Moroccan sugar that helped blacken their queen's teeth.

The wearing of Ottoman attire, however, did not mask English ignorance of Muslims and Islam or English fear of them. Only merchants, ambassadors, and a few unfortunate captives had occasion to visit Muslim lands and become acquainted with Muslims; even then, their ideas about the Islamic faith were distorted by the Christian prism through which they unavoidably viewed it. Islam was the traditional enemy of Christendom for

FIGURE 15.12 The Somerset House Conference, 1604, with Turkish carpet. Photograph provided by Wikimedia Commons under the CC-PD-Mark | PD-Art License.

most people in England, and no Muslim foe seemed more threatening than the Ottoman Turks. To his very popular work, *Acts and Monuments* (1563), which described the martyrdom of Protestants at the hands of Catholics, John Foxe added in 1570 a section entitled "The History of the Turks." It ends with a prayer beseeching God to grant his church "victory against the malicious fury of these Turks, Saracens . . . and all the malignant rabble of Antichrist."[3] Queen Elizabeth's diplomatic overtures to Sultan Murad would have done little to alter the opinions that Foxe's book engendered.

Captivity narratives solidified the association of Muslims with violence. Whether older English translations of the accounts of Hungarian Christians who had fallen into Ottoman hands or the original accounts of English captives, which began to be published in 1589, they told of the cruelty of Muslim captors and of the captives' strong Christian faith in the face of such adversity. However, in the account of the Englishman Richard Hasleton (1595), who had the misfortune of being taken captive first by Spaniards and then by corsairs from Algiers, the Muslims, who put him in "in most vyle slaverie and miserable bondage," were not as fearsome as the Catholics.[4]

The fear of and fascination with the Muslim world that the flood of eastern goods, visits of Moroccan diplomats, and tales of war and captivity inspired in the people of England were reflected on the Elizabethan stage. As a result of England's re-encounter with Islam, between 1576 and 1603 London's public theaters staged more than sixty plays with Turkish, Moorish, or Persian characters. The plays sent a mixed message to the audience, but since many plays featured despotic eastern rulers and turbaned figures brandishing scimitars, the image of Muslims was markedly negative and violent. Bloody episodes from Ottoman and Moroccan history provided some playwrights with their dramatic material. Robert Greene's play about the Ottoman sultan Selim I (1512–1520), *The First Part of the Tragicall Reign of Selimus*, showed Selim murdering his father and brothers and depicted Islam as akin to paganism. Composed around the time of the first Moroccan embassy to London, George Peele's *The Battle of Alcazar* dramatized the historic battle that had brought al-Mansur to the Moroccan throne in 1578. Of the three Sa'did princes involved in the battle, 'Abd al-Malik was portrayed as noble and tawny in color, while his nephew al-Mutawakkil (given the name "Muley Mahamet"), who had invited the Portu-

FIGURE 15.13 Sir Robert Shirley by Anthony Van Dyck, Rome, 1622. The Picture Art Collection / Alamy Stock Photo.

guese king Sebastian to invade Morocco, was played with his face made up with burnt cork and described as "Blacke in his looke, and bloudie [bloody] in his deeds." The third prince, "Muley Mahamet Seth"—none other than al-Mansur—is represented, of course, as victorious but also as potentially dangerous.[5] Some scholars think the play was intended as a warning against an English alliance with al-Mansur.

William Shakespeare (1564–1616) included Muslims in a number of his plays and, like other playwrights, distinguished between normally hostile "Turks" and potentially friendly North African "Moors." Shakespeare's Moors, however, were often more complex, even sympathetic figures whose portrayal seems to have been partly influenced by rumors of the queen's negotiations with al-Mansur. In *The Merchant of Venice*, written in 1596, Shakespeare includes a "Prince of Morocco" among the suitors of the Christian woman Portia from fictional Belmont. The Muslim prince boasts that he defeated the Ottoman "Sultan Solyman" in battle, but Portia still rejects him. Shakespeare began writing *The Tragedy of Othello, the Moor of Venice* in late 1601, months after the visit of the Sa'did ambassador al-Annuri, whom the playwright may well have seen. A mercenary general in the service of Venice against the Ottomans, Othello is portrayed as a Black Moor. Yet his bravery and earlier conversion to Christianity overcome concerns about his color, at least in the eyes of his White Christian wife, Desdemona. Still, Othello's past is mysterious, and his Christian faith ambiguous, not unlike that of al-Annuri, the ambassador of Morisco origins, or of al-Hasan al-Wazzan, the famous former convert whose geography of Africa was published in English in November 1600. Othello, who is tragically tricked into killing his wife, is an embodiment of the profound ambivalence with which the people of Elizabethan England viewed the Muslim world.

Discussion Questions

1. What common interests encouraged the development of connections between England and the Muslim world in the later sixteenth century?

2. How did the people of Elizabethan England acquire knowledge of Muslims, Islam, and Islamic culture, and how did an individual English person's social class affect his or her perception of Muslims and Islam?

3. How might one explain the almost contradictory feelings of fascination and fear that English people in Elizabeth I's day held in regard to the Muslim world?

Further Reading

Brotton, Jerry. *This Orient Isle: Elizabethan England and the Islamic World*. London: Allen Lane (Penguin Books), 2016.

Cory, Stephen. *Reviving the Islamic Caliphate in Early Modern Morocco*. Surrey: Ashgate, 2013.

MacLean, Gerald, and Nabil Matar. *Britain and the Islamic World, 1558–1713*. Oxford: Oxford University Press, 2011.

Matar, Nabil. *Britain and Barbary, 1589–1689*. Gainesville: University Press of Florida, 2005.

Notes

1. Brotton, 146.
2. Brotton, 151.
3. MacLean and Matar, 27.
4. MacLean and Matar, 135.
5. Brotton, 166–67.

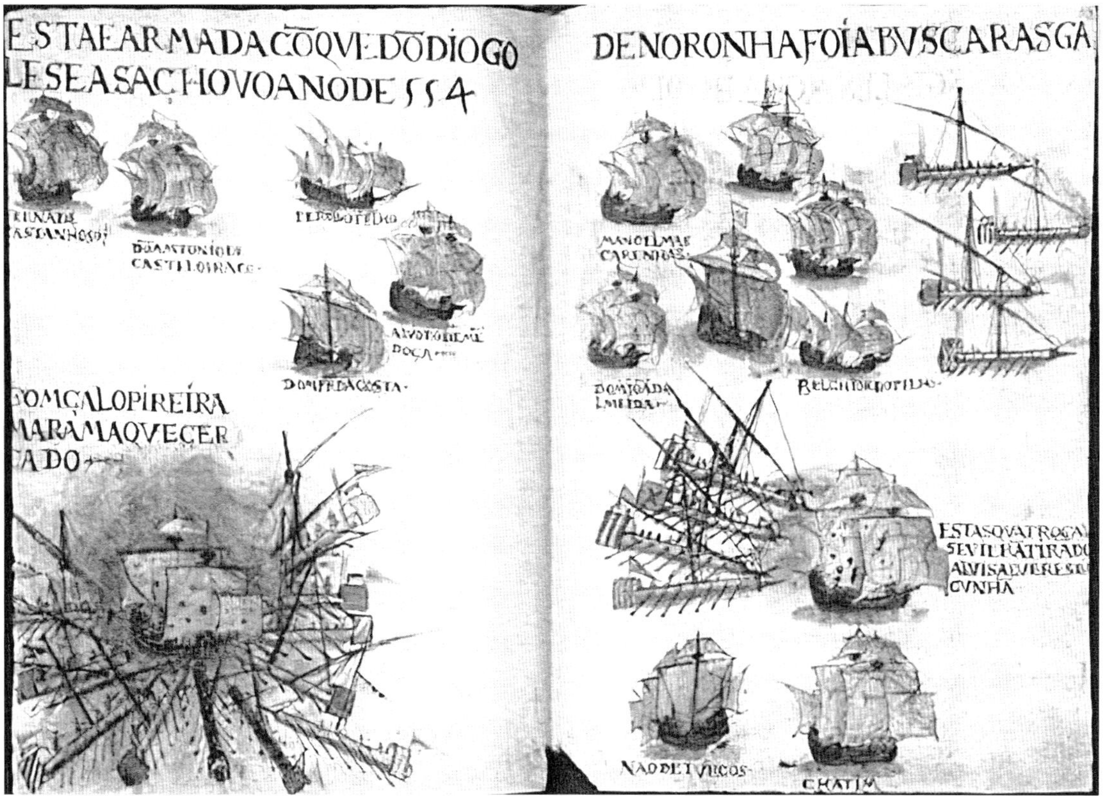

FIGURE 15.14 Ottoman galleys and Portuguese sailing ships in battle at Hormuz in the Persian Gulf, 1553. © Historical Views / agefotostock.

states still earned much of their profits from trading in the Middle Sea.

Empires, Entrepreneurs, and Newcomers

Selim I's conquest of Mamluk Syria and Egypt in 1516–1517 brought most of the eastern Mediterranean under Ottoman dominion and enhanced the region's economic integration. Ottoman merchants—Muslims, Greek and Armenian Christians, and Jews—broadened the scope of their trade with the sultans' backing, gaining entry into Christian ports eager to receive their business. The Adriatic port of Ancona, which was incorporated into the Papal States in 1532, thus became an important commercial center where a diverse cast of Ottoman merchants sold eastern goods and purchased from Florentine traders cloth produced in western European workshops. Catholic merchants from Ragusa, the Ottomans' protectorate, were able to move more easily across the Ottoman-Habsburg frontier and to extend their business beyond the Balkans and the Adriatic to Spain and even to England, where they sold Aegean wine and raisins and purchased English textiles. Ragusa's government at the same time encouraged Sephardi Jewish merchants to trade and settle in the city, a pragmatic policy befitting an Ottoman vassal.

With the conquest of Egypt and the Nile valley, the Ottomans acquired a major source of grain for provisioning Istanbul. The Alexandria-Istanbul route became a vital commercial artery. The Ottomans also won control of the Mediterranean hub of the immensely lucrative South Asian spice trade. The flow of spices to Cairo and Alexandria, however, had diminished considerably since 1501, when the Portuguese began shipping spices on an alternative Atlantic route from the Indian Ocean to Lisbon, and then on to Habsburg Antwerp for redistribution in northern Europe. The Venetians, who had been the main importers and distributors of eastern spices in Europe, were losing as much revenue as the Ottomans. Ottoman naval action against the Portuguese in the Indian Ocean and Persian Gulf brought about a revival of the Mediterranean spice trade—and the fortunes of Venetian merchants—in the mid-sixteenth century. For Venice, cooperation with the Ottomans remained essential for maintaining access to Egyptian and Syrian ports. Events surrounding the Battle of Lepanto in 1571 strained the relationship.

The western Mediterranean was less economically integrated than the eastern half of the sea in the sixteenth century because domination of it was hotly contested by the Ottoman empire with its North African regencies and a Spanish Habsburg monarchy intent on eradicating Islam from the Iberian Peninsula while hanging on to a few North African ports. Ottoman possession of Egypt, moreover, diverted to Istanbul eastern luxury goods that once would have been sent west from Alexandria to Maghribi markets. Trans-Saharan trade continued to be of major importance for the Maghrib, while the profits from piracy contributed increasingly to the economies of its cities. Merchants from France and England, the Habsburgs' enemies, did growing business in Maghribi ports, especially in the latter half of the century.

The needs and tastes of the growing number of Spanish colonists in America created opportunities for producers in Spain. Andalusian olive oil, wine, and grain were exported to America, as was Catalan cloth. Genoese merchants in Seville and Barcelona were active in this commerce. Yet as the sixteenth century progressed the Genoese invested less in trade and more in international finance. They began extending loans to Charles V in the 1520s to support his military campaigns and by midcentury they were the leading financiers of the Habsburg monarchy, a position they would occupy until 1627. The political alliance between the Genoese republic, which the admiral Andrea Doria restored in 1528, and the Spanish Crown solidified the financial relationship. The Genoese were partly reimbursed for their loans with the silver that Spain imported from America in growing quantities. The profits they earned were so large that they could absorb the losses incurred when Spanish kings declared bankruptcy. After the bankruptcy of 1627, however, Felipe IV's chief minister Olivares sought to loosen the hold of the Genoese on the Spanish treasury and so turned to Portuguese Converso bankers as a source of credit. The ability of these Conversos to amass funds through financial and kinship networks that extended from the Atlantic to the Mediterranean earned them the patronage of the Spanish monarchy.

If in the decades following the Battle of Lepanto English and Dutch merchants came to dominate long-distance trade in the Mediterranean, it was at least partly because the Spanish and Ottoman empires were disengaging from their struggle for Mediterranean supremacy and directing most of their military resources to other fronts. The imperial interests of the Sa'dids and Ottomans also facilitated the entry of these newcomers. The rulers of both Muslim states hoped that commercial and political agreements with Protestant England and Holland would help to counter the aggression of their common Catholic Habsburg enemies. England's trade in Morocco, ongoing since the 1550s, increased with its founding of the Barbary Company in 1585. The Sa'dids obtained war materials and cloth from the English and sold them Moroccan sugar and saltpeter. Consistent with the commercial treaty they had affirmed with their old ally France in 1569, the Ottomans extended trading privileges to England in 1580 and to the Netherlands in 1612. The sultans, moreover, were happy to reduce the role of Venice in eastern Mediterranean trade. English and Dutch merchants and the merchandise they carried were soon reshaping sectors of the Mediterranean economy.

A New Old World

During the sixteenth and seventeenth centuries Mediterranean rulers, producers, and entrepreneurs were operating in a world increasingly affected by the economic forces that European colonization of the Americas and penetration of South Asian markets had unleashed. They could not have foreseen, much less controlled, most of the economic transformations that ultimately gave northern Europeans a competitive edge in particular areas of commerce, industry, and agriculture. In the changing global environment they nonetheless made adjustments to their economic strategies that were logical and profitable, at least in the short term.

In sixteenth-century Venice, to take an important example, patrician merchants responded to the uncertainties of the spice trade and conflict with the Ottomans by reducing their direct participation and investment in international trade and instead investing more in real estate and industry, especially the manufacture of woolens. Venice's state-sponsored system of galley convoys thus came to an end in 1569. Non-noble Italians from Venice's peninsular domains, Greeks from its island possessions, and Jews took on the patricians' commercial role, often acting as their agents in foreign ports. After 1573, when Venice reaffirmed peace with Istanbul, Ottoman merchants—Muslims, Greeks, Armenians, and Jews—visited Venice in growing numbers, which led to the foundation of a Fondaco dei Turchi (Funduq of the Turks) to house them in 1621. By this time, however, the revived spice trade between Venice and Ottoman Egypt was finally being extinguished by the Dutch and English trading companies that were monopolizing commerce in the Indian Ocean and shipping spices to Europe on the Atlantic route.

English and Dutch merchants were especially effective competitors in international commerce because of their modes of marshaling capital and the unprecedented degree to which their governments supported their enterprises. The northern merchants formed joint-stock companies, such as the English Levant Company, which sold stock or ownership shares to scores of investors in order to accumulate the vast sums of capital needed for large-scale and long-term overseas trading. The governments of England and the Netherlands granted the companies a monopoly of trade in specific overseas territories. Furthermore, the companies possessed the resources to organize their own naval forces to protect their trade. Their ships were better armed and faster than the vessels of their rivals in the Mediterranean Sea and Indian Ocean.

The activities of English and Dutch traders contributed to the rapid rise of the ports of Livorno and Izmir (Smyrna) as major centers of Mediterranean commerce in the seventeenth century. Hoping to make the most of the changing economic environment, the Medici dukes of Tuscany in the 1590s established Livorno, on the northwestern Italian coast, as a "free port," offering foreign merchants of all backgrounds freedom of trade, tax exemptions, and protection from inquisitorial prosecution. The Medicis' approach differed from that of the Venetian government, for instance, which gave special protection only to its own merchants. Livorno thus became a trading hub for the English and Dutch, who brought northern European grain to provision Italian cities. They were joined by Sephardi, Armenian, Muslim, and Catholic merchants from most Mediterranean states. Aside from functioning as a key port for the transit trade between the Mediterranean and the Atlantic, Livorno forged commercial connections with North African ports, which made it a center for the redistribution of goods stolen by Muslim and Christian corsairs.

Ottoman Izmir, on the Anatolian coast, attracted a similar international cast of merchants. The Ottomans' seizure of the offshore island of Chios from the Genoese in 1566 had enabled the rise of the port. French, English, and Dutch merchants all secured trading privileges in Izmir from the sultans. Venetians traded there, too, but they did not fare well against their northern European competitors. Western merchants in Izmir purchased Anatolian cotton, fruit, nuts, and tobacco as well as the raw silk that Armenian traders brought from Iran. The silk fed their own countries' textile industries.

Mediterranean textile industries flourished through much of the sixteenth century, partly in response to the demand of growing populations. In the Ottoman empire Thessaloniki was a major center for the manufacture of woolens. The production of woolen and silk fabrics expanded significantly in northern Italy, especially in Venice, Florence, and Milan. Textile industries in Spain were less successful, however, because landowners and merchants exported so much of the country's famous merino (from "Marinids") wool to northern Europe and Italy, and because the Spanish government expended so much of its American gold and silver defending the empire.

Yet by 1650 the textile industries in Thessaloniki and northern Italy had declined dramatically in the face of northern European competition. English and French manufacturers produced quality woolens and silks at lower costs; their merchants flooded Mediterranean markets with the cheaper goods. The inflexibility of guilds in Italian cities and the higher wages they paid workers probably limited their ability to respond effectively.

Difficulties in the industrial sector were compounded by the growing tendency of families with monetary resources to invest in land rather than in industry. In the sixteenth century this was a sensible strategy for merchants, urban patricians, and even affluent Janissaries, since the growing demand for food made agriculture especially profitable. In Spain and Italy, moreover, landownership could lead to winning a noble title. Another conservative economic strategy was purchasing government bonds, especially Spanish imperial bonds, and living off the annuities. Aggressive competition from northern European industries and trading companies reinforced these tendencies. Increasingly the balance of trade was shifting, such that the Mediterranean was importing more manufactured goods from northern Europe and exporting more raw materials.

The development of northern European and Atlantic economies also had an impact on Mediterranean agriculture. On account of climatic disasters and the resulting dearth of grain, in the 1590s Mediterranean states, especially those in Italy, began purchasing Baltic cereals imported by Dutch merchants. Grown mostly by peasant serfs on aristocratic estates east of the Elbe River, Baltic grain was more plentiful and cheaper than that harvested by free Mediterranean peasants. The importation of northern European grain was so reliable that Mediterranean farmers began devoting less land to the cultivation of cereals. Sugar production in the Mediterranean also diminished, since the sugar imported from slave plantations in the Caribbean was abundant and cheaper. Instead of these crops, Mediterranean folk planted more vineyards and olive orchards, profiting from the increasing demand for wine and olive oil in northern Europe and the American colonies. By limiting the spread of vineyards northward, the "little ice age" favored Mediterranean wine-growers. At the same time, American crops, especially maize, began to dot the Mediterranean landscape and diversify the Mediterranean diet.

As the world around them changed, Mediterranean peoples, then, were adaptive and resilient, their economies still vital. Venetian and Florentine merchants, for instance, began expanding their business to more cities north of the Alps in the seventeenth century. Urban Italian industrialists began shifting textile production to the countryside, where, free of guild restrictions, the costs were lower. The cloth they manufactured helped supply local and regional markets. Italian glass, paper, and printing were still profitable and internationally competitive industries. The Ottoman empire was powerful enough to limit the penetration of northern European merchants, so that overland and short-distance coastal trade within the empire remained in the hands of Ottoman merchants of diverse backgrounds, especially Greek Christians. The Ottomans' loss of the Indian Ocean spice trade, moreover, was partially offset by their monopoly over the trade in coffee imported from Yemen. Cairo became the main center for the redistribution of coffee throughout the empire and Muslim world and to Europe as well. Spain still possessed its valuable American colonies, though northern European merchants were siphoning off an increasing share of the profits from the transatlantic trade.

The rise of the Atlantic powers—England, the Netherlands, and France—was fueled in part by their ability to exploit the economies of the Ottoman and Spanish empires, both licitly through commercial treaties and illicitly through contraband trade and piracy. These imperial economies, forged and expanded through centuries of conquest, were complex and productive international systems, generators of immense wealth. Yet the forces that brought about their creation led to their depletion, for with conquest came enemies and with enemies the high costs of imperial defense. We can only imagine how Mediterranean economies might have developed had Habsburg and Ottoman monarchs channeled more of their resources into industrial and agricultural innovation and expansion and less into perpetual warfare on multiple fronts. Yet in 1650 both empires were still intact and formidable, even though they stood on eroding economic foundations. It was their unraveling in the coming centuries that would give rise to large parts of the modern world as we know it. Born in the later Middle Ages on Mediterranean frontiers, the Ottoman and Spanish empires still had a major role to play in world history even as they waned.

Notes

1. Agnolo di Tura, as quoted in Robert Gottfried, *The Black Death: Natural and Human Disaster in Medieval Europe* (London: R. Hale, 1983), 45.

2. Ibn Khaldun, *The Muqaddimah: An Introduction to History*, trans. Franz Rosenthal (London: Routledge and Kegan Paul, 1958), 1:64.

EPILOGUE

Luís de Torres in Cuba, Ishmael in the South Pacific

A World Grown Larger, a Sea Grown Smaller?

The Earth turned out to be much larger than Christopher Columbus thought. Centuries earlier, Eratosthenes (ca. 276–194 BCE), a Hellenistic scientist, had calculated the circumference of the planet (24,900 miles) remarkably accurately (he was off by only .16 percent), and medieval scientists, such as the brilliant Muslim polymath Muhammad ibn Ahmad al-Biruni (973–1050), had confirmed his calculation. Yet Columbus's confusion about Arabic units of measure—the Arabic mile being much shorter than the Roman mile—and his adherence to a widely accepted view about the size of the Eurasian continent led him to reckon both that the Earth was about 25 percent smaller, and the coast of Asia far closer to Europe. Indeed, he was certain that the Canary Islands, his jumping-off place for his journey west, were only 2,300 miles from Japan. They are actually 12,400 miles away—and, of course, there were the huge landmasses of North and South America in between, about which he knew nothing.

As a result, Columbus was certain that he would find a familiar cultural reality when he reached the other side of the planet, and he had prepared himself: he had brought along one Luís de Torres, who, Columbus tells us in his *Diary* of his first voyage, "had been a Jew and knew... Hebrew and Chaldean and even a bit of Arabic."[1] This Converso (who had adopted Christianity only just before the voyage set sail) was to be Columbus's chief translator. Even on the far eastern margins of Asia, Columbus thought, he would find people—Jewish merchants perhaps—who spoke one of those Semitic languages. A Mediterranean *tarjuman/dragoman* would be just the right means for negotiating with the natives and contacting the Great Khan, whom he assumed ruled China.

Eventually even Columbus conceded that he had been wrong, and, as Eurasian civilizations gradually learned about and exploited this far bigger world, the Mediterranean seemed, in equal measure, to shrink in size and significance. With European commerce depending increasingly on Atlantic and Indian Ocean trade, the Sea in the Middle had turned in some ways into the Sea on the Margin. In actual size, of course, it had always been small as saltwater bodies go, and now the trajectories of world history after 1650 often seemed to pass it by entirely. In 2018 the ten largest economies in the world included only two (Italy and France) entirely or partially in the Mediterranean. Two more are in northern Europe (Germany and the United Kingdom), two in East Asia (China and Japan), and fully three in the Americas (the US, Canada, and Brazil). The top three—the US, China, and Japan—are at a vast distance from this Sea on the Margin.

Indeed, signs of Mediterranean decline appeared even before 1650. Though the Spanish empire imported vast amounts of silver from South America in the sixteenth and early seventeenth centuries, Felipe II's wars against Protestants and Turks ate up enormous quantities of it. Moreover, the flow of silver declined precipitously from the end of the sixteenth century on, leaving Spain virtually bankrupt by 1607. In addition, in the early nineteenth century, Spain lost most of its South American possessions to native-born independence movements, and when the United States wrested away its final colonies (Cuba and the Philippines) in the Spanish-American War in 1898, a wave of Spanish writers and intellectuals—the so-called Generation of '98—spent much of the next half century passionately debating the causes of their nation's decline from global supremacy in 1550 to near irrelevance on the eve of the twentieth century.

A similar national reckoning came even earlier in Ottoman lands. Though the sultans maintained a façade of invincibility, already in the late sixteenth century, the ruling Turks were no longer able to effectively govern their far-flung territories in the Maghrib. Moreover, they failed to keep up militarily with Europe, as their humbling defeat in the Ottoman-Russian War of 1768–1774 would make clear. Outgeneraled and outfought, the Ottomans were forced to hand over the Crimea. Just fourteen years later, Napoleon successfully invaded Ottoman territories in Egypt and Syria at the head of a French army and navy. Although the French presence lasted only until 1801, it was a horrifying shock. Politicians and scholars who believed that God's favor would never allow Ottoman defeat had to abandon this exceptionalism. The scholar-courtier Ahmed Vasif (ca. 1735–1806), who had seen the Russian victories at first hand, spent much of his career calling obsessively for reform of the empire to stave off further defeat. He saw it as necessary to imitate every European technological advance, a task that was, he argued, a *farz-i ayn* in Islamic terms—a duty incumbent upon each individual Muslim, not only the Ottoman rulers. But such radical proposals for reform had little effect, and by the nineteenth century the Ottoman realm was widely derided as the "sick man of Europe."

The decline of the Ottoman empire reflected an economic and military decline that spread across the whole Mediterranean, and was vividly obvious in the now empty docks and warehouses of Venice's once mighty Arsenal. Its name deriving from the Arabic *dar al-sina'a,* meaning "house of industry," the Arsenal was the great naval-military compound constructed and owned by the Venetian Republic, and the largest industrial complex in the premodern world. Now, all but abandoned, it is a stark reminder that although the Sea in the Middle once was the highway along which Arab engineering reached western Europe, it is now the home of neither the great navies nor the dominant economies of the wider world that Columbus's voyages revealed.

The cultural and intellectual history of the modern world could be told in similar fashion. The biggest stories seem to begin in northern Europe, run through the New World, and then on to the rest of the planet. The most famous figures of the eighteenth-century Enlightenment—Voltaire, Kant, Rousseau, Adam Smith—loudly proclaimed the universal authority of reason in Paris, Glasgow, and (in Kant's case) what is now Kaliningrad, a Russian possession on the cold Baltic Sea. Enlightenment political ideas, moreover, first found statutory form in the Constitution of the United States, and thereafter swept back through Paris in the French Revolution, and then on to—among other places—the South American colonies of Spain. Charles Darwin, educated in Scotland and England, propounded his theory of evolution after spending five years at sea doing biological research—not, however, in the Mediterranean, but in the South Atlantic, South Pacific, and Indian Oceans. Vienna, the home of both Carl Jung and Sigmund Freud, was the birthplace of psychoanalysis, while Einstein, a German, demonstrated that E = mc2, and developed the theories of special and general relativity in Bern, Switzerland, spending the last decades of his life in Princeton, New Jersey. In the twenty-first century, the great majority of the top twenty universities in the world—no matter who is making the list—are in the United States, with the remaining spread between the United Kingdom, northern Europe, and Canada. None are in the Mediterranean lands. In 1500 there were fewer than 5 million speakers of English; now there are some 350 million native speakers and anywhere from 500 million to a billion nonnative speakers, making English the most widely spoken language in the world.

From the point of view of those millions of English speakers, the medieval Mediterranean might well, therefore, seem little more than a distant irrelevance. Indeed, one of the greatest American writers, Herman Melville, alludes to the modern unintelligibility of the medieval Mediterranean in *Moby Dick,* his brilliant novel set on the deck of a nineteenth-century New England whaling ship. Near the center of the sprawling tale, the book's narrator, a Yankee sailor named Ishmael, muses upon the terrifying wonders of a vast sperm-whale head as it hung on the side of his vessel. Gazed upon from "the full front," he tells us, there is nothing that looks like a face, "only one broad firmament of forehead" so wrinkled that it seems "pleated with riddles." These wrinkled riddles on the face of this awesome creature, Ishmael reckons in his astonishment, must somehow speak of the mysterious presence of God himself. Yet, he wistfully asks:

How shall unlettered Ishmael hope to read the awful Chaldee of the Sperm Whale's brow?[2]

Here Aramaic ("Chaldee"), one of the three Mediterranean languages that Luís de Torres knew besides Spanish, is the ancient mystic tongue so obscure that one cannot possibly imagine deciphering it. For Ishmael, the premodern Mediterranean is so far beyond the knowledge of a humble sailor adrift in the vast South Pacific, that it is the apt metaphor for the utter unknowability of God.

The complex history of the lands surrounding the Sea in the Middle has indeed often seemed irrelevant—and has just as often been quite unknown—to modern Americans. Yet if we look more closely at the modern world, the powerful legacy of the medieval Mediterranean is visible on every side. The economic and political powerhouses of the modern world may not sit in Mediterranean harbors, but Mediterranean people—or at any rate people who in some way are deeply Mediterranean despite being born in Kaliningrad or Kansas City or Kolkata—made much of the modern world. Of the six most widely spoken languages in the world, three—Spanish, Arabic, and French—accounting for some 1.2 billion speakers, are thoroughly Mediterranean languages that spread with their speakers as they journeyed throughout the world. Moreover, while English is a Germanic tongue rooted deep in the northern European soil, its vocabulary is, nevertheless, 58 percent Latin or French in origin (plus a 1,000 words from Arabic), so that the most widely spoken language is a substantially Mediterranean instrument as well.

Indeed, the Mediterranean manufacture of the rest of world actually began much earlier than Columbus and his voyages, for Islam became a world civilization centuries before European Christendom. Though the Mongol sack of Baghdad in 1258 has often been seen as the beginning of a decline of Islamic civilization, in fact, Islam expanded ambitiously to both the south and east in the centuries thereafter. Muslim merchants, as we have seen, carried Islam to trading cities all along the east coast of Africa—Mogadishu, Mombasa, Zanzibar, Kilwa. Here they built mosques, and their Arab language mixed with local Bantu dialects to form the Swahili language. When Ibn Battuta, the world-traveling Moroccan, reached Kilwa in 1331 he met its pious Muslim sultan, Abu al-Muzaffar Hasan, who, in accordance with the Qur'an, generously gave a fifth of the booty won in war to charity—indeed, Ibn Battuta noted, he was "a man of great humility; he sits with poor brethren, and eats with them, and greatly respects men of religion and noble descent."[3]

The Islamic expansion to the east was even more impressive. Beginning about the same time as Ibn Battuta traveled the east coast of Africa, and continuing up through the early nineteenth century, conversion to Islam would make Muslims the majority religion in both the western and eastern flanks of the Indian subcontinent—what are today Pakistan and Bangladesh. Moreover, Muslims make up fully 14 percent of the vast 1.3 billion people of India proper. Indeed, modern India has more than 300,000 mosques, including magnificent structures such as the Masjid-I Jahan Numa (the "World-Reflecting Mosque") in Delhi, completed at the behest of the Mughal emperor Shah Jahan at the cost of 1 million rupees between 1644 and 1656, complete with three great gates and two minarets that are forty meters tall. A later Muslim ruler, Maharajah Jai Singh II (1699–1743), imported another important Islamic institution when he built observatories, modeled ultimately on the thirteenth-century observatory at Maragha, in several Islamic cities, including the massive Jantar Mantar, likewise in Delhi.

While always a minority in what is now the state of India, Islam as a religion, moreover, has exercised nevertheless a sustained influence on the non-Muslim Indian population, as the example of the great fifteenth-century Hindi poet Kabir (d. 1518) makes clear. Born into a Muslim family, and bearing an Arabic name (*kabir* means "big, grand"), he nevertheless was taught by a Hindu saint, Ramananda (d. <1475), adopted many aspects of Hindu devotional piety, and probably abandoned Islam formally. Yet his poetry has a strongly Sufi character, especially in its consistent emphasis on worshipping one God alone. At any rate, lines such as the following appealed to Indians of all religious persuasions:

My Lord brings to me words of sorrow
and words of joy and He Himself
heals their strife.
I will offer my body and mind to my Lord:
I will give up my life, but never can I
forget my Lord![4]

Indeed, Kabir's poems deeply impressed the founders of the Sikh religion, which began as a Hindu movement, and some of his poems made their way into Sikhism's scripture, the Guru Granth Sahib. In today's India and Pakistan Kabir's poems are both set to music by Sufi fusion bands and sung by Hindu vocalists.

But Islam spread even farther east. By Kabir's lifetime the Demak Great Mosque was being built in central Java in the modern country of Indonesia. Strikingly different from Middle Eastern mosques, it is constructed of wood, and, with its tiered roof, it resembles many Hindu and Buddhist sites in the same country. Islam traveled to this Southeast Asian island nation much as it did along the east coast of Africa, carried by far-flung Muslim traders, and the wandering Muslim scholars and Sufi masters who followed them. By the twenty-first century some 87 percent of the 260 million Indonesians are Muslims, making it by far the largest Muslim country in the world. Islam even reached what is the modern nation of the Philippines, well to the north of Indonesia and off the east coast of China, by as early as 1300. By the end of the fifteenth century Islam had a strong foothold in the Philippine region of Mindanao where 20 percent of the population are still Muslims. Indeed, only a small fraction of today's Muslims (14 percent) live in the Arabic-speaking lands of the Mediterranean, while fully 59 percent reside in sub-Saharan Africa and South and Southeast Asia. Islam was a world traveler before European Christianity was.

Christianity, though, traveled farther, following the shipping lanes established by Columbus and his successors, and wherever it went, this Mediterranean scriptural monotheism did just what another, Islam, did: brought much of the Mediterranean with it. When Hernán Cortés (1485–1547), the reckless, rebellious, but utterly successful conqueror of Mexico, traveled inland with his small army he saw Mediterranean realities everywhere. He praised the city-state of Cholula as "larger than Granada, and much stronger," and observed that "in its constitution of government . . . it resembles the states of Venice, Genoa, and Pisa." The exterior of the city of Talasca was "more beautiful than any in Spain." He had stood, he noted, on one "mosque"—the term he uses for native Aztec temples—and "counted . . . four hundred [other] mosques" and as many towers. Talasca, therefore, was "more suitable for the Spaniards to inhabit" than any other cities he had seen—Christian Spaniards being quite at home, apparently, with other religions' "mosques."[5]

The brutal European conquerors of the Americas killed many natives intentionally, but far more were massacred (probably some 90 percent of the native population) by the Old World diseases, such as smallpox, measles, and influenza, that they brought with them. Europeans, therefore, had something of a free hand to recreate the civilizations that they had left behind. In the writing of the Mexican nun and brilliant poet Sor Juana Inés de la Cruz (1648–1695), we find many of the features of contemporary Mediterranean culture thriving across the ocean in Mexico City: a humanist fascination with pagan Greek and Roman literature (she read the latter in Latin of course), an interest in experimental science, an abiding fascination with the long tradition of Aristotelian logic. Yet Sor Juana also had native blood (her mother was of mixed race), and she even knew Nahuatl and composed short poems in that Aztec tongue. There were other distinguished South Americans with similar backgrounds, including the Peruvian historian Garcilaso de la Vega (1539–1616). Known as "El Inca" because his mother was an Inca noblewoman, he wrote as both a Christian Spaniard content with the conquest and Christianization of his land, and a native who stoutly defended the sophistication of Inca civilization. In doing the latter, though, he relied heavily on the ancient Greek and Roman historians admired by Spanish humanists to argue that the Inca realms had been the Roman Empire of the New World, its rulers like the Caesars. Even a proud half Incan learned to think about the past from Mediterranean templates.

But what of English-speaking North America—a region dominated by Atlantic and Pacific trade, and steeped in an unstable mix of Protestant religion and Enlightenment thought? Of course, early English (and French, German, and Irish) settlers brought Christianity with them, imposing it no less ruthlessly than the Iberians in South America, and even in its (mostly) Protestant forms it is still recognizably the religion that came of age around the late ancient and medieval Mediterranean. But the imprint of the Sea in the Middle goes much deeper than that. In the United States, a land of massive immigration, the fourth largest ancestry group (after German, African American, and Irish) is Mexican, while the seventh and tenth are Italian and French, these comprising some 59 million Americans with deep cultural roots in the Mediterranean. Until the beginning of the twentieth century, going to college in the United States and Canada usually meant, even in the toniest of WASP circles, studying a curriculum of Latin and Greek languages and texts derived from Mediterranean humanism. Mark Twain modeled his literary career—and many of his characters—on *Don Quixote,* a novel written by the Spaniard Miguel de Cervantes (1547–1616), onetime combatant at Lepanto and inmate of a Muslim prison in North Africa at the height of the struggle between the Spanish and Ottoman empires. New York City's massive Central Synagogue, though founded by German-speaking Jews, was built in the Andalusi Mudejar style in 1872. The Sea in the Middle took up residence in the land of the brave.

Indeed, while Ishmael, on the hunt half a world away from the Mediterranean, may have been baffled by Aramaic riddles on a whale's head, *Moby Dick* is, nevertheless, awash otherwise in allusions to the Mediterranean past, beginning, of course, with the arresting name of its protagonist. Though Ishmael is originally a biblical personage—in Genesis 16:3 Ishmael is Abraham's son by Hagar, his wife Sarah's handmaiden—he also shows up repeatedly in the Qur'an as the firstborn of Abraham, and Arab Muslims have seen him as the ancestor of Muhammad himself. Aware of this, medieval Christians often called Muslims "Ishmaelites," and never named their own children Ishmael, though Muslims often did. From the first words of *Moby Dick* ("Call me Ishmael") on, therefore, the reader is entertained but permanently kept off-balance by this chatty, biblically literate Nantucketer who bears a Muslim name. But there is also mysterious Fedallah, captain of Ahab's private boat crew, a Persian with what seems to be an Arabic name meaning "sacrifice of God"; and Ishmael's description of the a right whale's tongue as like "a rug of the softest Turkey"; and his comment, as the nimble sailor Tashtego heads out along the yardarm to begin draining the oil from the sperm whale's head, that he "seems some Turkish Muezzin calling the good people to prayers"; and his whimsical philosophical conclusion, after contrasting the ominous heads of the right and sperm whales, that the first must have been a Stoic, the second a Platonist "who might have taken up Spinoza in his latter years."[6]

FIGURE E.1 Central Synagogue, New York City. Photo: Peter Horree / Alamy Stock Photo.

Even a nineteenth-century Yankee whaling ship carried a great deal of the premodern Mediterranean with it as it sailed across the vast South Pacific, and so it is with much of the twenty-first-century world as well. Indeed, if Columbus's flotilla had managed both to arrive where he thought he was going—the outer islands of Asia—and to jump miraculously across 500 years of time, he might have dropped anchor in the modern Philippine Islands. There he would have found a surprisingly familiar world. Overwhelmingly today's Filipinos are Catholics, the Spanish empire having conquered the islands in the sixteenth century and ruled them for more than 300 years.

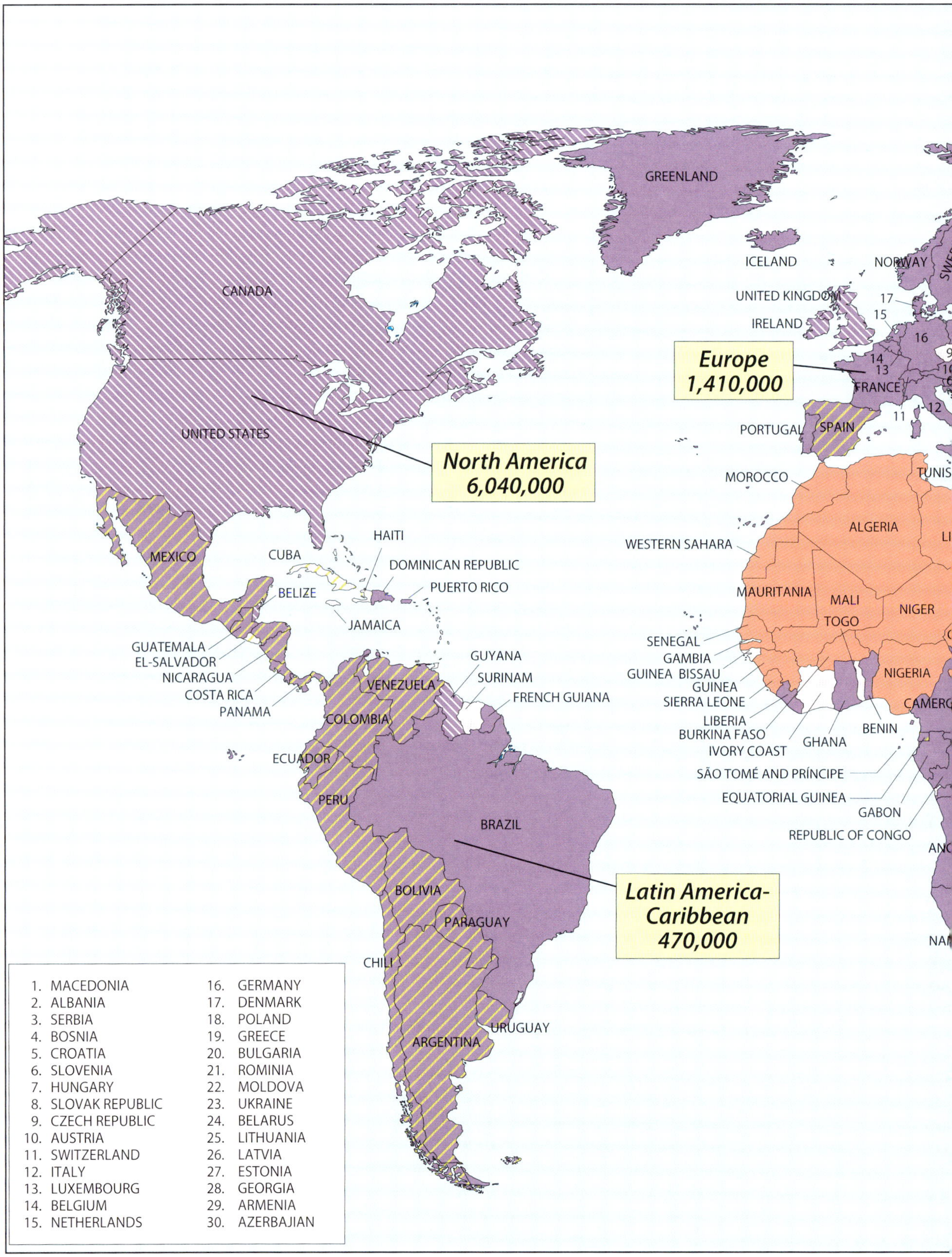

MAP E.1 The Mediterranean in the Modern World.

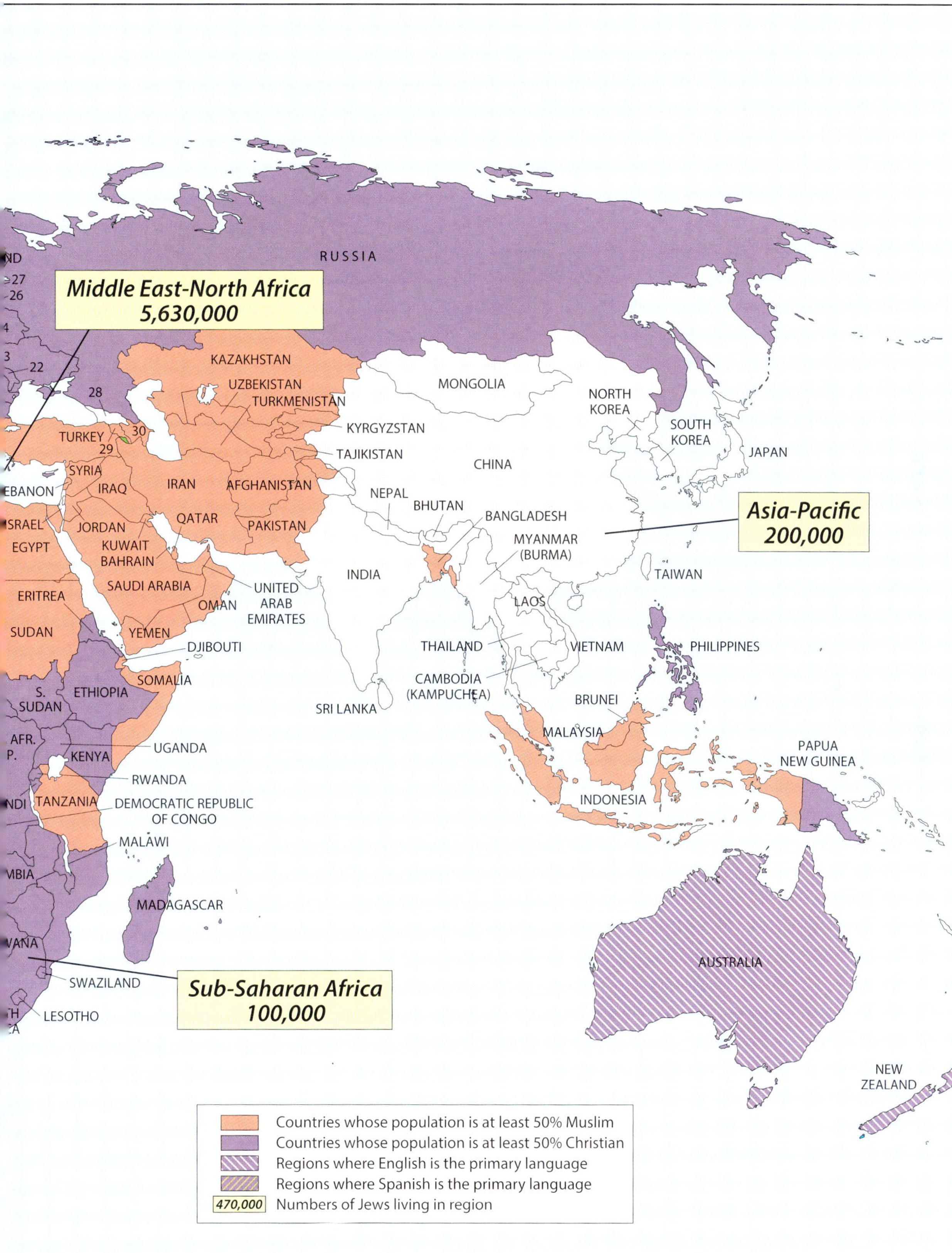
Middle East-North Africa
5,630,000
Asia-Pacific
200,000
Sub-Saharan Africa
100,000
RUSSIA
KAZAKHSTAN
UZBEKISTAN
TURKMENISTAN
KYRGYZSTAN
TAJIKISTAN
MONGOLIA
NORTH KOREA
SOUTH KOREA
JAPAN
CHINA
TURKEY
SYRIA
IRAQ
IRAN
AFGHANISTAN
JORDAN
QATAR
KUWAIT
BAHRAIN
PAKISTAN
EGYPT
SAUDI ARABIA
UNITED ARAB EMIRATES
OMAN
ERITREA
SUDAN
YEMEN
DJIBOUTI
SOMALIA
ETHIOPIA
S. SUDAN
UGANDA
KENYA
RWANDA
TANZANIA
DEMOCRATIC REPUBLIC OF CONGO
MALAWI
MADAGASCAR
SWAZILAND
LESOTHO
NEPAL
BHUTAN
BANGLADESH
MYANMAR (BURMA)
INDIA
TAIWAN
LAOS
THAILAND
VIETNAM
PHILIPPINES
CAMBODIA (KAMPUCHEA)
SRI LANKA
BRUNEI
MALAYSIA
PAPUA NEW GUINEA
INDONESIA
AUSTRALIA
NEW ZEALAND
22
26
27
28
29
30
Countries whose population is at least 50% Muslim
Countries whose population is at least 50% Christian
Regions where English is the primary language
Regions where Spanish is the primary language
470,000 Numbers of Jews living in region

FIGURE E.2 Golden Mosque, Manila. Photograph provided by Wikimedia Commons under the CC-SA-4.0.

But as we have seen, Islam has been present there from an even earlier period, and to this day between 6 and 10 percent of the Filipino population are Muslims (referred to, by the way, from the sixteenth century on as Moros by the Christian population), and Arabic is even taught in Muslim schools. Spanish used to be a lingua franca across the many-languaged archipelago, and though English serves that role now, the constitution still encourages its use. Though tiny, there is a Jewish community based in Manila. Luís de Tórres, a Spanish-speaking Converso dragoman specializing in Hebrew, Aramaic, and Arabic, would be right at home. The Sea in the Middle did, therefore, grow smaller in some respects after the middle of the seventeenth century, but in all sorts of ways it also grew larger as travelers, traders, missionaries, and conquerors, all deeply imprinted with the religious cultures of the Mediterranean, came to dominate, for good or ill, the modern world.

Notes

1. Oliver Dunn and James E. Kelley Jr., *The "Diario" of Christopher Columbus's First Voyage to America, 1492–1493, Abstracted by Bartolomé de las Casas, Transcribed and Translated into English with Notes and a Concordance of the Spanish* (1989; Norman: University of Oklahoma Press, 1991), 129.
2. Herman Melville, *Moby Dick or the Whale*, foreword by Nathaniel Philbrick (London: Penguin Books, 2009), 379–80.
3. *Travels of Ibn Battuta, A.D. 1325–1354*, trans. H.A.R. Gibb, B.R Sanguinetti, and C. Defremery (Cambridge: Published for the Hakluyt Society at the University Press, 1958–2000), 2:381.
4. *One Hundred Poems of Kabir*, 25, trans. Rabindranath Tagore (https://www.tagoreweb.in/Verses/one-hundred-poems-of-kabir-202/my-lord-hides-himself-3878).
5. Francis Augustus MacNutt, *Letters of Cortes to Emperor Charles V*, 1:209, 220–21 (consulted at https://en.wikisource.org/wiki/Letters_of_Cortes_to_Emperor_Charles_V_-_Vol_1/Second_Letter,_October_30,_1520).
6. Melville, *Moby Dick*, 366, 373, 367.

INDEX

Page references in italics refer to illustrations.

Founded in 1893,
UNIVERSITY OF CALIFORNIA PRESS
publishes bold, progressive books and journals on topics in the arts, humanities, social sciences, and natural sciences—with a focus on social justice issues—that inspire thought and action among readers worldwide.

The UC PRESS FOUNDATION
raises funds to uphold the press's vital role as an independent, nonprofit publisher, and receives philanthropic support from a wide range of individuals and institutions—and from committed readers like you. To learn more, visit ucpress.edu/supportus.